MARY: THE COMPLETE RESOURCE

MARY

The Complete Resource

EDITED BY

SARAH JANE BOSS

OXFORD

UNIVERSITY PRESS

OXFORD

UNIVERSITY PRESS

Oxford University Press, Inc., publishes works that further
Oxford University's objective of excellence
in research, scholarship, and education.

Oxford New York
Auckland   Cape Town   Dar es Salaam   Hong Kong   Karachi
Kuala Lumpur   Madrid   Melbourne   Mexico City   Nairobi
New Delhi   Shanghai   Taipei   Toronto

With offices in
Argentina Austria Brazil Chile Czech Republic France Greece
Guatemala Hungary Italy Japan Poland Portugal Singapore
South Korea Switzerland Thailand Turkey Ukraine Vietnam

Copyright © 2007 by Continuum International Publishing Group Ltd

Published by Oxford University Press, Inc.
198 Madison Avenue, New York, New York 10016
www.oup.com

Oxford is a registered trademark of Oxford University Press

Library of Congress Cataloging-in-Publication data
Boss, Sarah Jane.
   Mary: the complete resource / Sarah Jane Boss.
      p. cm.
   Includes bibliographical references.
   ISBN 978-0-19-533355-8 (cloth)
1. Mary, Blessed Virgin, Saint–History of doctrines. 2. Mary, Blessed Virgin,
Saint–Devotion to–History. I. Title.
   BT610.B65 2007
   232.91–dc22   2007017538

            ISBN-13: 978-0-19-533355-8 (cloth: alk. paper)

---

1 3 5 7 9 8 6 4 2

Typeset by BookEns Ltd, Royston, Herts.
Printed and bound in England by Antony Rowe Ltd, Chippenham, Wiltshire

CONTENTS

Contributors   ix
Abbreviations   xi

Editor's Introduction
Sarah Jane Boss   1

Part 1 The Virgin Mary in Earliest Christianity

1   Mary in the New Testament and Apocrypha
     Chris Maunder   11

     The Conception of the Virgin Mary
     from *The Protevangelium of James*   47

     The Annunciation
     from *The Protevangelium of James*   48

2   The Title Theotokos
     Sarah Jane Boss   50

3   Theotokos: The Title and its Significance in Doctrine and Devotion
     Richard Price   56

     Cyril of Alexandria on the title Theotokos
     from the *Third Letter to Nestorius*   74

4   Mary in Patristic Theology
     Tina Beattie   75

5   The Origins of Marian Art: The Evolution of Marian Imagery in
     the Western Church until AD 431
     Geri Parlby   106

6   Marian Liturgies and Devotion in Early Christianity
     Stephen J. Shoemaker   130

Part 2   The Cult of the Virgin Mary during the Middle Ages

7   The Development of the Virgin's Cult in the High Middle Ages
     Sarah Jane Boss   149

     The Vision of the Monk Robert
     translated by *Sarah Jane Boss*   173

8   Marian Devotion in the Latin West in the Later Middle Ages
     Eva De Visscher   177

     Miracles of the Blessed Virgin Mary
     from the Collection of *Johannes Herolt*   202

Part 3   Mariology

9   The Development of the Doctrine of Mary's Immaculate Conception
     Sarah Jane Boss   207

     Extract from a Medieval Sermon on the Conception of Blessed Mary   236

10   The English Reformers and the Blessed Virgin Mary
     Paul Williams   238

11   Francisco Suárez and Modern Mariology
     Sarah Jane Boss   256

     Extracts from Ineffabilis Deus
     Dogmatic Constitution on the Immaculate Conception   279

     Extracts from Munificentissimus Deus
     Apostolic Constitution on the Assumption   281

12   How to Think about Mary's Privileges: A Post-Conciliar Exposition
     Philip Endean   284

     The Fundamental Principle of Marian Theology
     Karl Rahner, translated and with an introduction by *Philip Endean*   292

13   Immaculate Mary: The Ecclesial Mariology of Hans Urs von Balthasar
     Francesca Murphy   300

14   The Virgin Mary in Anglican Tradition
     Paul Williams   314

15   Mary in Ecumenical Dialogue and Exchange
     David Carter   340

Part 4   Traditions of Devotion

16   Mary in Early Modern Europe
     Trevor Johnson   363

17   Telling the Beads: The Practice and Symbolism of the Rosary
     Sarah Jane Boss   385

18   Mary: Images and Objects
     Simon Coleman   395

19   Marian Consecration in the Contemporary Church
     Sarah Jane Boss   411

20   Apparitions of Mary
     Chris Maunder   424

21   Black Madonnas
     Sarah Jane Boss   458

Part 5   Mary in Art and Literature

22   Mary in Islam
     Tim Winter   479

23   Mary in Nineteenth-Century English and American Poetry
     Nancy de Flon   503

24   Mary in Modern European Literature
     Catherine O'Brien   521

25   Mary in Film
     Catherine O'Brien   532

26   The Iconographic Types of the Virgin in Western Art
     Maurice Vloberg   537

     Index   587

CONTRIBUTORS

Tina Beattie is Senior Lecturer in the Department of Theology and Religious Studies, Roehampton Institute, University of Surrey.

Sarah Jane Boss is Lecturer in Christian Theology and Director of the Centre for Marian Studies, University of Wales, Lampeter.

David Carter is a Member of the British Methodist/Roman Catholic Dialogue Group.

Simon Coleman is Professor of Anthropology, University of Sussex.

Philip Endean, SJ is a Fellow of Campion Hall, and Lecturer in Theology, University of Oxford.

Nancy de Flon is a writer and lecturer in New York, and academic editor at Paulist Press.

Trevor Johnson is Senior Lecturer in Modern European History, University of the West of England.

Chris Maunder is Senior Lecturer in the Department of Theology and Religious Studies, York St John University, York.

Francesca Murphy is Senior Lecturer in Theology, University of St Andrews.

Catherine O'Brien is Lecturer in French and German, University of Kingston.

Geri Parlby is Lecturer on Sacred Images of the Female, and a research student in the Department of Theology and Religious Studies, Roehampton Institute, University of Surrey.

Richard Price is Lecturer in the Department of Theology, Heythrop College, University of London.

Stephen J. Shoemaker is Associate Professor of Religious Studies, University of Oregon, Eugene.

Eva de Visscher is British Academy Research Fellow, Oriel College, Oxford.

Paul Williams is Vicar of Tewkesbury (Diocese of Gloucester), and former Adviser to the Anglican/Roman Catholic International Commission.

Tim Winter is Lecturer in Islamic Studies, Divinity Faculty, University of Cambridge.

ABBREVIATIONS

ACO   *Acta Conciliorum Oecumenicorum*, Eduard Schwarz, Berlin, 1927–
ARCIC   Anglican–Roman Catholic International Commission
CCSL   Corpus Christianorum Series Latina, Turnhout: Brepols.
DEC   Decrees of the Ecumenical Councils, ed. Norman Tanner
PG   *Patrologia Cursus Completus, Series Graeca*, 1857–91, ed. J.-P. Migne,
           166 vols, Paris: Garnier
PL   *Patrologia Curus Completus, Series Latina*, 1841–64, ed. J.-P. Migne,
           221 vols, Paris: Garnier
PO   *Patrologia Orientalis*

ILLUSTRATIONS

Figure   Page

#	Figure	Page
1	*Virgin Hodegetria*	107
2	*Isis nursing Horus*	112
3	*Isis with Harpocrates*	113
4	Figures from the Coemeterium Maius	116
5	Fresco, Catacomb of Priscilla	117
6	Triumphal arch, Santa Maria Maggiore	123
7	*Annunciation* mosaic, Santa Maria Maggiore	124
8	*Adoration* mosaic, Santa Maria Maggiore	124
9	Apex of *Mappa Mundi*, Hereford Cathedral	150
10	*Virgin in Majesty*, Clermont Cathedral	162
11	*Seat of Wisdom*, manuscript illumination	163
12	*Our Lady of Orcival*	165
13	Master Bertram, *Embrace of Saints Anne and Joachim*	222
14	Jusepe de Ribera, *Immaculate Conception*	223
15	The Virgin *Tota Pulchra*	226
16	The *Miraculous Medal*	228
17	*Our Lady of Lourdes*	229
18	Frontispiece to *Bavaria Sancta*	367
19	Woodcut by Pieter van der Borcht	372
20	*Immaculate Heart of Mary*	418
21	*Our Lady of Fatima* with Immaculate Heart	422
22	*Our Lady of Le Puy*	459
23	*Our Lady of Guadalupe*	462
24	*Notre-Dame de Bonne Délivrance*, Paris	467
25	*Ivory Virgin*, Villeneuve-lès-Avignon	538
26	*Marienklage*, South German	539

EDITOR'S INTRODUCTION

SARAH JANE BOSS

To understand the cult of the Virgin Mary is to understand the Christian religion. In part, this is because an understanding of the cult of the Virgin depends upon some understanding of other aspects of Christian practice. But the converse is also true. The many and various forms in which Christian people enact their relationship with Mary – including the suppression and rejection of her cult – are windows onto central features of Christianity. Not only is Mary the bearer of Christ, and therefore the unique holder of the title 'Godbearer', but as a consequence of this extraordinary status, Christian cult has also made her the bearer of all that centres on her Son. Much about Christian identity at a particular time and place can, as it were, be read off from the cult of the Virgin in that same time and place. This might seem to be an extravagant claim – one perhaps dreamt up by a Mariologist as a means of keeping herself in business, or by someone who has lost sight of Christianity's 'big picture'. But against this, it is not difficult to contend that it is only a highly distorted rendering of Christianity's history that could exclude Mary from its very heart. For this reason, a resource book in Marian studies provides soundings from many parts of the ocean of Christian practice.

In Athens, in the late fifth century before Christ, the citizens rebuilt their shrine to the Mother of the Gods. This deity was the guardian of the city's laws, and her shrine was the place where legal documents were stored and where people could go to seek justice if they had been wronged. The Mother of the Gods, however, was not just concerned with the administration of justice in Athens. She was understood to be more ancient than the gods of Mount Olympus – the children of Zeus – and was associated with the very foundations of the cosmos.[1] The Athenians thus saw her as the guardian of both the natural and the moral orders, and believed that their laws were not only good in the eyes of humanity, but were also in accordance with the deep ordering of the universe.

In the history of Christian culture, the Virgin Mary has sometimes performed a similar role. The French historian Dominique Iogna-Prat has made a study of the cult of the Virgin during the reign of Charles the Bald (840–77), Holy Roman Emperor and ruler of much of Western Europe.[2] Charles cultivated a devotion to Mary which was intimately bound up with his own sovereignty. He saw Mary as a royal figure of

---

1. Borgeaud 2004: 11–30.
2. Iogna-Prat 1996.

1

universal proportions: she was the queen who guaranteed the right ordering of the cosmos, and who was also the protectress of his own lineage – that is, of the kings who had been consecrated for the good governance of human affairs. Similar examples can be found elsewhere in the history of medieval Europe,[3] and their rationale seems somewhat similar to that of the Athenian devotion described above. In the case of Mary, however, the influence that led Christians to venerate her in this way may have come less directly from the ancient cult of the Mother of the Gods, and more immediately from ancient Hebrew practices in honour of divine Wisdom.

The British biblical scholar Margaret Barker has argued that the Temple cult in Jerusalem was once strongly tied to the figure of Wisdom. Through an analysis of biblical, apocryphal, patristic and later Jewish texts concerning the Jerusalem Temples (that is, the first and second Temples), Barker argues that the Temple, and in particular the Holy of Holies, was constructed and ordered in such a way that it expressed the order of God's creation. As with many sacred buildings throughout the world, the Temple architecture embodied an infinite mystery in a particular place. Thus the Tabernacle embodied Day One (Gen. 1.1–3), when creation began; the veil of the Tabernacle embodied Day Two, when the waters above were separated from the waters below, or heaven was separated from earth; and so on for the rest of the furnishings.[4]

Day One is the point that we are most concerned with here: the Spirit of God hovered over the waters at the dawn of creation, as the cherubim spread their wings over the Ark of the Covenant which was contained within the Tabernacle (1 Chron. 28.18). The Ark in turn contained the tablets of the Law (Exod. 25.10–22), and at an earlier period of Israel's history, David had carried it in procession to Jerusalem (2 Sam. 6). The Law came to be identified with the figure of Holy Wisdom, who, as we have seen, was present with God from before the foundation of the world, and who 'ministered before the Lord in his holy Tabernacle' (Ecclus 24.10). If Margaret Barker's understanding is correct, then the Tabernacle, because it is Day One of creation, is also the place from which the world issues forth.

When we turn to the presentation of Mary in Luke's Gospel, we find that she too is presented as if she were the Ark, or perhaps Tabernacle, of the Lord's presence, and that she may also be seen as the being out of whom the world is created, and certainly as the one in whom it is re-created. Luke presents Mary as the Ark, as we can see from the parallel that he draws with the narrative of King David taking the Ark to Jerusalem in 2 Samuel 6.

Under King David, Jerusalem becomes the dwelling place of God. Ever since the days of Moses, when the tribes of Israel were wandering in the wilderness, the people have carried with them the Ark of the Covenant, apparently surmounted by its cherubim throne. But David, amid much rejoicing and merrymaking, brings the Ark to Jerusalem, where David's son Solomon will eventually build a splendid temple to house it. On the way, however, as David and his men carry the Ark on an ox-cart to

---

3. In England, Richard II (d. 1399) seems to have had a devotion of this kind to Our Lady. See Boss 2004: 118–29.
4. This argument is developed throughout Barker 2003.

the holy city, one of the oxen transporting the sacred vessel stumbles in the road and one of the men present, by the name of Uzzah, puts out his hand and takes hold of the Ark. But, the narrator tells us, 'the anger of the Lord was kindled against Uzzah; and God smote him there because he put forth his hand to the ark; and he died there beside the ark of God' (2 Sam. 6.7).

David is frightened and angry that the Lord has treated Uzzah in this way. He asks, 'How can the ark of the Lord come to me?' (v. 9). And David takes the Ark aside to the house of a man named Obededom, where it remains for three months before continuing on its journey to Jerusalem.

Luke's account of Mary's visitation to her cousin Elizabeth (Lk. 1.39–56) seems to be strongly influenced by this narrative. Immediately after the Annunciation and the conception of Jesus, Mary goes to visit Elizabeth, who is also expecting a child, the future John the Baptist. When the two women greet one another, Elizabeth proclaims Mary 'blessed ... among women' and says, 'And why is this granted me, that the mother of my Lord should come to me?' (v. 43). Mary sings her great song of rejoicing, popularly known by its first word in Latin, the *Magnificat*, and at the end of the narrative we are told that 'Mary remained with her [Elizabeth] about three months'. Elizabeth's question as to why the mother of her Lord should come to her seems to echo David's question as to how the Ark of the Lord could come to him; and the time of Mary's stay at her cousin's is the same as the time that the Ark remains in the house of Obededom. Luke wants the reader to understand that Mary bears within her the word of the Lord, as does the Ark of God.[5]

Luke also tells us that Mary is 'overshadowed by the power of the Most High', and that the Holy Spirit came upon her, perhaps reminding the reader of the Lord on his cherubim throne. The consequence of this overshadowing, and of the action of the Holy Spirit, is that the new creation, who is Jesus Christ, is formed in her and of her. Indeed, Luke's account of the Annunciation by the angel Gabriel to the Virgin Mary draws strongly on the first three verses of Genesis. Luke 1.26–38 narrates the visit of the angel to Mary of Nazareth. He tells her that she is to be the mother of Jesus, 'the Son of the Most High', who will inherit the throne of his ancestor King David and will rule without end. Mary accepts the word of God that is given to her by the angel and, according to the traditional reading of the text, this is the moment at which Jesus is conceived in his mother's womb. The telling of this story seems intended to evoke the creation of the world: there are parallels between the creation and the Annunciation which suggest that the latter is a recapitulation of the former. As the earth at the dawn of the universe was 'without form and void', so Mary is a virgin; nothing has yet been created in her. As the Spirit of God hovers over the face of the waters, so, Mary is told, the manner of her conceiving will be that 'the Holy Spirit will come upon [her] and the power of the Most High will overshadow [her]' (Lk. 1.35). And as God accomplishes his first act (and, indeed, subsequent acts) of creation by means of speech, so it is by the angel's message that Mary conceives Christ: 'Let it be to me according to your word', she says (1.38). Jesus Christ is himself the new creation, in whom the universe is restored and fulfilled, and so it is only the language

---

5. See Saward 1993: 23–42.

of God's creation of the universe that can do justice to the cosmic significance of Christ's conception.[6]

So Mary is, in Barker's language, Day One, the Tabernacle. She is the one in whom the world is restored and fulfilled by the Son whom she conceives and bears. She is the dwelling place of Wisdom, who is Christ.

Yet on many occasions Mary herself has been identified with Wisdom. Margaret Barker suggests that the most ancient account of Mary's presentation in the Temple represents her deliberately as Wisdom.[7] According to the *Protevangelium* (or Gospel of James) – an apocryphal work which seems to have existed by the middle of the second century – Mary's parents took her to live in the Temple, and when she arrived, she danced on the steps 'and all Israel loved her'.[8] This seems to recall Proverbs 8.30, where Wisdom says she 'played before the Lord' before the beginning of creation.

In Catholic liturgy, from the High Middle Ages onwards, Wisdom texts were used to designate both Christ and Mary. Proverbs 8.22–31 and Ecclesiasticus 24, in particular, have been commonly used as the lections for the feasts of Mary's conception and her birthday. Under the influence of this liturgical use – and perhaps because Wisdom is portrayed as female – it became increasingly common to identify Mary, as well as Christ, with the biblical Wisdom.[9] Indeed, throughout the Church's history, Mary has intermittently appeared as Christ's female reflection or counterpart.

MARY AND THE CHURCH

It may in part be Mary's association with the Ark and the Temple which led early Christian writers to identify her readily with the Church. Just as the Temple had been the bearer of the Lord, so now the Church performed this task and had received its mandate to do so because Mary, as a living Temple, had borne the Lord incarnate. Thus Clement of Alexandria relates Marian language directly to the Church:

> There is but one Virgin Mother. I like to call her the Church. Alone this mother has not had milk, for she alone is not a woman but a virgin and a mother, immaculate as a virgin, loving as a mother; and she calls her children and feeds them with holy milk: the Word a child.[10]

Like Wisdom, the Church has been charged with the task of guiding men and women to live holy lives, and it also has the task of maintaining the sacred order of the world through prayer and the administration of the sacraments. Wisdom stands at the place where God the Creator holds and forms and animates the creation. She encompasses the intersection between God and the created universe; and the

---

6.   A short description of this theme in Christian writing is given in Boss 2000: 74–85.
7.   Barker 2003: 258.
8.   'Protevangelism' 7.3 Elliott 1993: 60.
9.   See Boss 2000: 139–46.
10.   PG 8:300–1; trans. in O'Carroll 1982: 103.

Church, likewise, is supposed to occupy this space. According to Christian teaching, the Church has been given the responsibility of rendering God's saving presence a thing of life and wonder in the world to which she ministers – for this is what Mary did, by conceiving and giving birth to the Word of God; and it is because one woman did this thing once, decisively, that Orthodox and Catholic Christians have confidence that human beings can mediate the divine presence to the rest of creation. Mary's role as mediatress is central to her identity. Of course, according to Christian doctrine, it is by the work of God in Christ that the human and divine natures are made as one; but Mary is the human person by whom and in whom a divine Person accomplishes that union, becoming one with the creation. Mary, like Wisdom, encompasses the intersection of God and the world.

Furthermore, if classical scholars are to be believed, then mediation may in fact be one of the attributes signified by Mary's virginity. The American classicist Mary Foskett has studied the portrayal of Mary's virginity in Luke's Gospel and the *Protevangelium* in the light of classical representations of virginity, such as would have been known to early Christians.[11] Foskett points out that virginity is often associated with the gift of prophecy (as in the famous example of the Pythian oracle at Delphi), and she accordingly understands Luke's portrayal of Mary singing the *Magnificat* as intended to indicate that Mary possessed prophetic power. However, the Swiss historian of religions Philippe Borgeaud has identified a deeper dynamic here. He contends that in late Roman antiquity, contemporaneously with early Christianity, a virgin could be considered to be especially suited to be a mediator between the realms of gods and mortals, or between heaven and earth.[12] The gift of prophecy, then, would be just one instance of this mediatorial power, and the significance of Mary's virginity runs far more deeply: it is the sign, and perhaps the facilitator, of the fact that the one who is born of her is God on earth, and that in him heaven and earth are united.

In the light of these considerations, it is not surprising to find that among Mariologists there used to be a saying, *De Maria, nunquam satis*, which meant that one could never find too much to say on the subject of the Blessed Virgin Mary. Although this notion fell into disrepute among Catholic theologians, one can easily gain the impression that the actual and possible literature on Marian matters, both by theologians and by scholars of many other disciplines, is infinite. Between 1949 and 1971, the French publisher Beauchesne brought out a series of eight very substantial volumes entitled *Maria: Etudes sur la Sainte Vierge*, edited by Hubert du Manoir; and even these cannot claim to exhaust the subject of the history of Marian doctrine and devotion. How much less, then, can the mere quarter of a million words that appear in the present volume do any kind of justice to their subject! But the authors hope that the essays presented here will open doors into a palace of riches that the reader will go on to explore more deeply.

This book is divided into five sections, according partly to chronological and partly to thematic considerations. There are a number of specially commissioned

11. Foskett 2002.
12. Borgeaud 2004: 127.

articles which give an overview of current scholarship on the subjects concerned, and some of these include new evidence and arguments. There are a number of extracts from important primary and secondary sources, and short articles to supply background information. There is also a detailed index. The book should be of use to the teacher or lecturer who is trying to construct a course in Marian studies; and to the student or researcher who is approaching the subject for the first time, or who needs to check information about, or gain an overview of, a particular topic or historical period.

The book is somewhat weighted towards the early centuries of the Christian era, since that is the period when the main lines of Marian doctrine and devotion were established, and which later centuries consistently refer back to. Chris Maunder gives an overview of the state of biblical scholarship concerning the figure of Mary in the New Testament and early apocryphal literature. Richard Price presents a discussion of the Christology and Mariology surrounding the Council of Ephesus, arguing that the council fathers themselves were concerned entirely with questions of Christology, and that a more full-blown Mariology emerged only some decades later. Stephen Shoemaker's essay on early Marian devotion, however, puts a different view, describing an already flourishing devotion to Mary in the fifth century and suggesting that this devotion probably formed part of the background to the important Christological discussions of that century. Tina Beattie – a Mariologist, rather than a Patristics scholar – provides an essay on Mary in the work of early Christian writers which not only gives an overview of the subject, but suggests that modern authors have too often read early writers' comments in the light of unwarranted modern presuppositions. And Geri Parlby's consideration of early Western images of figures who may or may not be Mary alerts again us to the danger of interpreting ancient images in the light of current concerns.

The Middle Ages receive fairly short, but condensed, treatment. Overviews are provided by Sarah Jane Boss and Eva da Visscher, and comprehensive bibliographies point the reader to further literature.

Marian doctrine and devotion in the early modern period has not been extensively treated in the literature available in English, and two essays in the present volume go a short way towards putting that right. Trevor Johnson makes available to the English reader a range of important material on the European background to modern Marian devotion, and Sarah Jane Boss considers the Mariology of Francisco Súarez and the subsequent development of the discipline in the later modern period. She also examines the development of the doctrine of the immaculate conception – a topic of sufficient importance to merit an essay of its own. Philip Endean introduces the Marian writing of Karl Rahner, and Francesca Murphy does the same for the very different Mariology of Hans Urs von Balthasar.

Paul Williams' article on Mary in the writings of the Anglican Reformers is a mine of information that has not previously been available to the general reader, as is his essay on Mary in Anglican–Roman Catholic dialogue. David Carter likewise presents a clear and thorough picture of recent ecumenical discussions about Mary. All these essays draw attention both to the fundamental difficulties that exist between Protestant and Catholic considerations of this subject, and to the enormous progress that has been made in recent years towards common understanding between the various Christian denominations.

Chris Maunder supplies a masterly overview of the subject of modern Marian apparitions, which is both sympathetic and critical towards the cults associated with them.

Several topics receive special treatment here because there is so little available literature which addresses the respective subjects. Simon Coleman casts an anthropological eye over the age-old use of images and objects in the cult of the Virgin Mary; Nancy de Flon examines Mary in nineteenth-century English and American poetry; Catherine O'Brien gives short considerations of the representation of Mary in film and in modern European literature; and Sarah Jane Boss provides an essay on the endlessly fascinating subject of Black Madonnas.

We have published for the first time in English a long article by Maurice Vloberg, the great French art historian, on the iconography of the Virgin in Western art from earliest times until the late Renaissance. Although some of his comments have been superseded by later research (such as the essay by Geri Parlby in the present volume), his overview of the subject is unsurpassed.

The only treatment of Mary in a religion other than Christianity occurs in Tim Winter's beautiful piece on Mary in Islam. This includes a large amount of poetry, and for that reason is placed under the section on 'Art and Literature'.

Throughout the centuries, and across the world, Christians have enacted in many different ways their relationships with Mary and their understandings of her agency in the work of the world's re-creation. The present volume is a small contribution to our attempt to understand the phenomena associated with Marian devotion.

BIBLIOGRAPHY

Barker, Margaret (2003) *The Great High Priest: The Temple Roots of Christian Liturgy*, London: T&T Clark.

Borgeaud, Philippe (2004) *Mother of the Gods: From Cybele to the Virgin Mary*, trans. Lysa Hochroth, Baltimore and London: Johns Hopkins University Press.

Boss, Sarah Jane (2000) *Empress and Handmaid*, London: Cassell.

Boss, Sarah Jane (2004) *Mary*, London: Continuum.

Elliott, J. K. (ed.) (1993) *The Apocryphal New Testament: A Collection of Apocryphal Christian Literature in an English Translation based on M. R. James*, Oxford: Clarendon.

Foskett, Mary F. (2002) *A Virgin Conceived: Mary and Classical Representations of Virginity*, Bloomington and Indianapolis: Indiana University Press.

Iogna-Prat, Dominique (1996) 'Le culte de la Vierge sous le règne de Charles le Chauve', in Dominique Iogna-Prat, Éric Palazzo and Daniel Russo (eds), *Marie: Le culte de la Vierge dans la société médiévale*, Paris: Beauchesne, 65–98.

O'Carroll, Michael (1982) *Theotokos: A Theological Encyclopedia of the Blessed Virgin Mary*, Dublin: Dominican Publications.

Saward, John (1993) *Redeemer in the Womb: Jesus Living in Mary*, San Francisco: Ignatius Press.

Part i

The Virgin Mary in Earliest Christianity

1

MARY IN THE NEW TESTAMENT AND APOCRYPHA

CHRIS MAUNDER

Studying Mary in the New Testament and Apocrypha in today's modern critical context provokes many interesting questions. Can we find out anything at all in these texts about the historical person who was the mother of Jesus? How exactly did the tradition of the virgin birth come about? What was her relationship to the shadowy figure of James, 'brother of the Lord'? Was she a female leader in the early Church, or did she look on, as in traditional images, quietly and reflectively? Did she really attend the crucifixion, given that three Gospels seem to leave this detail out? Why do Matthew, Mark, Luke and John have different ways of portraying her?

In this chapter, we consider (1) the name 'Mary' in the New Testament; (2) ways of approaching the ancient texts; (3) traditions about Mary that may lie behind the Gospels; (4) Mary as a literary character in the Gospel texts; (5) the ways in which the biblical Mary has inspired modern theology.

Yet if the written Gospels are already distant in time from Mary's life, and were not intended to present a history, why should we privilege them above the apocryphal writings of the following centuries? A Mary who is the basis for later doctrine and devotion can be found in them too. The apocryphal Mary lives in the Temple as a child; weaves the Temple veil; gives birth without pain; is upset by the boy Jesus' destructive antics; receives a resurrection appearance in the garden; dies and is taken up into heaven after a glorious visit from Jesus, and surrounded by the apostles (some of whom are raised from the dead for the event). This reflects a growing interest in Mary, who she was and what she meant to Christianity, a Mary whom Christians found it edifying to speculate upon and whose story merited expansion and proclamation. We therefore conclude the chapter with (6) a summary of the apocryphal, post-Gospel Mary.

(1) MARY

The name 'Mary' derives from 'Miriam' in Hebrew, or 'Mariam' in Aramaic, and is translated 'Maria' in Greek or Latin. It was a common name in first-century Israel/ Palestine, and it is the most frequently used woman's name in the New Testament. After Mary, the mother of Jesus, the most clearly identifiable Mary in the Gospels is Mary Magdalene, presumed to be from the village of Magdala, by the Sea of Galilee. All of the other Marys present something of a mystery; several are named in association with sons. At the cross and empty tomb are: Mary 'mother of James the younger and Joses' (in Mk 15.40; Mt. 27.56; also known as 'the other Mary' in

Matthew, 'Mary of James' in Mark and Luke, or 'Mary of Joses' in Mark) and Mary 'of Clopas' (in Jn 19.25). There is also Mary sister of Martha (in Luke and John), Mary 'mother of John Mark' (Acts 12.12) and the Mary of Romans 16.6.

There are two main tendencies in trying to resolve the question of the identity of the Marys. First, there is the tendency to conflate them: Catholic (but not Orthodox) tradition identified Mary Magdalene and Mary sister of Martha for many centuries, and Mary 'mother of James. . .' etc. has been thought to be the same person as 'Mary of Clopas'. Some people have identified Mary 'mother of James. . .' as Mary the mother of Jesus, although this is very much a minority view. On the other hand, modern writers are more than likely to distinguish them, in recognizing that the Gospel traditions derive in part from quite distinct sources, that the name was common enough at the time, and that the tendency to conflate is understandable but not necessarily accurate.

In this section we will consider those texts that relate to Mary the mother of Jesus. These texts have been the basis of a powerful and long-lasting devotion to her on the part of millions of Christians (note that she is also an important figure in the Qur'an). The modern tendency to elevate historical fact above allegory and legend was largely unknown before the Enlightenment, as was the attempt to test the historicity of the Gospel narratives, but in the wake of the birth of modern critical enquiry, one has to reappraise the texts about Mary in ways that make sense to a wide range of modern readers. In the academic context, critical enquiry is indispensable, but its limitations and presuppositions must also be recognized.

The New Testament texts that feature Mary the mother of Jesus are listed below.

Matthew 1.1–2.23: genealogy (parallel Lk. 3.23–38); conception of Jesus; Joseph's dream; birth of Jesus; flight to Egypt.

Luke 1.26–56: Annunciation; visit to Elizabeth and *Magnificat*.

Luke 2.1–52: Birth of Jesus; presentation of Jesus in Jerusalem; Jesus in Jerusalem at 12 years old.

Mark 3.31–5: Jesus contrasts his disciples with his family; see also 3.21; parallels Mt. 12.46–50; Lk. 8.19–21 (also 11.27–8).

Mark 6.3: Nazareth people identify the family of Jesus; parallels Mt. 13.55; Lk. 4.22; Jn 6.42.

John 2.1–12: The wedding at Cana.

John 7.41–2; 8.41: Jesus' origins.

John 19.25–7: women attend the crucifixion of Jesus; parallels Mt. 27.55–6; Mk 15.40; Lk. 23.49.

Acts 1.14: the community in prayer after the Ascension.

Revelation 12.1–6: the vision of the woman giving birth to the Messiah.

[**Galatians 4.4:** Paul refers to Christ as being 'born of a woman'; this is not a reference to Mary, but it links with the belief that Mary, as the human mother of Jesus, guarantees the reality of the incarnation.]

(2) WAYS OF APPROACHING THE NEW TESTAMENT

In examining the story of Mary in the New Testament, and using commentaries on it, the reader should take into account the different ways in which the texts may be approached.[1] Despite two hundred years of critical analysis of the New Testament – in which scholars dissect the texts and ask questions about their origins – people of devotion still read the texts literally, taking the meaning that appears 'on the surface'. However, this can be problematic if you begin to reflect, for example, on the apparent divergences between the Gospels, or on the role that tradition and the non-canonical (apocryphal) literature have played in colouring many people's reading of the Gospels. In academic study, you cannot avoid the critical questions, even if you start from a faith perspective.

The story of Mary that most people know is actually woven together from the different Gospel texts in which she is mentioned (listed above). The angel Gabriel visits her in Nazareth and tells her that she will become pregnant by the action of the Holy Spirit (Luke); the news worries Joseph, but he has a dream telling him to stand by her (Matthew); she visits Elizabeth, her kinswoman, and sings the *Magnificat* (Luke); she gives birth to Jesus (different accounts in Matthew and Luke); she presents her baby in the Temple (Luke); she flees with Joseph and Jesus to Egypt (Matthew); she is concerned when Jesus at twelve years old remains in the Temple (Luke); she encourages the adult Jesus to turn water into wine at Cana (John); Jesus refuses to be subject to family pressure (Mark, Matthew, Luke); Mary stands by the cross and is entrusted to the beloved disciple (John); she prays with the post-resurrection community after Jesus' Ascension (Luke-Acts). Outside the Gospels, there is a woman who gives birth to the Messiah in Revelation; while this is generally accepted as a visionary symbol, it has been assumed to be also an image of Mary that tells us something about her role in the Christian story of salvation.

This popular and well-known story is expanded upon in the apocryphal *Protevangelium of James*, which claims as author James the brother of Jesus, but which was written in the second century, according to most scholars.[2] Although the work was not included in the New Testament, and was not regarded highly by some early Christian theologians, nevertheless it has contributed some important details to the centuries-old tradition. Now we find that Mary was an extraordinarily holy child, the daughter of Anna and Joachim, and lived in the Temple until the time of her menstruation. Joseph, an elderly widower and father, took her as wife to protect her, with no intention of consummating the marriage. Mary gave birth while remaining a virgin, without any physical sign of her parturition. Thus the tradition of Mary as 'Ever Virgin' has its roots in this text. The *Protevangelium*, unlike the Gospels in which Jesus is the focal point, has Mary as its central character.

The biblical critic will notice how many of the units of the whole story of Mary occur in only one source. This is also true of other aspects of the gospel story

---

1. Useful, recent material on approaches to New Testament reading include: Green 1995; Shillington 2002; Thistleton 1992; Watson 1994.
2. See below, n. 54.

13

(although there are several elements, such as the feeding of the five thousand, the cleansing of the Temple, the anointing, the Passion and the empty tomb, which are present in all four Gospels, even if the details are different). Does this fragmentation of the story make it less convincing historically? Or is its historical accuracy important? So, to make sense of Mary's story from a critical perspective, we need to be more analytical and examine the story in more detail.

We can divide commonly used critical approaches into three main sections. First, there are the *historical* methods. In these, we look 'behind' the text, as it were, and try to uncover the actual history, in so far as it can ever be known. The first stage in this is to try to recover the development of the New Testament texts by concentrating on their differences. The assumption here is that the texts have histories; their divergence is due to several factors. One is that the evangelists had recourse to differing sources (*source criticism* attempts to uncover these). Another is that the evangelists chose aspects of the tradition that were important in the life of their community (the study of the relationship between text and its use in the community is called *form criticism*). Yet another is that they presented their material to audiences in their own style and with a specific theological emphasis in mind. So each evangelist edited the material available. The Gospels may have gone through one or more such processes of editing, or 'redaction', at the hands of one or more writers (which is the concern of *redaction criticism*).

In undertaking this kind of analysis, you may want to ask why a more positive and active portrait of Mary is apparently found in Luke or John than in Mark or Matthew, and may conclude that the communities represented by the former two Gospels had more interest in her than the latter. Their authors may have had recourse to traditions either not known to, or ignored by, the others. Whether you privilege the presentation in Luke/John or Mark/Matthew may depend on your own presuppositions in reading the texts. Historically, it is possible to assert either of two distinct possibilities (and there could be other answers that lie somewhere between them).

(a)   One or both of Luke/John had recourse to very reliable traditions about Mary, which takes us back close to the actual historical person, but which were not preserved or reckoned as important to the writers of Mark/Matthew and the communities which they represented.

(b)   Mark/Matthew show us that Mary was not particularly important in the very early Church, but legends about Jesus, either in oral form or invented by the evangelists themselves, led to an expansion of unhistorical material about his mother which was included in Luke/John (this legendary expansion then continued unabated in the *Protevangelium*).

These two strong positions will be favoured, respectively, by (a) those with a strong Marian devotion, especially Roman Catholics and Orthodox, and (b) critical thinkers, particularly those in the liberal Protestant community.

In trying to go far back beyond the texts to reconstruct the life of the individual woman Mary of Nazareth in any academic historical sense, one has very few resources; the task is impossible. Yet there are some general factors that might help narrow down the range of possibilities. Researchers can take into account the social and political history of Judaea and Galilee in the first century, and ask how far the text conforms to that understanding. It could be argued that the more it does so, the more likely it is to reflect a genuine situation. The social and political history may also fill in important background about the people, places and events mentioned in the New Testament texts, and enhance our knowledge of them. Extrabiblical material will also play its part in the task of reconstruction.

Second, there are *literary* methods. Scholars who choose these will examine the text itself, asking how it is constructed and what the author is trying to convey to the likely readers. There need be no attempt to discover a history that has given rise to it. These methods will be chosen, on the one hand, by those who do not think that the search for historical data behind the texts is likely to be very fruitful. They may conclude that the texts were created as faith documents, and were never intended to represent history in any literal sense; therefore, the history is largely unrecoverable. On the other hand, they may also be used alongside historical methods, in the recognition that the texts are derived in part from earlier sources, oral or written, but that this material has been shaped in such a way as to supply a literary expertise in the presentation of the written story.

Using literary methods in relation to the texts about Mary leads us to ask how she functions as a character in the narrative. What does the author want to communicate to the intended reader, and how does the figure of Mary help this to occur? Does she stand simply as a foil for readers to learn something about their faith in Jesus, or is she presented as a character in her own right? In Mark and Matthew, Mary hardly functions as a character at all, it would seem. In Luke she is the heroine of a story that tells us about God's purpose being fulfilled through the birth of Jesus. She stands at the beginning of both the Gospel of Luke and of his second volume in the Acts, spanning the whole life and resurrection of Jesus. In John, the presence of 'the mother of Jesus' also spans an important period, which is the length of Jesus' ministry, starting at Cana and ending at Golgotha. The link between these points in John serves to heighten the sense of expectation as the reader approaches Jesus' glorification, his 'hour', which comes on the cross.

Third, there are approaches that are more interested in the use of the texts in the Christian community than in their sources and original purpose. The *theological* approach relates New Testament texts to later theological developments. *Reader response* approaches concentrate on the ways in which the texts invoke reactions in modern readers. There is more interest here in the reader of today than in the reader the original author had in mind, based on a recognition that the responses in each case will be very different. Modern readers, too, will be very varied according to context and tradition. *Canon criticism* asks how the texts of the New Testament together make a whole, a 'canon'. The fact that the early Church chose these particular books is no accident, as they complement each other and express an orthodox theology as opposed to other, non-canonical or apocryphal texts. Who chose them, and why, and how do they interrelate?

Reader response approaches will include recognition of the importance of texts about Mary in feminist and liberationist circles. Whatever the original intention

15

behind Luke, Mary's *Magnificat* gives encouragement to those who seek a radical theological response to the Bible, and in John her presence at the cross will resonate in areas of the world where it is common for mothers to lose sons to violence. Feminists have differing assessments of the stress on Mary's virginity that has its basis in Matthew and Luke. For some it will emphasize her independence of male demands on a woman's body, while for others it represents an attitude which represses women's sexuality. Of course, many viewpoints stand in between these two and take them both into account.

Roman Catholic and Orthodox views of Mary seem to have incorporated the *Protevangelium* despite the fact that the book was not included in the New Testament canon. It is a question for debate as to whether its theology accords with that of the rest of the New Testament. This is a question that might be asked by Protestants. They will doubt the contention that later Roman Catholic theological doctrines about Mary, in particular the Ever-Virginity, Immaculate Conception and Assumption, can find a basis in the New Testament, whereas the Roman Catholic view is that tradition (as a reflection upon the biblical texts in the evolving life of the Christian community) has its own integrity and importance. This view is being challenged today within Roman Catholicism, as a more critical approach to biblical reading has become more established from the middle of the twentieth century.

This chapter will look at source material that covers the approaches to Mary in the New Testament in the next three sections: *historical*, *literary* and *theological*. They are not mutually exclusive, but draw on each other, and the boundaries between them are not clearly demarcated. Nevertheless, the categories help to distinguish between the types of biblical research that we are considering and to organize the diversity of material. To sum up, the sections will try to reach an understanding of the following points:

- how the New Testament texts about Mary came together from oral traditions and written sources;
- how the New Testament texts portray Mary as a literary character in the Gospel narrative;
- how the New Testament Mary is called upon to inspire groups of modern Christians, using her portrait in the Gospel narrative.

The source material will be presented with accompanying comments, some footnotes identifying other useful literature, and discussion of some of the major issues.

(3) THE HISTORICAL APPROACH [3]

The late Roman Catholic priest and scholar Raymond Brown was perhaps the greatest exponent of a critical approach to the New Testament texts that mention Mary. Brown was an academic biblical critic and did not take anything for granted

---

3. Recent commentaries which are helpful for this topic include Bovon 2002 and Keener 2003.

on the basis of his Church's theological perspective. He was prepared to accept that the narratives describing the birth of Jesus in Matthew and Luke were almost all created by the evangelists and/or their communities, in order to convey their theology and understanding of Jesus in story form. Their objective was to relate the birth narratives to themes in the Hebrew Scriptures, and to draw upon those themes. (At the time, the Scriptures were available in Hebrew or Greek and had not yet reached the final form now accepted in Judaism, or as the 'Old Testament' in the Christian Bible.) With these materials and this background, the birth narratives are vehicles for the expression of the gospel of Christ, using different strategies for the purpose.

> Just as Matthew and Luke approach the Old Testament differently, so also they handle the Gospel themes differently. Matthew chooses to dramatise Joseph who never appears in the ministry, except as the named father of Jesus. Luke chooses Mary and John the Baptist, using what is said of them in the Gospel accounts of the ministry as a guide to depicting them in the infancy narrative. The fact that the Lucan infancy narrative has a larger cast of characters means that the role of representing an obedient Israel responsive to God's revelation about His Son can be more widely distributed than in Matthew's infancy narrative where Joseph is the only major representative. In reading Luke, one gets the impression that most pious Jews were immediately attracted by Jesus...
> ... Luke is more interested in establishing the continuity of the Christian movement with Israel than in anti-synagogue apologetics. His heroine Mary will embody that continuity – she responds obediently to God's word from the first as a representative of the Anawim of Israel (1.38); she appears in the ministry as a representative of the ideals of true discipleship (8.19–21); and she endures till Pentecost to become a Christian and a member of the Church (Acts 1.14).[4]

In this commentary, *The Birth of the Messiah* (first published in 1977, updated 1993),[5] Brown analysed the texts from Matthew and Luke, and found a way of explaining the origin and creation of most of the narrative. Because of this work, Brown was criticized as a liberal; his approach is a long way from the traditional view that Luke used the reminiscences of Mary in his Gospel.[6] Yet, because he refused to rule out the possibility that the virgin birth was historical fact, he also attracted the charge that he was too accepting of Roman Catholic orthodoxy. He was unable to find a clear-cut explanation for the emergence of the virgin birth tradition that would contradict its historicity.

---

4. Brown 1993: 498–9.
5. For an influential analysis of Mary in the New Testament written before Brown's work referred to here, see McHugh 1975.
6. For example, Graef 1985: 1:6, drawing upon Laurentin 1957.

On purely exegetical grounds I came to the conclusion that the *scientifically controllable* biblical evidence leaves the question of the historicity of the virginal conception unresolved; yet there was better evidence for historicity than against. But as I noted, since this issue has repercussions for faith in Christ, many go beyond the limited results of exegesis and affirm the historicity of the virginal conception on theological grounds.[7]

This position was repeated in another volume, *Mary in the New Testament* (1978), the results of an ecumenical research project between Roman Catholics, Lutherans and other Protestants. Brown was one of four editors. The book took seriously what much devotional writing about Mary had overlooked: the fact that Jesus appears to distance himself from her in all four Gospels, although less so in Luke. It came to an important conclusion that has been influential in material on Mary since: that Matthew, Mark and John seem to imply that Mary's awareness of Jesus' mission was not fully formed until the crucifixion.

> While John sets the Cana story (2.1–11) within the ministry of Jesus, we have entertained the hypothesis that he built upon a story dealing with the pre-ministry period, in which Mary appeared as one who believed in Jesus, at least in him as a wonder-worker. The story as redacted by the evangelist probably retains that belief (cf. 2.3), although for him it is clearly a misunderstanding of Jesus. Jesus dissociates himself from his mother, who does not realise that the work which the father has given him takes precedence over the claims and interests of his natural family (2.4). But Mary's misunderstanding does not rank her with unbelievers (unlike the case of Jesus' brothers – 7.5). She will appear again in the Gospel at the foot of the cross, where she becomes the mother of the beloved disciple, who for the evangelist is the supreme model of Christian faith… [Mary] now becomes the mother of the disciples *par excellence*, and so becomes herself a model of belief and discipleship.[8]

The work of Ben Witherington III echoes this conclusion. In his *Women in the Ministry of Jesus* (1984), he places Mary and the other women in their social context. The sociological understanding of the New Testament, along with the literary one, has been especially important since the early 1980s. Witherington, more than Brown *et al.*, plays down the notion that the New Testament justifies the high Mariology that has developed over the centuries.

> What is particularly striking is that all four Gospels to one degree or another indicate both that Jesus' mother failed at some point to completely understand or honour her Son … and that Jesus distanced Himself from her in the process of distinguishing His physical family from His spiritual one … The overall

---

7. Brown 1993: 698.
8. Brown *et al.* 1978: 287–9.

impression left by the material in the Gospels about Mary is that no Evangelist made a concerted effort to give Mary more significance than she actually had in the ministry of Jesus; that no Evangelist attempted to paint a purely idealized portrait of her; and that no Evangelist attempted to portray a strictly Christian (i.e. non-Jewish) picture of Jesus' mother.[9]

Brown *et al.* and Witherington agree that Mary's post-resurrection discipleship was remembered in the early Church and may have influenced the portrait of her in the infancy narratives in Luke, but that the evidence for her fully matured belief in Jesus during the ministry is lacking. In this view, Jesus does not want to be tied to his natural family, but will only accept them in so far as they join other disciples in their assent to his true meaning and purpose.

> Mary learns that she is to be a mother as a disciple, not a mother and also a disciple. Discipleship must be the larger context in which her role as mother is delimited and defined. Mary responds in silence and submission. She obeys the word of the Lord and goes with the beloved disciple. In doing so she is the model woman – a testimony to a woman's new freedom in faith and also to a woman's traditional roles of serving under the authority and headship of man.[10]

This view of Mary corresponds to Witherington's social-historical reconstruction overall, in which he argues that the role and place of women in first-century Israel/Palestine was heavily circumscribed. Although women enjoyed a measure of equality in the early Christian movement, 'Jesus was attempting to reform, not reject, the patriarchal framework of His culture.'[11]

Meanwhile, the conclusion of Roman Catholic writers such as Brown and his co-writer Joseph Fitzmyer – that Mary's New Testament role derives more specifically from her status as disciple rather than as Jesus' mother – is consonant with the post-Vatican II understanding of Mary.[12] In this, she is situated more in a theology of Church, as prototype of all believers, and less as an exalted partner of Christ in the work of redemption, where her position as his mother is at the heart of her privileges (these are termed the *ecclesiotypical* and *christotypical* tendencies of Mariology, respectively). To say that the New Testament Mary is predominantly the first disciple corresponds with the first, and recently more popular, of these approaches (one which parallels a playing down of the Marian cult in the Catholic Church[13]). It becomes problematic in that the work of scholars like Brown *et al.* and Witherington may be taken even further and result in her not being the 'first disciple' at all. She fits this description only in the birth narratives in Luke, the historicity of which is in doubt.

---

9.   Witherington 1984: 99–100.
10.   Ibid.: 95.
11.   Ibid.: 129.
12.   The Second Vatican Council document on Mary is *Lumen Gentium* ('Dogmatic Constitution on the Church'), ch. 8. The text is given in Flannery 1996: 80–95.
13.   For a discussion of this issue, see Spretnak 2004.

Our contention, then, is that the Lucan annunciation message is a reflection of the christological language and formulas of the post-resurrection church … Now this Christology has been carried back to Jesus at the very moment of conception in his mother's womb … hence one ought not to assume that Mary had explicit knowledge of Jesus as 'the Son of God' during his lifetime. As we shall see, like other followers of Jesus, the Lucan Mary became part of the great eschatological family of Jesus … through obedient response to God's word and will (Luke 8.21). Presumably after the resurrection (see Acts 1.14) she came to vocalise her faith in Jesus in the christological language we have been discussing.[14]

So Brown *et al.* and Witherington stress the lateness of Mary's faith: 'it should be emphasised that this (the beloved) disciple's faith and his role as representative disciple, antedate Mary's role as spiritual mother'.[15]

This conclusion leads to a minimalization of the importance of Mary in the New Testament. It posits that she came to be a disciple at a late point in the ministry, and so the portrait of her as the believing 'handmaid of the Lord' is derived from a later memory; in reality, other disciples understood the mission of Jesus before she did. This minimalist view of Mary in the Gospels goes hand in hand with a diminution of her cultic status.

However, there are two prominent strands of critical thought that run counter to this tendency. These perspectives are less confident that the Gospel stories are true to the real situation in pre-Gospel Christianity going back to the ministry of Jesus. One asserts that the family of Jesus was probably more important than seems to be the case in the Gospels. Thus James, the brother of Jesus, has been the subject of several studies in recent years, and the picture of him that emerges may help in an historical reconstruction of the importance of Mary in the early Church. The second is the feminist view that women may have been more prominent in the development of pre-Gospel Christianity than the New Testament itself indicates. In both cases, the scholars concerned find many clues in the New Testament that might help to uncover the history behind the texts.

James and the Family of Jesus

Recent studies of the family of Jesus have shown how important James 'the brother of the Lord' was in the early Church.[16] They show how he could be regarded as the first 'pope' of the Church (an anachronism, but it makes the point). James does not appear much in the Gospels, and the general view in them is that the brothers of Jesus, even more than Mary, were dissociated from his mission. Despite this, however, James was a recipient of one of the founding resurrection appearances of Jesus (1 Cor. 15.7), the leader of the early Jerusalem Church (Galations 1–2; Acts 15), and very prominent as a Jewish Christian in Jerusalem. This is attested in non-

---

14. Brown *et al.* 1978: 118–19.
15. Witherington 1984: 96.
16. For example: Bauckham 1990; Bernheim 1997; Chilton and Neusner 2001.

biblical literature (Josephus; Clement of Alexandria; Eusebius, quoting Hegesippus; Jerome),[17] and the *Gospel of Thomas* describes James as Jesus' successor (12.1–2). It is difficult to imagine James evolving from outright disbeliever (Mk 3.21, 31–5; Jn 7.5) to the first Christian leader. Other members of Jesus' family were important in the early Church, and their lineage as descendants of David was influential for many years.

One plausible solution to this dilemma is that the Gospels, for some reason, play down the importance of James and other members of the family of Jesus in the early Church, and overemphasize – or even invent - their outsider status in the ministry. The possible reasons for this that have been suggested include:[18]

(a)   The Hellenistic Jewish and Gentile Christianity of Paul and his followers was antithetical to the Jewish orthodoxy of James (a Jewish zealot, according to one theory). This is attested in Galatians 2, and framed the writing of most of the New Testament, correspondingly belittling James's role in the gospel story of Jesus.

(b)   Furthermore, there may have been resistance on the part of the gospel communities to the Jerusalem Church's assertion of authority over the other Christian churches of the Empire.

(c)   The Gospels were written after James's death, and were written in communities that were more likely to remember Peter, as leader of the missionary movement (or, in the case of John, the 'beloved disciple', who has precedence over both).

(d)   The Gospel writers wanted to encourage Christians who were being ostracized by their families, and painted a picture of Jesus who had to wrestle with the same experience.

So any theory that sheds doubt on Mary's importance in early Christian tradition because of the gospel story has to account for this tendency of the Gospels to play down the importance of Jesus' family.

What is the relationship between James and Mary? Tradition gives us three alternative answers, named after their most influential supporters in the fourth and fifth centuries.[19] In the *Helvidian* view, Mary is James's natural mother, as Jesus is the firstborn of other children (listed in Mk 6.3). Those arguing for this alternative will suggest that this is the plainest reading of the text, and that any other theory is influenced by a later concern to proclaim the perpetual virginity of Mary. In the *Epiphanian* view (first stated in the second-century *Protevangelium*), Mary is James's stepmother, as he is a son of the widower Joseph by a previous marriage. In the

17.   Josephus, *Jewish Antiquities* 18; Clement of Alexandria, *Hypotypotes*; Jerome, *De Viris Illustribus* (all referred to in Bernheim 1997: 1–9); Eusebius 1965: *History*, 2.1 (72); 2.23 (99–103); 3.7 (118); 7.19 (302).
18.   These possibilities are amongst those explored in the sources cited in n. 16. For a more radical Jewish perspective on Jesus and James as zealots, see Eisenman 2002, who chooses to write from outside the academic community.
19.   For overviews, see Bernheim 1997: 11–29; Chilton and Neusner 2001: 2–23.

Hieronymian view (named after its author Jerome), Mary is James's aunt, and James and Jesus are cousins. This theory, which has several variants, was written to refute the Helvidian view and its corollary: that Mary did not remain a virgin. It became the traditional understanding in the Roman Catholic tradition, but is not popular among biblical scholars now, most of whom are content with the Helvidian, or occasionally the Epiphanian, answer.

Whichever of these viewpoints is chosen, it is reasonable to suppose that Mary's status in the early Church would have been associated with that of James, her son, stepson or nephew. She is mentioned as being present with the brothers of Jesus in all the Gospels and the Acts. If James were important to the early pre-Gospel Church (as its first leader), then she would likewise have been held in high regard.

The debate between the Helvidian, Epiphanian and Hieronymian viewpoints has led to attempts to explain the relationship between Mary the mother of Jesus and two other Marys: 'Mary mother of James the Less and Joses' and 'Mary of Clopas' in John 19.25 (the Greek wording 'of James' or 'of Clopas' could mean that the Mary in question is either the mother, wife or daughter of the named male person, which creates another ambiguity). The possibilities are as follows:[20]

(a) all three Marys are different people;
(b) 'Mary of James and Joses' is the same person as 'Mary of Clopas', but not Mary the mother of Jesus;
(c) all three names are different ways of describing the same person, Mary the mother of Jesus.

Option (b) is the more traditional view. It was suggested by Jerome, drawing on Hegesippus's testimony, in which Clopas was identified as Joseph's brother (presumably Mary, understood to be the wife of Clopas and described as Jesus' mother's sister in John 19.25, was thought more likely to have been her sister-in-law, because both were called Mary). Thus James and Joses are sons of Clopas and this other Mary, and cousins of Jesus. In this view, they are the same people as the James and Joses mentioned in Mark 6.3 as Jesus' brothers. To accept this answer, one would have to believe that the cousins were referred to as brothers, because of the closeness of the family. The problem here is the ubiquity of the description of the relationship between James and Jesus as 'brothers', when a common Greek word for 'cousin' was available.

Another explanation as to why the Mary 'of James' in Mark and Luke might have been described as Mary 'of Clopas' in John, as in option (b), could derive from the leadership succession in Jerusalem. Hegesippus relates how Symeon the son of Clopas was appointed bishop after the execution of James.[21] The traditions utilized by John, in which Mary was associated with the Jerusalem leader James, could have

---

20. For a discussion, see Brown *et al.* 1978: 68–72; Bauckham 2002: 203–53; the identification of the mother of James and Joses with the mother of Jesus does have early Church precedents, see Bauckham 2002: 253; option (c) is also endorsed by Eisenman 2002: 770–1.
21. Eusebius 1965: 3.11 (123–4); 3.32 (142–3); 4.21 (181–2).

been edited to establish the credentials of the new bishop Symeon as an apostle through his father Clopas (the father would have been more contemporary than the son with the events of Jesus' death). Clopas's name was therefore, perhaps, inserted into the Passion tradition in the place of James. Note that in Luke, also written during the period when Symeon would have been the leader in Jerusalem, a 'Cleopas' is named in the Emmaus resurrection narrative, at 24.18; he is not mentioned in Mark or Matthew. It is strange how scholars are quick to explain many Gospel passages in terms of later Church concerns, not regarding them as describing the historical ministry of Jesus, but do not see this as a possible answer when it comes to names like Clopas, which are usually regarded as belonging to an early stratum of tradition.

This could be regarded as tangential to our understanding of Mary's role. But if option (c) is possible, i.e. the Marys are all the same person, then it opens up a new dimension. Each Gospel would then identify, in a different manner, Mary the mother of Jesus as present at the crucifixion with Mary Magdalene. The differentiation of the three Marys could have occurred through the attempts to minimize the importance of James and his relationship to the Passion and resurrection tradition. If Mary 'mother of James and Joses', then 'of Clopas', is also Mary 'mother of Jesus', this would establish the importance of Mary to the pre-Gospel tradition of the Passion. It would mean that three important elements were brought together in early Christian tradition, and presumably, therefore, also in its liturgies of the Passion: the crucifixion and empty tomb; the leadership of the Church by James and then Symeon; and Mary as mother of the messianic family. The naming of the women is no accident, but points to the centrality of their status in the earliest memories of the Passion. The association of Mary, James (and other members of Jesus' family) and the crucifixion and resurrection would have presented a grave difficulty for those who wished to minimize the role of the family of Jesus. Any rewriting would therefore have played it down.

To conclude, the idea that Jesus initially distanced himself from Mary, or that her discipleship evolved only slowly, as emphasized in writers such as Brown *et al.* and Witherington, is rendered more doubtful as a true reflection of the earlier tradition by recent scholarly research on James. Perhaps the image of Mary, too, was affected by the trend of downplaying the family of Jesus, but in her case this was then reversed in Luke and John, perhaps because of their use of alternative traditions. This was sufficient to inspire many later writings and theological speculations about her. So the problem of James's prime position in a Church whose Gospels hardly remembered him is also an issue in the case of Mary, another member of the family of Jesus whose role in the Gospels is ambiguous.

The Status and Experience of Women in the Early Church

We saw above that, while Witherington accepted the radical nature of Jesus' movement in its greater freedom for women, he argued that it still remained within patriarchal boundaries, and this has influenced his reading of Mary. However, feminist scholars have carried out research that radically alters the common understanding of early Christianity. The seminal work is Elisabeth Schüssler

Fiorenza's *In Memory of Her: a Feminist Reconstruction of Christian Origins* (1983).[22] Fiorenza argues that the New Testament tradition represents a step away from a discipleship of equality between women and men, which existed in the period before the texts came to be written. In her view, the texts belong to a time of normalization, of accommodation to the prevailing culture in which gender roles were hierarchical and demarcated. Despite this, there are texts in which one can glimpse the earlier egalitarian praxis of the community of Jesus and the very earliest Church. The ministry of Jesus indicates a 'charismatic' or 'liminal' phase, where the ordinary structures of society were turned upside down among his followers. However, this radical period of the Church eventually gave way to the growing respectability of the movement, and thus became more accommodating to the social order. This coincided with the phase of the writing of its traditions. Such an analysis would have an impact on a historical understanding of Mary, in so far as we would then posit a stronger and more public role for Mary than the texts themselves indicate, perhaps a type of leadership.

Elsewhere, Elizabeth A. Johnson investigates the place of first-century Jewish women from a feminist perspective:

> There is no doubt that first-century Judaism, in tune with the rest of the ancient world, had its patriarchal, androcentric mores and that many, even the majority of women, were legally disadvantaged and powerless ... The sources we do have make clear, however, that no homogenous definition will fit all groups. Like their non-Jewish sisters in the empire, Jewish women in the first century engaged in a broader range of activity than that suggested by a narrow patriarchal stereotype. In the turbulent years leading up to the first war with Rome, women in Palestine may well have had more than the usual opportunities to assume nontraditional roles. Certainly the data suggest that one can find models for the leadership positions held by women in the early church both in Jewish and non-Jewish communities ... Comparison should then be made not between Jesus and Judaism but between, on the one hand, the Jesus movement as one of several prophetic emancipatory movements in Judaism and, on the other, entrenched systems of domination in antiquity that crushed human beings.[23]

Johnson also finds a different reading for the apparent rejection of Mary by Jesus. The distance between them, as in Mark 3.31–5, can be understood from a woman's and a mother's point of view. Aware of the inevitable consequences of Jesus' mission, her resistance to violence caused her anxiety, and she wished to persuade Jesus to seek safety. Thus Johnson refutes the suggestion that Mary misunderstood Jesus, and denies that her faith in him can be put into question.

---

22. Fiorenza 1983: *passim*.
23. Johnson 2003: 189.

Full of concern for the one she loves, Miriam of Nazareth does not have the New Testament to help her interpret God's designs. Embarking on a mission that ultimately fails, she stands 'outside' with an anxious mind and heart, the frustrated, angry mother of Elisabeth Moltmann-Wendel's image, maladapted to the shedding of blood. We should be wary of judging this scene as evidence of lack of faith. The scholars of *Mary in the New Testament* rather sweepingly declare that the event behind this scene took place *before* 'the time at which Mary's belief began', by which they mean more precisely the post-resurrection understanding of Jesus that she shared with the Jerusalem community. While this may be true in a Christian sense, her faith in God did not begin only after Easter, as witnessed by this scene, where her faith is at full pitch. Believing in God, Creator and Redeemer of the world, this Jewish woman partners the divine work of love by seeking to preserve and protect a precious life. No submissive handmaid, her memory moves in solidarity with women everywhere who act critically according to their best lights to seek the well-being of those they love.[24]

The *Feminist Companions* to the books of the Bible likewise seek out the story of the women in and behind the texts. Adele Reinhartz follows a line of research into John that posits women's leadership in the Johannine community (some, from Fiorenza onwards, have suggested female authorship of Johannine traditions). This is because of the strong and positive portraits of women in John, which seem to break with the patriarchal norms of the culture (one dissenter from this view is Adeline Fehribach – see below). For Reinhartz, the figure of the mother of Jesus in John represents the older women in the Johannine community.

> Within the Johannine story, Jesus' mother emerges as a figure of prophetic knowledge and authority. Her authority with respect to Jesus is expressed in her knowledge of him and her confidence in his abilities . . . If we transpose this picture to the story of a community, the mother emerges as a woman at its core. She is not necessarily a unique figure, but rather may signal the presence or prominence of elder wise women in the community. She has prophetic powers that stem from a profound knowledge of and faith in Jesus. She exercises leadership insofar as she teaches the importance of obedience and thereby facilitates the sort of events that will strengthen the faith of those who participate in and witness them . . . The suggestion that the mother of Jesus represents elder wise women in the community is supported by her anonymity in the two passages in which she appears. That the mother remains anonymous is often overlooked by readers who freely supply the name 'Mary' based on the gospels of Matthew and Luke. David Beck has argued that from a literary point of view the anonymity of this woman, as well as of other significant characters in the gospel, facilitates the readers' identification with these figures and thereby invites readers to place themselves within the narrative.[25]

---

24. Ibid.: 221.
25. Reinhartz 2003: 19–21. John is regarded here as originating in a community that valued the high status of women. Schneiders 1999 develops a theory of female authorship.

Therefore, the texts about Mary may point to women in the communities that wrote the Gospels, rather than telling us something about the history of the individual who was the mother of Jesus. In addressing Luke in another *Feminist Companion*, Turid Karlsen Seim posits an ascetic strain in the community due to its apocalyptic expectation (as also expressed by Paul in 1 Corinthians). The virginity of Mary has therefore a representative value in this case, too. In this excerpt, she reflects on the way in which Mary's motherhood is related to the 'hearing of the Word and doing it' in Luke:

> As Mary's prototypical role is converted from that of a mother with conventional rights to a motherhood constituted exclusively by the fruitful reception of the word of God, her role ceases to be limited to her; it becomes a possibility for all women who hear God's word and do it. Motherhood is dissociated from actual birth and the sexual role of women in reproduction. But at the same time, the reproductive role is metaphorically exploited as God is cast as the male agent who sows the seed of the word in the soil of her heart. The ascetic women bear the fruit of God's word implanted in them, and a scenario of ascetic discipleship framed as alternative and, in the end, spiritual motherhood is introduced.[26]

Research into the place of women in early Christianity has to take into account the circumstances of the time and place, including the fact of Roman military occupation. It is not possible to construct a portrait of Mary without recognizing the harsh realities of this and the consequences for women. Jane Schaberg's research in *The Illegitimacy of Jesus* (1987), another example of seeking a historical reality 'behind the text', is very controversial in this respect.[27] She picks up on the ancient Jewish claim that Mary's pregnancy with Jesus was not the result of a virginal conception, but rather came about through intercourse, perhaps due to rape by a Roman soldier. Where most Christian commentators have seen this as a slur by a rival religion, Schaberg takes it more seriously. She locates the tradition that the conception was illegitimate in the texts of Matthew and Luke themselves, using alternative but plausible translations and interpretations of the key texts. Mary's heroism consisted in believing God's promise that, from the 'lowliness' of her condition (i.e. a pregnancy forced on her by violence), something great would come. Her acceptance of this parallels Jesus' acceptance of the cup of sacrifice in Gethsemane. For Schaberg, only after the writing of the New Testament texts did Christians develop the doctrine that the conception was miraculous and that Mary as *parthenos* was a virgin in the biological sense, and not simply a young woman coming into puberty and not yet married.

Schaberg's feminist method is strictly biblical critical, but it has implications for an understanding of Mary. Mary suffers from injustice alongside the women of her day, just as Jesus also accepts defeat and suffering, thus aligning himself with the human

---

26. Seim 2002: 105.
27. The thesis was also repeated in Spong 1992 and Lüdemann 1998.

condition. Furthermore, the understanding of Mary as virgin mother is seen by feminists to distance her from ordinary women, but with the illegitimate conception idea this disappears: Mary experiences the things that are undergone by many women.

> The reading I have offered of the narratives as incorporating the tradition of the illegitimacy of Jesus supports and makes more precise the claim that Mary represents the oppressed who have been liberated; she becomes a symbol 'whose power is a power of access to reality'. In this case there is a subversion of the patriarchal family structures: the child conceived illegitimately is seen to have value – transcendent value – in and of himself, not in his attachment and that of his mother to a biological or legal father. Mary is a woman who has access to the sacred outside the patriarchal family and its control. The illegitimate conception turns out to be grace not disgrace, order within disorder. On the basis of belief in the Holy Spirit who empowers the conception of Jesus and his resurrection, and who creates and elects all, a community is believed possible.[28]

Schaberg's radical thesis has caused indignation and controversy. Even in feminist circles, it has not received acceptance; while many appreciate the method and purpose of her work, it is difficult for them to see how the writers of Matthew and Luke could, as Schaberg claims, have intended to convey anything other than virginal conception in the usual sense.[29] Schaberg is unlike other liberal critics in that she has taken the historicity of the conception narratives seriously, whereas most would see them as constructions based on myth and theological meaning of virtually no historical value.

However, writers like Johnson and Schaberg are together in following Fiorenza's lead in investigating the history behind the Gospel texts using a feminist biblical method, and they do this with a particular focus upon Mary. These works, in different ways, reconstruct the *status* of women in radical movements such as that of Jesus, and also the *experience* of women in difficult social circumstances. Once again, the Gospel texts are not regarded as giving us the whole story of the history of Christian origins. As in the case of James, the scholars attempt to give us a glimpse into the situation that existed before the Gospels were written, and the Gospel texts are expanded upon and, in some instances, put in doubt.

To conclude, these kinds of reconstructions have consequences for Mary as a figure in the early Church. These include the following possibilities.

- Her place was integrally linked to the Jewish–Christian leadership in Jerusalem based upon Jesus' family, in particular his brother James.
- Her place in the crucifixion scene may have been an important one, associated with the leadership, liturgy and memory of the Passion.

---

28.   Schaberg 1995: 199.
29.   See Johnson 2003: 229.

- Her representative role in the community may have been quite different from that expected in the patriarchal culture, i.e. one of leadership, or as an ascetic.
- Her experience as a woman in a territory occupied by a foreign military power will have been a harsh one, and cannot be idealized.

However, other work stems from a concern to deal with the texts as they appear in the form that we read them in the final canon of the New Testament, and how they have inspired reflection, doctrine and Christian life.

(4) THE LITERARY APPROACH

The literary approach is a more recent development than the historical one.[30] In applying literary theory to biblical texts, the critic is interested in the development of the narrative and its characters, the intended audience ('the implied reader') and the way in which the text may imply its authorship ('the implied author'). The implied reader and author can be deduced from the text in a way that the actual reader and author cannot. The implied reader in general terms is a first-century believer or enquirer who wished to know more about the identity of Jesus and the meaning of his ministry, death and resurrection, and how to live in the light of the faith that ensued. Many of the characters thus function as role models (all personalities in the text are characters, including God and the narrator). The implied author is someone who is already a believer and who has been the recipient of authoritative and reliable information about Jesus.

Beverly Roberts Gaventa, in *Mary: Glimpses of the Mother of Jesus* (1995), introduces the subject with the subheadings we have employed here: historical, theological, literary.[31] However, her work is original in that it develops the last of these approaches in relation to Mary, a task that had not been undertaken comprehensively before. For Gaventa, the connection between the varying portraits of Mary in the different Gospels is 'the scandal of the gospel'. In Matthew, this is shown in the association of Mary with the various subversive women in the genealogy. In Luke, Mary herself struggles to understand the challenge of Jesus, from the manner of his conception to the way in which he seems to reject his family at the age of 12. In John, she is present at the beginning of the ministry at Cana, and provokes a difficult exchange, and then also at the greatest scandal of all, the cross. Gaventa feels that the other major text featuring Mary, the *Protevangelium*, is different because it 'associates Mary with scandal, but it does so only to show, and with relentless insistence, that the scandal is a vicious lie'.[32]

So Gaventa concludes with three aspects of the Mary portrayed in the Gospel texts. She is 'vulnerable' (without being a helpless victim); she 'reflects on events', taking an active part as in the *Magnificat*; she is 'among the witnesses of Jesus'.

---

30. The seminal work is probably Alter 1981.
31. Gaventa 1999: 128–9.
32. Ibid.: 129.

What we do have in these glimpses of Mary are some important aspects of what it means to be a disciple of Christ: living with vulnerability, reflecting with care on the advent of Jesus Christ, and witnessing God's actions in the world. In that sense, Mary remains a model for all Christians.[33]

In the excerpt here, we reproduce Gaventa's summary of the picture of Mary in the different texts.

We began with the Gospel of Matthew, where Mary speaks not so much as a single word and is never addressed. She follows in the tradition of the other women in the genealogy, women who were perceived to threaten the Davidic line and who were threatened in return. Because he can only understand her pregnancy as a compromise of his righteousness, Joseph contemplates a divorce that would have grave consequences both for Mary and for her yet-unborn child. Herod sees in the infant Jesus a threat to his own power and therefore acts in a way that threatens both Jesus and his mother. Mary is confined to the role of mother, but in that role introduces an important dynamic in the Matthean Gospel.

In Luke-Acts, Mary plays a more extensive and complex set of roles (disciple, prophet, and mother) than in Matthew. Here she enters the story as a young unmarried woman selected by God to become the mother of Jesus. She consents to this responsibility with the words of a disciple, 'Let it be to me according to your word.' The story has only begun, however. With the triumphant lines of the Magnificat, Mary takes on the role of a prophet, anticipating leading themes in Luke's Gospel. During the events surrounding Jesus' birth, Luke draws attention to her reflection, anguish, and misunderstanding and anticipates the grief she will suffer at Jesus' death. Luke also insinuates here at the beginning some doubt about whether Mary will continue to be a disciple, a question that is resolved only when she appears in the company surrounding the apostles in Acts 1.

John introduces the mother of Jesus in two brief scenes. First, at the wedding at Cana, she announces to Jesus that the wine has run out, setting the stage for the startling miracle in which Jesus produces a large quantity of wine from water. Second, at the cross, she appears with other women and with the Beloved Disciple, whom Jesus declares to be her son and her to be his mother. These two scenes are connected to the evangelist's statement in 1.14 that the Word became flesh; that is, the mother's presence at Cana underscores the fact that Jesus is a real human being with a mother as well as a human father and brothers (1.45, 2.12). At the cross, when Jesus hands the Beloved Disciple to his mother and her to the Beloved Disciple, he surrenders these earthly relations.

By contrast with the minimal appearance of the mother of Jesus in the

---

33. Ibid.: 131.

Gospel of John, Mary occupies center stage throughout most of the Protevangelium. The author shows an interest in biographical details regarding Mary, particularly in those details that reinforce the sacred purity of Mary. In this narrative Mary herself is born as a result of divine intervention. Even in her infancy she is shielded from any impurity. She grows up living within the temple itself. The onset of puberty prompts a threat to the temple's purity and to Mary's own purity that is resolved when Joseph is selected, again by divine intervention, to be her husband. Her pregnancy prompts a more serious threat to her purity, and three times the story provides assurance that Mary's purity has not been violated. Even the birth of Jesus does not bring an end to Mary's sacred purity.[34]

In contrast to other feminist writers who see John as reflecting a positive view of women for its time, Adeline Fehribach's *The Women in the Life of the Bridegroom: a Feminist Historical-Literary Analysis of the Female Characters in the Fourth Gospel* (1998) does not.[35] Fehribach's thesis is that the core of John relates to Jesus' status as the heavenly Bridegroom; thus the women characters exist merely to heighten this image. For many other commentators, the mother of Jesus, the Samaritan woman, Mary and Martha and Mary Magdalene are regarded as strong portraits of women, and as indicative of the egalitarian community in which John was written and handed down; but for Fehribach this is not the case. Nevertheless, she concludes by stating that the reader of today can and should interpret the texts in more positive ways for women – her point is that researching the original intention of the text does not lend support to such interpretations. She understands the Cana text in the following way:

> The implied author of the Fourth Gospel characterizes the mother of Jesus at Cana along the lines of 'the mother of an important son' character-type from the Hebrew Bible. As such, she is assertive and her words and actions precipitate her son's fulfilling his destiny with regard to the promise God made to Abraham. Jesus meets his destiny by eventually responding to his mother's insistence that he do something about the lack of wine. The manner in which he provides the wine (i.e., providing quality wine in abundance by changing the water from purification jars into wine) would have been perceived by a first-century reader familiar with the Hebrew Bible as a sign that Jesus was accepting the role of messianic bridegroom, the one who would provide blessings in abundance. In this way, Jesus is portrayed as the representative of his heavenly Father, the bridegroom of Israel.
>
> Although the implied author constructs the character of the mother of Jesus along the lines of a 'mother of an important son', a first-century reader would have perceived the mother of Jesus as misunderstanding her son's importance. She approaches the need for wine as a means for her son to heighten his honor,

---

34. Ibid.: 126–7.
35. See also n. 25 above.

and thus her honor (a 'below' point of view). When Jesus responds with the words, 'Woman, what concern is that to you and me? My hour has not yet come' (2.4), a first time reader would not have understood that Jesus was raising the discussion to a higher level. Such a reader would have perceived the mother of Jesus as thinking Jesus' words meant, 'Woman, what concern is that to you and me? It's not my wedding.' Jesus' response would thus have been perceived as a rejection of the notion that he increase his earthly honor by providing wine for the bridegroom. Thus, a first-century reader, who was reading the Gospel for the first time, would have initially perceived the mother of Jesus as a non-believer who is simply not aware of her son's importance.

The character-type of the 'mother of an important son' from the Hebrew Bible is patriarchal because the mother is only important to the extent that she furthers the role of her son.[36]

The reading of John 2.1–11 as patriarchal is extended to other scenes from the Gospel, including the crucifixion at 19.25–7:

The characterization of the mother of Jesus at the cross supports the portrayal of Jesus as the messianic bridegroom. By having Jesus deemphasize his own matrilineal descent (calling his mother 'woman') and then deemphasize the beloved disciple's matrilineal descent (giving him a mother who was not his biological mother), the implied author used the characterization of the mother of Jesus to support the interpretation of Jesus' death as a blood sacrifice that establishes a patrilineal kinship group. By having Jesus give his mother to the beloved disciple, the implied author adapted the 'dying king' type-scene in such a way that the characterization of the mother of Jesus supports the concept of Jesus' establishing familial bonds with all those the beloved disciple represents. The use of such patriarchal type-scenes as the 'blood sacrifice' type-scene and the 'dying king' type-scene results in a very passive portrayal of the mother of Jesus at the cross, which is unlike her assertive portrayal at Cana. The two portrayals have the same purpose, however, that of helping to portray Jesus as the messianic bridegroom who has come to establish the family of God.[37]

Note here how the literary approach, in its interest in the implied reader, will turn to other ancient literature, including dramatic writing, to reconstruct the presuppositions that first-century readers might have brought to the text. Widely distributed literature and well-known drama would prepare them for particular motifs, scenes and narrative development.

Using this approach, Charles H. Talbert understands the virginal conception narrative as a construction meant to fulfil a particular theological purpose. He

---

36. Fehribach 1998: 42.
37. Ibid.: 142.

compares this motif, with its human mother and divine father, with four other mythological options drawn from ancient literature (human father and mother; no father and mother; divine father and mother; divine mother and human father).

> The option that regards origin in terms of a divine father and human mother apparently fits Luke's expectations on all counts. After all, this is the option he chose. Theologically, God is other than the world but acts directly in the world. Christologically, the one so produced shares in both divine and human spheres. Soteriologically, such a life is due to human submission to the divine will. Of the options available for speaking about Jesus' origins in order to explain how such a life was possible, Option Five functions best as a vehicle for Luke's Christian convictions. It is, then, no surprise that the Third Gospel tells the story of Jesus' birth in just the way that it does. The God who is other than the world intervenes in the world to create one who is both divine and human and whose birth models the means of salvation for all people: submission to the divine will. In only one area does the Lukan infancy narrative deviate from some of the Greco-Roman traditions that speak of an individual's being the offspring of a divine father and a human mother. Under no circumstances would Luke think of the conception of Jesus as occurring by means of sexual contact between God and the woman. Like Plutarch, Luke speaks in a way that has the conception take place by means of Spirit (Plutarch, *Is. Os.* 36). Mary asks: 'How shall this be, since I have no husband?' The angel says: 'The Holy Spirit will come upon you, And the power of the Most High will overshadow you' (Luke 1.34–35, RSV). The God who in Jewish tradition was transsexual remains so in the Christian story of Jesus' origins in the Lukan Gospel. A narrative told in terms of Option Five with the safeguards built in to avoid any inference about sexual contact between deity and woman would be heard by ancient auditors in a way that was consonant with the expectations of the Third Evangelist.[38]

Mark Coleridge, in *The Birth of the Lukan Narrative* (1993), finds Mary's characterization in Luke a model of faith. She is contrasted in Luke 1 with John the Baptist's father, Zechariah, in this respect. Coleridge's reading of the narrative supports a strong reading of Mary:

> Mary is unique among the characters for a number of reasons. For one thing, she is privileged over all other human characters in what she knows. She knows more of the identity of her son; yet strangely this becomes a problem, since it aggravates the sense of incoherence between his identity and the circumstances of his appearance. For Mary, then, unique privilege means unique pondering...
>
> In her initial act of faith in the promise and in her grappling with the signs of

---

38. Talbert 2003: 87–8.

fulfilment, Mary is the character in whom the narrator provides an answer to the question insinuated in the first episode: what does Abrahamic faith look like now? The question was discreetly put and the answer is discreetly given. Rather than tell the readers what the answer might be, the narrator prefers to show Abrahamic faith in Mary, and to do so not quickly but step by step in a process which begins in 1.26–38 and which remains unfinished even at the end of the infancy narrative.

Throughout the infancy narrative, Mary is cast in a receiving mode. Others take the initiative and she responds: Gabriel comes to her bearing the promise; an inspired Elizabeth speaks first in 1.39–56; the shepherds come with their announcement; Simeon and Anna do the same; and it is Jesus who takes the initiative in the final episode. It is also true that Mary is never responsible for the transmission of the news she receives: in that sense, she never proclaims. This might suggest that Mary is a wholly passive character; yet this is not so. From 1.26–38 until the end of the infancy narrative, there is in her a paradoxical interaction of the active and passive. Her activity is primarily at the point of epistemology, much of which is inward though no less active for that. This suggests that it is epistemology rather than mariology which provides the key for understanding how Mary functions in the narrative.[39]

In the literary approach, therefore, the scholar concentrates on the text and its implied readership. While historical approaches include the literary element, the literary approach tends to retain its tighter focus. In these examples, we have seen how the character of Mary, particularly in Luke and John, is situated in the text and, by implication, the context of the original readership. For Gaventa, Mary in Luke is a prophet, and Mary in John the guarantor of Christ's humanity; overall, she is a vulnerable yet active and reflective witness to the story of Jesus. Coleridge testifies to Mary in Luke being a model for a questioning and thoughtful faith. Fehribach sounds a feminist note of caution: the apparent strength of Mary in John can be misleading, as the female characters are there to supplement the image of Christ as Bridegroom, and their setting is wholly patriarchal. Talbert suggests that her virginal conception also serves a theological intention.

Overall, we can say that these and other readings of the Gospel texts do confirm the Christocentric nature of Mary's presence in them; she is there to tell us something about the Christian faith in the risen Jesus and his incarnation. However, she also acts as a strong role model of faith and reflection. These conclusions are not surprising, of course, and in both respects will accord with the way in which people have understood Mary through many centuries. The next section looks at how the figure of Mary as portrayed in the New Testament has been received in the faith community, to inform doctrine, prayer and action.

---

39. Coleridge 1993: 218–19.

(5) THEOLOGICAL APPROACHES

Theological approaches may draw upon historical or literary methods, but in this case, the main purpose is to ask: what does the text mean to the *present-day* community? Clearly, the New Testament texts about Mary have been the foundation for everything that is said about her in Mariological terms. So we start with the use of the New Testament in recent papal documents that discuss the role of Mary in Christian faith.

In *Marialis Cultus* (1974), Paul VI was eager to clarify the status of Marian devotion in the Roman Catholic Church in the wake of uncertainty and decline that had occurred after the Second Vatican Council. He emphasized the traditional association between Mary and the Church, and rooted this in the Gospel texts. This articulated the relationship between Mary and the Church's liturgy.

> Mary is *the attentive Virgin*, who receives the word of God with faith ... Mary is also *the Virgin in prayer*. She appears as such in the visit to [Elizabeth] ... Mary is also *the Virgin-Mother* – she who 'believing and obeying ... brought forth on earth the Father's son' (*Lumen Gentium*) ... Mary is, finally, *the Virgin presenting offerings*. In the episode of the Presentation of Jesus in the Temple (cf. Lk. 2.22–35), the Church, guided by the Spirit, has detected ... a mystery of salvation related to the history of salvation.[40]

He also addressed one of the reasons that some commentators gave for decline in Marian devotions: that the figure of Mary was an outmoded one, linked to notions of the role of women in society and the family, fast becoming obsolete. Therefore he identified Mary as an exemplar of faith, which could be linked to modern roles of women (the 'New Woman') and was not dependent on the social structures of any age in Christian history.

> First, the Virgin Mary has always been proposed to the faithful by the Church as an example to be imitated not precisely in the type of life she led, and much less for the socio-cultural background in which she lived and which today scarcely exists anywhere. She is held up as an example to the faithful rather for the way in which, in her own particular life, she fully and responsibly accepted the will of God (cf. Lk. 1.38), because she heard the word of God and acted on it and because charity and a spirit of service were the driving force of her actions. She is worthy of imitation because she was the first and most perfect of Christ's disciples. All of this has a permanent and universal exemplary value.[41]

John Paul II, in *Redemptoris Mater* (1987), was writing an encyclical letter that instituted a Marian Year (from Pentecost 1987). In establishing it, he was aware of

---

40. Paul VI 1974: paras 17–20 (31–5).
41. Ibid.: para. 35 (60–1).

the calls for an official celebration of the two-thousandth birthday of Mary, which would perhaps have been some 13 or so years before the birth of Christ. While John Paul II did not speculate on an appropriate date for this, he did link the Marian Year with the coming millennium, as Mary '*appeared* on the horizon of *salvation history before Christ*'.[42] He was also concerned to tie the Catholic Church in with celebrations of the thousandth-year anniversary of Christianity in Russia (1988), and emphasized the common ground in Marian devotion between Western and Eastern Churches. Finally, he wanted to relate the life story of Mary to the idea of the 'pilgrim people of God', i.e. Mary's pilgrimage is a forerunner and exemplar of the pilgrimage of the contemporary Church. Thus the whole encyclical is a meditation on the biblical texts concerning Mary.

> But above all, in the Church of that time and of every time Mary was and is the one who is 'blessed because she believed'; *she was the first to believe*. From the moment of the Annunciation and conception, from the moment of his birth in the stable at Bethlehem, Mary followed Jesus step by step in her maternal pilgrimage of faith. She followed him during the years of his hidden life at Nazareth; she followed him also during the time after he left home, when he began 'to do and to teach' (cf. Acts 1.1) in the midst of Israel. Above all she followed him in the tragic experience of Golgotha. Now, when Mary was with the Apostles in the upper room in Jerusalem at the dawn of the Church, *her faith, born from the words of the Annunciation, found confirmation*.[43]

More radical readings of Mary come from theologians who talk about the importance of the Bible in Christian communities of (a) the poor, and (b) women. Mary represents both groups. In Luke's *Magnificat* (1.46–55), she is the lowly servant who prophesies that the poor will be lifted up and the rich sent away empty; in Matthew and Luke, she is the woman under threat because of her pregnancy outside marriage. In John, she suffers the execution of her son.

For these reasons, Mary is important in the Roman Catholic liberation theology tradition. The Brazilians Ivone Gebara and Maria Clara Bingemer include a chapter on 'Mary in Scripture' in their *Mary, Mother of God, Mother of the Poor* (1987). The New Testament does not call Christians to reflect on other-worldly ideas or to promote resolutions of specific issues; rather, its whole directive is to the 'kingdom of God', a state of justice and love in human affairs, and one which we must strive to realize today.

> The New Testament, therefore, makes a theological re-reading of human-divine history. The sacred writers had no intention of copying models from Greco-Roman religion, which speak of gods marrying chosen women, nor of insisting on the superiority of the vow of virginity over marriage, nor of treating the problems faced by a Jewish single mother, nor of presenting the

---

42.   John Paul II 1987: para. 3 (7).
43.   Ibid.: para. 26 (58).

power of a woman who does not need the presence of a man in her life. All these interpretations, which have developed within different Christian communities at different periods, to some extent represent a turning away, albeit unconscious, from the theological and catechetical aim present in the New Testament texts.

What the New Testament strives to say is that God's gesture of love is repeated again in Mary and in Jesus, or in other words, is repeated in humankind as a new creation. For the sacred writers this is the great moment in human history, the moment when the human being is recreated, when it is love rather than the law that prevails, the moment when we touch the depths of the human mystery, mystery and dwelling-place of God. As the book of Genesis speaks of humankind's beginning, utilizing the mythical figures of Adam and Eve, the religious-symbolic expression of a people recognizing its origins in God, the Gospels speak of the beginning of a new humankind, built up from those who are most outcast from all nations.

This new humankind is no longer represented by mythical beings, but by historic beings who live concrete events, suffer the contingencies of specific economic, political, and social situations. Christianity accentuates and makes privileged the historic dimension present in Judaism, and goes further than Judaism in thinking about God's transcendence on the basis of the limited reality of human beings.[44]

From Sri Lanka, Tissa Balasuriya, in his controversial *Mary and Human Liberation* (1990), calls Mary 'a mature, adult woman'.[45] He wants to locate the figure of Mary in the story of her struggle in the Gospel texts, and not in subsequent Roman Catholic doctrine, which he regards as sexist and colonial. Balasuriya became entangled in a conflict with the Vatican, particularly because he denied the doctrine of original sin and used the story of Mary to support the cause for women's ordination.

> We can thus imagine the sort of woman Mary was in real life. It is this sort of woman who should be central to Christian spirituality. Mary belongs to the whole of humanity as a strong, dedicated woman and mother: one who was the closest associate of one of the greatest spiritual leaders of humanity. She was a mature, adult woman who was able to face life's problems along with Jesus. She was able to take up strong positions beside Jesus against all forms of exploitation. This portrayal of Mary is more faithful to the New Testament than the Mary of traditional Christian theology and spirituality.[46]

Elisabeth Schüssler Fiorenza likewise locates a radical image of Mary in the Gospel texts in her *Jesus, Miriam's Child, Sophia's Prophet* (1994). As in much feminist and liberation theology, the Mary of the New Testament is a role model just as she is in

---

44. Gebara and Bingemer 1989: 45–6.
45. Balasuriya 1997: 56–78.
46. Ibid.: 77.

more conservative circles, but with a different emphasis. The Mary described by Fiorenza is a realistic figure who inspires modern movements of liberation.

> The 'dangerous memory' of the young woman and teenage mother Miriam of Nazareth, probably not more than twelve or thirteen years old, pregnant, frightened, and single, who sought help from another woman, can subvert the tales of mariological fantasy and cultural femininity. In the center of the Christian story stands not the lovely 'white lady' of artistic and popular imagination, kneeling in adoration before her son. Rather it is the young pregnant woman, living in occupied territory and struggling against victimization and for survival and dignity. It is she who holds out the offer of untold possibilities for a different Christology and theology...
> ...feminist scholars in religion must firmly situate their theological discourses within the emancipatory movements of wo/men around the globe. Biblically based women's liberation movements have their historical roots in the liberation from slavery and oppression announced by Miriam, in the repentance preached by John, and in the *basileia* vision proclaimed by Jesus.[47]

The question as to how the events of the pregnancy of young Mary, or her visit to Elizabeth, came to be written into the Gospel texts is not the point here as it might be in the historical approaches. The texts in themselves have generated a whole system of theological thought, both conservative and radical.

The historical approach, which sheds doubt on the veracity of the Gospel stories, can threaten the symbolic power that these events contain. The critique of the texts from the theological point of view could also result in the unpacking of the symbol system that they represent; however, in many cases, it is not a rejection of the symbols, but instead their reinterpretation that constitutes the purpose of the work. Tina Beattie, in her *God's Mother, Eve's Advocate* (1999), explores the symbolism of the virginal conception of Jesus.

> Citing Nietzsche's work, *The Anti-Christ*, in which he refers to the 'Amphitryon story at the threshold of the Christian "faith",' [René] Girard argues, 'There is no more telling feature than the inability of the greatest minds in the modern world to grasp the difference between the Christian crib at Christmas-time and the bestial monstrosities of mythological birth.' Nor do theologians escape his criticism. Referring to Paul Tillich's dismissal of the virgin birth because of 'the inadequacy of its internal symbolism', he suggests, 'A great many modern theologians succumb to the terrorism of modern thought and condemn without a hearing something they are not capable of experiencing even as "poetry" any more – the final trace in the world of a spiritual intuition that is fading fast.'
> Girard's influence on Irigaray is clear in her reinterpretation of the Christian

---

47.   Fiorenza 1995: 187–9.

story in *Marine Lover of Friedrich Nietzsche*, in which she explores the possibilities of refiguring Marian symbolism around an ethic of peace and non-violence. She refers to 'the advent of a divine one who does not burst in violently, like the god of Greek desire. . .'. Inspired I think by Girard, she sees the possibility of interpreting the virgin birth as inaugurating a new relationship between the divine and women based not on the abusive violence of the gods of Greek mythology, but on the loving and fruitful encounter between Mary and the Spirit.

Girard's interpretation invites an understanding of the virginal conception of Christ as a response to the suffering that women experience in this world through the unholy alliance of sex, violence and power. It does not signal the end of sex, but the end of the association between sex and violence by which men exert their power over women, and by which sexual tyranny is perpetuated from generation to generation through family relationships and through the social order.[48]

The historical and literary approaches to the virginal conception often understand it in terms of its ancient Near Eastern context, in which biographical legend is common, and theological ideas rather than actual history are conveyed by it. The divergence between history and text that is thrown up by this kind of criticism was largely unknown before the eighteenth century. Many modern liberal Christians, of course, are able to hold in creative tension the belief that a text does not convey history, but is yet important symbolically. Nevertheless, this requires some theological sophistication, and it is understandable that many others suggest that historical criticism may damage or destroy the symbolic value of the text.

The image of Mary in the New Testament is a strong enough one for her to be the object of theological reflection in her own right; while this will always have a Christological reference, this does not necessarily mean that Mary serves only to tell the reader something about Jesus. Mariology with a biblical base is a worthwhile undertaking. As the prominent woman in the New Testament story, she has been considered to be the major female role model in the texts, and this requires critique and debate. Feminists have serious reservations about the consequences of Mary functioning in this way. If there is to be a female role model in the Gospels at all (and many would argue preferably not), then Mary the mother of Jesus need not be the only one; Mary Jo Weaver suggests that a 'garland of Marys', namely all the Marys of the New Testament, would give modern women a more varied set of images with which to work.[49]

Mary continues to inspire many contemporary Christians, both conservative and radical, and her New Testament presence will continue to be the source of discussion, debate and disagreement. The energy of a symbolic figure such as Mary can be judged from the amount of controversy that it causes; in this respect, we may conclude that the biblical Mary is still a dynamic force in contemporary Christianity.

---

48. Beattie 2002: 134–5.
49. Weaver 1985: 201–11.

(6) MARY IN THE APOCRYPHA

The apocryphal literature is extensive; here we will consider the most influential sources in which Mary is present. The name 'Mary' features a great deal in non-canonical literature that expands on the Gospel story. In some cases, this is not qualified by a description of which Mary is meant, but from the context it is fairly clear that the person implied is Mary Magdalene, rather than the mother of Jesus. Examples of the importance of Mary Magdalene in the Gnostic literature include (these probably originating in the second century): *The Gospel of Thomas*,[50] *The Dialogue of the Saviour*,[51] and *The Gospel of Mary*.[52] Mary Magdalene is also the prominent dialogue partner with Jesus in the *Pistis Sophia* (fourth century),[53] although Mary the mother of Jesus is also included in the cast of male and female disciples who speak with him (see below).

By far the most influential text on Mary in the Apocrypha is the above-mentioned *Protevangelium of James*, probably originating in the middle of the second century.[54] In it Mary is a central figure, and her holiness and virginity are major themes. The text is the first source in which we are told the names of Mary's parents: Anna and Joachim. Anna, like biblical characters before her, is barren, and this causes her and her husband some pain and embarrassment. However, after a visit from an angel, she finds she is pregnant. Mary is born, and her mother keeps her from the defilement of the world until she is two ('and so she turned her bedroom into a sanctuary, and did not permit anything profane or unclean to pass the child's lips'), in the company of 'the undefiled daughters of the Hebrews'. Then she is taken to live in the Temple. The text tells how 'she danced, and the whole house of Israel loved her'; she is fed by an angel.

At twelve years old, Mary has to leave the Temple to avoid the taboo of pollution due to menstrual blood. By the miraculous means of a dove emerging from his staff, Joseph is chosen to take her to his home. He is a widower with sons (thus the problem of the brothers of Jesus for the virginity of Mary is resolved). While Mary is helping to spin the veil of the Temple, having been allotted the purple and scarlet threads, she experiences the annunciation of the angel. The speech used in the meeting is similar to that in Luke, but is longer and more explanatory.

The visitation to Elizabeth follows, again adding speech, but omitting material too, such as the *Magnificat*. Joseph's dilemma over Mary's pregnancy follows (and so the text combines themes from Matthew and Luke). There is confrontation between Joseph and Mary, adding to the text in Matthew, resolved only by the more familiar angelic dream. There is public speculation, too; Joseph and Mary are tested for their honesty, by drinking 'the water of conviction of the Lord' (cf. Num. 5.11–31) and being sent into the wilderness, but they return unharmed and are therefore presumed innocent.

---

50.   For text and commentary, see Miller 1994: 301–22; Klauck 2003: 107–22. Another useful source for the apocryphal gospels is Elliott 1993. Note that the tentative dates for apocryphal texts given in this section are those most favoured by the commentaries.
51.   Miller 1994: 343–56; Klauck 2003: 185–91.
52.   Miller 1994: 357–66; Klauck 2003: 160–8.
53.   Hennecke 1963: 1:257–8.
54.   Miller 1994: 380–96; Klauck 2003: 65–72; Elliott 1996: 33–8.

The trip to Bethlehem follows, for the same reason as in Luke (the census), but with extra material. Joseph takes Mary into a cave for her to deliver and, while seeking a midwife, has a vision in which the world stands still. An intense light accompanies the birth. The midwife tells the story to Salome (introduced without comment, perhaps the woman at the cross in Mark is assumed; Salome is also a traditional name for a stepsister of Jesus). Salome doubts the unbroken virginity of Mary after giving birth and (Thomas-like) checks her physical condition. Her hand is consumed by flames because of her unbelief, but is restored when, on the instruction of an angel, she holds the hand out to the baby and picks him up. This is therefore Jesus' first healing miracle, according to the *Protevangelium*.

The Magi arrive, via Herod, as in Matthew. The massacre of the innocents that follows does not cause the flight to Egypt; rather, Mary 'took her child, wrapped him in strips of cloth, and put him in a feeding trough used by cattle', in order to hide him. Elizabeth returns to the action; a mountain splits open so that she and her son John are kept safe from Herod, and an angel protects them. However, Herod kills Zechariah for not giving up his son. His death is mourned by the priests, who appoint Simeon (the same as in Luke 2) high priest in his place. The text ends with a confirmation that its author is James (implying that this is either a son of Joseph - the one described as the 'Lord's brother' elsewhere – or James the Less, i.e. the younger), and that he wrote it at the time of the death of Herod.

The *Protevangelium* was probably the earliest articulation of the view that Mary was, in the physical sense, in a virginal state during and after the birth of Jesus. The earliest testimony to the associated belief that she gave birth without pain may come from an even earlier source, the *Odes of Solomon* (probably first-century), discovered in 1908, although here, it would seem, the 'Virgin' refers to Wisdom rather than the human mother of Jesus. Nevertheless, the text is vague enough for the association to be made.

And the womb of the Virgin [Wisdom] enfolded it [the milk of God], and she conceived and gave birth. And the Virgin became a mother with great compassion. And she entered labour and bore a Son without incurring pain, because it did not happen without divine purpose. Nor did she require a midwife, for He had caused her to give life. She bore, as it seemed, a man by the will of God; she bore him and made him manifest, and she received him, according to the great Power. And she loved him with affection, and guarded him with kindness, and made him known with majesty. Hallelujah.[55]

---

55. Davidson 2005: ode 19 (88). The original publisher of the manuscript did regard the reference to the 'Virgin' as meaning Mary. The consequent unexpectedly early date for this Mariological development led him to speculate a later, at least second-century, date for this passage; see Harris 1909: 114–16. His original translation for the text given here runs as follows: 'The Spirit opened the womb of the Virgin and she received conception and brought forth; and the Virgin became a mother with many mercies; and she travailed and brought forth a Son, without incurring pain; and because she was not sufficiently prepared, and she had not sought a midwife (for he brought her to bear), she brought forth, as if she were a man, of her own will; and she brought him forth openly, and acquired him with great dignity, and loved him in his swaddling clothes, and guarded him kindly, and showed him in majesty. Hallelujah.'

Texts that expand upon the childhood of Jesus include *The Infancy Gospel of Thomas* (probably second-century).[56] Jesus is a prodigious miracle-worker, creating birds out of mud, but not a very kind one, killing child companions who offend him. He also performs healing miracles. The theme seems to be that Jesus is human, a child with his wilfulness and lack of awareness of the consequences of his actions, but also divine, a life and death giver. His father Joseph is much embarrassed by these episodes and, as the main parental character, contends with Jesus. His mother (not named as Mary) enters the story at section 11, and she sends Jesus as a six-year-old to draw water; when he breaks the pitcher, he uses his cloak to carry the water. 'His mother, once she saw the miracle that had occurred, kissed him; but she kept to herself the mysteries that she had seen him do.' Section 19 echoes the story of Jesus in the Temple at the age of 12 in Luke. Now Mary is named. The story adds little to Luke 2.48–52, except that the scholars and Pharisees remark that Mary is to be congratulated, as the fruit of her womb is blessed.

Some apocryphal works pick up on the theme in the synoptic Gospels that contrasts Jesus' family and the disciples. *The Gospel of Thomas* and *The Gospel of the Ebionites* (the latter only known from disparaging quotations in Epiphanius)[57] do not add anything substantial to the text of Mark 3.31–5. In *The Secret Gospel of Mark*, a version of the canonical Mark known to Clement of Alexandria in the second century,[58] there is an extra section between 10.34 and 10.35 which parallels the raising of Lazarus in John, and an extra sentence in 10.46: 'Then they came to Jericho. The sister of the young man whom Jesus loved was there, along with his mother and Salome, but Jesus refused to see them.'

The Gospel of the Hebrews is known to us only through quotations in Cyril of Jerusalem, Jerome, Origen and Eusebius (third to fourth centuries).[59] This source, along with the above-mentioned *The Gospel of the Ebionites*, was Jewish-Christian, but the patristic writers used it to gain further information on Christian origins, and they support the text in places. The Holy Spirit is described as Christ's mother. The texts that refer to Mary are as follows:

> When Christ wanted to come to earth, the Good Father summoned a mighty power in the heavens who was called Michael, and entrusted Christ to his care. The power came down into the world, and it was called Mary, and Christ was in her womb for seven months. She gave birth to him... (*Gospel of the Hebrews*, paraphrased by Cyril of Jerusalem)[60]
>
> The mother of the Lord and his brothers said to him, 'John the Baptist baptized for the forgiveness of sins. Let's go and get baptized by him.' But he said to them, 'How have I sinned? So why should I go and get baptized by him?

---

56. Miller 1994: 369–79; Klauck 2003: 73–7.
57. Miller 1994: 435–40; Klauck 2003: 51–4.
58. Miller 1994: 408–11; Klauck 2003: 32–5.
59. Miller 1994: 427–34; Klauck 2003: 38–42.
60. Miller 1994: 430.

Only if I don't know what I am talking about.' (*Gospel of the Hebrews*, quoted by Jerome)[61]

The Gnostic *Gospel of Philip* (third-century?) has two references to Mary. The first seems to contrast her with Eve. As in the Jewish-Christian texts, the Holy Spirit is feminine, a heavenly mother of Christ.

> Some said, 'Mary conceived by the Holy Spirit.' They are in error. They do not know what they are saying. When did a woman ever conceive by a woman? Mary is the virgin whom no power defiled. She is a great anathema to the Hebrews, who are the apostles and the apostolic men. The virgin, whom no power defiled, reveals herself in order that the powers may defile themselves.[62]

The second reference identifies three Marys in intimate relationship with Jesus: 'There were three [women] who always walked with the Lord: Mary his mother and her sister and Magdalene, the one who was called his companion. His sister and his mother and companion were each a Mary.'[63]

The triple Mary may parallel the three Christs of the Gnostic Valentinian theology. If so, then the three Marys here would be allegorical figures for Sophia (Wisdom), the heavenly partner of the Redeemer, who is represented in each of them.

In the *Gospel of Bartholomew* (fourth-century?),[64] Mary speaks to Bartholomew, the representative of the apostles, about the birth of Jesus. This text derives in part from the *Protevangelium*, although there is additional material; for example, at the Annunciation, a cloud of dew descends on Mary, and the angel presents her with bread and wine. This is a eucharistic reference which is related to the incarnation of Jesus and may recall the feeding of the Israelites with manna. Later in the book, there is a resurrection appearance of Jesus to Mary, who has been in the garden with the other women, speaking to the gardener. The gardener, Philogenes, has been recounting the events of the resurrection. Jesus charges his mother with a message to the disciples; here she plays an almost identical role to that of Mary Magdalene in John. A resurrection appearance to Mary the mother of Jesus is attested to in Coptic, Syrian and Armenian traditions. In part, this may have arisen in connection with an identification of the 'other Mary' in the tomb tradition in Matthew with the mother of Jesus.[65]

In one of the dialogues in the *Pistis Sophia*, Mary talks to the risen Jesus about his childhood, and recounts a strange story in which she tells that the Spirit, resembling Jesus, visited her and asked to meet Jesus as his brother. Thinking him to be a ghost,

---

61. Ibid.: 430–1.
62. Klauck 2003: 128; see also Wilson 1962: 80–2.
63. Klauck 2003: 129.
64. Ibid.: 99–104.
65. Murray 1975: 329–35.

Mary trapped the Spirit and bound him to a bed, but when Jesus entered, the Spirit was freed, and Jesus and the Spirit merged into one being.[66] This seems to be a story that speculates on the coming of the Spirit upon Jesus, placing it earlier than the baptism story in the Gospels.

There are many legends about the death of Mary, and her *dormition* ('falling asleep'), or *transitus* ('passing'), or *assumption* ('being taken up'). Probably the oldest Greek narrative is *The Discourse of St John the Theologian about the Falling Asleep of the Mother of God* (fifth-century), although there are a few even earlier Syriac versions.[67] These texts arose in connection with Marian feasts and their liturgy. In the *Discourse*, there is the well-known motif of the gathering of the apostles in Jerusalem, some of whom have died and are raised from their tombs to be present. Paul, Mark and James are included along with members of the Twelve. Miraculous signs accompany the occasion, including the repulsion of 'the people of the Jews', who had come to burn the house. Christ descends riding upon the cherubim to bless Mary, and his words present a high Mariology:

> And when she had thus prayed, the Lord said to his own mother, 'Let your heart be glad and rejoice; for every grace and every gift has been given to you of my Father who is in heaven and of me and of the Holy Ghost. Every soul who calls upon your name shall not be put to shame, but shall find mercy and consolation and succour and confidence, both in this world and in that which is to come, before my Father who is in heaven.'[68]

There are also several other gospels about the infancy of Jesus that feature Mary. *Liber de Ortu Beatae Mariae et Infantia Salvatoris*, better known as *Pseudo-Matthew*, is a Latin work of probably the early seventh century.[69] It is partly drawn from the *Protevangelium*, with additions and amendments. One innovation is the ox and ass standing by the crib (a reference to Isaiah), an image that has been enduring in the Christmas tradition. The flight into Egypt has several new features. Jesus tames dragons and is served by wild beasts. A palm tree bends down so that Mary can take fruit, and water springs forth from its roots. This prefigures the story of Mary in the Qur'an (except that, there, this event happens as she is giving birth). The child Jesus also converts a city of Egypt by causing its idols to crash to the ground.

The sixth-century *Arabic Infancy Gospel*[70] draws from the *Protevangelium* and the *Infancy Gospel of Thomas*, and adds new and imaginative stories, such as the Magi taking one of Jesus' nappies, Jesus encountering the robbers of Golgotha, and accounts of Judas Iscariot and Bartholomew as children. Mary, carrying the infant

---

66. Hennecke 1963: 257–8.
67. Klauck 2003: 192–204; Elliott 1996: 40–4. The early history of the Dormition tradition is described in this volume in Stephen Shoemaker's article, 'Marian Liturgies and Devotion in Early Christianity' (00–00).
68. Klauck 2003: 196.
69. Ibid.: 78–80.
70. Ibid.: 80; Elliott 1996: 39–40.

Jesus and travelling with Joseph, cures a demoniac and saves a sick child with the water in which Jesus has been washed. Captives held by robbers are released as the Holy Family approaches. A later *Latin Infancy Gospel* (seventh- to ninth-century?) portrays Jesus being born from rays of light.[71]

Overall, the *Protevangelium* was the most influential apocryphal work that featured Mary. Its story found a place in Catholic tradition in, for example, the feast of the Presentation of Mary in the Temple and the doctrine of Mary's perpetual virginity. However, speculation about Mary's life, virginity, holiness and death, and about Jesus' childhood, continued to be expressed in various texts through the centuries.

Twentieth-century discoveries, such as that at Nag Hammadi in Egypt, and a modern critique of the politics behind the New Testament canon, have revived interest in the Apocrypha. They form alternative sources for understanding the development of Christian tradition in the first few centuries. Recently a musical work, *El Niño* by John Adams (2000), drew texts from the *Protevangelium, Pseudo-Matthew* and the *Latin Infancy Gospel* in its retelling of the infancy story.

BIBLIOGRAPHY

Primary Sources

Davidson, John (2005) *The Odes of Solomon: Mystical Songs from the Time of Jesus*, Bath: Clear Press.

Elliott, J. K. (ed.) (1993) *The Apocryphal New Testament: A Collection of Apocryphal Christian Literature in an English Translation based on M. R. James*, Oxford: Clarendon.

Elliott, J. K. (1996) *The Apocryphal Jesus: Legends of the Early Church*, Oxford: Oxford University Press.

Harris, J. Rendel (1909) *The Odes and Psalms of Solomon*, Cambridge: Cambridge University Press.

Hennecke, E. (1963) *New Testament Apocrypha*, ed. W. Schneemelcher, trans. R. McL.Wilson, London: Lutterworth.

Miller, Robert J. (ed.) (1994) *The Complete Gospels: Annotated Scholars Version*, 3rd edn, San Francisco: Harper.

Secondary Sources

Alter, Robert (1981) *The Art of Biblical Narrative*, New York: Basic Books.

Balasuriya, Tissa (1990, new edn 1997) *Mary and Human Liberation: The Story and the Text*, ed. Helen Stanton, London: Mowbray.

Bauckham, Richard (2002) *Gospel Women: Studies of the Named Women in the Gospels*, London: T & T Clark.

Bauckham, Richard (1990) *Jude and the Relatives of Jesus in the Early Church*, Edinburgh: T & T Clark.

Beattie, Tina (1999, new edn 2002) *God's Mother, Eve's Advocate*, New York: Continuum.

Bernheim, Pierre-Antoine (1997) *James, Brother of Jesus*, trans. John Bowden, London: SCM.

Bovon, François (2002) *A Commentary on the Gospel of Luke 1.1–9.50*, trans. Christine M. Thomas, ed. Helmut Koester, Minneapolis: Fortress.

Brown, Raymond E. (1977, updated 1993) *The Birth of the Messiah: A Commentary on the Infancy Narratives of Matthew and Luke*, London: Geoffrey Chapman.

---

71. Klauck 2003: 80.

Brown, Raymond E., Donfried, Karl P., Fitzmyer, Joseph A. and Reumann, John (eds) (1978) *Mary in the New Testament*, London: Geoffrey Chapman; Philadelphia: Fortress Press; New York/Ramsey/Toronto: Paulist Press.

Chilton, Bruce and Neusner, Jacob (eds) (2001) *The Brother of Jesus: James the Just and His Mission*, Louisville: Westminster John Knox.

Coleridge, Mark (1993) *The Birth of the Lukan Narrative*, in *Journal for the Study of the New Testament* Supplement Series, 88, Sheffield: Sheffield Academic Press.

Eisenman, Robert (2002) *James, the Brother of Jesus*, London: Watkins.

Eusebius (1965) *The History of the Church from Christ to Constantine*, trans. G. A. Williamson, Harmondsworth: Penguin.

Fehribach, Adeline (1998) *The Women in the Life of the Bridegroom: A Feminist Historical-Literary Analysis of the Female Characters in the Fourth Gospel*, Collegeville: Liturgical Press.

Fiorenza, Elisabeth Schüssler (1983) *In Memory of Her: A Feminist Reconstruction of Christian Origins*, London: SCM.

Fiorenza, Elisabeth Schüssler (1995) *Jesus, Miriam's Child, Sophia's Prophet: Critical issues in Feminist Christology*, London: SCM.

Flannery, Austin (ed.) (1996) *Vatican Council II: Constitutions, Decrees, Declarations*, rev. edn, Dublin: Dominican.

Foskett, Mary F. (2002) *A Virgin Conceived: Mary and Classical Representations of Virginity*, Bloomington and Indianapolis: Indiana University Press.

Gaventa, Beverly Roberts (1995, new edn 1999) *Mary: Glimpses of the Mother of Jesus*, Edinburgh: T & T Clark.

Gebara, Ivone and Bingemer, Maria Clara (1989) *Mary, Mother of God, Mother of the Poor*, trans. Phillip Berryman, Tunbridge Wells: Burns & Oates.

Graef, Hilda (1985) *Mary, A History of Doctrine and Devotion*, combined edn, London: Sheed & Ward.

Green, Joel (ed.) (1995) *Hearing the New Testament: Strategies for Interpretation*, Grand Rapids: Eerdmans.

John Paul II (1987) *Redemptoris Mater*, London: Catholic Truth Society.

Johnson, Elizabeth A. (2003) *Truly Our Sister: A Theology of Mary in the Communion of Saints*, New York: Continuum.

Keener, Craig S. (2003) *The Gospel of John: A Commentary*, 2 vols, Peabody: Hendrickson.

Klauck, Hans-Josef (2003) *Apocryphal Gospels: An Introduction*, London: T & T Clark.

Laurentin, René (1957) *Structure et Théologie de Luc I-II*, Paris: Gabalda.

Levine, Amy-Jill and Blickenstaff, Marianne (eds) (2002) *A Feminist Companion to Luke*, London: Sheffield Academic Press.

Levine, Amy-Jill and Blickenstaff, Marianne (eds) (2003) *A Feminist Companion to John, Volume II*, London: Sheffield Academic Press.

Levine, Amy-Jill and Robbins, Maria Mayo (eds) (2005) *A Feminist Companion to Mariology*, London: T & T Clark.

Lüdemann, Gerd (1998) *Virgin Birth? The Real Story of Mary and her Son Jesus*, trans. John Bowden, London: SCM.

McHugh, John (1975) *The Mother of Jesus in the New Testament*, Garden City: Doubleday.

Murray, Robert (1975) *Symbols of Church and Kingdom: A Study in Early Syriac Tradition*, Cambridge: Cambridge University Press.

Paul VI (1974) *To Honour Mary (Marialis Cultus)*, London: Catholic Truth Society.

Reinhartz, Adele (2003) 'Women in the Johannine Community: An Exercise in Historical Imagination', in Levine and Blickenstaff, *A Feminist Companion to John, Volume II*: 14–33.

Schaberg, Jane (1995) *The Illegitimacy of Jesus: A Feminist Theological Interpretation of the Infancy Narratives*, Sheffield: Sheffield Academic Press.

Schneiders, Sandra M. (1999) *Written that You may Believe: Encountering Jesus in the Fourth Gospel*, New York: Crossroad.

Seim, Turid Karlsen (2002) 'The Virgin Mother: Mary and Ascetic Discipleship in Luke', in Levine and Blickenstaff, *A Feminist Companion to Luke*: 89–105.

Shillington, V. George (2002) *Reading the Sacred Text: An Introduction to Biblical Studies*, London: T & T Clark.

Spong, John Shelby (1992) *Born of a Woman: A Bishop Rethinks the Birth of Jesus*, San Francisco: Harper.

Spretnak, Charlene (2004) *Missing Mary: the Queen of Heaven and Her Re-emergence in the Modern Church*, New York: Palgrave Macmillan.

Talbert, Charles H. (2003) *Reading Luke-Acts in its Mediterranean Milieu*, Leiden: Brill.

Thistleton, Anthony (1992) *New Horizons in Hermeneutics: The Theory and Practice of Transforming Biblical Reading*, London: HarperCollins.

Watson, Francis (1994) *Text, Church and World: Biblical Interpretation in Theological Perspective*, Edinburgh: T & T Clark.

Weaver, Mary Jo (1985) *New Catholic Women: A Contemporary Challenge to Traditional Religious Authority*, San Francisco: Harper & Row.

Wilson, R. McL. (1962) *The Gospel of Philip*, London: Mowbray.

Witherington III, Ben (1984) *Women in the Ministry of Jesus*, Cambridge: Cambridge University Press.

The Conception of the Virgin Mary

This is the account of Mary's conception given in The Protevangelium of James. *It casts the event in the mould of Old Testament conceptions, such as Sarah's conception of Isaac and Hannah's conception of Samuel.[1] In medieval and Renaissance painting, the conception of the Virgin is usually represented by an image of the meeting of Anne and Joachim at the Golden Gate of the Temple – a detail which is not included in the* Protevangelium, *but which does appear in the* Liber de Infantia, *or* Gospel of Pseudo-Matthew, *a medieval Latin work.[2] In the Western Church, the latter was the principal written source for the transmission of the stories of Mary's early life,[3] and it draws heavily upon the* Protevangelium.

And Anna saw a laurel tree and sat down beneath it and implored the Lord saying, 'O God of our fathers, bless me and heed my prayer, just as you blessed the womb of Sarah and gave her a son, Isaac.'

And Anna sighed towards heaven and saw a nest of sparrows in the laurel tree and she sang a dirge to herself:

'Woe is me, who gave me life
What womb brought me forth?
For I was born a curse before them all and before the children of Israel,
And I was reproached, and they mocked me and thrust me out of the temple of the Lord.
Woe is me, to what am I likened?
I am not likened to the birds of the heaven;
for even the birds of the heaven are fruitful before you, O Lord!
Woe is me, to what am I likened?
I am not likened to the beasts of the earth;
for even the beasts of the earth are fruitful before you, O Lord.
Woe is me, to what am I likened? I am not likened to these waters;
for even these waters are fruitful before you, O Lord.
Woe is me, to what am I likened?
I am not likened to this earth;
for even this earth brings forth its fruit in its seasons and praises you, O Lord.'

And behold an angel of the Lord appeared to her and said, 'Anna, Anna, the Lord has heard your prayer. You shall conceive and bear, and your offspring shall be spoken of in the whole world.' And Anna said, 'As the Lord my God lives, if I bear a child, whether male or female, I will bring it as a gift to the Lord my God, and it shall serve him all the days of its life.'

And behold there came two angels, who said to her, 'Behold, Joachim your husband is coming

---

1. The translation is taken from 'The Protevangelium of James', 2.4–4.4, in Elliott 1993: 58–9. The Greek text, with commentary indicating textual variants, is given in Smid 1965.
2. 'Gospel of Pseudo-Matthew', III, in James 1924: 73.
3. The detail of the Golden Gate, for example, is found in a thirteenth-century manuscript in Hereford Cathedral library. The Latin text is given in James 1927: 11.

with his flocks, for an angel of the Lord had come down to him and said to him, "Joachim, Joachim, the Lord God has heard your prayer. Go down from here; behold, your wife Anna shall conceive." ' And Joachim went down and called his herdsmen and said, 'Bring me here ten female lambs without blemish and without spot; they shall be for the Lord my God. And bring me twelve tender calves and they shall be for the priests and council of elders, and a hundred young he-goats for the whole people.' And, behold, Joachim came with his flocks, and Anna stood at the gate and saw Joachim coming and ran immediately and threw her arms around his neck saying, 'Now I know that the Lord God has greatly blessed me; for behold the widow is no longer a widow, and I, who was childless, shall conceive.'

And Joachim rested the first day in his house.

BIBLIOGRAPHY

Elliott, J. K. (ed.) (1993) *The Apocryphal New Testament: A Collection of Apocryphal Christian Literature in an English Translation based on M. R. James*, Oxford: Oxford University Press.

James, M. R. (trans.) (1924) *The Apocryphal New Testament: Being the Apocryphal Gospels, Acts, Epistles and Apocalypses*, Oxford: Oxford University Press.

James, M. R. (ed.) (1927) *Latin Infancy Gospels: A New Text, with a Parallel Version from Irish*, Cambridge: Cambridge University Press.

Smid, H. R. (1965) *Protevangelium Jacobi: A Commentary*, trans. G. E. van Baaren-Pape, Assen: Van Gorcum & Comp.

The Annunciation

The account of the Annunciation given below is that which is found in the Protevangelium.[1] *In Orthodox iconography, it is common for images of the Annunciation to include a skein of thread, as indicated in this narrative. The* Protevangelium *makes much of Mary's association with the Temple. As a small child, when she is taken by her parents to live in the Temple, she dances on the Temple steps. Margaret Barker has suggested that this is an allusion to the figure of Wisdom who, at the foundation of the world, 'was beside the Lord, like a little child rejoicing before him always' (Prov. 8.30).[2] The* Protevangelium's *emphasis on Mary's sexual purity and exceptional integrity seems intended to indicate that she is a suitable dwelling place for the Lord, and is thus herself another Temple. The motif of the spinning and weaving of the veil points to Mary's own role as the one who will both shelter and reveal the Lord who is about to dwell within her.*

Now there was a council of the priests saying, 'Let us make a veil for the temple of the Lord.' And the priest said, 'Call to me pure virgins of the tribe of David.' And the officers departed and searched and they found seven virgins. And the priest remembered the child Mary, that she was of the tribe of David and was pure before God. And the officers went

---

1. 'The Protevangelium of James', 1.3, in Elliott 1993: 61 (translation amended).
2. 'Wisdom, the Queen of Heaven', in Barker 2003: 229–61 (258).

and fetched her. Then they brought them into the temple of the Lord and the priest said, 'Cast lots to see who shall spin the gold, the amiantus, the linen, the silk, the hyacinth-blue, the scarlet, and the pure purple.' The pure purple and scarlet fell by lot to Mary. And she took them and went home. At that time Zacharias became dumb, and Samuel took his place until Zacharias was able to speak again. Mary took the scarlet and spun it.

And she took the pitcher and went out to draw water, and behold, a voice said, 'Hail, highly favoured one, the Lord is with you, you are blessed among women.' And she looked around to the right and to the left to see where this voice came from. And, trembling, she went to her house and put down the pitcher and took the purple and sat down on her seat and drew out the thread. And behold, an angel of the Lord stood before her and said, 'Do not fear, Mary; for you have found grace before the Lord of all things and shall conceive by his Word.' When she heard this she considered it and said, 'Shall I conceive by the Lord, the living God, and bear as every woman bears?' And the angel of the Lord said, 'Not so, Mary; for the power of the Lord shall overshadow you; wherefore that holy one who is born of you shall be called the Son of the Most High. And you shall call his name Jesus; for he shall save his people from their sins.' And Mary said, 'Behold, (I am) the handmaid of the Lord before him: be it to me according to your word.'

And she made ready the purple and the scarlet and brought them to the priest. And the priest blessed her and said, 'Mary, the Lord God has magnified your name, and you shall be blessed among all generations of the earth.'

BIBLIOGRAPHY

Barker, Margaret (2003) *The Great High Priest: The Temple Roots of Christian Liturgy*, London: T&T Clark.

Elliott (ed.) (1993) *The Apocryphal New Testament: A Collection of Apocryphal Christian Literature in an English Translation based on M. R. James*, Oxford: Oxford University Press.

2

THE TITLE THEOTOKOS[1]

SARAH JANE BOSS

We have already seen that Mary was written about in reverential terms during the second century of the Christian era. Christian authors developed their thinking about her over subsequent centuries, and by the time of the Council of Chalcedon (451), the main lines of Marian doctrine and devotion had been established. The teaching which was most important for subsequent Mariology is that which holds that she is correctly called 'Mother of God', or, more accurately, 'Godbearer'.

The belief that the Virgin Mary is the Mother of God is the corollary of the belief that her son, Jesus Christ, is God incarnate. A central tenet of the Christian faith is the doctrine of the incarnation. This teaches that the Word of God, who is God himself, through whom all things were created, became a part of his own creation when he was conceived, gestated and born of the Virgin Mary. The Word of God is simultaneously the man Jesus of Nazareth because he has a human mother. Theologians have generally agreed that this is an indispensable article of the Christian faith, although the exact reasons for its importance have been disputed. One classical version, however, runs as follows.

God created the world in a state of goodness, as a work of *grace* (something freely given), but sin entered the world when humanity disobeyed the Lord God. This goodness and its loss through human rebellion has traditionally been told through the narrative in which Adam and Eve, the first man and woman, disobeyed God when they ate the forbidden fruit of the tree of the knowledge of good and evil, in the Garden of Eden, and were expelled to a life of hardship (Genesis 3). This first sin led to men and women being estranged from God, from one another and from the earth with which they struggle for the food, clothing and shelter that sustains them. In theological language, when Adam and Eve ate the forbidden fruit, the consequence was that *nature* fell from *grace*. That is to say, the world as it was created by God (the world of nature) lost some – though not all – of the glory and holiness with which it was originally endowed (that is, grace). This was caused by human sin, but its effect touches all other creatures as well.

What counts here, of course, is not the detail of the putative first ancestors of the human race, but the representative function that they have always performed. They stand for a humanity which knows that men and women live disordered lives, in which our relationships with God, with one another and with other creatures –

---

1. Some of this chapter is an edited version of work that was previously published in Boss 2004.

minerals, plants and animals – are often harmful rather than joyful. As the poet
Gerard Manley Hopkins wrote in the nineteenth century,

> The world is charged with the grandeur of God.
> . . .[but] all is seared with trade; bleared, smeared with toil;
> And wears man's smudge and shares man's smell: the soil
> Is bare now, nor can foot feel, being shod.

Yet simultaneously with this awareness that the world is awry, Adam and Eve, who
once lived in Eden, represent men and women who know that the way the world is
now is not how it has to be: indeed, they have confidence that this is not what God
wills for it, and even now, that it is not the whole truth. As Hopkins continues,

> And for all this, nature is never spent;
> There lives the dearest freshness deep down things.[2]

The conception and birth of Christ from his mother Mary are cardinal moments in
God's redemption of the world from the sin that generates the state of malaise. For
God did not wish his creation to continue in its condition of suffering and
estrangement from him, and he sent Jesus into the world to save it from sin and
death. Jesus' own death – a violent death by crucifixion – was the only sacrifice which
was sufficient to atone for the sins of the world, just as his resurrection from the dead,
on the third day following his execution, was the only conquest that could restore
humanity to its right relationship with God: that could overcome death itself. The
resurrection constitutes the most fundamental tenet of the Christian faith, and
Christ's resurrection and eternal life will be shared by all those who have been
redeemed by him, when he returns in judgement on the Last Day and transforms the
whole created order into a state of glory.

Now, the reason why the crucifixion and resurrection of Jesus are able to have the
redemptive significance which Christians attribute to them lies in Jesus' identity. For
Jesus Christ is not only a human being who co-operates with the will of God for the
redemption of the world: he is himself divine. Since it was Adam – and with him, all
humanity – who sinned, it was necessary that a human being should make good what
had been damaged. Yet humanity alone is not capable of restoring the world to that
fullness of grace which comes from God alone. And so God redeemed the world by
uniting himself to human nature in Jesus and working the world's redemption as
God incarnate – that is, God made flesh.

We can be more specific on this point. In Christian teaching, the One God is also
Trinity. That is, God is both single and triune, three 'persons' who are nonetheless
one. Each person of the Trinity – the Father, the Son (or Word) and the Holy Spirit
– is God, and all three persons are present in the action of any one of the three. Thus
God the Father created the world through the eternal Word and in the power of the

---

2.   Hopkins 1963: 27.

Holy Spirit; but this is a single action of the one God. In the created world, number is applied to bounded objects conceptualized as separate from one another – three rabbits, twelve currant buns, or two hundred carrots, for example. And if there are three, twelve, or two hundred, then these are not simultaneously one. In God the Creator, however, there is no boundedness – no limit of any kind – and thus no contradiction between the single and the triune nature of the Godhead. The 'threeness' of the Deity is clearly something different from the threeness of the rabbits mentioned above. But this doctrine is too mysterious to be adequately grasped by human understanding, and for that very reason, meditation upon the Trinity provides a safeguard against imagining God to be in our own, or any other, image. The doctrine of the Trinity is the guarantee that humanity cannot comprehend or manipulate the Deity, but must always stand in awe of the God who is before and beyond the boundaries which characterize the created order.

So, to be more precise about the incarnation: since the One God is also Trinity, it was the eternal Word – or Son – of God, the Second Person of the Blessed Trinity, who became flesh in Mary's womb for the salvation of the world. Thus the means by which God chose to save the world from its sins was that he himself should take on human flesh, with all its sensual pleasures and pains; that the Creator should be one with a creature, as an embryo in a woman's entrails; that he who is eternal should take on transience, like the earth whose substance is shared by human flesh (Gen. 2:7); that he who is immortal should take on mortality, and that he should indeed suffer and die for the sake of his creation.

One of the greatest exponents of the theology of the incarnation is the fifth-century bishop Cyril of Alexandria (d. 444). Cyril teaches that the Word of God was conceived in Mary's womb in order to consecrate the human race from our very beginnings – that because God himself has been conceived in a woman's body, all human conception may now be sanctified.[3] And because the immortal God united himself to human flesh even in death, he accomplished 'the incorruptibility and imperishability of the flesh ... first of all in his own body', as we see in his resurrection from the dead, but also for the whole human race. By uniting himself to human death in Christ, God who is immortal overcame death itself and thus enabled all flesh to be 'set ... beyond death and corruption'.[4] 'In short, he took what was ours to be his very own so that we might have all that was his.'[5]

So Jesus' unique salvific power derives from his identity as both true God and true man, and for this reason Mary is essential to the Christian account of God and creation. For in the union of God and humanity, it is Mary who imparts the humanity. This belief is expressed in the teaching that Mary conceived Jesus by the power of the Holy Spirit when she was still a virgin (Lk. 1.26–38). Eternally begotten of God the Father, Christ was conceived and born on earth of his mother Mary. For this reason she is called by the paradoxical title of *Theotokos*, a Greek term meaning

---

3. 'Third Letter of Cyril to Nestorius', from the documents of the Council of Ephesus (431), in Tanner SJ 1990: 58.
4. St Cyril of Alexandria 1995: 57.
5. Ibid.: 59.

'Godbearer', or 'Mother of God'. Indeed, it was in order to explain and defend this title for Mary that Cyril of Alexandria wrote his Christology. God, of course, does not have a beginning: God is from all eternity, with no origin – no parent – outside Godself. But how else are Christians to express the wonder of the incarnation, whereby God and humanity are perfectly united, if not by the assertion that the human woman who is the mother of Christ is, by that token, the Mother of God? Furthermore, the Catholic, Orthodox and ancient Eastern churches have invariably held that Mary gave her free assent to the conception of Christ. If she had not consented to Gabriel's message, then the world's redemption would not have come about in precisely the manner in which it did: the redeemer would not have been the Jesus of Nazareth who in fact is God incarnate. So Mary is not only a physical, but also a moral, agent in the world's salvation.

The title *Theotokos* – the one who conceived or gave birth to God – is not without its difficulties, however; and it was in order to counter objections to this title that Cyril formulated his explanation of it. Cyril came from the oldest school of Christian theology, that of Alexandria, in Egypt. To understand the relationship that exists between the divinity and the humanity of Christ, Alexandrian theologians before Cyril had discussed the question, 'Did the Word of God die on the cross?' It should be immediately clear that there cannot be a simple 'yes' or 'no' answer to this. After all, since the Word of God is eternal, it seems incorrect to say that he died. Yet, as we have seen above, the doctrine of salvation demands that the human Christ's salvific work of life, death and resurrection should have been accomplished also by God. The technical solution to this conundrum was to say, 'In his humanity, the Word of God died on the cross; in his divinity, the Word of God did not die.' *The subject of both the dying and the not-dying is the same Word of God.* Thus it is appropriate to say, 'The Word of God died on the cross.' And more than this, Alexandrian theologians held that if one would not affirm this truth, then one had not properly grasped the reality of the incarnation, which, since it is the perfect union of God and humanity, entails that *everything that can truly be attributed to Christ's humanity can also be attributed to his divinity, and vice versa.* This principle is called the *communicatio idiomatum*, or 'communication of properties' (i.e. between Christ's divinity and his humanity).[6]

The principle of the *communicatio idiomatum* therefore entailed the possibility of saying, 'Mary gave birth to God', and so it was this principle which was used to justify honouring her with the title 'Godbearer'. However, a group of theologians who are sometimes called 'Antiochene', because many of them had been trained in the theological school of Antioch, opposed calling Mary the 'Godbearer'; and it was the dispute over this title which led to the calling of the Council of Ephesus in 431.[7]

---

6.   There is one exception to this principle, namely the statement, 'The Word of God was created.' This was not used by the Alexandrian theologians (and has not been used in 'mainstream' Christian theology since that time) because that formula had been specifically rejected at the Council of Nicaea (325), in opposition to the Arians, who held that the Word of God *in his divinity* had been created by God the Father.

7.   This is discussed in detail in Richard Price, 'Theotokos', in this volume (56–63). A somewhat different assessment of the council is offered in Stephen J. Shoemaker, 'Marian Liturgies and Devotion in Early Christianity', also in this volume (130–45).

The main objector was Nestorius, Bishop of Constantinople, and one of his concerns was that the title *Theotokos* implied that God had a beginning – as if he were a pagan god, or some other created being. The Word of God, he insisted, was eternal, and therefore without a beginning. Nestorius did not doubt that Christ was truly both divine and human, but Mary, he said, was the mother of Christ's humanity, not his divinity. But this concern was symptomatic of a more fundamental difference of approach between Nestorius and Cyril. Cyril subscribed to a Christology that is sometimes called *Logos/sarx*, or 'Word/flesh', Christology, because it flows from the verse in John 1, 'And the Word became flesh...' This Christology emphasizes the total union of the divine Word with the flesh of Christ, and holds that Christians in turn are sanctified because of their own union with Christ in the flesh. Cyril held that this union could be accomplished most fully by receiving the elements of the Eucharist – the body of Christ. Mary was therefore the mother of the Word made flesh.

Nestorius, on the other hand, held to a school of Christological doctrine that is sometimes called *Logos/anthropos*, or 'Word/human'. According to this understanding, it is important to emphasize that the Word of God was united not only to Christ's flesh – since this may mislead people into thinking that his divinity took the place occupied by the soul in other human beings – but that God was united to a whole human being, body and soul. Accordingly, Nestorius emphasized the importance of the imitation of Christ in one's actions, rather than just the sacramental reception of his body, for attaining the goal of the Christian life. Where Nestorius and the Antiochenes taught a strongly historical Christology, which focused on the life of Jesus as found in the Gospels, Cyril and the Alexandrians taught a much more cosmic Christology, focusing on the union of God with the whole of humanity and creation.

The main weakness of Nestorius's position was that it could not account adequately for the union of divinity and humanity in Christ, and gave the impression that the divinity and humanity were in some way stuck together without being properly united. If Mary did not give birth to God, then how and when did the Word of God unite himself to Christ's humanity? Crucially, of course, Nestorius's objection to the title *Theotokos* – to the assertion that Mary bore God – held equally well in the case of Christ's death: for just as God has no beginning, so he also has no end. And if we cannot say that the eternal Word of God died on the cross, then how is humanity redeemed? Cyril, by contrast, argued that the child to whom Mary gave birth was the one in whom 'the Word was flesh', and this made it clear that, in Christ, the two could not be separated.

Having said this, we should also note that when the *Theotokos* was victorious at the Council of Ephesus, and Nestorius was condemned as a heretic, Cyril may have been the general who won the war, but he did not win every battle in it. Where he had originally argued that there was only *one nature* in Christ, he eventually conceded Nestorius's point that Christ's humanity and divinity should indeed be considered as *two natures*. This formulation, together with the clear assertion that the child whom Mary bore was the one in whom these natures were united, provided the foundation for the Christological formula of the Council of Chalcedon (451), that Christ was 'one Person [i.e., the Word of God] in two natures [divine and human]'. This

Christology is that which is still held by the Catholic Church, and by most Orthodox and Protestant churches.

BIBLIOGRAPHY

Boss, Sarah Jane (2004) *Mary*, London: Continuum.
Hopkins, Gerard Manley (1963) *Poems and Prose*, ed. W. H. Gardner, Harmondsworth: Penguin.
St Cyril of Alexandria (1995) *On the Unity of Christ*, trans. John Anthony McGuckin, Crestwood, NY: St Vladimir's Seminary Press.
Tanner SJ, Norman P. (ed.) (1990) *Decrees of the Ecumenical Councils*, vol. 1, London: Sheed & Ward, and Washington: Georgetown University Press.

3

THEOTOKOS: THE TITLE AND ITS SIGNIFICANCE IN DOCTRINE AND DEVOTION

RICHARD PRICE

EARLY USES OF THE *THEOTOKOS* TITLE

In 1938 there was published a Greek text, written on an Egyptian papyrus, that was subsequently recognized as containing in only slightly damaged form the earliest known text of the Marian prayer known in Latin as *Sub tuum praesidium*. The restored text runs:

> Under your mercy we take refuge, *Theotokos*. Do not overlook our petitions in adversity but rescue us from danger, uniquely holy one and uniquely blessed one.[1]

Even though the style of the lettering on the papyrus pointed to a date in the third century, the original editor and some subsequent commentators have insisted on a later date on the grounds that both the title *Theotokos* and a prayer of intercession addressed to the Virgin exclude a date prior to the mid-fourth century.[2]

The title *Theotokos* means 'Godbearer', or 'the one who gave birth to God', and serves to express simultaneously that Christ is God and yet took on human nature in the womb of the Virgin Mary.[3] When did this title first come into use? The church historian Socrates, writing in the mid-fifth century, tells us that Origen (d. 254), in his now lost commentary on Romans, 'gave an ample exposition of the sense in which the term *Theotokos* is used' (*Ecclesiastical History* VII.32). Since, however, there is no instance of its use in surviving texts of Origen, it was clearly not in regular use in his day. The earliest undisputed use in an extant text is by Bishop Alexander of Alexandria in 325; only slightly later are the occasional uses of the word in Eusebius of Caesarea (d. *c.* 340) and other contemporaries.[4] It is striking that in all these instances the use of the word is incidental: it is not explained or justified, and no weight is placed upon it. The

---

1. John Rylands Papyrus 470. I follow the restoration of the text in Giamberardini 1975: 72–4. For an extensive bibliography relating to this papyrus, see Stephen J. Shoemaker, 'Marian Liturgies and Devotion in Early Christianity', in this volume, n. 6 (130).
2. See Shoemaker, ibid., n. 7 (131).
3. The favoured Latin translation was *Dei Genitrix*, from which the standard English rendering 'Mother of God' derives. This disguises the fact that 'Mother of God' (*mêtêr theou*) was a term that became widely used only much later. See Wright 2004.
4. For these and the following patristic references, see Campos 1970–85, vol. II, with *Indices*: 85.

implication is that by the time of the Council of Nicaea (325) the term was already in standard use. We must also remember that we have so little Greek patristic literature from the second half of the third century that the lack of attestation in this period does not prove that the term was not already in use. It seems reasonable to conclude that it was a novelty requiring explanation in the time of Origen, but had become standard by the end of the third century. Its use on the John Rylands papyrus is not therefore a ground for dating the papyrus later than the third century.

The objection that prayers of intercession were not addressed to the Virgin as early as the third century has more weight.[5] Invocation of the saints was an essential corollary of the cult of the martyrs, which started in the second century and expanded hugely in the fourth. But the lack of pilgrimage sites connected to the Virgin delayed the development of her cult. A text dating to 379 is cited as the first unmistakable reference to prayer to the Virgin: it is a passage of St Gregory the Theologian where he imagines the virgin Justina 'entreating the Virgin Mary to help a virgin in danger' (*Oration* 24.11): the wording does not suggest that prayers to the Virgin were a matter of course. Other evidence suggests that invocation of the Virgin became common practice not earlier than the late fifth or even sixth century. This date, however, is clearly too late for the John Rylands papyrus. It would appear to follow that it represents a development of the cult of Mary in Egypt that long preceded similar developments elsewhere; this could just as well have happened in the third century as in the fourth. In all, the slow development of the Marian cult does not exclude the third-century date for the papyrus suggested by the palaeographical evidence, though it does prevent us from treating the papyrus as representative of contemporary Christian piety.

Occurrences of the title *Theotokos* are fairly numerous in the fourth century. They are typically incidental and unemphatic. A few texts, however, are more significant, and illustrate important developments in fourth-century Mariology. One is the emphasis on Mary, in the literature of the monastic movement, as the supreme type of virginity and thereby a model for the celibate; we find this notably in Athanasius (d. 373) and Ambrose (d. 397). Another notable feature is the use of the title in Christological contexts to bring out the reality of the human nature of her son Jesus; this can already be claimed of the use of the title by Alexander of Alexandria in 325. Fifth-century debates were anticipated by Apollinarius (d. *c*. 390), who used the title to support his distinctive Christology, where all Christ's experience, including birth from a human mother, is immediately attributed to God the Word as the sole personal subject in Christ.

THE NESTORIAN CONTROVERSY AND MARIAN PIETY IN CONSTANTINOPLE

The title became the centre of a famous debate that reverberated round much of the Christian world in the second quarter of the fifth century. When in 428 the Syrian

---

5.   Gambero 2001 is striking for its failure to find any evidence apart from the John Rylands papyrus for the invocation of Mary prior to Nicaea.

monk Nestorius arrived at Constantinople as the newly appointed archbishop, he found the *Theotokos* title prominent in debate between the Apollinarians, who exploited it, and their opponents, who criticized it. He pointed out, logically enough, that to call Mary *Theotokos*, 'Godbearer', was an imprecise use of language, since she gave birth not to Christ's Godhead but to his humanity; strictly, Mary should be called *Anthropotokos* (Mother of the man) rather than *Theotokos*, but since Christ is one person, God and man, it would be best to call Mary *Christotokos* (Mother of Christ). Nestorius's reluctance to call Mary 'Mother of God' was widely interpreted to mean that he had doubts about the divinity of her Son. There resulted the celebrated 'Nestorian' controversy, in which Cyril of Alexandria (with Roman support) played a major role, and the bishops of Syria, led by their primate the bishop of Antioch, defended Nestorius with some reservations and attacked Cyril with none. The dispute came to a climax at the Council of Ephesus of 431 and was resolved for the time being by an accord agreed by Alexandria and Antioch in 433. It is manifest from the controversial literature generated by the dispute and from the Acts of Ephesus that the issue was primarily concerned with Christ. In what sense should he be called 'divine'? Are his human experiences, including being formed in Mary's womb with flesh taken from her flesh, to be attributed to the divine Logos as the personal subject who, in some sense, underwent them? Viewed from this perspective, the issue was simply the Christological implications of the title *Theotokos*, and not the dignity of the Virgin herself, even if a consequence of the debate was a stimulus to developments in Marian devotion that took place gradually after the immediate dispute had been resolved.

A number of recent writers have argued, however, that there had been significant developments in Marian devotion in the city of Constantinople in the period between the fall of John Chrysostom in 404 and Nestorius's arrival on the scene in 428, and that Nestorius's fall was due at least in part to the way in which he offended devotees of the Virgin. A prime role has been attributed to the empress Pulcheria, who was the unmarried sister of Theodosius II (408–50) and the spouse of his successor Marcian (450–7) in a marriage that was political and unconsummated. Already in her lifetime she was credited with having been one of Nestorius's keenest opponents and with having promoted Marian devotion. Under critical scrutiny, however, much of the evidence crumbles away. The date of the development of intense Marian piety in Constantinople was in fact the seventh and eighth centuries, starting with Mary's supposed role in a defeat of a siege of the city by the Avars and Persians in 626, and reaching its climax with the defeat of Iconoclasm. This was the period when Pulcheria became credited at Constantinople with dedicating to the Virgin churches that in fact were built after Pulcheria's time. Moreover, the weight of the evidence suggests that Pulcheria had at first actually supported Nestorius and that she deserted his cause only after the Council of Ephesus. Nevertheless, there is evidence that already in the period between the councils of Ephesus (431) and Chalcedon (451), belief developed that Pulcheria had been a determined opponent of Nestorius and, as a virgin, claimed a specially close relationship with both Christ and his mother. And there is contemporary evidence of a developing Marian cult at Constantinople prior to Ephesus, in surviving sermons by Bishop Atticus (406–25) and by Proclus, who was a notable preacher in the city from the time of Atticus and later its bishop (434–46).[6] Proclus's most famous sermon (Homily 1) was indeed preached on a feast day of the Virgin in the presence of Nestorius himself.

Only one of Atticus's sermons survives in an uncontaminated version. It contains one notable passage relating to the cult of Mary:

> And you, women, who have been renewed in Christ [in the Slavonic version: 'gave birth to Christ'] and have cast off every stain of sin and have participated in the blessing received by holy Mary, receive in the womb of faith the one who is today born from the Virgin; for holy Mary, having first purified by faith the temple of her womb, then received into this temple the King of the ages.[7]

The many sermons of Proclus also contain striking Marian passages, for example:

> The Virgin's festival, my brethren, summons us today to words of praise, and the present feast has benefits to bestow on those who assemble to keep it. And surely this is right, for its subject of chastity. What we celebrate is the pride of women and the glory of the female, thanks to the one who was at once both mother and virgin ... Let nature leap for joy, and let women be honoured! Let all humanity dance, and let virgins be glorified![8]

> Let women come running, because a woman ... is giving birth to the fruit of life. Let virgins also come running, because a virgin has given birth ... Let mothers come running, because by means of the Tree of Life a virgin mother has set right the tree of disobedience. Let daughters also come running, because a daughter's obedience has punished a mother's disobedience.[9]

The 'Virgin's festival' referred to in the first of these passages (not certainly identifiable, but probably 26 December) was also the occasion for Homily 5, which claims that Mary surpassed all the prophets of the Old Testament, for while they simply prophesied the coming of Christ, it was Mary who 'carried him incarnate in her womb':

> Traverse all creation in reflection, O man, and try to see if there is anything greater or even equal to the Holy Virgin *Theotokos* ... Marvel at the victory of the Virgin, for the one whom all creation praises in fear and trembling she

---

6.   For the supposed role of Pulcheria and development of Marian devotion in Constantinople in her time, see Holum 1982: 130–74; Limberis 1994; Cooper 1998 and 2004. For a sceptical reaction, see Price 2004.

7.   Francis J. Thomson, 'The Slavonic translation of the hitherto untraced Greek *Homilia in nativitatem Domini nostri Jesu Christi* by Atticus of Constantinople', *Analecta Bollandia* 118, 2000: 5–36.

8.   Homily 1.1, Constas 2003: 137.

9.   Homily 4.2, ibid.: 229 (revised).

alone admitted ineffably to the bridal chamber [of her womb]. On account of Mary all women are blessed.[10]

The curious language of the bridal chamber reappears in a panegyric of the empress Pulcheria contained in another homily by Proclus: 'Admire the empress's greatness of soul, pouring forth spiritual blessings to all . . . This virgin, after dedicating herself to Christ, depleted and spent riches, by reason of her piety. She made her own soul dead to passions, and admitted the crucified one into the bridal chamber of her soul' (12.1).

Do these passages amount to a policy of promoting Marian piety, through encouraging the women of Constantinople, led by Pulcheria, to take Mary as their model? The answer is yes, but with qualifications. It is to be noted that these passages occur in sermons that are uniformly Christological, not Marian, in their prime emphasis, and which have nothing to say about prayer to Our Lady or her powers of intercession. The heart of the message is not that women should focus their devotion on Mary, or pray to her, but that all faithful Christians need to get closer to Christ. Mary's role is primarily to symbolize in her divine motherhood the goal for all earnest Christians of union with her divine Son.

THE ECUMENICAL COUNCIL OF EPHESUS

Famously, the Nestorian controversy led to the Third Ecumenical Council, held at Ephesus in the summer of 431. We are constantly assured that this council formally defined that Mary is *Theotokos*. This is an excessively loose use of language: in fact the council issued no dogmatic decrees or definitions. It condemned Nestorius as a heretic, but not specifically for questioning Mary's dignity as *Theotokos*: his offence was to teach (allegedly) that Christ was a mere man; his criticisms of the *Theotokos* title were treated as evidence for the charge, but so were other extracts from his sermons that said nothing about Mary.[11] The nearest the Council of Ephesus came to defining that the Virgin is *Theotokos* was in a letter sent by Cyril of Alexandria to Bishop John of Antioch in 433 (*Letter* 39) which soon became known as one of the two 'conciliar' letters loosely associated with the council. In this letter Cyril accepted as orthodox an Antiochene Christological statement (known as the 'Formulary of Union' or 'Formula of Reunion') which included the *Theotokos* title:

> On the matter of how we think and speak concerning the Virgin the *Theotokos* and the manner in which the only-begotten Son of God became man, we must state briefly (not by way of addition, but in the form of giving an assurance) what we have held from the first . . . We acknowledge our Lord Jesus Christ, the only-begotten Son of God, perfect God and perfect man made up of a

---

10. Homily 5.2, ibid.: 261.
11. In a florilegium of 25 shocking extracts from Nestorius's writings which was read out at Ephesus, only the first three (which call Mary *Anthropotokos*, 'Mother of the man') relate directly to the *Theotokos* controversy; ACO, 1.1.7: 106–11.

rational soul and body, begotten from the Father before the ages in respect of the Godhead and the same on the last day for us and for our salvation from the Virgin Mary in respect of his manhood … By virtue of this understanding of the union which involves no merging, we acknowledge the holy Virgin to be *Theotokos*, because God the Word was enfleshed and became man and from the very conception united to himself the temple taken from her.[12]

The Antiochene approval of *Theotokos* was not a concession to Cyril, but simply reflected the fact that Nestorius's criticism of the title had never won the approval of his Syrian allies; John of Antioch had written to Nestorius before the council, pointing out that the title was sound and traditional, in response to which a humiliated Nestorius had declared in a sermon preached in December 430 his own acceptance of the title.[13] It was, therefore, the Antiochenes who were responsible for the nearest Ephesus got to 'defining' that Mary is *Theotokos*. And the Antiochenes were happy to accept the title because they appreciated its importance in bringing out the union of Godhead and manhood in Christ. In the words of Theodoret of Cyrrhus, the leading Antiochene theologian of the time: 'If anyone does not call the holy Virgin Theotokos, he is either calling our Lord Jesus Christ a mere man or separating into two sons the one who is both Only-begotten and Firstborn of all creation' (*Letter* 83).

To say that both Cyril and the Antiochene school approved the *Theotokos* title is not to say that they justified it in quite the same way. For Cyril, the rightness of the title followed from the fact that all the human experiences of Christ, including his birth from the Virgin, are to be ascribed to the divine Word as personal subject. But the Antiochenes recognized the humanity of Christ as itself a subject of attribution, and they therefore agreed with Nestorius that it was equally correct to call Mary *Anthropotokos* – the 'Mother of the man'. In the words of Theodore of Mopsuestia (d. 428), the true father of Antiochene Christology:

> Because they ask, 'Was Mary *Anthropotokos* or *Theotokos*?', let us say both – one by the nature of the reality, and other by relation. She was *Anthropotokos* by nature, because in the womb of Mary was a man, who also came forth from there, and she is *Theotokos*, because God was in the man who was born, not circumscribed in him according to nature but because he was in him through an affect of the will.[14]

What offended Cyril of Alexandria and his allies in such language was not any hint of disrespect towards the Mother of God in calling her also the 'Mother of the man'. Reverence towards the Virgin was common to both parties in the controversy; Theodoret hailed her as the model of virginity and superior to all other women in

---

12.   Ibid., 1.1.4: 17.
13.   For John's letter (*ep.* 4) see ibid., 1.1.1: 95, ll. 19–20), and for Nestorius's sermon see ibid., 1.4: 7, ll. 1–9).
14.   Ibid., 4.1: 61.

virtue.[15] What caused offence was the inadequate expression of the union of divinity and humanity in Christ. To treat the humanity of Christ as in any way a personal subject was seen to threaten this. Moreover, Cyril insisted that the language of indwelling, of Godhead residing in the human nature of Christ, which is how in the passage just quoted Theodore justifies the *Theotokos* title, fails to express the mystery: rather the Word *became* flesh – not that the Word changed, or that the flesh was not taken from Mary, but rather that it was God the Word who so 'emptied himself' (to use the language of Paul's letter to the Philippians 2.7) that he became the Son of a human mother and died on the cross.

The importance of acknowledging the Virgin as *Theotokos* was that it expressed the reality of the incarnation – that our Saviour is truly God and yet in the womb of Mary became truly man: it was because the Word truly became flesh in flesh that was taken from Mary, that Mary, in bearing and giving birth to Jesus, was *Theotokos*, the Mother of God. Cyril's championing of the dignity of Mary was motivated by his concern to uphold the true divinity of her Son. It was in this context that he pronounced at Ephesus, a few days after Nestorius's condemnation, a celebrated homily that begins with a notable section in praise of the Virgin:

> I see the resplendent assembly of all the saints who have eagerly gathered at the invitation of the holy and ever-Virgin Mary the *Theotokos*. My grief has been transformed into joy by the presence of the holy fathers. There has now been fulfilled in our case the sweet words of the psalmodist David, 'See how good and delightful it is for brothers to dwell together in unity.' We hail you, holy mystical Trinity, which has summoned us all to this church of Mary *Theotokos*. We hail you, Mary *Theotokos*, the venerable treasure of all the world, the inextinguishable lamp, the crown of virginity, the sceptre of orthodoxy, the indestructible temple, the container of the Uncontainable, the Mother and Virgin, the source of the one of whom it is said in the holy Gospels, 'Blessed is he who comes in the name of the Lord.'
>
> Hail to the one who contains the Uncontainable in her holy and virgin womb, through whom the holy Trinity is glorified and worshipped in all the world, through whom heaven is glad, through whom angels and archangels rejoice, through whom demons are put to flight, through whom the devil the tempter fell from heaven, through whom the fallen creature is received back into heaven, through whom the whole creation caught in idolatry has come to the knowledge of the truth, through whom holy baptism comes to believers, through whom is the oil of gladness, through whom churches have been founded throughout the world, through whom nations are led to repentance. Why should I say more? Through whom the only-begotten Son of God has shone as a light to those sitting in darkness and in the shadow of death, through whom the prophets spoke, through whom the apostles proclaim salvation to the nations, through whom the dead are raised, through whom kings rule.[16]

---

15. Campos 1970–85: IV.1, 3662, 3644.
16. ACO, 1.1.2: 102–4.

The message is that Mary, by giving birth to the one true Saviour, God and man, shares in the glory of the work of redemption that was initiated by his birth. Nothing is made of her personal holiness or of her status as the greatest of saints and a powerful intercessor in heaven. The accord of Cyril's Mariology with that in the Constantinopolitan sermons of Atticus and Proclus analysed above is clear: Christ is the unique Saviour and Advocate, and Mary's importance lies in the fact that it was Christ's birth from her that guarantees his renewal of the human race. Mary matters precisely as the *Theotokos*, the one who gave birth to Christ, God and man. She is not yet a theme in her own right.

MARY AND FEMININE WEAKNESS

One implication of this emphasis was that it was not necessary to insist that Mary was all-holy: her indispensable role in the history of salvation had indeed required her assent to the message of the angel, but this did not make it necessary to develop a Marian piety in which the Virgin is presented as the greatest of the saints and the model of all the virtues.

The episodes involving Mary in the Gospels, including her puzzlement at the Annunciation, the oddly testy dialogue between her and her Son at the marriage at Cana, her anguish by the cross, and her need to be entrusted to the beloved disciple, had received, and continued to receive in this period, an interpretation in which the theme of Mary's exemplary nature as the one who reversed the disobedience of Eve, failed to oust a traditional misogyny that treated Mary, just as it treated most other women in the Bible, as examples of feminine weakness. Perhaps it does not greatly surprise us to find this prominent in such Antiochene exegetes as John Chrysostom and Theodore of Mopsuestia. This is how Theodore interprets the role of Mary at the marriage at Cana, where she prompted Christ to turn the water into wine (Jn 2.1–4):

> When the wine ran short, the mother of Jesus said to him, 'They have no wine.' His mother, as is the wont of mothers, pressed him to perform a miracle, wanting to show off the greatness of her son immediately and thinking that the lack of wine was a good opportunity for a miracle. But the Lord said to her, 'Woman, what have you to do with me? My hour has not yet come' . . . In other words: 'Why do you solicit me and make a nuisance of yourself? Do not suppose that there are for me particular times for particular knowledge or works, as happened with Moses, who could produce now manna and now meat and then make water flow from the rock, according to the needs to the recipients . . . I possess the power to work always, whenever and however I choose; even without being pressed by the needs of recipients I am able to display my power. Therefore the excuse you allege of a lack of wine is an insult to me.'[17]

---

17. Campos 1970–85: II, 1310.

One may be more surprised to find Cyril of Alexandria giving a similarly unflattering interpretation of the Virgin's role at the foot of the cross according to St John (Jn 19.25):

> He introduces as standing by the cross his mother and the other women with her, and it is clear that they were weeping. The female sex is always somewhat tearful and particularly prone to lamentation when it has an abundant cause for the shedding of tears. What is it then that induced the blessed evangelist to go into trivial details and mention the transgression of the women? His reason was to show this – that the Passion in its unexpectedness had caused even the mother of the Lord to fall, as it appears, and that the death on the cross, being extremely bitter, made her depart to some extent from the thoughts that were fitting, as did also the insults of the Jews and the mocking of the one who had been hung by the soldiers stationed by the cross, and the way they dared to divide up his clothes in the very sight of his mother. For you need not doubt that she admitted into her mind thoughts of the following kind: 'I gave birth to the one who is mocked on the tree. Perhaps in saying that he was the true Son of almighty God he was mistaken. He was apparently in error when he said, "I am the Life." Why was he crucified? Why was he caught in some way in the snares of the murderers? Why did he not defeat the plots of his persecutors? Why does he not come down from the cross, even though he ordered Lazarus to come back to life and amazed all Judaea with his miracles?'
>
> It is extremely probable that a mere woman, ignorant of the mystery, was deceived into thoughts of this kind. For we must conceive in all justice that the nature of the events was sufficient to upset even a sober mind ... how then is it surprising if the delicate mind of a mere woman was seduced into thoughts that exhibit weakness? In saying this we are not guessing blindly, as someone might think, but proceeding to a surmise on the basis of what is written about the mother of the Lord. For we remember that the righteous Symeon, when he took the Lord as an infant into his arms, as it is written, gave thanks ... and said to the holy virgin, 'Behold this is for the fall and the raising of many in Israel, and a sign to be spoken against. And your own soul a sword shall pierce, so that the thoughts of many hearts will be revealed' [Lk. 2.34–5]. By 'sword' he meant the sharp onset of grief that cleaves the mind of a woman and stimulates misguided thoughts. For temptations test the heart of those who suffer, and reveal the thoughts within...
>
> I would add a further point: how could it not have been necessary for the Lord to make provision when his own mother had been made to fall and her thoughts had become disrupted and confused? Being true God and discerning the movements that occur deep in the heart, how could he be unaware of the ideas that upset her, at this time in particular, in relation to the venerable cross? Knowing, therefore, the thoughts in her mind, he entrusts her to the disciple as the best of teachers, well able to expound the profound mystery.[18]

---

18. *Commentary on John*, ibid.: IV.1, 3209–12, 3215.

By later standards, Cyril may seem to be lacking in respect towards Our Lady, but this is to judge him by an anachronistic standard. The Virgin *Theotokos* had indeed an indispensable role in his theology, but it was a more narrowly defined one than she was later to take on. The Mariology that is revealed to us by the Nestorian controversy, in both Cyril and his opponents, was firmly Christocentric. Its aim, as we said above, was to encourage the faithful to receive Christ 'in the womb of faith', in a spiritual imitation of Mary's giving birth. Her reception of the divine Word in her womb received great emphasis, both as indispensable for the incarnation and as a symbol of the spiritual parturition to which all are called. Supporters of Nestorius after the Council of Ephesus spread the story that Pulcheria had once said to Nestorius, 'Have I not given birth to God?'[19] The story was an invention, but it reflected accurately what lay at the heart of this spirituality: Mary was venerated simply for giving birth to Jesus, not because of her virtues. Her contribution to our salvation was seen to lie in her physical role in the incarnation of the divine Word; it was not necessary to suppose her to have been morally and spiritually perfect. Meanwhile, her role as a powerful intercessor in heaven received virtually no mention, and was clearly undeveloped in contemporary piety.

MARY AND DEIFICATION

In the two decades that followed the Council of Ephesus there occurred a notable shift in doctrinal loyalties: when we come to the next ecumenical council, that held at Chalcedon (across the Bosphorus from Constantinople) in 451, we find that Cyrillian Christology was treated as the yardstick of orthodoxy throughout the East and that Theodoret of Cyrrhus and other representatives of the Antiochene school found themselves, despite imperial support, in a tiny and unpopular minority. Cyril's emphasis on the full union of natures in Christ was linked to a view of human perfectibility that stressed the power of the Spirit to make us saints through a union with Christ in which our fallen natures become as passive and malleable as the human nature adopted by the incarnate Word of God. Christ, as God by nature, has the power to make us in our turn 'gods by grace'.

It was but natural that this found expression in a growing realization that Mary, as the human being most intimately united to Christ, had to be seen and presented, despite the frailty of woman, as a prime example of how union with Christ can liberate human nature from its limitations and enable it to partake of the holiness of the Godhead itself. This found classic expression in the greatest of the theologians who followed in Cyril's footsteps – Severus of Antioch (d. 538). Severus rejected the Chalcedonian definition, on the grounds that its teaching of two natures in Christ was Nestorian. He was therefore condemned as a heretic in the Byzantine tradition, and most of his writings survive only in Syriac translation. These facts have made him a fringe figure in the study of the Greek Fathers, but he remains the most striking

---

19.   Letter to Cosmas, PO 13: 279. See Price 2004: 32–3.

representative of the new current of Marian piety that developed during the century that followed Chalcedon.

Take, for example, his interpretation of the Cana story. We saw above how Theodore of Mopsuestia gave it a misogynist interpretation. Cyril of Alexandria in his own commentary on the passage avoided this extreme, but fails to develop any significant Marian theme:

> When the wine ran short for those who were feasting, his mother asked the Lord to exercise in his goodness his usual love of mankind, saying, 'They have no wine.' She urged him to perform the miracle since he had it in his power to do whatever he wanted. 'Woman, what have you to do with me? My hour has not yet come': this saying the Saviour devised most appropriately for us; for what was necessary was not to rush into action nor to seize the opportunity to show off as a miracle-worker, but to proceed reluctantly and only when requested, bestowing the favour in response to a need rather than to gratify the onlookers ... Moreover, Christ showed by this the greatness of the honour that is owed to parents, when out of respect for his mother he agreed to do what up to this point he had not wanted to do.[20]

Severus of Antioch's treatment represents a sea change in the presentation of the Mary of the Gospels:

> When Mary out of compassion condescended to the need of these people and presented a request, [Jesus] refused it, so as not to appear desirous of empty glory and aiming to share this glory with his mother, as if she had made this request as a contrivance while he was eager to display his miraculous powers. It was to keep his hearers far from this false impression and to show that he did everything for the sake not of glory but of utility that he replied to her severely, to instruct his hearers, as I have said, and teach the truth, and not out of contempt, 'Woman, what have you to do with me? My hour has not yet come.' That these words were not a rebuke but a mode of instruction for the benefit of strangers, was revealed by his mother. For it was not like one who had been reprimanded that she withdrew, and it was not like one who has suffered a rebuke that she did not answer back. But when she discerned in her spirit what had taken place, it was as if Jesus had said absolutely nothing that she said to the servants, 'Do whatever he tells you'...
>
> As we reflect on the text more carefully, we realize that the Mother of God, even after giving birth and thereby serving the mystery of salvation, was full of the Holy Spirit and knew in advance what was going to happen. She was indeed a prophetess, as Isaiah says, 'I approached the prophetess' [Isa. 8.3]. For if this had not been the case, she would have supposed that Jesus would produce wine before the eyes of all spontaneously, out of nothing, and from some invisible source. But because she knew in advance what was going to happen and that

---

20. *Commentary on John*, Campos 1970–85: IV.1, 3183–4.

Jesus would order the servants to draw water to be changed into wine, she too gave them an order in advance, saying, 'Do whatever he tells you.' In this way foreknowledge of what was to occur was shared in some way by both Jesus and Mary, by him as God and by her as someone who acted as a prophetess.[21]

We saw how Proclus lauded Mary as superior to the prophets in that she actually took part in the incarnation that they had merely foreseen. But Severus insisted that Mary surpassed the saints of both the Old and the New Testaments in their own roles:

It is right and fitting that we should offer words of praise to all the saints; let us then honour them by eulogy and festival, as those who have truly served their Master and faithfully contributed to the economy of our salvation . . . As for the Mother of God, the truly holy and ever-Virgin Mary, how could one not honour her as prophetess, as apostle, and as martyr. As prophetess according to the prophecy of Isaiah, who says of her, 'I approached the prophetess, and she conceived and bore a son' [Isa. 8.3] . . . Who is the prophetess mentioned in the divine books, if it is not the Mother of God, the Virgin who gave birth to Emmanuel. . .

Then again she is an apostle, as one will call her, and indeed one will rightly declare that she surpasses all the apostles, for from the first she was counted with the apostles, as is recounted in the Acts of the Apostles, 'They were gathered together and persevered in prayer together with Mary the mother of Jesus' [Acts 1.14]. Then again, if the saying that they heard from Our Lord, 'Go and teach all nations' [Mt. 28.19], had made them apostles, what nation is there that the Virgin has not taught and led to the knowledge of God, even though remaining silent, by means of her unique, exceptional and enduring parturition and her unmatched conception, which make her the mother and root of the preaching of the Gospel?

Then again let us not hesitate to acknowledge her as martyr in all sorts of ways – when she bore courageously the rash judgement of Joseph, who thought that the conception had taken place through adultery (before he discovered the mystery of childbirth through the revelation of the angel), and also when she fled into Egypt before the fury of Herod, and then returned from Egypt and departed for Nazareth, and yet again when she lived day by day among the murderous Jews and lived a life that was close to death.

Manifestly we are right to pay honour to her who is now honoured by the spirits of the just – by the patriarchs as the one who fulfilled the hope they had persevered in for so long, and who brought the blessing of the seed of Abraham, that is, the Christ, a blessing that has reached all peoples and all countries; by the prophets as the one who disclosed the meaning of their prophecies by giving birth to the Sun of Righteousness, and thereby revealed secret, hidden and unknown mysteries; by the apostles as the one they

---

21.   *Cathedral Homily* 119; PO 26: 379–84.

recognize to be the foundation of their preaching; by the martyrs as the first to give them an example of struggle and victory; and by the doctors of the Church and the shepherds of the spiritual flock of Christ as the one who shuts the mouth of heresy and who, like a pure and drinkable fountain, brings forth for us the streams of orthodoxy...

This is why we shower quite remarkable honours on the holy Mother of God and ever-Virgin Mary, as the one who is able, more than all the other saints, to send up prayers on our behalf, and as the one whom we boast of having acquired as the ornament of our race – as the earth endowed with reason from which the second Adam, who is neither fashioned nor created, formed himself according to the flesh, and as the virginal stem from which Christ, the heavenly ladder, was formed in the flesh by the Spirit, in order that we too, through following in his footsteps, might ascend to heaven.[22]

Mary's unique holiness was no longer open to question:

When I wish to lift my eyes to the Virgin Mother of God and touch simply on the thoughts about her, it at once seems to me that a voice comes from God to speak to me and cry loudly in my ears, 'Do not come near; put off your shoes from your feet, for the place on which you are standing is holy ground' [Exod. 3.5]. Truly in effect we must strip our minds not only of 'shoes' but of every mortal and fleshly imagination when we seek to attain the contemplation of any one of the things divine. And what could one contemplate that is more divine than the Mother of God, or which is higher than her? To come near her is to approach holy ground and reach to heaven. Certainly she belonged to the earth, was part of the human race by nature, and was of the same essence as ourselves, even though she was pure of all spot or stain. She brought forth from her own entrails, as well as from heaven, God made flesh, since she conceived and gave birth in a truly divine manner. It is not that she gave her Son his divine nature, since he already possessed it before every beginning and before all ages, but she gave him a human nature without involving him in change, and this out of herself and through the ineffable and mysterious coming of the Holy Spirit. If you want to discover how, your search stops short at the seal of virginity which this parturition did not violate, at that which is sealed and intangible, that remains an ineffable secret. As a result, astounded by this prodigy, one will exclaim like Jacob, 'How awesome is this place; it is the gate of heaven' [Gen. 28.17] ...

The God who is above everything descended also in days of yore, when he promulgated the law on Mount Sinai. 'The appearance of the glory of the Lord', says scripture, 'was like a devouring fire on the top of the mountain in the sight of the people of Israel' [Exod. 24.17] ... God wanted to instruct them by fear and correct them by the law ... There where was the spirit of servitude was a smoking mountain, because it received the mere appearance of the

---

22. *Cathedral Homily* 14; ibid. 38: 400–13.

Eternal in the form of a burning fire and Moses was the minister who played the part of an intermediary. But here in contrast, where is the grace of adoption, is the spiritual mountain, the Virgin, that is made to glitter and shine by the purity and coming of the Holy Spirit ...

The Mother of God is the yeast of the new creation, the root of the true vine of which we have become the branches through the germination of baptism. This is the goal of the reconciliation between God and mankind, on the occasion of which angels sang, 'Glory to God in the highest and peace to men on earth!' This is why memory of the Virgin awakens our souls, making us reflect from what irreconcilable enmity and from what state of war, so to speak, to what peace and to what divine fellowship and society we have been called through her mediation.[23]

The Christological foundation of Mary's unique importance is still clearly and rightly perceived, but she has now become more than simply the owner of the womb that bore Jesus. Mary is now the linchpin in the economy of salvation as the first and supreme instance of how the union between God and man in Christ makes possible the deification of each member of the human race. This led in Severus of Antioch, as in all subsequent theologians, to the elevation of Mary to the status of the most holy of all the saints; this in turn implied that she enjoys unrivalled powers of intercession. The cult of the Virgin in its classic form had now been born. To the development of that cult in liturgy and church dedications we shall now turn.

THE CULT OF THE VIRGIN

The peace of the Church in the fourth century saw a rapid development in the cult of the saints, centred on the shrines of martyrs. Among women saints, a prominent place was taken by St Thecla, whose shrine at Seleucia in Asia Minor was visited by the most famous of Western pilgrims, Egeria, in the 380s. It was partly the lack of any similar shrine that delayed the development of the cult of the Virgin. The earliest evidence for the dedication of a church to her is in the Acts of the Council of Ephesus, which regularly describe the church where the bishops assembled as 'the church called Mary'; the expression used in the Marian sermon preached there by Cyril of Alexandria (and quoted above) was 'this church of Mary the *Theotokos*'. Even if the building dedicated to the Virgin, whose ruins impress the pilgrim or tourist today, was built later (in *c.* 500), the literary evidence shows that the dedication is older;[24] it doubtless reflected the disputed tradition that the Virgin accompanied the

---

23. *Cathedral Homily* 67; ibid. 8: 349–53, 364–5.
24. It might be supposed that the holding of the council of 431 in a cathedral dedicated to the Virgin shows that her status was at the centre of the debate and that the emperor (Theodosius II) intended the council to condemn Nestorius (so Holum 1982: 164), but there are several indications that Theodosius favoured Nestorius at this stage, notably his appointment of one of Nestorius's allies, Count Candidianus, to represent himself at the council. The choice of Ephesus for the location of the council arose from practical considerations of easy accessibility.

apostle John to Ephesus and died there. Even though, as we have seen, it is a mistake to talk of the Council of Ephesus formally defining that Mary is *Theotokos*, the council appears to have acted as a spur for further dedications, the most famous of which is St Mary Major's in Rome, dedicated to Our Lady by Pope Sixtus (432–40). These dedications stimulated the development of the cult of the Virgin, involving invocatory prayer and the celebration of her intercessory power.

The cult was also assisted by the development (particularly in the sixth century) in the veneration paid to icons; this made up for the lack, manifestly, of major relics of the Virgin. An exceptionally fine sixth-century icon of the Virgin surrounded by angels and saints is still preserved in St Catherine's Monastery on Sinai.[25] There are notable references to images of the Virgin in the *Spiritual Meadow* of John Moschus, composed in Palestine in *c.* 600. We read, for example, of a hermit near Jerusalem, who on his frequent visits to distant shrines would entrust himself to the Virgin's protection and leave a lamp burning before an icon of the Virgin; each time he returned to his cell he found the lamp 'well cared for and alight' (ch. 180) – manifest proof of the Virgin's favour. Another story tells of how a hermit, plagued by the demon of fornication, received a promise from the demon to leave him alone if he stopped venerating an icon of the Virgin in his possession. The hermit consulted a senior monk, who replied, 'It would be better for you to leave no brothel in the town unvisited than to diminish your reverence to our Lord Jesus Christ and his mother' (ch. 45). In the West at around the same date, Bishop Gregory of Tours (d. 594) recounts a number of Marian miracles in his *Book of Miracles*, some of Palestinian and some of local Gallic origin, and associated with relics or shrines of the Virgin (I.1: 8–10). The development of Marian feasts also continued apace, with the feasts of the Annunciation, Nativity and Presentation appearing in the mid-sixth century, to which the Dormition was added on direct imperial initiative at the beginning of the seventh.[26] Meanwhile, Constantinople had come to house notable relics of the Virgin, her veil and her girdle, which increased in prominence throughout the sixth century. It was the defeat of the Avar and Persian siege of Constantinople in 626, after an icon of the Virgin had been hung on the gates of the city, that secured her status as the unrivalled protector and patron of the imperial city.

Our Lady's role in protecting the imperial city extended also to intercession on behalf of the needs of individuals. In the *Life of St Stephen the Younger*, his mother prays to the icon of the Virgin of Blachernae (in Constantinople) that she may conceive a son; the Mother of God promptly answers her prayer and Stephen is conceived shortly afterwards.[27] In one of the earliest homilies on the Assumption of the Virgin, dating to *c.* 600, Theotecnus of Livias (in Palestine) wrote of her:

> While she lived on earth, she watched over us all, and was a kind of universal providence for her subjects. Now that she has been taken up into heaven, she is

---

25.   Often reproduced – for example, in Cunningham 1988: 57.
26.   See Jugie 1944: 172–84. More details can be found in Shoemaker, 'Marian Liturgies and Devotion', in this volume, nn. 27 and 28 (135).
27.   PG 100: 1076.

an impregnable rampart for the human race and intercedes for us with God the Son.[28]

Patriarch Germanus of Constantinople, writing in the early eighth century, put the coping stone on the celebration of Mary's powers as an intercessor, as he insists that Mary's assumption into heaven in no way separates her from her devotees:

> You dwell among us still in the spirit; your great role as our protector is the chief mark of your presence among us. All of us hear your voice, and all of our voices come to your attentive ears. You know us because you care for us, and we know your constant patronage and protection. For there is no barrier to the mutual recognition between yourself and your servants ... You watch over us all, O Mother of God, and your care is for all people ... You were separated from the Christian people when you passed from us; you were not taken far off from this corruptible world, O life of our common incorruption, but you come close to those who call upon you, you are found by those who faithfully seek you ... Because you, then, are [Christ's] eternal place of rest, he has taken you to himself in his incorruption, wanting, one might say, to have you near to his words and near to his heart. So whatever you desire of him he gives you with a son's affection; and whatever you ask from him, he brings to fulfillment with a God's power – he who is blessed for all ages![29]

Such passages express a fully developed cult of the Virgin as heavenly intercessor. Her devotees now put particular petitions to her, and her cult has become the supreme example of that cult of the saints that had been developing apace since the beginning of the fourth century. Although the development was smooth and perhaps inevitable, one should note the change of emphasis. Cyril of Alexandria, Proclus of Constantinople and other champions of the full acknowledgement of Mary as Mother of God at the time of the Council of Ephesus took no interest in the intercessory power of Mary and her response to those in need of particular favours: what they were concerned to celebrate was instead the whole work of redemption that Christ had been able to achieve precisely because Mary had carried him in her womb and so united him to the human race. The Virgin was honoured in close union with her Son, in thanksgiving for her part in the greatest gift and miracle of all, the incarnation. The very title *Theotokos* expressed the fact that the cult of Mary was centred on her divine maternity, just as icons of Our Lady always represented her together with the Christ child. We have described the evolution by which the invocation of Mary as the all-powerful intercessor became prominent in her cult. Even so, she remained pre-eminently the *Theotokos*, the one whose supreme glory was to have given birth to God himself. This was faithful to the biblical witness to

---

28. Daley 1998: 80.
29. Homily 1, ibid.: 157–9.

Mary, and has served ever since to preserve in the Eastern tradition the sound doctrinal foundation of Marian devotion.[30]

BIBLIOGRAPHY

Primary Sources

Campos, Sergius Alvarez (1970–85) *Corpus Marianum Patristicum*, 6 vols (one in two parts) and *Indices*, Burgos: Aldecoa. A comprehensive collection of extracts relating to Mary from the Church Fathers of the first seven centuries. Latin texts are given in Latin only, Greek texts in Greek and Latin.

Constas, Nicholas (2003) *Proclus of Constantinople and the Cult of the Virgin in Late Antiquity: Homilies 1–5, Texts and Translations*, Leiden: Brill.

Daley, Brian E. (trans.) (1998) *On the Dormition of Mary: Early Patristic Homilies*, Crestwood NY: St Vladimir's Press.

Proclus of Constantinople (2001), *Homilies on the Life of Christ*, trans. with introduction and notes by J. H. Barkhuizen, Brisbane: Australian Catholic University.

Secondary Sources

Although all the items listed below are instructive, students should be aware that the history of the early cult of Mary has not yet been exhaustively explored, and that much of the literature is unguarded in its use of sometimes doubtful or ambiguous evidence. Items particularly recommended are starred.

Allen, Pauline (1996) 'Severus of Antioch and the Homily: the End of the Beginning?', in P. Allen and Elizabeth Jeffries (eds), *The Sixth Century: End of Beginning?*, Brisbane: Byzantina Australiensia 10: 163–75.

★Bardy, G. (1938) 'La doctrine de l'intercession de Marie chez les Pères grecs', *La Vie Spirituelle* 56, Supplément: 1–37.

Boss, Sarah J. (2000) *Empress and Handmaid*, London: Cassell.

Cameron, Averil (1978) 'The Theotokos in Sixth-century Constantiniople: A City Finds its Symbol', *Journal of Theological Studies* n.s. 29: 79–108.

★Cameron, Averil (2004) 'The Cult of the Virgin in Late Antiquity: Religious Development and Myth-Making', in Swanson (ed.), *The Church and Mary*: 1–21.

Cignelli, Lino (1966) *Maria Nuova Eva nella Patristica greca (sec. II-V)*, Assisi: Porziuncola.

Cooper, Kate (1998) 'Contesting the Nativity: Wives, Virgins, and Pulcheria's *imitatio Mariae*', *Scottish Journal of Religious Studies* 19 (1), Spring: 31–43.

Cooper, Kate (2004) 'Empress and *Theotokos*: Gender and Patronage in the Christological Controversy', in Swanson (ed.), *The Church and Mary*: 39–51.

★Cunningham, Mary B. (1988) 'The Mother of God in Early Byzantine Homilies', *Sobornost* 10.2: 53–67.

Cunningham, Mary B. (2004) 'The Meeting of the Old and the New: the Typology of Mary the Theotokos in Byzantine Homilies and Hymns', in Swanson (ed.), *The Church and Mary*: 52–62.

Gambero, Luigi (1999) *Mary and the Fathers of the Church: The Blessed Virgin Mary in Patristic Thought*, trans. Thomas Buffer, San Francisco: Ignatius Press.

Gambero, Luigi (2001) 'Patristic Intuitions of Mary's Role as Mediatrix and Advocate: The Invocation of the Faithful for her Help', *Marian Studies* 52: 78–101.

---

30. Contrast 'the modern aversion to Mary's physical motherhood' in recent Western piety, as identified by Boss 2000: 52–67.

Giamberardini, Gabriele (1975) *Il Culto Mariano in Egitto, I, sec. I–VI*, 2nd edn, Jerusalem: Franciscan Press.

Graef, Hilda (1963) *Mary: A History of Doctrine and Devotion*, vol. 1, *From the Beginnings to the Eve of the Reformation*, ch. 3, 'The Council of Ephesus and Afterwards', London: Sheed and Ward.

Holum, Kenneth G. (1982) *Theodosian Empresses: Women and Imperial Dominion in Late Antiquity*, esp. chs IV and V, Berkeley: University of California Press.

Jouassard, G. (1949) 'Marie à travers la Patristique: Maternité divine, Virginité, Sainteté', in Hubert du Manoir (ed.), *Maria: Etudes sur la Sainte Vierge*, vol. 1, Paris: Beauchesne: 69–157.

Jugie, M. (1944) *La Mort et l'Assomption de la Sainte Vierge: Étude historico-doctrinale*, Studi et Testi 114, Vatican City.

Klauser, Theodor (1972) 'Rom und der Kult der Gottesmutter Maria', *Jahrbuch für Antike und Christentum* 15: 120–35.

Limberis, Vasiliki (1994) *Divine Heiress: The Virgin Mary and the Creation of Christian Constantinople*, London: Routledge.

McGuckin, John A. (2001) 'The Paradox of the Virgin-Theotokos: Evangelism and Imperial Politics in the Fifth-Century Byzantine World', *Maria* 2.1: 8–25.

Nichols, Aidan (1993) *Byzantine Gospel: Maximus the Confessor in Modern Scholarship*, ch. 4, 'Michel van Esbroeck on Maximus' Mariology', Edinburgh: T & T Clark.

*O'Carroll, Michael (1983) *Theotokos: A Theological Encyclopedia of the Blessed Virgin Mary*, rev. edn, Wilmington, DA: Michael Glazier. This contains many excellent articles on early Mariology with useful bibliographies, e.g. 'Cyril of Alexandria', 'Intercession, Mary's', 'Sub Tuum, The', 'Theotokos, God-Bearer'.

Pelikan, Jaroslav (1996) *Mary through the Centuries: Her Place in the History of Culture*, New Haven, CT: Yale University Press.

Peltomaa, Leena M. (2001) *The Image of the Virgin Mary in the Akathistos Hymn*, Leiden: Brill.

Price, Richard M. (2004) 'Marian Piety and the Nestorian Controversy', in Swanson (ed.), *The Church and Mary*: 31–8.

Shoemaker, Stephen J. (2002) *Ancient Traditions of the Virgin Mary's Dormition and Assumption*, Oxford: Oxford University Press.

Swanson, Robert N. (ed.) (2004) *The Church and Mary*, Studies in Church History 39, Woodbridge: Boydell Press.

Vassilaki, Maria (ed.) (2005) *Images of the Mother of God*, Aldershot: Ashgate.

Wessel, Susan (1999) 'Nestorius, Mary and Controversy, in Cyril of Alexandria *Homily IV* (*De Maria deipara in Nestorium, CPG 5248*)', *Annuarium Historiae Conciliorum* 31: 1–49.

Wright, D. F. (2004) 'From "God-Bearer" to "Mother of God" in the Later Fathers', in Swanson (ed.), *The Church and Mary*, 22–30.

Young, Frances (2003) 'Theotokos: Mary and the Pattern of Fall and Redemption in the Theology of Cyril of Alexandria', in T. G. Weinandy and D. A. Keating (eds), *The Theology of St Cyril of Alexandria: A Critical Appreciation*, London: T & T Clark: 55–74.

Cyril of Alexandria on the Title Theotokos

Cyril's understanding of the significance of the title *Theotokos* is given succinctly in his *Third Letter to Nestorius*, which is included in the documents of the ecumenical Council of Ephesus.[1] In the passage quoted below, Cyril explains that the title indicates Mary's status as the one who conceived and bore the Word of God incarnate, in consequence of which all human life has the possibility of being sanctified from the moment of conception.

> Therefore, because the holy virgin bore in the flesh God who was united hypostatically with the flesh, for that reason we call her mother of God (*theotokos*), not as though the nature of the Word had the beginning of its existence from the flesh (for 'the Word was in the beginning and the Word was God and the Word was with God' [Jn 1.1], and he made the ages and is coeternal with the Father and craftsman of all things), but because, as we have said, he united to himself hypostatically the human and underwent a birth according to the flesh from her womb. This was not as though he needed necessarily or for his own nature a birth in time and in the last times of this age, but in order that he might bless the beginning of our existence, in order that seeing that it was a woman that had given birth to him, united to the flesh, the curse against the whole race should thereafter cease, which was consigning all our earthy bodies to death, and in order that the removal through him of the curse, 'In sorrow thou shalt bring forth children' (Gen. 3.16), should demonstrate the truth of the words of the prophet: 'Strong death swallowed them up' (1 Cor. 15.54 [see Isa. 25.8]), and again, 'God has wiped every tear away from all faces' (Isa. 25.8; cf. Rev. 7.17; 21.4). It is for this cause that we say that in his economy he blessed marriage and, when invited, went down to Cana in Galilee with his holy apostles (Jn 2.1–11).

---

1.   'Council of Ephesus – 431', DEC: 58.

4

MARY IN PATRISTIC THEOLOGY

TINA BEATTIE

INTRODUCTION

To evaluate the extent of Marian influence on the early Church is like putting together a jigsaw with many missing pieces. Although there is evidence of devotion to Mary prior to the Council of Ephesus (431),[1] her significance burgeoned after that time, when the title *Theotokos* ('Godbearer' or 'Mother of God') was officially endorsed for use by the whole Church. This accorded Mary a transcendent personal role in the story of salvation that is largely absent from theological texts of the first four centuries. The earliest Marian theology focuses on the significance of Mary's virginal motherhood for our understanding of the divine and human natures of Jesus Christ (Christology), and on her biblical significance as the New Eve with regard to the meaning and scope of salvation in Christ (soteriology). Only gradually did her personal holiness become a focus for theological reflection and veneration, so that, from the late fourth century, she began to acquire the kind of status that would make her a universal figure of devotion for Orthodox and Catholic Christians throughout the medieval and modern eras. Although it would be misleading to suggest a clear separation between theology and spirituality, particularly in the pre-modern Church, the focus of this chapter is early theological and doctrinal texts about Mary, since early Marian devotion has been dealt with elsewhere.[2]

Ante-Nicene theology took shape in a turbulent era when Christianity was a minority religion spread across the Roman Empire, representing a plurality of beliefs and devotions in different geographical and cultural contexts, with many of its followers being subjected to persecution and martyrdom. Early Christian doctrine was clarified through being challenged and defended in intense intellectual debates and cultural and political conflicts. Some of the Church Fathers, such as Justin Martyr (100/110–65), Clement of Alexandria (d. 215) and his successor in the Alexandrian

---

1. See Stephen J. Shoemaker, 'Marian Liturgies and Devotion in Early Christianity', in this volume, 130–45. See also Farrell 1997.

2. G. R. Evans points to the difficulty of discerning the relationship between popular Christianity and the writings of the Church Fathers; see Evans 2004, 'Introduction': 1–2. With regard to Marian devotion, the apocryphal literature suggests that Mary may have been a more significant figure in early popular Christianity than she was in early patristic writings. Indeed, Geoffrey Ashe has hypothesized that, alongside the masculine, Christ-centred Church, prior to the Council of Ephesus there may have been numerous Marian cults led by women, which were partially assimilated into mainstream Christianity after Ephesus; see Ashe 1976.

School, Origen (185–254), sought to emphasize the compatibilities between Christianity and Greek thought, while others such as Tertullian (*c.* 160–post-220) were vehemently opposed to such accommodations. Tertullian famously asked, 'What then do Athens and Jerusalem have to do with one another?'[3] Henry Chadwick suggests that 'he presupposes that the correct and indeed the only true answer to his question is "nothing whatever" '.[4]

While Greek philosophy had a formative influence on the development of Christian doctrine, the earliest patristic writings, including those on Mary, are rooted in Scripture as their primary theological resource. However, what counted as Scripture was still open to debate, and the boundaries between what would become the Christian Bible and other early Christian literature were fluid. So, for example, we see the influence of texts such as the second-century *Protevangelium of James* on the Marian writings of some of the Fathers, even though this was not included in the biblical canon. The early Fathers referred mainly to the Hebrew Scriptures and the Gospels, with the events and people of the Jewish Bible being read as allegories or types which anticipated the coming of Christ and were fulfilled in him.[5] This is particularly true of what would become known as the Alexandrian School, while the School of Antioch was more concerned with the language and grammar of Scripture. This difference in emphasis would have some influence on the development of Marian theology, which was more restrained in Antiochene theology than in the more symbolic and mystical interpretations of the Alexandrian School.

This complex background needs to be borne in mind in what follows, for any attempt to organize an ancient and diverse textual legacy into significant themes risks oversimplification. This is particularly true given the contested nature of Mariology and the effects of this on patristic scholarship. Scholars influenced by the Protestant tradition tend to minimize or even ignore the extent to which Mary features in the writings of the Fathers, while those in the Catholic tradition risk exaggerating her significance and projecting into patristic writings some of the devotional impulses which belong to a later era.

The readings in this chapter have been arranged to give a sense of the contours of the emergent Marian tradition and its development in the first five centuries of the Christian era. Topics have been arranged thematically, although there is also a chronological pattern to this, in so far as different aspects of the Church's beliefs about Mary emerged in response to various Christological controversies and debates, and in the context of changing social circumstances. It might therefore be helpful to begin by situating early developments in Marian theology in their historical and cultural contexts.

The New Testament says relatively little about Mary in comparison to the tradition

---

3. Tertullian, *De praescrip. haeret.* 7, quoted in Ramsey 1986: 210.
4. Chadwick 1966: 1.
5. See John W. Rogerson, 'The First Christian Writings', in Evans 2004. It should be noted that a strongly anti-Jewish bias informs some patristic writings on Mary, particularly in the appeal to Old Testament typology to argue that in Christ, God's promise to the Jewish people is fulfilled. There is still much scholarly analysis to be done in this area of early Marian writings.

that would later develop around her, and there are few references to her in the post-biblical writings of the apostolic Fathers (so-called because some believe they knew the apostles personally). Although some of the apocryphal literature of the second and third centuries points to popular interest in Mary, among the surviving theological and doctrinal literature of the apostolic era, the letters of Ignatius of Antioch (d. *c.* 110) are the earliest which contain references to Mary. Hilda Graef describes Mary as remaining 'in a kind of chiaroscuro'[6] in the Bible and the early Church.

The sparsity of early Marian theology might in part be attributed to the influence of the pagan cults with their maternal deities.[7] The first Christians shared the Jewish rejection of the cults, and they may have believed that drawing attention to Mary would have made Christianity susceptible to the influence of goddess worship. Allied to this, many early Christians had personal experience of the cults, and it is clear from their writings that, after conversion to Christianity, they developed a sense of revulsion over what they saw as the degenerate nature of cultic worship.

It is also possible that silence was an important dimension of early Christian reflection on Mary's role in the mystery of the incarnation. Luigi Gambero suggests that there might be 'an explanation of a "mystical nature" for the silence of Scripture and the ancient Fathers about Mary'. He quotes Ignatius of Antioch who 'affirmed that Christ himself "came forth from silence" '.[8] Moreover, a suggestion put forward by Ignatius and taken up by Origen, that the virginal birth of Christ had to be hidden from the devil,[9] might offer a further clue as to why early Christian writings rarely mention Mary.

Whatever the reasons for this initial silence, by the time of the post-apostolic Fathers there is more literature about Mary's doctrinal and biblical significance as the Virgin Mother of Christ and the New Eve. Among the second-century Apologists, the writings of Justin Martyr (d. *c.* 165) are the first to refer to Mary as the New Eve, a title which also features in the writings of Irenaeus (d. *c.* 202) and Tertullian. Mary is referred to in the surviving work of Clement of Alexandria and in the writings and homilies of Origen, who is the best-known representative of the so-called Alexandrian school of theology, noted for its combination of intellectual enquiry and mystical reflection. After a lull in the second half of the third century, increasing veneration of Mary during the fourth century is reflected in her growing significance in homilies, letters, biblical commentaries and theological writings, particularly those of the Greek and Syrian Fathers. The post-Nicene writings of Athanasius (295–373), also of Alexandria in Egypt, mark a significant development in Marian theology, with a style which suggests a personal devotion to Mary and a new emphasis on her personal qualities of silence and solitude as exemplary for consecrated virgins. This growing popularity of Mary might be understood in the context of two concurrent developments, both resulting from Christianity's new legitimacy in the Roman Empire.

---

6. Graef 1994: 132.
7. See ibid.: 32–3.
8. Gambero 1999: 28, quoting Ignatius of Antioch, *To the Magnesians*: 8, 2.
9. See Origen, 'Homily 6', in Lienhard SJ 1996: nos. 3–4 (24–5); PG 13, 1814–15.

The official toleration of Christianity by Rome dates from the edict of Milan in 313. After this, asceticism begins to take the place of martyrdom as a form of participation in the sufferings of Christ, and Mary's virginity becomes a model for the ascetic life. Her significance therefore expands to include ascetical and moral as well as Christological and soteriological aspects, so that her personal attributes of obedience, modesty and virginal purity begin to be emphasized, particularly with regard to female chastity. Graef points out that 'every age unconsciously forms its image of the Virgin according to its own ideal; and the age of the Fathers of the Desert could not conceive her otherwise than as a solitary, leading a life of the most exemplary austerity and consorting not even with her own brothers but only with angels.'[10]

One of the first challenges encountered by Christianity after it acquired imperial status was that posed by Arianism, which spread from the schools of Alexandria through the eastern Mediterranean. Arius (c. 250–336), a Christian priest in Alexandria, disputed a claim that would later inform the classic doctrine of the Trinity, by arguing that the Logos was not co-eternal and co-equal with God, but was created in time and was inferior to the Father. In order to quell the growing controversy, the Emperor Constantine I called an assembly of bishops at Nicaea (now Iznik in Turkey) in 325, at which Christ was confirmed as being 'of the same substance' or 'of one being' (homoousios) with God, and Arianism was condemned as a heresy.

In the fifth century, a movement known as Nestorianism provided the impetus for further refinement of Nicene Christology. Nestorius (c. 386–c. 451), Patriarch of Constantinople from 428, was associated with the School of Antioch under the tutelage of Theodore of Mopsuestia (352–428). Nestorius argued that the human and divine natures in Christ did not form a perfect unity, but were joined together while remaining separate. He rejected the popular title Theotokos, arguing that Mary should be known only as Christotokos ('Mother of Christ' or 'Christbearer'). Cyril, Patriarch of Alexandria (c. 375–444), took a stand against Nestorius, and the Emperor Theodosius II (c. 401–50) convened an ecumenical council at Ephesus in 431 to resolve the conflict. After a heated struggle with much political manoeuvring, Cyril's Alexandrian theology prevailed over that of Nestorius, the title Theotokos was adopted for use by the whole Church, and Nestorianism was condemned as a heresy. There were candlelit processions in the streets of Ephesus in honour of Mary, and in 432 Pope Sixtus III (d. 440) ordered the Basilica of Santa Maria Maggiore to be built on the Esquiline Hill in Rome, on the site of an earlier church dedicated to Mary, to commemorate the council. Given that this church, which is dedicated to the Mother of God, is built near the site of an earlier temple to the goddess Juno Lucina and may incorporate some of the marble columns from that temple, Santa Maria Maggiore might be seen as an enduring symbol of the assimilation of the Great Mother of the pagan cults to the cult of Mary after the Christianization of Rome.

Turning to the geographical spread of early Marian writings, prior to the late fourth century most of these are associated with the Greek- and Syriac-speaking

---

10. Graef 1994: 51.

churches of the Mediterranean basin and Asia Minor, although Irenaeus, originally from Asia Minor and later a priest – or possibly bishop – in Lyons, represents an early link between East and West. Syrian Christianity was closely associated with Antioch and Nestorianism, and today some Eastern churches are still described as Nestorian. Many consider that the hymns and other writings of Ephrem of Syria (306–73), sometimes referred to as 'the harp of the Holy Spirit', are unsurpassed in early Marian literature for their lyricism, symbolism and imagery.[11]

The influence of the Cappadocian Fathers on the theology of the Eastern Church was considerable, but their writings say relatively little about Mary. Gregory of Nyssa (d. 394) offers the most extensive reflections on Mary's virginity and her motherhood of God. She is also referred to in the writings of Basil of Caesarea (d. 379) and, to a lesser extent, in those of Gregory of Nazianzus (d. *c.* 390). Among the more significant Marian writings of the Greek-speaking world in the late fourth century are those of Epiphanius (d. 403), Bishop of Salamis, known for his refutation of heresies, including the cult of the Collyridians.[12] As well as consolidating and affirming the main features of the Eastern Marian tradition (Mary's perpetual virginity, the veneration owed to her as the *Theotokos*, the Eve/Mary parallel), Epiphanius is the earliest surviving source for the idea of Mary's bodily assumption into heaven. It is also worth mentioning the writings of John Chrysostom (d. 407), Patriarch of Constantinople, who was associated with the Antiochene school. While Alexandrian and Cappadocian theology emphasized the glory of the *Theotokos*, the Antiochene approach was more restrained and Mary was rarely referred to as *Theotokos*, reflecting the tendency expressed by Nestorius. John Chrysostom is a dissenting voice in fourth-century writings on Mary. Although he upholds the significance of Mary's virginal motherhood, he portrays her as ambitious, ignorant of her son's role, and obstructing his ministry in biblical accounts such as the description of Jesus' mother and brothers in Matthew 12.46–50, and the account of the wedding of Cana in John 2.1–11.

The Marian theology that emerges in the Latin Church from the mid-fourth century is more restrained and less speculative than that of the Greek Fathers, and tends to avoid reference to Mary as Mother of God (*Mater Dei* being the Latin equivalent of *Theotokos*), perhaps because of an ongoing resistance to the pagan cults. Hilary of Poitiers (315–67) is one of the first Latin theologians to accord significance to Mary's personal qualities as well as her virginal motherhood. However, the most significant early Latin writings on Mary are those of Ambrose (339–97), Bishop of Milan, who had studied the Greek Fathers and had a formative influence on the development of Western Mariology, including being the first to associate Mary with the Church; Jerome (*c.* 342–420), who placed considerable emphasis on the biblical significance of Mary, and Augustine (354–430), who consolidated a number of Marian themes – Mary's perpetual virginity, her personal sinlessness and her relationship with the Church. Augustine also emphasized the importance of both sexes being involved in the work of

11.   See Murray 1975: 142–150.
12.   Ashe 1976: 149–151. See also Shoemaker, in this volume, 132–4 and 137–8.

redemption, since both had played an active role in the fall. Buby describes Augustine's Marian doctrine as 'the crowning synthesis of what had been handed down from the Scriptures and what had been expounded, preached, and defended by the sub-apostolic writers and the theologians of the West and Alexandria who have preceded him'.[13]

The Council of Ephesus had a greater impact on the Marian theology of the East than on that of the West and, while Syriac and Greek writings on Mary proliferated, the Western Church struggled to survive in a climate of political and military upheaval which was hardly conducive to creative theological reflection. Latin doctrine on Mary was summarized by Leo the Great, pope from 440 to 461, in his famous Tome.[14] Eutyches (d. 454), an archimandrite of a monastery at Constantinople, opposed the dual-nature Christology of Nestorianism and proposed instead a single-nature Christology, which denied Christ's full humanity in favour of his divinity. Consulted by Flavius, the Patriarch of Constantinople, Leo wrote a letter in 449, subsequently approved at the Council of Chalcedon (451), in which he set out the Latin Church's position on Mary. Leo affirms the reality of Mary's motherhood of Christ, the conception of Christ by the Holy Spirit, Mary's virginity before and after his birth, and the unity of the two natures in the person of Christ, who descended from heaven and was born of Mary.

By the end of the fifth century all the main features of later Marian theology had been established, even if they would undergo considerable elaboration and development in the Western Church – less so in the Orthodox Church, whose liturgical life remains deeply rooted in the patristic age. Mary was the Virgin Mother of God, and; the New Eve in relation to Christ (the New Adam); she was worthy of veneration (*hyperdulia*), but not of adoration (*latria*), which was owed only to God; she was a model of the Christian life, particularly with regard to virginal asceticism; and she was symbolically associated with the motherhood of the Church. Although it would be many centuries before debates about the sinlessness of Mary would be resolved, some patristic writers had claimed that she was free from sin, thus paving the way for the doctrine of the immaculate conception. The idea of her bodily assumption into heaven at the end of her earthly life became a focus for early Marian devotion, with the first evidence for the Feast of the Dormition dating from 600 in Constantinople and about 50 years later in Rome.

Despite considerable variations in interpretation and emphasis, patristic thinkers of the first five centuries were refining and distilling a doctrinal tradition which would form the basis of all subsequent Christian orthodoxy. Catholics would argue that this is as true for Mariology as it is for all other aspects of theology, although Protestants would argue that Catholic Marian doctrines are an elaboration which do not reflect the teachings of Scripture and the early Church. In what follows I focus on central themes concerning Mary which emerge in the patristic era, and which have had a significant influence on subsequent Marian doctrine in Catholic and Orthodox Christianity.

---

13. DEC: 77–82.
14. Buby 1996: 171.

When Cardinal Newman sought to defend the Catholic Church's Marian teachings, he turned to the Church Fathers as an authenticating source for subsequent Catholic beliefs about Mary. I shall therefore end this brief introductory survey with an extract from Newman's *Letter to Pusey*.

> The Fathers made me a Catholic, and I am not going to kick down the ladder by which I ascended into the Church. It is a ladder quite as serviceable for that purpose now, as it was twenty years ago. Though I hold, as you know, a process of development in Apostolic truth as time goes on, such development does not supersede the Fathers, but explains and completes them. And, in particular, as regards our teaching concerning the Blessed Virgin, with the Fathers I am content; – and to the subject of that teaching I mean to address myself at once. I do so, because you say, as I myself have said in former years, that 'That vast system as to the Blessed Virgin ... to all of us has been the special *crux* of the Roman system.'
>
> Here, let me say, as on other points, the Fathers are enough for me. I do not wish to say more than they suggest to me, and will not say less. You, I know, will profess the same; and thus we can join issue on a clear and broad principle, and may hope to come to some intelligible result. We are to have a Treatise on the subject of our Lady soon from the pen of the Most Reverend Prelate; but that cannot interfere with such a mere argument from the Fathers as that to which I shall confine myself here. Nor indeed, as regards that argument itself, do I profess to be offering you any new matter, any facts which have not been used by others, – by great divines, as Petavius, – by living writers, nay, by myself on other occasions. I write afresh nevertheless, and that for three reasons; first, because I wish to contribute to the accurate statement and the full exposition of the argument in question; next, because I may gain a more patient hearing than has sometimes been granted to better men than myself; lastly, because there just now seems a call on me, under my circumstances, to avow plainly what I do and what I do not hold about the Blessed Virgin, that others may know, did they come to stand where I stand, what they would, and what they would not, be bound to hold concerning her.[15]

MARIAN THEMES IN PATRISTIC THEOLOGY

Virginal Motherhood

Some of the earliest disputes concerning the faith of the Christian Church arose with regard to the incarnation – the belief that Jesus Christ was fully God and fully human, and that the divine and human natures, although remaining distinct, were perfectly united in the one person of Christ. The movement known as Gnosticism, which encompassed a broad spectrum of religious and philosophical positions, rejected the idea that Jesus could have experienced all the material conditions of human life, such

---

15. Newman 1866.

as birth, suffering and death, while remaining divine. The polluting effects of the human body – particularly of the maternal body – were seen as incompatible with the divine incorruptibility of Christ. An early Gnostic teaching known as Docetism affirmed the divinity of Jesus but held that he could therefore only have appeared to be human, passing through Mary without taking anything from her and without his divinity being contaminated by her bodiliness. From a different perspective, a Judaic messianic sect known as the Ebionites denied the divinity of Jesus and claimed that he was the natural son of Mary and Joseph. Thus many early Christians had to defend their belief in both the divinity and the humanity of Christ, against those who would deny one or the other.

In response to these critics, the early Fathers insisted upon the virginal motherhood of Mary, which we might think of in terms of the horizontal and vertical axes of the doctrine of the incarnation. As mother, Mary guarantees the humanity of Jesus. He was born of her flesh, his story belongs within the history of the human race, and he participates fully in our humanity. As virgin, Mary is the guarantor of Christ's divinity. Her virginity signifies that the conception of Christ constitutes something new in creation, a cosmic event initiated by God which is outside all human power and initiative. When the Virgin assents to becoming the mother of Christ, and the Holy Spirit comes upon her, a rupture occurs in time and space, so that eternity breaks through into the human condition and renews the whole of creation from within matter itself.

Ignatius, Bishop of Antioch, was martyred early in the second century. The seven surviving letters to the churches which have been reliably attributed to him offer a defence of the incarnation against Docetism, and attest to the authority of the bishops and the apostolic foundations of the Church. His letters constitute the earliest extant writings on Mary after the New Testament. They include five references to Mary, which Buby suggests 'are best seen in a context of creed and mystery'.[16] The primary focus of these is the significance of Mary's virginal motherhood for the human and divine natures of Christ, although they also include a reference to the virginal conception of Christ being concealed from Satan, an idea which would be taken up and developed under the influence of Origen.

> And the prince of this world was in ignorance of the virginity of Mary and her childbearing and also of the death of the Lord – three mysteries loudly proclaimed to the world, though accomplished in the stillness of God! (Ignatius, *To the Ephesians* 19)[17]

> There is only one Physician, both carnal and spiritual, born and unborn, God become man, true life in death; sprung both from Mary and from God, first subject to suffering and then incapable of it – Jesus Christ our Lord. (Ignatius, *To the Ephesians* 7)[18]

---

16. Buby 1996: 10.
17. Kleist 1946: 67; PG 5, 753.
18. Ibid.: 63; PG 5, 737.

Stop your ears therefore when any one speaks to you that stands apart from Jesus Christ, from David's scion and Mary's Son, who was really born and ate and drank, really persecuted by Pontius Pilate, really crucified and died while heaven and earth and the underworld looked on; who also really rose from the dead, since His Father raised Him up, – His Father, who will likewise raise us also who believe in Him through Jesus Christ, apart from whom we have no real life. (Ignatius, *To the Trallians* 9)[19]

[Our Lord] is really *of the line of David according to the flesh*, and the Son of God by the will and power of God; was really born of a virgin, and baptized by John *in order to comply with every ordinance.* Under Pontius Pilate and the tetrarch Herod He was really nailed to the cross in the flesh for our sake – of whose fruit we are, in virtue of His most blessed Passion. (Ignatius, *To the Smyrnaeans* 1)[20]

Mary's virginal motherhood is a reference point for all the post-apostolic Fathers in their discussion of the incarnation, even if there are significant differences of emphasis and interpretation. A convert to Christianity, Justin is an early Christian apologist who set out to champion the Christian faith against its detractors. Of his many writings, only his two *Apologies* and his *Dialogue with Trypho the Jew* have survived. Many of Justin's arguments are based on appeals to Old Testament texts and Greek philosophy and mythology, in order to demonstrate that these are fulfilled in Christ. In the following quotation, he addresses the mystery of Christ's birth by referring to the prophecies of Isaiah:

But since the mystery of His birth now demands our attention I shall speak of it . . . And Isaiah said, Hear then, O house of David; Is it a small thing for you to contend with men, and how do you contend with the Lord? Therefore the Lord Himself will give you a sign. Behold, the virgin shall conceive, and shall bear a son, and his name shall be called Immanuel . . . Now it is evident to all, that in the race of Abraham according to the flesh no one has been born of a virgin, or is said to have been born [of a virgin], save this our Christ. But since you and your teachers venture to affirm that in the prophecy of Isaiah it is not said, 'Behold, the virgin shall conceive,' but, 'Behold, the young woman shall conceive, and bear a son;' and [since] you explain the prophecy as if [it referred] to Hezekiah, who was your king, I shall endeavour to discuss shortly this point in opposition to you, and to show that reference is made to Him who is acknowledged by us as Christ. (Justin, *Dialogue with Trypho*, XLIII)[21]

While insisting upon Christ's divine origination, Justin sees in Mary's virginal motherhood the affirmation of Jesus' physical and historical continuity with the

---

19.   Ibid.: 77–8; PG 5, 788–9.
20.   Ibid.: 90; PG 5, 840–1.
21.   Roberts and Donaldson (eds) 1996: 216; PG 6, 568–9. The reference to mystery might be further evidence that there was a reluctance to discuss the virgin birth in the early Church, for fear that it might lead to misunderstanding.

people of Israel, and confirmation of the fourth Gospel's claim that 'salvation is from the Jews' (Jn 4.22):

> Accordingly He revealed to us all that we have perceived by His grace out of the Scriptures, so that we know Him to be the first-begotten of God, and to be before all creatures; likewise to be the Son of the patriarchs, since He assumed flesh by the Virgin of their family, and submitted to become a man without comeliness, dishonoured, and subject to suffering. (Justin, *Dialogue with Trypho*, C)[22]

In Justin we find elements common to subsequent patristic writings on Mary. Although later language would evolve to include reflection on Mary's personal glory and holiness, the theological significance of her virginal motherhood, supported by appeals to Old Testament types and prophecies interpreted through the lens of the Christian faith, remains consistent. In the fourth-century writings of Athanasius, Mary's virginity is interpreted as proof of Christ's divinity:

> When He came among us, He formed Himself a body, taking it from a Virgin to offer a proof of His divinity which could not be ignored. It had to appear clearly that He who fashioned this body is the Maker of all things. For who, seeing a body being born of the Virgin alone, without the intervention of man, could fail to understand that He who appears in that body is the Maker and ruler of other bodies also? (Athanasius, *On the Incarnation of the Word*)[23]

In Ephrem of Syria we encounter a profound level of reflection on the ways in which three sources – the Old and New Testaments, and nature – illuminate one another in the incarnation. Kathleen McVey writes of Ephrem that 'the linchpin of his theological system is the paradox of the Incarnation, through which God has revealed the relation of the two Testaments to one another and to nature.'[24] Explaining the typological approach that enables him to see the promise of Christ throughout Scripture and in all creation, Ephrem writes,

> In every place, if you look, His symbol is there,
> and when you read, you will find His prototypes.
> (Ephrem, *Virg.* 20.12)[25]

In Ephrem's poetry and other writings, Mary's virginal motherhood becomes the focal point of some of the most eloquent early Christian reflections on the paradox and mystery of the incarnation. In one hymn, he represents Mary herself reflecting on Isaiah:

---

22. Ibid.: 249; PG 6, 709.
23. *On the Incarnation of the Word* 8, ed. Thomson, Oxford: Clarendon Press, 1971: 178, in Gambero 1999: 103; PG 25, 128.
24. McVey 1989: 43.
25. Ibid.: 41.

'Behold a virgin shall conceive and give birth'
without intercourse. Am I having a dream
or a vision that, behold, upon my lap
is Emmanuel? I shall cease all [else]
and give thanks to the Lord of the universe each day.
Whereas they despised virginity in Zion,
they honoured Your mother, O virginal Child
Who put on the evidence of the virginity of His mother
and emerged with it. To me You are Child,
Bridegroom and Son, even God.
(Ephrem, *Hymns on the Nativity* 19, 8–9)[26]

Elsewhere, the mystery of Mary's virginal motherhood is intrinsic to Ephrem's sense of the wonder of the incarnation:

Our Lord, no one knows
how to address Your mother. [I]f one calls her 'virgin',
her child stands up, and 'married' –
no one knew her [sexually]. But if Your mother is
incomprehensible, who is capable of [comprehending] You? ...

A wonder is Your mother: The Lord entered her
and became a servant; He entered able to speak
and He became silent in her; He entered her thundering
and His voice grew silent; He entered Shepherd of all;
a lamb He became in her; He emerged bleating.

The womb of your mother overthrew the orders:
The Establisher of all entered a Rich One;
He emerged poor. He entered her a Lofty One;
He emerged humble. He entered her a Radiant One,
and He put on a despised hue and emerged.
(Ephrem, *Hymns on the Nativity* 11, 1 and 6–7)[27]

The significance of Old Testament typology for the patristic understanding of Mary's virginal motherhood is also found in Gregory of Nyssa's association of the virgin birth with the burning bush:

What a marvellous happening! The Virgin becomes a mother and yet remains a virgin. Take note of this phenomenon. All other women if they remain virgin do not become a mother. Here, however, both words are applied to the same person Mary ... It was appropriate that the Redeemer, who participated in

---

26. Ibid.: 168.
27. Ibid.: 131–2.

human life to enable us to become incorruptible, himself possessed an incorruptible origin. In fact, in our manner of speaking, he comes purely from that woman who had no relations with a man.

It seems to me that already the great Moses had known of this mystery by means of that illumination in which God appeared to him, when he saw the bush burning without being consumed (Exod. 31ff.). Moses, in fact, said, 'I would like to approach to see what great mystery is here.' I believe that with the word 'approach' is not meant a local movement, but a perspective in time. That is what in fact was prefigured in the burning bush, once the intermediate elapsed, the mystery in the Virgin was fully manifested. As on the mountain the burning bush was not consumed, so the Virgin brought forth a child and did so without stain. This bush should not seem as an unlikely happening, but as something which prefigured the body of the Virgin who brought forth God. (Gregory of Nyssa, *On the Lord's Birthday*)[28]

The New Eve

When discussing Old Testament typology in relation to Mary, by far the most important title is that of the New Eve. There are several references in the Pauline epistles to Christ as the New Adam or the Second Adam (cf. Rom. 5.12–21; 1 Cor. 15.21–2, 45–9) and the comparison with Mary as the New Eve was a very early development, being referred to by Justin, Irenaeus and Tertullian. Irenaeus's *Against the Heresies* offers the earliest development of the Eve/Mary typology, and it had a formative influence on all subsequent Marian theology.

The story of creation and the fall in Genesis was seen as both type and antitype of the story of the incarnation, with Mary playing a role in the new creation analogous to that of Eve in the old creation – the one being a narrative of sin and fallenness, the other being a narrative of grace and redemption. This was given added impetus by a tendency among the Latin Fathers to translate Genesis 3.14–15 with a feminine pronoun – 'And the Lord God said to the serpent . . . I will put enmity between thee and the woman and thy seed and her seed: *she* [*ipsa*] shall crush thy head, and thou shalt lie in wait for her heel.' Today, the more commonly accepted translation is masculine, so that Christ rather than Mary can be understood to be the subject, although the Hebrew is most closely translated as 'it'.[29]

Also in Irenaeus we find the symbolic association of Mary's virginal motherhood with the virgin earth from which the first Adam was created. This too is a recurring theme in patristic and medieval writings. Augustine writes, 'The face of the earth, that is, the dignity of the earth, is correctly taken as the mother of the Lord, the Virgin Mary.'[30] This may have considerable significance for environmental theology, since it opens up modern anthropocentric readings of the significance of the

---

28. Buby 1996: 245–6; PG 46, 1136A–B.
29. For a helpful analysis of patristic translations of this text, see Livius 1893: 67–9. See also Brown *et al.* 1978: 29, n. 40.
30. Augustine, *Against the Manichees* 2.24.37, in Teske 1991: 134; PL 34, 216.

incarnation to a more cosmic vision in which all of creation is redeemed and renewed in Christ.[31]

Frances Young summarizes Irenaeus's Genesis typology as follows:

> Renewal and regeneration are key concepts, and they are achieved through 'recapitulation'. What Christ did was again to go over the ground trod by Adam, reversing his disobedience with obedience. Since all humanity is implicated in the Fall, so in Christ all humanity is potentially involved in the Redemption. Details of the correspondence and reversal are pressed: Adam was made through God's will and wisdom, from the virgin earth, so the Word, 'summing up Adam in himself, duly received from Mary, still a virgin, the birth of that nature in which Adam was summed up' (*Against the Heresies* 3.21.10; cf. *Demonstration* 32). Mary's obedience, in response to the angelic announcement reverses Eve's disobedience when seduced by the devil (*Against the Heresies* 3.22.3; 5.19.1; *Demonstration* 33). The transgression which occurred through a tree was undone by the obedience when Christ was nailed to the tree and hung from it (*Against the Heresies* 5.19.1; *Demonstration* 33–4). Thus Irenaeus develops the typology of Adam and Christ found first in St Paul's Epistle to the Romans, and briefly redeployed by Justin Martyr before him … The story of the old covenant prepared the way for the new. Prophecy and event foreshadowed the future. The Word to be incarnate was present already in the words of Scripture, its narratives and its prophecies.[32]

The following readings have been selected to give a sense of the ways in which these two themes from Genesis – Mary as the New Eve and Mary as the Paradise from which the Second Adam was created – inform patristic writings. Note that, as the tradition develops, the focus begins to encompass Mary's personal significance, alongside the Christological and soteriological concerns of the earliest writings.

> For as by one man's disobedience sin entered, and death obtained [a place] through sin; so also by the obedience of one man, righteousness having been introduced, shall cause life to fructify in those persons who in times past were dead. [Rom. 5.19] And as the protoplast himself, Adam, had his substance from untilled and as yet virgin soil ('for God had not yet sent rain, and man had not tilled the ground' [Gen. 2:5]), and was formed by the hand of God, that is, by the Word of God, for 'all things were made by Him', [Jn 1.3] and the Lord took dust from the earth and formed man; so did He who is the Word, recapitulating Adam in Himself, rightly receive a birth, enabling Him to gather up Adam [into Himself], from Mary, who was as yet a virgin. (Irenaeus, *Against the Heresies*, 3.21.10)[33]

---

31. In this respect, see Boss 2004.
32. Frances Young, 'The Interpretation of Scripture', in Evans (ed.) 2004: 26–7. As well as *Against the Heresies*, Young is referring to Irenaeus's work titled *Demonstration of the Apostolic Preaching*.
33. Roberts and Donaldson (eds) 1996: 454.

That the Lord then was manifestly coming to His own things, and was sustaining them by means of that creation which is supported by Himself, and was making a recapitulation of that disobedience which had occurred in connection with a tree, through the obedience which was [exhibited by Himself when He hung] upon a tree, [the effects] also of that deception being done away with, by which that virgin Eve, who was already espoused to a man, was unhappily misled, – was happily announced, through means of the truth [spoken] by the angel to the Virgin Mary, who was [also espoused] to a man. For just as the former was led astray by the word of an angel, so that she fled from God when she had transgressed His word; so did the latter, by an angelic communication, receive the glad tidings that she should sustain (*portaret*) God, being obedient to His word. And if the former did disobey God, yet the latter was persuaded to be obedient to God, in order that the Virgin Mary might become the patroness (*advocata*) of the virgin Eve. And thus, as the human race fell into bondage to death by means of a virgin, so is it rescued by a virgin; virginal disobedience having been balanced in the opposite scale by virginal obedience. For in the same way the sin of the first created man (*protoplasti*) receives amendment by the correction of the First-begotten, and the coming of the serpent is conquered by the harmlessness of the dove, those bonds being unloosed by which we had been fast bound to death. (Irenaeus, *Against the Heresies* 5.19.1)[34]

For it was while Eve was yet a virgin, that the ensnaring word had crept into her ear which was to build the edifice of death. Into a virgin's soul, in like manner, must be introduced that Word of God which was to raise the fabric of life; so that what had been reduced to ruin by this sex, might by the selfsame sex be recovered to salvation. As Eve had believed the serpent, so Mary believed the angel. The delinquency which the one occasioned by believing, the other by believing effaced. But (it will be said) Eve did not at the devil's word conceive in her womb. Well, she at all events conceived; for the devil's word afterwards became as seed to her that she should conceive as an outcast, and bring forth in sorrow. (Tertullian, *On the Flesh of Christ* XVII)[35]

In Athanasius of Alexandria's writings, Mary and Eve are endowed with personal characteristics which reflect the emergence of devotional themes associated with asceticism and female virtue, out of the early biblical typology:

Eve listened to the suggestion of the serpent and tribulations descended upon all. And you have inclined your ear to the supplications of Gabriel, and penitence flourished among the children of humankind. While Eve conversed with the serpent, the human race was affected by the venom of the serpent and tribulations came (*cum obtrectatione et gula adveneunt*). But Mary when she spoke

---

34. Ibid.: 547.
35. Roberts and Donaldson (eds) 1997: 536; PL 2, 827–8.

with Gabriel about how she would come to bear, the lips of the entire human race were cleansed through penitence and justification. Where Eve looked upon the tree with desire, lusts, voluptuousness, and impurity were multiplied upon the earth: All were 'like horses in heat and each one lusted after his neighbor's wife' (Jer. 5.8). But Mary speaking with sweetness looked upon Gabriel, and modesty together with temperance, and purity flourished in virginity upon all humankind. What a heavenly gift was obtained for you, O humankind, O true virgin! (Athanasius, *On Virginity*, MU 71, 212–19)[36]

As with many other themes in early Marian writings, in Ephrem of Syria we find a mystical rendition of the paradox of Mary's virginal motherhood, which exploits the contradictions and contrasts inherent in Christian interpretations of Genesis:

Man imposed corruption on woman when she came forth from him,
today she has repaid him – she who bore for him the Savior.
He gave birth to the Mother, Eve – he, the man who never was born;
how worthy of faith is the daughter of Eve, who without a man bore a child!
The virgin earth gave birth to that Adam, head of the earth;
the Virgin today gave birth to [second] Adam, head of heaven.
(Ephrem, *Nativity* 1, 14–16)[37]

Like Tertullian, Ephrem uses the imagery of the ear when comparing Eve and Mary:

Just as from the small womb of Eve's ear
Death entered in and was poured out,
so through a new ear, that was Mary's,
Life entered and was poured out.
(Ephrem, *Hymns on the Church*)[38]

Medieval artists allude to this imagery when they depict both Eve and Mary with one ear exposed. A more original and unusual symbol occurs in Ephrem's description of Mary and Eve as the two eyes of the world:

Behold the world! To it were given two eyes; Eve was the left eye, the blind eye; Mary instead is the right eye, the luminous eye. Because of the eye which became obscured, the world became dark. Then men, groping in the shadows, will discover the son of sin and will consider it a kind of divinity, calling lies the truth.

But when the world once more begins to shine, thanks to the other eye and to the heavenly light which will take its place in the cavity of this eye, then men

---

36. Buby 1996: 107.
37. McVey 1989: 65.
38. Brock 1992: 33.

will rediscover unity, perceiving that what they had found was causing the ruin of their lives. (Ephrem, *Hymns on the Church*)[39]

As Mariology developed in the Middle Ages and beyond, the contrast between Eve and Mary, which is a common feature of patristic writings, became highly dualistic, so that Eve came to stand unambiguously for sin, sexuality and death, and Mary, Eve's opposite, stood for grace, virginity and life. This is summed up in the popular patristic epithet, 'death through Eve, life through Mary', which is quoted in the Vatican II document on the Church, *Lumen Gentium*.[40] Feminists have pointed out that this dualistic imagery has been deeply detrimental in terms of the Christian representation of women, with Mary, 'alone of all her sex',[41] representing the impossible ideal of the Virgin Mother, while the female sex in general has more commonly been identified with Eve, the sinner and temptress.

However, in exploiting the contrasts between Mary and Eve, patristic writers were primarily concerned not with the condemnation of Eve, but with her redemption in Mary. This theme is clear in the following extracts, all of which make a particular connection between Mary and women's redemption. This aspect of patristic soteriology has been largely neglected by theologians, and it is a potentially rich area for further scholarship in the light of questions that feminism poses to the Marian tradition.

Mary, Eve and the Salvation of Women

In patristic thought, the redemption of Eve in Mary symbolizes the salvation of the whole female sex. When Ephrem of Syria writes 'You have conquered the death of Eve in the daughter of Eve,'[42] he is writing generically, with 'Eve' here signifying womankind in general. The following extracts make a particular connection between Mary and women's redemption.

> Elizabeth prophesies before John; before the birth of the Lord and Savior, Mary prophesies. Sin began from the woman and then spread to the man. In the same way, salvation had its first beginnings from women. Thus the rest of women can also lay aside the weakness of their sex and imitate as closely as possible the lives and conduct of these holy women whom the Gospel now describes. (Origen, *Homilies on Luke*, 8)[43]

---

39. Buby 1996: 320–1.
40. Vatican II, *Lumen Gentium,* Dogmatic Constitution on the Church, n. 57, in Flannery (ed.) 1992: 416.
41. This is the title of Marina Warner's (2000) critique of the cult of the Virgin Mary, *Alone of All Her Sex: The Myth and Cult of the Virgin Mary.* The title comes from the fourth-century writings of Caelius Sedulius.
42. 'Hymns on Virginity' 34.2, in McVey 1989: 412. This is a series of hymns by Ephrem which celebrate the redemption of women with reference to the women of the Old and New Testaments.
43. Lienhard 1996: 33.

At first, the feminine sex was obligated to give thanks to men, because Eve, born of Adam but not conceived by a mother, was in a certain sense born of man. Mary, instead, paid off the debt of gratitude; she did not give birth by means of a man, but by herself, virginally, through the working of the Holy Spirit and the power of God. (Cyril of Jerusalem, *Catecheses* 12, 39)[44]

On account of Mary all women are blessed. No longer does the female stand accused, for it has produced an offspring which surpasses even the angels in glory. Eve is fully healed [Gen. 3.17]; the Egyptian woman has fallen silent [Gen. 39.7–18]; Delilah is wrapped tightly in a shroud [Judg. 16.4–22]; Jezebel has fallen into oblivion [3 Kgs 16.31; 18.4]; and Herodias has been stricken from memory [Mk 6.14–29]. And now the assembly of women is admired: Sarah is praised as the fertile seedbed of nations [Gen. 17.15–20]; Rebeccah is honoured as a shrewd purveyor of blessings [Gen. 27.6–17]; Leah also is admired as the mother of the ancestor (of Christ) according to the flesh [Gen. 29.35; Lk. 3.30]; Deborah is praised because she overcame nature and fought as a leader in combat [Judg. 4.4–14]; Elizabeth is also called blessed because she conceived in her womb the leapings of the Forerunner of grace [Lk. 1.44]; and Mary is venerated for she became a mother, a servant, [Lk. 1.38] a cloud, [Isa. 19.1] a bridal chamber, and the ark of the Lord [Exod. 25.10]. (Proclus, *Homily* 5.3)[45]

For whereas the first virgin was hemmed in with troubles inflicted by the sentence of condemnation on account of her transgression, so that from her come so many groans, and by reason of her every woman has her lot in sorrow, and on her account every childbirth suffers bitterness; the Second Virgin, through the angelic salutation has banished all the misery of the female sex, and has closed up the entire source of sadness that is wont to be present in giving birth, and has dissipated the cloud of despondence with which women are oppressed in childbirth, and caused the light of gladness to shine in families. (Hesychius, *Oration in Praise of Virgins*)[46]

The Incorporeal finds His place on earth, the corporeal in heaven; God is made man, but is shown to be God. All that was done by Adam is washed out by Mary. Hence happy Eve, by whom was given the occasion; yea, rather happy Mary, by whom was offered the cure; happy Eve, by whom is born the people; happier Mary, by whom was born Christ. Hence, whilst He is better to one, both indeed are glorious; for Christ would not have made Mary glad, had He not deformed the former Eve from whom too Mary was herself born: nor would He have come to the people, had she not first sinned in the world. The one is called mother of mankind, the other of salvation. Eve taught us a lesson,

---

44.   Gambero 1999: 139; PG 33, 761 B–C.
45.   Constas 2003: 261–3. I have inserted Scripture references provided by Constas in footnotes into the text for ease of reference.
46.   Buby 1996: 222.

and Mary gave us strength. By Eve we grow, by Mary we reign: by Eve we were brought down to earth, by Mary we are raised to heaven; and with the view of briefly making plain the whole mystery of the Law, I shall show the intimate relation of these two women to one another, and with them of all: how of old Mary was in Eve, and afterwards Eve was revealed by Mary. (Attributed to Ambrose, *Sermon 155, On the First and Second Adam*)[47]

Augustine is sometimes held up as an example of the misogyny of early Christian writers, but in him we find one of the strongest patristic affirmations of the significance of woman's role in the incarnation. Rosemary Radford Ruether's question, 'Can a male savior save women?',[48] is often cited as a key question in feminist theology. Although Augustine had a hierarchical understanding of sexual difference – Christ had to be male because the man is the more perfect human being – he insisted that the participation of both sexes was necessary in the incarnation, because both were equally created and willed by God, and both had participated in the fall:

[H]e himself created both sexes, male and female; and that's why he wished to honour each sex in his birth, having come to liberate each of them. You know, of course, about the first man's fall, how the serpent didn't dare speak to the man, but made use of the woman's services to bring him down. Through the weaker he gained a hold over the stronger; and by infiltrating through one of them he triumphed over both. In order, therefore, to make it impossible for us with a show of righteous, horrified indignation, to put all the blame for our death on the woman, and to believe that she is irredeemably damned; that's why the Lord, who came to seek what was lost (Lk. 19.10), wished to do something for each sex by honoring them both, because both had got lost. In neither sex, then, should we wrong the Creator; the birth of the Lord encouraged each to hope for salvation. The male sex is honored in the flesh of Christ; the female is honored in the mother of Christ. (Augustine, *Sermon 190*)[49]

To show you that it's not any creature of God that is bad, but that it's crooked pleasures that distort them, in the beginning when I made man, I made them male and female. I don't reject and condemn any creature that I have made. Here I am, born a man, born of a woman. So I don't reject any creature I have made, but I reject and condemn sins, which I didn't make. Let each sex take not of its proper honor, and each confess its iniquity, and each hope for salvation. (Augustine, *Sermon 51*)[50]

---

47. Livius 1893: 53.
48. Ruether 1992: 116.
49. *Sermons 184–229Z*, in Hill and Rotelle 1993: 39; PL 38, 1008.
50. *Sermons 51–94 on the New Testament*, in Hill 1991: 22; PL 38, 335.

Just as death came to us through a woman, life was born to us through a woman. And so, by the nature of both one and the other, that is to say, female and male, the devil was vanquished and put to torture, he who had rejoiced in their downfall. It would have contributed little to his punishment if those two natures had been delivered in us without our being delivered by both of them. (Augustine, *On Christian Suffering*, 22, 24)[51]

For this cause did the Virgin Mary undertake all those functions of nature (conceiving, bringing forth, giving milk), with regard to Our Lord Jesus Christ, that she might succour all women who fly to her protection, and thus restore the whole race of women as the New Eve, even as the New Adam, the Lord Jesus Christ, repaired the whole race of men. (Attributed to Augustine, *Sermon 15, On the Birth of the Lord*)[52]

Mary, Eve and the Church

From about the tenth century, Mary's role became closely identified with that of the Church. However, in patristic writings, there is a subtle distinction in the use of the term 'New Eve', depending on whether it refers to Mary or to the Church. While the relationship between Eve and Mary is understood primarily in the context of Genesis 2 and 3 read from the perspective of Luke's annunciation narrative (Lk. 1.26–38), the relationship between Eve and the Church is understood in the context of the creation of Eve in Genesis 2, interpreted from the perspective of the piercing of Christ's side in John 19.34. From the time of Tertullian, this was understood as signifying the creation of the Church from the side of the dead Christ, just as Eve had been created from the side of the sleeping Adam in Genesis. As the mother of Christ, Mary is the perfect role model for the motherhood of the Church, but her maternal role is particular and historical, whereas that of the Church is universal because she is 'mother of all living', fulfilling the name given to Eve in Genesis 3.20. Describing these different meanings of the title 'New Eve', H. Coathalem writes,

[T]he one pronounces her 'fiat' at Nazareth, the other unites herself with the new Adam on the cross. The first capitulates the ancient Eve at the Annunciation, the second at Calvary ... [T]he new Eve-Mary always represents a particular and transitory act, the new Eve-Church, a state and a permanent function of the first Eve.[53]

The idea that Mary is a type of the Church finds its earliest expression in the writings of Ambrose and later, under the influence of Ambrose, Augustine:

Well [does the Gospel say]: married but a virgin; because she is the type of the Church, which is also married but remains immaculate. The Virgin [Church]

---

51. CSEL.41: 124, in Børresen 1995: 75.
52. Livius 1893: 74; PL 39, 1991.
53. Coathalem 1954: 20–1 (my translation).

conceived us by the Holy Spirit and, as a virgin, gave birth to us without pain. And perhaps this is why holy Mary, married to one man [Joseph], is made fruitful by another [the Holy Spirit], to show that the individual churches are filled with the Spirit and with grace, even as they are united to the person of a temporal priest. (Ambrose, *Exposition on Luke* 2, 7)[54]

Referring to those enrolled in the Church as catechumens, Augustine writes:

Perhaps you will say to me: If she is a virgin, how can she bear children? Or, if she does not bear children, why have we given her our names, in order to be reborn from her womb?

I answer: She is a virgin, *and* she bears children. Imitate Mary, who gave birth to the Lord. Did not holy Virgin Mary both give birth as a virgin and remain a virgin? So also the Church: she gives birth, *and* she is a virgin. And, if you think about it, she gives birth to Christ, because those who are baptized are his members. The apostle says: 'You are the body of Christ and his members' (1 Cor. 12.27). If the Church, then, gives birth to the members of Christ, then the Church greatly resembles Mary. (Augustine, *Sermon Guelferbytanus* 1, 8)[55]

However, Augustine was also at pains to emphasize that Mary's role was subordinate to that of the Church, of which she too was a member:

Mary is holy, Mary is blessed, but the Church is better than the Virgin Mary. Why? Because Mary is part of the Church, a holy member, an outstanding member, a supereminent member, but a member of the whole body nonetheless. If she is a member of the whole body, the body is undoubtedly greater than one of its members. (Augustine, *Sermon Denis* 25, 7)[56]

Moreover, Mary is not the only woman to serve as a type of the Church. Yves Congar writes, 'All the women of the Bible have, without doubt, been envisaged as types of the Church, under one aspect or another.'[57] While Mary's role is pre-eminent, she is closely identified with other biblical women, so that 'She has a place, a choice place, in an ensemble from which it seems arbitrary to extricate her.'[58] We see something of this association of all women with Eve as symbol of the redeemed community in the following text from Ambrose:

Come Eve, no longer one to be shut out from paradise, but rather to be rapt up to heaven. Come Eve, now Sara, since thou bearest children not in sorrow but in joy, not in grief but in laughter ... Come once more, Eve, now Sara, of

---

54. Gambero 1999: 198; PL 15, 1635–6.
55. *Miscellanea Agostiniana*, 447–8, in ibid.: 224.
56. *Miscellanea Agostiniana*, 163, in ibid.: 222.
57. Congar 1954: 21 (my translation).
58. Ibid.: 27.

whom may it be said to her husband: *Hearken to Sara thy wife* [Gen. 21.12]. Albeit thou art subject to a husband – for so it befits thee to be – yet soon hast thou loosed the sentence, seeing that thy husband is bidden to hearken to thee. Now if Sara by giving birth to a type of Christ, merits to be hearkened to by her husband, how great advantage accrues to the sex through its bringing forth Christ, and that without loss of virginity. Come then, Eve, now Mary, who hast not only given us an incentive to virginity, but also brought to us God ... By one woman He descended, but many women has He called. (Ambrose, *On the Institution of Virginity*)[59]

Mary, Death and Redemption

Closely related to the association of Eve with Mary and the Church is the theme of Christ's conquest of death, which is symbolized by virginity. Although, from the late fourth century onwards, Mary's virginity is increasingly interpreted in terms of sexual abstinence and moral purity, for the early Church Fathers its significance derives more from the belief that, in Christ, the cycle of sex and death has been broken. First in Mary, and then in the Church and her virgin members, virginity signifies Christ's triumph over the grave. This theme emerges clearly in the following extract from Gregory of Nyssa's writings on virginity:

It could not be indeed that death should cease working as long as the human race by marriage was working too; he walked the path of life with all preceding generations; he started with every new-born child and accompanied it to the end: but he found in virginity a barrier, to pass which was an impossible feat. Just as, in the age of Mary the mother of God, he who had reigned from Adam to her time found, when he came to her and dashed his forces against the fruit of her virginity as against a rock, that he was shattered to pieces upon her, so in every soul which passes through this life in the flesh under the protection of virginity, the strength of death is in a manner broken and annulled, for he does not find the places upon which he may fix his sting. (Gregory of Nyssa, *On Virginity*, 13)[60]

Some patristic writers see Christ's conquest of death as particularly significant for women's redemption, since it was Eve who was believed to have introduced death into the world. The following extract from a sermon by Peter Chrysologus on the resurrection of Lazarus represents Martha as symbolizing the woman's liberation from death and sin associated with Eve. The sermon describes Martha running to meet Christ after the death of Lazarus (Jn 11.20), and it goes on to make an elaborate association between the name of Mary, the sister of Martha, and the Virgin Mary:

The woman runs on account of a death, she who ran to death; she hastens to receive pardon, she who hastened to her guilt; she reaches her merciful

---

59.   Livius 1893: 259; PL 16, 327.
60.   Schaff and Wace (eds) 1994: 359–60; PG 46, 377–80.

Redeemer, she whom the very wicked seducer overcame; she looks for the resurrection, she who looked for destruction; and the very one who brought death to a man is all out of breath in her quest to restore life to a man. This is why Christ remained in that place, why Christ waited, why he did not enter the crowds, why he did not head for the house, why he did not stop off at the grave, and why he did not hasten to Lazarus, the very reason for his visit. But he takes time with the woman, he lingers with the woman, she is the first one he deals with, since she was the first one the tempter corrupted.

He banishes faithlessness from the woman, he calls her back to faith, so that the very same one who was the accomplice in destroying might assist in saving, and so that, in short, thanks to her faith she might be the mother of the living, who thanks to the devil was for so long the mother of the dead. And because a woman had been the origin of evil, the cause of death, he proceeds to wash away the offense before bestowing his favour; to remove the cause before overturning the sentence; and he takes the precautions necessary for man not to shun as his life-partner the woman through whom he had once been deceived.

And in short, woman would have perished if Christ the Lord had come to the man first. This is why, brothers, Christ is born by means of a woman; this is why the woman always awakens man from the tomb of her womb, so that she may call back with her pains the one whom she drove out with her enticements; so that she might restore through her morning sickness the one whom she ruined by eating.

And so when Martha professed her faith in Christ, and wiped out by her reverent confession whatever blame there was in womanhood, a message is sent to Mary, because without Mary death could not be banished, nor life be restored. Let Mary come, let the one who bears the name of his mother come, so that humanity might see that as Christ dwelt enclosed in the Virgin's womb, so too to that extent the dead will come forth from the underworld, the dead will come forth from the tombs. (Peter Chrysologus, *Sermon* 64, 2)[61]

Ever-Virgin

Although the belief that Mary remained a virgin *in partu* (during childbirth) occurs in the *Protevangelium of James* in the second century, its emergence in theological writings can only be traced with certainty back to the early third century, when it is referred to in the writings of Clement of Alexandria.[62] There is some debate as to whether or not Irenaeus can be interpreted as referring to Mary's perpetual virginity,[63] but it is explicitly denied by Tertullian, who, while affirming the virginal conception of Christ, denies that Mary remained a virgin during birth, and elsewhere claims that 'the brethren' referred to in Matthew 12.48 were Jesus' real brothers.[64]

---

61. Palardy 2004: 256–7.
62. See Graef 1994: 142–3.
63. See the discussion in ibid.: 42.
64. See Tertullian, 'Against Marcion', 4.19, in Roberts and Donaldson (eds) 1997: 377–8; PL 2, 434.

In 'On the Flesh of Christ', Tertullian refutes Marcion and others who would deny the reality of the incarnation, by giving a visceral account of Christ's birth which is unique among surviving writings on Mary's maternity, although it might represent a more widespread belief in the very early Church that Mary gave birth in the normal way. Tertullian argues that 'there is no nativity without flesh, and no flesh without nativity'.[65]

> Come now, beginning from the nativity itself, declaim against the uncleanness of the generative elements within the womb, the filthy concretion of fluid and blood, of the growth of the flesh for nine months long out of that very mire. Describe the womb as it enlarges from day to day, – heavy, troublesome, restless even in sleep, changeful in its feelings of dislike and desire. Inveigh now likewise against the shame itself of a woman in travail, which, however, ought rather to be honoured in consideration of that peril, or to be held sacred in respect of (the mystery of) nature. Of course you are horrified also at the infant, which is shed into life with the embarrassments which accompany it from the womb; you likewise, of course, loathe it even after it is washed, when it is dressed out in its swaddling-clothes, graced with repeated anointing, smiled on with nurse's fawns. This reverend course of nature, you, O Marcion, (are pleased to) spit upon; and yet, in what way you were born? You detest a human being at his birth; then after what fashion do you love anybody? ... Well, then, loving man [Christ] loved his nativity also, and his flesh as well. (Tertullian, *On The Flesh of Christ*, 4)[66]

In his treatise 'On Monogamy', Tertullian suggests that Mary would have entered into a normal marriage with Joseph after the birth of Christ, so that she signifies 'the two priestesses of Christian sanctity, Monogamy and Continence':

> And indeed it was a virgin, about to marry once for all after her delivery, who gave birth to Christ, in order that each title of sanctity might be fulfilled in Christ's parentage, by means of a mother who was both virgin, and wife of one husband. (Tertullian, *On Monogamy*, 8)[67]

Origen's writings, although ambivalent regarding the question of Mary's virginity *in partu*, affirm that she remained a virgin and did not enter into sexual relationships with Joseph after the birth of Christ.

The first known use of the title Ever-Virgin (*aeiparthenos*) is found in the writings of Peter of Alexandria (d. 311), and by the late fourth century, belief in Mary's perpetual virginity had spread to the Church in the West as well as being affirmed by the Cappadocian Fathers, Basil of Caesarea, Gregory of Nazianzus and Gregory of Nyssa. However, while Basil insists upon the necessity of Mary's virginity until the

65. 'On the Flesh of Christ', 1, in ibid.: 521; PL 2, 799.
66. Ibid.: 524; PL 2, 803–4.
67. Roberts and Donaldson (eds) 1994: 65; PL 2, 989.

time of Christ's birth, he is more pragmatic as to why she remained a virgin thereafter:

> For 'he did not know her' – it says – 'until she gave birth to a Son, her firstborn' (Mt. 1.25). But this could make one suppose that Mary, after having offered in all purity her own service in giving birth to the Lord, by virtue of the intervention of the Holy Spirit, did not subsequently refrain from normal conjugal relations.
>
> That would not have affected the teaching of our religion at all, because Mary's virginity was necessary until the service of the Incarnation, and what happened afterward need not be investigated in order to affect the doctrine of the mystery.
>
> But since the lovers of Christ [that is, the faithful] do not allow themselves to hear that the Mother of God (*Theotokos*) ceased at a given moment to be a virgin, we consider their testimony to be sufficient. (Basil of Caesarea, *On the Holy Generation of Christ*, 5)[68]

In the Church in the West, Ambrose was influenced by the teachings of the Greek Fathers in his highly influential writings on Mary. Although an early text suggests that he did not initially believe in Mary's virginity *in partu* – he writes that Christ 'opened his mother's womb'[69] – he later wrote in defence of her perpetual virginity *in partu* as well as *post partum*. In Ambrose's writings on virginity, we find an emphasis on Mary's moral purity as well as her physical virginity, so that she begins to acquire personal significance as a role model for female chastity:

> Let, then, the life of Mary be as it were virginity itself, set forth in a likeness, from which, as from a mirror, the appearance of chastity and the form of virtue is reflected. From this you may take your pattern of life, showing, as an example, the clear rules of virtue: what you have to correct, to effect, and to hold fast.
>
> The first thing which kindles ardour in learning is the greatness of the teacher. What is greater than the Mother of God? What more glorious than she whom Glory Itself chose? What more chaste than she who bore a body without contact with another body? For why should I speak of her other virtues? She was a virgin not only in body but also in mind, who stained the sincerity of its disposition by no guile, who was humble in heart, grave in speech, prudent in mind, sparing of words, studious in reading, resting her hope not on uncertain riches, but on the prayer of the poor, intent on work, modest in discourse; wont to seek not man but God as the judge of her thoughts, to injure no one, to have goodwill towards all, to rise up before her

---

68. Gambero 1999: 146; PG 31, 1468 B.
69. *Expositio in Lucam* 2.57; see Graef 1994: 179.

elders, not to envy her equals, to avoid boastfulness, to follow reason, to love virtue. (Ambrose, *Concerning Virgins* 2.2)[70]

In Ambrose's lengthy praise of Mary – her modesty, her domestic seclusion, her silence – we can learn much about emergent ideals of Christian womanhood, at a time when the conversion of Rome had contributed to the growing institutionalization and authority of the Church's male hierarchy. We find similar moralizing tendencies in Jerome's writings on virginity. He also vigorously defended the perpetual virginity of Mary in his tract *Against Helvidius*, in which he dismisses Tertullian's description of Christ's birth, saying that 'he was not a man of the Church'.[71]

Augustine not only affirmed Mary's perpetual virginity, but he is also the earliest known source for the belief that Mary had made a vow of virginity. He interprets this in the context of God's respect for Mary's freedom:

> Thus Christ, in being born of a Virgin who, before knowing to whom she was to give birth, had made up her mind to remain a virgin, preferred to show his approval of holy virginity rather than to impose it on her. Even so, in the woman within whom he took the form of a slave, he wanted her virginity to be freely chosen. (Augustine, *On the Holiness of Virginity* 2, 4)[72]

In a Christmas homily, Augustine gives eloquent expression to his belief in Mary's perpetual virginity:

> It was not the visible sun that made this day holy for us, but the sun's invisible Creator, when the Virgin Mother brought to light, out of her fruitful womb and virginal body, the Creator made visible for us, the same invisible God who had also created the Virgin. Virgin in conceiving, virgin in giving birth, virgin with child, virgin mother, virgin forever. Why do you marvel at this, O man? God had to be born in this way, when he designed to become man. Thus did he make her, who was made by her. (Augustine, *Sermon* 186)[73]

Mary's Sinlessness

The question of whether or not Mary was entirely without sin would eventually be resolved in the doctrine of the immaculate conception,[74] at least as far as the Roman Catholic Church is concerned, but patristic texts suggest diverse views on this issue. For example, while Augustine affirms Mary's personal holiness, there is considerable debate as to whether or not he believed that she was free from original sin:

---

70.   Schaff and Wace (eds) 1997: 374.
71.   Hritzu 1965.
72.   Ibid.: 221; PL 40, 398.
73.   Ibid.: 220; PL 38, 999.
74.   See Sarah Jane Boss, 'The Development of the Doctrine of Mary's Immaculate Conception', in this volume: 207–35.

With the exception of the holy Virgin Mary, in whose case, out of respect for the Lord, I do not wish there to be any further question as far as sin is concerned, since how can we know what great abundance of grace was conferred on her to conquer sin in every way, seeing that she merited to conceive and bear him who certainly had no sin at all? (Augustine, *On Nature and Grace*, 36, 42)[75]

While most patristic writers affirm Mary's sinlessness during her life, even if they do not agree that she was conceived without sin, there are some exceptions to this belief. Among second-century writers, both Irenaeus and Tertullian attribute fault to Mary. Irenaeus suggests that she showed 'untimely haste' during her intervention at the wedding at Cana,[76] and Tertullian takes an even harsher view of her failings. In his interpretation of the reference to Christ's mothers and brothers in Matthew 12.48 and Luke 8.20–1, he represents Jesus as disowning his natural family, who are lacking in belief, in favour of those disciples who follow him and do God's work. He goes on to suggest that 'in the abjured mother there is a figure of the synagogue, as well as of the Jews in the unbelieving brethren'.[77]

However, Augustine interprets Matthew 12.48 as an affirmation of Mary's faith. She is one who does the will of God and therefore a true disciple of Christ. Here as elsewhere, Augustine insists that Mary's personal faith and holiness are more significant than her physical motherhood in her relationship with Christ:

Should the Virgin Mary not have done the will of the Father, she, who by faith believed, by faith conceived, who was the chosen one from whom our salvation should be born among men, who was created by Christ before Christ was created in her? Indeed, the holy Mary obviously did the will of the Father: and therefore it is greater for Mary to have been Christ's disciple than to have been his Mother ... The truth of Christ is in the mind of Mary, the flesh of Christ in her womb; greater is what she bears in her mind, than what she bears in her womb. (Augustine, *Sermon Denis*, 25, 7)[78]

While Athanasius does not attribute sin to Mary, he does suggest that she was susceptible to 'bad thoughts'.[79] Basil of Caesarea suggests that Mary suffered doubt on Calvary, and this was the sword to which Simeon referred (Lk. 2.35):

Indeed, every soul, at the moment of the Passion, underwent a kind of doubt, just as the Lord said: 'You will all be scandalized because of me' (Mt. 26.31). Therefore Simeon prophesies that Mary herself, while standing by the Cross

---

75. Gambero 1999: 226; PL 44, 267. For a bibliography on the debate about Mary's sinlessness in Augustine's writings, see ibid.: 226, n. 25. See also Graef 1994: 198–100.
76. See Graef 1994: 40, referring to Irenaeus, *Against the Heresies* 3, 10, 2.
77. Tertullian, 'On the Flesh of Christ', 7, Roberts and Donaldson 1869: 528–9.
78. Quoted in Graef 1994: 196.
79. See ibid.: 53.

observing what was happening and hearing what was being said, after the witness of Gabriel, after the secret revelation of the divine conception, after the great showing of miracles, would have known some wavering in her soul. Indeed it was necessary that the Lord should taste death for all and that, having become a sacrificial victim for the world, he should justify all by his blood.

Even you [O Mary], who learned about the Lord from above, will be affected by doubt. This is the sword. (Basil of Caesarea, *Letter* 260)[80]

However, the most emphatic condemnation of Mary is found in the writings of John Chrysostom, who represents a singular exception to the thinkers of his time in his negative representation of Mary. In his homilies on Matthew, he suggests that Mary might have been tempted to kill herself when she found she was pregnant.[81] In a homily on the wedding at Cana in John's Gospel, he explains why Mary waited until then to speak out:

Before this time He lived as one of the many, and therefore His mother had not confidence to say any such thing to Him; but when she heard that John had come on His account, and that he had borne such witness to Him as he did, and that He had disciples, after that she took confidence, and called Him, and said, when they wanted wine, 'They have no wine.' For she desired both to do them a favour, and through her Son to render herself more conspicuous; perhaps too she had some human feelings, like His brethren, when they said, 'Show thyself to the world', desiring to gain credit from his miracles. Therefore He answered somewhat vehemently, saying 'Woman, what have I to do with thee? Mine hour is not yet come' … though he was careful to honor His mother, yet He cared much more for the salvation of her soul, and for the doing good to the many, for which He took upon Him the flesh.

These then were the words, not of one speaking rudely to his mother, but belonging to a wise dispensation, which brought her into a right frame of mind, and provided that the miracles should be attended with that honor which was meet.[82]

However, although debates about the immaculate conception would rage for many centuries, the relationship between Mary's virginal motherhood of Christ and her personal purity and holiness become ever more pronounced as Marian devotion began to flourish from the late fourth century on. Ephrem of Syria sees Mary as uniquely sharing in the sinlessness of Christ:

---

80.   Quoted in Gambero 1999: 148.
81.   See John Chrysostom, 'Homily IV, 9', in Schaff (ed.) 1991: 24.
82.   'Homily XXI, 2–3', in Schaff (ed.) 1996: 74–5.

You and Your Mother are the only ones who are perfectly beautiful in every respect; for there is no spot in You, O Lord, nor any taint in Your Mother. (Ephrem of Syria, *The Nisibis Hymn* 27)[83]

CONCLUSION

To end this section on Mary in patristic theology, I shall quote at some length from Proclus (d. 446), a famous orator and later Patriarch of Constantinople, whose sermons represent the beginnings of a high Mariology associated with the Byzantine Church. Sometime between 428 and 429, Proclus preached a homily in honour of Mary, in the presence of the patriarch Nestorius, and his affirmation of the title *Theotokos* sparked the Nestorian controversy which led to the Council of Ephesus. Nicholas Constas describes this homily as 'perhaps the most famous sermon on the Mother of God in the history of Christianity'.[84] Although the focus of Proclus's homily is Christological – he is concerned to affirm the significance of Mary's virginal motherhood for the incarnation – the rhetorical flourish of his language suggests the extent to which Mary's personal qualities of holiness and purity had also acquired significance. In this extract, we see all the foregoing themes brought together in a lavish celebration of the redemptive significance of the Virgin:

The Virgin's festival, my brethren, summons us today to words of praise, and the present feast has benefits to bestow on those who assemble and keep it. And surely this is right, for its subject is chastity. What we celebrate is the pride of women and the glory of the female, thanks to the one who was at once both mother and virgin. Lovely is the gathering! See how both the earth and the sea serve as the Virgin's escorts: the one spreading forth her waves calmly beneath the ships, the other conducting the steps of travelers on their way unhindered. Let nature leap for joy, and let women be honoured! Let all humanity dance, and let virgins be glorified! For 'where sin increased, grace abounded yet more.' [Rom. 5.20] She who called us here today is the Holy Mary; the untarnished vessel of virginity; the spiritual paradise of the second Adam; [cf. Rom. 5.14; 1 Cor. 15.21–2, 45–9] the workshop for the union of natures; the market-place of the contract of salvation; the bridal chamber in which the Word took the flesh in marriage; the living bush of human nature, which the fire of a divine birth-pang did not consume; [Exod. 3.2] the veritable swift cloud [Isa. 19.1] who carried in her body the one who rides upon the cherubim; the purest fleece [Judg. 6.37–8] drenched with the rain which came down from heaven, whereby the shepherd clothed himself with the sheep; [cf. Jn 10.11] handmaid and mother, [cf. Lk. 1.38, 43] virgin and heaven, the only bridge for God to

---

83.   Paul F. Palmer, *Mary in the Documents of the Church*, Westminster, MD: Newman, 1952: 23, in Buby 1996: 331.
84.   Constas 2003: 128. As well as parallel texts of the homilies of Proclus, Constas offers an excellent study of the context in which they were delivered, and an analysis of their imagery, typology and symbolism.

mankind; the awesome loom of the divine economy upon which the robe [Jn 19.23] of union was ineffably woven. The loom-worker was the Holy Spirit; the wool-worker the overshadowing power from on high. [Lk. 1.35] The wool was the ancient fleece of Adam; the interlocking thread the spotless flesh of the Virgin. The weaver's shuttle was propelled by the immeasurable grace of him who wore the robe; the artisan was the Word who entered in through her sense of hearing. . .

As man, Emmanuel opened the gates of human nature; as God, he left the bars of virginity unbroken. As he entered through the ear, so too did he come out from the womb; as he was conceived, so was he born. His entering in was altogether without passion, and his coming out was altogether beyond understanding – as the prophet Ezekiel said: 'The Lord brought me back by the way of the outer gate of the sanctuary, which faces east; and it was shut. And the Lord said to me, "Son of man, this gate shall be shut; it shall not be opened. No one shall pass through it, but the Lord, the God of Israel, he alone shall enter and come out, and the gate shall be shut."' [Ezek. 44.1–2] There you have a clear testimony to the Holy and 'God-bearing' [*theotokos*] Mary.[85]

BIBLIOGRAPHY

Primary Sources
Buby SM, Bertrand (1996) *Mary of Galilee, Vol. III: The Marian Heritage of the Early Church*, New York: Alba House.
Constas, Nicholas (2003) *Proclus of Constantinople and the Cult of the Virgin in Late Antiquity: Homilies 1–5, Texts and Translations*, Supplements to *Vigiliae Christianae*, formerly *Philosophia Patrum*: Texts and Studies on Early Christian Life and Language, Vol. LXVI, Leiden and Boston: Brill.
Gambero, Luigi (1999) *Mary and the Fathers of the Church*, trans. Thomas Buffer, San Francisco: Ignatius Press.
Hill OP, Edmund (trans.) (1991) *The Works of Saint Augustine – a Translation for the 21st Century III*, Vol. 3, under the auspices of the Augustinian Heritage Institute.
Hill OP, Edmund and Rotelle OSA, John E. (trans.) (1993) *The Works of Saint Augustine – a Translation for the 21st Century III*, Vol. 6, under the auspices of the Augustinian Heritage Institute.
Hritzu, John N. (trans.) (1965) *St Jerome, Dogmatic and Polemical Works*, in *The Fathers of the Church, a New Translation*, Vol. 53, Washington DC: The Catholic University of America Press.
Kleist, James A. (trans.) (1946) *The Epistles of St Clement of Rome and St Ignatius of Antioch*, in *Ancient Christian Writers: The Works of the Fathers in Translation*, No. 1, Washington DC: The Catholic University of America; Westminster, Maryland: The Newman Bookshop.
Lienhard SJ, Joseph T. (trans.) (1996) *Homilies on Luke* and *Fragments on Luke*, in *The Fathers of the Church, a New Translation*, Washington DC: The Catholic University of America Press.
Livius, Thomas (1893) *The Blessed Virgin in the Fathers of the First Six Centuries*, London: Burns and Oates Ltd; New York, Cincinnati, Chicago: Benziger Brothers.
McVey, Kathleen E. (1989) *Ephrem the Syrian: Hymns*, New York, Mahwah: Paulist Press.

---

85.   Proclus of Constantinople, 'Homily I', in ibid.: 137–47; Schwartz 1960: I, I, I (103–7); PG, 65, 680C–692B.

Palardy, William B. (trans.) (2004) *St Peter Chrysologus: Selected Sermons, Volume 2*, in *The Fathers of the Church, a New Translation*, Vol. 109, Washington DC: The Catholic University of America Press.

Roberts, Alexander and Donaldson, James (eds) (1869) *The Writings of Tertullian*, Vol. I, *Ante-Nicene Christian Library* XI, Edinburgh: T&T Clark.

Roberts, Alexander and Donaldson, James (eds) (1994) *The Ante-Nicene Fathers*, Vol. IV, *Fathers of the Third Century: Tertullian, Part Fourth; Minucius Felix; Commodian; Origen, Parts First and Second*, Edinburgh: T & T Clark; Grand Rapids, Michigan: Wm. B. Eerdmans Publishing Co. (reprint).

Roberts, Alexander and Donaldson, James (eds) (1996) *The Ante-Nicene Fathers*, Vol. I, *The Apostolic Fathers with Justin Martyr and Irenaeus*, Edinburgh: T & T Clark; Grand Rapids, Michigan: Wm. B. Eerdmans Publishing Co. (reprint).

Roberts, Alexander and Donaldson, James (eds) (1997) *The Ante-Nicene Fathers*, Vol. III, *Latin Christianity: Its Founder, Tertullian*, Edinburgh: T & T Clark; Grand Rapids, Michigan: Wm. B. Eerdmans Publishing Co. (reprint).

Schaff, Philip (ed.) (1991) *A Select Library of Nicene and Post-Nicene Fathers of the Christian Church*, First Series, Vol. X, *The Homilies of St John Chrysostom, Archbishop of Constantinople, on the Gospel of St Matthew*, Edinburgh: T & T Clark; Grand Rapids, Michigan: Wm. B. Eerdmans Publishing Co. (reprint).

Schaff, Philip (ed.) (1996) *A Select Library of Nicene and Post-Nicene Fathers of the Christian Church*, First Series, Vol. XIV, *Saint Chrysostom: Homilies on the Gospel of St John and the Epistle to the Hebrews*, Edinburgh: T & T Clark; Grand Rapids, Michigan: Wm. B. Eerdmans Publishing Co. (reprint).

Schaff, Philip and Wace, Henry (eds) (1994) *A Select Library of the Nicene and Post-Nicene Fathers of the Christian Church*, Second Series, Vol. V, *Gregory of Nyssa: Dogmatic Treatises etc.*, Edinburgh: T & T Clark; Grand Rapids, Michigan: Wm. B. Eerdmans Publishing Co. (reprint).

Schaff, Philip and Wace, Henry (eds) (1997) *A Select Library of Nicene and Post-Nicene Fathers of the Christian Church*, Second Series, Vol. X, *St Ambrose: Select Works and Letters*, Edinburgh: T & T Clark; Grand Rapids, Michigan: Wm. B. Eerdmans Publishing Co. (reprint).

Schwartz, Eduard (1960) *Acta Conciliorum Oecumenicorum*, Berlin: De Gruyter (reprint).

Teske SJ, Roland T. (trans.) (1991) *On Genesis: Two Books on Genesis. Against the Manichees and on the Literal Interpretation of Genesis: an Unfinished Book*, in *The Fathers of the Church, a New Translation*, Washington DC: The Catholic University of America Press.

Secondary Sources

Ashe, Geoffrey (1976) *The Virgin*, London and Henley: Routledge & Kegan Paul.

Børresen, Kari Elisabeth (1995) *Subordination and Equivalence: The Nature and Role of Woman in Augustine and Thomas Aquinas*, Kampen: Kok Pharos Publishing House (first published 1968).

Boss, Sarah Jane (2004) *Mary*, London: Continuum.

Brock, Sebastian (1992) *The Luminous Eye: The Spiritual World Vision of Saint Ephrem the Syrian*, Kalamazoo, Michigan: Cistercian Publications.

Brown, Raymond, Donfried, Karl P., Fitzmyer, Joseph A. and Reumann, John (eds) (1978) *Mary in the New Testament*, London: Geoffrey Chapman; Philadelphia: Fortress Press; New York/Ramsey/Toronto: Paulist Press.

Chadwick, Henry (1966) *Early Christian Thought and the Classical Tradition – Studies in Justin, Clement, and Origen*, Oxford: Clarendon Press.

Coathalem SJ, H. (1954) *Le Parallelisme entre la Sainte Vierge et l'Église dans la Tradition Latine jusqu'à la Fin du XIIe Siècle*, Analecta Gregoriana, Cura Pontificiae Universitatis Gregorianae edita, Vol. LXXIV, Series Facultatis Theologicae Sectio B, n. 27, Romae: Apud Aedes Universitatis Gregorianae.

Congar, M-J, Yves (1954) 'Marie et l'Église dans la Pensée Patristique', in *Revue des Sciences Philosophique et Theologique* 1: 3–38.

Evans, G. R. (ed.) (2004) *The First Christian Theologians: An Introduction to Theology in the Early Church*, Oxford and Malden, MA: Blackwell Publishing.

Farrell RSM, Marie T. (1997) *The Veneration of the Blessed Virgin Mary in the Church Prior to the Council of Ephesus AD 431*, Wallington: The Ecumenical Society of the Blessed Virgin Mary.

Flannery OP, Austin (ed.) (1992) *Vatican Council II: The Conciliar and Post Conciliar Documents*, Vol. 1, Dublin: Dominican Publications; New Town, NSW: E. J. Dwyer (first published 1974).

Graef, Hilda (1994) *Mary: A History of Doctrine and Devotion*, London: Sheed and Ward (first published 1963 [Part 1] and 1965 [Part 2]).

Murray, Robert (1975) *Symbols of Church and Kingdom: A Study in Early Syriac Tradition*, Cambridge: Cambridge University Press.

Newman, John Henry (1866) *A Letter Addressed to the Rev. E. B. Pusey, D.D., on His Recent Eirenicon*, London: Longmans, Green, Reader and Dyer.

Ramsey OP, Boniface (1986) *Beginning to Read the Fathers*, London: Darton, Longman & Todd.

Ruether, Rosemary Radford (1992) *Sexism and God-Talk: Towards a Feminist Theology*, London: SCM Press (first published 1983).

Warner, Marina (2000) *Alone of All Her Sex: The Myth and Cult of the Virgin Mary*, London: Vintage (first published 1976).

5

THE ORIGINS OF MARIAN ART: THE EVOLUTION OF MARIAN IMAGERY IN THE WESTERN CHURCH UNTIL AD 431

GERI PARLBY

In a recent article, 'The Cult of the Virgin in Late Antiquity' Averil Cameron wrote despairingly about how much of our understanding of the early development of Marian veneration had been shaped by 'later ideas, wishes and religious agendas'. As an eminent historian of the period she has been attempting to unravel the textual evidence on the cult of Mary for decades; she ruefully admits to being even less certain about the subject now than she was 20 years ago.[1]

There is no doubt that unravelling the visual evidence is an equally frustrating experience. In part this is because most of the evidence we have does not come from the days of the earliest Christian artists. Instead, we are presented with a plethora of polemics from ninth- and tenth-century iconophiles defending their right to worship holy images, and sixteenth-century Catholic scholars fighting against the devastating effects of the Reformation. Add to this the inevitable myths and legends that grow up around any religious cult, and it is easy to see how later researchers might lose sight of both the wood and the trees.

LEGENDARY PORTRAITS

One legend that purports to explain the origin of Marian art has been remarkably persistent. The story of the multi-talented St Luke – apostle, evangelist, Gospel writer, doctor and portrait painter to the Mother of God – has become so ingrained in Church tradition that it now forms part of the liturgical texts of the Orthodox Church. Although the details vary with the telling, the basic premise of the story is that after the crucifixion, Mary went to live with the 'beloved disciple', John. There she met Luke and, knowing he was an artist, asked him to paint a portrait of her with Jesus as a young child. In order to make the portrait all the more poignant, she suggested he use the top of a cedar or cypress table that had been made by Jesus when he worked as a carpenter in Joseph's workshop. While being painted, Mary is said to have told Luke the stories of Jesus' life that he later incorporated into his Gospels.[2]

---

1. Cameron 2004: 1.
2. Carroll Cruz 1993: 380–3. This version of the legend forms an integral part of the history of the Polish 'Black Virgin of Czestochowa'. For more information on this icon, see Maniura 2004.

Fig. 1. *Virgin Hodegetria*. Paint on parchment. *c.* 1300 (?). Cyprus. Staatliche Museen, Berlin, Kupferstichkabinett, 78 A 9 (Hamilton 119).

Mary was said to have been so pleased with the painting that she asked Luke to paint several other similar portraits of her with the young Jesus. Even after her death, the Evangelist continued to paint the holy couple from memory and, according to other legends, also carved several statues of mother and son. After Luke's death, several of the paintings remained hidden in Jerusalem, until they were rediscovered by a Byzantine empress several centuries later. In some versions of the story the empress is Helena, mother of the first Christian emperor Constantine, while others suggest that it was Eudocia, wife of Theodosius II, who ruled over the Eastern empire during the lead-up to the Council of Ephesus in the fifth century.[3] Eudocia is said to have discovered at least one of the paintings while on pilgrimage in the Holy Land; having sent it to her sister-in-law Pulcheria, a special church was built to house it.[4] Known as the Hodegetria, or 'pointer of the way', this icon went on to become the palladium of Constantinople, revered by all and regularly paraded around the city (Fig. 1). It survived right up until the fall of Constantinople in 1453, when it was finally destroyed by the invading Ottomans.[5]

Although the Hodegetria is now lost, we know what the icon looked like from the hundreds of copies made, and through several depictions of the original in manuscript illuminations and other icons. In these images the Virgin is always portrayed heavily draped and veiled, her head covered by a dark, often purple-coloured *maphorion*, or veil. She gestures to her son with her right hand, an unusual pose that has been interpreted as symbolizing Mary pointing to her son as 'the way'.

The Hodegetria was just one of many icons circulating during the medieval period that claimed to be an authentic representation of the appearance of Mary painted by Luke, and this is how she continues to be portrayed in the artistic tradition of the Orthodox Church.[6] Of course the legend is unlikely to have any historical basis. Eusebius of Caesarea, the fourth-century Church historian, tells us that Luke died around AD 150, aged 74, so this dating makes it hard to prove that Luke could ever have painted Mary from life.[7] There are also other legends that suggest that Luke painted several more portraits of the Virgin after she appeared to him in a vision, and even today, from as far afield as Moscow and Montserrat, Lukan images of the Virgin and Child are deeply revered as holy relics even if they are 'authorized copies' rather than 'originals'.[8]

It was during the medieval period that the legend of St Luke as an artist became especially popular, and many scholars believe that this was the time that the

---

3. Theodorus Lector, *Hist. Eccles.* (sixth century), claims that Eudocia sent to Pulcheria from Jerusalem an image of the Mother of God painted by the apostle Luke. The authenticity of this reference is now disputed as it is only known from the writings of the fourteenth-century writer Nikephoros Kallistos Xanthopoulous; see Bacci 2000.

4. This legend may also be a later addition as there is no textual reference to the church, known as the Hodegoi, before the ninth century and it only becomes famous from the twelfth century onwards. The two other Constantinopolitan churches dedicated to the Virgin Mary and said to have been built by Pulcheria are the Blachernai and the Chalkoprateia. These two churches were in fact probably built after the death of Pulcheria by the empress Verina around 475; the former housed the relic of the *maphorion* of Mary, while the latter reputedly held her girdle or cincture – an aspect of the story which may have been added in the early eighth century; see Mango 2000: 19.

5. Bacci 2000. In the same volume, Cyril Mango disputes the dating of the building of the Hodegoi; see Mango 2000: 17–25.

6. Rather confusingly, most of these other icons also claim to have been discovered by either Helena or Eudocia in the Holy Land.

7. Eusebius, *Hist. Eccl. III*, iv, 6. The 'Prefatio vel Argumentum Lucæ', possibly by Julius Africanus (b. AD 164), states that Luke was unmarried, that he wrote the Gospel in Achaia, and that he died at the age of 74 in Bithynia.

8. By the Middle Ages it was believed that by duplicating an original image its power could be extended. Belting 1995: 57–9; Oikonomides 1991.

Byzantine Hodegetria was first attributed to the hand of the Evangelist.[9] During the Renaissance, Luke became the patron saint of painters and some of the greatest artists of the time, such as Leonardo da Vinci, Raphael and Jan Vermeer, belonged to the Guild of St Luke.

There is no doubt that Luke has been inextricably linked with the image of Mary both as her artist and as the Gospel writer who described her life in the most detail. However, it seems that the Evangelist was not the first artist to paint Mary, and his story may have replaced a much older legend dating to as early as the fifth century - ironically, one that credits the first portrait of the Virgin and Child to a pagan artist. The story links the first portrait with the pagan Magi, or three wise men, who travelled from the East to pay tribute to the Christ child. The tale claims that at the moment Christ was born, a star appeared above the goddess's statue in the temple of Hera or Fons in the Persian capital; this same star then led the Magi to Jerusalem on a journey that took two years. The Magi had the presence of mind to take with them their own artist to record the event; he painted a portrait of the holy couple, and on their return to Persia, the Magi placed the painting in their temple as a tribute to the holy family.[10]

There is no suggestion that copies of this Persian painting were made or that it found its way back to the West. However, two eleventh-century illustrated manuscripts survive that show the Magi's artist at work painting an image of the Virgin and Child. In one of the manuscripts, the scene is so similar to medieval paintings of St Luke as an artist that it is still regularly misattributed.[11]

Whether or not the pagan Magi artist was the inspiration for the Luke legend, most scholars nowadays agree that the Luke version of the story is no older than the eighth or ninth century. In all likelihood, it was developed during or after Iconoclasm, as a way of emphasizing the legitimacy of the icons of the Virgin Mary and Jesus by proving they were actual portraits rather than idolatrous images. The Byzantine Church, ever watchful against the return of iconoclasm, clung on to the idea that an authentic portrait of the Virgin Mary had been painted during her lifetime.

Iconoclasm had barely affected the West, and initially the Luke legend seems to

---

9.   Pentcheva 2000: 392 suggests that the legend of St Luke was first associated with the Hodegetria at the end of the eleventh century.

10.   The most detailed version of this story has been found in a homily on the Nativity attributed to John of Damascus in the eighth century. His source appears to be the *Narratio de Rebus Persicis*. This text is said to have come from a religious conference at the court of a Sassanid king called Arrinato, held between Christians, Jews, pagans and a Persian magus. Although it has been attributed to Anastasius 1 of Antioch or Anastasius the Sinaite, it has also been suggested that a pagan Persian wrote it as a way of demonstrating that paganism had made a valuable contribution to the growth of Christianity. Some of the information for the *Narratio de Rebus Persicis* may have been drawn from an earlier text by Philip of Side (434–9), the author of the *Historia Christiana*. There is no record of any king Arrinato in the annals of the Sassanid rulers. See Scorza Barcellona 1991: 582.

11.   Pentcheva 2000: 392. The manuscripts contain two illustrated editions of the homily on the Nativity by the Syrian theologian John of Damascus (*c.* 675 – *c.* 749). The illustration of the Magi's artist in the Taphou 14 manuscript, now in the Greek Patriarchal Library of Jerusalem, is the one most commonly confused with the Luke scene.

have been given little credence in the Western Church. An extract from the late-eighth-century Frankish treatise on the issue of sacred images, known as the 'Libri Carolini', shows how unclear the whole issue of Marian art was at this time. The author wrote:

> How can we recognize her [Mary] or distinguish her from other women who look like her? When we look at a picture of a beautiful woman with a baby on her lap, how can we be sure, if there is no inscription, that the subject is not Sarah and Isaac, Rebecca and Jacob, Bathsheba and Solomon, Elizabeth and John, or simply any woman with her child? Or, if we turn to the pagan myths that are so often depicted, how can we be sure that this woman is not Venus with Aeneas, Alcmene with Hercules or Andromache with Astyanax?[12]

This wary approach to identifying images of the Virgin Mary started as early as the fifth century, when St Augustine made it clear that there were no records, either in writing or art, of how Mary looked, and in his opinion an artist could only guess at her appearance.[13]

CATACOMB PAINTINGS

Although most of Augustine's ministry took place in North Africa, he did live in Rome at a time when the catacombs had become a pilgrimage centre for the newly developing cult of martyred saints.[14] It is in the catacombs that the oldest examples of Marian art are said to be found; but although these images have been dated stylistically from the second to the fourth centuries, they lack inscriptions and were not formally identified as Marian images until the catacombs were rediscovered at the height of the Counter-Reformation. We will be looking more closely at these interpretations later, but before we leap ahead to the sixteenth century, it is worth looking more closely at the origins of Christian art as a whole.

Although there are examples outside the capital, the Roman catacombs hold the largest surviving collection of early Christian images, none of which has been dated to earlier than the late second century.[15] In the past, scholars have given the Church's hostility to religious artistic representation as the reason for the late arrival of art; it is

---

12. Paraphrased extract of the 'Libri Carolini', from Winston 2002: 289, n. 8.
13. Augustine, 'De Trinitate', Book VIII, Cap. V, cited in Winston 2002. In spite of this early scepticism, by the end of the sixth century and during the devastations of iconoclasm, Rome started to acquire its own collection of Lukan icons. Many of these ancient icons still adorn churches around the capital.
14. Augustine ran a school of rhetoric in Rome in 383. Pope Damasus (366–84) spent his pontificate fostering a new cult of the martyrs, centred on pilgrimages and devotional visits to their tombs in the catacombs.
15. Some of the earliest examples of Christian art, together with a remarkable series of synagogue frescoes dating to the middle of the third century, were discovered in the Roman garrison town of Dura Europos in Syria. Weitzmann and Kessler (1990) have written the definitive guide. The definitive study on the subject of early Christian art is still Grabar 1969, although a more up-to-date overview of the interpretation of early Christian art can be found in Jensen 2000.

now accepted that there are far more complex issues surrounding the whole subject of the development of early Christian art, not least the suggestion that pagan and Christian art was often indiscernible in the pre-Constantine period.[16]

The theory that Christian art absorbed and adapted pagan artistic traditions was first mooted in the nineteenth century,[17] but it has recently received an enormous boost from the mainstream world of popular fiction. Dan Brown's *Da Vinci Code* states in a wonderfully matter-of-fact manner that the Egyptian goddess Isis suckling Horus was the inspiration behind the first images of Mary and the infant Jesus.[18] It is interesting that, whenever this idea is mooted, the evidence usually presented to support the theory is the traditional stylized image of Isis and Horus from ancient Egyptian art (Fig. 2). It is hard to see a real link between this version of Isis and Horus and the more humanized images of Mary and Jesus. However, it was a rather different Isis who went on to become one of the most widely venerated goddesses of the Graeco-Roman world in late antiquity. The Hellenized Isis and her son Horus, who by then had evolved into Harpocrates, bear a far closer resemblance to the later images of Mary with her son (Fig. 3).

This version of Isis continued to be venerated in Egypt long after the Emperor Theodosius's ban on paganism in the late fourth century. The temple of Isis at Philae remained open for another two centuries, when it was eventually converted into a Christian church. Throughout this time, Isis and Mary continued to be equally revered, and there is strong evidence that Mary absorbed many of Isis's attributes in Egypt, including her imagery and the title *Theotokos*, or 'Mother of the God'.[19]

The image of Mary nursing Jesus seems to have been especially popular among Egyptian Christians, perhaps because of its striking similarity to the Hellenized iconography of Isis. Known as the Galaktotrophousa, or 'she who nourishes with milk', this was an image that did not acquire popularity in the West until the later medieval period. Unfortunately, none of the Egyptian Galaktotrophousa frescoes can be dated to earlier than the sixth century, so it is hard to chart how the early imagery may have evolved.[20] It has been suggested that there may be another subtle clue as to a link between Isis Galaktotrophousa and the later Marian iconography outside Egypt. This can be found in the unusual hand gesture of Mary in the Hodegetria

---

16.   For a detailed analysis of the arguments surrounding the late development of Christian art, see Murray 1977, and her subsequent paper *Rebirth and Afterlife* (1981). Finney 1994 provides an excellent overview of early Christian attitudes towards art up until the late third century, and Mathews 1998 provides some compelling evidence of the crossover between pagan and Christian artistic traditions.
17.   Jameson 1890: xx.
18.   Brown 2003: 314.
19.   McGuckin 2001. For an excellent analysis of the reasons for the popularity of the Coptic Galaktotrophousa, see Bolman 2005.
20.   Some of the earliest Christian paintings in Egypt are dated to the end of the third century and were found in the catacombs of Karmuz in Alexandria. Although these images no longer exist, we have records that several New Testament scenes were depicted, included the wedding feast at Cana, with the Virgin Mary identified via an inscription. The earliest frescoes of the Virgin Galaktotrophousa date from around the sixth century and have been found on the walls of monks' cells in the desert monasteries of Middle Egypt. For an interesting interpretation of the significance of these images, see Bolman 2005.

Fig. 2. *Isis nursing Horus.* Etching from A. Jameson, *Legends of the Madonna as Represented in the Fine Arts*, London: Longmans, 1867: xxii.

icon. Rather than Mary pointing to her son, another interpretation is that she is actually holding out her hand to cup her breast, mimicking the same gesture as both the Isis and the Mary Galaktotrophousa images. The Byzantine artists who developed the Hodegetria icon may well have used the Egyptian Galaktotrophousa as a prototype, but decided to cover the breast both out of modesty and to distance themselves from any pagan link.[21]

Besides Isis, there were several other goddess-mother cults still popular in the early centuries of Christianity that may have influenced Mary's developing iconography. The Eastern 'mother of the gods', Cybele, was venerated in Phrygia, but also had a cult centre in Rome, where she was described as 'Magna Mater' and depicted seated on a lion throne. Like many of her predecessors, Cybele was a chaste virgin goddess whose son/lover Attis was sacrificed and reborn in the spring as a

---

21.   Parlby 2002: 25; Mathews and Muller 2005: 9.

Fig. 3. *Isis with Harpocrates*. Decoration from bowl. Egypt, first century CE. British Museum, GR1938 3–14. Photo by Geri Parlby.

symbol of renewal. Her cult, with its orgiastic rituals and eunuch priests, continued into the Christian era right up until the time of the Roman Emperor Julian the Apostate in AD 363. Romans adorned her statues with roses, a symbol which represented resurrection. They also regarded the rose garden as a sacred world or hidden dimension of the goddess, an attribute similar to some that were later associated with Mary. The goddess Diana of Ephesus was known as 'the virgin all mother', and her cult was at the height of its popularity in the third century. Mary was herself closely linked with Ephesus, which became one of the traditional sites of her Dormition and Assumption, as well as providing the venue for the Church council that promulgated her title *Theotokos*. In Rome, the goddess Juno, the mother of the gods, was a great favourite among women. Her festival, the Matronalia, was celebrated on 1 March. She also appeared under various guises and titles, such as Juno Lucina, goddess of childbirth; Juno Sospita, saviour of women in distress; and Juno Regina, Queen of Heaven. Vesta and Tellus Mater were also still powerful goddesses in the late antique period. Tellus Mater was depicted on Augustus's Ara Pacis as a seated woman embracing two children.[22]

---

22.   For a thorough study of the pagan roots of Mariology, see Benko 2004.

The argument that existing pagan goddess art may have influenced the developing iconography of Mary is certainly persuasive. However, this may have been more out of necessity and habit than as a calculated system for absorbing a rival cult's iconography. Certainly in the Roman catacombs, much of the artistic influence seems to have come from an existing repertoire of funerary art.[23] Many of the sculptors and fresco painters commissioned to produce commemorative art would have been either pagan or recently converted Christians, so it would have been perfectly natural for them to work with the images familiar to them. Indeed, many of these may have come from an existing template or pattern book.[24] These early artists did not feel the need to identify their figures by inscriptions and, as we have already seen, this ambiguity was already causing confusion as early as the eighth century. By the time the catacombs were rediscovered in the sixteenth century, the frescoes were already badly disintegrated, making it even harder to interpret their original meaning.

The rediscovery came at a time when the religious agenda of the Catholic Church was especially tense. Proving that the early Christians used art as part of their religion was a hugely important piece of evidence to add to the Counter-Reformation's arsenal, so uncovering the catacombs must have seemed like a sign from heaven for the Church. They sponsored various explorers to work at uncovering the catacombs' secrets, but in the main, their efforts were fairly haphazard and inevitably damaging, and it took a Maltese lawyer by the name of Antonio Bosio (c. 1576–1629) to create some system for this new discipline of Christian archaeology.[25] Bosio interpreted his findings in the catacombs as hard evidence of a link between the early Christian communities and the later Roman Catholic Church. Through the catacomb images, the Church was now able to vindicate its reverence for art and rituals, and, more importantly, thanks to Bosio's identification of images of Mary and Jesus, they were able to prove that the veneration of the Virgin Mary was not a recent Catholic invention. He and a team of artists very carefully reproduced all the frescoes he uncovered, and each image of a mother and child was duly identified as a Virgin and Child. However, the yardsticks that Bosio and his fellow explorers used for identifying these early images have never really been challenged.

Bosio's research was published after his death in 1629. Called *Roma Sotterranea*, it continued as the main point of reference for the catacombs and their art until the nineteenth century, when Giovanni Battista de Rossi (1822–94) continued the work of Bosio, rediscovering many more catacombs in the process. Although de Rossi brought a more scientific method to the study of the catacombs, claiming that he was 'an archaeologist not a theologian', he did not contradict any of Bosio's assumptions about the identification of the Marian images.[26]

These assertions were continued with some gusto by the members of the clergy

---

23.   Finney (1994: 151) suggests that to search for a single point of origin for early Christian art 'is an exercise in futility', as the early artists were either from pagan workshops in the first place or turned to 'existing iconographic repertoires' for inspiration.
24.   Mathews (1998: 32) provides a fascinating example of how a sarcophagus carving of Endymion was rebranded as Jonah.
25.   Bosio 1632. A full history of the rediscovery of the catacombs can be found in Nicolai *et al.* 2002.
26.   de Rossi 1994.

who took up Christian archaeology in the late nineteenth century, the most prominent of these being the German Jesuit, Father Joseph Wilpert. He became one of the most prolific writers on the subject of Christian art and the first to use photographs of the art of the catacombs.

Christian iconographers had long stressed the importance of the imagery of the Virgin holding the child Jesus as a representation of the incarnation, the key tenet of the Christian faith. However, Wilpert himself appears never to have considered any other interpretation of the mother and child images from the catacombs. 'These paintings,' he says, 'better than any written document from the period of the persecutions, characterise the position of Mary in the Church of the first four centuries and show that, in terms of substance, she was the same person then that she would later become.'[27]

Wilpert continued his work into the twentieth century, and many of his successors followed a similar agenda. By the end of the century, three catacomb frescoes first discovered by Bosio had been singled out as representing the earliest images of Mary and Jesus in the intimate pose of a mother and son. Art historians now agree that one of these images, part of a much larger tableau in an area of the catacomb of Priscilla, was wrongly identified. Even so, up until as recently as 1999, the mother and child section of the tableau was being reproduced in isolation and erroneously identified as 'a very early Virgin and Child'.[28]

The other famous early image of Mary from the catacombs can be found in the lunette of the arcosolium of a chapel in the Coemeterium Maius cemetery in Rome (Figs 4a and 4b). The painting shows a richly dressed, lightly veiled woman in an orans, or praying, position with the head and shoulders of a boy resting against her chest. On either side of her are painted Chi-Rho monograms with the χ (Rho) symbols unusually mirroring each other.

This fresco is still identified as the Virgin and Child, despite being flanked by two orans figures of an older man and woman facing each other. Considering the bigger picture, it may therefore be more appropriate to suggest that these figures represent members of the same family all buried within the chamber. The Chi–Rho symbols would indicate their religious beliefs, rather than singling them out as Mary and Jesus.[29]

The second mother and child fresco from the catacomb of Priscilla is still widely regarded by art historians and theologians as the earliest extant representation of Mary

---

27. Wilpert 1903: 197.
28. Beckwith 1970 identified the fresco as 'possibly a very early Virgin and Child', and this photo caption was still in place in the 1993 reprint. Even more recently, the book accompanying Melvyn Bragg's ITV series *Two Thousand Years* (1999) confidently refers to the image as part of 'a third–century fresco showing the Virgin Mary as Theotokos'. The most recent consensus of opinion is that the fresco is an anecdotal narrative portraying scenes from the life of the deceased, a very popular form of funerary art in the late antique period. See Toynbee 1996 and Zanker and Ewald 2003 for a thorough study of Roman burial practices and funerary art.
29. Mother and child images were a common type of funerary art used across the Empire. See Thomas 2000 for some examples and discussion.

Fig. 4a. Illustration of Coemeterium Maius – Greater Cemetery of St Agnes – from Antonio Bosio, *Roma Sotterranea. Opera postuma di A. Bosio, compita dispossta, ed accrescuita da G. Severanti da D. Severino*, Rome, 1632. Photo by Geri Parlby.

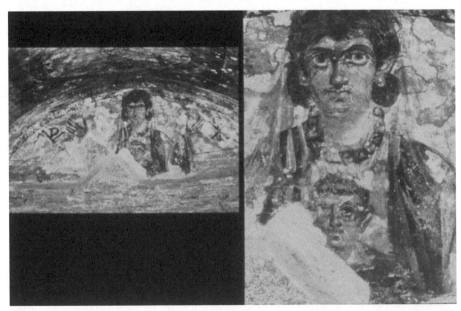

Fig. 4b. Orans figures from the Coemeterium Maius. (Copyright Pontificia Commissione di Archeologia Sacra, Rome.)

Fig. 5. Fresco taken from Joseph Wilpert's *Die Malereien der Katakomben Roms Freiburg* (1903). Catacomb of Priscilla. (Copyright PIA.)

(Fig. 5). It is usually dated to between AD 230 and 240.[30] However, this is yet another image that tends to be published out of context. Few people realize, when seeing it reproduced in books, that the photograph they are looking at is actually an upended version of the original painting. The image was originally painted vertically in an inconspicuous corner of one of the oldest parts of the catacomb, at the end of the vaulted roof of an arcosolium in the Greek Chapel. It appears alongside a stucco image of two Good Shepherd figures, each flanked by a pair of sheep and skeletal trees bearing red flowers or fruit. The fresco, painted uniformly in a pinkish-brown pigment, represents a seated mother and child. The mother wears a short-sleeved tunic and has her head covered with a light veil; the child she is holding has turned its head to look towards the viewer. In front of the couple stands a figure pointing to a star hovering below a branch of the tree above them. He appears to be holding a large book and wearing a pallium, with one shoulder exposed in the style of a philosopher. Although it is hard to pick out individual details from the painting, the difference in the quality of the two figures is still apparent. While the pointing figure is now little more than a daub of paint, the woman and child show some remarkably sophisticated shading and highlighting. This style of painting is very reminiscent of Pompeiian art, such as the second-century frescoes from the House of Adonis. Indeed, this similarity has led many in the past to date the fresco as early as the second century.[31]

Although the painting was first identified in the sixteenth century as the Virgin and Child, with the pointing figure seen as the prophet Balaam, and has continued to

---

30.   The dating of this has long been debated. Recent restoration work is reviewed by Bisconti (1996).
31.   Northcote and Brownlow 1879: 134. Bisconti (1996) has identified four different phases of work: phase 1, 'Shepherd and sheep' (stucco relief): 220–30; phase 2, Madonna: 230–40; phase 3, full figure orants: 240–50; phase 4, orant bust: 290–310.

be linked with the idea of Old Testament prophecy, there is strong evidence that there may have been some substantial changes to the fresco since the seventeenth century.[32]

So if these frescoes are not the Virgin Mary, where else within the catacombs can we find her image? It seems that we need to look at the New Testament narrative scenes for a more likely source for Marian images. The first time we meet Mary in the New Testament is at the Annunciation, and this scene is only referred to by Luke in a fairly sketchy fashion. He writes that the angel Gabriel was sent from God to a town in Galilee called Nazareth, to a virgin engaged to a man whose name was Joseph, of the house of David. The virgin's name was Mary.[33]

For a more detailed description of this event, we have to turn to the non-canonical text known as the *Protevangelium of James*. Normally dated to the second century, this text was originally ascribed to the authorship of James, brother of Jesus, or alternatively to James the Less.[34] Scholars have long disregarded this attribution, and the text's real author is still unknown. The *Protevangelium* describes how a council of Jewish priests decided to make a new veil for the Jerusalem Temple and various colours of thread were allocated to seven virgins, including Mary, who was given the 'true purple and the scarlet'. While she was spinning the scarlet, she went out to draw a pitcher of water and heard a voice saying, 'Hail, you that are highly favoured', but returned in fear to the house and began to spin the purple thread. Then the angel appeared and delivered his message, after which 'she made the purple and scarlet and brought them to the priest'. The priest blessed her and said, 'Mary, the Lord God has magnified your name.'[35]

The existence of the *Protevangelium* during the creation of the earliest Christian images provides us with a real dilemma. The texts would have been familiar to both the leaders of the Roman Church and educated Christians in the capital. As the descriptions of key events such as the Annunciation are far more colourful than in the Gospels, it would be logical to see some influence on the developing Christian iconography in the catacombs. Indeed, in later Christian art the *Protevangelium* becomes one of the key sources for imagery and, although less popular in the West, in the early Italian, as well as Eastern, churches it was hugely influential in the development of Christian art.[36]

So far, only two early examples of this scene have been identified in the

---

32. The figure has been variously identified as Balaam, who claimed that 'A star shall come forth out of Jacob and a sceptre shall rise out of Israel' (Num. 24.15–17), as well as Isaiah, or even a generic personification of a prophet, intended to emphasize the prefiguring of the New Testament by the Old. See Nicolai *et al.* (2002): 124–5. An analysis of the evidence of a series of later restoration work forms part of my PhD research paper.

33. Lk. 1:26–38.

34. See Chris Maunder, 'Mary in the New Testament and Apocrypha', in this volume: 39–46.

35. Book of James, or *Protevangelium*, XI–XII, from James 1924.

36. In the West, from the early medieval period onwards, the Annunciation was usually portrayed with Mary seated and reading the text from Isaiah 8.14, '*Ecce virgo concipiet, et pariet filium* ...' ('Behold a virgin shall conceive and bear a son ...'); see Murray and Murray (eds) 1996: 23–4.

catacombs, and neither appears to follow either Luke's or the *Protevangelium*'s description. The older portrayal can be found on the ceiling of a chamber in the catacomb of Priscilla. The 'angel' is dressed in the robes of a Roman senator, and he stands before a seated woman with his right hand raised as a sign that he is speaking. Neither Luke nor the author of the *Protevangelium* suggests the angel appears in 'the guise of a man', a phrase used to describe the angels that appeared to Abraham in the Old Testament.[37]

The second fresco identified as representing the Annunciation can be found in the catacomb of Peter and Marcellinus. This fresco appears in the context of other narrative scenes from the early life of Jesus and presents a far more complex interpretation. The central figure in the ceiling is the image of Christ teaching the apostles; the four main scenes in the sections surrounding the central image appear to show events from the life of Christ, featuring the three Magi following the star, and two Magi presenting gifts in an Adoration scene. Opposite the Adoration is a scene of the baptism of Christ, and above is the Annunciation scene. In the four corners of the ceiling are images of two male orant figures and two Good Shepherds. These frescoes are generally dated to between the second and fourth centuries; however, during the fourth century the catacomb was enlarged and embellished by Pope Damasus, and then again in the fifth and sixth centuries, with the final improvements taking place under the pontificate of Honorius I (625–38).[38]

It is obviously hard to know whether the iconography of this ceiling fresco was changed during the different stages of restoration work. It is certainly unusual to find a fresco featuring the Magi in two different scenes so close together before the fifth century.[39] It seems, therefore, that there is still room for doubt when recognizing early images of the Annunciation, so a firm identification of Mary in this context is not possible.

Perhaps a safer context in which to find Mary would be the Nativity, yet surprisingly, the early Christian artists seemed remarkably uninspired by what nowadays we regard as one of the key moments in the Christian story. From before the sixth century, the only extant examples of the baby Jesus resting in his manger are found in a handful of sarcophagi carvings, the most prominent being on the Syracuse

---

37. Mazzei 1999: 233–80. Some scholars have suggested that the reason why the angel is unwinged is that the artist is following the pagan tradition of portraying angels in this way. There is indeed a good example of this stylistic peculiarity in the pagan cubiculum of Vibia; here we can see a fresco portraying the dead woman Vibia being escorted into paradise by a male figure, also dressed in senatorial robes; he is identified by an inscription as an 'Angelus Bonus', or good angel. Some pagan and Jewish sects believed that after death their 'good angel' would lead them to the banquet of the eternally happy.
38. Mancinelli 1981: 39.
39. An exception to this rule can be found in the intricate carvings on the Adelphia sarcophagus, dated to around 340 and said to have come originally from Rome, but now lodged in the Syracuse National Museum in Sicily. Both the lid and the base of the sarcophagus have carvings featuring the Magi. The lid also shows a Nativity scene and some images that may represent scenes inspired by the *Protevangelium*; these have been interpreted as showing the first meeting between Mary and Gabriel while she is drawing water from a stream, and her presentation in the Temple. The unusual iconography of this sarcophagus is almost unique and certainly merits far more study. See Cartlidge and Elliot 2001: 78; and Volbach and Hirmer 1961: fig. 37.

Adelphia sarcophagus (see n. 38). But once again the iconography is far from clear: Mary is often featured seated apart from Christ and looking away from him. He appears as an overlarge mummified figure lying in a tomb-shaped manger which seems to be prefiguring his own death.[40]

However, there is another moment in the birth story of Jesus that seems to have really caught the imagination of the early artists, and that is the Adoration of the Magi.

The appearance of the three 'wise men' is an episode that only appears in the Gospel of Matthew and the *Protevangelium*. Despite this paucity of references, from as early as the middle of the third century it became one of the most popular tableaux, both in the catacomb frescoes and in sarcophagus carvings. The iconography of the scene is quite simplistic. It shows a woman seated in a high-backed chair holding a young child on her lap. The couple are usually depicted in profile with three male figures approaching on foot and holding a variety of objects which they are preparing to present to the seated child. These figures are normally dressed in pointed Phrygian caps and wear leggings, tunics and billowing cloaks.[41]

Although the numbers and the gifts they carry may vary, the Magi are almost always identically dressed in the type of clothes contemporary Roman artists used to illustrate barbarians from the East. So why did the early Christians portray the Magi as Eastern barbarians paying tribute to an enthroned Mary and Jesus? One of the most logical and least contentious suggestions is that these early artists were working with existing iconographic repertoires. They needed images of men from the East, so they used the 'off-the-shelf' figure of an Eastern barbarian. There was no shortage of iconographic repertoires among the sculpted friezes of the triumphal arches of Rome. The Victory Arch of Septimus Severus, dedicated in 203 to commemorate the emperor's defeat of the Parthians, clearly shows how similar the dress of the Eastern barbarians was to that of the Magi. In one key scene we see a Parthian prisoner kneeling in submission before a seated female figure representing Roma.[42]

It has been suggested that an actual historical event of imperial tribute may have inspired Matthew's writings. This was the visit to the Emperor Nero of the

---

40. Apart from the Adelphia sarcophagus, another famous example is a large marble tomb from St Ambrogio in Milan, which is dated to the late fourth century and shows a heavily swaddled baby Jesus in a manger, flanked by an ox and an ass. Neither Mary nor Joseph features in this scene. There is an interesting comparison between this scene and the representations of the miraculous birth of Alexander the Great from a pavement mosaic in Lebanon. Olympias his mother, allegedly impregnated by Zeus, sits apart from her newborn son while his father Philip turns his back on his wife and son. Later icons of the Nativity often show Joseph in a similar pose. See Grabar 1969: 130.

41. The billowing cloak or robe is a clever artistic device to indicate motion or recent arrival. It was also used in later depictions of the Annunciation to indicate that the angel Gabriel had just arrived before Mary.

42. The Parthian Empire arose in the third century BC, and at its height it occupied all of modern Iran, Iraq and Armenia, parts of Turkey, Georgia, Azerbaijan, Turkmenistan, Afghanistan and Tajikistan, and – for brief periods – territories in Pakistan, Syria, Lebanon, Israel and Palestine. The end of this loosely organized empire came in AD 224, when the last king was defeated by one of his vassals, the Persians of the Sassanid dynasty. See Ferris 2000: 120.

Armenian prince Tiridates in AD 66. Tiridates was a follower of the pagan god Mithras and was said to have initiated Nero into the religion during the visit.[43]

From a theological point of view, the Adoration scene is generally regarded as a representation of the conversion of the first Gentiles to Christianity, thereby making it an exceptionally important moment in the development of the Christian faith. It can also be seen as symbolizing the suppression of paganism and heretical sects, on the basis that several pagan gods were portrayed in the same dress as the Magi, as were members of the Gnostic sect of Manichaeism.[44]

Whatever the origin or true meaning of the Adoration may have been, it must surely offer us the earliest verifiable image of the Virgin Mary. Here we have a seated Mary portrayed in a variety of guises, sometimes with her head covered by her pallium, or a flimsy diaphanous veil; sometimes with her head completely bare, her dark hair elegantly coiled into the latest fashion. But once again, second-guessing the minds of the early Christian artists may not be that straightforward. There was another very popular artistic style that may have inspired this representation, and that was the art of *personification* – the use of allegorical figures to represent cities, states, rivers, seasons and other abstract ideas in human form. A famous example of this was the Roma imagery, a familiar and much revered representation of the enduring power of the city and her protective divinities, that continued to be popular throughout the early centuries of Christianity. She was usually portrayed in a seated position and, as shown on the triumphal arch of Severus, would also be seen receiving tributes from vanquished enemies.[45]

It is altogether possible that, rather than being part of a simple narrative scene, the seated female figure was intended to have a far more abstract meaning. One possible interpretation is that she is Roma presenting the new religion of Christianity to the Gentiles, the Christ figure representing the essence of the new cult. Alternatively, she may have been created to represent an entirely new personification, that of the Church itself, a role that Ambrose, Bishop of Milan, would link firmly with Mary by the latter half of the fourth century.[46]

If this image of Mary and Jesus was regarded as no more than a shorthand reference to the new religion, then it might explain some of the actions of the early Christians that today we would regard as being completely sacrilegious.

In the fourth century the Cult of the Martyrs was at its height, with the catacombs transformed into a centre for pilgrimage. Devout Christians were clamouring to be buried as close to the tombs of the martyred saints as they could get. The *fossores*, or gravediggers, were paid handsomely to free up space in the tombs, and in the process

---

43.   Trexler 1997: 15.
44.   God heroes such as Mithras, Attis and Orpheus were all depicted in the same dress as the Magi. Manichaeism was an Eastern Gnostic sect that became enormously popular in Rome in the third and fourth centuries. It was founded by the Persian Mani in the latter half of the third century and was said to be a synthesis of all the religious systems then known, consisting of Zoroastrianism, Dualism, Babylonian folklore, Buddhist ethics and Christianity. For an updated study of Manichaeism, see Lieu 1993.
45.   Beard *et al.* 1998: 158–60, 257–9; Stafford and Herrin (eds) forthcoming.
46.   Graef 1985: 1: 77–89.

hacked their way through scores of earlier frescoes. One engraving from Bosio's *Roma Sotterranea* illustrates part of an Adoration scene, with Mary's head completely replaced by a gaping hole where a new loculus had been dug out. This example shows just how little regard the *fossores* and their clients had for images – an attitude that might be more understandable if we accept that the frescoes depicted allegorical figures rather than divine portraits.

REPRESENTATIONS IN CHURCHES

Above ground, Christian art was evolving at a rapid pace, having now been given the support of the Emperor Constantine. After the Edict of Milan in 313, the emperor actively encouraged the building of churches for worship, and art became a means of linking the Bible and liturgy. It is from this time that a more formalized repertoire of images started to develop and yet, rather frustratingly, only a handful of Marian art survives from this period, giving us an iconography that is still confusingly ambiguous.

One of the earliest examples of non-funerary art was part of a gift to Ambrose of Milan. In around 382 Pope Damasus sent the bishop a set of relics of the apostles. Ambrose had them enshrined in a specially designed silver reliquary casket which now resides in St Nazaro Maggiore in Milan. The casket was decorated with scenes from the Old Testament and the life of Christ, with an especially unusual Adoration scene. Here Mary is represented enthroned in a frontal position with a naked Christ child, and she is flanked by two Magi dressed as Cynic philosophers, rather than Persian priests. This fascinating reliquary provides us with the earliest example of Mary wearing the style of dress that, by the next century, was to become her trademark – tightly fitting veil falling low onto her forehead, and full length, all-encompassing robes, very much in the style of Roman bridal dress. In the traditional pre-Christian wedding ceremony, the bride would wear a flame-coloured mantle known as a *flammeus*. This was pulled forward to hide half the face.[47] Ambrose seems to have drawn heavily on the bridal references found in The Song of Songs, said to signify the Church whom Christ had taken as his bride. He developed the theme into a treatise on the life of a Christian virgin who had consecrated herself to Christ as her spouse.[48] It is conceivable that this treatise had been inspired by his own sister Marcellina, who was one of the first virgins to take part in a formal consecration, making her devotion sometime between 352 and 354 before Pope Liberius, who is said to have given her a veil of 'sombre colour'.[49]

As well as describing Mary as a model of the Church, Ambrose also describes her as a model of virginity and an example to which all good Christians should aspire. It is tempting to think that the bishop may also have designed the iconography for the

47. Sebesta and Bonfante 2001: 54.
48. Hunter 1993: 54–5.
49. Wright 1991: 485. A possible interpretation of the 'sombre' colour is that it was created as an antithesis to the vibrant flame colour of the traditional bridal veil.

Fig. 6. Santa Maria Maggiore, Rome: Triumphal arch.

casket, in the process creating the prototype of Marian art – a combination of Mary as the mother of Christ and a personification of the Church.

Perhaps the most important monument to Mary was the church of St Maria Maggiore in Rome, built 50 years or so after Ambrose's reliquary was created. It was decorated and dedicated to Mary by Pope Sixtus III after the Council of Ephesus in 431, and has one of the oldest surviving sets of images of Mary outside the catacombs. Her likeness appears in mosaic in four different narrative scenes on the triumphal arch (Fig. 6), namely the Annunciation (Fig. 7), Adoration (Fig. 8), Presentation in the Temple, and Flight to Egypt. The original apse, destroyed at the end of the thirteenth century, was said to have held an image of the Virgin enthroned, although there is no firm evidence to support this idea.

Scholars have suggested that the unusual themes illustrated in these tableaux indicate a heavy apocryphal influence. The Annunciation features a seated Mary unravelling a skein of scarlet thread, part of her task of spinning a new veil for the Temple, as referred to in the *Protevangelium*. However, she is also surrounded by five angels and an overly large dove. The scene of the Presentation in the Temple shows Mary and Joseph with Jesus meeting the prophetess Anna and Simeon; this story forms part of Luke's Gospel (2.22–38), but does not feature in the *Protevangelium*.[50]

---

50. *Protevangelium*, ch. 10, in James 1924.

Fig. 7. Santa Maria Maggiore, Rome: *Annunciation* (mosaic, fifth century).

Fig. 8. Santa Maria Maggiore, Rome: *Adoration of the Magi* (mosaic, fifth century).

Various different interpretations have been advanced for the scene that is usually referred to as 'The Flight to Egypt'. The most common suggestion is that it represents an apocryphal story of the Holy Family meeting Aphrodosius, the pagan governor of Sotinen-Hermopolis in Egypt. However, the storyline does not appear to tally with the images in the mosaic, and the strange bare-chested man alongside Aphrodosius has never been properly identified.[51]

In these three tableaux, Mary is dressed in a style that has been described as falling somewhere between a Byzantine empress and a *clarissima femina*, or high-born woman. She is depicted wearing a long tunic with full sleeves and jewelled cuffs. On top of the tunic is a gold overgarment, with a large brooch pinned under her breasts attached by a double strand of pearls. Around her neck is a heavily jewelled collar with matching earrings and hair decoration. There has been a considerable amount of

---

51. The problem with the identification is that the source of the legend was the *Gospel of Pseudo-Matthew*, a Latin compilation based on the *Protevangelium* and the *Gospel of Thomas*, but not usually dated to earlier than the end of the sixth century, and more often to the eighth or ninth centuries. Spain (1979) suggests that the figures are in fact David and Isaiah, and reinterprets all the other iconography of the arch, suggesting that the bejewelled woman is in fact Sarah.

debate as to whether this is indeed an imperial version of Mary, the suggestion being that her outfit is too understated to represent the dress of an empress.[52] However, imperial art in the late antique period was almost as complex as religious art. Even though statues of empresses would have been a familiar sight in Constantinople between the fourth and fifth centuries, it was their imperial, rather than feminine, identity that was their most distinctive attribute. But although these sculptures were likely to have been idealized images, rather than portraits, the message being conveyed was not one of imperial wealth and extravagance; rather, they were intended to represent an idealistic image of perfection, both physical and moral.[53] The empress's modesty was represented by her dress as a dignified *clarissima femina*, rather than an overtly regal figure. The art of personification was used even in imperial imagery; for example, a popular image from the fourth century was that of the empress as a personification of chastity, with her *palla* pulled up over her elaborately dressed hair.[54]

The fourth scene on the arch is perhaps the most puzzling of all, and once again it represents the Adoration, but with an entirely new iconography. Here we can see the elaborately dressed Mary seated on the right of the enthroned Christ child. Two Magi approach from the other side of the throne, while the third stands between her and another figure, normally identified as Joseph. Seated on the left of Christ, in a strikingly more prominent position, is a mysterious, heavily veiled woman, her chin resting on her right hand in an attitude of deep thought, her other hand clutching a consular *mappa*. A pair of red shoes peep from beneath her dark purple robes and, like the Mary figure in the St Nazaro Maggiore reliquary, her veil is pulled far over her forehead.[55] All the signs indicate that this is a very important figure, and some scholars have identified her as Sophia, or Divine Wisdom, or even the Old Testament Sarah.[56]

The most important study of the mosaics at St Maria Maggiore was conducted in 1975 by the German art historian Beat Brenk. He concluded that the main theme of

---

52.   One piece of evidence to suggest that these are not imperial images is the lack of a diadem with jewels or pendilia hanging from the side. However, there is still considerable debate as to when this form of imperial dress was first adopted. See A. M. Stout, 'Jewelry as a Symbl of Status in the Roman Empire', in Sebesta and Bonfante 2001: 77–100. For an excellent overview on the imagery of early empresses, see McClanan and Wheeler 2002.

53.   McClanan and Wheeler 2002: 3–4.

54.   E. Gittings, 'Civic Life, Elite Women', in Kalavrezou 2003: 35, 86.

55.   The *mappa* was a folded cloth. It was originally used by the emperor as part of the ceremony to start the gladiatorial games. When the cloth was dropped the games would commence. Later it was adopted as part of the regalia of the Roman consuls who took on the responsibility for organizing the games. Its incorporation into female representation in art seems strange, but it must also have been used as a way of indicating high rank. The red shoes were also a sign of high, usually imperial, rank, as was the colour purple.

56.   Oakeshott 1967: 73. Spain (1979) suggests a completely different reading for this scene, with the bejewelled woman being Sarah, and the veiled woman the real Mary. It is important to note that between the Middle Ages and the late twentieth century there has been a considerable amount of alteration and restoration work, with the whole of the apse mosaic being entirely replaced in the thirteenth century. The latest restoration work took place in the 1990s.

the arch mosaics was the Universal Church combining the Church of the Jews and the Church of the Gentiles. He saw these two aspects of the early Church represented in the different mosaic scenes which, he argued, depicted the divinity of Christ being recognized by believing Jews and Gentiles, and denied by unbelieving Jews.[57] Based on this conclusion, Brenk proposed that the mystery woman in the Adoration scene was a personification of the Church of the Gentiles.

The Church of St Sabina, built just a few years before St Maria Maggiore, provides some support for this idea. The original dedication of the church has survived, and on either side of the Latin inscription are two mosaic female figures. Both are shown heavily veiled and draped, each holding a book in her left hand and performing a blessing with her other hand. The figure on the right wears a tight-fitting cap under a dark veil, and a tightly wrapped robe. She is identified by an inscription as *Ecclesia Ex Circumcisione*, or Church of the Jews, whereas the woman on the left wears a looser robe in the style of a Roman *stola* and *chiton*, and in her left hand she holds a white *mappa*. This figure is identified as *Ecclesia Ex Gentibus*, or the Church of the Gentiles.[58]

These two figures were intended to represent the two different branches of the early Church, evolving as it did from the Jewish and Gentile traditions. There is no doubt that the mystery woman of St Maria Maggiore looks remarkably similar to these personifications, but rather than restricting her to the Church of the Gentiles alone, I would suggest that she is in fact a merger of both Churches – a true Universal Church incorporating the attributes of both her forerunners.[59]

There is no doubt that the mosaics of St Maria Maggiore present us with a key moment in the development of the imagery of the Virgin Mary. At first glance she appears as a powerful and independent *clarissima femina*, bedecked in rich robes and elaborate jewellery, taking a prominent role in the four scenes in which she is depicted. This imagery would have been entirely appropriate as a tribute to her newly elevated role as *Theotokos* after the Council of Ephesus. As the Mother of God, she had now become a powerful force within Christianity, but a force that might be dangerous if controlled by powers outside the Church. During the fourth and fifth centuries, an increasing tension had been growing between the imperial family and the leaders of the Church. The emperors, in the time-honoured tradition, continued to believe they had the divine right to control their empire's religion, but the bishops had other ideas.[60]

---

57. For a thorough analysis, see the monograph on St Maria Maggiore by Brenk (1975). Brenk sees the whole pictorial theme of the arch as representing the Universal Church, consisting of the Church of the Jews and the Church of the Gentiles under the peaceful rule of Christ.

58. There is only one other extant example of these two figures, and these are in the much restored apse mosaic of the church of Santa Pudenziana, dated to the late fourth century. However, there is still considerable debate as to whether this is the correct identification, as there are no identifying inscriptions; see Oakeshott 1967: 65.

59. The imagery of *Ecclesia Gentibus and Circumcisione* disappeared at about this time, only to resurface in the West in the medieval period, when sculptures of Church and Synagogue often appeared in cathedrals across Europe. They were always portrayed as women, Church crowned triumphant with her cross and chalice, and Synagogue blindfolded and defeated, with her sceptre broken and her tablets of law cracked.

60. Cooper 1998: 31–43.

The mosaics of St Maria Maggiore seem to show that Mary's iconography was becoming dangerously similar to that of the idealized empress imagery. We have no surviving images of Mary from Constantinople from this time, but it is telling that the mosaicists of the Church may well have been from the Eastern capital.[61] At this time the emperor's sister Pulcheria held sway, an empress who had dedicated her virginity to Christ at the age of 14. Pulcheria believed herself to be Mary's living image, and had her own portrait, rather than Mary's, hung in the great church above an altar bedecked with her imperial robe. This was a woman in control of her church.[62]

Religious wars have been won and lost through the power of images; the bishops knew that they had to reclaim control over the image of Mary, one of their most important assets since the ruling of the Council at Ephesus. The mystery woman in the Adoration scene was their solution: she exhibited all the attributes of Bishop Ambrose's ideal Mary – modest and demure, swathed from head to toe in dark robes, and exhibiting only the subtlest signs of her rank. Mary became the visual representation of both the Mother of God and the Church, but rather than a regal and powerful empress figure, she evolved into the epitome of a modest and obedient Virgin Bride – a woman under the control of men. The stage was set for the next 1,500 years of Marian art.[63]

BIBLIOGRAPHY

Bacci, M. (2000) 'With the Paintbrush of St Luke', in Vassilaki (ed.), *Mother of God*: 79–89.

Beard, M., North, J. and Price, S. (1998) *Religions of Rome. Vol. 1: A History*, Cambridge: Cambridge University Press.

Beckwith, J. (1970) *Early Christian and Byzantine Art*, reprinted 1993, New Haven: Yale University Press.

Belting, H. (1995) *Likeness & Presence: A History of the Image before the Era of Art*, Chicago: University of Chicago Press.

Benko, S. (2004) *The Virgin Goddess*, Leiden: Brill.

---

61. Kitzinger 1995: 73. There is one other surviving piece of art contemporary with the St Maria Maggiore mosaics that shows Mary portrayed in this way. An ivory diptych, discovered in Milan but possibly originating in Ravenna, shows Mary being surprised by an angel while she is drawing water, and being shown the Temple by the same angel. In both these scenes, as if to indicate that they took place before the birth of Christ, she is dressed as a *clarissima femina*. What is particularly interesting is that in the two other scenes, featuring the Nativity and Adoration, she is shown robed in the style of the mystery woman from St Maria Maggiore.

62. Cooper 1998: 31–43. The Patriarch Nestorius had Pulcheria banished from the Church and her image and robe removed. He refused to acknowledge that Mary was *Theotokos*, and it is likely that Pulcheria was a key player in the Council of Ephesus that brought about his ultimate downfall. For further details of the dispute between Nestorius and Cyril of Alexandria, see Richard Price, 'Theotokos: The Title and its Significance in Doctrine and Devotion', in this volume: 56–73.

63. The imperial Mary has been revived from time to time, but under the control of the Church. In the seventh and eighth centuries, the popes used Maria Regina as Queen of Heaven imagery for political ends, as a means of endorsing their claim that Rome, and not Constantinople, was the centre of the Christian faith. This version of Mary was a far more regal image than the *clarissima femina* figure portrayed on the St Maria Maggiore mosaics. This Western Mary was portrayed crowned and carrying imperial regalia; see Osborne 2003.

de Berardino, A. (ed.) (1991) *Encyclopedia of the Early Church*, trans. Adrian Walford, Cambridge: James Clarke.

Bolman, E. S. (2005) 'The Enigmatic Coptic Galaktotrophousa and the cult of the Virgin Mary in Egypt', in Vassilaki, *Images of the Mother of God*: 13–22.

Bosio, A., *Roma Sotterranea*, Rome, 1632.

Brenk, B. (1975) *Die frühchristlichen Mosaiken in S. Maria Maggiore zu Rom*, Stuttgart: Steiner Verlag.

Brown, D. (2003) *The Da Vinci Code*, London: Corgi.

Cameron, A. (2004) 'The Cult of the Virgin in Late Antiquity: Religious Development and Myth-Making', in Swanson (ed.), *The Church and Mary*: 1–21.

Carroll Cruz, J. (1993) *Miraculous Images of Our Lady*, Illinois: Tan Books.

Cartlidge, D. R. and Elliot, J. Keith (2001) *Art and the Christian Apocrypha*, London: Routledge.

Eastmond, A. and James L. (eds) (2003) *Icon & Word*, Aldershot: Ashgate.

Ferris, I. M. (2000) *Enemies of Rome: Barbarians through Roman Eyes*, Stroud: Sutton Publishing.

Finney, P. C. (1994) *The Invisible God*, Oxford: Oxford University Press.

Grabar, A. (1969) *Christian Iconography: A Study of its Origins*, London: Routledge.

Graef, H. (1985) *Mary: A History of Doctrine and Devotion*, combined edn, London: Sheed & Ward.

Holum, K. G. (1982) *Theodosian Empresses: Women and Imperial Dominion in Late Antiquity*, Berkeley: University of California Press.

James, L. (2001) *Empresses & Power in Early Byzantium*, London: Continuum.

James, M. R. (trans.) (1924) *The Apocryphal New Testament*, Oxford: Clarendon Press.

Jameson, A. (1890) *Legends of the Madonna as Represented in the Fine Arts*, London: Longmans.

Jensen, R. M. (2000) *Understanding Early Christian Art*, London: Routledge.

Kalavrezou, I. (2003) *Byzantine Women and Their World*, New Haven: Yale University.

Kitzinger, E. (1995) *Byzantine Art in the Making*, Cambridge, MA: Harvard University Press.

Lieu, S. N. C. (1993) *Mesopotamia and the Roman East*, Religions in the Graeco-Roman World, Leiden: Brill.

Limberis, V. (1994) *Divine Heiress: The Virgin Mary and the Creation of Christian Constantinople*, London: Routledge.

Mancinelli, F. (1981) *Catacombs and Basilicas: The Early Christians in Rome*, Florence: Scala.

Mango, C. (2000) 'Constantinople as Theotokoupolis', in Vassilaki (ed.), *Mother of God*.

Maniura, R. (2004) *Pilgrimage to Images in the Fifteenth Century: The Origins of the Cult of Our Lady of Czestochowa*, Woodbridge: Boydell Press.

Mathews, T. F. (1998) *The Clash of the Gods: A Reinterpretation of Early Christian Art*, Princeton, NJ: Princeton University Press.

Mathews, T. F. and Muller, N. (2005) 'Isis and Mary in early Icons', in Vassilaki, *Images of the Mother of God*.

McClanan, A. L. and Wheeler, B. (2002) *Representations of Early Byzantine Empresses: Image and Empire*, New York: Palgrave Macmillan.

Murray, Sister C. (1981) *Rebirth and Afterlife: A Study of the Transmutation of Some Pagan Imagery in Early Christian Art*, Oxford: BAR Int. Series.

Murray, P. and Murray, L. (eds) (1996) *Oxford Companion to Christian Art and Architecture*, Oxford: Oxford University Press.

Nicolai, V. C., Bisconti, F. and Mazzoleni, D. (2002) *The Christian Catacombs of Rome*, Regensburg: Schnell & Steiner.

Northcote, J. S. and Brownlow, W. R. (1879) *Roma sotterranea*, Vol. 2, London: Longmans.

Oakeshott, W. (1967) *The Mosaics of Rome*, Greenwich, NY: New York Graphic Society.

Osborne, J. (2003) 'Images of the Mother God in Early Medieval Rome', in Eastmond and James, *Icon and Word*.

Parlby, G. (2002) 'St Luke as an artist: the evolution of a legend and its relevance to the development of the iconography of the Virgin and Child', MA dissertation, London: Courtauld Institute.

Partner, P. (1999) *Two Thousand Years, The First Millennium: The Birth of Christianity to the Crusades*, London: Granada Media.

Pentcheva, B. (2000) 'Miniature of St Luke Painting the Icon of the Virgin and Child', in Vassilaki (ed.), *Mother of God*.

de Rossi, G. B. (1994) *Giovannie Battista de Rossi e le catacombe romane. Mostra fotografica e documentaria in occasione del I Centenario della morte di Giovanni Battista de Rossi (1894–1994)*, Citta del Vaticano.

Rutger, L. V. (2000) *Subterranenan Rome*, Louvain: Peeters.

Scorza Barcellona, F. (1991) 'Narratio de Rebus Persicis', in Berardino, *Encyclopedia of the Early Church*.

Sebesta, J. L. and Bonfante, L. (eds) (2001) *The World of Roman Costume*, Wisconsin: University of Wisconsin Press.

Stafford, E. and Herrin, J. (eds) (2005) *Personification in the Greek World from Antiquity to Byzantium*, Aldershot: Ashgate.

Stevenson, J. (1978) *The Catacombs: Rediscovered Monuments of Early Christianity*, London: Thames & Hudson.

Swanson, Robert N. (ed.) (2004) *The Church and Mary*, Studies in Church History 39, Woodbridge: Boydell Press.

Thomas, T. K. (2000) *Late Antique Egyptian Funerary Sculpture*, Princeton, NJ: Princeton University Press.

Toynbee, J. M. C. (1996) *Death and Burial in the Roman World*, Baltimore, MD: Johns Hopkins University Press.

Trexler, R. C. (1997) *The Journey of the Magi, Meanings in the History of a Christian Story*, Princeton, NJ: Princeton University Press.

Vassilaki, M. (ed.) (2000) *Mother of God: Representations of the Virgin in Byzantine Art*, Milan: Skira.

Vassilaki, M. (ed.) (2005) *Images of the Mother of God*, Aldershot: Ashgate.

Volbach, W. F. and Hirmer, M. (1961) *Early Christian Art*, New York: Abrams.

Weitzmann, K. and Kessler, H. L. (1990) *The Frescoes of the Dura Synagogue and Christian Art*, Dumbarton Oaks Studies 28, Dumbarton Oaks: Dumbarton Oaks Publication Service.

Wilpert, J. (1903) *Die Malereien der Katakomben Roms*, Vol. 1, Freiburg im Breisgau: Herclersche Verlags Handlung.

Wright, F. (1991) *Selected Letters of St Jerome*, Loeb Classical Library, Cambridge, MA: Harvard University Press.

Zanker, P. and Ewald, B. C. (2003) *Mit Mythen Leben. Die Bilderwelt der römischen Sarkophage*, Munich: Hirmer Verlag.

Journals

Bisconti, F. (1996) 'La Madonna di Priscilla: interventi di restauro ed ipotesi sulla dinamica decorativa', *Rivista di Archeologia Cristiana* LXXII, 1–2: 7–34.

Cooper, K. (1998) 'Contesting the Nativity: Wives, Virgins and Pulcheria's *imitatio Mariae*', *Scottish Journal of Religious Studies*, 19 (1), Spring: 31–43.

Hunter, D. G. (1993) 'Helvidius, Jovinian, and the Virginity of Mary in late fourth century Rome', *Journal of Early Christian Studies*, Vol. 1: 54–5.

Mazzei, B. (1999) 'Il cubicolo dell'Annunciazione nelle catacombe di Priscilla. Nuove Osservazioni all luce dei recenti restauri', *Rivista di Archeologia Cristiana* 75: 233–80.

McGuckin, J. (2001) 'The Paradox of the Virgin-Theotokos: Evangelism and Imperial Politics in the Fifth Century Byzantine World', *Maria: A Journal of Marian Theology*, 2.1.

Murray, Sister C. (1977) 'Art and the Early Church', *Journal of Theological Studies*, N.S. XXVIII: 303–45.

Oikonomides, N. (1991) 'Holy Icon as an Asset', *DOP*, vol. 45: 35–44.

Spain S. (1979) 'The Promised Blessing: The Iconography of the Mosaics of S. Maria Maggiore', *The Art Bulletin*.

Winston, J. (2002) 'Describing the Virgin', *Art History*, Vol. 25, No. 3, June: 275–92.

6

MARIAN LITURGIES AND DEVOTION IN EARLY CHRISTIANITY

STEPHEN J. SHOEMAKER

It is perhaps somewhat surprising, given the central position that the Virgin Mary eventually came to occupy in the Christian tradition, that Marian piety and veneration developed only relatively late in the history of Christianity. To be sure, Mary was an important focus of Christian theology and even devotion already in the second century, as Irenaeus of Lyons and the *Protevangelium of James* attest,[1] but it is not until the later fourth century that we first encounter unambiguous evidence of cult and prayer offered to the Virgin herself. This circumstance is not altogether unusual, however, in as much as it is around this same time that the veneration of so many other saints first becomes visible and organized.[2] Although it has recently been suggested that Marian cult developed more slowly than did the veneration of several other early saints,[3] a complete survey of the earliest available evidence reveals that this is not the case. Testimony from a variety of different sources, including early liturgical manuals, homiletics, archaeology, hagiography, papyrology, and especially the early Dormition apocrypha, witnesses to a thriving cult of the Virgin in the east Roman provinces already at the end of the fourth century. That Marian piety first develops only somewhat later than the earliest veneration of certain martyr saints, such as St Menas in Egypt,[4] comes as no great surprise, in as much as it is well known that the veneration of martyrs preceded – and eventually gave rise to – the cult of saints.[5]

The earliest clear indication of Marian piety would appear to be an intercessory prayer addressed to the Virgin preserved on a fragmentary papyrus from late ancient Egypt. Now identified as an early version of the prayer '*Sub tuum praesidium*', the reconstructed text is as follows: 'We take refuge in your mercy, Theotokos. Do not disregard our prayers in troubling times, but deliver us from danger, O only pure one, only blessed one.'[6] Although the precise date of the papyrus remains somewhat

---

1. See, for example, Gambero 1999: 51–8; Foskett 2002: 141–64; Pelikan 1996: 39–50; Knight 2002; Zervos 2002.
2. Brown 1981: 7–8, 50 *et passim*; Maraval 1985: 12, 23 *et passim*.
3. Averil Cameron makes this point in a pair of recent articles in comparison with the cult of Thecla, which she holds to have developed earlier; see Cameron 2000: 5; Cameron 2004: 5–6.
4. See, for example, Maraval 1985: 319–22.
5. See, for example, Delehaye 1927; Delehaye 1933; Brown 1981; Février 1991; Cunningham 2005: 5–27.
6. The text was first published in Hunt *et al.* 1911–52: 46–7. The best reconstruction of the text is in Stegmüller 1952. See also Giamberardini 1974–5, vol. 1: 69–97; Giamberardini 1969: 324–62; Triacca 1989; Förster 1995.

in question, most scholars are agreed that it was written in the latter part of the fourth century at the latest. In fact, the document's palaeography is most consistent with an even earlier dating, around the turn of the fourth century, but most interpreters have cautiously followed the judgement of the text's initial editor in assigning it to the end of the fourth century, when evidence of prayer to the Virgin first begins to appear in other sources.[7]

Some of the earliest indications of Marian cult come from the writings of the two great Cappadocian Gregorys, Gregory of Nyssa and Gregory of Nazianzus. The latter, in his *Oration 24*, affords an important witness to the practice of Marian prayer in Constantinople during the late fourth century. In this rather peculiar work, a panegyric on 'Cyprian', Gregory freely mixes traditions about Cyprian of Carthage with those of Cyprian of Antioch (in Pisidia), whose feast the oration was presumably intended to commemorate.[8] Cyprian of Antioch was, according to legend, a magician who sought with his spells to seduce a beautiful Christian virgin named Justina. Justina, however, successfully defended herself by calling on her 'husband', Christ, as well as by praying to the Virgin Mary for her aid, since she too was a virgin who had once faced danger.[9] Whether or not a virgin named Justina actually sought the Virgin's assistance and protection through prayer in the early fourth century, as the legend suggests, is really beside the point: the primary significance of this passage lies in its witness to the practice of intercessory prayer to the Virgin among the Nicene Christians of Constantinople by 379, when Gregory delivered this oration.[10] From Gregory's representation of Justina, we may assume that such Marian prayers were fairly common practice in the community that he led, which included, we should note, a number of aristocratic women who were devoted to the cult of the saints and their relics.[11]

Only a year later, in the fall of 380, Gregory of Nyssa delivered his panegyric on yet another Gregory, the third-century Gregory Thaumaturgus. In this biography, Gregory of Nyssa describes a waking vision of the Virgin experienced by Gregory Thaumaturgus, who received a trinitarian creed directly from the apostle John at the Virgin's command.[12] This would appear to be the earliest account of a Marian apparition, and while Gregory of Nyssa's account of the episode is no guarantee that Gregory Thaumaturgus ever had such an experience, it attests that such appearances of the Virgin Mary were familiar to the Nicene Christians whom Gregory of Nyssa shepherded.[13] Indeed, back in Constantinople, if we may believe the fifth-century Church historian Sozomen, such Marian apparitions were a fairly regular occurrence in Gregory of Nazianzus's church of Anastasia.

7.   Hunt *et al.* 1911–52, vol. 3: 47; Stegmüller 1952: 78. See also Giamberardini 1974–5, vol. 1: 95–7, but see the dissenting opinion of Förster 1995.

8.   Mossay (ed.) 1981: 9–27.

9.   Gregory of Nazianzus, *Oration 24*, 9–11, in ibid.: 54–61. English translation in Gambero 1999: 166–7.

10.   Mossay (ed.) 1981: 25; Stegmüller 1952: 78; Peltomaa 2001: 75.

11.   McGuckin 2001: 252.

12.   Gregory of Nyssa, *Life of Gregory Thaumaturgus*, in Heil *et al.* (eds) 1990: 16–18.

13.   See Starowieyski 1990.

Gregory of Nazianzen presided over those who maintain the 'consubstantiality' of the Holy Trinity, and assembled them together in a little dwelling, which had been altered into the form of a house of prayer, by those who held the same opinions and had a like form of worship. It subsequently became one of the most conspicuous in the city, and is so now, not only for the beauty and number of its structures, but also for the advantages accruing to it from the visible manifestations of God. For the power of God was there manifested, and was helpful both in waking visions and in dreams, often for the relief of many diseases and for those afflicted by some sudden transmutation in their affairs. The power was accredited to Mary, the Mother of God, the holy virgin, for she does manifest herself in this way. The name of Anastasia was given to this church.[14]

The fact that both Gregory of Nazianzus and Gregory of Nyssa would refer to these events in such a matter-of-fact manner suggests that Marian prayer and even apparitions were not particularly uncommon in their communities.[15] As Nicholas Constas observes, even though these are the first reports of such phenomena, 'these accounts do not have the air of novelty or innovation',[16] and presumably they reflect what were already well-established practices.

A somewhat different sort of evidence is afforded by Epiphanius of Salamis, who in his 'medicine-chest' against heresies, the *Panarion*, describes the heresy of the 'Kollyridians'. According to Epiphanius, the Kollyridians were a group of women, first in Thrace and Scythia and then in Arabia, who worshipped the Virgin Mary and allowed women to serve as priests, both practices that he vigorously condemns. These women, he explains, 'prepare a certain carriage with a square seat and spread out fine linens over it on a special day of the year, and they put forth bread and offer it in the name of Mary, and they all partake of the bread'.[17] Although it has recently been suggested that we 'should probably leave aside' Epiphanius's reference to this group of women who venerated Mary,[18] I see no compelling reason to doubt his report in this instance: it is not clear what is to be gained by inventing such a group. In any case, whether or not the Kollyridians actually existed or were simply the product of Epiphanius's (admittedly active) imagination is largely immaterial for the present purpose. Their alleged practice of worshipping the Virgin is of primary interest, and even if the Kollyridians are Epiphanius's own creation, surely he has not also fabricated the worship of Mary merely to refute it. While the Kollyridians might serve as useful 'straw women' for Epiphanius to use in addressing the issue of Marian cult, it would make little sense for him completely to invent the worship of Mary only to condemn something that no one actually did. Furthermore, Epiphanius's

14. Sozomen, *Ecclesiastical History* 7.5.1–3, in Bidez and Hansen (eds) 1995: 306; trans. Schaff and Wace (eds) (1891), vol. 2: 378–9.
15. Kelly 1978: 498.
16. Constas 2003: 246.
17. Epiphanius, *Panarion* 79.1.7, in Holl and Dummer (eds) 1915, 1980, 1985, vol. 3: 476.
18. Cameron 2004: 6–7.

concerns in this section are not limited to the Kollyridians alone, or even to their veneration of the Virgin; rather, he addresses the issue of Marian cult more broadly within the context of a general critique of the veneration of saints and angels. His persistent complaint is that such holy persons, among whom he includes the Virgin Mary, may not receive our worship (*proskunēsis*) but only our honour (*timē*): 'Let Mary be held in honor, but let the Father, the Son, and the Holy Spirit be worshipped: let no one worship Mary.'[19]

Consequently, it would be a mistake to interpret the Kollyridians, as some have done, as worshipping Mary 'as a goddess', or as 'eager to put Mary in the place of God'.[20] To a large extent such assessments fall victim to Epiphanius's rhetoric, undoubtedly with encouragement from an older view of the cult of Mary and the saints as a vulgar intrusion of Graeco-Roman 'paganism' into the Christian faith.[21] It is true that Epiphanius first introduces these women as having 'done their best and doing their best, in the grip both of madness and of folly, to substitute her for God',[22] but he almost immediately situates these remarks within the context of a broader critique of any sort of veneration offered to saints:

> The words, 'Some shall depart from sound doctrine, giving heed to fables and doctrines of devils,' apply to these people as well. For as the scriptures say, they will be 'worshipping the dead' as the dead were given honors in Israel. And the timely glory of the saints, which redounds to God in their lifetimes, has become an error for others, who do not see the truth.[23]

Nowhere does Epiphanius indicate that the Kollyridians actually went so far as to identify Mary with the deity, in the way that Christians came to understand her son, for instance. He does not attack them for advancing a theological belief in Mary's divinity, but rather for their practice of offering cult to the Virgin and venerating her in a manner that *he* considers entirely inappropriate for a human being. Such ritual activities in his view are tantamount to 'substituting her for God', involving worship of a creature in the place of God, regardless of intention.

Yet it is doubtful that the Kollyridians (or whoever's practices Epiphanius is attacking) understood their actions in this way. To the contrary, it appears that the Kollyridians offered Mary the kind of veneration that was increasingly directed towards Christian saints during the late fourth century. Reading between the lines suggests that the Kollyridians were no more interested in replacing God with Mary or elevating her to a divine status than the early devotees of St Thecla or St John were intent on divinizing the subjects of their devotion. Such, at least, is how Epiphanius represents their practice in opposing it through a general critique of the cult of the saints:

---

19. Epiphanius, *Panarion* 79.7.5, in Holl and Dummer (eds) 1915, 1980, 1985, vol. 3: 482.
20. For example, Limberis 1994: 118; Benko 1993: 170–95.
21. For example, Benko 1993: 1–5; see the excellent critique of this view in Brown 1981: 4–22.
22. Epiphanius, *Panarion* 78.23.3, in Holl and Dummer 1915, 1980, 1985, vol. 3: 473; trans. Williams 1987, 1994, vol. 2: 618.
23. Epiphanius, *Panarion* 78.23.5, in Holl and Dummer, ibid.; trans. Williams, ibid.: 618–19.

Which scripture has spoken of it? Which prophet permitted the worship of a man, let alone a woman? The vessel is choice but a woman, and by nature no different [from others]. Like the bodies of the saints, however, she has been held in honor [*timē*] for her character and understanding. And if I should say anything more in her praise, she is like Elijah, who was a virgin from his mother's womb, always remained so, and was taken up, but has not seen death. She is like John who leaned on the Lord's breast, 'the disciple whom Jesus loved.' She is like St Thecla; and Mary is still more honored than she, because of the providence vouchsafed her. But Elijah is not to be worshipped [*proskunētos*], even though he is alive. And John is not to be worshipped, even though by his own prayer – or rather, by receiving the grace from God – he made an awesome thing of his falling asleep. But neither is Thecla worshipped, nor any of the saints. For the age-old error of forgetting the living God and worshipping his creatures will not get the better of me. 'They served and worshipped the creature more than the creator,' and 'were made fools.' If it is not his will that angels be worshipped, how much more the woman born of Ann?[24]

Here and elsewhere in discussing this 'heresy', Epiphanius reveals himself not only as a critic of the Kollyridians and their Marian devotions, but also as an opponent of the veneration of saints in general. Epiphanius apparently refused to allow for any distinction between the worship offered to God and that offered to God's saints, a conservative tendency that also expressed itself through his early opposition to the cultic use of images of Christ and the saints.[25] These principles, of course, applied no less to the *Theotokos*, and in this particular section of the *Panarion*, we find Epiphanius extending his wholesale rejection of the cult of the saints to the Kollyridian veneration of Mary. Thus Epiphanius bears witness to the existence of Marian cult situated within the context of the broader veneration of the saints already by 377, when he most likely completed the *Panarion*.[26] Even if, as some would suggest, the Kollyridians never actually existed as a clearly defined group in the way that Epiphanius presents them, his attack on the veneration of Mary as a particular variant of the emergent cult of the saints reveals that by this time such practices were already sufficiently well established to arouse opposition from a 'watchdog' such as Epiphanius.

Further evidence for the cult of the Virgin around this time comes from the earliest traditions of the Virgin Mary's Dormition and Assumption. Although frequently overlooked and misinterpreted, this collection of traditions about the end of Mary's life offers important confirmation of Mary's veneration in the later fourth century, including what is more than likely the earliest direct evidence of annual liturgical commemorations in her honour. This corpus is extremely complex and variegated, and uncertainties regarding the dates and literary relations of the earliest

24. Epiphanius, *Panarion* 79.5.1–4, in Holl and Dummer, ibid.: 479–80; trans. Williams, ibid.: 624–5.
25. Quasten 1950, vol. 3: 390–3. See also Clark 1992: 103–4.
26. Quasten, ibid.: 388.

narratives have no doubt discouraged scholars from paying them much attention. Thanks largely to the work of Antoine Wenger and especially Michel van Esbroeck, these traditions are now more clearly understood, and the different literary traditions can be delineated.[27] Continued research on these traditions has established that the oldest narratives were almost certainly composed by the later fourth century, and some may in fact be even earlier.

Of the two major literary traditions, the so-called Palm of the Tree of Life narratives appear to be the oldest.[28] Fragments of a late-fifth-century Syriac manuscript preserve the earliest extant narrative from this family, and since this version has been translated from a Greek original, we may be assured that this apocryphon, known as the *Obsequies of the Virgin* or the *Liber Requiei*, was already in existence by the early fifth century.[29] Yet other factors suggest an even earlier composition. The likely dependence of the *Apocalypse of Paul* (written around 400) on the *Obsequies of the Virgin* indicates the circulation of this Dormition apocryphon already by the later fourth century,[30] and the prominence of some rather 'unorthodox' theological concepts, many of which appear to be associated with Gnostic Christianity, suggests an even earlier date, perhaps as early as the third century.[31]

This earliest narrative yields only rather limited indications of Marian veneration, and this probably is yet another sign of its early composition. For instance, when the apostles arrive through miraculous means to attend her funeral, they do not offer her any special kind of veneration either before or after her death. There is little that would suggest the existence of an organized cult of the Virgin, but these early apocrypha clearly mark the beginnings of a theological interest in the Virgin herself, as figure of religious significance in her own right and not just focus of Christology. They also present clear evidence of Marian intercession, which may rival the '*Sub tuum praesidium*' in its antiquity. For example, on the night before Mary's death, Peter delivers a sermon in which he refers to Mary's intercessory powers, telling the crowd, 'The light of our sister Mary's lamp fills the world and will not be extinguished until the end of days, so that those who have decided to be saved will receive assistance from her. And if they receive the image of light, they will receive her rest and her blessing.'[32]

Mary's intercession appears again at the narrative's conclusion, when the resurrected Mary and the apostles are taken on a tour of the heavenly realms that concludes with a visit to hell. There they observe several sinners in their torments, and the damned cry out for mercy, first asking Michael to intercede on their behalf. Yet when Michael's pleas prove ineffective, they appeal to the apostles, who reply, 'Where did you place our doctrine that we taught you?' Hearing this, the damned

---

27. See especially Wenger 1955; van Esbroeck 1981; van Esbroeck 1995.
28. See Shoemaker 2002: 32–46.
29. Wright 1865a: 42–51; Arras 1973, vol. 1; trans. Shoemaker 2002: 290–350.
30. Bauckham 1998: 344–6; Shoemaker 2002: 42–6.
31. Shoemaker 2002: 205–56.
32. *Liber Requiei* 55, Arras 1973, vol. 1: 33; trans. Shoemaker 2002: 321.

'were very ashamed and could not reply to the apostles'.[33] They also pray to Mary, saying, 'Mary, we beseech you, Mary, light and the mother of light; Mary, life and mother of the apostles; Mary, golden lamp, you who carry every righteous lamp; Mary, our master and the mother of our Master; Mary, our queen, beseech your son to give us a little rest.'[34] In the end their pleas are successful, and as a result of the intercessions of Mary, Michael and the apostles, Christ grants a respite of nine hours each Sunday for the damned. While Mary is admittedly not the only advocate for the dead in this scene, it is clearly implied that her intercessions were the most effective.[35]

A rather different account of the end of Mary's life emerges from the earliest narratives of the Bethlehem tradition, the various early versions of the 'Six Books' apocryphon. Although these narratives appear to be somewhat later than the earliest Palm narratives, they most likely originated during the late fourth century, if not perhaps slightly earlier.[36] Their existence by the early fifth century at the latest is in any case quite certain: considerable fragments of two different Syriac versions of the Six Books survive in late-fifth-century manuscripts, both of which were translated from Greek originals.[37] This somewhat later dating is consistent with the relatively more developed Marian piety evidenced in these early narratives; the early Six Books apocrypha are replete with evidence of Marian cult, and many of the phenomena already seen from other sources appear in much greater relief in these early Dormition narratives.

The power of Marian intercession is a frequent theme of the Six Books narratives, which extensively describe the numerous miracles worked by the Virgin in the days prior to her death. After the apostles had gathered to her in Bethlehem, its citizens were witness to a parade of miraculous healings effected by the Virgin Mary. Women travelled from all over the Christian world seeking Mary's miraculous assistance: 'from the towns and from distant regions; and from Rome, and from Alexandria, and from Egypt, and from Athens; daughters of kings, and daughters of the magnates of nations. And daughters of Procurators and of rulers; and they brought honors and offerings, and they came and adored the Lady Mary. And whosoever had an affliction, she healed it.'[38] The stories of several individual women follow, and the scene concludes with Mary healing almost three thousand people at once with only a single brief prayer.[39] Later in the narrative, after Mary returns from Bethlehem to Jerusalem, she heals the Roman governor's son, which initiates another catalogue of her miracles. In this instance, each of her miracles was occasioned by an apparition of the Virgin, of which she made several in Rome, Egypt and elsewhere, even to ships at sea – all the while simultaneously remaining in the company of the apostles in

---

33. *Liber Requiei* 99, Arras, ibid.: 58; trans. Shoemaker 2002: 345.
34. *Liber Requiei* 99, Arras, ibid.; trans. Shoemaker, ibid.
35. See also the same account as preserved in Donahue 1942: 52–5; Herbert and McNamara 1989: 130; Wenger 1955: 258–9.
36. See Shoemaker 2002: 54–7; van Esbroeck 2001; Bauckham 1998: 346–60, esp. 358–60.
37. Shoemaker 2002: 46–9.
38. Smith Lewis 1902: 33–4; Wright 1865b: 141.
39. Smith Lewis 1902: 34–5; Wright 1865b: 141–2.

Jerusalem![40] Other examples of Mary's intercessory prayer abound throughout the narrative, including, for example, the scene in which the Jew who attacks her funeral procession is healed: his arms are restored when both he and Peter invoke the name of Mary.[41]

Perhaps the most remarkable feature of the Six Books apocrypha, however, is their liturgical programme outlining the commemoration of a feast of the Virgin Mary on three separate occasions during the year. Although there is some slight variation in regard to the exact dates of these liturgical feasts, their approximate times and significance are quite uniform across the early versions of the Six Books. First there is to be a feast of Mary two days after the Nativity (celebrated 24 December or 6 January in the different manuscripts), followed by a second on 15 May and a third on 13 August. Each feast has strong agricultural associations and is meant to ensure Mary's protection of the crops.[42] Yet none of the feasts is identified either with a commemoration of Mary's death or any other event from her life, which seems indicative of a very primitive stage in Marian cult, before any of the specific occasions in her life came to be memorialized liturgically. Yet the most extraordinary aspect of this brief liturgical handbook from the early Dormition apocrypha is the rather explicit set of instructions for how each of these feasts is to be celebrated:

> And the apostles also ordered that any offering offered in the name of my Lady Mary should not remain overnight, but that at midnight of the night immediately preceding her commemoration, it should be kneaded and baked; and in the morning let it go up on the altar whilst the people stand before the altar with psalms of David, and let the New and Old Testaments be read, and the volume of the decease of the blessed one [i.e. the Six Books apocryphon]; and let everyone be before the altar in the church, and let the priests celebrate (the holy Eucharist) and set forth the censer of incense and kindle the lights, and let the whole service be concerning these offerings; and when the whole service is finished, let everyone take his offerings to his house. And let the priest speak thus: 'In the name of the Father, and of the Son, and of the Holy Spirit, we celebrate the commemoration of my Lady Mary.' Thus let the priest speak three times; and (simultaneously) with the word of the priest who speaks, the Holy Spirit shall come and bless these offerings; and when everyone takes away his offering, and goes to his house, great help and the benison of the blessed one shall enter his dwelling and stablish it for ever.[43]

The similarity of this ritual to the practices ascribed to the Kollyridians certainly should not be overlooked. A special bread is prepared and offered to the Virgin, and

---

40. Smith Lewis 1902: 49–50; Wright 1865b: 146–8.
41. Wright 1865b: 149.
42. Smith Lewis 1902: 59–61; Wright 1865b: 152–3; the fifth-century palimpsest fragments from Sinai also refer to the three feasts, although this particular section is lacking: see Smith Lewis 1902; trans. Shoemaker 2002: 371–2. See also Mimouni 1992: 157–74.
43. Wright 1865b: 153.

after a ceremony in her honour (during which the Six Books apocryphon is read), the participants take home the consecrated bread and 'all partake of the bread'. These liturgical instructions combined with the narrative's constant reference to 'worship' offered to the Virgin Mary add considerable credibility to Epiphanius's complaints against such practices. While there is no indication of women serving as priests, nor any direct link with the 'Kollyridians', the Six Books apocrypha confirm that by the late fourth century certain groups were regularly venerating (or 'worshipping') the Virgin Mary using a ritual that looks very much like the one Epiphanius attributes to the Kollyridians. In addition, this passage further attests to the early liturgical usage of the ancient Dormition apocrypha as well as to the rise of the Dormition traditions within the context of the emerging cult of the Virgin.[44]

By the opening of the fifth century, the veneration of Mary had become a much more organized and public phenomenon, as evidenced in the earliest official Marian feasts, celebrated in Jerusalem and Constantinople from the beginning of the fifth century and perhaps even somewhat earlier. Known by the title 'the Memory of Mary', as well as 'the Memory of the Virgin' and 'the Memory of the *Theotokos*', this early feast was originally a commemoration of Mary's divine maternity and her virginity, often celebrated in close proximity to the feast of the Nativity of the Lord. The early Dormition traditions and other related sources suggest the possibility of a similar Marian feast in Syria and Egypt by this time, but this remains very uncertain.[45] Although Simon Mimouni posits the existence of such a feast in Egypt by the beginning of the fifth century, his claim rests on evidence that even he himself acknowledges is rather dubious.[46]

In the imperial capital, the feast of the Memory of Mary is first attested in the famous homily on the *Theotokos* by Proclus of Constantinople, a future bishop of Constantinople and one of Nestorius's most ardent opponents.[47] Delivered in 430 at the height of the Nestorian controversy in the presence of Nestorius himself and his main supporters, Proclus's homily responded directly to Nestorius's attacks on Marian piety and in the process 'established the veneration of the Theotokos upon theological and exegetical principles which defined the rhetoric and rationale for the cult of the Virgin Mary throughout the Byzantine period'.[48] The occasion for this homily, as Proclus himself informs us, was 'the Virgin's festival', a recently established feast in Mary's honour celebrating her divine maternity and virginity, most likely observed on 26 December (on which date the Eastern churches still celebrate a similar Feast of the Theotokos). As Constas observes in his recent study of Proclus, this new feast of the Virgin had almost certainly been established by one of Nestorius's immediate predecessors as Bishop of Constantinople, and for a variety of reasons Atticus of Constantinople, bishop from 406 to 425, stands out as a likely

44.   See also Mimouni 1993a: 403–25; Mimouni 1993b.
45.   Mimouni 1992: esp. 159–62.
46.   Mimouni 1991: esp. 123–33, 127 n. 243; Mimouni 1995: 413–20, esp. 418 n. 20.
47.   Proclus of Constantinople, *Homily I: On the Holy Virgin Theotokos*, in Constas 2003: 128–56.
48.   Constas 2003: 128.

suspect.[49] In any case, Proclus's homily assures us that prior to the Council of Ephesus – and more than likely before the arrival of Nestorius – the incipient Marian piety witnessed by Gregory Nazianzus and other late-fourth-century sources had found formal expression in the imperial capital through an official, annual feast of the Virgin.

The same is true of Jerusalem, where by approximately the same time a similar commemoration of the Virgin Mary had developed.[50] The Jerusalemite feast of the Memory of Mary, observed on 15 August, is attested by a number of early-fifth-century witnesses, including liturgical manuals and homilies for the feast, as well as the archaeological remains of the church where the feast was originally observed. The most direct evidence for this annual Marian feast comes from the Jerusalem Armenian Lectionary, a manual outlining the yearly liturgical celebrations of the Holy City sometime between 417 and 439. Among its commemorations is an annual feast of the Memory of Mary, celebrated on 15 August at the third mile from Bethlehem, midway between Jerusalem and Bethlehem.[51] The prescribed lectionary readings for the feast all refer to Christ's birth from Mary, indicating a commemoration of Mary's role in the Nativity similar to the feast of the Virgin celebrated by Proclus in Constantinople. This is not at all surprising, since the site itself is also connected with the events of the Nativity: according to the second-century *Protevangelium of James*, Christ was born not in the city of Bethlehem, but halfway between Jerusalem and Bethlehem in a cave located just off the main road, the precise location of this early Marian feast.[52] Although there are some indications that in its earliest history both this site and its feast were identified with the Nativity itself, by the early fifth century it had become the scene of an annual commemoration of Mary.[53]

By the beginning of the fifth century, this site boasted an important church, the church of the Kathisma, or 'Seat', of the *Theotokos*, which, according to tradition, stood over the spot where the Virgin had sat to rest briefly before giving birth in the nearby cave. Over the past several decades, two fifth-century churches have been unearthed at this location, and their relations to one another and to the traditions of the Kathisma and the Memory of Mary remain somewhat uncertain. The most likely explanation is that the smaller church and its monastery were constructed in the late fourth or early fifth century to serve as the earliest site of this Marian feast, while the larger church, some 300 metres to the south-west at the bottom of the hill, is a more recent construction that was probably built during the later fifth century to accommodate increasing pilgrimage traffic.[54] In any case, whatever the solution to this liturgical and archaeological puzzle may be, it is quite certain that at least one of

---

49.   See ibid.: 31–5, 56–9; Constas 1995: esp. 172–6.

50.   See Shoemaker 2001.

51.   Renoux 1971, vol. 2: 354–7; regarding the date, see vol. 1: 166–72.

52.   *Protevangelium of James* 17.1.3, in Tischendorf (ed.) 1876: 33.

53.   Ray 2000; Capelle 1943; some rather different speculations on the origin of the feast, also connected with the birth of Christ, are offered in Verhelst 2001: 161–91.

54.   Shoemaker 2002: 81–98; Shoemaker 2001: 23–36. The newly discovered church is well presented by its excavator in Avner 2003.

these two churches stood at this location by the beginning of the fifth century, housing an altar for the annual observance of Mary's feast.

In addition to these material remains from the nascent cult of the Virgin, several early homilies for the feast of the Memory of Mary also survive from the Jerusalem church. The earliest of these are two homilies in honour of Mary by Hesychius, a priest in Jerusalem during the early fifth century. Hesychius delivered his *Homily V* to commemorate the Memory of Mary sometime between 431 and 433, and *Homily VI* was most likely for the same occasion sometime before 428.[55] Presumably, both homilies were pronounced in the church of the Kathisma, and even if by some chance the shrine was not yet so named, it is safe to assume that Hesychius spoke in one of the two churches standing at the site identified by the Armenian Lectionary. In any case, these homilies by Hesychius confirm the existence of this Marian feast in Jerusalem by the early fifth century, adding precision to the witness of the Armenian Lectionary in affirming the observance of the Memory of Mary before 428. A similar homily for this feast delivered by Chrysippus of Jerusalem around the middle of the fifth century bears further witness to the importance of this feast in the liturgical life of Jerusalem during the early fifth century.[56]

It is important to note, however, that Egeria does not mention the Memory of Mary in her description of Jerusalem's annual liturgical practices, made during her pilgrimage to the Holy City in 383.[57] Yet this silence offers no assurance that the establishment of this Marian feast post-dates her visit, in as much as her account is almost certainly incomplete, focusing only on certain major feasts. Although Egeria rather extensively describes the observances surrounding Epiphany, Lent, Holy Week, Easter and Pentecost, during the period of 'ordinary time' she notes only the dedication feast of the Holy Sepulchre in mid-September. Egeria 'describes only dominical feasts and does not mention any commemorations of saints',[58] which severely limits the usefulness of her account for understanding liturgical practices outside the Epiphany to Pentecost cycle. As John Baldovin cautions,

> The liturgical data provided by Egeria must be considered carefully in contrast with the A[rmenian] L[ectionary]. Since she does not pretend to give a complete liturgical calendar for Jerusalem but only describes major feasts, one cannot tell how many individual saints were honored by the Christian community in Jerusalem in the late fourth century. On this level, that of a more complete sanctoral calendar, we must overlook differences with the A[rmenian] L[ectionary].[59]

Consequently, Egeria's failure to mention the Memory of Mary does not indicate the absence of this feast from Jerusalem's liturgical calendar in the later fourth century. It

---

55. Aubineau 1978, vol. 1: 117–205; see also Mimouni 1995: 392–5, especially in regard to *Homily VI*.
56. Jugie 1926: 293–7, 336–43; Mimouni 1995: 395–7.
57. Pétré (ed.) 1971. On the date, see Devos 1967; Devos 1968: 87–108.
58. Ray 2000: 6.
59. Baldovin 1987: 94.

seems likely that many of the sanctoral commemorations described by the Armenian Lectionary extend back into the fourth century, and it is certainly possible that the feast of Mary was among these. Nevertheless, only the observance of this feast prior to 428 is certain, as evidenced by the homilies of Hesychius of Jerusalem.

By the middle of the sixth century, this 15 August celebration of Mary's virginity and divine maternity had changed into a commemoration of the end of Mary's life, her Dormition and Assumption. When this transformation occurred is not precisely known, but around the turn of the sixth century seems to be a reasonable estimate. The context for this transformation may very well have been the church in Jerusalem commemorating her tomb, built most likely between 440 and 450. The Memory of Mary was probably celebrated in this early Marian shrine as well as at the Kathisma, and at her tomb the feast perhaps took on new significances relating to the end of her life. Moreover, this shift brought the Memory of Mary into greater conformity with the commemorations of other saints, whose feast days generally fell on the day of their departure from this world into the next.[60] By the seventh century, the August commemoration of Mary in Jerusalem had grown to encompass several days, which were observed in stational liturgy that united all of the Holy City's Marian shrines: the Kathisma, the Tomb of the Virgin, the Nea and, eventually, Mount Zion.[61]

Several other important early Marian feasts also originated during the sixth century, including the feasts of the Annunciation (25 March),[62] the Nativity of Mary (8 September)[63] and the Presentation of Mary (21 November).[64] Nevertheless, Jerusalem's 15 August commemoration of the Memory of Mary, as transformed into a celebration of her Dormition and Assumption, emerged from antiquity as perhaps the single most important Marian feast. According to a fourteenth-century source, the Emperor Maurice established the observance of this feast throughout the Empire at the end of the sixth century.[65] In spite of understandable concern at the lateness of this report, the information generally comports with indications from other sources that the observance of Mary's Dormition and Assumption on 15 August had spread from Jerusalem to other major centres of the early Byzantine Empire by the end of the sixth century, reaching Rome and the Western Church shortly thereafter, most likely around the middle of the seventh century.[66]

It was in the later fourth century, however, that Marian veneration first developed within the 'orthodox' Christian communities of the Eastern empire, emerging against the larger backdrop of the rise of the cult of the saints at this time. This, of course, is well before the Council of Ephesus's vindication of Mary as *Theotokos* in 431 and, consequently, the origins of Marian piety should not be linked too tightly with the council's outcome. Admittedly, the Council of Ephesus contributed

---

60. Shoemaker 2002: 120–3.
61. Shoemaker 2001: 56–71; Shoemaker 2002: 123–40.
62. First attested in Abraham of Ephesus, *Homily on the Annunciation*, in Jugie 1926: 442–7. See also Fletcher 1962; van Esbroeck 1968.
63. Taft and Carr 1991. The origins of this feast need further study.
64. Bouvy 1897; Vailhé 1901–2; Bouvy 1902; Vailhé 1903; Mimouni 1995: 377, 512–14.
65. Nicephorus Callistus, *Ecclesiastical History* 17.28, PG 147.292.
66. Shoemaker 2002: 73, 116; Wenger 1955: 141.

dramatically to the spread of Marian piety in the middle of the fifth century, and following the council, expressions of Marian devotion proliferated throughout the Roman Empire.[67] Yet it would be a mistake to see Ephesus as the primary catalyst behind the veneration of Mary, as is often popularly maintained.[68] The origins of Marian piety clearly lie in the fourth century and, as we have seen, a number of different sources converge towards the end of that century to make the cult of the Virgin visible for the first time. It is likely, however, that Marian devotion was practised even earlier, existing somewhere along the margins of proto-orthodox Christianity, as the ancient Dormition narratives in particular appear to indicate. Jaroslav Pelikan even suggests that there is 'plausible' evidence for the observance of a commemoration of Mary in Egypt at the time of Athanasius.[69] In light of this, it may perhaps be time to reconsider the date of the 'Sub tuum praesidium' papyrus and the significance of its palaeography. In any case, it seems rather certain that the cult of Mary was already well established before Nestorius stood against it – indeed, before Epiphanius stood against it. When viewed against this backdrop, Kenneth Holum's innovative and influential hypothesis that the Nestorian controversy revolved as much around Mariology as Christology appears all the more convincing.[70] The Council of Ephesus should thus be understood as just as much a product of Marian piety as it was its vehicle, and the roots of Marian devotion are to be found instead in beliefs and practices of fourth-century Christianity, where the cult of the Virgin first developed within the broader context of the emerging cult of the saints.

BIBLIOGRAPHY

Primary Sources

Arras, Victor (1973) *De transitu Mariae apocrypha aethiopice*, Corpus Scriptorum Christianorum Orientalium, 342–3, 351–2, 2 vols, Louvain: Secrétariat du Corpus SCO.
Bidez, Joseph and Hansen, Günther Christian (eds) (1995) *Sozomenus: Kirchengeschichte*, Griechischen christlichen Schriftsteller der ersten Jahrhunderte, Neue Folge, 4, 2nd edn, Berlin: Akademie Verlag.
Constas, Nicholas (2003) *Proclus of Constantinople and the Cult of the Virgin in Late Antiquity: Homilies 1–5, Texts and Translations*, Supplements to *Vigiliae Christianae*, 66, Leiden: Brill.
Donahue, C. (1942) *The Testament of Mary: The Gaelic Version of the Dormitio Mariae together with an Irish Latin Version*, New York: Fordham University Press.
Heil, Gunterus, Cavarnos, Johannes P. and Lendle, Otto (eds) (1990) *Gregorii Nysseni Opera*, vol. 10.1, *Gregorii Nysseni Sermones, Pars II*, Leiden: E. J. Brill.
Herbert, Máire and McNamara, Martin (1989) *Irish Biblical Apocrypha: Selected Texts in Translation*, Edinburgh: T & T Clark.
Holl, Karl and Dummer, Jürgen (eds) (1915, 1980, 1985) *Epiphanius*, Griechischen christlichen

---

67. See, for example, Cameron 2004: 8–14.
68. See, for example, Benko 1993: 257–62; and the rather prejudicial study by von Campenhausen 1964: 66–70.
69. Pelikan 1996: 60–1.
70. Holum 1982: esp. 147–74. See also Limberis 1994: 53–61; Constas 2003: 46–73; Peltomaa 2001: 54–77; Cooper 1998: 31–43; Cooper 2004. For alternative views, see Price 2004; Benko 1993: 253–9.

Schriftsteller der ersten drei Jahrhunderte, 25, 31, 37, 3 vols, 2nd edn, Leipzig, Berlin: J. C. Hinrichs; Akademie-Verlag.

Hunt, Arthur S., Johnson, John de Monins and Roberts, Colin H. (1911–52) *Catalogue of the Greek Papyri in the John Rylands Library, Manchester*, 4 vols, Manchester: University Press.

Jugie, Martin (1926) *Homélies mariales byzantines (II)*, Patrologia Orientalis, 19.3, Paris: Librairie de Paris/Firmin-Didot et Cie.

Mossay, Justin (ed.) (1981) *Grégoire de Nazianze: Discours 24–26*, Sources chrètiennes, 284, Paris: Les Éditions du Cerf.

Renoux, A. (1971) *Le codex arménien Jérusalem 121*, Patrologia Orientalis, 35.1 and 36.2, 2 vols, Turnhout: Brepols.

Schaff, Philip and Wace, Henry (eds) (1891) *A Select Library of Nicene and Post-Nicene Fathers of the Christian Church, Second Series*, 14 vols, New York: The Christian Literature Company.

Smith Lewis, Agnes (1902) *Apocrypha Syriaca*, Studia Sinaitica, 11, London: C. J. Clay and Sons.

Tischendorf, Constantin (ed.) (1876) *Evangelia Apocrypha*, 2nd edn, Leipzig: H. Mendelssohn.

Secondary Sources

Aubineau, Michel (1978) *Les homélies festales d'Hésychius de Jérusalem*, Subsidia Hagiographica, 59, 2 vols, Brussels: Société des Bollandistes.

Avner, Rina (2003) 'The Recovery of the Kathisma Church and Its Influence on Octagonal Buildings', in G. C. Bottini, L. D. Segni and D. Chrupcala (eds), *One Land – Many Cultures: Archaeological Studies in Honor of Stanislao Loffreda, OFM*, Studium Biblicum Franciscanum Collectio major, 41, Jerusalem: Franciscan Printing Press.

Baldovin, John Francis (1987) *The Urban Character of Christian Worship: The Origins, Development, and Meaning of Stational Liturgy*, Orientalia Christiana Analecta, 228, Rome: Pont. Institutum Studiorum Orientalium.

Bauckham, Richard (1998) *The Fate of the Dead: Studies on Jewish and Christian Apocalypses*, Supplements to Novum Testamentum, 93, Leiden: Brill.

Benko, Stephen (1993) *The Virgin Goddess: Studies in the Pagan and Christian Roots of Mariology*, Studies in the History of Religions, 59, Leiden: E. J. Brill.

Bouvy, E. (1897) 'La fête de l'Εισοδος ou de la Présentation de la Vierge au Temple dans l'Église grecque', *Bessarion* 1: 555–62.

Bouvy, E. (1902) 'Les origines de la fête de la Présentation', *Revue augustinienne* 1: 581–94.

Brown, Peter (1981) *The Cult of the Saints: Its Rise and Function in Latin Christianity*, The Haskell Lectures on History of Religions, New Series, 2, Chicago, IL: University of Chicago Press.

Cameron, Averil (2000) 'The Early Cult of the Virgin', in Vassilaki (ed.), *Mother of God*.

Cameron, Averil (2004) 'The Cult of the Virgin in Late Antiquity: Religious Development and Myth-Making', in Swanson (ed.), *The Church and Mary*.

Capelle, Bernard (1943) 'La fête de la Vierge à Jérusalem au Ve siècle', *Le Muséon* 56: 1–33.

Clark, Elizabeth A. (1992) *The Origenist Controversy: The Cultural Construction of an Early Christian Debate*, Princeton, NJ: Princeton University Press.

Constas, Nicholas (1995) 'Weaving the Body of God: Proclus of Constantinople, the Theotokos, and the Loom of the Flesh', *Journal of Early Christian Studies* 3: 169–94.

Cooper, Kate (1998) 'Contesting the Nativity: Wives, Virgins, and Pulcheria's *imitatio Mariae*', *Scottish Journal of Religious Studies*, 19 (1) Spring: 31–43.

Cooper, Kate (2004) 'Empress and *Theotokos*: Gender and Patronage in the Christological Controversy', in Swanson (ed.), *The Church and Mary*.

Cunningham, Lawrence S. (2005) *A Brief History of Saints*, Blackwell Brief Histories of Religion, Oxford: Blackwell Publishing.

Delehaye, Hippolyte (1927) *Sanctus: essai sur le culte des saints dans l'antiquité*, Subsidia Hagiographica, 17, Brussels: Société des Bollandistes.

Delehaye, Hippolyte (1933) *Les origines du culte des martyrs*, Subsidia Hagiographica, 20, 2nd edn, Brussels: Société des Bollandistes.

Devos, Paul (1967) 'Le date du voyage d'Égérie', *Analecta Bollandiana* 85: 165–94.

Devos, Paul (1968) 'Égérie à Bethléem; Le 40ᵉ jour après Paques à Jérusalem, en 383', *Analecta Bollandiana* 56: 87–108.

van Esbroeck, Michel (1968) 'La lettre de l'empereur Justinien sur l'Annonciation et la Noël en 561', *Analecta Bollandiana* 86: 356–62.

van Esbroeck, Michel (1981) 'Les textes littéraires sur l'assomption avant le Xe siècle', in François Bovon (ed.), *Les actes apocryphes des apôtres*, Geneva: Labor et Fides.

van Esbroeck, Michel (1995) *Aux origines de la Dormition de la Vierge: Etudes historique sur les traditions orientales*, Brookfield, VT: Variorum.

van Esbroeck, Michel (2001) 'Some Earlier Features in the Life of the Virgin', *Marianum* 63: 297–308.

Felici, S. (ed.) (1989) *La mariologia nella catechesi dei padri (età prenicena). Convegno di studio e aggiornamento, Facoltà di Lettere cristiane e classiche, Pontificium Istitutum Altioris Latinitatis, Roma, 10–11 marzo 1989*, Biblioteca di scienze religiose, 95, Rome: LAS.

Février, Paul-Albert (1991) 'Martyre et sainteté', in Jean-Yves Tilliette (ed.), *Les Fonctions des saints dans le monde occidental (IIIe–XIIIe siècle): actes du colloque organisé par l'Ecole française de Rome avec le concours de l'Université de Rome 'La Sapienza', Rome, 27–29 octobre 1988*, Collection de l'École française de Rome, 149, Rome: École française de Rome.

Fletcher, R. A. (1962) 'Celebrations at Jerusalem on March 25 in the Sixth Century AD', *Studia Patristica* 5: 30–4.

Förster, Hans (1995) 'Zur ältesten Überlieferung der marianischen Antiphon "Sub tuum praesidium"', *Biblos: Österreichische Zeitschrift für Buch- und Bibliothekwesen, Dokumentation, Bibliographie, und Bibliophilie* 44.2: 183–92.

Foskett, Mary F. (2002) *A Virgin Conceived: Mary and Classical Representations of Virginity*, Bloomington and Indianapolis: Indiana University Press.

Gambero, Luigi (1999) *Mary and the Fathers of the Church*, trans. Thomas Buffer, San Francisco, CA: Ignatius Press, 1999.

Giamberardini, Gabriele (1969) 'Il "Sub tuum praesidium" e il titolo "Theotokos" nella traditzione egiziana', *Marianum* 31: 324–62.

Giamberardini, Gabriele (1974–5) *Il Culto Mariano in Eggito*, Pubblicazioni dello Studium Biblicum Franciscanum, Analecta, 6–8, 3 vols, 2nd edn, Jerusalem: Franciscan Printing Press.

Holum, Kenneth G. (1982) *Theodosian Empresses: Women and Imperial Dominion in Late Antiquity*, Berkeley: University of California Press.

Jones, F. Stanley (ed.) (2002) *Which Mary? The Marys of Early Christian Tradition*, Society of Biblical Literature Symposium Series, 19, Atlanta, GA: Society of Biblical Literature.

Kelly, J. N. D. (1978) *Early Christian Doctrines*, rev. edn, New York: Harper & Row.

Knight, Jonathan (2002) 'The Portrait of Mary in the Ascension of Isaiah', in Jones (ed.), *Which Mary?*.

Limberis, Vasiliki (1994) *Divine Heiress: The Virgin Mary and the Creation of Christian Constantinople*, London: Routledge.

Maraval, Pierre (1985) *Lieux saints et pèlerinages d'orient: Histoire et géographie des origines à la conquête arabe*, Paris: Les Éditions du Cerf.

McGuckin, John (2001) *Saint Gregory of Nazianzus: An Intellectual Biography*, Crestwood, NY: St Vladimir's Seminar Press.

Mimouni, Simon C. (1991) 'Genèse et évolution des traditions anciennes sur le sort final de Marie: Etude de la tradition littéraire copte', *Marianum* 42: 69–143.

Mimouni, Simon C. (1992) 'La fête de la dormition de Marie en Syrie à l'époque byzantine', *The Harp* 5: 157–74.

Mimouni, Simon C. (1993a) 'La lecture liturgique et les apocryphes du Nouveau Testament: Le cas de la Dormitio grecque du Pseudo-Jean', *Orientalia Christiana Periodica* 59: 403–25.

Mimouni, Simon C. (1993b) 'Les Transitus Mariae sont-ils vraiment des apocryphes?', *Studia Patristica* 25: 122–8.

Mimouni, Simon C. (1995) *Dormition et Assomption de Marie: Histoire des traditions anciennes*, Théologie Historique, 98, Paris: Beauchesne.

Pelikan, Jaroslav (1996) *Mary through the Centuries: Her Place in the History of Culture*, New Haven, CT: Yale University Press.

Peltomaa, Leena Mari (2001) *The Image of the Virgin Mary in the Akathistos Hymn*, The Medieval Mediterranean, 35, Leiden: Brill.

Pétré, Hélène (ed.) (1971) *Éthérie: Journal de voyage*, Sources chrétiennes, 21, Paris: Éditions du Cerf.

Price, Richard M. (2004) 'Marian Piety and the Nestorian Controversy', in Swanson (ed.), *The Church and Mary*.

Quasten, Johannes (1950) *Patrology*, 3 vols, Westminister, MD: Newman Press.

Ray, Walter D. (2000) 'August 15 and the Development of the Jerusalem Calendar', Ph.D. dissertation, University of Notre Dame.

Shoemaker, Stephen J. (2001) 'The (Re?)Discovery of the Kathisma Church and the Cult of the Virgin in Late Antique Palestine', *Maria: A Journal of Marian Studies* 2: 21–72.

Shoemaker, Stephen J. (2002) *Ancient Traditions of the Virgin Mary's Dormition and Assumption*, Oxford Early Christian Studies, Oxford: Oxford University Press.

Starowieyski, M. (1990) 'La plus ancienne description d'une mariophane par Grégoire de Nysse', in H. Drobner and C. Klock (eds), *Studien zu Gregor von Nyssa und der christlichen Spätantike*, Leiden: Brill.

Stegmüller, Otto (1952) 'Sub tuum praesidium: Bemerkungen zur ältesten Überlieferung', *Zeitschrift für katholische Theologie* 74: 76–82.

Swanson, Robert, N. (ed.) (2004) *The Church and Mary*, Studies in Church History 39, Woodbridge: Boydell Press.

Taft, Robert F. and Carr, Annemarie Weyl (1991) 'Birth of the Virgin', in A. Kazhdan (ed.), *The Oxford Dictionary of Byzantium*, 3 vols, New York: Oxford University Press.

Triacca, Achille M., '"Sub tuum praesidium": nella "lex orandi" un'anticipata presenza della "lex credendi." La "teotocologia" precede la "mariologia"?', in Felici (ed.), *La mariologia nella catechesi dei padri (età prenicena)*.

Vailhé, S. (1901–2) 'La fête de la Présentation de Marie au Temple', *Echos d'Orient* 5: 221–4.

Vailhé, S. (1903) 'La dédicace de Sainte-Marie-la-Neuve', *Revue augustinienne* 2: 136–40.

Vassilaki, Maria (ed.) (2000) *Mother of God: Representations of the Virgin in Byzantine Art*, Milan: Skira.

Verhelst, Stéphane (2001) 'Le 15 août, le 9 av et le kathisme', *Questions liturgiques* 82: 161–91.

von Campenhausen, Hans (1964) *The Virgin Birth in the Theology of the Ancient Church*, trans. Frank Clarke, Studies in Historical Theology, 2, London: SCM Press.

Wenger, Antoine (1955) *L'Assomption de la T. S. Vierge dans la tradition byzantine du VIe au Xe siècle; études et documents*, Archives de l'Orient chrétien, 5, Paris: Institut français d'études byzantines.

Williams, Frank (1987, 1994) *The Panarion of Epiphanius of Salamis*, Nag Hammadi Studies, 35–6, 2 vols, Leiden: E. J. Brill.

Wright, William (1865a) *Contributions to the Apocryphal Literature of the New Testament*, London: Williams and Norgate.

Wright, William (1865b) 'The Departure of My Lady Mary from This World', *The Journal of Sacred Literature and Biblical Record* 6–7: 417–48, 108–60.

Zervos, George T. (2002) 'Seeking the Source of the Marian Myth: Have We Found the Missing Link?', in Jones (ed.), *Which Mary?*.

Part 2

The Cult of the Virgin Mary during the Middle Ages

7

THE DEVELOPMENT OF THE VIRGIN'S CULT IN THE HIGH MIDDLE AGES

SARAH JANE BOSS

INTRODUCTION

The famous *Mappa Mundi* at Hereford Cathedral was made around the year 1260, but it encapsulates in a single, complex image a world view (though not necessarily a world model, in the physical sense) that would have been held by many people for many hundreds of years between the early Middle Ages and the Renaissance. It depicts the earth spread out as a circle, and includes not only all the important places, but also many of the events, recounted in the Bible and in classical literature. Jerusalem, the site of the Lord's crucifixion and resurrection, is at the centre. Bethlehem is shown, as are Mount Etna and the Cretan labyrinth. At the top of the map, reigning over all time and space, sits Christ in judgement (Fig. 9). He shows the viewer the five wounds that he suffered on the cross. For those who repent of their sins and are faithful Christians, these are the wounds by which one is saved. The same wounds, however, condemn to damnation those who refuse to repent and who reject the Christian gospel, since these are the people whose sins continue to inflict suffering on Christ. Beneath Christ, his mother Mary kneels, her crown removed, beseeching her Son for mercy on behalf of the world which lies spread out before them. She is pulling back her robes to reveal her breasts, thus reminding the viewer of the incarnation of God in the Son whom she carried in her own body. The Word of God became so truly human that he was an infant who depended on his mother's milk; and that is why humanity can be confident that he understands what it is to be feeble and frail, and hence that he will take pity on human beings in their weakness and be willing to forgive them their sins. Mary thus occupies the place next to that from which all time and space is governed.

Several features of the *Mappa Mundi* are peculiar to a fairly short historical period. The depiction of Mary revealing both breasts was commonly represented during the fourteenth century (the *Mappa Mundi* is a particularly early example of the motif), but is rarely found in the art of earlier and later periods.[1] The image of Christ holding up his wounds was very common throughout the later Middle Ages, but did not appear in earlier periods of Christian art. Nonetheless, the idea of Christ as Lord of all time and space, and of his mother as heavenly queen and as the most powerful intercessor,

---

1.   An exception to this is given in the present volume, in Trevor Johnson, 'Mary in Early Modern Europe': 372.

Fig. 9. Apex of the *Mappa Mundi* made by Richard of Haldingham (Hereford Cathedral). Drawing by Dominic Harbour. Copyright (Dominic Harbour).

were dominant among the Christians of Western Europe for the greater part of a millennium.

Originally, the term 'Middle Ages' was a somewhat pejorative one, signifying the period between the fall of the Roman Empire – and hence the end of the great age of classical civilization – and the Renaissance, with its revival of classical learning. In the nineteenth century, Romantic artists and poets viewed the Middle Ages more favourably, turning for inspiration to this period as a time before the evils of the industrial revolution. During the twentieth century, however, it came to be increasingly realized that the foundations of many of the accomplishments of the modern world – in engineering, for example – were laid precisely during these 'interim' centuries; and in recent decades, many scholars have argued that the scholarship and spirituality of the Middle Ages often contained a wisdom that has been lost in modernity. Yet however one views the many centuries between – on the one hand, the fall of the Roman Empire, and on the other, the gradual emergence between the fifteenth and seventeenth centuries of a more bourgeois and scientific society in Western Europe – it cannot be denied that the Virgin Mary was omnipresent in the Christian culture of this period. The American author Henry Adams, in his masterly work *Mont Saint Michel and Chartres*,[2] contrasts 'the Virgin'

---

2.   Adams 1986.

with 'the dynamo', arguing that, where modern culture is dominated by machinery and machine-like processes, signified by the dynamo, so medieval culture was dominated by spiritual and artistic concerns, signified by the figure of the Blessed Virgin Mary, patroness of Chartres Cathedral and of all the great French Gothic cathedrals. Notwithstanding the fact that Gothic cathedrals are masterpieces of engineering technique, their spiritual meaning overrides all other concerns, and Adams' thesis still deserves serious consideration.

IMAGES AND ICONOCLASM

In the history of Marian devotion, the use of images has been immensely important. In the Eastern Church, the All Holy One is an exceptionally important subject for icon makers, and is depicted in some of the most sacred and miraculous icons; while in the West, the Virgin's cult is frequently focused on miraculous statues, and has contributed subject matter for the greatest artists of all periods. Yet throughout the history of Christianity, the use of images has provoked controversy.[3] As a monotheistic religion, Christianity professes belief in a single God who is infinite and eternal, and thus beyond representation. God is the Creator of all things, and to offer to created beings the adoration due only to God is condemned as idolatry (i.e. 'the worship of an idol', from the Greek words *eidol* and *latreia* [worship]). There have always been Christians who have feared that the veneration of images leads too easily to the adoration of created things, rather than their Creator – that the images become idols. This concern seems to underlie the third commandment of the biblical decalogue (Exod. 20.4; Deut. 5.8), which forbids the making of graven images.[4]

Perhaps the Christian Church's greatest dispute over the use of images occurred in the Eastern Church during the eighth and ninth centuries, in the Iconoclast dispute, which continued from 726 until 843. For the student of the cult of the Virgin Mary, a brief outline of this dispute may be helpful, both because of the importance of visual images in Marian devotion and because of the importance of Marian images for the defenders of icons.[5]

The dispute concerned the use of images of human beings – of Christ and the saints – in Christian devotion. On the one side there were those who were opposed

---

3. An excellent anthropological discussion of the meanings of human images is given in Freedberg 1989. Freedberg includes many examples of Marian representation.

4. We might also suspect that there is another concern here, namely that of what might loosely be termed 'witchcraft'. It is a common belief that if one has an image of a person, then one can exercise power over them. For example, people may try to bring harm to another person by injuring a doll which represents that person. Likewise, one may believe that one can gain influence over a supernatural being by acting in specified ways towards a representation of that being: by reciting certain prayers or making certain offerings before a sacred image, it may be possible to secure what one desires. But the God worshipped by Christians, Muslims and Jews is the God who is the maker and governor of all powers, who cannot be controlled by any of them. To make an image of God may therefore mislead the worshipper as to the nature of the Deity.

5. For what follows on the subject of icons and iconoclasm, see Pelikan 1977: 91–145; Cormack 2000: 86–129; Louth 2002: 193–222; Bryer and Herrin (eds) 1977.

to the use of such images at all, and who destroyed the images and attacked those who made or promoted them. These were the *iconoclasts* (from the Greek words *eikon* [image] and *klasmo* [break]). On the other side, there were the *iconodules* (from *eikon* and *doulia* [service]) or *iconophiles* (from *eikon* and *philia* [affection]), who believed that it was right and even dutiful for Christians to venerate suitable images. It should be stated at the outset that this dispute was not concerned with the capacity of the material world as such to be a bearer of God's grace. Both sides in the argument agreed that Christ as God incarnate was present in the consecrated elements of the Eucharist, and that God's grace was bestowed in other sacraments, such as baptism; both sides also agreed that the veneration of the cross was a good and ancient Christian practice. Likewise, the veneration of the relics of saints was not contested. The point at issue was only the use of images of the human form.

Earliest Christian practice with regard to the use of images is not well attested. The oldest images are those from the Roman catacombs, but it is not always easy to identify the figures represented in these, and when an image clearly represents Christ or the Blessed Virgin, there is no way of knowing how the image was used. It may have been for decoration or instruction, or it may have had some specifically devotional purpose.[6] Evidence from the fourth century suggests that at that time there was some use of the images of saints for purposes of devotion. It was argued that a saint bears 'the image of the heavenly man' – i.e. the human person in the state of perfection, who is Christ – and that it is therefore good to look upon an image of the saint. Something of the saint's holiness will be conveyed to the devout viewer. Conversely, local church synods sometimes condemned the use of images. The Council of Elvira (Spain), for example, banned devotional images from churches in the early fourth century.[7] During the periods of iconoclast rule in the East, most devotional images were destroyed, which means that little evidence of early Christian iconography survives from Byzantium.

There seem to have been several factors which brought the iconoclast dispute to a head, although historians are uncertain as to which of these was most important. The Emperor Leo III, the Isaurian, had to contend with attacks from invading Muslim Arabs, and this is a significant consideration. Leo was concerned as to why God had allowed Christianity's Muslim enemies to attain the success which they had already achieved, and he believed that God had acted in this way partly in order to punish Christians for their use of images – something that was entirely forbidden in Islam. Leo therefore believed that the destruction of Christian images was clearly indicated by this sign from God, and in 726 he imposed iconoclasm – the destruction of icons and the persecution of those who continued to make and use them – and, as it happens, was successful in protecting the Empire against Arab incursions.

Jaroslav Pelikan argues that there was also another, internal, political conflict at stake in the iconoclast dispute. This concerned the relative authority of the emperor

6. See Geri Parlby, 'The Origins of Marian Art: The Evolution of Marian Imagery in the Western Church until ad 431', in this volume: 106–29.
7. The council's main concern was to distinguish Christians clearly from non-Christians, both pagans and Jews, and to strengthen distinctively Christian practices. See de Luis 1992.

and the clergy in religious matters. The emperor was keen that the only public images that people should see would be of himself, thus ensuring that the image of the emperor would be uppermost in the mind of the populace. The clergy, on the other hand, wanted there to be images of saints in churches, which would naturally be controlled by Church authorities and thereby guarantee the clergy's influence over the people who offered veneration to these icons. The terms of the dispute, however, were entirely theological.

The question was whether the power that was communicated through the sacraments was exclusive to them, or whether sacred power might also be contacted through the images of Christ and the saints. It was agreed that only the Eucharist is identical with the essence of that which it signifies, but there might nonetheless be a more general principle of sacramental mediation that could be effected through icons. The defenders of icons argued that images instruct the simple. For the unlettered, venerating images is a substitute for reading, or attending to readings of, the Scriptures. The iconclasts, on the other hand, argued that simple people might be deceived into thinking that matter is divine, if images were objects of devotion.

More theological issues were also involved in the dispute, however. Human beings are made in the image of God, and the iconophiles argued that an image of a human being can portray that divine likeness. Since the fall, the divine image in the human person has been tarnished. However, it is fully present in Christ, and is restored in the saints, who are rightly venerated. Hence the image of a saint is an image of the divine image, and to honour the icon of Christ or a saint is thus a proper thing to do. The close connection of the icon to the humanity of Christ led iconophiles to maintain that to deny the rightness of venerating icons was tantamount to denying Christ's very humanity. Since it was possible to portray the likeness of a human being, to say that this could not be done in the case of Christ was to say that he was not properly human. The iconoclasts, on the other hand, contended that godlikeness is precisely that quality of human existence which cannot be conveyed in representations. Therefore the veneration of an icon is a misplaced activity. So to the iconophiles, the iconoclasts appeared to be too much like Jews and Muslims, while to the iconoclasts, the iconophiles appeared too similar to pagans. A particularly important defender of icons was St John Damascene (*c.* 675–*c.* 749), who was also a great devotee of the Mother of God. He is notable for his preaching on Marian themes,[8] and argued for the connection of icons to Christ's humanity.

Because of the importance of the icon in conveying the presence of the sacred, it was important that it should be properly constructed. That is to say, not just any image could serve for such a holy purpose. The convention which came to be accepted in the East was that the icon must be a portrait, with recognizable characteristics of the holy person which it portrayed, but distinguished from its subject – which is to say that it should not be possible to confuse the image with its original, as may happen in the case of a pagan idol. Subsequently, this definition gave

---

8.   English texts of St John's homilies for the Dormition are contained in Daley 1998: 203–48; the original Greek, with French translations, of homilies on both the Nativity and the Dormition, is given in Damascène 1961.

rise to the rubrics that the image should be flat, that it should have non-realistic proportions, and that the use of colour should be governed by symbolic meaning.

In the year 729, as part of the iconoclast campaign, Leo the Isaurian forced the resignation of Germanus, the Patriarch of Constantinople, who was another strong defender of icons. St Germanus (d. 733) also had a great veneration for the Blessed Virgin Mary, presenting himself as her slave, and considering her to be the Refuge of Christians and the Mediatress through whom redemption is given. According to Germanus, the Mother of God has authority even over Christ.[9] Although all Christians involved in the dispute over icons held the Blessed Virgin in great honour, it is not by chance that such strongly marked Marian devotion should have characterized a leading iconophile, for Christ's human mother Mary guarantees his true humanity, and, according to the iconophiles, the icon of the Lord is likewise a sign of that divine humanity. Indeed, they argued that the icon of Christ brings the benefit of his humanity to the world again. The fact that Mary is always associated with Christ's humanity made her a particularly suitable subject for icons.

When Leo III died in 741, he was succeeded by his son Constantine V, known as Kopronymos, who continued his father's policy of iconoclasm. In 780, however, he was succeeded by Constantine VI, who was too young to rule and whose mother Irene acted as regent. The Empress Irene was an iconophile, who reversed the iconoclasm of the previous two emperors. She summoned the Second Council of Nicaea, which met in 787 to rule on the question of the use of icons. This council was attended only by Eastern bishops, although it is generally judged to be an ecumenical council of the whole Church. The council ruled in favour of the use of icons, declaring:

> The production of representational art is quite in harmony with the history of the spread of the gospel, as it provides confirmation that the becoming man of the Word of God was real and not just imaginary, and as it brings us a similar benefit. For, things that mutually illustrate one another undoubtedly possess one another's message.[10]

In the year 815, iconoclasm was again imposed, and all icons condemned as pagan idols. In 843, another minor ascended the imperial throne and, again, his regent mother, the Empress Theodora, lifted the ban on icons. She immediately summoned the Synod of Constantinople, which reinstated the veneration of icons. This brought an end to the iconoclast controversy.

ART IN THE WEST

In the Western Church, there was not a dispute over the use of images as such. Indeed, some iconophiles who were persecuted in the East took refuge in the West.

---

9. Germanus of Constantinople, 'On the Most Venerable Dormition of the Holy Mother of God', in Daley 1998: 153–68 (161).
10. Tanner (ed.) 1990, vol. 1: 135.

(The lovely church of Santa Maria in Kosmedin, in Rome, was founded by iconophiles fleeing from persecution.) Other discussions were afoot, however.

In 794, the Emperor Charlemagne (Charles I, the Great) established his court at Aachen (Aix-la-Chapelle). Charlemagne wished to restore the Christian Roman Empire, conquering and imposing political unity on a huge swathe of Western Europe, and making himself the Holy Roman Emperor who ruled in the realm of the temporal, while the Pope held authority over Christendom in matters spiritual. A great reformer and promoter of many aspects of European culture, Charlemagne based his religious and cultural reforms on the principle of the *renovatio*, that is, the revival of the Christian Roman Empire of Constantine. The art that is called 'Romanesque' was inspired by this vision.

Following the Second Council of Nicaea, a four-volume work known as the *Libri Carolini* was published, which challenged the council's decrees concerning the use of images. The authorship of the work is disputed: Alcuin of York and Theodulph, Bishop of Orleans, have both been suggested. It is sometimes held that the reason for the work's disagreement with the decisions of Nicaea was that the Latin version of the text was badly translated from the Greek, containing several mistakes. However, the *Libri*'s own views are so strikingly different from those of the council that it is hard to see that even an accurate translation would have yielded much agreement between Nicaea and Aachen on this matter. The *Libri Carolini* follow the teaching of Pope Gregory I, that images may be used to embellish churches and to instruct the illiterate. It is a pragmatic theory of art, which allows no room for supernatural elements. This view was put before the Council of Frankfurt in 794, which ruled that a Christian image may be used for didactic purposes, aesthetic adornment or moral inspiration, but not for adoration. Popes, however, were more inclined to accept the rulings of Nicaea.

Perhaps the Western Church's 'low' theory of sacred art had ironic consequences. The Eastern Church, with its belief in the power of the image to convey some essential quality of the original, was careful to specify that only certain types of image – flat ones, such as paintings and mosaics – could be deemed suitable for devotional use, thus trying to ensure that, on the one hand, the image would direct the viewer's mind to heavenly contemplation, and, on the other, that the icon would not be confused with that which it represented. By contrast, the Western Church's less lofty view of art meant that artistic forms were much less tightly regulated, with the consequence that images which really looked rather like pagan idols came into use as popular objects of veneration – something that was guarded against in the East.

In fact, there was concern in the West about the use of free-standing statues of the saints. The enthusiasm for all things Roman was in practice directed not only towards the Christian culture of Constantine, but also towards aspects of classical antiquity that were not Christian. Free-standing statues had often been considered to be something used only by pagans. However, they seem to have been used in central southern France from the high Middle Ages, and it may be that they were permitted for use in Christian devotion if they were reliquaries. In this way, it would be the relic, and not the image, that was being venerated. The use of such statues was not ubiquitous, however, until very late. In the year 1015, a young man called Bernard –

a native of Angers, in northern France, who was a student at Chartres – travelled with a friend to the south, and was shocked when he found Christians kneeling before statues, such as those of St Gerard at Aurillac, St Faith at Conques, and the 'golden majesty' of the Virgin near the shrine of St Sernin. It seems he had previously supposed that it was only pagans who prayed before statues in this way.[11] By the twelfth century, however, the use of free-standing statues – with or without relics – was widespread in northern European Christianity, having become officially acceptable because of the secular custom of using a statue – for example, of the emperor – to stand in for a person of official importance during the absence of the person represented.[12] Some of the statues which are of greatest importance, from the point of view both of art history and of the history of devotion, are Romanesque images of Mary that were sculpted in the tenth to twelfth centuries.

THE DEVOTION DUE TO THE SAINTS

From the point of view of Marian devotion, it is worth noting that the dispute over images helped to clarify the terminology which is used to indicate the measure of veneration that is due to those persons to whom Christians offer devotion. In the Eastern Church, the term *latreia* was used to refer to the worship that was due to God – to Christ and the Trinity – and the term *proskynesis* (which literally means 'bowing' or 'prostration') was used for the devotion that should be offered before holy icons. One of the areas in which the Latin translation of the decrees of Nicaea was deficient was the rendering of these terms, and this led to misunderstanding as to what the council really intended. However, the Western Church followed St Augustine's teaching that the honour due to the saints, who are human beings, is *doulia* – a Greek word which literally means 'service' – while *latreia* designates the adoration that is due to God alone. The Blessed Virgin Mary, however, is owed a type of devotion that is somewhat greater than that due to the other saints. This is called *hyperdoulia*, which means something like 'super-service', or 'more-than-service'. Thus she is not to be offered the worship that is owed to God alone, but her unique status as Mother of God means that she is marked out above other holy men and women.

THE VIRGIN'S QUEENSHIP

Throughout the early and high Middle Ages, the Virgin's queenship[13] was a central aspect of her cult. This had a political aspect to it, since earthly rulers associated their own authority with hers, linking their own rule with the providential order of the world. During the Carolingian court of the ninth century, an empress would be crowned as such only after giving birth to a child, thus making motherhood, and not marriage alone, the condition for the emperor's wife to hold full imperial status. Furthermore, the rites for the crowning of empresses made allusion to the Virgin

---

11. Mâle 1982: 32–3; references scattered in Forsyth 1972. See also Bouillet 1897.
12. Forsyth 1972: 84–5.
13. For a study of the development of the motif of Mary's sovereignty, see Roschini 1949.

Mary, who herself was queen and empress in virtue of her motherhood.[14] She could also be the model of Christian queenship that was to be imitated by earthly queens.[15] The role of the empress as mother was not just a private matter, but concerned the whole governance of the realm, and so it is not surprising to find that, during the reign of Charles the Bald (840–77), the king made reference to his lineage and his kingdom when he founded the royal monastery of Sainte Marie de Compiègne in the Virgin's honour, and in this way he associated his own title to kingship with 'the glorious Mother of God and perpetual Virgin Mary'.[16] As Mary was the Mother of God, and thus incorporated into the most regal household possible, so the emperor associated his lineage with her in order to guarantee the sacred ordinance of his own rule. Mary stands as the bridge between heaven and earth, and is thus the doorway for earth-dwellers who seek access to the divine, for the purposes of either the present time or the hereafter. Mary's queenship, however, is a more complex affair than the sacred undergirding of earthly rule.

In the first place, Mary is physically the mother of God incarnate. It was her flesh which became the body of Jesus Christ: which is to say that her flesh was united to the Word of God in the incarnation within her own body, and that the body which was formed from her was the same body which suffered, died and rose from the dead for the salvation of the world.

The art historian Yrjö Hirn has drawn attention to another aspect of Mary's physical motherhood which has been important within Catholicism since the early centuries of the Church, namely her condition of being the sacred vessel which, like the Ark of the Covenant, was incomprehensibly the bearer of the true God.[17] In contemporary Europe it is common to regard a vessel as something which is purely functional. For example, people buy milk in cartons, and when the milk is finished the carton is thrown away as rubbish. Yet until recently in Britain, milk always came in glass bottles which were returned to the dairy to be used again, an action which already suggests a more respectful attitude towards milk-bearing vessels than is expressed by throwing cartons into the bin. And there will be people reading this book who will remember a time when they took their own china or earthenware jug to the milk cart, to have it filled from a churn. That jug may have been cared for through many generations, and may have been of great sentimental value – a simple container which was a small treasure. Beyond this secular example, the awareness that vessels have the capacity to be infused with holiness has permeated Catholic consciousness for many centuries, and was certainly a dominant motif of liturgical piety in the high Middle Ages, remaining so until the early modern period. Reliquaries containing the remains of saints, and altars, which themselves are vessels containing relics, are among the most obvious examples of sacred containers; but eucharistic chalices and patens, which must be lined with the most precious materials and purified with cloths set aside for that purpose, have perhaps been the most

---

14. Iogna-Prat 1996a.
15. Corbet 1996: 110 *et passim*.
16. Quoted in Iogna-Prat 1996b: 67.
17. Hirn 1958.

common. The font, likewise, is the precious bearer of the waters of rebirth for all who are baptized into Christ. All these things are holy objects in themselves, because of the precious contents which they may bear. Mary's body, therefore, which carried God incarnate, and part of whose very substance became God's flesh, is necessarily the most sacred of all vessels.

In some places, the importance of Mary's physical motherhood was underlined by the placing of an image of the Virgin and Child above the altar, so that she was seen immediately above the eucharistic elements during the celebration of Mass. This is probably a deliberate device which is intended to remind the worshipper that the bread and wine on the altar are truly the body and blood of Christ. During the eleventh century, the Western Church had settled on a realist interpretation of the consecrated elements of the Eucharist: that is to say, the bread and wine over which the priest proclaimed the words 'This is my body' and 'This is my blood' were in some physical sense the body and blood of God incarnate. The bread and wine did not have a purely mystical relationship to the body and blood of Jesus of Nazareth, but were turned into those very things.[18] During the late twelfth century, it also became common for the priest to elevate the chalice (containing the wine) and the paten (containing the bread) after he had spoken the words of consecration.[19] Now, the image of the Virgin and Child is an image of the original incarnation of Christ, and the placing of such an image above the altar therefore provided a strong visual reminder that the bread and wine of the Mass became the body and blood of that same Christ who took his human flesh from his mother Mary – that the eucharistic elements participate in the original incarnation.

During the twelfth and thirteenth centuries, Christians universally believed that, in addition to these physical aspects of Mary's motherhood, there was also a strong moral element to her participation in the incarnation: that she became Jesus' mother through an act of her free will, so that God did not force her to be the mother of Christ, but sought her consent. Mary is not merely the instrument of God's will in the world, nor simply the vessel through whom he realized the beginning of the world's salvation, but is also a participant who actively agreed to co-operate with God's plan. Now, this view of Mary's part in the drama of salvation is, as has already been seen, one which dates back to the early centuries of the Christian Church. Irenaeus, in the second century, took up St Paul's motif of Christ as the second Adam, and extended it to render Mary the second Eve. He contrasted Eve's disobedience to God with Mary's free obedience, the former having brought death to the world, whereas the latter restored life.[20] This view of Mary is the one which held sway throughout Christendom until the time of the Protestant Reformation. It is based on the story of Jesus' conception as it is recounted in the first chapter of Luke's Gospel (1.26–38), in which the angel Gabriel appears to Mary and tells her that she is to conceive the Son of God, and Mary responds with the words, 'Behold the handmaid of the Lord; be it unto me according to thy word.' Thus the incarnation is

18. Rubin 1991: 14–28.
19. Ibid.: 55–7.
20. Irenaeus of Lyons, 'Adversus Haereses III', 22:4; PG 7.958–60.

a consequence of Mary's deliberate action. This is seen most vividly in one of St Bernard's homilies on the Annunciation. The Marian devotion of St Bernard of Clairvaux (1090–1153) had great influence on subsequent Catholic devotion to Mary, and in the fourth of his homilies, 'In Praise of the Virgin Mother', he lays the greatest possible emphasis on the contingency of Mary's response to the angel and consequently on the dependence of the world's salvation upon the Virgin's word. Addressing Mary, Bernard says:

> Since you have heard joyous and glad tidings, let us hear the joyous reply we long for … The angel is waiting for your reply. It is time for him to return to the one who sent him … The price of our salvation is being offered you. If you consent, we shall immediately be set free … Doleful Adam and his unhappy offspring, exiled from Paradise, implore you, kind Virgin, to give this answer … For it the whole world is waiting, bowed down at your feet.[21]

Mary is therefore a moral as well as a physical agent in the incarnation, and so is doubly active in the process of humanity's redemption from sin and death. It is for this reason that she is honoured above all other saints. In part, Mary's regal status can therefore be read as a sign of her supereminent position among the saints of the Church – a position of such central importance that she can be portrayed as holding the office of highest authority after that of Christ.

In addition to indicating Mary's personal merits and the dignity of the divine motherhood, however, the portrayal of her as Queen of Heaven also reflects something of the Christian Church's understanding of its own nature and mission in the world. As far back as St Ambrose (339–97), Mary is explicitly said to be the *type* or *figure* of the Church, which in effect means that she is the Church's pattern or model, both actual and ideal.[22] Mary's willing co-operation with God's plan of salvation is the model for the Church's own relationship to her Maker. The Church, like the Virgin, is bride of Christ;[23] each is mother of Christians and bearer of Christ to the world. Indeed, sometimes it seems that the Christian imagination has in some sense rendered the Virgin and the Church almost identical with one another, and in painting, this identity may date back to the second century, to the art of the catacombs.[24] The authority attributed to Mary is in part an expression of the power wielded by the institutional Church.[25]

In the Western Europe of the high Middle Ages, the power of the Church was felt in many areas of social and economic life and, by the time of the Canfield Virgin, the cult of Mary's queenship was firmly established and flourishing in Western

---

21.   St Bernard 1979: 53–4.
22.   Ambrose of Milan, 'De Institutione Virginis', 1:XIV.89; PL 16.326C.
23.   Examples given in Warner 1978: 121–4.
24.   Vloberg 1952: 486–93. This is disputed, however; see Parlby, 'The Origins of Marian Art', this volume: 14–19.
25.   A detailed discussion of the relationship between the development of Marian iconography and ecclesial politics is given in Russo 1996.

Christendom. The many visual representations of Mary as queen bear witness to this. At the beginning of the thirteenth century, references to Mary's queenship include Pope Innocent III calling her 'Empress of Angels' and 'Queen of Heaven',[26] while in the same period, the *Salve Regina* was becoming increasingly popular throughout the Latin Church.[27]

It is sometimes remarked that the image of Mary as queen was softened during the later Middle Ages by the increasingly widespread representation of her as a mother. Certainly, it is not until the eighth or ninth century that we find her represented in a devotional context as a mother to the worshipper (as distinct from being the mother of Christ), when the expression '*Monstra te esse matrem*' – 'Show yourself a mother' – appears in the anthem *Ave Maris Stella*.[28] Origen (*c.* 185–254), commenting on John 19.25–7, had written of Mary as mother of Christians,[29] but this exegesis is exceptional in patristic writing, and seems not to have been taken up again until Rupert of Deutz (*c.* 1075–1130) wrote his commentary on the same passage.[30] Likewise, the most popular of the Western Marian hymns, the *Salve Regina*, originally addressed Mary with the words 'Hail, queen of mercy', and was subsequently amended to 'Hail, Queen, mother of mercy'.[31] We should, however, consider the possibility that the change that is manifest here is not a shift away from perceiving Mary as a queen to perceiving her as a mother, so much as a change in the perception of motherhood itself. That is to say, it may be that the social changes which included the rise of the bourgeoisie during the later Middle Ages were accompanied by a corresponding change in the cultural understanding of motherhood, so that the mother ceased to be a figure characterized principally by the power to command, and became a figure characterized more often by domesticity and tenderness.[32] Differences of emphasis notwithstanding, however, Mary is certainly both queen and mother for the whole period designated by the term 'later Middle Ages'.

THE VIRGIN IN MAJESTY[33]

In the statues known as the 'Seat of Wisdom' or 'Virgin in Majesty', Mary is associated both with queenship and with the figure of Wisdom. The German scholar Leo Scheffczyk has argued that it was during the reign of Charlemagne that Mary first became a focus of devotion and theological consideration in her own right, and not purely as the Mother of God incarnate.[34] The incarnation, however, remained the

---

26. Roschini 1949: 604.
27. Graef 1985, 1: 229.
28. Ibid.: 174.
29. O'Carroll 1982: 275, citing Origen's *Commentary on John*, 1.4; PG 14.32A–B.
30. Ibid.: 315, citing Rupert's *In Jo. 13*; PL 169.789–90.
31. Miller n.d.
32. Boss 2000: 45–52.
33. This section is an amended version of work that has previously appeared in Boss 2004.
34. Scheffczyk 1991. Scheffczyk's major work on this subject was done in the 1950s, but a more recent consideration can be found in Scaravelli 2001.

predominant focus of Mary's cult for several more centuries, as the iconography of the Virgin in Majesty testifies.

One of the most ancient images in Christian art is that of the Adoration of the Magi. It appears in the catacombs in Rome, probably painted in the third century,[35] being an image that is taken in the first instance from the Gospels. The visitation of the Magi to the infant Jesus is recorded in Matthew 2.11: 'and going into the house [where the child was], the magi saw the child with Mary his mother, and they fell down and worshipped him'.

The Gospel text does not tell us anything about Mary's posture or demeanour at the time of the visit, but in ancient and medieval art, she is always enthroned and has a regal bearing, with her son seated on her lap. In fact, this is not out of keeping with the narrative of Matthew's Gospel, which begins with Christ's genealogy in which King David is identified as one of Jesus' ancestors. Matthew clearly does want the reader to understand that Jesus is descended from the royal line of David, of the house of Judah. Indeed, it is possible that the reference to Mary in this verse (Mt. 2.11) is intended to be a reference to the office of Queen Mother, which seems to have been held by the mothers of the kings of Judah. But from earliest Christianity, Jesus' kingship was associated not only with that of the royal line of Judah, but, more importantly, with the governance of the universe – of the whole created order, moral and physical. In Christian tradition, the Magi, or 'wise men', are also kings; so the three kings are earthly rulers who have come to pay homage to the Lord under whose authority all temporal rulers hold their respective offices.

During the seventh and eighth centuries, it became common to represent the Virgin and Child in the same posture of enthronement in which they are shown in Adoration scenes, but without the Magi. Mosaics of this kind exist in Rome and Constantinople, and, stripped now of the narrative element of the visitation, form a clear focal point for devotion. From the tenth century, starting in the Auvergne region of France, images of this kind began to be made as free-standing statues. A statue of this type is known as a Virgin in Majesty, or Seat of Wisdom.

The Iconography of the Incarnation
The earliest recorded free-standing statue of the Virgin Mary was made in 946 for the cathedral at Clermont (now Clermont-Ferrand) in south-eastern central France. The statue is depicted in a manuscript written by Arnold the Deacon (Fig. 10).[36] After the cathedral had been destroyed by Norman invaders, Bishop Etienne II had it rebuilt and commissioned a statue of the Virgin and Child to stand over the main altar. The statue was made by Aleaume, the cathedral architect, who was also a goldsmith, and it contained relics of Christ and Our Lady. The picture shows a statue made according to a model that continued to be used by artists who carved other, wooden, statues that still exist, both in Auvergne and elsewhere, and which is also seen in flat representations, such as manuscript illumination. Christ is shown here not as an

---

35.   Parlby, 'The Origins of Marian Art', this volume: 120.
36.   Bibliothèque Municipale de Clermont-Ferrand, ms. 145. Translated in this volume as 'The Vision of the Monk Robert': 173–6.

Fig. 10. *Virgin in Majesty* of Clermont Cathedral (tenth century). Bibliothèque municipale de Clermont, ms. 145.

infant, but as a child with rather adult features. Behind his head there is a cruciform halo, and his right hand is raised in blessing. He bears a cross in his left hand, and his feet are bare. His mother Mary is enthroned, with one hand around her son's chest, and the other extended so that it curls slightly around in front of him. Similar iconography can be seen in an illuminated manuscript from Eynsham Abbey, Oxfordshire, in which Christ's left hand holds a book (Fig. 11). In this case, Mary holds a rod of Jesse, with a bird that possibly signifies the Holy Spirit.

It seems very likely that Majesty statues were influenced by older pagan images,

Fig. 11. *Seat of Wisdom* (*c*. 1130–40). Manuscript of Augustine's *Commentary on Psalms 101–50*, probably from Eynsham Abbey (Bodleian Library, Oxford). Drawing by Neil Walmsley.

but, as we have seen, this type of iconography is found in representations of the Adoration of the Magi, and it is certainly the Adoration that is the principal Christian source for these figures. So the statue is, as it were, taken out of the context of the visit of the Magi. The word 'Magi' is the plural of 'magus' (from which we get the word 'magic'), and we often refer to the Magi as the 'wise men'. So in its origins, this type of image is associated with wisdom. Furthermore, liturgical texts from the twelfth century indicate that statues of this kind were actually used in dramatic performances representing the visitation of the Magi.[37] At Epiphany – the feast of the Three Wise Men, on 6 January – it was the custom in some places to perform a play in which clerics who were dressed up as the three kings would go in search of the

37.   Forsyth 1972: 49–59.

baby Jesus, and would find him in the form of a statue of the Virgin in Majesty, and then would fall down and worship Christ before it. So when worshippers look upon an image of this kind, they are being enjoined to stand in the place occupied by the Magi in Matthew's Gospel – to fall down and worship the child and offer him their gifts.

Let us consider, then, the symbolism encoded in these representations of the Seat of Wisdom. Christ has adult proportions, yet he is only a child in his mother's lap. He raises his hand in a gesture of authority, yet has the bare feet of a pauper. In the illuminations, he also has a cruciform halo behind his head. This collection of attributes is intended to tell us that the boy is God incarnate. The fact that he is a mature figure with his hand raised signifies his regal, or imperial, authority. The cruciform halo carries a similar indication of authority, since it is a symbol that was already used in representations of Christ as the Pantocrator, or Ruler of All. The book in Christ's left hand signifies that he is the Word of God, the Second Person of the Trinity. In the statue of Our Lady of Orcival (Fig. 12), a magnificent Virgin in Majesty in the diocese of Clermont, the book Christ holds in his left hand is marked with the Greek letters Alpha and Omega, the Beginning and the End, showing clearly the sacred and cosmic significance of the book's bearer. Yet, in the words of John's Gospel, 'the Word was made flesh and dwelt among us', meaning that Jesus is not only God eternal, but is also a human being who is present in time as one of us. And that is why he is only a small child on his mother's knee. The child's bare feet likewise signify his humanity. In symbolic commentaries on the Scriptures, the Church Fathers teach that references to Christ's head are references to Christ in his divinity, and references to his feet are references to his humanity.[38] In later Renaissance paintings, it is common to find that one of the three kings is kissing the bare foot of the infant Lord. This is because the event depicted here is the Epiphany, or Showing, that is, the showing of God in human form. The kings therefore venerate the humanity in which divinity is miraculously present. So the bare feet of the child in the Majesty statues points us to his real humanity. Thus the God through whom all things were created has become one of his own creatures in Mary's womb.

Now, the corollary of all this is, as we have seen in a previous chapter, that Mary, who is the mother of Christ, is simultaneously the Mother of God. This is the highest honour which could be bestowed upon any creature: other than being God incarnate, there is no superior condition which any human being could attain, because no one could ever be more intimately united with the Godhead than this – to conceive and bear God in her very body. So, in the traditions of both the Catholic and Eastern Orthodox Churches, the Virgin is said to be higher than the angels, and is crowned and enthroned as the Queen of Heaven.

It would be hard to overstate the extent of Mary's power and majesty in the culture of Western Europe in the eleventh and twelfth centuries. There has been no time in the history of Western Christianity when she has been accorded a higher status than she was during this period. For example, Eadmer of Canterbury, a pupil of

---

38. For example, Maximus the Confessor, 'Liber Ambiguorum', PG 91.1379C. Other references are given in Steinberg 1983: 143–4.

Fig. 12. *Our Lady of Orcival*. From *Histoire d'un Sanctuaire d'Auvergne, Notre-Dame d'Orcival*, Paris: Desclée, de Brouwer et Cie, 1984, frontispiece.

St Anselm who is best known for having written the *Life of Anselm*, also wrote a work entitled *Tractate on the Conception of Saint Mary*,[39] a defence of the doctrine of Mary's immaculate conception. Writing in the late eleventh century, the language in which Eadmer writes of the privileges that accrue to Mary in virtue of her being the Mother of God is almost entirely that of supreme authority. More than once he calls her 'mistress of the world and empress of the universe', and the reader is left in no doubt as to her cosmic dignity.

A very different example of Mary being accorded extreme authority in the

---

39. See Eadmer of Canterbury 1904.

eleventh century is furnished by St Peter Damian (d. 1072), of Ravenna. He tells of a man who was visited in a dream by his deceased godfather and, with the following words, was invited to follow him:

'Come see a spectacle that cannot fail to move you.' And he led him to the basilica of Saint Cecilia in the atrium of which he saw Saints Agnes, Agatha, and Cecilia herself in a choir of numerous resplendent holy virgins. They were preparing a magnificent throne which stood on a higher plane than those around it, and there the Holy Virgin Mary with Peter, Paul, and David, surrounded by a brilliant assemblage of martyrs and saints, came to take her place. While silence reigned in this holiest of gatherings and all respectfully remained standing, a woman who, though a pauper, wore a fur cloak, prostrated herself at the feet of the immaculate Virgin and implored her to have pity on the dead patrician, John. When she had repeated her prayer three times and received no answer, she added, 'You know, my lady, queen of the world, that I am that unfortunate woman who lay naked and trembling in the atrium of your great basilica [Santa Maria Maggiore]. That man [the patrician John] saw me and immediately took pity on me and covered me with the fur that I am wearing.' Whereupon Mary, blessed of God, said: 'The man for whom you are pleading was crushed by a great weight of crimes. But he had two good points: charity toward the poor and devotion, in all humility, to the holy places. In fact he often carried oil and kindling on his own shoulders for the lights of my Church.' The other saints testified that he did the same for their churches. The queen of the world ordered that the patrician be brought before the assembly. At once he was dragged in, bound and chained, by a horde of demons. Whereupon Our Lady ordered that he be delivered, and he went to swell the ranks of the saints [the elect]. But she ordered that the bonds from which he had just been set free be kept for another man, still living.[40]

Here, the Queen of Heaven has the power to save and to damn; she exercises that power to both ends, and she does so without direct reference to Christ.

What we see here is a certain symmetry between Christ and the Virgin. The Second Person of the Trinity, who has all things subject to him, descends to become a small creature in the Virgin's womb; and the Virgin, who is only a human woman, is elevated to share the power and authority of Christ himself. In an elegant movement of descent and ascent, the God who becomes human enables the woman who gave him his humanity to rise up and be enthroned on the seat which is next to the Deity.

Seat of Wisdom

In an image of the Seat of Wisdom, however, the Virgin is not just enthroned: she is herself a throne. For Christ is enthroned on her lap, and this is the primary meaning

---

40. Peter Damian, 'De diversis apparitionibus et miraculis', tract 34.2; *PL* 145.188; quoted in Le Goff 1984: 179.

of the title 'Seat of Wisdom' as it is applied to the Virgin in Majesty. So let us turn now to think about the figure of Wisdom.

In the Hebrew Scriptures, Wisdom as a personal figure – as distinct from wisdom as a human attribute – should perhaps be understood in the first instance as an attribute of God.[41] Wisdom directs men and women to lead good lives, and thus is associated with specifically moral action. But the workings of Wisdom are also perceived in the natural order of the non-human world: animals know how to build themselves homes, when the mating season is, and so on. The seasons likewise come in an ordered cycle. If human beings attend to the teachings of Wisdom, then our lives will be similarly properly ordered, in accordance with God's intention. Wisdom, then, governs the natural and the moral orders, and wisdom is often personified as a female figure.

Some books of the Bible are known as 'Wisdom writings' – for example, the Hebrew books of Proverbs, Ecclesiastes and the Song of Songs, and the Greek books of the Wisdom of Solomon, Ecclesiasticus and Baruch. Much of this literature is attributed to King Solomon. Just as the first five books of the Bible, the Torah, are attributed to Moses, the great teacher and law-giver, and the Psalms are attributed to King David, the musician, so the biblical literature that is concerned with right living and with the discernment of Wisdom is attributed to King Solomon, reputedly the wisest of all men and women. One text that is particularly important when considering the Catholic cult of the Virgin Mary is Proverbs 8.22–31. In this numinous speech, Wisdom herself declares, 'The Lord created me at the beginning of his works, the first of his acts of old.' She then goes on to say that she was present before anything else was created – the earth, the sea, and so on. She says she was present with God, delighting in his works.

In the New Testament, Christian authors apply Old Testament texts about Wisdom to Christ. In 1 Corinthians, St Paul refers to Christ as 'the Wisdom of God' (1.24), and sees the world as existing through him (8.6). In John 1.1–5, the Word, who is Christ, is described in language that draws heavily upon Wisdom imagery. Christians have always continued to see Christ as Wisdom incarnate, but, as we shall see, it was not only Christ, but other figures also, who came to be seen as endowed with the attributes of Holy Wisdom.

For the moment, however, let us ask why it is that the figure of Wisdom should be enthroned, as Christ is, seated upon his mother's lap in the Majesty statues? What is the significance of Wisdom's enthronement? Well, part of the reason is that Mary is the place in whom Christ resides, and for that reason she is often given titles such as 'altar', or 'throne of Grace'. But there is a more particular symbolism involved here. I have already mentioned that Solomon is seen in Scripture and tradition as one who is uniquely wise among men and women; and the books of 2 Kings and 2 Chronicles make much of Solomon's splendid throne:

---

41.   It is disputed how exactly the figure of Wisdom should be interpreted in the Hebrew Scriptures. See, for example, Camp 1985; Barker 2003.

The king also made a great ivory throne, and overlaid it with pure gold. The throne had six steps and a footstool of gold, which were attached to the throne, and on each side of the seat were arm rests and two lions standing beside the arm rests, while twelve lions stood there, one on each end of the steps on the six steps. The like of it was never made in any kingdom. (2 Chron. 9.17–19)

In the Eynsham manuscript illumination (Fig. 11), the Virgin and Child are enthroned, and the Virgin is seated on a lion throne – intending you to call to mind King Solomon, and therefore Wisdom. To Christian authors of the twelfth century, the Old Testament was filled with 'types' of characters from the Gospels. The word 'type' is derived from the Greek word *tupos*, meaning a blow, or strike. In English, the word is used in relation to printing, where we have the words 'typeface' and 'typewriter', since these make an imprint by striking a blow. A biblical *type*, therefore, is a person or action that bears a likeness, or imprint, of some other person or action. In particular, the men and women of the Old Testament were (and sometimes still are) seen to foreshadow the greater figures of the New – and especially Christ and the Virgin. So, for example, Abraham's sacrifice of Isaac is a type of the Father's sacrifice of the Son on the cross. Likewise, Solomon, the wise ruler, is a type of Christ, and the splendid throne on which he sits is a type of the Virgin, in whose body Christ resided.

The spiritual writer Adam of St Victor (d. 1180) wrote a hymn to the Virgin in which he says, 'You are the throne of Solomon . . . white ivory foretells your chastity, red gold foretells your charity.'[42] So every detail of the throne becomes a type of some quality of the Blessed Virgin.

Sometimes the Queen of Sheba is seen as a type of the Magi. She was a ruler noted for her wisdom and learning, who came to visit King Solomon (1 Kgs 10.1–13). She asked him many questions, and, finding he could answer them all, had to acknowledge his superior wisdom. As the Queen of Sheba came to pay homage to Solomon on his throne, so the Magi are similarly wise rulers who come to pay homage to Christ in the lap of the Virgin.

A sermon attributed to Peter Damian identifies Mary with Solomon's throne, and continues:

> Our Solomon [Christ], [who is] not only wise but [is] indeed the Wisdom of the Father . . . has prepared a throne, manifestly the womb of the chaste Virgin, in which sat that Majesty which shakes the world with a nod.[43]

This sermon says that the ivory of Solomon's throne is an image of Mary's virginity; and it then describes the gold with which the throne was covered, concluding: 'In like manner, God clothed the Virgin and was clothed in the Virgin.' Some of the Majesty statues are indeed gilded. The statue of Our Lady of Orcival (Fig. 12), for example, is clothed in silver gilt. It is a carved wooden figure, covered in pieces of

---

42. The hymn is discussed in Forsyth 1972: 26–9.
43. Ibid.: 25.

gilded silver, and seated upon a throne which is also covered in silver gilt. The Virgin is herself Solomon's throne; she is covered in the gold of majesty and honour which God has bestowed upon her, as he himself was covered by the womb which she bestowed upon him.

Maria Sapientia

So far, we have seen several examples of a certain symmetry between Our Lord and Our Lady. He takes her human condition, and she shares his heavenly one. She gives him the throne of her body, and he gives her the throne of judgement. She clothes him with flesh, and he clothes her with honour. But the most important symmetry that I am going to refer to here is still another one: namely that Mary, like Christ, is identified with the Wisdom of God.

As we have seen, in the statues which are called 'Seat of Wisdom', it is not only Christ who is seated, or enthroned, but also Mary, and during the high Middle Ages, biblical texts concerning Holy Wisdom were used to refer to Mary herself. An identification between Mary and Wisdom became common in this period because of the use of Wisdom texts in Marian liturgies – a usage which seems to dates back at least to Alcuin of York (d. 804), who was official liturgist at the court of the Emperor Charlemagne, and whose work was influential in much subsequent Western liturgy. By Alcuin's time, it was not uncommon for texts concerning Holy Wisdom to be used in the liturgies for the feast days of virgins. Alcuin himself probably used a Wisdom text in the Mass for the feast of St Agatha, the virgin martyr. And in this instance, the reference being made is principally to the Wise Virgins of the gospel: the virgin saint is the one who has chosen the path of wisdom and kept her lamp ready to welcome the bridegroom.[44] However, Alcuin uses Wisdom texts in several more contexts than this. He wrote a complete set of prayers for a Mass in honour of Holy Wisdom, and in these prayers Wisdom seems to be attributed with characteristics of both the Second and Third Persons of the Blessed Trinity. Elsewhere, in a non-liturgical text, Alcuin identifies Wisdom explicitly with each of the three Persons of the Trinity.[45] It is therefore most interesting that he wrote two votive Masses of the Blessed Virgin – which were used on Saturdays, since Saturday came to be the day set aside in Mary's honour – and that in one of these Masses Alcuin includes the text beginning at Ecclesiasticus 24.14 (Vulgate), 'From eternity, in the beginning, he created me, and for all the ages I shall not cease to be', referring to Wisdom dwelling with the Lord. It seems clear that the use of these verses is intended in some way to designate Mary. Certainly, that is how it came to be understood within a very short space of time. In 853, Haymon, Bishop of Halberstadt, preached on Ecclesiasticus 24.14 as applied to Mary. His homily explains that the Wisdom of God took flesh of the Virgin, but that it is not unsuitable to apply this text to the Mother of God herself, since the Wisdom of God was created from her, 'that

44.   Catta 1961: 694.
45.   Meyers 1995.

through her the Son of God might be created without human concupiscence, to ransom human nature'.[46]

A Vatican manuscript of the tenth century includes a Mass for Our Lady's Birthday in which one of the lections is Proverbs 8.22ff: 'The Lord possessed me at the beginning of his ways ...' and so on. The Gospel reading which is given for the same Mass is Christ's genealogy from the beginning of Matthew. One modern commentator, Etienne Catta, describes this combination of readings as 'striking',[47] since it seems to suggest that the birth of the Virgin is analogous to Christmas, with Mary's creation from the beginning of time being rendered parallel to the Prologue to John's Gospel, whose opening words are 'In the beginning was the Word', referring to Christ. As Christ was present from eternity, and in the fullness of time became flesh in his mother's womb, so Mary was in some manner present from the foundations of the world, and likewise was born when the time was right for her part in the fulfilment of God's plan. Proverbs 8.22–31 in fact came to be the standard reading at Mass for the feasts of Mary's Birthday (8 September) and of her Conception (8 December).

Whether this association of Wisdom with Mary is an example of imaginative hyperbole, or whether it has some theological substance, is a matter for debate. When Wisdom readings were first applied to Mary, it was not claimed that they applied to her in the direct manner in which they applied, for example, to Christ – only that the language used in them could also be seen to be true in some sense of Mary as well. The Wisdom texts referred to Mary not literally, but by 'accommodation', or suitability. However, during later centuries, it came to be generally accepted that these texts could be taken to signify Mary directly, and the liturgical use of Wisdom texts played a part in the development of the doctrine of the immaculate conception.

BIBLIOGRAPHY

Primary Sources

St Bernard (1979) 'Four homilies in praise of the Virgin Mother', IV:8, in Marie-Bernard Saïd and Grace Perigo (trans.), *In Praise of the Blessed Virgin Mary*, Kalamazoo: Cistercian Publications.

Daley, Brian E. (trans.) (1998) *On the Dormition of Mary: Early Patristic Homilies*, Crestwood, NY: St Vladimir's Seminary Press.

Damascène, S. Jean (1961) *Homélies sur la Nativité et la Dormition*, trans. Pierre Voulet, 'Sources Chrétiennes', Paris: Les Editions du Cerf.

Eadmer of Canterbury (1904) *Eadmeri Monachi Cantuariensis Tractatus de Conceptione Sanctae Mariae*, ed. H. Thurston and Slater, Freiburg-im-Breisgau: Herder.

Goullet, Monique and Iogna-Prat, Dominique (1996), 'La Vierge en Majesté de Clermont-Ferrand', in Iogna-Prat *et al.* (eds), *Marie*: 382–405.

Tanner, Norman (ed.) (1990) *Decrees of the Ecumenical Councils*, 2 vols, London: Sheed & Ward.

---

46. Haymon, Bishop of Halberstadt, 'Homilia V. In Solemnitate Perpetuae Virginis Mariae', PL 118.765D.
47. Catta 1961: 696.

Secondary Sources

Adams, Henry (1986) *Mont Saint Michel and Chartres: A Study of Thirteenth-century Unity*, Harmondsworth: Penguin.

Barker, Margaret (2003) 'Wisdom, the queen of Heaven', in *The Great High Priest: The Temple Roots of Christian Liturgy*, London: T & T Clark: 229–61.

Boss, Sarah Jane (2000) *Empress and Handmaid: On Nature and Gender in the Cult of the Virgin Mary*, London: Cassell.

Boss, Sarah Jane (2004) *Mary*, London: Continuum.

Bouillet, Auguste (1897) *Liber miraculorum Sancte Fidis: Collection de textes pour servir à l'étude et à l'enseignement de l'histoire*, Paris.

Bryer, Anthony and Herrin, Judith (eds), *Iconoclasm*, Birmingham: University of Birmingham, Centre for Byzantine Studies.

Camp, Claudia V. (1985) *Wisdom and the Feminine in the Book of Proverbs*, Sheffield: Almond Press.

Catta, Etienne (1961) 'Sedes Sapientiae', in du Manoir (ed.), *Maria*, vol. 6: 689–866.

Corbet, Patrick (1996) 'Les impératrices ottoniennes et le modèle marial: Autour de l'ivoire du château Sforza de Milan', in Iogna-Prat *et al.*, *Marie*: 109–35.

Cormack, Robin (2000), *Byzantine Art*, Oxford: Oxford University Press.

Forsyth, Ilene H. (1972) *The Throne of Wisdom: Wood Sculptures of the Madonna in Romanesque France*, Princeton, NJ: Princeton University Press.

Freedberg, David (1989) *The Power of Images: Studies in the History and Theory of Response*, Chicago, IL, and London: University of Chicago Press.

Le Goff, Jacques (1984) *The Birth of Purgatory*, trans. Arthur Goldhammer, Aldershot: Scolar Press.

Graef, Hilda (1985) *Mary: A History of Doctrine and Devotion*, combined edn, London: Sheed & Ward.

Hirn, Yrjö (1958) *The Sacred Shrine: A Study of the Poetry and Art of the Catholic Church*, London: Faber & Faber.

Iogna-Prat, Dominique (1996a) 'La Vierge et les *ordines* de couronnement des reines au IXe siècle', in Iogna-Prat *et al.* (eds), *Marie*: 100–7.

Iogna-Prat, Dominique (1996b) 'Le culte de la Vierge sous le règne de Charles le Chauve', in Iogna-Prat *et al.* (eds), *Marie*: 65–98.

Iogna-Prat, Dominique, Palazzo, Éric and Russo, Daniel (eds) (1996) *Marie: Le culte de la Vierge dans la société médiévale*, Paris: Beauchesne.

Louth, Andrew (2002) *St John Damascene: Tradition and Originality in Byzantine Theology*, Oxford: Oxford University Press.

de Luis, P. (1992) 'Elvira, Council of', in Angelo Di Berardino (ed.), *Encyclopedia of the Early Church*, vol. 1, trans. Adrian Wolford, Cambridge: James Clarke: 270.

Mâle, Émile (1982) *Religious Art from the Twelfth to the Eighteenth Century*, Princeton, NJ: Princeton University Press (first English edn 1949).

du Manoir, Hubert (ed.) (1949–71) *Maria: Etudes sur la Sainte Vierge*, 8 vols, Paris: Beauchesne.

Meyers, Ruth A. (1995) 'The Wisdom of God and the Word of God: Alcuin's Mass "of Wisdom"', in Martin Dudley (ed.), *Like a Two-edged Sword: The Word of God in Liturgy and History*, Norwich: Canterbury Press: 39–59.

Miller, Desmond (n.d.) 'The origin and practice of the *Salve Regina*', Wallington: Ecumenical Society of the Blessed Virgin Mary.

O'Carroll, Michael (1982) *Theotokos: A Theological Encyclopedia of the Blessed Virgin Mary*, Collegeville: The Liturgical Press.

Parlby, Geri (2007) 'The Origins of Marian Art: The Evolution of Marian Imagery in the Western Church until ad 431', in this volume: 106–29.

Pelikan, Jaroslav (1977) *The Christian Tradition: A History of the Development of Doctrine*, vol. 2, *The Spirit of Eastern Christendom (600–1700)*, Chicago, IL, and London: University of Chicago Press.

Pelikan, Jaroslav (1990) *Imago Dei: The Byzantine Apologià for Icons* New Haven and London: Yale University Press.

Piastra, Clelia Maria (ed.) (2001) *Gli Studi de Mariologia Medievale Bilancio Storiografico*, 'Millennio Medievale 26, Atti de Convegni 7', Bottai, Tavarnuzze-Firenze: SISMEL-Edizioni del Galluzzo: 65–85.

Röckelein, Hewig, Opitz, Claudia and Bauer, Dieter R. (1990) *Maria: Abbild oder Vorbild? Zur Sozialgeschichte mittelalterlicher Marienverehrung*, Tübingen: Edition Diskord.

Roschini, G.-M. (1949) 'Royauté de Marie', in du Manoir (ed.), *Maria*, vol. 1, 601–18.

Rubin, Miri (1991) *Corpus Christi: The Eucharist in Late Medieval Culture*, Cambridge: Cambridge University Press.

Russo, Daniel (1996) 'Les représentations mariales dans l'art d'Occident: essai sur la formation d'une tradition iconographique', in Iogna-Prat *et al.*, *Marie*: 173–291.

Scaravelli, Irene (2001) 'Per una mariologia carolingia. Autori, opere e linee de ricerca', in Piastra (ed.), *Gli Studi de Mariologia Medievale Bilancio Storiografico*: 65–85.

Scheffczyk, L. (1991) 'Karolingerzeit. I. Mariologie', in Remigius Bäumer and Leo Scheffczyk (eds), *Marienlexikon*, vol. 3, St Ottilien: EOS Verlag: 512–13.

Steinberg, Leo (1983) *The Sexuality of Christ in Renaissance Art and Modern Oblivion*, London: Faber & Faber.

Vloberg, Maurice (1952) 'Les types iconographiques de la Mère de Dieu dan l'art Byzantin', in du Manoir (ed.), *Maria*, vol. 2, 403–44.

Warner, Marina (1978) *Alone of All Her Sex: The Myth and Cult of the Virgin Mary*, London: Quartet Books.

The Vision of the Monk Robert

Translated by Sarah Jane Boss

This is the earliest record of a free-standing statue of the Virgin Mary (see Fig. 10). It was written sometime after 984, and refers to the construction of the new cathedral of Clermont by Bishop Stephen II (937–84) in 946. The account is contained in a manuscript in the Bibliothèque Municipale in Clermont-Ferrand, ms. 145. The Latin text, with French translation, is published in Monique Goullet and Dominique Iogna-Prat, 'La Vierge en Majesté de Clermont-Ferrand', in Dominique Iogna-Prat, Éric Palazzo and Daniel Russo (eds) (1996), *Marie: Le culte de la Vierge dans la société médiévale*, Paris: Beauchesne: 383–405.

In the name of the holy and undivided Trinity. Here begins the vision of the devout monk Robert, which took place, as is known, on the XVI of the Kalends of September, concerning the basilica of St Mary, Mother of God, situated in Auvergne. This vision is related by Arnold, a deacon.

Brothers, I report a matter which has occurred in our days and will arouse the astonishment of those who hear of it. It is an apparition that was seen recently in a nocturnal vision that was had by the abbot of Mozat, a man of venerable life by the name of Robert. At the time when the excellent bishop Stephen had charge of the Arverna [inhabitants of the Auvergne region], he displayed a great concern for the conservation of holy relics. He was indeed a man of illustrious birth, who, in the exercise of his functions, took care to introduce the sons of the Church to the best examples, to give good governance to the Church herself, who is the spouse of Christ, and to uphold it by that governance. He therefore had a basilica built in the place where he had acceded to the episcopate – that is, in the city of Arverna – in honour of the perpetual Virgin, Mother of God. This basilica is so amazing that nothing like it would be seen or undertaken in our time, in the whole world. For it is a beautiful sight, and wonderful to behold. From this evidence, I think it is without doubt that the very Virgin of God, in whose praise and honour he had it raised and consecrated, is the helper and guardian of his soul. For, as I have said above, he honoured the bodies of the saints with devotion, and conserved their relics wonderfully – those of the Mother of God, amongst others, which he venerated with a wonderful affection.

He had in his service a cleric, a certain Aleaume, of very noble birth, whom all our neighbours know as very gifted in goldsmithing and stone-carving. Even if we go back a long way into the past, we cannot find his equal in working gold, stone or any other material. It is he who measured out the said church with the reed [i.e., drew up the plans] and wonderfully completed it. The venerable bishop, wishing to honour the Virgin's relics, charged Aleaume with the execution of a chair in gold and precious stones. He ordered that a representation of the Mother of God should be placed on it, wonderfully worked in the purest gold, with the figure of her son, our Lord, on her knees; and in that ornament the said relics would be most honourably laid. The cleric worked at it with zeal and without respite.

173

The work was not yet completed, when the abbot Robert testified that during his sleep, he had seen this vision. He found himself in a workshop with the goldsmith and his brother Adam, who, through the teaching of his brother, had also become a goldsmith; and they had met together there to assemble the marvellous majesty. Adam advised his elder brother that it would not be appropriate to fashion the statue in the bishop's absence. Complying with the counsel of his younger brother, Aleaume sent a messenger to the prelate straight away, to ask him to come as quickly as he could. The latter did not delay, but, filled with great charity, and, for the love of the Mother of God, desirous of taking every encouragement to the artists, he hurried to get himself to the piece of work which had been started. During this time, the goldsmith Aleaume and his assistants, as well as the abbot Robert, seated at their side, awaited the arrival of the holy pastor. Suddenly they saw the bishop entering, holding hands with his patron, who was now deceased. The man who accompanied the prelate was the predecessor of Robert, who spoke of seeing this vision. Those who knew this man say that, during his monastic life, he was seen to exercise patience and humility at all times. While he was on this earth, his name was Drucbert. Seeing these venerable men, worthy of God, enter and seat themselves on benches, the goldsmiths and their assistants wanted to finish the work of sacred service that they had begun. But when they had taken up the things that were necessary for the marvellous work, they suddenly saw at this point that they were surrounded by flies that they were quite unable to drive away. The pontiff was angry and had the idea of cleaning the workshop of this infection by waving what is commonly called a fan. But the venerable Drucbert indicated to him that he would never get rid of them without the assistance of God. Pleased with this advice, the bishop put on the white stole, blessed the water, and, following the ritual, intoned the anthem, 'Asperges me domine hysopo et mundabor', and then the collect, 'Exaudi nos Deus salutaris noster et mitere digneris sanctum angelum tuum', etc. When the assembled company had responded, 'Amen', the flies disappeared. I think it is without doubt that he by whose counsel, with divine assent, the scourge of flies disappeared, was an envoy from God. Indeed, what else should we see in the flies but the snares of the enemy? What else but the invasion of sin? We read of the Prince of darkness that he is called the Prince of flies. For in the fly we can see the ancient Enemy. The Devil, indeed, is night to the man of goodness, not only in himself, but also through the snares in which he ceaselessly attempts to capture God-fearing souls, especially those of the faithful whom he sees living in conformity with the divine will. This is why he could not bear to see the work that the goldsmith had undertaken, and why he had wished to prevent its realization in sending a swarm of flies.

But let us leave this question there and return to our story. As it was told by the venerable Robert, who had this vision, once the workshop was cleared of flies, the goldsmiths could not continue their work immediately, because they suddenly saw about three hundred bees enter through the east window. Surrounding the statue and landing on the precious stones, they stood on the pearls like gentle and docile animals. The artists were astonished by this and wanted to chase them off, but the bishop said to them: 'Do not harm them, I beg you. These little birds are fed by us. Let them go without doing them harm.' We profess that this vision had the following significance: the bees had come down to bear witness to the Virgin's merits. For, just as the Virgin gave birth and remained a virgin after childbirth – a fact unique among women – in the same way, bees constitute a unique phenomenon amongst birds. Indeed, Gregory, the famous doctor, judges the race of bees blessed and admirable amongst all birds, saying that their sex is not violated by the male nor injured by the foetus, and that the infants do not cause any rupture to their chastity. But, since it would take too long to treat of their chastity in detail, let us content ourselves with saying that the aggression from the impure flies that was undergone by the devotees of the Mother of God had to be effaced by virgin animals. Seated on their benches, these blessed men, as was told by Robert himself, the abbot of happy memory, saw that the undertaking was accomplished. The marvellous statue, placed on a pedestal so that everyone might see it, aroused general admiration.

Drucbert, whose name I have heard much praised – the very same who had entered with Bishop Stephen – admiring the majesty and holding the prelate's right hand, was saying to him: 'Dear Bishop, where do you intend to place such a beautiful majesty? It is fitting, for the love of God and the respect due to his Mother, that these relics should be conserved worthily. Where have you prepared the home which should receive them?' Astonished by the abbot's remarks, the bishop replied: 'What is this, father? What is this, brother? What are you saying? Don't you know the house that I have had built for God and his Mother, the perpetual Virgin?' Since the venerable priest confirmed that he did not know it, the lord Stephen hurried to guide him and, the two men holding hands, he said to him: 'Come, most holy brother, let us hurry, so that you too might be able to see the grandeur and beauty of the places that I have prepared for these relics. For you claim to be ignorant of that which is known to all the inhabitants of Auvergne.'

[Bishop Stephen then takes Drucbert on a dream-like tour of a building of extraordinary size, wealth and beauty, filled with gemstones and precious metals, containing images of Christ, the apostles and the Virgin Mary. Finally ...]

... before the Holy of Holies, there was a raised altar, which was reached up three steps. Robert affirmed that it was so admirable that he could not describe its richness. He told of how, on the altar, he had seen a majesty of the Redeemer of the human race, magnificently painted in many colours. To its right was the representation of the Virgin Mary; to its left, that of the archangel Michael. All around, with wings outstretched, were cherubim and seraphim, who enfolded the scene with all their splendour. Behind the altar there stood erect a column of wonderful marble; at its top, in the manner of jasper, was a capital of wonderful size, destined by the pontiff to become the plinth of the saving image that I have described above.

[Stephen tells Drucbert that this building was painstakingly constructed by human labour and became so fine by the help of God. The narrator concludes that the bishop must have been chosen by Christ before the meeting with the venerable Drucbert, and benefited from divine protection.]

On waking, Robert did not think he had been asleep, but, preoccupied with his vision, he had the bells rung and, when he had sung the psalms and said the morning office, he called a few of the monks in whom he confided, and told them what was in his heart. They were filled with amazement and said that this vision was revealed by God. After holding council, they asked to convey to the bishop what they considered to be the cause of the vision. The prelate was filled with cheer, delighted by the vision, happy at the revelation of the temple, burning with the fire of charity. The love that he bore for the Mother of God increased still more; he commanded that the said majesty should be accomplished with the greatest speed and, with the help of God, that the precious relics should be given a fitting position behind the altar. In all the world, one could not find relics more precious than these. The bishop, a president worthy of God, loved them to the point of venerating them and honouring them more than all the others. Indeed, he enclosed the bodies of several saints in coffers of gold and silver; these particular relics, however, he wanted to honour in a different way.

This account was composed to the praise of Our Lord Jesus Christ, to whom are honour and glory, world without end. Amen.

8

MARIAN DEVOTION IN THE LATIN WEST IN THE LATER MIDDLE AGES

Eva De Visscher

Throughout the Middle Ages, Mary appears as a central figure in devotional theory and practice. As the subject of countless doctrinal treatises, prayers, songs, sermons, legends and works of art, she emerges in the roles of mother and virgin, bride and second Eve, type of the Church, divine intercessor and Throne of Wisdom. While occupying a place at the heart of clerical as well as lay religious devotion, over time the emphases on her roles have shifted, focuses have changed. In this chapter I aim to explore the general directions in which Mariology developed from *c.* 1000 to *c.* 1500 and, more specifically, to examine how Mary was portrayed by theologians, exegetes, preachers, poets and visionaries of the time. This chapter will first deal with the sources which helped to shape medieval thought on and expression of Marian devotion; second, it will study the medieval treatment of separate aspects of Mary, concentrating on her various roles as well as on the miracles through which these roles were defined: the immaculate conception, the incarnation, the virgin birth and the assumption.

The cult of the Virgin in the Middle Ages relied first of all on the New Testament tradition, and on its exposition by the Church Fathers. Mary is not a prominent figure in the New Testament.[1] The Gospels of Mark and John refer to her only twice each: Mark 3.31–5 relates how she sends for her son in vain while he is surrounded by a crowd; a little later, in Mark 6.3, she is simply mentioned as Christ's mother. In John she appears at the wedding feast at Cana (2.1–11) and, memorably and movingly, at the foot of the cross together with the apostle John 'whom Jesus loved' (19.25–7). Although the few references to Mary in the fourth Gospel (John) lie at the basis of several major aspects of her cult, to be discussed below, the New Testament accounts which provide the most extensive material on Mary's life are those of Matthew and Luke. Both establish a strong connection between Old Testament dynastic history and Christ by tracing his lineage to King David, albeit through the paternal and not the maternal line. Since Matthew and Luke indicate that Joseph is not Christ's biological father (Mt. 7.20; Lk. 1.34–5), although Luke calls him Christ's father 'by repute' (3.23), this genealogy posed a problem. Patristic authority

---

1. For a more elaborate discussion of Mary in the Gospels, see Chris Maunder, 'Mary in the New Testament and Apocrypha', in this volume: 11–38. For briefer discussions, see Graef 1985, vol. 1; Pelikan 1996; Warner 2000.

therefore developed the explanation that Mary was in fact Joseph's cousin, and thus also of the House of David.[2] The apocryphal tradition also straightens out this contradiction by making Mary a kinswoman of Joseph.[3] Throughout the Middle Ages, Mary is generally considered to be of Davidic descent and her image is included in biblical genealogies. The notable Suger, abbot at the monastery of St Denis in the mid-twelfth century, is credited with developing the iconography of the root of Jesse, from which Mary and Christ sprout as descendants of a line of kings.[4]

Both evangelists further take great pains to present Christ's coming as the fulfilment of messianic prophecy, and interwoven in their accounts are several references to the prophets. The most influential one in the development of the doctrine of the Virgin Birth is Matthew's rendering of Isaiah 7.14, 'Behold a young woman [*'almah*] shall conceive', according to the Greek Septuagint tradition, which has 'Behold a virgin [*parthenos*] shall conceive'. The Latin *virgo* (virgin), so close in sound and orthography to *virga* (rod), smoothed a further exegetical link between Mary and another prophecy: 'a rod shall come forth from the root of Jesse and a flower shall arise from its root' (Num. 17.1; Isa. 11.1). The twelfth-century Cistercian abbot Bernard of Clairvaux, with characteristic rhetorical flourish, calls Christ 'a virgin born of a rod that was a virgin' (*virgo virga virgine generatus*).[5] Hildegard of Bingen, a German contemporary of Bernard and abbess of the Benedictine monasteries at Disibodenberg and Rupertsberg, dedicated several hymns and musical compositions to the Virgin. Two of the better-known ones begin with a reference to her title of 'virga': 'O greenest rod' (*viridissima virga*) and 'O rod and diadem' (*O virga ac diadema*).[6]

To the Gospel of Luke we owe the accounts of the Annunciation, the Visitation, the Nativity and the Presentation of Christ in the Temple. These stories depict crucial events in Mary's life partly through her own words (to the angel Gabriel, to Elizabeth, to her son) and reveal more about her in relation to others than any other New Testament narrative. The combination of these mostly domestic scenes and the divine message revealed in them has proven extremely fertile ground for the expression of devotion to the Virgin in medieval theology, art and literature. Mary's unquestioning, obedient co-operation in God's plan, both at the incarnation with the words 'Behold the handmaid of the Lord. Be it unto me according to thy word' (Lk. 1.38), and in silence during the crucifixion, lifted her above all other faithful.

Religious authors of the late eleventh and twelfth centuries describe her as the most blessed of the saints.[7] In his *Office of the Blessed Virgin Mary*, dating from the mid-eleventh century, the Italian theologian and cardinal-bishop of Ostia Peter Damian (d. 1072) states, 'Blessed Virgin, [you possess . . .] singular privilege of merits, so that as you do not know a peer among human beings, you also surpass the dignity of the

---

2. Clayton 1998: 14; Warner 2000: 20.
3. 'The Protevangelium', in Elliott 1993: 61.
4. Warner 2000: 114.
5. *Sermones super cantica canticorum*, sermon 47.2.5, in Bernard of Clairvaux 1957–77, vol. II: 64.
6. Hildegard of Bingen 1983: 24, 27.
7. Guibert of Nogent, *De Laude Sanctae Mariae*, 1, PL 156: 539; Richard of Saint Victor, *De Emmanuele*, 2.31, PL 196: 664.

angels.'[8] Bernard of Clairvaux, who was a great advocate of her cult, called her 'more precious than any, more holy than all'.[9] He placed her at the very summit of the hierarchy of life, stating that, while God existed in all creatures, more particularly in those endowed with reason, and especially in those who were good and holy, he was present in Mary as in no other. For she is the only one who can claim that Christ had been formed of God's substance and of hers.[10]

Mary's vigil at the cross as described in the fourth Gospel has given rise to her identification with several different roles: that of *Mater Dolorosa* and of *Divine Mother*, and that of the *type of the Church* (*Ecclesia*). Her presence at the world's redemption, interpreted as full acceptance of God's will, forms the basis of the idea that Mary is the perfect type of both the Church and of every individual soul within it. The fact that 'church' and 'soul' are feminine nouns in many languages, most prominently in Greek and Latin, facilitates this association which is so pervasive in medieval exegesis. The image of Mary as *Ecclesia* gains further support through the brief mention in Acts 1.14 that she was present in Jerusalem 'in the upper room' with the apostles and several women after the Ascension. Since the descent of the Holy Spirit, described in the next chapter, was believed to have taken place in the same room, it was assumed that she was part of this event as well.[11]

In his commentary on the woman of the Apocalypse, the twelfth-century regular canon and mystic Richard of St Victor elaborates on the comparison in the following way:

[...] *Sancta Ecclesia totis viribus laborat ut faciendo voluntatem summi Patris Christi matris fiat* [...] *Sancta nimirum Ecclesia, quae Patri sunt placita perficiendo mater Christi efficitur, quia concipit eum, fecundante eam gratia per fidem, parturit per bonam voluntatem, parit per bonam actionem.*[12]

The holy Church is striving with all her might to do the will of the Father most high, in order to become the mother of Christ [...] For the Church all-holy becomes Christ's mother, whenever she strives to do what is pleasing to the Father: she conceives him in her womb through the power of grace in the faith, she gives him birth through her holy desire, she has him as her child through her good works.[13]

As Marina Warner has pointed out, the importance given to the cult of *Maria Ecclesia* varies over the centuries and seems very much dependent upon fluctuations in the Church's self-image.[14] This is particularly noticeable during the eleventh and twelfth

---

8.   PL 145: 935.
9.   *Advent Sermons*, 2.4, in Bernard of Clairvaux 1957–77, vol. IV: 173.
10. *In Laudibus Virginis Matris*, 3.4, in ibid.: 38.
11. Warner 2000: 18.
12. *Apocalypsim Joannis*, PL 196: 798.
13. Rahner 1961: 79.
14. Warner 2000: 103.

centuries, a period marked by a tendency of the Church to consolidate its power and institutionalize its doctrine. While existing in the Latin West since at least the sixth century, it is in the course of the eleventh and twelfth centuries that depictions of *Maria Ecclesia* as triumphant queen become highly prominent. Crowned, dressed in splendour and often seated on a throne, she represents the power of the Church in general and of the papacy in particular. Her portrayal should not just be understood in an eschatological sense, as a vision of her future supremacy in the New Jerusalem. It expressed her very real aim for contemporary society. As *Ecclesia*, Mary captures the medieval Church's highest aspirations for itself: to be nearest to Christ, to be loved by him above all and to reign supreme, both in this world and in the world to come. In the West, building upon the classical tradition of personifying cities and institutions, she embodies Rome. Further, as a multi-layered figure and magnificent piece of propaganda, she symbolizes the Church as theocracy, with the Papal See as its centre and the Pope as its representative.[15]

Several other developments influenced the association of the Virgin with the Church, one of which is the cult of her assumption. While the notion of her bodily ascension into heaven did not become firmly established until the fourteenth century,[16] the idea of Mary as Queen of Heaven (*Maria Regina*), crowned, radiant and surrounded by angels, was commonly accepted and intertwined itself with the idea of the triumphant Church. Connections have been drawn also between the figure of *Maria Ecclesia* and that of the secular female ruler, acting as queen-regent to her son. From the tenth until the late twelfth centuries we find several queens and empresses who, legitimately and relatively unchallenged, held their own court while their sons were under-age. One such example is Theophano, mother of Otto III, later Emperor of the Holy Roman Empire (d. 1002), who, having become a widow when her son was three years old, ruled in his stead until he came of age. Similarly, among the Norman kingdoms, Roger II's mother Adelaide ruled Sicily before her son ascended the throne in 1130. In other parts of the Norman territories, widows such as Adela of Flanders in Naples and Constance of France in Taranto held court as well at that time. For both the Ottonians and the Norman kings, the Virgin was a special patron. Since Otto III's mother was Greek and since Roger II grew up among oriental, including Greek, courtiers, this particular devotion to Mary could have been partly influenced by the Byzantine concept of the emperor as God's representative on earth, which would draw together the notions of the emperor's mother and the mother of God. One of the most prominent female regents at the end of the twelfth century was Blanche of Castile, mother of future king (and saint) Louis IX. It is under her and her son's rule, and to an extent through their lavish endowments, that the cathedrals of Chartres and Paris display such glorious devotion. One gift of Blanche warrants our attention in particular. It is a rose window of the north transept to Chartres Cathedral proclaiming Mary Queen of Heaven. Both Blanche and her son stood under the cultural influence of Suger, referred to earlier, who has been considered instrumental to the development of the Gothic image as carrier of a theological message. He was

---

15. Ibid.: 103–4.
16. The development of the doctrine of the assumption is discussed in Mayr-Harting 2004.

an adamant devotee of the Virgin Mary and around 1150 he donated to the old church of Notre Dame in Paris a stained-glass window representing the triumph of the Virgin. The window was irretrievably lost during the French Revolution, but it is believed that it showed Mary in heaven, already crowned, seated at the right hand of her son. Émile Mâle argues that Suger's innovative portrayal of the Virgin sparked similar depictions on the portals of other French Gothic cathedrals, such as Senlis, Mantes and Chartres. In thirteenth- and fourteenth-century religious art we see a transition of the theme of the triumphant, crowned Virgin to that of the coronation itself. In these scenes appearing, for example, in England in the glass of Canterbury Cathedral and in Italy on later medieval altarpieces, Mary bows down to receive her crown from Christ or from an angel.[17] Emphasis here lies not so much on the Virgin's glory as on her acceptance and humility.

The borrowing of imagery also worked the other way: not only did the Church clothe itself with secular *regalia*, but secular rulers sought to identify themselves with the King and Queen of Heaven. Warner draws attention to a *Bible moralisée*, a richly illuminated work offering a moralized reading of the Scriptures, commissioned *c.* 1235 by Blanche of Castile. It shows her enthroned on the right side of her son, raising her hands in a pleading (*orans*) gesture identical to that of the Virgin in scenes of the Last Judgement on contemporary portals of French cathedrals. By imitating the Virgin's pose, the illumination presents Blanche as the earthly representative of Mary as Divine Intercessor.[18]

Mary's coronation in heaven and seat on Christ's right side was considered as justified on account of her part played in the redemption of humankind. She had, through her obedience to God at the incarnation and the death of Christ, become the *Mediatrix* of Divine Grace. Because of her son, she had been exalted above all, as the early-twelfth-century Guibert, abbot of Nogent, states, 'There is nothing in heaven that is not subject to the Virgin through her son.'[19] While the term *Mediatrix* in association with Mary crops up as early as the eighth century, it gained widespread acceptance only during the central Middle Ages.[20] Peter Damian calls her 'the gate of Paradise, which restored God to the world and opened heaven to us'.[21] Bernard of Clairvaux describes her in her unique position between the human sphere and the divine as '[the one] through whom we ascend to him who descended through her to us'.[22]

Apart from giving rise to the concept of *Maria Ecclesia*, the scene at the cross as described in the fourth Gospel also became the foundation for the cult of a less triumphant, more human face of Mary. However brief, this passage inspired

---

17.   Mâle 1949: 57, 81; Warner 2000: 105–13.
18.   Warner 2000: 114, plate 15.
19.   *De Virginitate*, 5, PL 156: 585, '*Virgo, cui per Filium nil coeleste non subjectum.*'
20.   Pelikan 1978: 165.
21.   *Carmina sacra et preces*, PL 145: 933: '*Haec Virgo verbo gravida fit paradisi janua, quae Deum mundo reddidit, coelum nobis aperuit*'; trans. Pelikan 1978: 166–7.
22.   *De adventu domini* 2.5, in Bernard of Clairvaux 1957–77, vol. IV: 174: '[. . .] *nos, dilectissimi, ad ipsum per eam ascendere qui per ipsam ad nos descendit*'; trans. Pelikan 1978: 165.

theologians, biblical commentators and artists throughout the medieval period and is powerfully evoked through the connection of this scene with Simeon's prophecy to Mary in Luke 2.35: 'A sword shall pierce through your soul also' (*et tuam ipsius animam pertransiet gladius*). Mary's grief at the sight of her son's crucifixion found its way into poetry, taking the form of passionate and bitter laments.[23] The best-known one, in an acrostic scheme called *kontakion*, was written for Emperor Justinian I (d. 565) for inclusion into the official liturgy for Good Friday.[24] In the West, even though elements of this tradition, such as the Eastern liturgical *Kontakion*, had been trickling in before, it was only during the period of the Crusades that the veneration of Mary as mother of sorrows, or *Mater Dolorosa*, began to flourish. There was a tradition of describing Mary as both lamenting and welcoming her son's death. She lamented him as her son, but welcomed him as Saviour of humankind, including her.[25] However, from the late eleventh until well into the fifteenth centuries, when contacts with the East intensified through both military operations and pilgrimage, we see a growing attention to Mary's experience of sorrow parallel to that of Christ's passion. Devotion to this cult seems to have risen first in Italy and France, spreading to Spain, England and Flanders during the twelfth century.[26]

One of the first to dedicate a series of prayers to the Virgin as grieving mother is Anselm of Canterbury (d. 1109). 'My most merciful Lady,' he exclaims in his second prayer (*Oratio 2*), 'what do I know of the flood that drenched your matchless face, when you beheld your Son? [...] How can I judge what sobs troubled your most pure breast when you heard, "Woman, behold your son." '[27] This more expressive and emotional form of piety, which encouraged identification with the wounded Christ and his grief-stricken mother, infused the works of mystical authors of the time. In the works of Bernard of Clairvaux (d. 1153) and other Cistercians in the twelfth century, and in those of Francis of Assisi (d. 1226) and the Friars in the thirteenth to fifteenth centuries, the humanity of Christ and the reality of his suffering lie at the very heart of Christian faith. Every Christian is encouraged to envisage Christ's wounds, to imagine his pain, and to empathize with those who witness his Passion. As his mother, Mary is seen as the one who feels his pain most overwhelmingly. Bernard states in his sermon on Mary's experience under the cross,

Tuam ergo pertransivit animam vis doloris, ut plus quam martyrem non immerito praedicemus, in qua nimirum corporeae sensum passionis excesserit compassionis effectus.[28]

Therefore, the power of grief pierced through your soul, so that not without merit we call you more than a martyr, since without doubt the effect of compassion exceeded the sensation of corporeal passion.[29]

---

23. Warner 2000: 209.
24. Pelikan 1996: 125–6; Warner 2000: 209.
25. Pelikan 1978: 169.
26. Warner 2000: 209–10.
27. *Oratio 2*, in Anselm of Canterbury 1946–61, vol. III: 8; Anselm of Canterbury 1973: 96.
28. Bernard of Clairvaux, *Dominica infra octavam Assumptionis*, 14, PL 183: 437–8.
29. Trans. Fulton 2002: 425.

Amadeus of Lausanne (d. 1159), one of Bernard's protégés, elaborates on this theme of Mary's spiritual martyrdom and self-effacing empathy with her son:

> *Torquebatur namque magis, quasi torqueretur ex se, quoniam supra se incomparabiliter diligebat id unde dolebat.*[30]

She was more tortured than if she was suffering torture in herself, since she loved infinitely more than herself the source of her grief.[31]

Mary therefore becomes the ideal figure with whom to identify oneself. In order to reach up to Christ and sincerely contemplate his Passion, one should aspire to imitate her in both her love and her pain. In his *Sermons on the Song of Songs* Bernard exhorts his audience to emulate Mary's spiritual martyrdom and confesses that he has often tried in vain:

> *Ego vero me felicem putaverim, si summa saltem quasi cuspide hujus gladii pungi inter me sensero, ut vel modico accepto amoris vulnere, dicat etiam anima mea: Vulnerata charitate ego sum (Cant.II:5). Quis mihi tribuat in hunc modum non modo vulnerari sed et expugnari omnino usque ad exterminationem coloris et caloris illius, qui militat adversus animam?*[32]

I would reckon myself happy if at rare moments I felt at least the prick of the point of that sword. Even if only bearing love's slightest wound, I could still say: 'I am wounded with love' (Song 2.5). How I long not only to be wounded in this manner but to be assailed again and again till the colour and heat of that flesh that wars against the spirit is overcome.[33]

While the Cistercians produced some of the most eloquent and sophisticated evocations of the cult of the *Mater Dolorosa*, its popular dissemination was to a large extent instigated by the Franciscan movement. In order to reach the poorest who, ignorant of Latin and often overlooked by the clergy, had had little access to the gospel before, Francis and his followers preached in public, using simple language and imagery. Deeply influenced by this new form of intensified, affective piety, the cult reached its peak during the fourteenth and fifteenth centuries. In that period we see the growing popularity of Passion plays, which centre not just on the death and resurrection of Christ, but also give dramatic expression to the feelings of anguish and suffering of the Passion's protagonists.

Pilgrims returning from the Holy Land brought back accounts of the *Via Dolorosa* in Jerusalem, the path Jesus himself was believed to have trodden on his way to Calvary. This spurred Franciscans to develop the so-called Stations of the Cross, a

---

30. *Homilia V: De mentis robore seu martyrio beatissimae virginis*, PL 188: 1328.
31. Amadeus of Lausanne 1979: 39–47; see also Fulton 2002: 304.
32. *Sermones super cantica canticorum*, sermon 29.8, in Bernard of Clairvaux 1957–77, vol. I: 208–9.
33. Bernard of Clairvaux 1976, vol. 3: 110; see also Fulton 2002: 305.

cycle of various stages of the Passion, usually established in churches; these Stations, inviting the onlooker to meditate upon and empathize with Christ's suffering and death, formed in effect a small-scale popular equivalent to foreign pilgrimage.[34] The tradition of Passion plays and Stations of the Cross in turn inspired – and were possibly inspired by – Passion sermons, which centred on both the bodily agony of Christ and the emotional martyrdom of those who witnessed him die.

The thirteenth to fifteenth centuries saw the composition of numerous hymns and poems, many in the vernacular, which focused on the suffering of Christ and Mary, and on their almost symbiotic relationship. An anonymous mid-fourteenth-century English lyric describes Mary's wish to share her son's pain:

> *Why have ye no reuthe on my child?*
> *Have reuthe on me, full of murning.*
> *Taket down on Rode my derworthy child*
> *Or prek me on Rode with my derling*
>
> *More pine ne may me bendon*
> *Than laten me liven in sorwe and shame.*
> *Als love me bindet to my sone*
> *So lat us deiyen bothen isame.*[35]

> Why do you not have any pity on my child?
> Have pity on me, full of mourning.
> Take my precious child down from the Cross,
> Or impale me on the Cross together with my darling.
>
> I could not have been subjected to a bigger torment
> Than being left to live in sorrow and in shame.
> Since love binds me with my son,
> Let us die both together.[36]

Another, slightly earlier lyric takes the form of a dramatic dialogue between mother and son, in which Jesus attempts to comfort a grieving Mary by pointing out the ultimate purpose of his suffering. The first two couplets run:

> *'Stond well, moder, under Rode.*
> *Behold thy sone with glade mode–*
> *Blithe moder might thou be.'*
> *'Sone, how shulde I blithe stonde?*
> *I se thine fet, I se thine honed*
> *Nailed to the harde Tre.'*

---

34. Ellington 2001: 80–2; Sticca 1988: 11–15; Warner 2000: 210–11.
35. Davies (ed.) 1963: 119.
36. Trans. Geert De Wilde.

'Moder, do wey thy wepinge.
I thole deth for monkinde-
For my gult thole I non.'
'Sone, I fele the dedestounde:
The swerd is at mine herte grounde,
That me bihet Simeon.'[37]

'Mother, stand composedly under the Cross.
Look at your son with a joyful heart –
You should be a delighted mother.'
'Son, how should I stand up and be delighted?
I see your feet, I see your hands
Nailed to the hard tree.'

'Mother, stop your weeping.
I suffer death for mankind –
It is not for my own sins that I suffer.'
'Son, I feel the moment of death [approaching]:
The sword is sharpened against my heart,
That Simeon promised me.'[38]

The dialogue continues with Jesus emphasizing Mary's double state as a 'pure virgin' (*clene maiden-mon*), who nevertheless, being a mother herself, should understand a mother's grief (*rew of moder care, for now thou wost of moder fare*). That this should move Mary to have mercy on all sinners is suggested by the further affirmation of her status as intercessor for all those in need, be they 'virgin, wife or prostitute' (*Sone, help at alle need / Alle tho that to me grede, / Maiden, wif and fol wimmon*).

Mary's historical function as *Mediatrix* by virtue of being Christ's mother transforms itself here into a spiritual role as *Intercessor* between God and humankind. Increasingly from the twelfth century onwards, she appears as merciful advocate of her faithful, but sinful, devotees. Saints' lives, folktales and miracle stories frequently show her untiring willingness to plead the cause of lapsed human beings before her son. One of the most popular medieval tales is that of Theophilus ('lover of God'), the central theme of which resurfaces throughout Western literature and has formed the inspiration for the figure of Dr Faustus. Theophilus, allegedly a historical figure, served as treasurer and archdeacon to the Bishop of Ardana, Asia Minor, and died around 538. As the story goes, after the death of his patron Theophilus is elected as his successor. Feeling too humble, he declines the offer. A different candidate is chosen, who, having accepted the post, promptly dismisses the former treasurer. Angry and envious, Theophilus engages the skills of a Jewish necromancer and signs away his soul to the devil, in exchange for wealth and success. Proof of this pact is a

37. Davies (ed.) 1963: 86–8.
38. Trans. Geert De Wilde.

deed, written in Theophilus's own blood. Being still a man of conscience, however, worldly riches fail to bring him any happiness. He begs the devil to reverse the bargain, but to no avail. One day, falling asleep while praying to the Virgin, he dreams that she appears to him and hands him back his deed. She explains to him that she herself has forcibly retrieved it from the devil and that he is pardoned. He wakes up to find his dream come true, and dies in peace shortly afterwards.[39]

This story circulated in the West in Latin translation from the late eighth century onwards, was two centuries later adapted in verse form by Hroswitha of Gandersheim (d. 975), and in the eleventh century became included in the office of Our Lady in France. In the twelfth century we find it visualized in the portal of the abbey church of Souillac, a century later it is the subject of stained-glass windows, illuminated manuscripts, paintings and Books of Hours.[40] Other stories describe how Mary helps runaway nuns by taking their place in the cloister, so they would not be missed, pardons fornicating monks, and rescues thieves and liars who seek refuge in the *Ave Maria*.[41] More than those of every other saint, the miracles of the Virgin dominated monastic as well as lay piety throughout medieval Europe. As Benedicta Ward has argued, two factors underlie the universal and unlocalized devotion to Mary. First, as the mother of Christ and divine Intercessor, her claim to sanctity was well established and did not need additional miracles to be proven. Second, she was increasingly believed to be assumed into heaven, leaving behind only secondary relics, such as breast milk and clothing; therefore her miracles did not predominantly occur around shrines of her relics, as was the case with most other saints.[42]

The Virgin's ability and readiness to take pity upon the lowest of sinners springs forth from her own experience of immense suffering. The mystic Bridget of Sweden (d. 1373) calls Mary 'the most afflicted of all mothers' because of her foreknowledge of Christ's Passion. Therefore the sword that pierces through her heart at the same time causes her mercy to flow.[43] One of the most widely read works of that period was Ludulphus of Saxony's *Mirror of Human Salvation* (*Speculum humanae salvationis*), composed in 1324 at Strasbourg. Ludulphus dedicates a whole chapter to Mary's lament alone. It was common for copies of this work to include miniature Marian offices for the seven sorrows or 'swords'.[44]

The cult of Mary as *Mater Dolorosa*, who shared her son's torments and grieved over his death, also seems to have resonated with communities which had been particularly affected by the Black Death epidemic of 1347–50. In Germany, where some areas lost more than half of their population to the epidemic, her cult seems to have taken on a particularly morbid form. Left to us are countless images and statues of Mary displaying 'unfettered goriness and anguish'.[45] Flagellants also included

39. Warner 2000: 323.
40. Mâle 1902: 297–300.
41. One example of a late medieval collection is Johannes Herolt Discipulus, *Miracles of the Blessed Virgin Mary* (trans. 1928).
42. Ward 1982: 132–3.
43. Warner 2000: 216.
44. Sticca 1988: 62.
45. Mackay with Ditchburn (eds) 1997: 209–10; Warner 2000: 217.

prayers to the Virgin at the beginning and the end of their processions. During flagellations they would sing of the sufferings of Christ and Mary.[46]

Various religious orders and confraternities were drawn towards the human aspect of Mary and dedicated themselves to the contemplation of her 'sorrows'. These sorrows, which varied in number between five and fifteen, were eventually fixed at seven: the prophecy of Simeon, the flight into Egypt, the loss of Jesus in the Temple, Mary's meeting with her son on the road to Calvary, the crucifixion, the deposition of the body, and the entombment. The Order of the Servites, originating in mid-thirteenth-century Florence, believed that the Virgin had revealed her seven sorrows to their seven founder saints. In Flanders at the end of the fifteenth century we see the first confraternity dedicated to the Sorrows: the Confrérie de Notre Dame de Sept-Douleurs. The cult was ratified in 1423, when Thierry de Meurs, Archbishop of Cologne, introduced a Feast of Our Lady of Sorrows, which eventually received a fixed date of 15 September. As an art form, the Pietà became popular during this period.[47]

Towards the end of the medieval period the tide of Marian devotion seems to turn away somewhat from this portrayal of a mother lamenting her son. Before the thirteenth century some theologians portrayed Mary as a stoic figure who willingly and tearlessly carried out the will of God.[48] In the fifteenth century the question rises again whether Mary, elevated as she is above all women, and knowing that her son would rise from the dead, would be given to such sorrow and tears. Indignant that some harbour such doubts, Bernardino of Busti, an Italian Franciscan, composed a collection of sermons dedicated to Mary in which he provides a strong set of arguments in favour of the image of a human, suffering Virgin who is an example to us all:

> *Tunc menti virginee nulla ratio occurrebat de filio nisi in ratione amaritudinis et transfigentis doloris* [. . .] *ideo ipsa est speculum et exemplum* [. . .] *omnium lamentantium mortem Christi, et archa et armarium dolorum corporis boni Yesu.*[49]

Then no thought concerning her son occurred to her virginal mind unless transfixed by bitterness and grief [. . .] She is therefore a mirror and example of all those lamenting the death of Christ and she is the ark and chest of the bodily sorrows of the good Jesus.[50]

---

46. Leff 1967, vol. II: 486–7; Ellington 2001: 80–1, n. 13.
47. Ellington 2001: 80; Warner 2000: 217–18.
48. Ambrose of Milan, *De obitu Valentiniani consolation*, PL 16: 1371: '*Durum quidem funus videtis; sed stabat et sancta Maria iuxta crucem Filii, et spectabat Virgo sui unigeniti passionem. Stantem illam lego, flentem non lego*'; see also Ambrose, *De institutione virginis liber unus*, PL 16: 318: '*Stabat ante crucem mater, et fugientibus viris, stabat intrepida. Videte utrum pudorem mutare potuerit mater Jesu, quae animum non mutavit. Spectaculo piis oculis filii vulnera, per quem sciebat omnibus futuram redemptionem. Stabat non degeneri mater spectaculo, quae non metuebat peremptorem*'; in the same vein, see Richard of St Victor, *De differentia sacrificii Abrahae a sacrificio Beatae Mariae Virginis*, PL 196: 1047–8; Arnauld Bonnaevallis, *Tractatus tertius de vii verbis Domini in cruce*, PL 189: 1693–4; Ellington 2001: 81.
49. Bernardino of Busti (1493) *Mariale*, Milan: Leonardus Pachel, quoted in Ellington 2001: 82.
50. Trans. in ibid.: 82.

Apart from the (relatively scarce) New Testament tradition, there are two other sets of sources on which medieval Christians drew in their contemplation of the Virgin: the Apocrypha and the Song of Songs. With its sensuous language and powerful erotic imagery, the Song of Songs came to be seen as the perfect allegory of Mary's relationship with Christ; on a different level the Apocrypha gave much-desired factual information on Mary's life and death.

Literally meaning 'secret' or 'hidden' books, the Apocrypha are writings relating to the New Testament but not included in the canon. They fill in what were perceived as gaps in the existing narratives, interweaving the accounts of the canonical infancy gospels with Old Testament material and Jewish lore. Surfacing in Asia Minor, Egypt and Syria in the second century, the apocryphal tradition on Mary contains elaborations on her birth, childhood, death and assumption. While not officially endorsed, many of these apocryphal stories were used with great enthusiasm in medieval art and literature, and played a crucial role in the doctrinal and liturgical development of the notions of her immaculate conception, perpetual virginity and corporal assumption into heaven or paradise.[51] Significantly, in the Western tradition the trend of the apocryphal texts goes towards a greater degree of conformity. Underlying this trend is a process through which successive versions either suppressed or satisfactorily explained the more theologically problematic elements of previous texts. Apocryphal narratives became therefore increasingly absorbed into mainstream Christian thought.[52]

The oldest apocryphal account, and the one on which much of the medieval Latin tradition is based, is known as the *Protevangelium of James* (*Protevangelium Iacobi*). It describes Mary explicitly as of Davidic descent, and in some of the oldest manuscripts suggests that she was conceived in the absence of her father. The work further narrates that she was brought up in the Temple and paid great attention to her purity and virginity before, during and after the birth, culminating in the episode of Salome, the woman whose hand withered when she dared to test Mary's virginity *post partum*. It straightens out the question of the four siblings of Jesus, mentioned in Mark 6.3, by explaining them as Joseph's children by his deceased first wife. The idea of Mary as second Eve, who reverses the sins of the first, also appears here.[53]

Latin extracts of the *Protevangelium* were present in the West from the fifth or sixth centuries onwards. Its most substantial translation seems to date from the Carolingian period and fragments and adaptations of it are extant in several French and German manuscripts of the thirteenth to fifteenth centuries.[54]

However, much more influential than any of these translations was a new text, titled the *Gospel according to Pseudo-Matthew* or, in some of the earliest manuscripts, *On the Birth of Saint Mary* (*De nativitate sanctae Mariae*). Attributed to Jerome but in fact composed between 550 and 700 in a monastic environment, it intertwines material from the *Protevangelium* with that of other accounts on the Virgin. It is clear that the

---

51. For further discussion, see Clayton 1998: 6–18; Elliott (ed.) 1993; Warner 2000: 25–33.
52. Clayton 1998: 99–100.
53. Ibid.: 15.
54. Ibid.: 16–18; Elliott (ed.) 1993: 51–67.

monastic ideal of chastity, humility and piety takes up a central place in the work. It contains, for example, the first explicit description of Mary taking a voluntary vow of virginity. While the idea of her taking such a vow already existed in patristic literature, notably in the West in Augustinian thought, it was not present in the *Protevangelium*. In *Pseudo-Matthew* Mary discovers for herself a new order (*novus ordo*) of virginity. Her adolescence spent in the Temple becomes an example for religious women: she leads a cloistered existence, and her time is regulated in such a way as to reflect the daily division between work and prayer of monastic rule:

> *Hanc autem sibi ipsa regulam statuerat ut a mane usque ad horam tertiam orationibus insisteret, a tertia uero usque ad nonam textrino se in opere occupabat. A nona uero hora iterum ab oratione non recedebat, usque dum illi dei angelus appareret de cuius manu escam acciperet, et ita melius atque melius in dei timore proficiebat.*[55]

She had set out for herself the following rule: from early morning until the third hour she would dedicate herself to prayer; but from the third until the ninth hour she would occupy herself with weaving. From the ninth hour she would again not withdraw from prayer until the angel of God appeared to her. From his hand she would receive food, and so she progressed more and more in her awe for God.

Even later on when married to Joseph, she remains surrounded by five virgins, as if following a quasi-monastic communal lifestyle. She is also described as possessing miraculous healing powers and an extraordinary knowledge of divine law.[56] Thus aspects previously the prerogative of Christ and the Old Testament prophets only are attributed to her as well.

In the tenth or very early eleventh century the early chapters of *Pseudo-Matthew* were further revised or, as Mary Clayton calls it, 'sanitized', into the *On the Birth of Mary* (*De nativitate Mariae*) to bring them more into line with Jerome's views. One major change to this version is that Joseph is said to be an unmarried man, and not a widower. This conforms to Jerome's belief that the 'brothers of Jesus' in the Gospels are not to be explained as Jesus' stepbrothers, but rather as his cousins. As the period of composition of this work is also marked by a growing concern about clerical marriage and concubinage, one of its purposes might have been to present a narrative propagating the ideal of male chastity.[57]

Since there is no mention in the New Testament of Mary maintaining her virginal state during or after the birth of Christ, the translations and adaptations of the *Protevangelium of James* were crucial in consolidating the notion of Mary as *Perpetual Virgin*. It ingrained into medieval consciousness vivid scenes, such as Mary's personal vow of virginity, or the miracle of Salome's withered hand. On a second level, it

---

55.   Clayton 1998: 20.
56.   Warner 2000: 30–1; Clayton 1998: 18–21.
57.   Clayton 1998: 20–3. Irenaeus, *Adversus Haereses* V.19.1, PG 7: 1175–6; see also Newman 1987: 167.

fostered the rise of the cult of the Virgin in general, for through these narratives, which supported or elaborated upon the canonical accounts, or which explained 'what happened before', some attention is diverted from Christ to Mary. While it is impossible to see Mary as separate from Christ and from the purpose of his death and resurrection, the tradition sprouting from the *Protevangelium* has been instrumental to the development of the cult of Mary as Perpetual Virgin and, to some extent, as immaculately conceived. Theologians and poets of the central and later Middle Ages exulted over Mary's miraculous status as Virgin-Mother, or, as Bernard of Clairvaux calls it, 'fertile virgin, chaste child-bearer, untouched mother' (*Virgo fecunda, casta Puerpera, Mater intacta*).[58] The miracle of the Virgin Birth was a recurring theme of contention in medieval Jewish–Christian polemic. An anonymous *Dialogue between a Christian and a Jew* dating from the early twelfth century expresses the Jewish dismissal of the miracle as follows:

> *Dic mihi quomodo contra naturam parere potuit, quae, sicut ipse dicis, auctorem naturae generavit: non enim usitatum imo contra naturam est, quod sine virili semine de Maria filius natus est, et si virgo concepit et peperit, illud tamen quod vos additis, propheta non addidit, id est, post partum virgo permansit.*[59]

Tell me, how could she of whom you say that she is the mother of the author of nature, give birth in a way that is contrary to the laws of nature, for it is not common, no, rather contrary to nature that a son was born to Mary without the seed of a man. But, even if she as virgin conceived and gave birth, the prophet (Isaiah) never added what you add, that is, that she would remain a virgin after giving birth.[60]

Many of these polemical texts, including the one containing the passage above, were dialectical exercises written by Christian authors. The arguments of the Jew, brought on stage to defend his own religion and attack Christianity, only to admit defeat in the end, served to pre-empt possible Christian doubts on central matters of faith and to consolidate Christian doctrine.

As a perpetual virgin, Mary was the guiding light for advocates of clerical celibacy. Peter Damian states in his treatise on the subject (*Opusculum contra intemperantes clericos*):

> *Nam quia Dominicum corpus in virginalis uteri templo coaluit, nunc etiam ministris sui continentis pudicitiae munditiam quaerit.*[61]

Because the Lord's body grew together in the temple of the Virgin's womb, he now requires of his ministers the purity of sexual continence.[62]

---

58. *De laudibus Virginis Matris*, 3.8, in Bernard of Clairvaux 1957–77, vol IV: 198; Pelikan 1978: 163.
59. Anonymous, *Dialogue between a Christian and a Jew*, PL 163: 1054.
60. Translation partly based upon Abulafia 1989: 105–25, 114–15.
61. PL 145: 388.
62. Trans. Pelikan 1978: 163–4.

Indirectly, Hildegard of Bingen seems to give her nuns the same message in one of her songs. This responsory, consisting of a respond, verse and partial respond, and probably meant to be performed at Matins (early morning), glorifies the mother of God's perpetual virginity:

R.: *O quam preciosa est*
Virginitas virginis huius
Que clausam portam habet,
Et cuius viscera sancta divinitas
Calore suo infudit
Ita quod flos in ea crevit
Et Filius Dei per secreta ipsius
Quasi aurora exivit.

V.: *Und dulce germen*
Quod Filius ipsius est,
Per clausuram ventris eius
Paradisum aperuit.
R.: *Et Filius Dei per secreta ipsius*
Quasi aurora exivit.[63]

R.: How precious is
The maidenhood of this Virgin,
She of the shut door
Whose womb the holy Godhead
Filled with His fire
So that a flower bloomed in her
And the Son of God From that secret place
Went forth like the dawn.

V.: Thus the sweet seed,
who was that Son,
Through the shut door of her womb
Unlocked paradise.
R.: And the Son of God From that secret place
Went forth like the dawn.[64]

Images such as 'the shut door' (Song 8.9) and the portrayal of the Virgin's womb as an enclosed garden (Song 4.12), and of her son as a flower blooming in it, were traditional and referred to Mary's unique role in the divine plan. On a tropological (moral) level, Mary in her virginal state would have served as an example for the nuns

---

63.   *Symphonia*, responsory 63, in Newman 1987: 276.
64.   Trans. Flanagan 1989: 114.

to imitate.[65] In another passage Hildegard describes the virgin birth in detail, in an interesting parallel to the creation of Eve:

> When the blessed Virgin was a little weakened, as if drowsy with sleep, the infant came forth from her side – not from the opening of the womb – without her knowledge and without pain, corruption, or filth, just as Eve emerged from the side of Adam. He did not enter through the vagina, for if he had come out that way there would have been corruption; but since the mother was intact in that place, the infant did not emerge there. And no placenta covered the infant in the Virgin Mother's womb, in the manner of other infants, because he was not conceived from virile seed.[66]

The birth of Christ in Hildegard's vision is as far removed from a natural birth as possible. Exempt from the curse of Eve after the fall, Mary does not suffer painful labour, but only feels 'a little weakened'; there is no afterbirth. The miracle of Mary's intact virginity during and after the birth receives its own partially logical explanation, as the child emerges from her side. The comparison with Eve's 'birth' out of Adam's side draws attention to God's role as direct *auctor* of both events. Instead of presenting Christ as the New Adam and the Virgin as the New Eve, the vision forms an unusual correlation between Adam and Mary on the one hand, and Eve and Christ on the other.

While the transmission of the apocryphal tradition on Mary's birth and childhood is relatively straightforward, the texts relating to her death and assumption pose greater problems. These texts, also called *Dormition*, *Obsequies* or *Transitus* narratives, find their origins in largely Greek and/or Syriac sources. They affirm the belief that Mary's body and soul ascended to paradise. While the Greek and Syriac sources in general add an apocalypse element to the assumption narrative, the Latin tradition does not.

The most streamlined and probably most influential of Latin *Transitus* texts is the *Transitus of Pseudo-Melito*. The work has come down to us in two versions which differ in many (often minor) details. The original is generally assumed to have been composed in the same period as the *Gospel of Pseudo-Matthew* and might even have served as a basis for it. The number of manuscripts we possess of this particular *Transitus* shows that it must have been relatively well known and popular from the eighth till the fifteenth century. Its importance lies in its tightness of style and structure. By smoothing out or suppressing theological ambiguities of earlier sources, the *Pseudo-Melito* arrives at presenting a clear, focused account of Mary's assumption.[67] It is the apocryphon which gives most weight to her corporal assumption both in its actual description and in its attention paid to the theological necessity for it. For, prior to the assumption itself, Christ asks the apostles what to do with Mary's body:

---

65. See also Flanagan's discussion, ibid.: 114–15.
66. *Fragment* IV.7, ed. Schipperges 1956: 68, quoted from Newman 1987: 176.
67. Clayton 1998: 99–100; for a fuller discussion of the Latin tradition, see 66–100.

Then the Saviour spoke to them, saying, 'Before I ascended to my Father I gave you a promise, saying that you who have followed me, in the regeneration when the Son of man shall sit on the throne of his majesty, you also shall sit on twelve thrones, judging the twelve tribes of Israel. Now this woman I chose out of the twelve tribes of Israel by the commandment of my Father, to dwell in her. What then do you wish me to do to her?'

The apostles reply:

'Lord, you chose this your handmaid to become your immaculate chamber, and us your servants for your ministry. All things you foreknew before the worlds with your Father, with whom to you and the Holy Ghost there belong equal Godhead and infinite power. If therefore the power of your grace can bring this about, it has happened right to us your servants that, as you having overcome death reign in glory, so you should raise up the body of your mother and take her with you rejoicing into heaven.'
Then the Saviour said: 'Be it done according to your will.'

Christ then commands the archangel Michael to bring Mary's soul and after the stone of her grave has been rolled away, he addresses her:

'Rise up, my love and my kinswoman: you who did not suffer corruption by union of the flesh shall not suffer dissolution of the body in the sepulchre.'[68]

Angels then bear Mary's reunited body and soul into paradise, which in this context is probably synonymous with heaven, Christ's destination after his mother's assumption.[69] By having the apostles pronounce the arguments for her bodily assumption, the *Pseudo-Melito* emphasizes that the assumption of Mary is part of the apostolic faith.

While throughout the medieval period we encounter theological discomfort with these non-canonical narratives, they nevertheless became absorbed into mainstream religious thought. Since through Mary, and through her alone, divinity has become incarnate, the state of purity of her body and soul were of great religious concern. By emphasizing her bodily purity and portraying her as untouched by worldly desires, the apocryphal narratives respond to a real preoccupation with issues relating to the divinity of Christ. We find references to the apocryphal stories in the liturgy in the West from the seventh century and images of the *Transitus* narrative, possibly imported from Eastern exemplars, from *c.* 872.[70]

In the late tenth century the nun Hroswitha of Gandersheim, who was a playwright and poet, composed the first Latin verse narrative of Joachim and Anna and the birth of Mary. She admits in her introduction that she had started on her

---

68.   Elliott (ed.) 1993: 713–14; Tischendorf (ed.) 1866: 124–36, version B1.
69.   Clayton 1998: 94.
70.   Ibid.: 106–7.

work not knowing that the authenticity of her material had been questioned; nevertheless, this discovery did not change her mind and she continued to draw extensively upon the apocryphal tradition in her poems.[71] Around the same time, the Anglo-Saxon monk Ælfric warned against the 'heretical content' of *Transitus* narratives in his Catholic homilies. However, he seems to be the only Anglo-Saxon vernacular witness opposing the apocrypha and we have little evidence that his warnings achieved anything. We have evidence of knowledge of the apocryphal tradition from the ninth century onwards. Vernacular translations and adaptations of the birth and *Transitus* narratives circulated in Anglo-Saxon England from at least the late tenth century onwards.[72] One of the reasons why, in spite of opposition from some corners, the narratives were so readily absorbed into medieval religious culture may be that they were considered to be hagiographical rather than apocryphal.[73] This may explain why accounts of the birth, purification and bodily assumption of the Virgin are also included in a highly popular collection of Saints' Lives, titled *The Golden Legend* (*Legenda Aurea*) and composed *c.* 1260 by the Dominican friar Jacobus de Voragine (d. 1298). This work became one of the most widely read in the later Middle Ages and was translated into every Western European language.[74]

The transmission of the apocrypha on Mary in written and visual form has greatly nurtured, and has been nurtured by, the cult of the Virgin, encouraging belief in and the celebration of her immaculate conception and assumption. The conception of Mary was celebrated as a feast in the West as early as the ninth century. It was instituted in Winchester, which was a centre of Marian devotion, in 1030. Yet theologians such as Anselm of Canterbury in the eleventh and Bernard of Clairvaux in the twelfth century rejected the idea of her conception as being free of sin. Anselm writes in his theological treatise *Cur Deus homo?* (*Why did God become man?*):

> *Virgo tamen ipsa* [. . .] *est in iniquitatibus concepta, et in peccatis concepit eam mater ejus, et cum originali peccato nata est.*[75]

The virgin herself [. . .] was conceived in iniquity and in sin did her mother conceive her and with original sin was she born.

Others disagree, among them Anselm's nephew, Eadmer, and another English theologian, Osbert of Clare (fl. 1137). They advocated enthusiastically the Feast of the Conception on 8 December and argued that as John the Baptist leapt in his mother's womb when Mary came to visit, this was a sure sign he had been freed from the burden of sin by her pure presence. Mary, Eadmer argues, was born without sin, not because it was necessary but because it was fitting (*quia decebat*).[76]

---

71. See Hroswitha of Gandersheim 1923: xxxii–iii.
72. Clayton 1998: 110–16.
73. Mimouni 1993: 128; see also Clayton 1998: 1.
74. Introduction to de Voragine 1993, vol. I: xiii–xiv.
75. PL 158: 416.
76. Eadmer, *De conceptione beatae Mariae virginis*, PL 159: 303.

From England the cult spread to France and from there to Italy, where by the end of the twelfth century a few monasteries and towns celebrated the Feast of the Immaculate Conception. It was not before the second half of the thirteenth century, however, that Rome celebrated Mass for her on that day. The Italian theologian Peter Lombard (d. 1164) developed a compromise on the matter: as a human being Mary was conceived in sin, but as mother of God she was not. A century later, Thomas Aquinas (d. 1274) partly agreed with this, but pointed out that she could not have been free from original sin at her conception as no one could have been redeemed before redemption. The great sacrifice of the cross, he argued, would be diminished if it were superfluous in the case of Mary. Dominicans followed Thomas in this doctrine, but the Franciscans endorsed the immaculate conception. Duns Scotus (d. 1308) at the end of the thirteenth century turned around Thomas's argument, instead claiming that the Virgin's immaculate conception did not belittle the sacrifice on the cross, but rather enhanced it, as prevention is better than cure. She was *prevented* from sin *before*, but only really *saved* at the redemption.[77]

Mary's roles as Mother of God, Perpetual Virgin and Intercessor bring her into linear opposition to that other pivotal figure in the divine plan, Eve. Just as Christ is the New Adam, Mary is the New Eve. Where Adam and Eve caused the fall of humankind, Christ and Mary represent restoration. As *Second Eve* Mary is chaste while Eve is not; she brings eternal life while Eve brings sin and sorrow.[78] This reversal is seen to be symbolized in the angel Gabriel's greeting of her at the Annunciation with *Ave*, or *Eva* back to front. Hildegard of Bingen expresses this notion in one of her *Symphonia* (no. 13):

> *1a O virga ac diadema*
> *Purpure regis,*
> *Que es in clausura tua*
> *Sicut lorica.*
> *1b Tu frondens floruisti*
> *In alia vicissitudine*
> *Quam Adam omne genus humanum*
> *Produceret.*
>
> *2a Ave ave, de tuo ventre*
> *Alia vita processit*
> *Qua Adam filios suos*
> *Denudaverat*
> *2b O flos, tu non germinasti de rore,*
> *Nec de guttis pluvie*
> *Nec aer desuper te volavit,*

---

77. Warner 2000: 241–2.
78. For patristic precedent, see Ambrose, *In Lucam* IV.7, in Ambrose ed. Adriaen 1957: 108; Irenaeus, *Adversus Haereses* V.19.1, PG 7: 1175–6; for a more detailed overview, see Newman 1987: 167; Warner 2000: 50–67.

Sed divina claritas
In nobilissima virga te produxit.

3a O virga, floriditatem tuam
Deus in prima die creature sue
Previderat.
3b Et de verbo suo quream materiam,
O laudabilis virgo,
Fecit

4a O quam magnum est in viribus suis
Latus viri de quo Deus
Formam mulieris produxit,
Quam fecit speculum
Omnis ornamenti sui
Et amplexionem omnis creature sue.
4b Inde concinunt celestia organa
Et miratur omnis terra,
O laudabilis Maria,
Quia Deus te valde amavit.

5a [O] quam valde plangendum
Et lugendum est
Quod tristicia in crimine
Per consilium serpentis
In mulierem fluxit.
5b Nam ipsa mulier,
Quam Deus matrem omnium posuit,
Viscera sua cum vulneribus ignorantie
Decerpsit,
Et plenum dolorem gneri suo protulit.

6a Sed, o aurora,
De ventre tuo novus sol processit
Qui omnia criminal Eve abstersit
Et maiorem benedictionem
Per te protulit
Quam Eva hominibus nocuisset.
6b Unde, o salvatrix,
Que novum lumen
Humano generi protulisti,
Collige membra filii tui
Ad celestem armoniam.

1a O rod and diadem of royal purple,
You are like a breastplate unbroached.
1b Your branching flowered in contradiction
To the way Adam brought forth all mankind.

2a Hail! Hail! From your womb
A different life came forth
From the life that Adam denied his sons.
2b O flower, you were not budded by the dew
Nor drops of rain, nor the circumambient air,
But divine light brought you out
From this most noble stem.

3a O stem, your flowering
God foresaw on the first day of his creation.
3b and from his Word made you the golden matter,
O praiseworthy virgin.

4a O great is the strength of man's side,
From which God took the form of woman,
And made her the mirror of all adornments,
The clasp of his entire creation.
4b Then the celestial harmony sounded
And all earth marvelled,
O praiseworthy Mary,
Because God loved you so.

5a O plangent and doleful it is
That sadness and crime at the serpent's word
Flowed into a woman.
5b For that woman, whom God placed as mother of all,
Ruined her womb with the wounds of ignorance
And brought great sorrow on her children.

6a Yet, O dawn, from your womb
A new sun came forth, who cleaned away all Eve's sin
And through you brought a greater blessing
To mankind than all Eve's harm
6b Whence O saving lady, who brought a new light
To human kind
Unite the members of your Son
In celestial harmony.[79]

---

79. Hildegard of Bingen 1983: 27; trans. Flanagan 1989: 121–3.

Since Paul had called the Church the Bride of Christ (Eph. 5), Mary's identity as type of the Church also associated her with the image of Christ's *Bride*. The biblical book which most closely expressed Mary's feelings of love and longing for her son, the heavenly Bridegroom, was the Song of Songs. Although the Marian reading of the Song dates from patristic times, it is in the twelfth century that it comes to be interpreted as an expression of the *historical* relationship between Mary and Christ. This new mode of exegesis of the Song, Fulton argues, does not have a patristic precedent. It did not result directly from previous allegorical and tropological interpretations of the Song's Bride as a type of either the Church or the soul. Instead, it developed out of the liturgies of the Assumption and the Nativity of the Virgin, emerging in the seventh to ninth centuries. The 'historical' reading of the Song as relating to Mary's life and death is therefore indirectly influenced by apocryphal narratives.[80]

Rupert of Deutz (d. 1129) was the first exegete to consider the Song exclusively as such; later followed the commentaries of, among others, Philip of Harvengt (d. 1183), Alan of Lille (d. 1202) and Alexander Neckam (d. 1217), and the *Sermons on the Song of Songs* by Bernard of Clairvaux. As Ann Astell observes, this type of Marian exposition of the Song encompasses two histories: that of Mary's life according to the Gospels, and that of the content of the Song itself. For monastic and secular clergy at the time, the reading of Scripture and biblical commentary (*lectio divina*) was far more than passively absorbing its content; it constituted an act of devotion.[81] Here, the readers or auditors are invited to imagine and participate in Mary's experience and to 'become her extended self'.[82] For example, Rupert of Deutz associates 'My beloved is for me a bundle of myrrh; he will dwell between my breasts' (Song 1.13) with the joy and grief of Mary when nursing her son:

> *Prophetissa namque eram et ex quo mater ejus facta sum, scivi eum ista passurum. Cum igitur carne mea taliter progenitum, talem filium sino meo foverem, ulnis gestarem, uberibus lactarem, et talem ejus futuram mortem semper prae oculis haberem, et prophetica, imo plusquam prophetica mente praeviderem, qualem, quantam, quam prolixam me putatis materni doloris pertulisse passionem? Hoc est quod dico: 'Fasciculus myrrhae dilectus meus mihi, inter ubera mea commorabitur.' O commoratio, dulcis quidem, sed plena gemitibus inenarrabilibus!*[83]

For I was a prophetess, and because I was his mother, I knew he was going to suffer these things. When, therefore, I fondled such a Son, born of my flesh, at my bosom, carried him in my arms, nursed him at my breasts, and had always before my eyes such a death as was destined for him, and foresaw everything with a prophetic, nay more than a prophetic, mind, what kind of passion of maternal grief, how much and how extensive, do you imagine me to have

---

80. Fulton 1996: 86; see also Leclercq 1979: 37–8.
81. Leclercq 1961: 87–109.
82. Astell 1990: 45.
83. *In Cantica Canticorum*, PL 168: 856.

endured? This is what I mean when I say: 'My Beloved is for me a bundle of myrrh; he will dwell between my breasts.' O sojourn, sweet indeed, but filled with inutterable groanings![84]

The first verse of the Song, 'Let him kiss me with the kisses of his mouth', is read as relating to the Annunciation in Alan of Lille's *Elucidation on the Song of Songs*:

> *Gloriosa igitur Virgo sponsi optans praesentiam, desiderans gloriosam conceptionem ad angelo nuntiatam, affectans divinam Incarnationem, ait sic: 'Osculetur me osculo oris sui.'*[85]

The glorious Virgin, therefore, hoping for the presence of the bridegroom, desiring the glorious conception announced by the angel, eagerly wishing for the divine Incarnation, speaks thus: *Let him kiss me with the kiss of his mouth.*[86]

Mary, as Bride thirsting for, and rejoicing and grieving over, her son, embodies several of the roles previously discussed in this chapter: she is at different stages Perpetual Virgin, Divine Intercessor and *Mater Dolorosa*. She is not the quiet, or even mute, character of the Gospels; through the Song, she acquires a voice. As Fulton states, 'the "historical" Marian interpretation of the Song gave the commentators access to her most closely guarded secret: the tender reality of her physical and emotional relationship with Christ. Through the Song, Mary opens her heart and describes her beloved.' This new mode of reading the Song of Songs responded to a need for greater proximity to Mary and Christ and more intimate knowledge about their relationship than was offered by the Gospels. While the apocryphal narratives fulfilled part of that need, the Song had the advantage of canonical authenticity.[87]

Throughout the central and later Middle Ages the veneration of Mary dominates religious culture. The different facets of her role, although their presence fluctuates depending on time period and geographical area, do not exclude one another. While the preoccupation with Mary's body persists, we do see, from the twelfth century onwards, a clear development in biblical commentary, poetry and religious literature overall towards meditation upon her experiences and emotions, and eager identification with her as a human being. This correlates with a general emergence of a more personalized, affective piety in the medieval West.

---

84.   Astell 1990: 64.
85.   PL 210: 53.
86.   Astell 1990: 61.
87.   Fulton 1996: 105.

BIBLIOGRAPHY

Primary Sources

Amadeus of Lausanne (1979) *Eight Homilies on the Praise of the Virgin Mary*, trans. Grace Perigio, Cistercian Fathers Series 18B, Kalamazoo: Cistercian Publications.

Ambrose of Milan (1957) *Opera IV: Expositio evangeli secundum Lucam*, ed. Marcus Adriaen, CCSL 14, Turnhout: Brepols.

Anselm of Canterbury (1946–61) *S. Anselmi Cantuariensis archiepiscopi Opera Omnia*, ed. F. S. Schmidt, 6 vols, Edinburgh: Nelson and Sons.

Anselm of Canterbury (1973) *The Prayers and Meditations of Saint Anselm*, ed. Benedicta Ward, Harmondsworth: Penguin.

Bernard of Clairvaux (1957–77) *S. Bernardi opera*, ed. Jean Leclercq *et al.*, 8 vols, Rome: Editiones Cistercienses.

Bernard of Clairvaux (1976) *On the Song of Songs I–IV*, trans. Kilian J. Walsh, Cistercian Fathers Series 4, Kalamazoo: Cistercian Publications.

Davies, R. T. (ed) (1963) *Medieval English Lyrics: A Critical Anthology*, London: Faber and Faber (reprinted 1991).

Elliott, J. K. (ed.) *The Apocryphal New Testament: A Collection of Apocryphal Christian Literature in an English Translation based on M. R. James*, Oxford: Clarendon.

Hildegard of Bingen (1983) *Abbess Hildegard of Bingen (1098–1179): Sequences and Hymns*, ed. Christopher Page, Lustleigh: Antico.

(H)roswitha of Gandersheim (1923) *The Plays of Roswitha*, trans. Christopher St John, London: Chatto and Windus.

Jacobus de Voragine (1993) *The Golden Legend: Readings on the Saints*, trans. William Granger Ryan, 2 vols, Princeton NJ: Princeton University Press.

Johannes Herolt Discipulus (1928) *Miracles of the Blessed Virgin Mary*, trans. C. C. Swinton Bland, London: Routledge.

Tischendorf, C. (ed.) (1866) *Apocalypses Apocryphae*, Leipzig: Mendelssohn.

Secondary Sources

Abulafia, Anna Sapir (1989) 'Jewish-Christian Disputations and the Twelfth-Century Renaissance', *Journal of Medieval History* 15: 105–25.

Astell, Ann A. (1990) *The Song of Songs in the Middle Ages*, Ithaca: Cornell University Press.

Clayton, Mary (1998) *The Apocryphal Gospels of Mary in Anglo-Saxon England*, vol. 26, *Cambridge Studies in Anglo-Saxon England*, Cambridge: Cambridge University Press.

Ellington, Donna Spivey (2001) *From Sacred Body to Angelic Soul: Understanding Mary in Late Medieval and Early Modern Europe*, Washington DC: The Catholic University of America Press.

Flanagan, Sabina (1989) *Hildegard of Bingen, 1098–1179: A Visionary Life*, London and New York: Routledge.

Fulton, Rachel (1996) 'Mimetic Devotion, Marian Exegesis, and the Historical Sense of the Song of Songs', *Viator* 27: 85–116.

Fulton, Rachel (2002) *From Judgment to Passion: Devotion to Christ and the Virgin Mary 800–1200*, New York: Columbia University Press.

Graef, Hilda (1985) *Mary: A History of Doctrine and Devotion*, combined edn, London: Sheed and Ward.

Leclercq, Jean (1961) *The Love of Learning and the Desire for God: A Study of Monastic Culture*, trans. Catherine Misrahi, New York: Fordham University Press (rev. edn, London: SPCK, 1974).

Leclercq, Jean (1979) *Monks and Love in Twelfth-Century France: Psycho-Historical Essays*, Oxford: Clarendon Press.

Leff, Gordon (1967) *Heresy in the Later Middle Ages*, 2 vols, New York: Barnes and Noble.

Mackay, Angus with Ditchburn, David (eds) (1997) *Atlas of Medieval Europe*, London and New York: Routledge.

Mâle, Émile (1902) *L'art réligieux du 13ième siècle*, Paris: Colin.

Mâle, Émile (1949) *Religious Art from the Twelfth to the Eighteenth Century*, London: Routledge.

Mayr-Harting, Henry (2004) 'The Idea of the Assumption in the West, 800–1200', in R. N. Swanson (ed.), *The Church and Mary*, Studies in Church History 39, Woodbridge: Boydell Press: 86–111.

Mimouni, S. C. (1993) 'Les *Transitus Mariae* sont-ils vraiment des apocryphes?', *Studia Patristica* 25: 122–8.

Newman, Barbara (1987) *Sister of Wisdom: St Hildegard's Theology of the Feminine*, Aldershot: Scolar Press.

Pelikan, Jaroslav (1978) *The Christian Tradition: A History of the Development of Doctrine*, vol. III, *The Growth of Medieval Theology (600–1300)*, Chicago, IL, and London: University of Chicago Press.

Pelikan, Jaroslav (1996) *Mary through the Centuries: Her Place in the History of Culture*, New Haven, CT: Yale University Press.

Rahner, Hugo (1961) *Our Lady and the Church*, trans. Sebastian Bullough, London: Darton, Longman & Todd.

Schipperges, Heinrich (1956) 'Ein unveröffentlichtes Hildegard-Fragment', *Sudhoffs Archiv für Geschichte der Medizin* 40: 41–77.

Sticca, Sandro (1988) *The 'Planctus Mariae' in the Dramatic Tradition of the Middle Ages*, trans. Joseph R. Berrigan, Athens: University of Georgia Press.

Ward, Benedicta (1982) *Miracles and the Medieval Mind: Theory, Record and Event 1000–1215*, London: Scolar Press (reprinted Wildwood House, 1987).

Warner, Marina (2000) *Alone of All Her Sex: The Myth and Cult of the Virgin Mary*, 3rd edn, London: Vintage (first published 1976).

Miracles of the Blessed Virgin Mary
from the Collection of Johannes Herolt

The following two accounts are taken from the fifteenth-century book of *Miracles of the Blessed Virgin Mary*, by Johannes Herolt, called Discipulus (1435–40),[1] and are typical of the genre. Some miracle books pertain to particular shrines, while others are general collections of Marian miracles; some of the miracles occur in nearly all the collections, and others are peculiar to a specific group or volume. Both of the following appear in different forms in many collections.[2]

L

There was a certain man who was religious in name only, but, wherever true religion was concerned, hard-hearted and careless. He was, however, in the habit of praying to the Blessed Virgin and saying once every day a hundred 'Hail, Mary's'. Coming near his end, he was caught away in an ecstasy, and devils charged him before the Great Judge seeking a sentence that would adjudge him to be theirs. God, therefore, knowing his manifold sins, said that he must be condemned.

Meantime the Blessed Virgin came offering schedules in which were contained all the 'Hail Mary's', and begging her Son to allow him to receive a milder sentence. But the devils brought many books full of his sins. The books on both sides were put into the scales, but the sins weighed most. Then the Blessed Virgin, seeing she was doing no good, earnestly besought her Son, saying: 'Remember, Beloved, that Thou didst receive of my substance, visible, tangible and sensible substance; give to me one drop of Thy blood shed for sinners in Thy passion.' And he replied: 'It is impossible to deny thee anything. Yet know that one drop of my blood weighs heavier than all the sins of the whole world. Receive therefore thy request.' Receiving it, she placed it in the scales, and all those sins of the religious weighed against it as light as ashes.

Then the devils departed in confusion, crying out and saying: 'The lady is too merciful to Christians; we fail as often as she comes to contend with us.' And so the man's spirit returned to his body, and on recovery he related the whole tale and became a true monk.

XC

A woman who was in peril of childbirth for seven days and turning black had been given up by everyone, made a vow to the Blessed Francis and with her dying breath began to implore his aid.

Now after uttering this prayer she fell asleep, and in her sleep she saw the Blessed Francis addressing her with kindly words and asking whether she knew his face and if she knew how to recite the 'Salve Regina' in honour of the Glorious Virgin. When she replied that she had knowledge of both, St Francis began that antiphon of the Glorious Virgin that is the 'Salve Regina'. And as she uttered in prayer the words: 'The fruit which the Virgin brought forth', at once she was delivered from all her pains, and she brought forth a fine child and

---

1. Johannes Herolt Discipulus, trans. 1928: 76–7, 118–19.
2. Other collections that have been published with English-language introductions include Nigel of Canterbury, ed. 1986; *The Myracles of Oure Lady*, ed. 1990; Marcus Bull, trans. 1999.

she offered thanksgiving to the Queen of Heaven who through the merits of the Blessed Francis deigned to pity her.

BIBLIOGRAPHY

Johannes Herolt Discipulus (1928) *Miracles of the Blessed Virgin Mary*, trans. C. C. Swinton Bland, London: Routledge.

Marcus Bull (1999) *The Miracles of Our Lady of Rocamdour: Analysis and Translation*, Woodbridge: Boydell Press.

The Myracles of Oure Lady (1990), ed. Peter Whitford from Wynkyn de Worde's edition, Middle English Texts 23, Heidelberg: Carl Winter/Universitätsverlag.

Nigel of Canterbury (1986) *Miracles of the Virgin Mary, in verse. Miracula Sancte Dei Genitricis Virginis Marie, versificie*, ed. Jan Ziolkowski, Toronto Medieval Latin Texts 17, Toronto: Pontifical Institute of Medieval Studies.

PART 3

MARIOLOGY

9

THE DEVELOPMENT OF THE DOCTRINE OF MARY'S IMMACULATE CONCEPTION

SARAH JANE BOSS

The doctrine of Mary's immaculate conception teaches that she was conceived without original sin, and the history of the dispute over this doctrine is one of the most interesting in the history of the Christian Church.[1] During the Middle Ages, the doctrine was strongly promoted by the Franciscan order, and supported by most other religious orders, such as the Carmelites. Opposition came most strongly from the Dominicans, who continued their struggle against it into the seventeenth century.

That Mary was conceived without the stain of original sin was defined as an article of faith for Roman Catholics in the papal bull *Ineffabilis Deus* in 1854, although by that time there were few Catholics who dissented from it. The doctrine had already been promulgated at the Council of Basel in 1439,[2] and many bishops and secular rulers at the time had presumed that the council's injunction to observe the feast was binding upon them. However, the Church subsequently ruled that the Council of Basel at this date was not an ecumenical council of the Church, so its decree on the immaculate conception carried no legal force.[3]

It has sometimes been asserted that the doctrine's final acceptance by Church authorities was a victory for popular devotion over the opinions of theologians. However, this idea has reasonably been called into question, since – by the later Middle Ages, at least – the strong Marian devotion which it undoubtedly expressed was evidently felt by the theologians who promoted the doctrine in academic and official circles.[4]

This article considers the changing interpretation of the doctrine among Catholics through the centuries.

---

1.   A collection of papers presenting a history of the doctrine can be found in O'Connor (ed.) 1958. A discussion of the development of the doctrine of the later Middle Ages can be found in Lamy 2000.
2.   The case in favour of the immaculate conception was prepared for the Council of Basel in 1436 by the Franciscan John of Segovia; see Ioannis de Segovia 1965 (facsimile edn). The case against was prepared by the Dominican John of Torquemada in 1437, and was published in 1869 by E. B. Pusey, an Anglo-Catholic opponent of the doctrine; see Pusey 1966 (facsimile edn).
3.   Sebastian 1958: 228–34. Note the typographical error on 232, which gives the year of the decree as 1438 instead of 1439.
4.   Lamy 2001.

207

FOUNDATIONS

The story of Mary's conception is told in the so-called *Gospel of James*, or *Protevangelium*, which is thought to date from the second century.[5] It describes Mary's parents, Anne and Joachim, as righteous Jews who were distressed by the fact that they were childless. In her desolation, Anne cried out a prayer to God for the gift of a child, vowing that any child she bore in answer to this prayer would be consecrated to the Lord's service. The Lord heard her appeal, and while Joachim was tending his flocks in the fields, an angel appeared to him to announce that his wife would conceive a child. At the same time, an angel appeared to Anne in her house and delivered the same message. On hearing the news, Anne and Joachim both left their work, each running to find the other. They met at the Temple gate – which in other versions of the story is identified as the Golden Gate[6] – and embraced one another there. The couple then returned home, and nine months later Anne gave birth to a daughter, Mary. This story was the focus of the earliest liturgical feast in honour of Mary's conception, and scenes from it became standard features of the devotional art of the Middle Ages and Renaissance. It seems to have been celebrated first in the Eastern Church, at the end of the seventh century.[7] It is possible that there was a feast of Mary's Conception in eighth-century Ireland, but the earliest well-attested record of such a celebration in the West comes from England during the early eleventh century, when it was kept on 8 December, that is, nine months before Mary's birthday on 8 September.[8] After the Norman Conquest, the feast of Mary's Conception was suppressed, and it was in protest against this suppression that the first thorough account of the doctrine of Mary's immaculate conception was expounded.

From the early centuries of Christianity it was widely believed that Mary never committed any actual sins during her life, and this became the Church's universal teaching. However, the doctrine of the immaculate conception states that even at the first moment of her existence, Mary was free of the condition of original sin which is the inheritance of humanity in general. Since the fifth century, the Western Church had considered the doctrine of original sin to be orthodox teaching. In most traditional accounts, original sin is the wickedness to which all humanity has been subject since Adam's and Eve's fall from grace. It is a condition which affects everyone from the moment of conception, regardless of what actual sins they may or may not commit during their lifetime; but it is washed away by the waters of baptism, since baptism accomplishes the remission of all sins. The doctrine's great champion was Augustine of Hippo (354–430), who taught that original sin was transmitted through sexual intercourse and was connected to the lust which necessarily

---

5.   See Chris Maunder, 'Mary in the New Testament and Apocrypha', in this volume: 39–40, and extracts from the *Protevangelium*: 47–9.
6.   *Gospel of Pseudo-Matthew* 3: 88.
7.   O'Carroll 1982: 180.
8.   Clayton 1990: 40–3.

accompanies sexual union.[9] Only Christ was free of original sin: and he, of course, was conceived without sexual intercourse. Augustine taught that human passions should always be ordered by the faculty of reason, and that reason in turn should be subordinated to the will of God. For Augustine, it is the irrational and uncontrollable nature of sexual desire which is its sinful aspect. He noticed that even in people who had been baptized, feelings of sexual lust and other inclinations towards sin remained present. From this, Augustine concluded that the general tendency to sin, known as *concupiscence*, was a vestige of original sin which baptism did not remove.

Yet Augustine's principal intention was not to denigrate the human condition, but to emphasize that men and women are totally dependent upon God for their salvation. In particular, he attacked the doctrine of Pelagius, an ascetic teacher who believed that human beings could accomplish their own salvation by the living of holy lives. Against this, Augustine taught that it is only the grace of God which can bestow salvation, and that the fallen, sinful condition of humanity (apart from the limitations of created beings in general) prevents men and women from achieving for themselves the redemption which that condition requires. The doctrine of original sin makes clear humanity's inability to save itself. Pelagius pointed out that the logic of Augustine's argument was that even the Blessed Virgin must once have been in a state of sin, yet piety demands that we confess her to have been sinless. In reply to this, Augustine made the non-committal assertion: 'Where sin is concerned, I wish to have no question with regard to Mary.'[10] Thus right at the beginning of the Western Church's discussion of original sin, the doctrine seemed to be confronted with a difficulty in the case of the Lord's mother.

Although Western Christianity was rapidly converted to belief in original sin, not everyone accepted Augustine's theory that it was transmitted in the procreative seed. Most notably, a different view was advanced by Anselm (1033–1109), the great scholar and Archbishop of Canterbury. He taught that original sin was the absence of the original justice with which the world was created: it is a lack of justice brought about by Adam's disobedience. The main consequence of original sin is that it impedes humanity's free will, giving the will a propensity towards evil. Therefore, argued Anselm, although the potential for original sin is present in everyone from conception, it does not take effect until a child has reached the age at which it should have the possibility of exercising free will. It was Anselm's understanding of original sin which came to be used as the foundation for intellectual defences of the immaculate conception.

---

9.   An account of, and references for, Augustine's understanding of the transmission of original sin are given in Pelikan 1971: 299–301.

10.   *De Natura et Gratia*, 36:42, PL 44: 267. The Pelagian Julian of Eclanum also took issue with Augustine over the question of Mary's sinlessness; see *Opus Imperfectum contra Julianum* 4:CXXII, PL 45: 1417–18.

THE FEAST OF THE CONCEPTION AND ITS DEFENCE

Discussion over Mary's freedom from original sin was initiated by liturgical practice, rather than by problems of theory. In general, Christians did not celebrate the saints' birthdays, but only their death days – that is, the day on which the saint was reborn into heaven. However, there were two exceptions to this, namely St John the Baptist and the Blessed Virgin Mary, whose birthday had been celebrated in some places since the sixth century.[11] Since Christians could not celebrate the birthdays of people who were born in a state of sin, it was argued that these two, who in any case were pre-eminent among the saints, must have been sanctified (i.e. freed from sin) before birth. In the case of John the Baptist, this sanctification would have taken place at the time of the visitation of Mary to his mother Elizabeth, when the Holy Spirit came upon her and the child leapt in her womb (Lk. 1.41). However, in the case of Mary there was disagreement and doubt about the time of her sanctification, and the majority of theologians did not favour the view that she was conceived without original sin. Yet, as we have already noted, a feast of Mary's Conception was being celebrated in parts of the Western Church from at least the eleventh century.

The celebration of Mary's conception met with considerable opposition, and initially the opponents' main objection was that, since a normal human conception is sinful, to celebrate Mary's conception was to celebrate a sinful event. The most famous example of such an objection is the letter which St Bernard of Clairvaux wrote to the canons of Lyons Cathedral in 1125. The cathedral had started to observe the feast of the Conception, and Bernard wrote to express his surprise and disapproval at this innovation. In this letter he asks rhetorically, 'How indeed was sin not present where lust was not absent?'[12]

This seems to have been the theological content of the Norman Church's objection to the feast of the Conception in Anglo-Saxon England. Eadmer of Canterbury (1060/64–1141), a former pupil of St Anselm, wrote a treatise against the suppression of the feast. It is entitled *Tractate on the Conception of Saint Mary*,[13] and argues that it is legitimate to observe the feast of the Virgin's Conception because she was conceived without original sin. Thus the first thorough apologia for the belief that Mary's conception was immaculate (i.e. 'without stain') seems to have been written out of a desire to defend a liturgical celebration whose origin lay in devotion rather than Marian doctrine.

The structure of Eadmer's argument is important, because it was followed by subsequent proponents of the teaching. It falls into three parts. Eadmer wants to show, firstly, that an immaculate conception is possible in principle. To do this he uses an analogy which corresponds to Anselm's understanding of original sin. He gives the example of a chestnut tree. Its seed is a thorny shell surrounded by thickest prickles. Yet the centre is a milky liquid, and the chestnut which eventually bursts

---

11. O'Donnell 1988: 158.
12. Letter 174, PL 182: 335C, cited in Balić 1958: 173, n. 60. A full translation is given in *The Letters of St Bernard of Clairvaux* (1998), Letter 215.
13. Eadmer of Canterbury 1904.

out is without any thorns.[14] And this, he suggests, is the sort of thing we mean when we say that Mary is conceived without original sin: like the unharmed chestnut in its prickly covering, Mary is sinless in a world overrun with the sin of Adam.

However, the fact that an immaculate conception is possible does not demonstrate that God would ever have wanted to bring about such a thing, and hence does not show that he would have done it for Mary. So the second part of Eadmer's argument is to show that God would have wanted Mary to be preserved from original sin. Eadmer starts from the point that Mary is the Mother of God. This is the greatest gift ever bestowed upon any creature, and God's wish to give her the highest of honours is seen also in the fact that he has made her mistress of the world and empress of the universe. From this, we can know that God does not wish to withhold from her any good thing that is possible, and consequently, he must have given her the gift of freedom from original sin. Furthermore, Eadmer argues, Mary is higher than the angels, who are not tainted with sin of any kind, and in this respect God would not wish to treat her less favourably than he treats them.

Now, for God to will something is the same as for him to accomplish it. As human beings, we may will something and not have the power to realize it; or we may will something which is evil, or may change our minds. But in the classical Christian understanding of God, none of these limitations applies to him. So if God willed that Mary should be immaculately conceived, then indeed she was. Thus Eadmer's argument follows three stages: first, it addresses the question of *how* God could cause someone to be exempt from the sin of Adam, and thus tries to show that Mary's immaculate conception is *possible*; second, the argument deals with the question of *why* Mary would have been conceived without sin, and tries to show in what way such a conception would *accord with divine providence*; and from this the argument concludes that *God did it*.

The celebration of Mary's conception spread rapidly during the later Middle Ages, gradually gaining official recognition. This led to a reversal of the earlier situation: where Eadmer had defended the feast of the Conception with an argument for the event having been sinless, later authors who wrote in support of the immaculate conception would sometimes appeal to the practice of keeping the feast of the Conception as evidence for the sanctity of the event which was celebrated. For example, in 1436 the Spanish Franciscan John of Segovia submitted to the ecumenical Council of Basel a series of arguments in favour of the immaculate conception. Among these, he contended that

the Church would not institute a celebration to solemnize a work of nature, but a heavenly miracle: not a sin, but grace. It is right to understand that in the Conception there is some mystery of a singular and heavenly virtue.[15]

The liturgical observance of Mary's conception thus added weight to the belief that the conception was sinless.

---

14.   Ibid., 10: 10–11.
15.   Ioannis de Segovia 1965: 23.

The fact that the doctrine was expounded in defence of the feast, and that the feast continued to spread in the face of strong theological objections, means that popular celebration was taking precedence over technical argument.

DUNS SCOTUS'S ARGUMENT FOR THE POSSIBILITY OF CONCEPTION WITHOUT SIN

The most important theological objection to the doctrine of the immaculate conception had been raised by the Dominican Thomas Aquinas (1225–74). He argued from the fact that Christ alone did not need to be redeemed, while all other children of Adam stand in need of salvation. Hence Mary too must have been saved by Christ. Thomas argued that to be redeemed meant to be 'snatched from the devil's power', like a kingdom which has fallen into enemy hands and whose king wins it back by means of battle. Therefore Mary must at some time have been within the power of the devil, i.e. in a state of sin. Since Mary did not commit any actual sins, the only sin from which she could be saved would be that which she inherited from her forebears. So if she was not tainted even by this, then she did not need Christ's salvific work, and he is not the universal Redeemer whom Christians believe him to be. Consequently, Thomas argued, Mary cannot have been conceived without original sin.[16] St Thomas's importance as a theologian in his own religious order had the consequence that his argument on this point carried much weight among Dominicans for several centuries. Yet the immaculate conception did not lack intellectual proponents, and the theological defences of the doctrine reveal an understanding of the human condition which emphasizes its capacity for goodness and salvation. Aquinas's opposition was contested early on by the English Franciscan William of Ware (d. *c.* 1305), who used the analogy of debt, rather than military capture, to understand the condition of bondage to sin. Following Augustine, William argued that there are two kinds of debt: that which is contracted and must be paid, and that which is not contracted when it could have been. The sinfulness of most of humanity means that they fall into the first of these two categories, while Mary, who was always sinless, falls into the second. Nevertheless, it is only the Passion of Christ which remits Mary's debt of sin before it is incurred.[17] This type of argument was followed by William's pupil, John Duns Scotus (1266–1308), who argued that preservation from sin is better than deliverance. Consequently, to claim that Mary was preserved from contracting original sin is to say not that she did not need to be redeemed, but on the contrary, that she was the object of Christ's most perfectly redemptive action. Thus the doctrine of the immaculate conception teaches that Christ's salvific power reaches to the fullest possible extent.

When Duns Scotus defended the doctrine of Mary's immaculate conception, there was a second major objection which he addressed. It concerned the mechanism by which original sin is transmitted, and was a more detailed version of the Augustinian type of argument which had already been raised in the twelfth century. It

---

16. Balić 1958: 192–6.
17. Ibid.: 203.

went as follows: Mary's procreation by her parents came about through sexual intercourse, and was therefore subject to the law of sin which affects humanity in general since the fall of Adam. This means that her body must have been formed from contaminated seed from which her soul in turn would have been contaminated when it was infused into her body.[18]

I have mentioned above that arguments in favour of the immaculate conception depended upon an Anselmian doctrine of original sin. This was true of Scotus's argument for how a sinless conception would be possible, and it became a standard defence of the doctrine ever afterwards. The inheritance of Anselm, in its Franciscan transformation, indicates an important aspect of the Immaculists' spiritual orientation, namely a strong conviction that the material world has the capacity for goodness and redemption. Contrary to those who thought that original sin was transmitted in the procreative seed, Anselm argued that the seed which generates new human life is intrinsically neither sinful nor meritorious. Rather, the absence of justice affects the human will by weakening it, but does not have an immediate effect on any other part of the person. It is the will, not the seed, which is subject to sin. And the will pertains to the rational soul, and not to the body as such.[19] Before Duns Scotus, it had been more commonly believed that sin resided in human flesh from conception and that the newly created soul was tainted with this sin when it was infused into the body some weeks later. Since the sin in the flesh was a consequence of the lust experienced during sexual intercourse, anyone conceived in the normal way – including Mary – was bound to inherit original sin. Anselm's teaching that the seed and the flesh were not intrinsically sinful broke this immediate connection between procreation and original sin, and made plausible the idea that a soul might be united to a seminally conceived body, but nonetheless be saved from subjection to the guilt of Adam's offspring. Nevertheless, Anselm thought that it was not wrong to speak of someone being 'conceived in sin', not least because this is a phrase found in Scripture. This means that since the fall, one's flesh is destined from conception to become part of a human being who will lack original justice. Sin is said to be present at conception because the necessity for future sin is carried in the seed.[20]

Duns Scotus points out that when a person is baptized, original sin is removed (i.e. the guilt of not possessing original justice is forgiven), but the 'contamination of the flesh' (*infectio carnis*) remains as before, without reinfecting the soul. Consequently, it cannot be the case that the contamination of the flesh necessarily gives rise to a state of sin in the soul. For this to be the case, baptism would either have to remove the contamination of the flesh, or else not remove original sin permanently from the soul. The fact that it accomplishes the sanctification of the soul but not the purification of the flesh means that the former does not depend upon the latter; more specifically, Duns Scotus is saying that the state of original sin as such pertains only to the soul, and not to the body. Therefore God could have sanctified Mary's soul at the

---

18. Duns Scotus 1933, III.3.1: 21–2. A good account of Duns Scotus's defence of the immaculate conception is given in Wolter and O'Neill 1993: 54–84.
19. Anselm 1946, 7: 147–9.
20. Ibid., 7–8: 148–9.

first moment of her conception notwithstanding the fact that she had been engendered by her parents in the natural way.[21] Duns Scotus thus uses an example taken from sacramental teaching to support Anselm's doctrine of original sin, in which moral qualities such as evil are located in the will (which is a property of the soul), not in the seed (which belongs to the flesh).

Anselm himself had taught that natural procreation by the children of Adam always conferred upon the offspring the necessity for future sin. He argues that all things are made, or brought about, by one or more of three 'courses', namely by the will of God, by nature, or by the will of a creature. The generation of humanity by procreation is a work of both nature and human will.[22] Furthermore, it is in the natural and wilful propagation of humanity that men and women pass on to their offspring the evils which Adam took upon himself when he rejected the good things that he had received from God. By contrast, the virginal conception of Christ was something which occurred only by the will of God, so the lack of original justice which afflicted the rest of Adam's and Eve's offspring was not passed on to him.[23] Yet in contending that the physical creation could not of itself be sinful, Anselm had opened the route by which later theologians could argue that Mary's conception was immaculate as well as being the result of sexual intercourse. If sin pertained to the will – and thus to the soul – and not to the flesh, then there was no reason why God should not have sanctified Mary's soul at the moment of its creation and infusion into her body. This is what God did for John the Baptist in his mother's womb, and what he does for anyone at baptism: he did it for Mary at the moment of her soul's creation.

By thus making a separation between the moral and physical orders, John Duns Scotus makes it possible, in the first place, not to maintain that the physical conception of a child is intrinsically evil, and, in the second place, to show how Mary could have been preserved from original sin. In this way, the seed of procreation and the flesh which it engenders are freed from condemnation as evil, and gain the potential to be freed from any guilt of sin even in a post-lapsarian world. Furthermore, although Anselm had claimed that in principle Adam and Eve might have begotten sinless children through sexual intercourse, he believed that because of the fall, the only people who had in fact been created without sin were those who had come into the world by means of a miracle (i.e. the will of God), and not because of nature and the will of a creature. Duns Scotus, on the other hand, showed that even in a fallen world, a human being conceived through sexual union could be created sinless, and he offered Mary as the example in whom this possibility had been realized.

THE IMMACULISTS' THEOLOGICAL ANTHROPOLOGY

Duns Scotus's defence of the immaculate conception expresses an optimistic understanding of humanity's, and the physical world's, capacity for goodness and

---

21. Duns Scotus 1933, III.3.1: 27–8.
22. Anselm 1946, 11: 153–4.
23. Ibid., 12: 154–5.

redemption. It is not surprising that such a defence should have been proposed by a Franciscan, since the Franciscan way of life had at its heart a reverence for even the humblest aspects of the created order. Over the next few centuries, proponents of the immaculate conception continued to be men and women who held a strong belief in the goodness of God's creatures, and Franciscans were in several respects the most important promoters of the doctrine.

St Bridget of Sweden (1303–73), a relative of the Swedish monarch, was a lay member of the Franciscan order who received a great number of revelations – or visions – of Christ, the Virgin and other sacred figures. Her revelations were generally considered to be reliable and were sometimes cited by theologians as authoritative. On one occasion, the Mother of God spoke to her, saying:

> Supposing a man wishes to fast when he feels the desire to eat, but his will resists the desire; but he has already been told by a superior, to whom he owes obedience, that out of obedience he should eat, and he – out of obedience but against his own will – does eat. That eating would be worthy of greater reward than a fast would be. The union of my parents was like this when I was conceived. And on that account it is the truth that I was conceived without original sin, and not in sin; because just as my Son and I never sinned, so no marital union would be more honourable than that from which I came forth.[24]

This text may seem humorous to modern readers, but it illuminates a point which is important for understanding the meaning of the immaculate conception to the doctrine's medieval protagonists. First, the doctrine was spoken about in terms which expressed a belief that the physical creation could be the bearer of goodness and grace. Duns Scotus had rescued Mary's conception from the imputation of wickedness by separating the moral condition of her soul from the physical act by which her parents conceived her. St Bridget, on the other hand, not only presents Mary's passive conception in the womb as sinless, but also sees the active union of Mary's parents as meritorious. Indeed, Bridget suggests that the sinlessness of Mary's conception was in some measure caused by the honourable character of her parents' union; and in making this connection she restores the natural integrity of procreative intercourse and conception which had been betrayed in the subtlety of Duns Scotus's argument. Where Augustine had argued that both sexual intercourse and conception were in some measure sinful, Duns Scotus separated the two events, retaining a weakened notion of the sinfulness transmitted in procreation, but making it possible that at least in one case the conception which resulted was sinless. Bridget, however, claims both that the parents' intercourse was honourable and that the child's conception was free of original sin.

What Bridget really implies is that the sexual union of Anne and Joachim was restored to the condition which would have pertained to sexual relations had

---

24.   St Bridget of Sweden 1680, 6.49: 507 (my own translation).

humanity not fallen from grace. For they come together not because they are driven by desire (although that is something which they feel), but out of obedience to the will of God; so their pleasure now serves God's purpose, and nature is in harmony with grace.

A bolder statement of the connection between Mary's conception and her parents' sexual intercourse is made in another fourteenth-century text, the *De Concepto Virginali* attributed to the Catalan philosopher and theologian Ramon Llull (*c*. 1232–1317).[25] Llull believes that, in many circumstances, an actor's intention is all-important in determining the outcome of an action. In the case of the conception of a child, he believes that if a couple sincerely desire to conceive a child who will know and love God, a child whose human condition they desire to be united to that of Jesus Christ, then the child conceived of that union will be morally superior to a child conceived out of less noble motives. Now, just as the builder who builds a palace for a king chooses only the finest materials and the best workmen, so God will have willed that the woman who was to be the mother of his Son should be the worthiest human being possible. Accordingly, Llull argues that when Anne and Joachim conceived the child who was to be the Mother of the Son of God, they must have had the holiest of intentions; and the purity of the parents' desire would then have ensured the moral purity of the child whom they conceived. This general line of thought is consistent with that expressed by St Bridget. However, Llull differs from Bridget in contending that the exceptional holiness of this Mary's conception would have meant that Anne and Joachim enjoyed greater carnal pleasure than any other couple have ever enjoyed during sexual intercourse.[26]

Llull's argument has the virtue of restoring a unity to the physical and the spiritual – a unity that is lost in the formulation of Duns Scotus. Parental motives, sexual pleasure and the moral character of the child conceived are all tied to one another in a manner that implies the necessary integrity of the human person and of people's relationships with one another. Llull's case – like Bridget's – also has the virtue of tying the doctrine of the immaculate conception to the wider question of humanity's capacity for holiness: it is because that capacity is already there that Anne and Joachim can respond to God's grace and conceive a sinless infant.

Ramon Llull's and St Bridget's accounts suggest that the exemption from Adam's sin which applies to Mary is partially extended to her parents, and this seems to support an anxiety about the immaculate conception which was expressed by some of the doctrine's later opponents, to wit, that it was the thin end of the wedge. After all, if there is even one exception to the law of original sin, then already it is not universal, and who knows how far this undermining of the doctrine of humanity's inherent wickedness might not go? One Protestant commentator, Giovanni Miegge – an opponent of the immaculate conception – observes: 'There is evidently a sort of elective affinity between this theory [Pelagianism] that reduces the seriousness of the original fall and the doctrine of the Immaculate Conception

---

25. Lulio 1664. There is dispute as to whether this work was actually written by Llull, or by a later author. See Peers 1929: 315, n. 2.
26. Lulio 1664: 112–14.

that wants to exempt Mary from it.'[27] And indeed, there is ample evidence that the medieval defenders of the immaculate conception held a rather low doctrine of original sin. This is a further indicator of the Immaculists' optimism about the condition of created beings.

One may be tempted to think that belief in Mary's unique sinlessness can be sustained only to the detriment of the rest of humanity, with whom she is contrasted. That is to say, one might think that if Mary is seen as being exempt from sin, then the sin of other people will appear to be correspondingly more serious, and the difference between Mary and the rest of humanity will be strongly emphasized. Yet evidence from the doctrine's medieval protagonists suggests the very opposite to be the case. William of Ware, for instance, argued that the feast of Mary's Conception should be celebrated even if she contracted original sin, because her flesh is the 'original principle' of the body of Christ.[28] Now, if William had held a 'high' doctrine of original sin – that is, if he had placed great emphasis on its severity – then the fact of original sin would have made it improper to celebrate Mary's conception, as St Bernard and others had already argued was the case. The fact that William is willing to promote the feast regardless of whether or not Mary's conception was sinless indicates that he takes a relatively light view of original sin. Yet the argument just cited follows on immediately from arguments in favour of the immaculate conception.

As we have seen, original sin was often defined as the absence of 'original justice' or 'original righteousness', which was the term for the condition of grace in which Adam and Eve lived before the fall. During the early fourteenth century, there was discussion of this topic among Spanish Franciscans, in which most argued that men and women have an obligation to possess original justice, so that failure to do so constitutes a *sin* in the proper sense of the word. However, one of their number, William Rubio, considered that there was no obligation to possess original justice; and consequently, original sin is not properly called 'sin', but is rather the *poena damni* or 'penalty of the condemned'.[29] This seems to be a very weak reading of the doctrine of original sin; and Rubio, its proponent, was another defender of the immaculate conception.

The examples given above suggest that the intention of the medieval promoters of the immaculate conception was not to draw attention to humanity's sinfulness: on the contrary, this was a subject in which they had relatively little interest. Rather, they were concerned with the glorification of the Virgin and of God's generosity to her.

MARY'S BODILY CONCEPTION

Defenders of the immaculate conception saw humanity as inherently capable of great goodness, and Mary as the human person in whom this capability was realized. Moreover, the commemoration of Mary's sinless beginning had as its object her body

---

27.   Miegge 1955: 111.
28.   Balić 1958: 203, n. 205.
29.   Sebastian 1958: 219.

as well as her soul. The Immaculists stressed that what was being celebrated on the feast of the Conception was not only Mary's spiritual sanctification, but also her beginning as a human being, including her flesh. The immaculate conception's opponents, on the other hand, argued that where the Church approved the celebration of the feast of the Conception, then the proper object of the celebration was the sanctification of Mary's soul in her mother's womb, and not her physical origin. The Immaculists rejected this. John of Segovia pointed out that the feast of 8 December is called the Conception, not the Sanctification. As with the Assumption, this feast must be concerned with the glorification of the body, and not with the soul alone:

> Since on that day in the church's office [i.e. the prescribed prayer for the hours of the day], and even in the homily from the Fathers, mention is made of the glorification of the body, so [the feast] cannot refer only to the sanctification.[30]

St Robert Bellarmine (1542–1621), the Jesuit cardinal, likewise referred to liturgical practice when he responded to the contention that it was Mary's sanctification, not her conception, which the Church celebrated. He observed that the term 'holy Conception' is used in the divine office and wrote, 'but it is not a conception unless [it occurs] in the first instant, when the soul is infused in the body, when in the nature of things the Virgin's whole person began its existence'.[31] Bellarmine thus argues that Mary's immaculate conception is the beginning of the unity of her body and soul.

Three centuries earlier, William of Ware had laid emphasis on the importance of Mary's bodily existence. His contention that Mary's flesh is the 'original principle' of the body of Christ, and its conception a cause for celebration, shows that William held Mary's physical conception in high esteem. When the eternal Word of God was 'made flesh', it was Mary's flesh that he took, and hence her conception is the beginning of the flesh that will be united to God in the incarnation. William's interest is in the physical connection between Mary's conception and the incarnation of Christ.

The continuity between the Virgin's body and Christ's went on being alluded to in later defences of the immaculate conception. In one of the *Revelations* of St Bridget, God the Father tells her that Mary had been conceived without sin in order that the Son should be born without sin.[32] Elsewhere, the Blessed Virgin says to Bridget: '[The Son of God in me] came with honour, since all sin of Adam was separated from me. Whence the most honourable Son of God took on most honourable flesh.'[33]

---

30. Ioannis de Segovia 1965: 21.
31. 'Sententia Roberti Bellarmini pro Immaculata Conceptione Sanctissimae Virginis Mariae', in Brodrick 1928, vol. 1: 513. Although St Robert supported the doctrine, he argues elsewhere that, since the Church allows either opinion on the immaculate conception, there is at least a doubt as to whether it is right to celebrate the feast of the Conception; see 'De Ecclesia Triumphante' 3:16, in Bellarmine 1721: 514.
32. *Revelations* 5, Interrog. 16, in St Bridget of Sweden 1680: 440.
33. *Revelations* 6, 12, in ibid.: 456.

An association between the immaculate conception and the incarnation is expressed also in a poem on the immaculate conception by the English Jesuit Robert Southwell (1560–95). In 'The Conception of Our Ladie' he writes, 'Earth breedes a heaven for God's new dwelling-place.'

A similar association seems to underlie the vow taken by the Jesuit scholastic John Berchmans in 1621. He died in August of that year and was later canonized. The seventeenth century saw a great movement for the promotion of the immaculate conception to the status of official Catholic teaching, and it was not uncommon for the doctrine's protagonists to make dramatic gestures in support of their cause. The most celebrated – or infamous – of such gestures was the 'vow of blood' (*votum sanguinis*), by which one vowed to defend the doctrine of the immaculate conception 'even to the shedding of blood'.[34] John Berchmans does not seem to have taken this controversial vow, but after his death a piece of paper was found on which he had written the following words:

> I, John Berchmans most unworthy son of the Society of Jesus, do declare before you and before your Son, whom I believe and confess to be here present in the most glorious sacrament of the Eucharist, that always and everywhere, in so far as a decision of the Church does not oppose it, I will profess and defend your Immaculate Conception. As testimony to this, I have signed in my own blood, and traced below, the sign of the Society of Jesus. The year 1621. John Berchmans, IHS.[35]

St John's vow points to the integrity of the various elements of his faith, and especially to the link between Mary's conception and the incarnation. Mary's conception is the beginning of the soul who will freely accept Christ into the world for the world's salvation. And her conception is equally the beginning of the flesh which is eventually to be united with the eternal Word of God in Christ. It is this flesh of Christ which is again made real in the host on the altar, in whose presence St John wrote his profession of faith. Moreover, the letters IHS are the first three letters of Jesus' name in Greek, so that the sign of the Society of Jesus at the end of John Berchmans's declaration enhances the connection between Mary's conception and the incarnation. The conception of the Virgin, the eucharistic host and the name of the incarnate Lord are all constituent parts of a single mystery whose unity can be traced to the conception of the Virgin: Christ's first earthly dwelling place, whose flesh and blood he took for his own.

It must be acknowledged that it is not always clear what kind of anthropology underlies the Immaculists' insistence that the feast of Mary's Conception refers to her body as well as her soul. Duns Scotus's demonstration of how an immaculate conception would be possible refers back to Anselm's teaching that sin resides in the will rather than the seed, and it may be that for some authors, this understanding was

---

34.   O'Carroll 1982: 363.
35.   Quoted in Villaret 1952: 948–9.

itself sufficient to legitimate the celebration of a bodily conception. But even for Anselm, the body of someone conceived through nature and human will carried a propensity for the flowering of sin in the soul to which it would be united; and the fact that some of the Immaculists, such as St Bridget, imply that there is a causal link between Mary's immaculate conception and the flesh from which the body of Christ is made, may suggest that some of the defenders of the doctrine believed that not only Mary's soul but also her body was sanctified. Certainly, some later authors, such as Jean-Jacques Olier (1608–57), believed both that original sin was transmitted in the flesh and that Mary was immaculately conceived.[36]

However, there is a defence of the immaculate conception which would be consistent with Duns Scotus's understanding and which would also explain why the doctrine's protagonists might have insisted that the immaculacy of Mary's conception included both body and soul. This argument holds that since the flesh of the incarnate Word was taken from the flesh of the Virgin, it is inconceivable that the Virgin's flesh would ever have been united to a soul contaminated by sin.[37] This might suppose an action which is the reverse of that described in the Augustinian view: it is not that the soul is contaminated by the flesh, but that the flesh may in some way be adversely affected by the soul. It seems possible that what underlies the argument is a notion of ritual pollution; that is to say, when something which is ritually clean comes into contact with something which is unclean, then that which is clean becomes contaminated. Since everything about Christ must be as holy (and therefore as clean) as possible, the flesh from which he is made must never have been bound to anything impure. It is true that the idea that the body of Christ might in principle be subject to pollution is one which has rarely been given houseroom in Catholic theology; since Christ is God, it is not possible for him to be ritually polluted. But Christian sentiment is not always congruent with academic argument.

In any event, what seems clear is that, in the hands of its medieval and Renaissance promoters, the doctrine of the immaculate conception was concerned with the sanctification of Mary's whole humanity, including her flesh – flesh which in turn would be united to the Word of God in Christ.

MARY'S PREDESTINATION TO DIVINE MOTHERHOOD

The Immaculists' optimistic understanding of the human condition can be seen in the further connection which they made between the immaculate conception and Mary's predestination to be Mother of God. In Christian theology, there have been two classic ways of understanding the relationship of the incarnation to human salvation. The first of these holds that the world's salvation was accomplished in the crucifixion and resurrection of Christ, and that this was effective because he was both divine and human. The incarnation was the necessary condition for the work of redemption. The second view does not deny the first, but adds to it, stating that God was already redeeming the world in the act of taking flesh in Mary's womb. The

---

36.   Olier 1866, vol. 1: 88–9.
37.   This argument is given in Roschini 1948, vol. 2, par. 11: 82.

incarnation is not just a preparation for salvation, but is itself salvific. Duns Scotus – notably, but by no means uniquely – went beyond both these views, claiming that the incarnation would have taken place even if Adam had never sinned, which is to say that although the incarnation did indeed bring about the world's salvation, this was not the primary purpose for which it was ordained.

Duns Scotus taught that before the sin of Adam was foreseen, God intended that the Word should become flesh in Christ in order that human nature should be glorified.[38] Later Scotists argued that if God willed from eternity that the Word should take human flesh, then the woman from whom that flesh was to be taken must likewise have been predestined from eternity to be the Mother of God. Mary therefore shares in the predestination of Christ. Since Mary was predestined to her sacred office prior to Adam's fall, it was argued that her humanity was ordered in the first instance to her divine motherhood; so if the existence of original sin meant that there would be some tension between Mary's descent from Adam and her office as Mother of God, then – provided it was possible – the former must be subordinated to the latter.[39]

I have described this Scotist understanding as 'optimistic' because it sees the immaculate conception as deriving in the first instance from God's intention to glorify human nature, and because it is tied to an anthropology which holds that the predestination to glory is prior to any human wickedness.

HOLY WISDOM IN THE LITURGY OF THE CONCEPTION

The association between Mary's predestination and her conception may have been influenced by the liturgy, which in most rites employed a Wisdom text as the lection, or first reading, for the Mass of the feast.[40] After the Council of Trent (1545–63), Proverbs 8.22–31 was the standard lection for both the Conception and Nativity of the Virgin. The Gospel for the same feasts was usually the genealogy of Christ from Matthew 1. These readings give the impression of God's goodness being present in creation from the beginning, and of his plan being fulfilled in Christ through Mary.

THE ICONOGRAPHY OF MARY'S CONCEPTION: CHANGING INTERPRETATION

The motif of Mary's predestination was also taken up in the iconography of the immaculate conception.

The medieval understanding of Mary's immaculate conception as a physical, and not purely a spiritual, event was expressed in the art as well as the theology of the period. The most common representation of the Virgin's conception showed her parents, Anne and Joachim, embracing at the Golden Gate (Fig. 13). This did not

---

38. Wolter and O'Neill 1993: 49–54.
39. Lamy 2001: 257–8.
40. See Sarah Jane Boss, 'The Development of the Virgin's Cult in the High Middle Ages', in this volume: 69–70.

Fig. 13. Master Bertram of Minden, *Anne and Joachim embrace at the Golden Gate*. Buxtehuder Altarpiece, c. 1400. (Copyright Hamburg Kunsthalle.)

necessarily indicate a conception without sin, and was acceptable to both the supporters and the opponents of the immaculate conception. Images which were expressly concerned with the conception's sinlessness included representations of St Anne with the Virgin visibly present in her womb; although here again, the image was sometimes used by those who believed that Mary was sanctified by the Holy Spirit after conception, rather than that she was conceived immaculately.

In the modern period, by contrast, and especially from the seventeenth century, the images of parental embrace and infant presence in the mother's womb have been supplanted by a type of image which is intended to represent a simply spiritual aspect of the Virgin's conception. This type of image shows the Virgin as a young girl

Fig. 14. Jusepe de Ribera, *Virgin of the Immaculate Conception* 1635, Salamanca. (Photograph Museo del Prado, Madrid.)

standing alone, sometimes at prayer, sometimes treading on a serpent, sometimes standing on the moon, sometimes crowned with stars – not in physical contact with another human being, although having some association with those aspects of the physical creation which appear alongside her (Fig. 14). This iconography signifies that Mary was conceived in the mind of God before the foundation of the world, and associates her with the figure of Wisdom. The association of Mary with Wisdom shows that thoughts of the Mother of God permeated the Christian understanding of creation and redemption. But the image which alludes to Proverbs 8 bears many other connotations as well. Some of these carry an open reference to warfare within creation and associate Mary with the victorious side in its defeat of evil.

The representations of the immaculate conception by such artists as Diego Velàzquez (1599–1660) and Bartolomé Esteban Murillo (1617–82) draw on older iconography. When Adam and Eve are expelled from Eden, God says to the serpent, 'I will put enmity between you and the woman, and between your seed and her seed; he shall bruise your head, and you shall bruise his heel' (Gen. 3.15). In Christian exegesis, the woman and her seed had long been understood as the Virgin and Christ, crushing the devil in the person of the serpent.[41] In the Latin Vulgate, however, the second half of the prophecy was rendered: 'She will crush your head, and you will lie in wait for her heel.' Thus in the usual Catholic reading it was the woman, rather than her seed, who would be at war with the serpent. So the verse was read as a prophecy principally concerning Mary: Mary is the second Eve, and by her the devil will be destroyed. In both art and theology, the motif of the woman trampling the serpent underfoot was applied to Mary's immaculate conception, since her freedom from sin was a sign of the devil's total defeat.

During the Counter-Reformation period, Catholic scholars addressed the question of the Latin Bible's mistranslation of the Hebrew, and argued that although the primary meaning of the text was that Christ, that is, the woman's seed, would crush the serpent, nevertheless, since Christ imbues his saints – and pre-eminently his mother – with the grace to share in this work of destroying evil, it is right to apply the text to Mary as well.[42]

In art, the image of the woman crushing the serpent was sometimes combined with the image of the woman in the Book of the Apocalypse (or Revelation) 12.1–6. The latter is described as 'clothed with the sun, with the moon under her feet, and on her head a crown of twelve stars'. The passage continues:

> And the dragon stood before the woman who was about to bear a child, that he might devour her child when she brought it forth; she brought forth a male child, one who is to rule all the nations with a rod of iron, but her child was caught up to God . . . and the woman fled into the wilderness, where she has a place prepared by God.

41. For example, Gregory of Nyssa (c. 335–95), *Homily on the Annunciation*, PG 62: 765–6. English translation in Berselli and Gharib (eds) 1981: 24–6, 100.
42. This is the argument of Peter Canisius; see Brodrick 1963: 646.

Then there is war in heaven, with the archangel Michael fighting against the dragon. The dragon is defeated: 'And the great dragon was thrown down, that ancient serpent, who is called the Devil and Satan' (12.9).

Over the centuries, there has been general agreement that the woman in this passage at least partly signifies the Church, or the righteous people of Israel. However, exegesis from at least the fourth century down to the present day has frequently maintained that she is also Mary, the mother of Christ, who is herself the Church's principal type.[43] The battle which is described here is the final battle of God's angels against the devil, and the defeat of the dragon can thus be read as the fulfilment of the prophecy of Genesis 3.15, since the woman's offspring crushes the serpent. The perfect redemption of Mary in the immaculate conception is the first fruit of Michael's triumph over the serpent, who is the devil, as it is recounted in the Book of the Apocalypse.

The art historian Maurice Vloberg considers that the earliest certain representation of the Virgin of the Immaculate Conception trampling underfoot the head of the serpent is a wooden statue which was ordered for the church of St Mary of Cremona in 1407. The statue was to be 'crowned with twelve stars and with the ancient serpent under her feet', thus drawing together the imagery of Genesis 3.15 and the Apocalypse 12.1.[44] From the end of the fourteenth century onwards, there are also representations from Germany and the Low Countries in which the Virgin and Child are shown standing on the moon, as is the woman of the Apocalypse.[45] An English missal of the same period shows the Virgin clothed with the sun and standing on the moon, with the Blessed Trinity above her.[46]

A further contribution to the iconography of the immaculate conception was made by the *tota pulchra* image (Fig. 15). This probably had its source in German representations of Mary as she lived in the Temple as a young girl, the *Ährenkleidjungfrau* – so called because she was shown with ears of wheat on her dress.[47] The basic image was taken up and used to illustrate a text from the Song of Songs: 'You are all fair, my beloved, and there is no stain in you [Latin: *macula non est in te*]' (Song 4.7). Christians had always interpreted the Song as a love song between Christ, who is the groom, and the Church, who is the bride. In the high Middle Ages it became customary to accord Mary the part of the bride, or the beloved. So, for example, the 'sealed fountain' and 'garden enclosed' (4.12) became figures for her unbroken virginity, and sometimes for her freedom from sin, which found no place by which to enter her. Not surprisingly, then, the quotation 'there is no stain in you' seemed to invite an immaculist interpretation. Commenting on the many fifteenth- and sixteenth-century book engravings which represent the Beloved of the Song, the art historian Suzanne Stratton writes:

---

43. O'Carroll 1982: 375–7.
44. Vloberg 1958: 471.
45. A synopsis of some of the art-historical research is given in de Suduiraut 1998: 11–13.
46. Rickert 1952: 46–7 and Plate D. The illumination is for the votive Mass of the Holy Trinity, not the feast of the Immaculate Conception.
47. Stratton 1994: 40.

Fig. 15. The Virgin *Tota Pulchra*. Woodcut used in a number of books of Hours printed in Paris, including that of Thielman Kerver, c. 1500.

The presence of God the Father above the banderole that reads 'Tota pulchra es. . .' in the engravings emphasizes the creation of the Virgin in the mind of God, before all things, reflecting the new theological emphasis on the Immaculacy of her spiritual rather than physical conception.[48]

Compared with the embrace at the Golden Gate, or the infant in her mother's womb, the image of the pure young girl was indeed a long way from the physical details discussed by medieval theologians of the doctrine. Yet this was only one image of the immaculate conception, and when taken with the others it contributed to a richness of iconography which enhanced the variety of meanings that were to be found in liturgy, theology and devotion. However, during the sixteenth and seventeenth centuries, Spanish painters who were promoting the doctrine formulated an iconography which drew upon certain of the earlier types of image but excluded others. The iconography which they developed has remained the standard representation of the immaculate conception down to the present day, so its character is of more than historical interest.

Francisco Pacheco, in his influential *Art of Painting* (1649), rejected the embrace at the Golden Gate as a representation of Mary's conception, on the grounds that many people misinterpreted the image to mean that Mary was conceived miraculously at the time of her parents' embrace, rather than through sexual intercourse. This is a very reasonable objection, but it is not one which could apply to an image of the unborn Mary in her mother's womb – yet this image also failed to find favour with the great Spanish painters and fell out of use. It was at this time that the image of the Virgin and Child was also removed from the iconography of the immaculate conception. Commenting on an image which shows the Virgin without Christ, Vloberg says: 'The Blessed Virgin appears alone, without her Son, as befits her who is not yet the Mother of God, but has been prepared for that unique dignity by the unique privilege of exemption from original sin.'[49] Yet this is a strange line of reasoning, for it is the divine motherhood which provides the starting point for every medieval argument that Mary was immaculately conceived, and it is in virtue of her son's merits that the grace of sinlessness is bestowed upon her. Accordingly, it could be argued that any symbolic depiction of the immaculate conception should incorporate a representation of Christ; but Spanish artists opted instead for the *tota pulchra* image of the young girl standing alone.

Pacheco, drawing on the visions of Blessed Beatrice de Silva (d. 1490), foundress of the Conceptionist order of nuns, judged that the Virgin of the Immaculate Conception should be shown crowned with twelve stars, clothed with the sun, and standing on the moon. He also wrote: 'This lady should be shown in the flower of age, as twelve or thirteen years old, as a very beautiful *niña*.'[50] All these directions were followed by later painters, and most of them by sculptors as well. The insistence on extreme youth may derive from a Hispanic belief in childhood goodness and

---

48.   Ibid.: 43.
49.   Vloberg 1958: 471.
50.   Cited ibid.: 493.

Fig. 16. The *Medal of the Immaculate Conception*, known as the 'Miraculous Medal'.

innocence,[51] although the international popularity of the iconography requires some other explanation.

THE IMMACULATE CONCEPTION IN THE NINETEENTH AND TWENTIETH CENTURIES

The new image of the immaculate conception was used as a battle standard in the campaign to have the doctrine defined as part of the Catholic Church's official teaching. It spread throughout the Hispanic world and is found, for example, in the images of Our Lady of Guadalupe – patroness of Mexico and the Americas – and Nossa Señora Aparecida, the patroness of Brazil. But it did not become dominant in the devotion of Western Europe until the nineteenth century.

In 1830, Catherine Labouré, a novice in the Daughters of Charity, had a series of visions of the Virgin in the chapel of the sisters' convent in the rue du Bac in Paris. In one of these, Mary asked Sister Catherine to have a medal struck (Fig. 16). On the obverse side is an image of the Virgin with her arms outstretched and rays of light emanating from her hands. She is standing on a globe, but this is not understood to be the moon. Rather, it is the whole world, receiving the graces which are signified by the rays of light. The image usually includes a snake which the Virgin is treading underfoot. The tableau is placed against an oval background around whose edge are inscribed the words: 'O Mary conceived without sin, pray for us who have recourse

---

51. See Christian, Jr 1981: 215–22. St Teresa of Avila imagined the Blessed Virgin 'with the grace of a young girl, *niña*' (see Vloberg 1958: 493) and, according to legend, Juan Diego, the visionary of Our Lady of Guadalupe, saw the Virgin as a young girl of 'about fourteen years old' (sources cited in Carroll 1986: 182).

Fig. 17. Statue of Our Lady of Lourdes, in the grotto at Lourdes. (Photo Doucet)

to thee.' The reverse of the medal shows the hearts of Jesus and Mary, surmounted by a cross intertwined with a letter M, surrounded by twelve stars. The medal was first distributed in 1832 and was called the Medal of the Immaculate Conception. It was immediately popular, and the large number of miracles attributed to it led to its being known unofficially as the Miraculous Medal – the title by which Catholics throughout the world know it today.[52]

In 1854, Pope Pius IX issued the Bull *Ineffabilis Deus*, which declared the doctrine of Mary's immaculate conception to be the faith of the Church. Less than four years later, in 1858, Bernadette Soubirous of Lourdes received visions of a lady who said that she was the Immaculate Conception. The lady's appearance was very similar to that of the Virgin on the Miraculous Medal, the most notable difference being that in Bernadette's vision Mary held her hands together in prayer and that the cosmic symbols of globe and stars were missing (Fig. 17). Through thousands of copies, the statue of Our Lady of Lourdes, derived from Bernadette's vision, is now familiar to people across the world.

---

52.   Laurentin 1983; Dirvin 1984.

Subsequent apparitions of Mary have often manifested her in a similar form. The most famous of these is probably that which was seen by three children at Fatima in Portugal in 1917. The principal seer, Lucia dos Santos, later said that she had had visions in which Christ and the Virgin requested devotions to her Immaculate Heart,[53] and consecration to the Immaculate Heart forms an important aspect of the cult of Our Lady of Fatima.

In the modern period, the image of the Virgin of the Immaculate Conception has displaced the regal Virgin and Child as the dominant visual focus for Catholic Marian devotion, so that Mary as mother seems to have been supplanted by Mary as virgin. Yet despite the fact that the less maternal image of Mary enjoyed increasing popularity during the eighteenth and nineteenth centuries, much that was written about the immaculate conception during this period continued to follow the medieval pattern of argument, associating the Virgin's sinless conception with her divine motherhood. For example, Alphonsus Liguori's popular work *The Glories of Mary*, first published in 1750, gives as the principal reason for the immaculate conception that Mary was predestined to be the Mother of God.[54] Likewise, Pope Pius IX's Bull *Ineffabilis Deus* begins with an account of God electing Mary from before all time to be mother of the incarnate Word. Her immaculate conception is then related back to this.[55] But in the nineteenth and twentieth centuries, the divine motherhood has been reinterpreted in ways which have led to its definitive position being undermined.

The very slight shift in this direction is seen in the writing of Karl Rahner. In his important essay 'The Immaculate Conception', Rahner ties the doctrine to an anthropological position which holds that God's love for humanity is more funda-mental and important than the consequences of human sin, and he thus echoes the medieval approach to the doctrine's interpretation.[56] Rahner also follows a Scotist line in arguing that the distinctiveness of Mary's sanctification follows from her predestination to be Mother of God. He acknowledges that both the physical and the moral aspects of the divine motherhood are necessary, but he parts company with his medieval predecessors in the particular emphasis which he places upon her assent. It is because of her exceptional state of grace that Mary is able to consent fully and freely to a vocation which demands the participation of her whole person, and it is in this respect that Rahner understands Mary's immaculate conception to have a direct bearing on her motherhood. The possibility of full and free consent, rather than the requirement for purity or fittingness, is what makes Mary's radical sinlessness a necessary precondition for her divine motherhood.

However, more recent Mariological authors have almost abandoned references to Mary's motherhood in their own accounts of the immaculate conception. The

---

53. Zimdars-Swartz 1991: 69.
54. de' Liguori 1937: 19.
55. Latin text given in Gousset 1855: 761–75; English translation given in *Apostolic Constitution of Pius IX*, n.d. The understanding of Mary's predestination which the Bull presents is not the Scotist one outlined earlier in this chapter. Rather, it holds that the incarnation and divine motherhood were predestined because Adam's sin was foreseen from eternity.
56. Rahner 1961.

Spanish theologian Joseph Paredes gives four reasons why the Church teaches that Mary was immaculately conceived. Two of the reasons make no reference to her motherhood, although one of these is concerned with her *fiat* – her acceptance of God's will. The argument seems to be influenced by Rahner, claiming that Mary's consent would have embraced her whole life and must therefore have its roots deeply laid in her. But where Rahner speaks of Mary's active choice, Paredes says that she was 'utterly open and docile to God'.[57] Both here and throughout the book, Mary's motherhood is subordinated to a notion of her vocation as something which is principally concerned with spiritual attitude, to the point at which her physical maternity becomes more or less incidental. Thus it is not the divine motherhood, but 'Mary's personal act of faith and the believing attitude she maintained all her life [which] was the cause of salvation for the whole human race'.[58] Of the reasons Paredes gives for the immaculate conception, the two which do allude to Mary's motherhood describe her not as Mother of God, but as 'the Holy Mother of Jesus', and as mother of 'the "new Humanity"'.[59] The divine motherhood has slipped from view.

Another recent work, Kathleen Coyle's *Mary in the Christian Tradition*, makes no attempt to account for why the immaculate conception is necessary or fitting. So notwithstanding references to Eadmer and Duns Scotus,[60] the divine motherhood is not mentioned. Coyle presents Mary's sinlessness as the realization of that holiness to which all Christians are called and to which the Church is destined, but no explanation is given as to why Mary should be the one in whom this perfection is already accomplished.[61]

So in the iconography of the immaculate conception, the motif of physical motherhood has been lost, and in recent Mariological writing, the divine motherhood has also tended to disappear. At the same time, changes to the Mass of the Immaculate Conception in the Roman rite since the Second Vatican Council encourage a different reading of the doctrine from that which had been promoted in the liturgy for the previous 800 years. For the reading from Proverbs 8 has been removed and replaced by Genesis 3.9–15 and 20, which includes the prophecy of the woman's seed crushing the head of the serpent, and Eve being designated 'Mother of All the Living'. So a reading which invited the hearer to see the immaculate conception in the light of God's entire work of creation has been supplanted by one which sets the doctrine within a strongly anthropocentric perspective, implying that it should be understood in relation to sin and redemption, rather than to the foundations of the cosmos.

Yet the major changes to the interpretation of the immaculate conception, apart from those of visual representation, seem to have occurred only recently, in the twentieth century. This may be because the doctrine contains an inherent

---

57.   Paredes 1991: 228.
58.   Ibid.: 151.
59.   Ibid.: 228.
60.   Coyle 1996: 37–8.
61.   Ibid.: 35–44.

antagonism to the sorts of development which have occurred in the Virgin's cult more widely, so that the doctrine's reinterpretation has been retarded.

Evidence that the doctrine is interpreted in terms of God's care for the human body is provided by Andrea Dahlberg's anthropological study of three English pilgrimages to Lourdes, conducted in the 1980s. The shrine at Lourdes centres upon its healing spring and is particularly associated with prayer for the sick. Dahlberg examined the way in which bodily suffering is interpreted by sick and healthy pilgrims, and by staff at the shrine. The focus of devotion at Lourdes is care for those who are suffering illness or injury, and prayer for physical healing, but Dahlberg found that the healthy human body became a metaphor for other kinds of wholeness. For example, one pilgrim said that she was not sick but she had 'come to pray for "healing for all and especially for the sick"'.[62] Thus 'healing' was sought even for those who did not suffer physical ailments. Conversely, the moral perfection which is realized in Mary's sinlessness is seen as a source of physical health. Dahlberg argues that the pilgrims' behaviour revealed two distinct understandings of bodily suffering. The first of these she calls the Miracle discourse, and the second the 'Sacrificial discourse'. Both discourses make an association between sin and physical suffering, but they deal with them differently. The attitudes of most ordinary pilgrims towards bodily suffering constitute the Miracle discourse, which focuses upon the image of Our Lady of Lourdes. Pilgrims say that she is 'beautiful' – a whole body without imperfection of any kind. The aim of the Miracle discourse is to obtain miraculous healing,

> to eliminate sin in the body and so effect a cure. It is chiefly identified with Mary as Our Lady of Lourdes; Mary herself exemplifies the human being without sin by her perfect body and is also the source of the power the people hope to contact and thereby perfect themselves. The Miracle discourse is oriented to life in this world and in this body; it is premised upon the hope that the divine will intervene positively in the life of a person as God intervened in the life of Mary from the moment of her conception.[63]

So an image whose ostensible meaning is one of specifically spiritual perfection becomes simultaneously a symbol of hope for physical health. Perhaps this is not surprising, since the cult of a healing spring is founded upon the belief that divine power may work through material things, and since the Virgin of the Immaculate Conception is associated with Holy Wisdom, who directs both the natural and moral orders of the world.

By contrast, the 'Sacrificial discourse' sanctifies bodily suffering itself by construing it as a participation in the suffering of Christ:

> As a means of expiation, atonement and of achieving personal sanctity bodily suffering is valued. This discourse draws its power from the sacrifice of Christ. It

---

62. Dahlberg 1991: 45.
63. Dahlberg 1987: 286.

is Christ in the passion, an image of death and of the shattering of the unity of His two natures which provides an image for it. This discourse emphasises the redemptive power of the suffering of the innocent. It is oriented to the other-world where the sacrificial victim is rewarded and in relation to which bodily suffering is meaningful and valuable. This discourse teaches transcendence; this world is passed through and authentic existence is realised in the next.[64]

The Sacrificial discourse is that which is promoted by the clergy and lay officials at the shrine, who try to avoid talk of miracles, and who focus their attention on Christ at the expense of Mary.

Christianity has always contained the two dynamics exemplified in Dahlberg's study: on the one hand, the redemptive power of suffering, and, on the other, delight and rejoicing in God's work of creation and redemption. The doctrine of the immaculate conception is one of the strongest expressions of the latter of these two dynamics.

BIBLIOGRAPHY

Primary Sources
Anselm (1946) 'De conceptu virginali et de originali peccato', in *S. Anselmi Opera Omnia*, ed. F. S. Schmitt, vol. 2, Edinburgh: Thomas Nelson.
Bellarmine, Robert (1721) *De Controversiis Christianae Fidei*, vol. 2, *De Conciliis, et Ecclesia*, Prague: Wolffgang Wickhart.
Bernard of Clairvaux (1998) *The Letters of St Bernard of Clairvaux*, trans. Bruno Scott James, Stroud: Alan Sutton (first published Burns & Oates, 1953).
Berselli, Costante and Gharib, Giorgio (eds) (1981) *In Praise of Mary: Hymns from the First Millennium of the Eastern and Western Churches*, trans. Phil Jenkins, Slough: St Paul Publications.
St Bridget of Sweden (1680) *Revelationes Caelestes Seraphicae Matris S. Birgittae Suecae*, Gelder: Sebastian Rauch.
Duns Scotus, John (1933) *Opus Oxoniense*, in Ioannis Scoti, *Theologiae Marianae Elementa*, ed. P. Carolus Balić, Sibenik, Yugoslavia: Typographia Kačić.
Eadmer of Canterbury (1904) *Eadmeri Monachi Cantuariensis Tractatus de Conceptione Sanctae Mariae*, ed. H. Thurston and T. Slater, Freiburg-im-Breisgau: Herder.
Elliott, J. K. (ed.) (1993) *The Apocryphal New Testament: A Collection of Apocryphal Christian Literature in an English Translation based on M. R. James*, Oxford: Clarendon.
Gousset, Cardinal (1855) *La Croyance Générale et Constante de l'Eglise Touchant l'Immaculée Conception de la Bienheureuse Vierge Marie*, Paris: Jacques Lecoffre.
[John of Segovia] Ioannis de Segovia (1965) *Allegationes et Avisamenta pro Immaculata Conceptione Beatissime Virginis* (for the Council of Basel, 1436), facsimile edn of that by Balthasar Vivien, Brussels, 1664, Brussels: Culture et Civilisation.
de' Liguori, Alphonsus (1937) *The Glories of Mary*, trans. Anon., 2 vols, London: St Peter's Press.
[Ramon Llull] B. Raymundo Lulio (1664) *Libro de la Concepcion Virginal*, Latin text with Spanish translation by Alonzo de Zepeda, Brussels: Balthasar Vivien.
Miegge, Giovanni (1955) *The Virgin Mary: The Roman Catholic Marian Doctrine*, trans. Waldo Smith, London: Lutterworth Press.

---

64. Ibid.

Olier, M. (1866) *Vie Intérieure de la Très Sainte Vierge*, collected from Olier's writings, 2 vols, Rome: Salviucci.

Paredes, Joseph (1991) *Mary and the Kingdom of God: A Synthesis of Mariology*, trans. Joseph Davies and Josefina Martinez, Slough: St Paul Publications.

[Pius IX] (n.d.) *Apostolic Constitution of Pius IX Defining the Dogma of the Immaculate Conception*, Boston, MA: St Paul Books & Media, (reprinted from *Our Lady*, Papal Teachings Series).

Pusey, E. B. (1966) *Tractatus de Veritate Conceptionis Beatissimae Virginis, facienda relatione coram Patribus Concilii Basileæ, compilatus per Reverendum Patrem, Fratrem Joannem de Turrecremata*, facsimile of the 1869 edn, Bruxelles: Culture et Civilisation.

Rahner, Karl (1961) 'The Immaculate Conception', in *Theological Investigations*, trans. Cornelius Ernst, vol. 1, London: Darton, Longman & Todd: 201–13.

Rickert, Margaret (1952) *The Reconstructed Carmelite Missal: An English Manuscript of the Late XIV Century in the British Museum (Additional 29704-05)*, London: Faber & Faber.

Roschini, Gabriel M. (1948) *Mariologia*, 4 vols, Rome: Angelus Belardetti.

Suárez, Francisco (1860) *De Mysteriis Vitae Christi: Commentarii et Disputationes in Tertiam Partem D. Thomae*, in *Opera Omnia*, ed. Charles Berton, vol. XIX, Paris: Vivès.

Secondary Sources

Balić, Carlo (1958) 'The Medieval controversy over the Immaculate Conception up to the death of Scotus', in O'Connor (ed.), *The Dogma of the Immaculate Conception*: 161–212.

Brodrick, James (1928) *The Life and Work of Blessed Robert Francis Cardinal Bellarmine, SJ*, 2 vols, London: Burns, Oates & Washbourne.

Brodrick, James (1963), *Saint Peter Canisius, SJ*, London: Geoffrey Chapman (first published 1938).

Carroll, Michael (1986) *The Cult of the Virgin Mary: Psychological Origins*, Princeton, NJ: Princeton University Press.

Catta, Etienne (1961) 'Sedes Sapientiae', in du Manoir (ed.), *Maria*, vol. 6: 689–866.

Christian, Jr, William A. (1981) *Apparitions in Late Medieval and Renaissance Spain*, Princeton, NJ: Princeton University Press.

Clayton, Mary (1990) *The Cult of the Virgin Mary in Anglo-Saxon England*, Cambridge: Cambridge University Press.

Coyle, Kathleen (1996) *Mary in the Christian Tradition from a Contemporary Perspective*, Leominster: Gracewing.

Dahlberg, Andrea (1987) *Transcendence of Bodily Suffering: An Anthropological Study of English Catholics at Lourdes*, London School of Economic and Political Science, PhD thesis.

Dahlberg, Andrea (1991) 'The body as a principle of holism: three pilgrimages to Lourdes', in John Eade and Michael J. Sallnow (eds), *Contesting the Sacred: The Anthropology of Christian Pilgrimage*, London and New York: Routledge: 30–50.

Dirvin, Joseph I. (1984) *Saint Catherine Labouré of the Miraculous Medal*, Rockford, IL.: Tan Books (first published 1958).

Lamy, Marielle (2000) *L'Immaculée Conception: Etapes et Enjeux d'une Controverse au Moyen Âge (XIIe–XVe siècles)* Paris: Institut d'Études Augustiniennes.

Lamy, Marielle (2001) 'Les plaidoiries pour l'Immaculée Conception au Moyen Age (xiième-xvème siècles)', in Clelia Maria Piastra (ed.), *Gli Studi de Mariologia Medievale Bilancio Storiografico*, 'Millenio Medievale 26, Atti di Convegno 7', Bottai, Tavarnuzze-Firenze: SISMEL-Edizioni del Galluzzo: 255–74.

Laurentin, René (1952) *Marie, l'Eglise et le Sacerdoce: 1. Essai sur le Développement d'une Ideé Religieuse*, Paris: Nouvelles Editions Latines.

Laurentin, René (1983) *The Life of Catherine Labouré, 1806–1876*, trans. Paul Inwood, London and Sydney: Collins.

du Manoir, Hubert (ed.) (1949–71) *Maria: Etudes sur la Sainte Vierge*, 8 vols, Paris: Beauchesne.

O'Carroll, Michael (1982) *Theotokos: A Theological Encyclopedia of the Blessed Virgin Mary*, Dublin: Dominican Publications.

O'Connor, Edward Dennis (ed.) (1958) *The Dogma of the Immaculate Conception: History and Significance*, Notre Dame, IN: University of Notre Dame Press.

234

O'Donnell, Christopher (1988) *At Worship with Mary: A Pastoral and Theological Study*, Wilmington, DE: Michael Glazier.

Peers, E. Allison (1929) *Ramon Lull: A Biography*, London: Society for Promoting Christian Knowledge.

Pelikan, Jaroslav (1971) *The Christian Tradition: A History of the Development of Doctrine*, vol. 1, *The Emergence of the Catholic Tradition (100–600)*, Chicago, IL: University of Chicago Press.

Sebastian, Wenceslaus (1958) 'The controversy over the Immaculate Conception from after Duns Scotus to the end of the eighteenth century', in O'Connor (ed.), *The Dogma of the Immaculate Conception*: 213–70.

Stratton, Suzanne L. (1994) *The Immaculate Conception in Spanish Art*, Cambridge: Cambridge University Press.

de Suduiraut, Sophie Guillot (1998) *La Vierge à l'Enfant d'Issenheim: Un chef d'oeuvre bâlois de la fin du Moyen Age*, ?.

Villaret, E. (1952) 'Marie et la Compagnie de Jesus', in du Manoir (ed.), *Maria*, vol. 2, 935–73.

Vloberg, Maurice (1958) 'The iconography of the Immaculate Conception', in O'Connor (ed.), *The Dogma of the Immaculate Conception*: 463–506.

Wolter, Allan B. and O'Neill, Blane (1993) *John Duns Scotus: Mary's Architect*, Quincy, IL: Franciscan Press.

Zimdars-Swartz, Sandra (1991) *Encountering Mary: Visions of Mary from La Salette to Medjugorje*, Princeton, NJ: Princeton University Press.

Extract from a Medieval Sermon on the Conception of Blessed Mary[1]

May your charity, venerable brethren, deign to listen to me, as I tell how it has been shown, by many signs that have been observed in England, France and other parts of the world, that the Conception of the venerable Mother of God and ever Virgin Mary ought to be celebrated.

For in the days when God, in His goodness, saw fit to correct the evils of the English people and to bring them to a more strict fulfilment of the duties pertaining to His service, the most glorious duke of the Normans, William, subdued their land by warfare. Having become King of the English, William reformed the entire ecclesiastical hierarchy (*ecclesiasticae dignitatis honores*) by the power of God and his own zeal. The devil, the enemy of all good things, hated the works undertaken in this pious intention and often attempted to obstruct the King's success, through the treachery of his associates, and the attacks of outsiders. But the Lord protected and glorified this king who feared Him, and 'the hateful one was brought to nothing' (Ps. 14.4).

When the Danes, however, heard that England had been subjected to the Normans, they were deeply angered, as if an hereditary right had been taken from them. They prepared their arms and made ready their fleet in order to go and expel the Normans from the land which they felt had been given them by God. When William heard of this, being a very prudent man, he sent for a certain monk (Helsin), abbot of the monastery (of Ramsay) and sent him to Denmark to seek out the truth of the matter. The latter, a man of keen intelligence, carried out the King's mission vigorously, and, with his task faithfully accomplished, set sail again for England.

At first the trip went well, and he had crossed the greater part of the sea, when strong winds suddenly arose on all sides, and a terrible storm agitated both the sea and the sky. With the oars broken, the ropes snapped and the sails fallen, all hope was lost by the sailors, who were too exhausted to make any further effort, and were wretchedly waiting to be drowned. Despairing of saving their bodies, they loudly commended to their Creator the salvation of their souls alone, and they called upon the most Blessed Virgin Mary, Mother of God, the refuge of the miserable and the hope of the desperate. Suddenly they saw, in the midst of the waves not far from the ship, a man rather majestically garbed, and wearing a bishop's mitre.

He called the abbot (Helsin) to him, and began to address him in these words: 'Do you

---

1. This work, of unknown authorship, was for centuries attributed to St Anselm, who for this reason was frequently cited among the authorities favouring the doctrine and the feast of the Immaculate Conception. We reproduce here the legend of Helsin. Our translation (taken from Edward D. O'Connor (ed.), *The Dogma of the Immaculate Conception: History and Significance*, Notre Dame, IN: University of Notre Dame Press, 1958: 522–4) has been made from the text printed in Migne, PL 159: 319–24 (entire sermon, which includes two other legends in favour of the feast of Mary's Conception). The names Helsin and Ramsay, which we give in parentheses, are given in parentheses in Migne, PL, without any further explanation. Another account of the Helsin legend, closely parallel to the present one, has been edited by H. Thurston and Th. Slater in *Eadmeri Cantuariensis Tractatus de Conceptione Sanctae Mariae*, Freiburg im Breisgau, 1904: 88–92, followed by two other accounts which are not so similar. A fifth redaction is given by Migne immediately following the one here translated.

wish to escape from the peril of the sea? Do you wish to return to your country safe and sound?' When the abbot had tearfully[2] replied that he desired this with all his heart, and looked for nothing more than this, the stranger declared, 'Know that I have been sent to you by Our Lady Mary, the Mother of God, to whom you have so readily appealed: and if you are willing to do what I tell you, you and your companions will be saved from the danger of the sea.'

The abbot at once promised that he would obey in everything if he should escape this shipwreck.

'Then promise,' said the stranger, 'to God and to me, that you will solemnly celebrate the day of the conception and creation of the Mother of Our Lord Jesus Christ, and that you will exhort others to celebrate it.'

At this, the abbot, being a most prudent man, inquired, 'On what day is this feast to be celebrated?'

'You are to celebrate[3] this feast on December 8 (*sexto Idus Decembris*),' was the rejoinder.

'And what office,' asked the abbot, 'shall we use in the Church services?'

'The entire office of her Nativity is to be recited for the Conception, except that instead of the word *Nativity*, you are to read *Conception*.'

With this he disappeared, and in less time than it takes to tell, the storm died down. A breeze arose and the abbot safely reached the English shore, and made known what he had seen and heard to whomever he could. Moreover, he directed that this feast be celebrated in the monastery (of Ramsay), and until the end of his life celebrated it devoutly.

Therefore, dearly beloved brethren, if we wish to reach the port of salvation, we will celebrate the feast of the Conception of the Mother of God with fitting rites and services, so that we may be rewarded by her Son with a fitting recompense.

---

2. Reading *fletu* instead of the *fietu* which occurs in Migne, PL.
3. Reading *tenebis* instead of the *tenebris* which occurs in Migne, PL.

10

THE ENGLISH REFORMERS AND THE
BLESSED VIRGIN MARY[1]

PAUL WILLIAMS

INTRODUCTION

The writing of the sixteenth-century Reformers is characterized by strong reactions against contemporary Catholic Marian piety. The positive Marian teaching of Anglican Reformers concentrates on the incarnation and is summed up in the acceptance of Mary as the *Theotokos*, because this is seen to be profoundly scriptural. The immaculate conception was rejected by some Reformers who wrote strongly against the sinlessness of Mary, though some accepted that her sinlessness was now a part of the *consensus fidelium* and, therefore, to be believed. All stress Mary's need for a Saviour (cf. Lk. 1.47) – for some Reformers this can also mean preservation from sin – the agency of the Holy Spirit in the conception of Jesus, and Mary's real motherhood of her son. In the writers consulted, there is an absolute consensus about the perpetual virginity of Mary. Where the Assumption is discussed, it is either rejected or held to be of the *adiaphora*. From 1561, the Anglican calendar contained five Marian feasts (Conception, Nativity, Annunciation, Visitation and Purification, with no feast on 15 August for the assumption), but the Elizabethan *Book of Common Prayer* (1559) is almost devoid of specific Marian texts, and what there are stress only her purity and that the Son took human nature 'of her substance'. The basic shape of sixteenth-century Anglican teaching about Mary was avowedly that of the Scriptures and the first four General Councils. Only in the seventeenth century was there a richer recovery of Anglican reflection on Mary's place in the tradition of the Church.

THE SIXTEENTH-CENTURY DRIVE FOR REFORM

In the early sixteenth century, criticism of exaggerated Marian devotion[2] did not lead Catholics like Erasmus (1466/9–1536) and More (1478–1535) to consider breaking

---

1. This paper was prepared in collaboration with Nicholas Sagovsky and Michael Nazir-Ali, as a background document for the Anglican group of the Anglican/Roman Catholic International Commission, in its discussions concerning the Blessed Virgin Mary. As a study on the theological writings of the English Reformers, it is heavily indebted to the meticulous editing of classic Anglican sixteenth-century texts for the Parker Society. This doughty series gives to the authors and texts it includes a kind of 'canonicity' which has influenced not only the content of this paper but also the self-understanding of Anglicanism. *Caveat lector*: one has in addition to look elsewhere to capture the flavour of popular devotion, as has been so convincingly demonstrated by Duffy 1992, and by others.
2. For a brief account of late medieval Marian devotion, see Duffy 1992: 256–65.

with Rome. Erasmus visited Walsingham twice in 1512 and 1514. He criticized the Christians of his time because they never seemed to address themselves to God, but only to Our Lady and the saints. Thus in *The Shipwreck*, from his *Familiar Colloquies*, the sailors called on Mary, chanting the *Salve Regina*:

> They implored the Virgin Mary, calling her Star of the Sea, Queen of Heaven, Mistress of the World, Port of Salvation and many other flattering titles which Holy Scripture nowhere applies to her.

Thomas More wrote in his *Dialogue Concerning Heresies*:

> The people in speaking of our lady: Of al our Ladies, saith one, I love best our Lady of Walsingham, And I, saith the other, our Lady of Ipswich. In whiche woordes what meanth she but her love and her affeccion to the stocke that standeth in the chapel of Walsingham or Ippiswiche? ... Doth it not plainly appeare that either thei trust in the images of Christes stede and our Ladies, letting Christ and our Lady go, or take at lest wise those ymages that thei wene thei were verily the one Christ, the other our Lady her self.

There were, however, other, more radical reformers, influenced from the 1520s by Lutheranism, for whom such criticism was integral to a much wider theological and practical drive for reform. Hugh Latimer (*c.* 1485–1555), known for his powerful preaching, is typical of such critics, when he comments in a sermon for the First Sunday after the Epiphany on the wise men's worship of Jesus:

> Here is confounded and overthrown the foolish opinion and doctrine of the papists, which would have us to worship a creature before the Creator; Mary before her Son ... Mary was a blessed woman, above all women, and yet not such a one as should be called upon and worshipped.

Of the sixteenth-century Anglican writers, John Jewel (1522–71), Bishop of Salisbury, is one who returns frequently to this issue:

> That blessed mother of our Saviour Christ hath been openly blasphemed in the church: she was called *spes, vita, dulcedo*, 'our hope, our life, and our sweetness'. And further: *Salva omnes sperantes in te*: 'Save all them that trust in thee.' Thus have men openly prayed unto her, to the great blaspheming of her holy name.

Or, in similar vein:

> I beseech you, mark the form and fashion of their prayers. To the blessed virgin they said: *Ave Maria, salus et consolatrix vivorum et mortuorum*: 'Hail Mary, the saviour and comforter both of quick and dead.' And again: *O gloriosa virgo Maria, libera nos ab omni malo, et a poenis inferni*: 'O glorious virgin Mary, deliver

us from all evil, and from the pains of hell.' Again: *Monstra te esse matrem*: 'Show that thou art a mother.' Thy call her *regina coeli, domina mundi, unica spes miserorum*; 'queen of heaven, lady of the world, the only hope of them that be in misery'. It were tedious and unpleasant to recite the like their blasphemies . . . How foul a kind of idolatry was it to worship the image with the self-same honour wherewith they worship the thing itself that is represented by the image!

Jewel is thought to have been the author of the homily 'Against Peril of Idolatry':

> When you hear of our Lady of Walsingham, our Lady of Ipswich, our Lady of Wilsdon, and such other, what is it but an imitation of the Gentiles idolaters' Diana Agrotera, Diana Coryphea, Diana Ephesia, &c. . . . Whereby is evidently meant, that the Saint for the image sake should in those places, yea, in the images themselves, have a dwelling: which is the ground of their idolatry; for where no images be they have no such means.

This whole lengthy homily bears witness to the continuing fear among those of a reforming disposition of the idolatrous use of religious images:

> Wherefore the images of God, our Saviour Christ, the blessed Virgin Mary, the Apostles, Martyrs, and other of notable holiness, are of all other images most dangerous for the peril of idolatry; and therefore greatest heed to be taken that none of them be suffered to stand publicly in churches and temples. For there is no great dread lest any should fall to the worshipping of the images of Annas, Cayphas, Pilate, or Judas the traitor, if they were set up. But to the other, it is already at full proved, that idolatry hath been, is, and is most like continually to be committed.[3]

Though they firmly reject the invocation of saints, the *Homilies* say nothing specifically about the invocation of Mary,[4] but the Reformers' continuing concern about 'idolatry' and the 'invocation of Saints' is evident in the miscellaneous rejection of 'Romish Doctrine' in Article XXII:

> The Romish Doctrine concerning Purgatory, Pardons, Worshipping and Adoration, as well of Images as of Reliques, and also invocation of Saints, is a fond thing vainly invented, and grounded upon no warranty of Scripture, but rather repugnant to the Word of God.[5]

---

3. *Certain Sermons or Homilies*, 'The Third Part of the Homily Against Peril of Idolatry': 259.
4. Invocation of the Saints (without specific mention of Mary) is strongly rejected in 'The Second Part of the Homily concerning Prayer', *Certain Sermons or Homilies*: 348.
5. Article XXII, 'Of Purgatory', composed in 1553. 'Romish doctrine' was substituted for 'The Doctrine of the school authors' in 1563.

Latimer defended his critical attitude to the *Ave Maria* in the following terms:

> As for the *Ave Maria*, who can think that I would deny it? I said it was a
> heavenly greeting or saluting of our blessed lady, wherein the angel Gabriel,
> sent from the Father of heaven, did annunciate and shew unto her the goodwill
> of God towards her, what he would with her, and to what he had chosen her.
> But I said, it was not properly a prayer, as the *Pater noster*, which our Saviour
> Christ himself made for a proper prayer ... So that I did not speak against well
> saying of it, but against superstitious saying of it, and of the *Pater noster* too.[6]

Much of the invocation of Mary to which Jewel and others referred came from the
commonplaces of popular piety (for example, *spes, vita, dulcedo*) in primers and other
prayer books, some of which gave particular offence. Thomas Rogers (d. 1616)
refuted 'the Romish doctrine concerning pardons' by quoting 'a further manifestation of the vanity and impieties of the Romish pardons' from the *Horae beatissimae
Virginis Mariae secundum usum Sarum*:[7]

> Whosoever devoutly will say the prayer following shall merit (thereby) eleven
> thousand years of pardons; 'Hail, Lady, saint Mary, mother of God, queen of
> heaven, the gate of paradise, the lady of the world, the light eternal, the empress
> of hell, &c. Pray unto thy beloved Son Jesus Christ for me, and deliver me
> from all evils, pray for my sins. Amen.'

A number of the Reformers specifically criticized Bonaventura's composition of
'Our Lady's Psalter'[8] in which the word 'Lady' is substituted for 'Jahweh', as in
'*Domina mea, in te speravi: de inimicis libera me, Domina*: O my Lady, in thee have I put
my trust; deliver me from mine enemies, O Lady.'[9] Among those who cite
Bonaventura are William Tyndale (1494?–1536), William Fulke[10] and John
Jewel.[11] Another of Jewel's targets was Cardinal Bembo, 'sometime the pope's
secretary', who called 'the same blessed virgin *dominam et deam nostram*, "our lady

---

6.   Latimer to Morice, *Works*, vol. 2: 360. Latimer's remarks were probably occasioned by the rosary
which consists of 15 decades of *Ave Marias*, each decade being followed by a *Pater Noster*.
7.   Rogers 1854: 220–1.
8.   This work is no longer believed to be by St Bonaventure.
9.   Tyndale 1848: 150, note.
10.   Fulke 1843: 528: 'I have seen that horrible blasphemous Psalter of Bonaventure, perverting all
the psalms unto the honour of the virgin Mary, with intolerable blasphemy against God and the holy
mother of Christ, whose greatest honour is the kingdom of her Son, and in his infinite glory.'
11.   Jewel, 'Upon the Second Epistle to the Thessalonians', *Works*, vol. 2: 900: 'They turn all that is
spoken of in the whole book of the psalms of the prophet David either of God or of Christ, and apply
it to the virgin Mary, and call that psalter *psalterium beatae Mariae*, "the psalter of blessed Mary". Who
will take the pains to peruse it shall find that comfortable speech of our Saviour, "Come unto me, all
ye that are weary and laden, and I will ease you," thus blasphemously abused in the second psalm:
Venite ad eam, omnes qui laboratis et tribulati estis; et refrigerium et solatium dabit animabus vestris: "Come unto
her, all ye that travail and be heavily loaden; and she will give rest and comfort to your souls."' See also
'On Luke 10.23–4': 1083.

and goddess" '.[12] This was the kind of overblown language which generated the hostility of the Reformers to the rosary, also known as the 'Lady-Psalter'. Grindal's Visitation Articles (1576) for the Province of Canterbury enquire of the parishes:

> Whether any your parsons, vicars, curates, or ministers be favourers of the Romish or foreign power, letters [i.e. hinderers] of true religion, preachers of corrupt and popish doctrine, or maintainers of sectaries, or do set forth and extol vain and superstitious religion, or be maintainers of the unlearned people in ignorance and error, encouraging or moving them rather to pray in an unknown tongue, than in English, or to put their trust in a certain number of prayers, as in saying over a number of beads, Lady-Psalters, or other like?[13]

In the fervid atmosphere of the mid-1570s, Anglican divines were quick to see an integral connection between treason, impiety, Roman Catholic doctrine, super-stition, ignorance, the liturgical use of Latin, and Marian devotion, especially the rosary.

Against this background, it is entirely understandable (however shocking it might be to contemporary liberation theologians) to find Mary twice extolled in the *Book of Homilies* for her obedience to the political authorities. The 'Sermon on Obedience' tells how:

> We read that the holy Virgin Mary, mother to our Saviour Christ, and Joseph, who was taken for his father, at the Emperor's commandment went to the city of David, named Bethleem, to be taxed among other, and to declare their obedience to the magistrates for God's ordinances' sake. And here let us not forget the blessed Virgin Mary's obedience...[14]

In the 'Sermon against Wilful Rebellion', the point is made even more forcefully:

> In the New Testament the excellent example of the blessed Virgin Mary, the mother of our Saviour Christ, doth at the first offer itself . . . This obedience of this most noble and most virtuous lady to a foreign and pagan prince doth well teach us, who in comparison to her are most base and vile, what ready obedience we do owe to our natural and gracious Sovereign.[15]

However politically tendentious, this way of putting things serves to illustrate a fundamental polemical stance that characterizes the drive for reform: all the Reformers were concerned for the proper reading and use of Scripture as a critical principle against teaching which they found offensive because it obscured or distorted the gospel. It is typical that this passage should begin: 'In the New Testament, the

---

12. Jewel, 'Defence', *Works*, vol. 3: 577.
13. 'Articles to be Enquired of within the Province of Canterbury', from Grindal 1843: 163.
14. 'The Third Part of the Sermon on Obedience': 120.
15. 'The Second Part of the Sermon against Wilful Rebellion': 607.

excellent example of the blessed Virgin Mary ... doth at the first offer itself.' Miles Coverdale (1487/8–1569) is representative of the radical, reforming movement of the early sixteenth century when he expresses against Roman Catholicism his concern that teaching about Mary should be based not on the authority of the Church alone, but on the witness of Scripture:

> Doth not the scripture affirm this doctrine, that the mother of our Saviour is the purest virgin that ever God created? If she had any need of you, ye show her but a faint friendship in reporting that her most pure virginity hath none other ground but the authority of your church.[16]

THE MARIAN TEACHING OF THE ANGLICAN REFORMERS

The central affirmation of Anglican teaching about the Blessed Virgin Mary is expressed in Cranmer's (1549) Collect for Christmas Day:

> Almighty God, who hast given us thy only-begotten Son to take our nature upon him, and as at this time to be born of a pure Virgin: Grant that we being regenerate, and made thy children by adoption and grace, may daily be renewed by thy Holy Spirit; through the same our Lord Jesus Christ, who liveth and reigneth with thee and the same Spirit, ever one God, world without end. *Amen.*

The focus is Christological: Mary's significance as a 'pure Virgin' is determined by the significance of the incarnation. This, like the collects for the Annunciation and the Purification, is a prayer about fruitful participation in the Christian life, not about Mary.

In his 'Lesson of the Incarnation of Christ', John Hooper (*c.* 1495–1555) argues closely from Scripture that the humanity of Jesus Christ was formed from the humanity of the Virgin:

> And this way, wrought God Almighty the humanity of his only Son, our Saviour, Jesus of Nazareth, without the knowledge of man, using the blessed Virgin by the operation of the Holy Ghost to conceive and bring forth this blessed seed, which was made of her, *and took the original of his humanity of and in her,* by the operation of the Holy Ghost; and neither nourished in her womb, neither brought forth she the humanity of Christ, as a thing that God had given Christ from heaven, or else from some other where; but nourished in her, and brought forth the blessed seed that God had made by his holy power of her own substance.[17]

He then deals with a number of objections, perhaps the most significant being, 'If

16. Coverdale 1846: 415.
17. 'A Lesson of the Incarnation of Christ', Hooper 1852: 5 (our emphasis).

Christ took his flesh of a woman, then were he a sinner, and partaker of the sin that naturally dwelleth in every [one] of Adam's posterity.' What Hooper does not say in his answer is that Mary was preserved from sin at or after her conception: on this he remains silent. Nor does he associate the sinlessness of Jesus with the virginity of Mary. His line is strictly scriptural ('This testimony of the will of God in the scripture should suffice the people of God'):

> The scripture declareth not only Christ to be the seed and fruit of the Virgin, but also a seed and fruit without sin, saying, 'The thing that shall be born of thee is holy, and shall be called the Son of God.'[18]

Not all early Anglican writers stick as closely to the text of Scripture as Hooper. Jewel's *Apology of the Church of England* and his *Defence of the Apology* are central texts for the establishment among Anglicans of the authority of the tradition affirmed by the first four General Councils. He rejects the appeal of heretics like Arius, Nestorius and Eutyches to the Scriptures, because they were not reading the Scriptures as 'the holy fathers' had done:

> In the third council kept at Ephesus ... the heretic Nestorius boasted, as ye do, of the scriptures, saying they were of his side, and would neither speak nor hear ought but scriptures, scriptures; and alleging a place or two out of the gospel, where Mary is called the mother of Jesus, stoutly: 'Find me in all scripture,' quoth he, 'where Mary is called the mother of God.' Hereto what said that holy and learned bishop Cyrillus chief in that council? ... 'This faith,' saith he, 'the disciples of God have by tradition left unto us. And although they made no express mention of this word *deipara* yet so to think we have been taught by the holy fathers.'[19]

Jewel's controversy with the Roman Catholic Harding turns on what he sees as the departure of Roman Catholic teaching from 'the authority of the holy fathers':

> We despise them [the fathers] not therefore, but rather give God thanks in their behalf, for that it hath pleased him to provide so worthy instruments for his church; and therefore we justly reprove you, for that so unadvisedly and without cause ye have forsaken the steps of so holy fathers. The four general councils wherein you dwell so long, as they make nothing against us, so in sundry points they fight expressly against you.[20]

Jewel's standard is clearly the teaching that is common to the Scriptures, to the Fathers of the Church, and to the first four General Councils. All three converge in

---

18. Ibid.: 13.
19. Jewel, 'Defence', *Works*, vol. 3: 224.
20. Ibid.: 225.

his vigorous defence of *Theotokos*, the term used at the Council of Ephesus to define Mary's role in the incarnation.[21]

There is an important point about language here, made very clearly by Whitaker:

> We readily receive even new terms, provided they are such as expound the genuine sense of scripture. Such are *consubstantial, Trinity, person, supposition, unbegotten, theotokos,* and the like, which are convenient exponents of the meaning of scripture. But we should cautiously avoid those terms which are foreign from the scriptures, such as *transubstantiation, consubstantiation, concomitance, ubiquity,* and the like.[22]

The controversy about the reading of Scripture, and especially the role of the Church in the reading of Scripture, which is central to the whole Reformation dispute, is exemplified perfectly by the controversy over Marian teaching and devotion.

Some Anglican writers are united in their rejection of the immaculate conception. Tyndale, with typical irony, points out the division of opinion between Thomas Aquinas and Duns Scotus on this issue:

> And of your dead saints let us take one for an example. Thomas de Aquino is a saint full of miracles, as friars tell; and his doctrine was, that our lady was born in original sin. And Duns, doing no miracle at all, because, I suppose, no man wotteth where he lieth, improveth that with his sophistry, and affirmeth the contrary. And of the contrary hath the pope, for the devotion of that the grey friars gave him, ye may well think, made an article of the faith.[23]

Arguing on the same grounds as Jewel – that the reason why the immaculate conception cannot be an article of faith is its *novelty* – Whitaker writes,

> But the papists affirm that the church can now prescribe some new article of faith, which had not been esteemed in former ages as a necessary dogma. That the virgin Mary was conceived without original sin, was formerly thought a free opinion, not a necessary part of faith … But, at present, it is not permitted amongst papists to retain the ancient liberty of opinion on this subject; and he

---

21. The *Theotokos* is also defended by Whitaker as 'grounded upon the scriptures'. See 'The First Controversy', in Whitaker 1849: 538–9.

22. Ibid.: 603. It is clear from the terms mentioned that Whitaker is differentiating his position not only from Roman Catholic theological terminology, but also from Lutheran. On 'transubstantiation', compare Article XXVIII, 'Of the Lord's Supper' (1553, significantly amended 1563): 'Transubstantiation (or the change of the substance of Bread and Wine) in the Supper of the Lord, cannot be proved by Holy Writ; but is repugnant to the plain words of Scripture, overthroweth the nature of a Sacrament …'

23. Tyndale 1850: 131–2; see also, 'Obedience of a Christian Man', in Tyndale 1848: 159, 313, 316; 'The Answer to the Preface', in Fulke 1843: 35–6; Rogers 1854: 100, commenting on Article IX, 'Of Original or Birth-sin' (1553), against 'the Papists, who say, that original sin was not at all, much less remained in the Virgin Mary'; Jewel, 'Defence', *Works*, vol. 3: 611.

is hardly deemed a catholic, who ascribes any even the slightest taint of sin to Mary.[24]

The assertion by the Council of Trent that, in speaking of original sin, it did not intend to include 'the blessed and immaculate virgin Mary, who gave birth to God'[25] increased the pressure on Anglican theologians to distance themselves from teaching which they saw as going beyond the witness of Scripture. In commenting on Article XV, 'Of Christ alone without Sin' (1553), Rogers began by presenting Roman Catholic doctrine:

> The Papists say that the blessed virgin was pure from all sin, both original and actual. For (these are their own words) 'Our Lady never sinned;' Our Lady 'sinned not so much as venially in all her life;' she exactly filled the whole law, that is, was without sin.[26]

The 'Papists', who teach this, are listed first among 'the adversaries' of the truth that 'All men besides Christ, though regenerate, be sinners'.

The rejection of the immaculate conception by some Anglican writers was supported by the critical reading of the text of the Vulgate. Whitaker was only one of a number of Reformers[27] who drew attention to the corruption of the Vulgate text at Genesis 3.15:

> *Ipsa conteret caput tuum.* So it is wrongly and corruptly read in the Vulgate. For the reading ought to be *Ipse* or *Ipsum*, so as to make the reference to the Seed of the woman, not to the woman herself. ... Though all the fathers were to say that we should read *Ipsa*, yet it should by no means be admitted or approved. For the Hebrew copies constantly read *Hu*; the Septuagint exhibits *autos*; the Chaldee Paraphrase confirms the same reading; and lastly, some copies of the Vulgate edition retain *ipse*, some *Ipsum*. Finally, the very drift of the sentence requires that we should understand it of the Seed of the woman, not of the

---

24. Whitaker 1849: 504.
25. Council of Trent, *De Pecc. Orig.*, 6. Richard Hooker (*c.* 1554–1600) gives a careful reading of the council's teaching in his 'Answer to Travers' (see Hooker 1888, vol. 3: 579–83.): 'In the end, they did wisely cut out their canon by a middle thread, establishing the feast of the Virgin's conception, and leaving the other question [that of Mary's sinlessness] doubtful as they found it; giving only a caveat, that no man should take the decree which pronounced all mankind originally sinful, for a definite sentence concerning the Blessed Virgin' (581). He concludes, 'The Fathers of Trent have not set down any certainty about this question, but left it doubtful and indifferent' (582). Hooker discusses the question no further.
26. Rogers 1854: 134.
27. See also Fulke 1843: 74, 532. That the 'seed' referred to is Christ not Mary is taught in the Catechism of Edward VI (*The Two Liturgies*: 503); by Thomas Becon (*c.* 1511–67), though he takes 'an woman' to be 'the most pure and blessed virgin Mary' (Becon 1843: 71); by Alexander Nowell (*c.* 1507–1602, Nowell 1853: 151); and by the Swiss Reformer Heinrich Bullinger (1504–75), whose translated sermons (1577) had a wide circulation in Elizabethan England (see Bullinger 1851, vol. 3: 13–14).

woman. What woman could crush the serpent's head? Was it Mary? I am well aware that this is what is said by them. But how? When she bore Christ? But to bear Christ is not to crush the head of the serpent: ... Was it when she believed in Christ? But this applies to all believers. Christ therefore, and Christ only, is he who by his power could crush and destroy the head of the infernal serpent, and rescue and deliver us out of his jaws.[28]

However, Latimer in his *Articles untrully, unjustly, uncharitabily imputed to me by Dr Powell of Salisbury* seems to accept Mary's sinlessness as part of the *consensus fidelium*:

> ... foresomuch as now it is universally and constantly received and applied that she was no sinner, it becometh every man to stand and agree the same, 'and so will I,' quoth I ... Good authors have written that she was no sinner; but good authors never wrote that she was not saved: for though she never sinned, yet she was not so impeccable, but she might have sinned, if she had not been preserved: it was of the goodness of God that she never sinned ...[29]

Again in Latimer's *Letter to Morice*, a future secretary to Archbishop Cranmer, concerning Dr Powell's accusation he could also be equivocal:

> Occasioned of some, not only laymen, but also priests and beneficed men, which gave so much to our lady of devotion without judgment, as though she had not needed Christ to save her: to prove Christ her Saviour, to make Christ a whole Saviour of all that be or shall be saved, I reasoned after this manner: that either she was a sinner, or no sinner: there is no mean. If she were a sinner, then she was redeemed or delivered from sin by Christ, as other sinners be: if she were no sinner, then she was preserved from sin by Christ; so that Christ saved her, and was her necessary Saviour, whether she sinned or no.[30]

When on the defensive, Latimer was careful not to emphasize his belief that Mary could be said to be a sinner, though he clearly accepted and taught this. At such times, he returned to his primary emphasis on Christ as Saviour:

> It hath been said in times past, without sin, that our lady was a sinner; but it was never said, without sin, that our lady was not saved, but a Saviour. I go not about to make our lady a sinner, but to have Christ her Saviour ... To make a pernicious and damnable lie, to have our lady no sinner, is neither honour nor yet pleasure to our lady; but great sin, to the dishonour and displeasure both of God and our lady.[31]

---

28.   Whitaker 1849: 163–4.
29.   Latimer, *Works*, vol. 2: 226–7.
30.   Ibid.: 225–6; cf. Letter of Latimer to Morice: 358–9.
31.   Ibid.: 228.

It is not absolutely clear, but Nowell's Catechism can be read as affirming Mary's sinlessness – which is significant because it was approved in Convocation in 1563, though not printed until 1570:

> *M*. But why was [Jesus] conceived of the Holy Ghost, and born of the Virgin Mary, rather than begotten after the usual and natural manner?
>
> *S*. It behoved that he that should and could satisfy for sins, and entirely restore wicked and damned persons, should not himself be defiled or blemished with any stain or spot of sin … Therefore, when the seed of man was wholly corrupt and defiled, it behoved that in conception of the Son of God, there should be the marvellous and secret working of the Holy Ghost, whereby he might be fashioned in the womb of the most chaste and pure Virgin, and of her substance that he should not be defiled with the common stain and infection of mankind.[32]

Nowell appears to attribute this sinless conception jointly to the operation of the Holy Spirit and to Mary's purity ('fashioned in the womb of the most chaste and pure Virgin … of her substance').[33]

The Anglican Reformers were also much concerned with the translation of *kecharitomene* as *gratia plena* in Luke 1.28. Wycliffe and Tyndale translated the angel's greeting to Mary 'Hail, full of grace', but in the Geneva Bible of 1557 this became 'Hail, thou that art freely beloved', and in the Authorized Version of 1611, 'Hail, thou that art highly favoured'. Fulke commented:

> That we have translated 'Hail, Mary, freely beloved,' or, 'that art in high favour', we have followed the truth of the Greek word, not so denying thereby, but that the virgin Mary, of God's special goodness without her merits, as she confesseth, was filled with all gracious gifts of the Holy Spirit, as much as any mortal creature might be, except our Saviour Christ, *whose only privilege it is to be free from sin*, and to have received the gifts of the Holy Ghost without measure in his manhood.[34]

The issue of Mary's peccability was debated hotly by the early Reformers, particularly Latimer and Tyndale. Both found in Chrysostom support for the position that Mary was 'taken with a little vain-glory' (cf. Lk. 8.19–21);[35] and Latimer claimed that

---

32. Nowell 1853: 152–3.
33. Compare Roger Hutchinson (d. 1555, 'The Image of God, a Layman's Book', in Hutchinson 1842: 147): 'But albeit he took flesh of his mother, yet it was holy flesh, not sinful flesh, that he took; forasmuch as it was conceived and wrought by the overshadowing of the Holy Ghost. Albeit the seed and flesh of other be sinful, yet hers was not so; but sanctified by the Holy Spirit, and most clean. For to her it was said, *Benedicta tu inter mulieres*.' This would suggest that the 'sanctification' of Mary took place in the conceiving of Jesus, a position commonly taken by the Reformers.
34. Fulke 1843: 528 (our emphasis); cf. 149–50.
35. Tyndale 1850: 207; Latimer, citing Augustine and Chrysostom: 'pricked with a little vain-glory' ('The Fourth Sermon on the Lord's Prayer', *Works*, vol. 1: 383); 'pricked with vain-glory' (*Works*, vol. 2: 117).

Chrysostom and Augustine 'plainly affirm that Mary was somewhat arrogant' (cf. Jn 2.3–4). He went on to note Jesus' sharp words to his parents, 'Know ye not that I must be in the business of my Father?' (Lk. 2.49), concluding, 'Now, in all these places, as the writers say, *Passa est humanum*; "She hath shewed her frail nature." '[36] The thinness of the evidence is, however, palpable:

> On a time when our Saviour was preaching, his mother came unto him, very desirous to speak with him, insomuch that she made means to speak with him, interrupting his sermon which was not good manners. ... She would have been known to be his mother, else she would not have been so hasty to speak with him. And here you may perceive that we gave her too much, thinking her to be without any sparkle of sin; which was too much: for no man born into this world is without sin, save Christ only.[37]

There was universal agreement that Mary needed Christ as her Saviour. Thomas Becon (*c.* 1511–67) links this affirmation with the famous words of Augustine, refusing to entertain the question of Mary's being a sinner:

> I answer with St Austin: 'Whensoever there is disputation of sin, all must needs confess themselves sinners, *except the holy virgin Mary*, of whom, for the honour of the Lord, I will have no question at all when we entreat of sin. For we know there was given to her more grace than to any other creature for to overcome sin on every part, forasmuch as she deserved to conceive and bring forth him, whom it is evident to have had no sin. Therefore, *this virgin except*, if we could gather all the saints both men and women ... if they might be asked this one thing, they would surely cry with one voice, 'If we should say that we have no sin, we deceive ourselves and the truth is not in us.' ... Yet this dare I boldly affirm and say, that this most holy, pure, and glorious virgin disdained not to confess Christ to be also her Lord and Saviour.[38]

Not all Anglican writers, then, are as outspoken against Mary's sinlessness as Tyndale and Latimer, though it cannot be said they explore the matter with any depth or unanimity. Anglican writers are, however, unanimous in asserting Mary's need of a Saviour (although not pursuing the debate as to whether Mary was 'sanctified' at the conception of Jesus, or rather preserved from sin from her mother's womb, or even

---

36.   Latimer, *Works*, vol. 1: 515–16.

37.   Ibid.: 383; cf. 514: 'We ought not to live after any saint, nor after St Paul, or Peter, nor after Mary the mother of Christ, to follow them, I say, universally: we are not bound so to do, for they did many things amiss'; also vol. 2: 117–18, 157–8, 163–5. Latimer refers to Augustine, *Epistle 243, In Joan. Evangel. c. 1 Tract VIII* and Chrysostom, *Hom XLV in Matt. XII, In Joan. Hom. 22.*

38.   'A New Year's Gift', from Becon 1843: 317 (our emphasis); cf. Becon 1844: 170: 'The glorious virgin Mary, although of all creatures most holy, most pure, most innocent (Christ Jesus her Son only excepted), in her song, considering certain imperfections to remain and abide in her, which she received of old Adam from her father and mother ... calleth God her Saviour, to declare that there was somewhat in her, from the which she must be saved by the mercy and goodness of God.'

from her conception, some do raise these views). They are also unanimous in affirming Mary's virginity both before and after the birth of Christ. Little is said specifically about her being *virgo in partu*, but a great deal is said, both explicitly and implicitly, about Mary as *semper virgo*.

Cranmer, in correcting Henry VIII's *Institution of a Christian Man* (1538), records:

> And I beleve also, that this child Jesu Christ was not only thus conceived without sin, but also that he was born in like manner of the said most blessed mother: and that she, both in conception, and also in the birth and nativity of this her child, and ever after, retained still her virginity pure and immaculate, and as clear without blot, as she was at the time that she was first born and ever after also we verily believe.[39]

Whitaker acknowledges that the belief that 'the blessed Mary was always a virgin' was a matter of faith, though it was supported by Jerome, Ambrose and Epiphanius.[40] He also notes the opinion of Basil who thought it 'no article of faith'. Whitaker is one of a number of Anglican writers who mention the rejection of Mary's perpetual virginity by Helvidius[41] – and the opposition of the Fathers to Helvidius's position. On the use of Scripture to refute Helvidius, he is engagingly frank:

> As to the perpetual virginity of Mary, it is no business of mine to meddle with that dispute. I content myself with saying, that the fathers, who managed the controversy with Helvidius, adduced not only some obscure traditions, which no one would rank very high, but made use also of testimonies from scripture . . . Therefore, if these fathers determined aright, this opinion is not absolutely without scriptural authority.[42]

Tyndale takes a modified version of Basil's line on the perpetual virginity of Mary 'which, though it be never so true, is yet none article of our faith, to be saved by. But we believe it with a story faith, because we see no cause reasonable to think the contrary'.[43] Latimer asserts:

> [Mary] had no more, neither before nor after, but was a clear virgin before she brought forth, and after she brought forth him she remained a virgin.[44]

---

39. Cranmer 1846, vol. 2: 88.
40. 'The First Controversy', in Whitaker 1849: 502; cf. 539.
41. Helvidius (a fourth-century Latin theologian, against whom Jerome wrote *De perpetua virginitate B. Mariae adversus Helvidium*) is also explicitly refuted by Latimer, *Works*, vol. 2: 105; Hooper 1843: 161; Thomas Cranmer (1489–1556), Cranmer 1846: 60; Jewel, 'Defence', *Works*, vol. 3: 440–1); John Philpot (1516–55), Philpot 1842: 427. Helvidius is also refuted by Bullinger (*Works*, vol. 4: 437).
42. Whitaker 1849: 539.
43. Tyndale 1850: 96; cf. 33. Tyndale repeats his opinion in his Marginal Notes on St Matthew's Gospel, from Tyndale 1849: 227.
44. Latimer, *Works*, vol. 2: 105.

Cranmer also accepts, with 'Cyprian, Chrysostom, Jerome, Ambrose, Austin and all other speaking thereof', that 'the perpetual virginity of our lady is to be believed of necessity', and that this is to be defended as 'written in scripture':

> All the said authors prove her perpetual virginity by this text of scripture: 'This door shall be still shut, and not opened for any man to go through it, but only for the Lord God of Israel; yea, he shall go through it, else shall it be shut still.' For if these and such other fathers had not judged her perpetual virginity to have been written in the scriptures, they would never have judged it a thing to be believed under pain of damnation.[45]

Where Anglican writers discuss the doctrine of the assumption, it is either rejected or held to be of the *adiaphora*. Tyndale several times wrote in knockabout style about his rejection of this and other Marian doctrines:

> Of what text thou provest hell, will another prove purgatory; another *limbo patrum*; and another the assumption of our lady: and another shall prove of the same text that an ape hath a tail. And of what text the gray friar proveth that our lady was without original sin, of the same shall the black friar prove that she was conceived in original sin.[46]

Whitaker is more restrained:

> The papists celebrate the feast of the assumption of the blessed virgin Mary with the utmost honour, and the Rhemists in their notes on Acts I praise this custom exceedingly: yet Jerome, in his book to Paula and Eustochium, concerning the assumption of the blessed virgin, says that 'what is told about the translation of her body is apocryphal'. Erasmus, indeed, writes that that book is not by Jerome, but by Sophronius, who, however, was contemporary with Jerome.[47]

Yet Tyndale can also write:

> As pertaining to our lady's body, where it is, or where the body of Elias, of John the evangelist, and many other be, pertaineth not to us to know. One thing we are sure of, that they are where God hath laid them. If they are in hyevaen, we have never the more in Christ: if they be not there, we have never the less ... as for me, I commit all such matters unto those idle bellies, which have nought else to do than to move such questions; and give them free liberty to hold what they list, as long as it hurteth not the faith, whether it be so or no ...[48]

---

45.   Cranmer 1846, vol. 2: 60. Cf. Ezek. 44.2.
46.   'Obedience of a Christian Man', Tyndale 1848: 158–9; cf. 313, 316; Tyndale 1850: 28.
47.   Whitaker 1849: 667; cf. 579–80.
48.   Tyndale, *Works*, vol. 1: 315f. A similar argument is forwarded in Tyndale 1850: 28.

One other line of criticism is exegetical: of the 'woman clothed with the sun' in Revelation 12.1, John Bale (1495–1563) writes, 'Not Mary, Christ's mother, is this woman, though many hath so fantasied in their commentaries; but it is the true christian church, of whom Mary is a most notable member.'[49]

Finally, we need to note that an embryonic Eve/Mary parallel is found in *The King's Book*.[50] Commenting upon *The Salutation of the Angel to the Blessed Virgin Mary*, it records:

> And also how high grace was this, that after the default made through the persuasion of the first woman, our mother Eve, by whom Adam was brought into disobedience, this blessed virgin was elect to be the instrument of our reparation, in that she was chosen to bear the Saviour and Redeemer of the world?[51]

Noting the above arguments surrounding the mistranslation of Genesis 3.15, some Anglican writers could still associate Mary with this text. Heinrich Bullinger's *Decades*, first published in 1577, were held in high regard by members of the Church of England. Not only did he provide a haven for those who fled the persecution under Queen Mary, but also the Convocation of Canterbury in 1586 commended the reading of the *Decades* to every minister having the cure of souls. Commenting on Genesis 3.15, Bullinger writes:

> God in these words promiseth seed: the seed, I say, not of man, but of woman; and that too, of the most excellent, to wit, that most holy virgin Mary, the women that was blessed among women.[52]

And more explicitly Hutchinson observes:

> The seed which is promised unto Adam is named to be *semen mulieris*, 'the seed of a woman:' the same seed of Eve; the selfsame afterward is called the seed of Abraham, of Jacob, the seed of David, and the blessed virgin.[53]

CONCLUSION: THE BLESSED VIRGIN MARY IN ANGLICAN DEVOTION AND TEACHING

The broad lines of Anglican teaching about the Blessed Virgin Mary were clearly established in the sixteenth century, though Anglican devotion to Mary was much enriched in the seventeenth. Despite the continuation of theological controversy

---

49.   Bale 1849: 404.
50.   *The King's Book*, published in 1543, was a revision of the *Bishops' Book* and issued under the sanction of the King in Convocation.
51.   *The King's Book*: 137.
52.   Bullinger 1851, vol. 3: 14.
53.   Hutchinson 1842: 146.

about doctrine, liturgy and devotion throughout the sixteenth century, there were no major changes to Anglican liturgical or doctrinal expressions of Marian teaching and devotion after the publication of the 1561 Calendar, which through the reign of Elizabeth accompanied the 1559 *Book of Common Prayer*. The content of the 1662 *Book of Common Prayer* was largely completed 100 years earlier.

In the Prayer Books of 1549 and 1552, the Calendar was greatly simplified. Of the Marian feasts, only the Annunciation and the Purification were retained by Cranmer in 1549. The Conception, the Nativity, the Visitation and the Assumption were removed. However, in 1561, the Conception (*sic*) of the Blessed Virgin Mary, the Nativity of the Blessed Virgin Mary and the Visitation were all restored to join the Annunciation and the Purification as Marian feasts. The one, conspicuous, continuing omission was the Assumption, which disappeared from Anglican worship in 1549, only partially to return in some twentieth-century Anglican calendars.[54]

For some 400 years, the Anglican calendar had five Marian feasts. However, only for the Annunciation were a collect, epistle and Gospel prescribed: until 1662, for the Purification there was only a collect and Gospel. What is striking about the collects for these feasts (which were simple translations from the Missal) is the absence of specific reference to Mary. The collect for the Annunciation reads:

> We beseech thee, O Lord, pour thy grace into our hearts; that, as we have known the incarnation of thy Son Jesus Christ by the message of an angel, so by his cross and passion we may be brought unto the glory of his resurrection; through the same Jesus Christ our Lord. *Amen.*

And that for the Purification:

> Almighty and everlasting God, we humbly beseech thy Majesty, that, as thy only-begotten Son was this day presented in the temple in substance of our flesh, so we may be presented unto thee with pure and clean hearts, by the same thy Son Jesus Christ our Lord. *Amen.*

The relatively generous provision in the Calendar for the celebration of Mary after 1561 is as striking as the relative absence of specific Marian texts not just for those feasts, but throughout the *Book of Common Prayer*. This was the Elizabethan sequel to an interrupted official programme of 'reform within the shell of traditional forms'[55] that had begun with the production of the King's Primer in 1545. Diarmaid MacCulloch comments that this officially sponsored Primer contains 'none of the exuberant conversations of medieval liturgy with Our Lady or the saints'.[56] Though the book contained none of the traditional prayers to the Virgin, it did, however,

---

54. Not until recent liturgical revisions has there been within Anglicanism a Marian feast on 15 August, and then not of the Assumption. In England this is now a non-specific feast of the Blessed Virgin Mary. In some Anglican provinces it is celebrated as the feast of the Dormition.
55. MacCulloch 1996: 335; cf. Duffy 1992: 446–7.
56. Ibid.: 336.

contain the Litany, which was first translated in 1544, with the petition: 'Holye Virgin Mary mother of God our Savyoure Iesu Christ *Praye for us.*'[57] This petition was removed in the *Prayer Book* of 1549. The 1549 *Prayer Book* nevertheless retained the Eucharistic Canon, with the conclusion,

> And here wee doe give unto thee most high prayse, & heartye thankes, for the wonderfull grace and vertue, declared in all thy sainctes, from the beginning of the world: and chiefly in the glorious and most blessed virgin Mary, mother of thy sonne Iesu Christ our Lord and God . . .[58]

This was removed in 1552. From 1552, in the *Book of Common Prayer*, with the exception of the Creed, the Collect (already mentioned) and the proper Preface for Christmas Day ('who, by the operation of the Holy Ghost, was made very man of the substance of the Virgin Mary, his mother, and that without spot of sin, to make us free from all sin'), there was no mention of Mary in the Communion. The 39 Articles of Religion (1563), though, as we have seen, they mark out certain theological positions which directly reflect controversy over Mary, contain, from start to finish, only one explicit, central, non-controversial Marian statement: 'The Son . . . took Man's nature in the womb of the blessed Virgin, of her substance.'[59]

This austerity in the Prayer Book, the Ordinal (including the Litany) and the Articles speaks volumes about the extent to which in the sixteenth century Anglican Marian devotion was 'cauterized' by the climate of reaction to the overblown Marian piety of the late Middle Ages. Much of that piety was, however, contained in devotions, prayers and iconography which were not integral to the Liturgy. From 1561, the Anglican Prayer Book left considerable space for Marian piety (for example, at the five Marian feasts), but the explicit focus remained determinedly Christological and determinedly scriptural. Not until the seventeenth century did Anglicans again become creative in their reflection on Mary as a type of the Church's delight in God's Word and of the Church's obedience to God's Spirit, a creativity that was only possible when it was not immediately equated with ill-informed popular religion.

BIBLIOGRAPHY

Primary sources which are cited in the article but are not in the Bibliography are published by the Parker Society.

Primary Sources
Bale, John (1849) *Select Works*, Cambridge: Parker Society.
Becon, Thomas (1843) *Early Works*, Cambridge: Parker Society.
Becon, Thomas (1844) *The Catechism, with other pieces written by him in the reign of Edward VI*, Cambridge: Parker Society.

---

57. See Brightman 1915, vol. 1: 174.
58. Ibid., vol. 2: 690.
59. Article II, 'Of the Word or Son of God, which was made very Man' (1553, slightly expanded 1563).

Bullinger, Heinrich (1851) *Decades*, Cambridge: Parker Society.
Certain Sermons or Homilies Appointed to be Read in Churches (1938), London: SPCK.
Coverdale, M. (1846) *Remains*, Cambridge: Parker Society.
Cranmer, Thomas (1846) *Works*, 2 vols, Cambridge: Parker Society.
Fulke, William (1843) *A Defence of the Sincere and True Translations of the Holy Scriptures into the English Tongue, against the Cavils of Greg. Martin*, Cambridge: Parker Society.
Grindal, E. (1843) *Remains*, Cambridge: Parker Society.
Hooker, Richard (1888) *Hooker's Works*, 4 vols, Oxford: Clarendon.
Hooper (1843) *Early Writings*, Cambridge: Parker Society.
Hooper (1852) *Later Writings*, Cambridge: Parker Society.
Hutchinson, Roger (1842) *Works*, Cambridge: Parker Society.
Jewel, John, *Works*
The King's Book (1865), ed. T. A. Lacey, London: R. Browning.
Nowell, Alexander (1853) *Catechism*, Cambridge: Parker Society.
Philpot, John (1842) *Examinations and Writings*, Cambridge: Parker Society.
Rogers, T. (1854) *The Catholic Doctrine of the Church of England, an Exposition of the Thirty-Nine Articles*, Cambridge: Parker Society.
The Two Liturgies (1844), Cambridge: Parker Society.
Tyndale, W. (1849) *Expositions and Notes on Sundry Portions of the Holy Scriptures*, Cambridge: Parker Society.
Tyndale, W. (1850) *An Answer to Sir Thomas More's Dialogue*, Cambridge: Parker Society.
Tyndale, W. (1848) *Doctrinal Treatises and Introductions to Different Portions of the Holy Scripture*, Cambridge: Parker Society.
Whitaker (1849) *A Disputation on Holy Scripture against the Papists*, Cambridge: Parker Society.

Secondary Sources

Brightman, F. E. (1915) *The English Rite*, 2 vols., London: Rivingtons.
Duffy, E. (1992) *The Stripping of the Altars: Traditional Religion in England, 1400–1580*, New Haven, CT, and London: Yale University Press.
Graef, H. (1985) *Mary: A History of Doctrine and Devotion*, vol. 2, London: Sheed & Ward.
MacCulloch, D. (1996) *Thomas Cranmer, a Life*, New Haven, CT, and London: Yale University Press.

11

FRANCISCO SUÁREZ AND MODERN MARIOLOGY

SARAH JANE BOSS

FRANCISCO SUÁREZ

Throughout the Tridentine era, the name of Francisco Suárez was commonplace in Catholic educational institutions and beyond, and he is a figure of outstanding importance in European intellectual history. He was born in Granada in 1548 and joined the Society of Jesus at the age of 16. He then spent the rest of his life in Jesuit academic institutions, including Rome – where he worked out much of his thinking on the Virgin Mary – and Coimbra, where he spent the longest period of time, and where he died in 1617. So his work took place in the decades immediately following the Council of Trent (1545–63).[1] Suárez was a man of many parts: most famously, perhaps, he was an extremely important legal theorist. He is often thought of as the founder of international law; and the Hispanic countries of the world still have legal systems that draw heavily on Suarezian principles. He was also an important philosopher: his moral theology and theory of canon law was employed in Catholic ethical thinking until very recently, and his *Metaphysics* was a standard work in European universities – both Catholic and Protestant – for the better part of two centuries.[2]

Suárez's view of the human condition is favourable and hopeful. In the Foreword to his major work on law, *De Legibus*, he asks why a theologian should be concerned with laws. In reply, he argues that the theologian is concerned with God as, among other things, 'the final end to which rational creatures are striving', and in whom is their ultimate happiness; and the function of legal systems is to help those creatures attain their end in God, who is also himself the legislator.[3] So the purpose of law is not merely the correction of sinfulness, but primarily the generation of righteousness and the attainment of heaven. Suárez's ethical theory and his understanding of God's general dealings with humanity assume that God has ordered the world in such a way that it is always within the grasp of a man or woman to increase in merit and come nearer to perfection.[4] Suárez's teaching on the Blessed Virgin Mary presents her as the one who reaches humanity's final destination by following the most perfect path that is possible for a human being.

---

1. The most substantial biography of Suárez is de Scoraille 1912.
2. The importance of Suárez's thought for the whole development of Western metaphysics has been brilliantly argued by Courtine 1990.
3. *De Legibus*: 2–3.
4. An overview of Suárez's work in several fields is given in Razón y Fe 1948.

Suárez's Mariology

The earliest existing example of the use of the word 'Mariology' comes from a text dated 1602, where its use is defended, evidently because it was a neologism.[5] The activity which it designates, however, had been practised for two decades previously; and among Suárez's theological writings, his longest text on the Virgin Mary, composed mainly in the 1580s, is generally reckoned to be the first of its kind.[6] That is to say, it is the first systematic treatment of Marian doctrine as a whole. Earlier authors had dealt with particular Marian questions, such as those concerning the immaculate conception; but Suárez organized the various topics of Marian doctrine into a coherent whole – each part being linked to the others by means of neo-scholastic argument, and the entire treatise being set within the wider body of Christian theology.

Suárez's treatment of Marian doctrine begins by establishing that she is the Mother of God, and everything else that he says about her follows from this office, from the honour intrinsic to it, and from the Virgin's predestination to it.[7] Suárez establishes the truth of the divine motherhood (i.e. that Mary is the mother of God) by arguing from the Scriptures – in which Mary is the mother of Christ, who is God – and then from the teaching of the ecumenical Council of Ephesus (AD 431). At Ephesus, Mary was proclaimed to be the Godbearer – or Mother of God – in accordance with the arguments of Cyril, Bishop of Alexandria (d. 444), who defended this title for the Blessed Virgin. Cyril contended that to deny that the human woman Mary was the mother of God was in effect to deny that humanity and divinity were properly united in her son Jesus Christ. Conversely, to affirm that Mary is the Godbearer is to assert the full humanity and the full divinity of the one whom she conceived and bore. So, having established the truth of the divine motherhood – on the basis of Scripture, the authority of a Church council and rational argument – Suárez then has a foundation on which to construct other lines of argument about Mary. For example, he argues that God bestowed upon her an exceptional degree of grace from the moment of her conception. And his main argument for this is related directly to the divine motherhood. This is how the argument goes: As a general principle – apart from his Mariology – Suárez argues that God gives us the grace that is necessary for us to perform the task to which God calls us: if God requires me to visit the sick, or if God requires me to die as a martyr, or whatever it may be, God

---

5.   Nicolas Nigido, *Summa Sacrae Mariologiae*, Palermo: J. A. de Franciscis, 1602, cited in Laurentin 1952: 211.

6.   It is contained in a work popularly known as *De Mysteriis Vitae Christi*, which is part of Suárez's commentary on the *Summa Theologica* of Thomas Aquinas, *Commentarii et disputationes in Tertiam Partem D. Thomae*, in Berton (ed.) 1860, vol. 19, Disputations I–XXIII: 1–337. This work first appeared in print in Alcalá in 1592 (a short discussion of the dating of Suárez's principle writings on the Virgin Mary can be found in de Aldama 1952: 978–9). An English translation of Disputations I, V and VI can be found in Suarez 1954.

7.   *De Mysteriis*, Disp. I: 3. The eminent Mariologist José de Aldama, writing in the 1950s, claimed that Suárez's raising of the question as to the first principle of Mariology, and his systematic working out of a Marian theology from a first premise, was his main legacy to modern mariology; de Aldama 1950: 55–73.

will give me the grace sufficient to that task. Now, in Mary's case, she was called to be the Mother of God. That, according to Suárez, is the greatest task which any simple human being (i.e. one who is not God incarnate) ever has been or could be called upon to perform. Accordingly, the grace that Mary received, being commensurate with the task and the office (Latin: *dignitas*) to which she was called, was the greatest that anyone has ever received.[8]

Moreover, following the teaching of John Duns Scotus (1266–1308), the great thirteenth-century Franciscan, the incarnation of the Word of God in Christ was predestined from before the foundation of the world, and not only as a response to human sinfulness;[9] and since the incarnation consisted in part, at least, in Mary giving Christ his humanity – in her being the mother of God – Mary's divine motherhood must have been predestined in the same act by which God predestined the incarnation.[10] That means that there was never a time when Mary was not going to be the mother of God.[11] So from the moment of Mary's conception, God called her to the divine motherhood. Since her whole life would have been ordered to this supreme dignity, according to Suárez we can be sure that God will have bestowed upon Mary an exceptional degree of grace from the very first moment of her life.[12]

The divine motherhood, and Mary's predestination to it, is the reason of all the other blessings which she receives, and the doctrine that she is the mother of God informs everything else that systematic theology can say about her.

The Divine Motherhood in Relation to Mary's Free Will

What, then, does Suárez say is the character of Mary's divine motherhood? What does he tell us about her being the mother of God? Well, there are, of course, two principal elements to it: on the one hand, Mary makes a *moral* contribution to the incarnation. She freely assents to God's will. She makes an act of free will, and says,

---

8. *De Mysteriis*, Disp. I, sect. II:7: 9–10.
9. A short account of Scotus's Christology is given in Wolter and O'Neill 1993: 49–54. Wolter and O'Neill consider that 'Scotus was not primarily concerned with what God might have done … if Adam had not sinned'; rather, 'he began with … the fact of the Incarnation as it actually occurred in all its details. And thus Scotus also takes into account that the complete motive for Christ's Incarnation includes also the prevision of Adam's fall and his subsequent redemption' (49). The more usual reading of Scotus highlights his teaching that the incarnation was predestined from before the prevision of Adam's fall, and this is the teaching that appears in Suárez's teaching on the Blessed Virgin's predestination to be Mother of God. It should be noted that Duns Scotus was not by any means the only advocate of this doctrine, but is certainly one of the most eminent.
10. '*Secundo probatur, quia Christus Deus homo praedestinatus est, seu electus ante prævisum originale peccatum; ergo et ejus mater*', *De Mysteriis*, Disp. I, sect. III:4: 11.
11. Ibid., Disp. I, sect. III:1–4: 10–11.
12. Suárez argues that at her conception, the Virgin received a greater intensity of grace than the consummate grace of humanity and the angels (*De Mysteriis*, Disp. IV, sect. I:3–4: 56–7). This argument went back to Suárez's earliest engagements in theological argument. At the Jesuit College in Salamanca he had presented a dissertation which argued that Mary's graces and merits outweighed those of all other creatures put together (de Scoraille 1912: 107). He subsequently defended the supereminence of Mary's grace in a university disputation (ibid.: 113–14).

'Let it be to me according to your word', thus consenting to the earthly conception of Christ.[13] So Mary is a moral agent in the incarnation.

But that moral agency – Mary's act of free will – would be of purely private interest – it would not be of universal importance – if it did not lead to the bodily conception of the world's Redeemer, of the eternal Word. Christ redeemed us in his flesh: in his Passion and death on the cross, but also in his carnal human life in general and in his bodily resurrection; Christ redeemed us in the flesh, and it was Mary who gave him that flesh. So Mary is not only a moral but also a physical agent in the incarnation.

Now, in general, Christian theologians, including Suárez, have argued that an act of the will – a conscious decision or attitude – carries a moral weight that a purely physical action does not. For example, St Bernard of Clairvaux (1090–1153), in one of his homilies in praise of the Blessed Virgin Mary, enjoins his audience to take note of both her virginity and her humility. Mary's virginity is a physical state and her humility a condition of the soul. Bernard says that both these things are praiseworthy. But, he says, if you are a virgin and are *proud* of your virginity – if you boast about it – then it is of little moral worth. Furthermore, not everyone is called to be a virgin; but even people who are not virgins are called to be humble, and humility is a great virtue whatever one's physical state may be. So although the physical state of virginity is good, the moral state of humility takes precedence.[14]

If we follow this line of thought, then we might be inclined to say that Mary's moral consent to be the mother of Christ is of greater worth than her physical conception of God incarnate in her womb. She hears the word of God and keeps it, and surely that is what counts the most? But Suárez points out that in the case of Mary's conception of Christ we are dealing with a matter that is of a completely different order from that which is at issue with other people under different circumstances. All God's saints 'hear the word of God and keep it', as Mary did. But Mary also conceived and gave birth to God incarnate, the Saviour of the world, which the others did not. So her physical act of conceiving and bearing Christ is a unique, miraculous and indispensable element in God's redemption of the world, and, as such, it cannot properly be compared to an ordinary moral assent to God's will. Ordinary obedience to the will of God, and conceiving God incarnate, are not commensurable activities. Moreover, all human co-operation with the will of God is possible only because of the grace which God has already given us; and in Mary's case, the grace to do God's will follows precisely from the grace which enables her to be the Godbearer and the grace which follows from that task and office. So the physical act of Godbearing takes priority over everything else that a theologian might want to consider in Mary's life, including her moral virtues.[15]

---

13.   *De Mysteriis*, Q.XXX, art. I, Comm.:5: 130. Suárez argues here that although the incarnation is predestined, so that the Virgin's free will is not a *cause* of the event, God nevertheless seeks the consent of those whose co-operation is required for a predestined act.

14.   Bernard of Clairvaux, (Homily on the Annunciation) Homily I:5–6, in Bernard of Clairvaux and Amadeus of Lausanne 1979: 9–10.

15.   *De Mysteriis*, Disp. I, sect. II: 7–10.

At this point, one might ask how it is that Mary could both have been predestined to be the mother of God and at the same time have exercised free will in consenting to Gabriel's announcement of the conception of Christ. Does the one not preclude the other? This question is of particular interest in relation to the thought of Suárez, since he was one of many Jesuits during this period who, in the debate over how to reconcile divine foreknowledge with created free will, argued for the strongest possible understanding of freedom of the will. Writing in relation to Mary, Suárez observes that, in the history of the world, there are a very, very few cases in which human choice is predestined. Christ's consent to be crucified, and Mary's to conceive the Saviour, are two of these. So in the case of Christ's conception, God did not merely have foreknowledge of Mary's assent to be the mother of Christ; the matter was pre-ordained, and Mary's exercise of free will was not, strictly speaking, the *cause* of the incarnation, but her *consent* to it. Suárez observes that when something is predestined, the human will that is necessary to its realization will freely move to consent, and he comments, 'Such is the mystery before us.'[16]

Suárez provides encyclopaedic material relating to every topic he discusses, citing the works of all major, and many minor, patristic and medieval authors, and assessing their arguments. His discussions provide interesting, and sometimes corrective, reading. For example, following Augustine and Anselm, he contends that Adam's culpability for the fall was greater than Eve's. For Anselm, the reason given for this assertion is that the whole seed of humanity resided in Adam, the male, and not in Eve, the female.[17] Thus, if Eve alone had sinned, then the ensuing guilt and other consequences would have been hers alone; but since the whole human race was contained in Adam, it was his sin which led to the fall of all humanity. For Suárez, being a political and legal theorist, the reason for Adam's greater culpability is that he is the head of the human race in the way in which a king is head of a people, or a father is head of a family. Adam thus has a representative function which Eve does not, and, like the king who brings good or bad fortune to his subjects, Adam's actions bring consequences upon all those whom he represents. Eve, however, plays a contributory role in the fall; and Mary, likewise, working with Christ who is the Second Adam, contributes to the world's salvation, and may be said to be a 'cause' of it, in a non-technical sense.[18]

Suárez also surveys the medieval literature concerning the question as to whether Mary made a physiologically active contribution to the conception of Christ, or whether her contribution to the physical act of conception was purely passive. He points out that most earlier theologians and philosophers subscribed to a theory of human conception attributed to Galen, according to which the male parent's contribution to a couple's offspring is to provide active seed, while the female parent provides both active seed and passive matter. The Aristotelian theory of conception, by contrast, holds that the male provides the active seed and the female provides passive matter alone. The Aristotelian view was promoted mainly by Thomas

16. *De Mysteriis*, Q.XXX, Art. I.5: 130, '*quale est praesens mysterium*'.
17. St Anselm 1946.
18. *De Mysteriis*, Disp. XXIII, sect. 1.4: 331.

Aquinas and his followers, and was the minority opinion. According to the dominant Galenic view, then, Mary contributed both active seed and passive matter to the generation of God incarnate. A different view, however, was provided by Duns Scotus, who held that the Aristotelian understanding of conception was correct in the natural course of things – that is to say, the father normally contributes active seed to the conception of a child, and the mother contributes only passive matter – but that the situation could not have been quite like this in the case of the conception of Christ. For if Mary had provided only passive matter to the generation of her son, and he also had no human father, then there would have been no active human principle involved in his conception, and hence he could not have been fully human. Yet Christ's full humanity is an essential aspect of the doctrine of the incarnation, and Duns Scotus therefore contended that, in the unique case of the conception of Christ, his mother Mary must have contributed active seed as well as passive matter. Suárez, however, disagrees with the majority opinion and with Duns Scotus, holding instead that – regardless of what happens in normal acts of conception – Mary contributed only passive matter to the conception of Christ. His discussion seems to be premised upon the view that female physiology is analogous to male physiology, such that any active contribution that the female might make to a conception would be similar to that which is made by the emission of the male seed;[19] and the emission of seed in some measure compromises bodily integrity, and thus virginity. Suárez takes the view that the emission of seed of any kind would undermine Mary's perfect virginity, and he is determined that she maintained the absolute integrity of her virginal state.[20]

SUÁREZ AND HIS MARIOLOGICAL SUCCESSORS

Writing in the 1580s, Francisco Suárez stated that 'by reason of her dignity as mother', the Virgin Mary 'has a singular right to the goods of her son',[21] who is God.[22] That is, Mary has rights in those things which belong to Christ because she is his mother. Some decades later, Jean-Jacques Olier (1608–57), founder of the seminary of Saint Sulpice and a highly influential figure in the development of European Catholic spirituality,[23] contended that since Mary was elected to be mother of God the Son, she was therefore chosen to be spouse of God the Father.

---

19.   For example, Disp. V: 78.
20.   Elsewhere, I have argued that the reason for Suárez's insistence on Mary's absolute physical virginity is that he understands the relationship between Mary and Christ to be the created image or counterpart to the eternal relationship between the first and second Persons of the Blessed Trinity. As the generation of the Son by the Father effects no change in the Father, so the generation of the incarnate Son by his mother brings about no change in her.
21.   *De Mysteriis Vitae Christi*, Disp. I, sect. II:7: 10, '*ratione maternae dignitatis habet singulare jus ad bona filii*'.
22.   Ibid.: Disp. I, sect. II:2: 8, '*singulare jus habeat ad bona Dei filii sui*'.
23.   An overview of the Mariology of the so-called 'French School' is given in Graef 1985, vol. 2: 31–43; Olier's work is described on 35–41. See also Wright 2004: 271–9. Selections from the writings of the French School can be found in Thompson (ed.) 1989.

Olier describes a literal, albeit idealized, marital relationship between the Father and the Blessed Virgin,[24] and specifies:

> The spouse [i.e. Mary], who enjoys the rights and prerogatives of ordinary spouses, enters into possession of her spouse [i.e. the Father], who becomes hers; and then [she enters] into a perfect commonwealth of all the goods which he possesses.[25]

Thus, while Suárez and Olier both hold that Mary has an entitlement to the goods of God, the basis for this claim is different in the two authors. For Suárez, it is Mary's status as mother which accords her this right, while for Olier, it is her status as spouse.

As we have seen, in the Mariology of Suárez, Mary's position as mother of God determines everything else that can be said of her; and this marks Suárez off clearly from what has become the mainstream of Mariological writing in the nineteenth and twentieth centuries, which, following Olier, presents arguments founded less often on the basis of her motherhood, and frequently on the assertion that she is the spouse or bride of God. The purpose of the present chapter is to show that Suárez's 'maternal' Mariology provides an interpretative model by which the relationship between God and humanity is understood without recourse to gender as a primary category, and in which emphasis is given to unity between Creator and creation, and correspondence between heaven and earth. It will be suggested that this is theologically and anthropologically superior to more recent, 'spousal' Mariologies, which involve a new emphasis on sexual difference, and which prevent a proper grasp of the implications of the hypostatic union for Christian anthropology.

The Relationship of Mother and Son: Perfect Union
In his principal work of Marian theology, then, Suárez states at the outset that everything which he will say of the Virgin rests on the divine motherhood, its dignity (*dignitas*) and the Virgin's predestination to it.[26] He uses the Scriptures and Church Fathers to argue the case that Mary is truly the Mother of God, and then adds 'a conjecture, or congruence', as follows:

> For doubtless God wished to communicate himself to people by all kinds of means, and, so to say, to contract with them all kinds of kinship, by blood and by affinity, that tend towards perfection; yet one kind [of kinship], and one which is exceedingly perfect, exists that God may not so much be man but even the son of man, and that some created human person may be joined together with God [*conjuncta Deo*], in so far as is possible with regard to a person. Whence indeed it is accomplished that not only human nature in

---

24. Olier 1966, vol. 1: 53–66.
25. Ibid.: 60: '*L'épouse, qui jouit des droits et des prérogatives des épouses ordinaires, entre en possession de son époux, qui devient sien; et ensuite en communauté parfaite de tous les biens qu'il possède.*'
26. *De Mysteriis*, Disp. I: 3.

Christ, but also a created person in the Virgin, will have been exalted above all the choirs of angels.[27]

Thus the divine maternity is not merely an implicit adjunct to the incarnation, but is an end in itself, because it is the one relationship in which a human person is joined to God in the most complete manner possible. At first glance, one might think that this is a mistake, since it is the humanity of Christ, not of Mary, that is joined to God most perfectly. But although in Christ the human and divine natures are perfectly united, Christ's *person* is divine and not human.

The Christological definition of Chalcedon states that Christ is 'one person in two natures'. The natures are human and divine, but the person, being the Second Person of the Trinity, is only divine. When the Council of Chalcedon met in 451, the term 'person' had been employed for many decades to designate a member of the Blessed Trinity; and in the case of Christ, Chalcedon ruled that the Second Person – the eternal Word – was the principle uniting the divine and human natures, and this did not compromise Christ's full humanity. In his discussion of the Persons of the Trinity, Suárez follows Thomas's account of Boethius in holding that 'a person is an individual substance of a rational nature'.[28] In defending the view that a person is a substance, and not a quality, Suárez points out that the term 'person' can signify a human being, but not a part of a human being, such as a hand or a head. Likewise, he says Christ's humanity 'is not a person, because with respect to substance, it is not at all complete'.[29] A human person is constituted of a body and a soul, and in the incarnation, the Word of God took both of these and was thus fully human. But the Church's definition of the union of Christ's natures holds that they are united in a single person, and that the one person is divine. Suárez thus employs a Mariological device to show how something which might superficially be seen as a deficiency in the Chalcedonian definition is implicitly made good by Mary's person being joined as closely as possible to the Deity. And this move of Suárez's has felicitous consequences, which I shall consider at various points below.

In Suárez's thought, Mary's being uniquely joined to God corresponds to, and is a consequence of, a similarly unique closeness which exists between her and Christ in the incarnation. For in the human flesh which he shares with his mother, Christ is bound to her in an altogether singular way. Suárez quotes Peter Damian as saying, 'Whilst God may be present in other things in three ways, in the Virgin he was present in a fourth, special way, namely, by identity, because he is the same as that

---

27.   Ibid., Disp. I, sect. I:9: 5, '*Quia nimirum voluit Deus sese omnibus modis hominibus communicare, et (ut ita dicam) omnes cognationis et affinitatis modos perfectionem importantes cum illis contrahere; unus autem, et valde perfectus, est, ut Deus non tantum sit homo, sed etiam filius hominis, et ut quaedam persona humana creata sit conjuncta Deo, quantum esse potest in ratione personae. Unde etiam factum est, ut non solum humana in Christo natura, sed etiam persona creata in Virgine super omnes Angelorum choros fuerit exaltata.*'

28.   Suárez, *Commentarii et Disputationes in Primam Partem D.Thomae*, Liber 1: 'De Trinitate Personarum', cap. I, sect. 2: 533: '*Persona est rationalis naturae individua substantia.*'

29.   Suárez: 'De Trin. Pers.', cap. I, sect. 4: 534: '*nullus enim partes hominis, caput, aut manus, personam appellavit, et ipsamet Christi humanitas, persona non est, quia in ratione substantiae non est omnino completa*'.

which she is.'[30] Suárez also observes that 'some substance of her virginal body, from which Christ's body was [taken] and first formed, and afterwards grew, for as long as it was nourished by his mother's blood or milk, would be hypostatically united to the Word of God'.[31] Moreover, since Augustine claims that the flesh of Christ which is transformed by the glory of the resurrection nevertheless remains the same flesh which was taken from Mary, Suárez thinks that as the human Christ matured, the substance of flesh which he originally assumed from the Virgin was never entirely lost, but was always conserved, united to the Word of God.[32]

Mary's bodily assumption is the occasion for special comment upon the shared flesh of mother and son. Summing up the rationale which the Fathers give for Mary's assumption, Suárez writes:

> Because the body of Christ was taken from the body of the Virgin, they can be said in some manner to be one flesh. For this reason, just as Adam said: 'This now is bone of my bones and flesh of my flesh', so Christ can say the converse: 'This now is flesh of which is my flesh.' Therefore, just as it befits the flesh of Christ to be blessed and incorrupt *omni ex parte*, so is this also the case for the flesh of his mother, whose glory abounds in this honour.[33]

Kinship and Gender

That Mary is honoured because of her fleshly union with the Word of God is mentioned by Suárez in more than one place, and I shall return to it below. For the present, let us note Suárez's allusion to the motif of Christ as the New Adam and Mary the New Eve. The focus here is not the spousal image of Eve as Adam's wife, with its mystical reunion of flesh through bodies joined in sexual intercourse (Gen. 2.23). Rather, it is the substantial union of the flesh of which one body has its origin in the other (Gen. 2.21–2): Christ's body taken from Mary is the reciprocal of Eve's body taken from Adam. It is the substantial union of shared flesh, not the nuptial joining of otherwise separate bodies, which Suárez sees as fundamental to Mary's relationship with God and to her part in God's plan of salvation. In this respect, Suárez's Mariology stands in the sharpest contrast to the tradition of Mariology which emerged out of nineteenth-century German romanticism. Matthias Scheeben, for example, argued that the basic principle of Mariology – the foundation on which

---

30. *De Mysteriis*, Disp. I, sect. II:2: 7, '*Cum Deus in aliis rebus sit tribus modis, in Virgine fuit quarto speciali modo, scilicet, per identitatem, quia idem est quod ipsa.*'

31. Ibid.: '*aliqua substantia virginei corporis, ex qua fuit Christi corpus et in principio constitutum, et postea auctum, quandiu sanguine vel lacte matris nutritum fuit, unita sit hypostatice Verbo Dei.*'

32. Ibid. Suárez argues that the 'resolution', or dissolution, which normally occurs, through the action of heat, to the flesh that one receives initially from one's mother, may have been prevented in the case of Christ: '...*nulla illius resolutione facta. Probabile denique est, ex speciali providentia et voluntate ipsius Christi hoc fieri potuisse.*'

33. *De Mysteriis*, Disp. XXI, sect. II:6: 317, '*quia cum corpus Christi ex corpore Virginis sumptum sit, dici possunt quodammodo esse una caro. Quare, sicut Adam dixit*: Hoc nunc os ex ossibus meis, et caro de carne mea, *ita e contrario Christus dicere potest*: Haec nunc caro, de qua est caro mea; *sicut ergo decuit carnem Christi omni ex parte esse beatam et incorruptam, ita etiam et carnem matris, cujus gloria in illius honorem redundat.*'

all other Marian truths rest – is the 'bridal motherhood' (*gottesbräutliche Mutterschaft*), which is the state which Mary entered at the Annunciation, when, according to this theory, she became simultaneously Christ's mother and his spouse.[34]

This theme was taken up in the 1950s by Otto Semmelroth, who argued that the basic principle of Mariology is that Mary is 'archetype of the Church', which is to say that everything that the Catholic faith proclaims about Mary is true because she was ordained by God to be the pattern of the Church's own existence.[35] Semmelroth does not reject Scheeben's concept of the 'bridal motherhood', but sees it as itself being accounted for by the principle of the archetype: that is to say, it is because the Church is both bride of Christ (see Eph. 6:31–2) and mother of the members of his body, producing his body again in the sacrament of the Eucharist, that Mary, as the Church's archetype, is both mother and bride. Semmelroth draws on the writings of Church Fathers in support of his view, suggesting that since Mary is seen as the 'New Eve', she must correspondingly be the wife of the New Adam, who is Christ. The idea that Mary's relationship to Christ or to God is centrally a spousal one has been taken up by Joseph Ratzinger[36] and is a theme in the writings of Hans Urs von Balthasar.[37] But none of this has any part to play in the Mariology of Suárez. Why not?

From the point of view of theology as such, the reason for Suárez's focus upon Mary's motherhood and his ignoring of spousal motifs can perhaps be understood as an important technicality. Working with a traditional, though previously ill-defined, distinction between the literal and spiritual senses of Scripture, Thomas had contended that 'no arguments could be drawn from the spiritual senses, but only from the letter'.[38] Thus we can argue as a point of doctrine that Mary is the Godbearer, because it can be shown from the literal interpretation of Scripture that she is the mother of Jesus Christ, and because the literal reading of Scripture also shows Christ to be God incarnate. From knowing that Mary is the Godbearer, we may then be able to deduce other truths about her.

Thomas included in the 'literal' sense of a text the whole intention of an inspired writer, regardless of whether the text was written as a bald narrative or factual list, or whether it was symbolic or metaphorical. The 'spiritual' senses were derived from sacred history as a whole, and were not known to the writer as he was writing, but only to God. These senses are found in events, not in the letter, and this is why no arguments can follow from them.[39] For example, the spiritual sense of Judith's slaying of Holofernes may be that it is a type of the Virgin's defeat of Satan, prophesied in Genesis 3.15, but it does not follow that from reading about Judith we can deduce anything further about Mary. For example, Judith pretends that she wishes to seduce Holofernes, but there is no point at which Catholic teaching

---

34. Scheeben 1946/7, esp. vol. 1: 154–83.
35. Semmelroth 1964.
36. Ratzinger 1983; Ratzinger 1988.
37. Highly competent criticism of von Balthasar's use of spousal metaphors is given in Beattie 2002: 56–7.
38. Smalley 1983: 300.
39. Ibid.

presents Mary as deliberately tempting the devil in order to destroy him. The spiritual meaning of the Scripture resides in Mary's co-operation in the work of redemption, not in the details of the narrative about Judith.

Even allowing for Thomas's highly inclusive understanding of the 'literal', it is hard to see how arguments about Mary's bridal status could follow from it. The claim that Mary's motherhood of the divine Son renders her literally the spouse of the Father depends upon one of two considerations. It either denies the virginal conception and effectively rewrites the narrative of Jesus' conception so that it involves a pagan-type sexual union between a male god and a human woman; or else it makes an imaginative addition to Scripture in which, as part and parcel of the conception of Christ, Mary and the First Person of the Trinity undertook a mutual commitment of the type undertaken in marriage. In either case, the argument does not follow from the text. Furthermore, to hold that Mary is the bride of Christ is no less probematical than to hold that she is the spouse of the Father. St Paul refers to the Church as the bride of Christ, and extrabiblical sources refer to Mary as a type of the Church. But even if we were to accept that there are some texts in Scripture itself in which the author intends us to understand Mary in a typological manner (for example, Jn 19.25–7), no logical deduction follows from it. In this sense, a type is like a metaphor. I may say that it is 'raining cats and dogs', but it does not follow that there are fur and whiskers all over the ground. Likewise, nothing follows systematically from the figurative relationship of one event to another. Again, what counts here are the events – not the picturesque language by which they are indicated.

Suárez follows these precepts strictly, always keeping to the sobriety of the literal and the logical. And since the language of Mary as bride of Christ or of God – whether it occurs in Scripture or later authors – depends upon her being a type of the Church and has no literal purchase whatsoever, Suárez never follows this line of argument in his commentary on the *Summa*. Indeed, the modern theologians who write about Mary in a manner that systematizes the symbolic do seem to engage in a certain amount of epistemological confusion, so that it is not clear what counts as an argument – or rather, what would *not* count as an argument; and at the side of such authors, Suárez offers a refreshing clarity of thought.[40]

A further methodological difference between Suárez and many of his successors is found in the direction of approach that the respective authors take to the construction of a Mariological system. Suárez begins with the first principle of the divine motherhood, and then constructs arguments that follow from that principle, according to accepted rules. Theologians of the nineteenth and twentieth centuries, on the other hand, often start by taking for granted 'everything that is legitimately believed to be true' concerning the Blessed Virgin Mary, and then try to find an underlying principle that can account for all these teachings. That is, they work in the opposite direction from Suárez.

---

40. I have in mind here the Mariology of Hans Urs von Balthasar. For a sympathetic treatment of his work on Mary, see Francesca Murphy, 'Immaculate Mary: The Ecclesial Mariology of Hans Urs von Balthasar', in this volume: 300–13.

In addition to these methodological considerations, Suárez's emphasis on Mary's motherhood, and later authors' interest in a bridal or spousal Mariology, can be understood against a background of social and economic change affecting the institutions of kinship and a corresponding shift of emphasis in the perceived importance of gender for social relationships.

The cult of St Anne, mother of the Blessed Virgin, was a dominant feature of Catholic piety in the fifteenth and sixteenth centuries,[41] and one of its forms of expression was the representation of the 'Saint Anne Trinity',[42] depicting St Anne – usually as the largest figure in the group – with the Virgin and the Christ child. Another popular iconographic type was the Holy Kinship, that is, the infant Jesus with his blood relatives on his mother's side,[43] in some instances including the women's husbands, and in other instances including only the women. The dominant figure in such a group was usually St Anne, and her daughter Mary was of course invariably featured, as was Anne's legendary mother Esmeria. During the latter part of the fifteenth century, the cult of St Joseph, husband of the Virgin Mary, was gaining in popularity, and as devotion to Joseph became widespread, representations focusing on St Anne began to decline in number as another type of image, that of the Holy Family, began to become more popular.[44] The Holy Family typically includes the Christ child with the Blessed Virgin and St Joseph, and it has sometimes been suggested that St Joseph in effect came to replace St Anne in the popular perception of Jesus' immediate kin group. Thus the Virgin's husband replaced her mother. This iconographic change may reflect changes that were taking place in bourgeois domestic life.[45] The household was gradually ceasing to be the focus of economic activity, as men increasingly went to run their businesses outside the home; and, consequently, the wife's role as business partner (for example, as book-keeper to her merchant husband) dwindled away as she was left at home to manage a seemingly economically unproductive household. With the loss of her economic power and the increasing separation between her and the economically active male members of the household, the wife lost some of her public status and central position in the life of the kin group. The woman's social status now resided more in the husband upon whom she was dependent than in her office as mother of children over whom she had authority. The kin group was increasingly seen as consisting of a man with his dependent wife and children, so that the economically all-powerful husband and father came to replace the matrilineal arrangement found in earlier representations of kin groups.[46]

Having said that, it may be that the differences that are involved here are as much

41.   See Nixon 2004.
42.   There is not a recognized English term for this type of representation, but the French term is 'Sainte Anne Trinité' and the Spanish is 'Santa Ana Trinitas'. The perhaps more familiar German term is 'Anna Selbdritt'.
43.   Sheingorn 1990: 173. See also Brandenbarg 1987: 101–28.
44.   A discussion of the representation of these figures in northern Europe at the beginning of the sixteenth century can be found in Arnold 1993: 153–74.
45.   Sheingorn 1990: 182–4.
46.   Economic and social changes of this kind in England are described in Clark 1919; and Stone 1977. A wider list of sources is given in Sheingorn 1990: 196–7.

to do with place as they are with time. The difference between Suárez's emphasis on Mary's motherhood and Olier's shift to the spousal motif may relate not so much to the decades that separated them in history as to the fact that Suárez was the product of Spain and Olier of France, and to the differing cultures of the two areas of Europe. Nevertheless, over time and across geographical boundaries, an interest in Mary as bride or spouse eventually became common in Mariological writing, and was finally most marked in nineteenth- and twentieth-century Germany, where, as we shall see, it is also associated with a particular ideology of gender.

To the modern reader, one of the striking features of Suárez's Mariology may be its lack of interest in Mary's womanhood or femaleness as such. But in fact this is common to most medieval and Renaissance writings on Mary. The relative lack of importance that was often attributed to sexual difference in the fifteenth and sixteenth centuries is nicely illustrated by the following example. On the walls of Eton College chapel there is a set of fifteenth-century paintings of Miracles of the Virgin.[47] This was a popular subject in both the printed word and the visual arts of late medieval and Renaissance Europe, and the Eton College set is typical of the genre. One sequence of the paintings is concerned with a story of a woman whose life was endangered in childbirth and who was saved because of the Blessed Virgin's miraculous intervention.[48] To the twentieth-century mind it may seem curious that a drama that is so clearly concerned with the particular needs of the female sex should be depicted in a chapel given over entirely to the use of men and boys, for in the nineteenth and twentieth centuries it was common in European culture to accord gender difference a high priority. But for previous generations of Christians, the condition of each sex was an aspect of the human condition *per se*. So the woman in childbed or the soldier on the battlefield were undergoing experiences that were essentially human, and hence of concern to other human beings, regardless of their sex. The Mariology of Francisco Suárez, I suggest, bears witness to this older view of the human condition, in which the shared humanity of Christ and the Virgin is the guarantee of the possibility of redemption and glorification for the whole human race.

It is reasonable to think that Suárez's lack of concern with questions of gender is related to his interest in Mary's maternal status and to his silence on any notion that she may be the bride of Christ or of God. For an anthropological emphasis on gender as such seems to be tied to a placing of marriage or sexual relationships at the forefront of human relationships in general.

In medieval scholastic texts, the female as such is almost invariably presented as inferior to the male as such, typically being seen as deficient in qualities that the male possessed.[49] However, in real human interactions, male and female very rarely encounter one another in their 'undiluted' state. Rather, in almost all social relationships, a variety of moral and social factors come into play between the parties involved. For instance, when answering the question as to whether one ought to love

---

47. James 1907.
48. Cf. the Herolt miracle XC, reproduced in this volume: 202–3.
49. MacLean 1983; Allen 1997.

one's mother more than one's father, Aquinas argues that the father as such contributes to his child something that is of greater value than that which is contributed by the mother as such. This is, first, because Aquinas follows Aristotle's biology on this point, and believes that the mother contributes passive matter to the infant in the womb, whereas the father contributes the active form which organizes the matter; and, second, because Aquinas values the active form as being superior, in the sense of being closer to God, than the passive matter. However, Aquinas notes that in real relationships between parents and children, an actual mother may on other grounds be more worthy of love than an actual father: a good mother is better than a bad father.[50] So although the father *per se* is owed more than the mother *per se*, in particular relationships this debt may be overruled by other considerations.

This pattern of understanding moral relationships as an interplay between a variety of factors is characteristic of scholastic thinking. So although the male as such is judged to be superior to the female as such, in practice there are relationships in which gender is of only marginal importance, including some in which a woman may hold a position of authority over a man. Perhaps the clearest example of this is the relationship between mother and son. The commandment to honour one's father and mother was taken with the utmost seriousness, and until the modern period seems to have been widely assumed to apply to adults as well as to children who had not attained the age of majority. Suárez argues that the relations of mother and son remain between Mary and Christ for all time and even in the state of glorification; and the reason for this is not principally the exceptional character of their physical connection, but the universally valid consideration that 'it is always true to say that this man was born of that woman; the said relations follow intrinsically from this'.[51]

The relationship in which male superiority as such most clearly encountered female inferiority as such was that of marriage. Marriage was concerned with the union of man as such with woman as such, and Renaissance authors generally considered that in a married couple, the male should possess typically 'masculine' characteristics to a greater degree than the female, and vice versa. It was recognized, however, that in practice this may be hard to attain. Intelligence was perceived to be naturally stronger in the male than the female, but everyone knew that there were many intelligent women and many stupid men. Theorists therefore advised that an intelligent woman should marry a man more intelligent than herself, thus preserving the proper balance of the two sexes. Within any particular marriage, this right ordering of gender differences would include the subordination of wife to husband.[52]

Now, in a society in which marriage was the institution in which the articulation of gender differences was seen to occur most clearly, but in which marriage – understood as an alliance between one man and one woman – was not the most overwhelmingly important of human relationships, gender was not necessarily central to people's understanding of human relationships in general, including

---

50. Aquinas, *Summa Theologiae* 2a2ae, 26:10; vol. 34: 146–9.
51. *De Mysteriis*, Disp. 12, sect. 3:3: 208, '*Quia semper est verum dicere hunc hominem fuisse genitum ab illa muliere; ex hoc autem intrinsece sequuntur dictae relationes.*'
52. McLean 1983: 57–8.

relationships between people who were men and people who were women. But when the institution of marriage as a contract between one man and one woman (as distinct from an alliance between families) gained in cultural importance, and kin groupings across generations became less dominant, the ideology of gender that was supposed to be enshrined in marriage gained enormously in social significance.

Studies in the history of medicine show a huge tendency towards polarizing the sexes in the modern period, so that by the nineteenth century, the medieval recognition that a woman may have strong 'masculine' characteristics and a man have strong 'feminine' ones had been superseded by a view which held that male and female were radically different from one another. Women, for example, were portrayed as being dominated by their nervous systems and organs of generation, and men by their brains and musculatures.[53]

This polarization of gender was found throughout the cultural life of Western Europe in the nineteenth century, being manifested in such details as changes in styles of dress. For example, the practice of men dressing in plain, sombre costume to show off the brilliance of women's appearance began in the early nineteenth century. The polarizing trend was especially marked in Germany, where romanticism concentrated on the union of the supposed opposites of male and female. Eva Rieger's essay on the changing situation of women in Western classical music points out that in nineteenth-century Germany, even the analysis of musical structure could be conducted in terms of gender and relations between the sexes.[54] This is the background out of which Jungian psychology eventually developed, and it is perhaps not surprising that it gave rise to a Mariology of the type written by Scheeben.

More recently, this fascination with sexual difference has been influential not only among thinkers who are frankly misogynistic, but also among some feminists, such as the philosopher Luce Irigaray. Irigaray has written:

> Sexual difference represents one of the questions or the question which has to be thought about in our era. Each era – according to Heidegger – has one thing to think about. Only one. Sexual difference is probably the one for our age. The thing of our age which, thought, would bring us 'salvation'?[55]

Irigaray's concern is to undermine the tendency of dominant groups – in this case, men – to cast the rest of the world in their own image, whereby they suppress alternative ways of acting or the acknowledgement that such ways exist. When men do not allow women to speak, they refuse to admit of difference. Irigaray's cause, then, is the rejection of 'the same'. The difficulty with this approach is that it does not entirely get away from a romantic fascination with 'otherness' and difference that is fraught with difficulty and danger for those who are 'other' and 'different'. The feminist writer Sheila Jeffreys has pointed out that when people in modern Britain

---

53. A brief description of some of the literature concerning attitudes towards sexual difference in the history of medicine is given in Boss 2000: 96–7, 118.
54. Rieger 1995: 135–49 (139–40).
55. Irigaray 1984: 13.

and North America praise 'difference', this almost always turns out to refer to a difference of power in a relationship of domination. This imbalance of power is precisely the disparity that is praised in the expression '*vive la différence*'. The 'differences' between men and women are differences that are so bound up with inequalities of power that under present conditions of social and economic domination, it is impossible for us to know what might turn out to be our respective qualities or how we might relate to one another in a just world.[56] Hence, if we are to speak at all of the 'differences' between men and women, this must be done only in the context of criticizing the social and psychological construction of such differences.

Thomas Laqueur, writing about the history of medicine, put forward the now well-known argument that until the modern period, women's physiology was widely understood to be analogous to that of men.[57] In the words of Laqueur's dictum, 'There was one sex, and that was male.' Thus the female was an adaptation of the male original. We have already seen that this assumption may underlie some of Suárez's thinking about Mary's conception of Christ; and clearly, it raises the possibility that the language of unity, continuity and identity, on at least some occasions, may mark the assumption that differences between dominant and subordinate parties in a social relationship can be ignored because the subordinate is simply subsumed by the identity of the dominant actor. This concern is a factor underlying that wave of feminist thought represented by Irigaray, which asserts the importance of recognizing and understanding the differences between the sexes, so that women are not just assumed to be like men, but have their own distinctive voices heard in both private and public spaces.

The lesbian theologian Elizabeth Stuart considers that the language of unity or sameness that is found in the phrase 'one flesh' makes many women uncomfortable, since marriage is a relationship in which many women 'appear to find their passion captured, constrained and narrowly channelled'.[58] It is in the context of a discussion of marriage that Stuart makes this observation, but, as I have already shown, in Suárez's Mariology marriage is not the phrase's primary point of reference. Unity of flesh is maternal/filial, not nuptial. I suggest that looking back to Suárez's Mariology of identity and continuity helps us to see some of the respects in which contemporary discussion about 'difference' and 'the other' is itself constrained by social relations of domination; a looking back encourages the present-day theologian to take up the more ancient task of seeking that which transcends, undergirds and is common to all beings who are different from one another.

Now, to make use of maternal/filial, rather than supposedly sexual or marital, aspects of the relationship between Christ and Mary does not of itself do away with questions about the abuse of power in the ideal that is envisaged here. Mothers can exercise terrifying domination over their offspring (something that German romanticism has not been good at coming to terms with), and one might well ask

---

56. Jeffreys 1991.
57. Laqueur 1990.
58. Stuart 1995: 187–8.

whether Suárez's portrayal of an 'identity' between Christ and Mary does not serve to idealize or reinforce a more primitive mode of refusal to recognize alterity and difference. Suárez certainly portrays the Virgin's maternal office in very august terms, referring frequently to her maternal dignity (*dignitas matris*); and the merits and graces which accrue to her from this office are such that she merits *de congruo* the world's salvation.[59] However, Suárez states that although she prays to Christ on our behalf, she does not command him.[60] In fact, Christ's ontological status as God and Mary's own sinlessness must guarantee that no abuse occurs between them, while the very distinctiveness of this relationship from all others ensures that it does not act as a cover for, or idealization of, those which do not conform to such perfection.

Although later Mariologists paid lip service – or pen service – to Suárez, his maternal Mariology was progressively undermined, so that the sexual differences assumed by nineteenth-century German romanticism were taken lock, stock and barrel into an influential strand of contemporary Mariology, where any transcendence of those differences is achieved by means of a union in which the differences are simultaneously retained.[61] In the Renaissance theology of Suárez, on the other hand, differences are subverted, overcome and minimized, so that the purely ontological distinction between Creator and creature, and those differences which necessarily follow from it, are all that count when considering Mary in relation to her Maker and Christ in relation to his mother.

THE GLORIFICATION OF CREATION

A deep interest in unity and continuity between creation and God and between created beings themselves is a feature of other noteworthy authors of the fifteenth and sixteenth centuries. The European Renaissance produced Christian thinkers who were concerned with the task of looking beyond the limited world of boundedness, incommensurability and opposition, to a vision of something – or rather, someone – in whom these limitations not only did not exist, but in whom they would also find their resolution. Most striking, perhaps, is the sustained attempt by Nicholas of Cusa (1401–64) to find language to speak of God that focused precisely on integrity and the transcendence of limit. Thus in *De Docta Ignorantia*,[62] Nicholas famously promulgated the doctrine of the 'coincidence of opposites' in the Deity; while in his later work *De Non Aliud*,[63] he teases out a way of speaking of God as 'not other' (than created beings, persons of the Trinity, and so on). Suárez, who was acquainted with Nicholas's work, wrote a Marian theology that was firmly in this tradition.

We have seen above that Suárez considers one purpose of the incarnation – or,

59.   *De Mysteriis*, Disp. 23, sect. I:4: 331, '*Beata Virgo . . . merendo de congruo . . . ad nostram salutem . . . cooperata est.*'
60.   Ibid., sect. I:1, '*Addunt [haeretici] etiam nos dicere Virginem, non tantum orare Christum, sed etiam ei imperare. Hic tamen error nullum habet fundamentum.*'
61.   An honourable exception to this trend is the Mariology of Karl Rahner, which seems to have been strongly influenced by Suárez.
62.   English translation can be found in *Selected Spiritual Writings*, trans. Bond 1997.
63.   See *On God as Not Other*, ed. and trans. Hopkins 1979.

more properly, the divine motherhood – to be 'that some created person may be joined together with God [*conjuncta Deo*], in so far as is possible with regard to a person'. Although the adjectival participle *conjuncta* is a form of the same word as the noun *conjunx*, which has the derivative meaning of 'spouse', there is nothing to indicate that Suárez intends a narrowly marital connotation here, and I suggest that the model of kin relations that underlies his understanding of Mary's union with God is one that belongs to the same kind of older world view as that which I have argued is represented by his emphasis on the maternal/filial relationship between the Virgin and Christ.

It seems to have been a common practice among European aristocracy to regard a married woman as belonging fully to her husband's family only when she conceives his child. That is to say, it is not the marriage ceremony or sexual union which bestows upon her the status of a full family member: it is conceiving, gestating and bearing a child of the family's stock. Conversely, when the woman conceives and bears the husband's child, she enters fully into his household and kin group. I have observed elsewhere:

> Textual evidence suggests that at the Carolingian court in the ninth century, an empress would be crowned as such only after giving birth to a child, thus making motherhood, and not marriage alone, the condition for the emperor's wife to hold full imperial status. Furthermore, the rites for the crowning of empresses made allusion to the Virgin Mary, who herself was queen and empress in virtue of her motherhood.[64]

This seems to be the sort of model of kin relations that underlies Suárez's understanding of Mary's closeness to God. In the passage quoted above, when he writes of Mary being joined together with God, he presents this connection as a consequence of a relationship that is more excellent than other forms of consanguinity and affinity. Because she is the Godbearer, Mary is, as it were, taken into the household of the Blessed Trinity, and enjoys a unique intimacy with the Godhead.[65] And we can note something of theological importance about this analogy. For the woman who becomes fully a member of her husband's family does not thereby cease to be a member of her natal kin group. She is a member both of her family of origin and of her child's paternal family. This example provides not a perfect correspondence, but point of comparison, by which it can be seen how the Blessed Virgin may be a member of the divine household without ceasing to be fully human. So – against those who assert that the Virgin's glorification removes her from the human condition – I suggest that in Suárez's understanding of the

---

64.   Boss 2000: 46. The source for this observation is Iogna-Prat 1996. A modern example of this attitude was given by the novelist Lisa St Aubin de Terán, who in a radio interview explained that when she married her wealthy Argentinian husband, she was not regarded as being fully a 'de Terán' until she had become pregnant with his child.

65.   The twentieth-century Mariologist C. X. J. M. Friethoff speaks directly of Mary as related to the Blessed Trinity by consanguinity and by affinity; Friethoff 1958: 11–13.

Godbearer, we are presented with an image of human glorification which shows us precisely that it is possible for a creature to enjoy the most perfect closeness to God without her humanity being compromised, and we thus have a sign of hope for our own destiny.

Suárez's picture of Mary as the human person most closely joined to God follows a long tradition of describing the incarnation in terms of a movement of mirroring: the Word 'descends' into flesh so that those who are made of flesh may 'ascend' to be with God in glory. Mary, whose flesh was the particular flesh assumed by the Word, is the principal example of human ascent to heaven mirroring the divine descent to earth.[66] For Suárez, Mary's glorification is articulated in particularly strong language, thereby emphasizing the creature's potential to reflect and be united to divinity.

If we return now to consider the motif of Mary's flesh being always present in the body of Christ, I suggest that this too is a teaching which at root is concerned with the rendering of earth as a counterpart to heaven. Taken on its own, Suárez's proposal that the flesh of Mary always remains in Christ's body seems eccentric and even bizarre. But perhaps its theological purpose is to present the relationship between Christ and his earthly mother as a created counterpart to and reflection of the relationship that exists between Christ and God the Father in eternity. For if Christ and Mary share 'one flesh', then they have a substantial union which may be seen as an echo of the consubstantiality of the persons of the Trinity.[67]

Many patristic homilies for Christmas take up the theme of the 'double nativity', that is, the eternal begetting of the Son by the Father and his human birth from Mary. Suárez refers to this idea at the very beginning of the Marian section of his commentary, as part of his apologia for devoting so much space to questions concerning the Blessed Virgin. He writes:

> There was indeed the greatest necessity that this matter [i.e. knowledge of the Godbearer] should be treated fully. For just as the eternal procession of Christ cannot be believed without faith in the eternal Father, so his generation in time, which had its beginning from a mother without a father, cannot be grasped without prior knowledge of the Godbearer.[68]

That this is Suárez's opening consideration suggests that it should be understood as colouring or guiding much of what follows, and so it seems quite justified to interpret his suggestion that the flesh of Mary remained always in Christ as implying a

---

66. See Boss 2000: 34–6.
67. I am grateful to John Montag SJ for pointing out to me that Suárez's assertion of the continued union of Christ's and Mary's flesh is probably a point about substance.
68. *De Mysteriis*, Praefatio, 1: 1, '*Erat enim haec tractatio ad hujus materiae complementum maxime necessaria. Nam, sicut aeterna Christi processio absque aeterni Patris fide credi non potest, ita temporalis ejus generatio, quae ex matre sine patre initium habuit, sine praevia ejusdem Deiparae cognitione comparari non poterat.*'

certain parallel between Christ's relationship with his human mother and his relationship with his eternal Father.[69]

The doctrine of shared flesh and consequent identity between human mother and human-divine Son, lasting into the condition of glorification, indicates the capacity of the material creation to be glorified and joined together with God.[70] In Mary, the physical creation becomes the image and counterpart to the glory shared by the angels and saints in God's immediate presence. As God comes to earth, the earthly is joined to God, and earth is the reflection of heaven. The possible ramifications of this strong reading of the incarnation and divine motherhood are enormous. For example, the Muslim writer Seyyed Hossein Nasr has argued that one of the causes of the world's current ecological crisis is that humanity has forgotten that earth must be understood in relation to heaven. He contends that for humanity to have a proper respect for the earth (understood to mean the material creation as a whole), we have to understand the earth as having a relationship to heaven, and hence as being sacred. It is because we no longer have a belief in heaven that we are destroying the earth.[71] Suárez's contention that in the union of God and creation, things of earth become a counterpart to the divine, seems to imply that the earth possesses the capacity for glorification and therefore the kind of sanctity that Nasr argues it is imperative for us to recognize.

Suárez thus presents a picture in which, in the incarnation and divine motherhood, differences are transcended to the maximum possible degree. The dominant model of human relationship in his understanding is that of mother and son – a relationship of identity, unity and continuity. This understanding of the relationship between Christ and Mary not only has better theological grounding than an understanding based upon a metaphor of marriage, but it also enables us to see the potential of creation for a far more radical union with God. For the 'one flesh' of heterosexual union is the coming together of separate bodies which always retain their different sexes; while the 'one flesh' of mother and child is a unity prior to differentiation which can therefore provide confidence that the social injustices which are signified by natural difference can finally be overcome. In particular, the play on the paradox that mother and son are also human and God, respectively, tends to undercut assumptions about male dominance and female subordination.

We cannot – and would not wish to – return to the world inhabited by the Spanish upper classes of the sixteenth century. But to recover a little of Suárez's theological understanding gives a perspective on contemporary theology from which

---

69.   In Renaissance painting, the St Anne Trinity is sometimes depicted as St Anne and the Virgin seated with Christ between them, and directly above him are shown God the Father and the Holy Spirit. Christ thus simultaneously forms part of a vertical and of a horizontal triad, indicating both his human and divine origins. The visual correspondence between the two 'Trinities' gives a strong sense of there being a parallel between the divine and the earthly. See Sheingorn 1990: 176–8.

70.   The focus of Suárez's own interest is the material creation in so far as it constitutes a part of the human condition. However, because God united himself to human flesh, and flesh is what humanity has most in common with the rest of the physical world – and perhaps because the human person is seen as a microcosm of the universe – there is a strong patristic and medieval tradition of understanding the incarnation as initiating the redemption of the whole created order. See Boss 1999; Sherrard 1992.

71.   Nasr 1996.

we might discover some of the latter's weaknesses. In the light of such considerations, we can go on to ask questions as to how we might regain those strengths of Suárez's theology that have been somewhat overshadowed in more recent centuries.

BIBLIOGRAPHY

Primary Sources

St Anselm (1946) 'De conceptu virginali et de originali peccato', in *S. Anselmi Opera Omnia*, ed. F. S. Schmitt, vol. 2, Edinburgh: Thomas Nelson.

Aquinas, Thomas (1975) *Summa Theologiae*, vol. 34, Blackriars; London: Eyre & Spottiswoode; New York: McGraw-Hill.

Bernard of Clairvaux and Amadeus of Lausanne (1979) *Magnificat: Homilies in Praise of the Blessed Virgin Mary*, trans. Marie-Bernard Saïd and Grace Perigo, Kalamazoo, Michigan: Cistercian Publications.

Friethoff, C. X. J. M. (1958) *A Complete Mariology*, trans. A Religious of the Retreat of the Sacred Heart, London: Aquin Press.

Irigaray, Luce (1984) *Ethique de la Différence Sexuelle*, Paris: Les Editions de Minuit.

Nasr, Seyyed Hossein (1996) *Religion and the Order of Nature*, New York and Oxford: Oxford University Press.

[Nicholas] Nicolai de Cusa (1977) *De Docta Ignorantia*, 3 vols, *Schriften des Nikolaus von Kues*, Heft 15a–c, Latin with German trans., ed. Hans Gerhard Senger, Hamburg: Felix Meiner.

Nicholas of Cusa (1979) *On God as Not Other: A translation and an appraisal of De Li Non Aliud*, with Latin text, ed. and translation Jasper Hopkins, Minneapolis: University of Minnesota Press.

Nicholas of Cusa: Selected Spiritual Writings (1997) Classics of Western Spirituality, trans. H. Lawrence Bond, Mahwah, NJ: Paulist Press.

Olier, Jean-Jacques (1966) *Vie Intérieure de la Très-Sainte Vierge*, collected from the writings of M. Olier, 2 vols., Rome: Salviucci.

Ratzinger, Cardinal Joseph (1983) *Daughter Zion: Meditations on the Church's Marian Belief*, trans. John H. McDermott, San Francisco, CA: Ignatius Press.

Ratzinger, Cardinal Joseph (1988) 'On the position of mariology and Marian spirituality within the totality of faith and theology', trans. Graham Harrison, in Helmut Moll (ed.), *The Church and Women: A Compendium*, San Francisco, CA: Ignatius Press.

Scheeben, Matthias (1946/7) *Mariology*, 2 vols, trans. T. L. M. J. Geukers, St Louis and London: Herder Book Co.

Semmelroth, Otto (1964) *Mary: Archetype of the Church*, trans. Maria von Eroes and John Devlin, Dublin: Gill and Son.

Sherrard, Philip (1992) *Human Image, World Image: The death and resurrection of sacred cosmology*, Ipswich: Golgonooza Press.

Stuart, Elizabeth (1995) *Just Good Friends: Towards a Lesbian and Gay Theology of Relationships*, London: Cassell.

[Suárez] C. Berton (ed.) (1860) *Opera Omnia*, Paris: Vivès.

[Suárez: *De Mysteriis Vitae Christi*] Franciscus Suarez e Societate Jesu, *Commentarii et Disputationes in Tertiam Partem D. Thomae* [questions 27–59], Disp. I, II:7, in Berton (ed.), *Opera Omnia*, vol. 19.

[Suárez] Franciscus Suarez e Societate Jesu, *Commentarii et Disputationes in Primam Partem D.Thomae*, Liber 1: 'De Trinitate Personarum', in Berton (ed.), *Opera Omnia*, vol. 1.

Suarez, Francis (1954) *The Dignity and Virginity of the Mother of God*, trans. Richard O'Brien, West Baden Springs, IN: West Baden College.

Suárez, Francisco (1971) *De Legibus*, vol. I: *De natura legis*, ed. Luciano Pereña et al., Latin text with Spanish translation, Madrid: Consejo Superior de Investigaciones Cientificas (vol. XI of Corpus Hispanorum de Pace).

Thompson, W. M. (ed.) (1989) *Bérulle and the French School: Selected Writings*, trans. L. M. Glendon, New York and Mahwah: Paulist Press.

Secondary Sources

de Aldama, J. A. (1950) 'El sentido moderno de la mariología de Suárez', in *Actas del IV Centenario del Nacimento de Francisco Suárez, 1548–1948*, vol. II, Madrid.

de Aldama, J. A. (1952) 'Piété et système dans la mariologie du "Doctor Eximius"', in Hubert du Manoir (ed.), *Maria: Etudes sur la Sainte Vierge*, vol. 2, Paris: Beauchesne: 975–90.

Allen, Prudence (1997) *The Concept of Woman: The Aristotelian Revolution, 750 BC–AD 1250*, Grand Rapids, MI; Cambridge: Eerdmans.

Arnold, Klaus (1993) 'Die Heilige Familie: Bilder und verehrung der Heiligen Anna, Maria, Joseph und des Jesuskindes in Kunst, Literatur und Frömmigkeit um 1500', in C. Opitz, H. Röckelein, G. Signori and G. P. Marchal (Hg.), *Maria in der Welt: Marienverehrung im Kontext der Sozialgeschichte 10.–18. Jahrhundert*, Zürich: Chronos Verlag: 153–74.

Beattie, Tina (2002) *God's Mother, Eve's Advocate: A Marian Narrative of Women's Salvation*, London: Continuum.

Boss, Sarah Jane (2000) *Empress and Handmaid: On Nature and Gender in the Cult of the Virgin Mary*, London: Cassell.

Boss, Sarah Jane (1999) 'Mary at the Margins: Christology and ecclesiology in modernity', in Geoffrey Turner and John Sullivan (eds), *Explorations in Catholic Theology: Papers from the Catholic Theological Association*, Dublin: Lindisfarne Books: 47–77.

Brandenbarg, Ton (1987) 'St Anne and her family. The veneration of St Anne in connection with concepts of marriage and the family in the early-modern period', in *Saints and She-devils: Images of Women in the 15th and 16th centuries*, trans. from Dutch, C. M. H. Sion, London: Rubicon Press: 101–28.

Clark, Alice (1919) *Working Life of Women in the Seventeenth Century*, London: George Routledge & Sons.

Courtine, Jean-François (1990) *Suárez et le Système de la Métaphysique*, Paris: Presses Universitaires de France.

Graef, Hilda (1985) *Mary: A History of Doctrine and Devotion*, combined ed., London: Sheed & Ward.

Iogna-Prat, Dominique (1996) 'La Vierge et les *ordines* de couronnement des reines au IXe siècle', in Dominique Iogna-Prat, Éric Palazzo and David Russo (eds), *Marie: Le culte de la Vierge dans la société médiévale*, Paris: Beauchesne: 100–7.

James, M. R. (1907) *Frescoes in the Chapel at Eton College: Facsimiles of the drawings by R. H. Essex, with explanatory notes*, London: Spottiswoode & Co.

Jeffreys, Sheila (1991) *Anticlimax: A Feminist Perspective on the Sexual Revolution*, London: Women's Press.

Laqueur, Thomas (1990) *Making Sex: Body and Gender from the Greeks to Freud*, Cambridge, MA, and London: Harvard University Press.

Laurentin, René (1952) *Marie, l'Eglise et le Sacredoce: I. Essai sur le développement d'une idée religieuse*, Paris: Nouvelles Editions Latines.

MacLean, Ian (1983) *The Renaissance Notion of Woman: A study in the fortunes of scholasticism and medical science in European intellectual life*, Cambridge: Cambridge University Press.

Nixon, Virginia (2004) *Mary's Mother: Saint Anne in Late Medieval Europe*, University Park, PA: The Pennsylvania State University Press.

Razón y Fe, Collaboradores de (1948) *Francisco Suárez: El Hombre, La Obra, el Influjo* Madrid: Editorial Razón y Fe.

Rieger, Eva (1995) '"Dolce semplice"? On the changing role of women in music', in Gisela Ecker (ed.), *Feminist Aesthetics*, trans. Harriet Anderson, London: The Women's Press.

de Scoraille, Raoul (1912) *François Suarez de la Compagnie de Jésus, d'après ses lettres, ses autres écrits inédits et un grand nombre de documents nouveaux*, 2 vols, Paris: Lethielleux.

Sheingorn, Pamela (1990) 'Appropriating the Holy Kinship: Gender and family history', in Kathleen Ashley and Pamela Sheingorn (eds), *Interpreting Cultural Symbols: St Anne in Late Medieval Society*, Athens, GA, and London: The University of Georgia Press.

Smalley, Beryl (1983) *The Study of the Bible in the Middle Ages*, Oxford: Basil Blackwell.

Stone, Lawrence (1977) *The Family, Sex, and Marriage in England, 1500–1800*, New York: Harper and Row.

Wolter, Allan B. and O'Neill, Blane (1993) *John Duns Scotus: Mary's Architect*, Quincy, IL: Franciscan Press.

Wright, A. D. (2004) 'Bérulle and Olier: Christ and the Blessed Virgin Mary', in R. N. Swanson (ed.), *The Church and Mary*, Studies in Church History 39, Woodbridge: Boydell Press: 271–9.

Ineffabilis Deus
Dogmatic Constitution on the Immaculate Conception

By the nineteenth century, the Catholic Church almost universally celebrated the feast of Mary's Conception, and the dispute over her immaculate conception had effectively been resolved in favour of the doctrine. However, in the 1850s Pope Pius IX thought that the time may be right for the doctrine's official formulation and promulgation, and he accordingly commissioned theologians to investigate the matter,[1] and canvassed the opinions of the world's bishops. As a result of this, the Pope declared the doctrine *de fide*. This was the first time that an article of faith had been defined by a Pope independently of an ecumenical Church council. At the First Vatican Council (1869–70), the Pope was officially recognized as having the power to make infallible pronouncements on matters of faith and morals. Pius IX considered that his promulgation of the doctrine of the immaculate conception had been a *de facto* exercise of infallible power, and he thereby used *Ineffabilis Deus* to support the doctrine of papal infallibility.[2] From a historical perspective, there was a certain irony in this; for a previous attempt had been made to formalize the Church's teaching and practice with regard to the immaculate conception, at the Council of Basel (1431–49),[3] and on that occasion, the supporters of the doctrine had consisted largely of conciliarists – i.e. those who thought that the powers of the Pope should be constrained by Church councils – while the doctrine's opponents had been predominantly papalists – i.e. those who favoured the Pope having an authority above that of the councils. The political significance of the immaculate conception had thus shifted from one side of the debate to the other.

EXTRACTS FROM *INEFFABILIS DEUS*, APOSTOLIC CONSTITUTION ISSUED BY POPE PIUS IX ON 8 DECEMBER 1854

God Ineffable – whose ways are mercy and truth, whose will is omnipotence itself, and whose wisdom 'reaches from end to end mightily, and orders all things sweetly' – having foreseen from all eternity the lamentable wretchedness of the entire human race which would result from the sin of Adam, decreed, by a plan hidden from the centuries, to complete the first work of his goodness by a mystery yet more wondrously sublime through the Incarnation of the Word. This he decreed in order that man who, contrary to the plan of Divine Mercy had been led into sin by the cunning malice of Satan, should not perish; and in order that what had been lost in the first Adam would be gloriously restored in the Second Adam. From the very beginning, and before time began, the eternal Father chose and prepared for his only-begotten Son a Mother in whom the Son of God would become incarnate and from whom, in the blessed fullness of time, he would be born into this world. Above all creatures did God so love her that truly in her was the Father well pleased with singular delight. Therefore, far above all the angels and all the saints so wondrously did

---

1. These investigations resulted in, among other works, Carlo Passaglia's very impressive three-volume survey of the history of Christian teaching on the subject of the immaculate conception, *De Immaculato Deiparae semper Virginis Conceptu* (1854).
2. Hasler 1981: 45, 81.
3. Sebastian 1958: 213–70 (228–32).

God endow her with the abundance of all heavenly gifts poured from the treasury of his divinity that this mother, ever absolutely free of all stain of sin, all fair and perfect, would possess that fullness of holy innocence and sanctity than which, under God, one cannot even imagine anything greater, and which, outside of God, no mind can succeed in comprehending fully.

Supreme Reason for the Privilege: The Divine Maternity

And indeed it was wholly fitting that so wonderful a mother should be ever resplendent with the glory of most sublime holiness and so completely free from all taint of original sin that she would triumph utterly over the ancient serpent. To her did the Father will to give his only-begotten Son – the Son whom, equal to the Father and begotten by him, the Father loves from his heart – and to give this Son in such a way that he would be the one and the same common Son of God the Father and of the Blessed Virgin Mary. It was she whom the Son himself chose to make his Mother and it was from her that the Holy Spirit willed and brought it about that he from whom [the Spirit] himself proceeds should be conceived and born.

The Definition

Wherefore, in humility and fasting, we unceasingly offered our private prayers as well as the public prayers of the Church to God the Father through his Son, that he would deign to direct and strengthen our mind by the power of the Holy Spirit. In like manner did we implore the help of the entire heavenly host as we ardently invoked the Paraclete. Accordingly, by the inspiration of the Holy Spirit, for the honour of the Holy and undivided Trinity, for the glory and adornment of the Virgin Mother of God, for the exaltation of the Catholic Faith, and for the furtherance of the Catholic religion, by the authority of Jesus Christ our Lord, of the Blessed Apostles Peter and Paul, and by our own: **We declare, pronounce, and define that the doctrine which holds that the most Blessed Virgin Mary, in the first instance of her conception, by a singular grace and privilege granted by Almighty God, in view of the merits of Jesus Christ, the Saviour of the human race, was preserved free from all stain of original sin, is a doctrine revealed by God and therefore to be believed firmly and constantly by all the faithful.**

BIBLIOGRAPHY

Hasler, August Bernhard (1981) *How the Pope became Infallible: Pius IX and the Politics of Persuasion*, trans. Peter Heinegg, New York: Doubleday & Co.

Passaglia, Carlo (1854) *De Immaculato Deiparae semper Virginis Conceptu*, 3 vols, Rome: Congregation for the Propagation of the Faith.

Sebastian, Wenceslaus OFM (1958) 'The Controversy over the Immaculate Conception from after Scotus to the end of the Eighteenth Century', in Edward Dennis O'Connor (ed.), *The Dogma of the Immaculate Conception: History and Significance*, Notre Dame, IN: University of Notre Dame Press.

Munificentissimus Deus
Apostolic Constitution on the Assumption

The following material consists of extracts from the formal definition of the doctrine of Mary's Assumption, issued by Pope Pius XII on 1 November 1950.

3. God, who from all eternity regards Mary with a most favourable and unique affection, has 'when the fullness of time came' [Gal. 4.4] put the plan of his providence into effect in such a way that all the privileges and prerogatives he had granted to her in his sovereign generosity were to shine forth in her in a kind of perfect harmony. And, although the Church has always recognized this supreme generosity and the perfect harmony of graces and has daily studied them more and more throughout the course of the centuries, still it is in our own age that the privilege of the bodily Assumption into heaven of Mary, the Virgin Mother of God, has certainly shone forth more clearly.

4. That privilege has shone forth in new radiance since our predecessor of immortal memory, Pius IX, solemnly proclaimed the dogma of the loving Mother of God's Immaculate Conception. These two privileges are most closely bound to one another. Christ overcame sin and death by his own death, and one who through Baptism has been born again in a supernatural way has conquered sin and death through the same Christ. Yet, according to the general rule, God does not will to grant to the just the full effect of the victory over death until the end of time has come. And so it is that the bodies of even the just are corrupted after death, and only on the last day will they be joined, each to its own glorious soul.

5. Now God has willed that the Blessed Virgin Mary should be exempted from this general rule. She, by an entirely unique privilege, completely overcame sin by her Immaculate Conception, and as a result she was not subject to the law of remaining in the corruption of the grave, and she did not have to wait until the end of time for the redemption of her body.

17. In the liturgical books which deal with the feast either of the dormition or of the Assumption of the Blessed Virgin there are expressions that agree in testifying that, when the Virgin Mother of God passed from this earthly exile to heaven, what happened to her sacred body was, by the decree of divine Providence, in keeping with the dignity of the Mother of the Word Incarnate, and with the other privileges she had been accorded. Thus, to cite an illustrious example, this is set forth in that sacramentary which Adrian I, our predecessor of immortal memory, sent to the Emperor Charlemagne. These words are found in this volume: 'Venerable to us, O Lord, is the festivity of this day on which the holy Mother of God suffered temporal death, but still could not be kept down by the bonds of death, who has begotten your Son our Lord incarnate from herself.' [*Sacramentarium Gregorianum*]

18. What is here indicated in that sobriety characteristic of the Roman liturgy is presented more clearly and completely in other ancient liturgical books. To take one as an example,

the Gallican sacramentary designates this privilege of Mary's as 'an ineffable mystery all the more worthy of praise as the Virgin's Assumption is something unique among men'. And, in the Byzantine liturgy, not only is the Virgin Mary's bodily Assumption connected time and time again with the dignity of the Mother of God, but also with the other privileges, and in particular with the virginal motherhood granted her by a singular decree of God's Providence. 'God, the King of the universe, has granted you favors that surpass nature. As he kept you a virgin in childbirth, thus he has kept your body incorrupt in the tomb and has glorified it by his divine act of transferring it from the tomb.' [*Menaei Totius Anni*]

33. In the fifteenth century St Bernardine of Siena collected and diligently evaluated all that the medieval theologians had said and taught on this question. He was not content with setting down the principal considerations which these writers of an earlier day had already expressed, but he added others of his own. The likeness between God's Mother and her divine Son, in the way of the nobility and dignity of body and of soul – a likeness that forbids us to think of the heavenly Queen as being separated from the heavenly King – makes it entirely imperative that Mary 'should be only where Christ is'. [*In Assumptione B. Mariae Virginis, Sermo 11*] Moreover, it is reasonable and fitting that not only the soul and body of a man, but also the soul and body of a woman should have obtained heavenly glory. Finally, since the Church has never looked for the bodily relics of the Blessed Virgin nor proposed them for the veneration of the people, we have a proof in the order of sensible experience. [*Ibid.*]

39. We must remember especially that, since the second century, the Virgin Mary has been designated by the holy Fathers as the new Eve, who, although subject to the new Adam, is most intimately associated with him in that struggle against the infernal foe which, as foretold in the protoevangelium [Gen. 3.15], would finally result in that most complete victory over the sin and death which are always mentioned together in the writings of the Apostle of the Gentiles [Rom. 5–6; 1 Cor. 15.21–6, 54–7]. Consequently, just as the glorious resurrection of Christ was an essential part and the final sign of this victory, so that struggle which was common to the Blessed Virgin and her divine Son should be brought to a close by the glorification of her virginal body, for the same Apostle says: 'When this mortal thing hath put on immortality, then shall come to pass the saying that is written: Death is swallowed up in victory.' [1 Cor. 15.54]

40. Hence the revered Mother of God, from all eternity joined in a hidden way with Jesus Christ in one and the same decree of predestination [*Ineffabilis Deus*], immaculate in her conception, a most perfect virgin in her divine motherhood, the noble associate of the divine Redeemer who has won a complete triumph over sin and its consequences, finally obtained, as the supreme culmination of her privileges, that she should be preserved free from the corruption of the tomb and that, like her own Son, having overcome death, she might be taken up body and soul to the glory of heaven where, as Queen, she sits in splendor at the right hand of her Son, the immortal King of the Ages. [1 Tim. 1.17]

44. For which reason, after we have poured forth prayers of supplication again and again to God, and have invoked the light of the Spirit of Truth, for the glory of Almighty God who

has lavished his special affection upon the Virgin Mary, for the honor of her Son, the immortal King of the Ages and the Victor over sin and death, for the increase of the glory of that same august Mother, and for the joy and exultation of the entire Church; by the authority of our Lord Jesus Christ, of the Blessed Apostles Peter and Paul, and by our own authority, we pronounce, declare, and define it to be a divinely revealed dogma: **that the Immaculate Mother of God, the ever Virgin Mary, having completed the course of her earthly life, was assumed body and soul into heavenly glory.**

12

How to Think about Mary's Privileges: A Post-Conciliar Exposition[1]

Philip Endean

> Mary Immaculate,
> Merely a woman, yet
> Whose presence, power is
> Great as no goddess's
> Was deemèd, dreamèd.

One of Gerard Manley Hopkins' most striking poems compares Our Lady 'to the air we breathe'. The image provokes Hopkins into some wonderfully evocative, creative writing, and rather diverts our attention from what he is saying doctrinally. Mary 'mothers each new grace / That does now reach our race'; she continues to conceive Christ in us; she herself is not merely our almoner, but is identified with God's 'sweet alms'.

> Through her we may see him
> Made sweeter, not made dim,
> And her hand leaves his light
> Sifted to suit our sight.

In these beautifully paced lines, Hopkins is seducing us into an account of Mary's role in the life of all believers that many would instinctively qualify or reject were it put in a more prosaic form: everything we know of the light of God comes to us refracted through Mary. Mary's presence is greater than had ever been attributed to any of the pantheon of goddesses, because the life of the one true God is a life of self-giving, a self-giving into which Mary is mysteriously and uniquely incorporated, a self-giving of which she becomes in some way a part.

Hopkins was, of course, an imaginative genius; he was also given to original theological speculation. But the instinct to assign a special role to Mary was one that he shared with the ordinary Roman Catholic piety of his day. Mary was Mother of God, not simply 'St Mary the Virgin':

---

1.   This article first appeared as as 'How to Think about Mary's Privileges', *Priests and People*, 7/5, May 2003: 190–5.

> The saints are high in glory
> With golden crowns so bright;
> But brighter far is Mary
> Upon her throne of light.

The invocations of the Litany of Loreto were common coin – 'tower of David, house of gold, ark of the covenant'. Catholics were proud of their devotion to Mary, and prepared to defend it against hostile Protestant criticism:

> When wicked men blaspheme thee
> I'll love and bless thy name.

PERFECT DISCIPLESHIP

In the 1960s, following Vatican II, this exuberance began to feel awkward, and therefore to vanish. The downplaying of devotion to Mary was one of the most obvious effects of the council on mainstream Catholic life, rivalled perhaps only by the disappearance of the Latin liturgy. The council's decision – one which was quite controverted on the council floor – not to write a decree specifically about Mary, but to deal with her in a chapter of its Constitution on the Church, was taken only very narrowly: a large number of the council Fathers wanted indeed to make a dogmatic proclamation of Mary as mediating all graces.[2] What prevailed, however, was a more ecumenically sensitive presentation, avoiding new titles, and setting Mary within the perspective of salvation history. It became fashionable to base any account of what we might want to say about Mary on what Christianity must say about human beings in general. In such a light, the dogma of the assumption appears simply as an affirmation that Mary models (perhaps by anticipation) what will ultimately be true of all of us. Similarly, the immaculate conception appears as an affirmation that grace prevails over original sin even at the origins of the human race. Influentially, Raymond E. Brown, the noted Roman Catholic biblical scholar, often centred his account of Mary in the Bible on the concept of the 'perfect disciple'.

This tendency influenced even official teaching. Paul VI's 1974 Apostolic Exhortation on Mary, *Marialis cultus*, acknowledged the difficulties which many – especially Christians of other Churches – had with devotion to Mary. Paul was aware of 'the discrepancy existing between some aspects of this devotion and modern anthropological discoveries and the profound changes which have occurred in the psycho-sociological field in which modern man lives and works'. In authentic Roman Catholic devotion to Mary, 'every care should be taken to avoid any exaggeration which could mislead other Christian sisters and brothers about the true doctrine of the Catholic Church'. When Paul describes an authentic devotion to Mary for his time, he stresses how she can serve as a model for Christian humanity:

---

2. See the discussions by Alberto Melloni and Evangeilista Vilanova in Alberigo and Komonchak (eds) 2000: 95–8, 367–72, 425–8.

She is worthy of imitation because she was the first and the most perfect of Christ's disciples. All of this has a permanent and universal exemplary value.

The excesses complained about by Christians of the Reformation 'are not connected with the Gospel image of Mary nor with the doctrinal data which have been made explicit through a slow and conscientious process of drawing from Revelation':

> The reading of the divine Scriptures, carried out under the guidance of the Holy Spirit, and with the discoveries of the human sciences and the different situations in the world today being taken into account, will help us to see how Mary can be considered a mirror of the expectations of the men and women of our time. (nn. 35–7)

A contemporary theologian sees a theology of Mary as indicating

> ... that God's redemption in Jesus Christ has taken root and has started in the rest of humanity which is not Jesus Christ, so that affirmations about Mary are actually also affirmations about the nature of human salvation.[3]

This approach to Mary – Mary as the pre-eminent hearer and keeper of the Word – may have served a useful, even necessary purpose in the period immediately following the council. Many were helped by the encouragement to think of Mary in less obviously exalted terms, to imagine her as a human being, faced with the normal challenges of the human condition. Preconciliar accounts of original sin certainly needed to be complemented by a doctrine of an even more original grace, and it may be that the traditions of Mary's immaculate conception were indeed a useful pointer. Similarly, heaven was all too easily spoken of in terms of an unreal and inhumane beatific vision; perhaps the doctrine of the assumption, dogmatized as it was in 1950, had some effect in encouraging us to take seriously the communion of saints and the resurrection of the body, and to recognize that our glorified life must still – whatever we want to say about divinization – be a *human* life. Some, like the German theologian Wolfgang Beinert, lamented how 'the choral praise of the mother of God in the days of Pius XII' had been 'succeeded by a deep silence';[4] certainly the relative eclipse of Marian devotion in the period was not the intention of the council, of Paul VI, or of the theologians most influential over the council's Marian statements. Others, however, saw this eclipse of Marian rhetoric as salutary, an ecumenically sensitive corrective to earlier exaggeration. It was high time we learned to focus on the woman of Nazareth; we needed to divest her of a greatness associated with goddesses, and see her instead as a human being under God. If the rhetoric of Marian privilege – of immaculate conception and assumption into heaven body and soul – helped us understand better what it was to be human under God, well and good; if not, then it was ripe for demythologization.

---

3. Johnson 1984: 155–82 (181).
4. Quoted in Stefano de Fiores, 'Mary in Postconciliar Theology', in Latourelle (ed.) 1988: 469–539 (474).

JESUS, MARY, AND SALVATION HISTORY

The changes in the Church's Marian devotion and rhetoric can never, of course, be understood in isolation. As we have already noted, ecumenical considerations played a part; perhaps feminism too, and more generally the profound changes in gender relations in the twentieth century, had some influence. Here, however, I want to concentrate on how these changes in Mariology connect with broader trends in the history of theological ideas. Vatican II was concerned to situate the distinctive elements in Christian revelation – Jesus, Scripture, Church – within the whole sweep of salvation history, presenting the Church as the sacrament of salvation. Theologians might then tease out what this must imply for our understanding of Christian uniqueness: the Church is not the ark in which alone God's grace can be found, but something at once more richly generous and more unassuming: the definitive presence of a grace diffused over the whole creation.

Such an approach leads some to hesitate and others to criticize. Precisely because it tries to understand the central elements of Christianity in terms of what we must say about human beings at large, it can never – so it is claimed – do justice to a Jesus who claims to be not simply the 'real and proper man' of the 1970s liturgical ditty, but rather, uniquely and singularly, '*the* way, *the* truth and *the* life'.[5] The Church is surely instituted 'from above'; it is not simply a matter of devout human beings organizing themselves. And Mary is *Mother of* God: Catholic tradition requires that we not simply understand her as the model of human *response to* God. The Church's liturgy – particularly the Marian solemnities – seem to imply something stronger than a Mariology of perfect discipleship.

There are different possible responses to such criticisms. One is simply to accept them, and hence conclude that much post-conciliar theology is misguided, a sell-out of Christianity to the spirit of the 1960s. Another denies their validity: religious maturity consists precisely in our abandoning any sense of Christian pre-eminence, precisely in our replacing the language of special divine initiative in Jesus with that of an ever more authentic commitment to serve the world in humane partnership. Both of these approaches, however, violate a fundamental principle of Christian theology. Both proceed as if you resolve the tensions in the Christian message by opting either for an approach 'from above', prioritizing the 'divine', or from below, prioritizing the 'merely human'. Central to Christianity's witness is that such ways of thinking miss the point. Claims about the divinity of Jesus are not made *at the expense of* claims about his humanity; claims about Scripture's divine inspiration must not imply a *denial* of the human agencies through which it came to be. We must therefore not understand 'Mary woman of Nazareth' and 'Mary Mother of God' as somehow in competition, as though one of these descriptions is true only to the extent that the other is false. We have to find ways of understanding them together, as complementary truths. This suggests, then, the need for a third and rather different response. This understands the divine *and* human life of Jesus (and therefore also of Mary) within the context of the divine life given to all human beings in grace. But it

---

5. A particularly trenchant, logically clean advocacy of this principle comes in Marshall 1987.

also attempts to do justice to rooted intuitions about their *special role within* this universal grace, to a sense that they represent the presence of God among us in a particular and distinctive way.

KARL RAHNER AND THE IMMACULATE CONCEPTION

At this point, I introduce the figure of Karl Rahner, and in particular one idea from an essay which he wrote in 1954 in honour of its being a Marian year, marking the centenary of Pius IX's proclaiming Mary's immaculate conception as a dogma.[6] Rahner never had a special interest in Mary; he may well have regarded the more extravagant forms of Marian devotion with some disdain; some of his writings on Mary express quite simply a Mariology of perfect discipleship. But this particular essay points us to a way of thinking about Mary that enables us to strike the necessary balances. It helps articulate why Mary, though subordinate to Christ, nevertheless plays a uniquely special role in God's dealings with the creation.

Taken at face value, the doctrine of Mary's immaculate conception seems to tell a story of Mary's being privileged with regard to just when the life of grace began in her. Pius IX, in proclaiming the tradition of the immaculate conception to be a dogma, declares that 'from the first moment of her conception' Mary was 'preserved from all stain of original sin'. This occurred through a 'singular grace and privilege of almighty God'; by implication, the rest of us are conceived and born in sin, and grace is given to us only later, when we are baptized (at least by desire). Politely, Rahner points out that there are problems with such a way of thinking, because it seems unduly pessimistic about the unbaptized infant:

> This child ... is already, as unbaptized an object of God's infinite mercy, in spite of original sin; it is included in God's vision of God's only-begotten Son, and thus it has, if not yet a realized, at least a 'remote' claim to inheritance with the Son.

Simply by virtue of its existence, its creation, the child is 'already comprehended within God's grace and love' (207). It is only because this love of God is already there that the child's salvation 'takes a sacramentally visible form'. It follows that nothing of decisive significance turns on just when baptism takes place – as Rahner asks ironically, '[H]as anyone ever seriously regretted having been baptized after a fortnight instead of as a two-day-old?' And hence,

> ... the whole mystery of Mary's Immaculate Conception cannot simply consist in the fact that she was graced a little earlier, temporally speaking, than we were. The distinction must lie deeper, and this deeper distinction must condition the temporal difference. (208)

---

6. 'The Immaculate Conception', Rahner (1954), trans. Ernst 1961: 201–12. See also 'The Fundamental Principle of Marian Theology', *Maria*, 1, August 2000 (1954): 86–102. References to the first essay are henceforth made simply by page number in the text, and the translation is occasionally modified.

Rahner is writing diplomatically here, but the force of his argument is that the idea of a temporal difference between when grace begins in Mary and when it begins in the rest of us must be merely a figure of speech pointing to something much more significant. If the doctrine of the immaculate conception is to mean anything significant, it must point to some stronger sense in which Mary's relationship to sin and grace differs from that of human beings at large.

Rahner, good Thomist that he is, can simply assume that divine grace and human freedom are compatible: to say that God wills Algernon to perform an action is not to deny that Algernon freely performs that action. Thus Mary's free response to God's call, expressed in Luke's Annunciation story, is nevertheless – for Rahner – something which is predestined in the designs of God, just as is Jesus' free acceptance of his mission even unto death. It is in this context, of freedom and predestination, that Rahner makes what he sees as the necessary distinction. God's predetermining will to become incarnate in Christ entails that 'an earthly Mother of the Son was likewise predestined' – an earthly Mother who gives free consent; and for her, 'the divine purpose of salvation' is 'the predestination of Christ himself':

> That is to say, if she had not been willed as the Holy one and the perfectly Redeemed, then Christ himself would not have been willed by God in just the way he stands before us. (210)

Had Mary said 'no' to the invitation represented by Luke's angelic message to her, had God's saving will not included Mary's consent, Jesus Christ quite literally would not have existed. This cannot be said of any other creature. Peter and Judas, to say nothing of countless later Christians, may reject Christ, be ambivalent about him, and in an extended sense, therefore, affect who Christ is. But their rejection would not bring about the withdrawal of the promise which Christ, crucified and risen, represents for us: 'in every other case Christ could exist and be predestined by God without its being necessary for the individual concerned to be one of the redeemed'. Mary, by contrast, 'stands within the circle of Christ's own predestination':

> and thus she is different from us not merely through her having become the graced one at a temporally earlier point in her existence. The mystery that really gives the temporal difference between her and us in the mystery of her immaculate conception its proper meaning is, rather, the mystery of her predestination. (210–11)

Christ incarnate, crucified and risen represents to us a promise that a life without sin is possible. Christ embodies the promise; the rest of us receive it and hand it on. We are not talking here about a divine reality being communicated to human beings. We are talking, rather, about a God who exists in self-giving to the creation, about all humanity (not just that of Jesus) caught up in the very life of Christ – 'I am all at once what Christ is, since he was what I am', as Hopkins reminds us. What makes Jesus distinctive is not that God is somehow 'more' present in him than in the rest of creation, but rather that he alone reveals that presence definitively. He assures us that sin will be overcome. Rahner's rather abstract argument about Mary's predestination in connection with Christ's then amounts to the claim that Mary is not simply a recipient of this message: her saying 'yes' is, rather, a constitutive – if duly subordinate – element within the message.

The ideas in Rahner's 1954 essay on the immaculate conception need to be linked with what Rahner wrote elsewhere about salvation. In the 1954 essay, Rahner talks about redemption in rather conventional terms that he elsewhere challenged.[7] There are powerful reasons for asserting that the primary agent in our salvation is the love of God, which is eternal and changeless. Christ's death and resurrection must not be understood as if they made any difference to that – as if, for example, they could somehow convert the anger of God into graciousness. Christians have all too easily used religious language as a vehicle for expressing their own hostilities, and forgotten that – as Julian of Norwich so memorably put it – 'it is the greatest impossibility conceivable that God should be angry, for anger and friendship are two contraries'.[8] Christ causes God's will to be salvific only in a very carefully qualified, transferred sense of the term 'cause'. 'Cause' here simply means that in Christ's death and resurrection, God's salvific will is expressed as an irrevocable promise to us who must accept it and work it through in faith; his uniqueness consists in his embodying the promise, whereas we must receive it.[9] If we combine this idea with what Rahner wrote in 1954, the conclusion is clear: within this properly Christian (more so than most conventional ones) understanding of redemption, Mary is Co-Redemptrix. The promise of sin's being overcome that God made in Christ involved her too in a subordinate way that was quite unique to her. It would obviously be crassly offensive were Roman Catholic authority to make a dogma out of this title. But that does not mean that there is no truth in the idea. Christ transforms us by giving us in his person, his message, his death and his resurrection, God's assurance that what we call sin is overcome. In so far as he is essentially dependent for his very existence on Mary, she too is not merely the most perfect recipient of redemption, but rather part and parcel of its proclamation. Feminist theology has, happily, begun to reform our conceptions of God, and to deconstruct the use of Mary in Catholic Christianity as a safety-valve within an inhumanly patriarchal system. But the abuses are rooted in something positive, something which it would be a pity to lose completely.

Too easily Christians are trapped in ways of thinking that will not allow them to express Christian truth. Too easily, we think we need to choose between Christ as divine and Christ as human, Mary as Mother of God or Mary of Nazareth, the perfect disciple. One of the reasons why standard Mariologies appear either too

---

7. The fullest statement of Rahner's views comes in 'The One Christ and the Universality of Salvation', in Rahner (1975), trans. Moreland 1979: 199–224; another late statement comes in Rahner (1976), trans. Dych 1978: 282–5. But the ideas were in place much earlier; see, for example, the 1959 essay, 'Dogmatic Questions on Easter', in Rahner (1959), trans. Smyth 1975: 121–33, and Rahner 1949/1958, trans. Henkey 1961. Rahner tended to be innovative in only one area of theology at any one time, and while doing so to presuppose standard positions on other topics – even if elsewhere he had already given good grounds for moving beyond those positions.
8. Julian of Norwich 1998: 112 (Long Text, ch. 49).
9. Rahner (1976), trans. Dych 1978: 284, 202.

extravagant or too reductive is that we imagine revelation as a divine message to a godless humanity. We need, instead, to think of the world as bathed in grace from the start; revelation in one sense changes nothing, although by giving us assurance of God's irrevocable love it also changes everything. As Christina Rosetti's hymn reminds us, the effect of Christ's coming is to shatter conventional cosmology:

> Heaven and earth shall flee away
> When he comes to reign.

Mary is 'great as no goddess', because she is one factor defining a world in which powers and dominations are overcome and being a god or a goddess has ceased to have meaning, a world in which the only God there is lives in irrevocable solidarity with creatures, even the lowest and most despised. Christ's manifestation of this mysterious truth inevitably involves his mother, and that is why she will always have a special place in any healthy Christian theology. As Hopkins put it, Mary's 'presence, power' has 'this one work' to do:

> Let all God's glory through,
> God's glory which would go
> Through her and from her flow
> Off, and no way but so.

BIBLIOGRAPHY

Alberigo, Giuseppe and Komonchak, Joseph A. (2000) *History of Vatican II*, vol. 3, Leuven: Peeters.

Johnson, Elizabeth A. (1984) 'Mary and Contemporary Christology', *Église et théologie*, 15.

Julian of Norwich (1998) *Revelations of Divine Love*, trans. Elizabeth Spearing, London: Penguin.

Latourelle, René (ed.) (1988) *Vatican II: Assessment and Perspectives Twenty-Five Years After (1962–1987)*, vol. 1, Ramsey, NJ: Paulist.

Marshall, Bruce D. (1987) *Christology in Conflict: The Identity of a Saviour in Rahner and Barth*, Oxford: Blackwell.

Rahner, Karl (1949/1958), trans. Charles H. Henkey (1961) *On the Theology of Death*, Edinburgh and London: Nelson.

Rahner, Karl (1954), trans. Cornelius Ernst (1961) 'The Immaculate Conception', *Theological Investigations*, vol. 1, London: Darton, Longman and Todd.

Rahner, Karl (1959), trans. Kevin Smyth (1975) 'Dogmatic Questions on Easter', *Theological Investigations*, vol. 4, London: Darton, Longman and Todd.

Rahner, Karl (1975), trans. David Moreland (1979) 'The One Christ and the Universality of Salvation', *Theological Investigations*, vol. 16, London: Darton, Longman and Todd.

Rahner, Karl (1976), trans. William V. Dych (1978) *Foundations of Christian Faith*, London: Darton, Longman and Todd.

The Fundamental Principle of Marian Theology

Karl Rahner
translated and with an introduction by Philip Endean

INTRODUCTION: THE MARIOLOGY OF KARL RAHNER

Karl Rahner (1904–84) was one of the most influential Catholic theologians of the twentieth century. However, unlike many of the theologians discussed in this book, he was not an enthusiastic Mariologist, and Mary was not a major focus of his extensive publications. His most substantial work on Mary was written in the context of the papal Marian initiatives of the 1950s: the Marian year of 1954 marking the centenary of the proclamation of the immaculate conception as a dogma, and, above all, the dogmatization of the Assumption in 1950. Rahner's reaction to these events was complex. On the one hand, he was a responsible and respectful Catholic theologian, and certainly had a personal devotion to Mary; on the other, he was concerned that much Marian devotion of the 1950s was theologically irresponsible. It is – as the text which follows states at the outset – Christ who is at the centre of Christianity, and what is said about Mary must respect that principle.

Rahner reacted to the Marian celebrations of 1950 and 1954 by taking his own misgivings seriously, rather than repressing them in a misguided loyalty, and letting them stimulate him to constructive and creative theological work: notably, a long monograph on the assumption that nevertheless contained much valuable reflection on general principles of Mariology. Many modern Catholic writers on Mary, particularly after Vatican II, have been rather crudely revisionist in their approach. Taking a lead from the council's decision to incorporate Mary within the Dogmatic Constitution on the Church, they have tended simply to present Mary as the pre-eminent Christian disciple, effectively as St Mary the Virgin rather than as Mother of God. That kind of reaction against undisciplined exuberance here was one that Rahner shared, and indeed some of his later occasional writings on Mary follow this trend. But such writing is often overreactive. In the 1950s, Rahner saw clearly that mainstream Catholic tradition required a subtler vision, one that might indeed subordinate Mary to Jesus Christ, but which still assigned her a distinctive and unique role in the history of God's dealings with the creation. Rahner's attempt to answer this theological need was original, one from which we can learn today. His slightly later essay on the immaculate conception, which is concerned with Mary's predestination, has been discussed above (288–290).

Rahner's monograph on the assumption has only recently been published in the original German, as part of a project to make available all Rahner's writing in a 35-volume standardized edition. In the 1950s, the text encountered problems with the censor appointed by Rahner's Jesuit superiors, and only short excerpts were published. After the council, there was a demand for a quite different kind of theological writing, and the highly wrought scholastic subtlety of the argument in the Mariology monograph would probably have been incomprehensible. Rahner thus let the matter lapse.

Rahner's wider work on the theology of grace led him to adopt what he refers to here, rather off-puttingly, as a 'historico-theological personalism': under God, the life and death of each of us conditions the context in which we all live. Thus the way is opened for conceiving the uniqueness of Christ not in terms of some unique divine identity (for indeed, all of us are children of God), but in terms of a decisive historical effect, a transformation of the historical context in which we all live. God's self-gift is directed to the whole cosmos as it evolves in history; the incarnation's uniqueness consists not in its amounting to an exclusively unique manifestation of that gift, but rather in its being the historical moment when the divine self-gift is manifest in a way that is irrevocably assured. Mary's *fiat*, Mary's saying 'yes', is unique, not because it represents some privileged retroactive effect of the salvation wrought by Christ (that much, in Rahner's theology, applies to all history prior to Christ), but because it is itself essential to the definitive sign of the salvation wrought by God's love which is the Christ-event. Had Mary not freely, under God's grace, said 'yes' to the angel's invitation, Christ would have been a different person: her predestination in grace to say 'yes' is the predestination of Christ himself.

Rahner's 'historico-theological personalism' enables him to move beyond a crude distinction between 'subjective' and 'objective' redemption, between the redemption objectively established by God in Christ and the redemption that people at large can, with greater or lesser degrees of success, appropriate subjectively. Within such a framework of thought, Mary can only appear as one holy person among others in the Church, as a high-class manifestation of 'subjective holiness', or else as an element in 'objective redemption', as herself implicitly a divine co-redeemer with the divine Son in an unacceptable sense. But for the Jesuit censor, Rahner's avoidance of this latter tendency was seriously problematic; Rahner did not respect sufficiently papal teaching about how 'the Blessed Virgin Mary was united with her Son to the closest possible degree in the struggle that was to lead to the complete victory over sin and death'. Rahner's work on Mary was thus published only in attenuated form. In the post-conciliar reaction, Rahner's inventive attempt to develop a theology of Marian privilege which avoided excess remained lost. Perhaps it is time now to retrieve it.

Bibliographical Note

What follows is based on Karl Rahner, 'The Fundamental Principle of Marian Theology', *Maria*, 1, August 2000: 86–102, a translation by Sarah Jane Boss and Philip Endean SJ from a 1954 French publication of an extract from the Assumption monograph. The monograph itself has now been published in volume 9 of the *Karl Rahner Sämtliche Werke: Maria, Mutter des Herrn – mariologische Studien*, ed. Regina Pacis Mayer, Freiburg: Herder, 2004, and the extract given here comes on pages 253–61. Philip Endean has revised the original translation in the light of the newly available German original, omitting some peripheral and very technical material. Mayer's introduction is an invaluable guide to the troubled history of the monograph. The other essay quoted above, 'The Immaculate Conception', in *Theological Investigations*, vol. 1, trans. Cornelius Ernst, London: Darton, Longman and Todd, 1961: 201–12, is important; as is an attractive collection of sermons from the 1950s, *Mary, Mother of the Lord*, trans. W. J. O'Hara, 1963, and published over the following years by several firms. For a relatively painless piece in English offering some further background information, readers may like to consult Philip Endean, 'How to Think about Mary's Privileges', *Priests and People*, 7/5, May 2003: 190–5, reproduced in this volume: 284–91. Important work has been published in German by the Polish Jesuit theologian Jacek Bolewski: 'Das Assumptio-Dogma und seine Bedeutung für die Eschatologie nach Karl Rahner', *Collectanea Theologica*, 58, 1988; and *Der reine Anfang: Dialektik der Erbsünde in marianischer Perspektive nach Karl Rahner*, Frankfurt: Knecht, 1991. Other Mariological work of

Rahner's that is available in English includes two essays on the *in partu* virginity: 'Virginitas in partu', in *Theological Investigations* 4, trans. Kevin Smyth, London: Darton, Longman and Todd, 1961: 201–13; and 'Human aspects of the birth of Christ', in *Theological Investigations* 13, trans. David Bourke, London: Darton, Longman and Todd, 1975: 189–94. There is also a clear interpretative exposition of the dogma of the Assumption in *Theological Investigations* 1: 215–27. This list is not exhaustive.

EXTRACT FROM 'THE FUNDAMENTAL PRINCIPLE OF MARIAN THEOLOGY'

A sense that theological meaning comes through persons, persons at specific places in history (*ein geschichtstheologischer Personalismus*), is one of the fundamental structures of the order of salvation. That point can here be taken as read. But we still need to ask what this means with regard to Mary.

Our salvation is Jesus Christ. And in the end, it is him alone. In him, the trinitarian God has given himself to humanity; in him, God has revealed himself; he has come into the world as grace, reconciliation and salvation. Speaking abstractly, and a priori, the incarnation could be represented as follows: the Word of God took upon himself a human nature taken from a woman (in a manner that was in some way purely 'biological'). According to this account, the importance of this woman for the salvation of the world would be limited to this material and biological fact; essentially, in relation to the incarnate Word, she would be of the same order as, for example, the fact that, to accomplish our salvation, he had to be nourished by the bread and wine of this wretched and guilty earth. It is true that this would not deny the Blessed Virgin's divine motherhood: we should still have to confess that Mary is truly mother of the divine Person, mother of God; we should not cease to maintain the teaching of faith of the Council of Ephesus, the '*theotokos*', in an 'ontological'[1] and objective sense. Nevertheless, this divine motherhood would remain extrinsic with regard to what is truly personal, and to the history of salvation; it would not go beyond a purely biological domain[2] in which Mary would not necessarily have any further interest for us from a religious point of view or with regard to our faith.[3]

Were all this the case, Scripture could have told us that Jesus' mother according to the flesh was such-and-such a woman who had this or that name – as is done, for example, in the case of the apostles James and John – and we would then be able to register this 'historical information' as a 'very interesting' enrichment of our secular historical knowledge

---

Editors' footnotes are given in square brackets. Some technical bibliographical references in the footnotes have been tacitly omitted.

1. ['Ontological' does not have here the technical, sub-Heideggerian sense that it has in Rahner's other writings.]

2. Of course, for a metaphysical anthropology and ethics, the reality of the 'mother–child' relationship among humanity is and must be something other than a purely biological question. When it descends to this level, it becomes perverse. But we can leave this question aside here, because the totally human and personal element that is inherent in a woman's human motherhood and that cannot be reduced to biological categories would nevertheless not alone be sufficient to prove, in the case of Jesus, that Mary's motherhood belongs to the dimension of salvation history as such.

3. More precisely: if Mary were seen in terms of her motherhood in respect of Jesus, the only theological interest she would have for us would be from the point of view of her membership of the human race. Her motherhood would show that Jesus also is truly of our race: he has the 'same nature' as we do. Mary's interest for us would not come from her being precisely the particular person that she was, with particular concrete power to make a free decision.

about Jesus, before we then just filed it away. The relevance of this information for salvation history as such would be even less than the significance for world history as such of the fact that Napoleon's mother was a specific woman called Maria Letizia Ramolino from Ajaccio. In the end, one would just have to put this information in a 'biography' of Jesus (supposing that it were possible and sensible to write such a thing), and Mary could be judged by 'the standards of the world' as are other 'mothers of great men'; but the historical information in question would not belong to the history of salvation, of the 'gospel' *as such*. Indeed it would be a matter of indifference for our faith in this perspective whether Jesus had become 'Son of God' from the beginning of his existence, or whether he became such (ultimately in a docetist sense) only during the course of his own personal history. In fact, his divine sonship would no longer have any really essential relationship to the earthly origin of his existence, in so far as the latter is the act of a mother.

Yet according to the witness of Scripture, it is precisely not in this manner that faith should conceive of Mary's motherhood. Scripture places us at the outset before the alternative which decides in advance the whole of Mariology: whether we take seriously, as believers, what it tells us about the entry of the Word into his earthly existence, or whether we explain it in 'history of religion' terms, seeing in the story an embellishment added after the event, poetically transforming the beginning of the life of a man whose importance for our salvation lies only in what he himself 'consciously' experiences for us in his later life, in the words he addresses to his fellow men and women, and in the actions which he accomplishes on their behalf. On such an account, Jesus' coming into the world and his 'earlier life' would only be a preliminary condition for salvation – neutral, purely objective, and without interest for us.

But if we approach the witness of Scripture in the obedience of faith, we arrive at a quite different result. Mary is not only the mother of the Lord 'biologically'. Her motherhood as such is essentially salvation history. The holy thing born from her is, from the beginning, the Son of God (Lk. 1.35). It is upon *her* that the Holy Spirit comes, and the Power of the Most High takes her under his shadow (Lk. 1.35); it is she who is full of grace and the Lord is with her (Lk. 1.28). She is the blessed woman (Lk. 1.42); she conceives through her *faith* (Lk. 1.45) and through her obedient *saying yes* (Lk. 1.38) the incarnate Word of the Father for the world. This conception is virginal (Lk. 1.34–5; Mt. 1.16, 18–20, 25) so as to make us understand that already this singular event between mother and child, and not just, so to speak, what Jesus subsequently is and does of himself, is from the outset and in itself an act of God. It is something beyond the profane course and earthly chains of world history; in short, it is the history of salvation. Thus, Scripture itself has breached unequivocally the only conceivable boundary that could be erected against a Mariology that was in the full sense theological and dogmatic. It does not consider the bodily conception of the Son of God as a purely biological event, as a fact whose character is exclusively private and human, concerning at most Jesus' private existence and his mother only in relation to this. Rather, this very act of becoming is already a supernatural divine act of salvation – a work of his power in the Spirit, accomplished in a virgin; and in this event a human being says yes in faith. Scripture itself already contains a theology of the incarnation, and not just a theology of the cross. And in this incarnational, salvific act of God, Mary plays the only role that could be available to a human creature: she conceives (*empfängt*)[4] the Son in the

---

4. [It may be worth noting that the German *empfangen* means both 'to receive' and 'to conceive'.]

obedience of faith.[5] She opens the doors into the world for him; she conceives him for the world.

Of course, we must not think of this act of Mary's as if it were a 'synergism', as if the sovereign power of God's grace – of this grace that Mary has found in his sight (Lk. 1.31) – did not dispose causelessly the very act of her free obedience, but rather just constrained itself to 'concur' with an act which would not of itself be a grace. No, the free 'yes' that she gives itself belongs to the grace that she has found from God – like everything that a human being can do in the order of salvation. But it is precisely this which gives her 'yes' its salvific significance, which makes of it an event in the history of salvation as such. Thus, Mary does not enter into equal partnership with God. But then again, nor does HE, who brings about human activity and 'passivity' in grace alike – because his grace, being that of God, 'transcends' human activity just as much as passivity – enter into an equal partnership with humanity. Rather, he gives us what is precisely our free and saving action, and gives it *in such a way* that this action can be significant for salvation.[6] It is a gift of this kind which, according to Scripture, God gave to Mary: that her 'yes' conceived the Son of God in the flesh for the salvation of the world. Her 'yes' is taken up into the history of salvation.

If this is true, it follows simply and straightforwardly that Mary – as far as mere human beings are concerned – stands with her God-wrought 'yes' at *the decisive* place in salvation history, one that cannot be surpassed. For she does not accept any old word from God which might be of importance for all; in her and through her, it is not just any old salvific action of God in history that occurs; she accepts the Word of the Father absolutely; in her, passing through her and her freedom, the central act of God in the world is accomplished: the irrevocable acceptance of the world in the incarnation of the Son, the act to which all the previous history of salvation led unambiguously, and in which the whole future was already at root decided, however much that salvation thus established still needed through the death of the incarnate Word to be realized in the world and to receive its definitive consummation. Seen scripturally – the point is to be noted – Mary occupies this central place precisely not in so far as she *is* the Lord's mother passively, but in so far as she

---

5. This obedience of faith is not attested in Scripture among the generations preceding Mary, enumerated in Jesus' genealogy, and nor can it just be presumed to have been there. So it *cannot* be held that we should make the same claim concerning Jesus' grandparents, etc., *mutatis mutandis*, as we do for the Blessed Virgin because of her motherhood. They do not necessarily constitute a part of salvation history as such; this latter is a history of believers, brought about by their acts of faith in the flesh, however much the genealogy of Jesus quite properly attests that the Lord is of our race, and however much this is a fundamental truth of salvation.

6. We do not need here specifically to highlight and demonstrate that we are here bringing out the decisive difference from the Protestant conception of grace. The Catholic Church also insists on *sola gratia* in the event of salvation; but it refuses to see in the grace that brings about all that is salvific a correlative concept which is logically the opposite of human passivity. Rather, the grace which brings about all things brings about precisely the human agent's free consent; this consent is and remains the human agent's responsibility. If it is lacking, then the fault is human; if it is given, it is a grace of God. From this point of view, one can understand that a genuine Protestantism – whatever the case with Lutheranism in the past – cannot have a Mariology; Catholic teaching, on the other hand, must have one. In the last analysis, constructing a Mariology does not mean giving information about an individual human being and her private distinctions, but rather the expression of what Mary means for the salvation of the world. When this salvation is only passively received and imputed, it can be described in its pure origin from God, and as though it were still floating above humanity. If it comes as a pure grace of God, while also being freely enacted by humanity without it ceasing to be a grace, then it cannot be fully described without also saying how it is something done by the human agent: both for him- or herself and for others.

becomes his mother actively, in so far as she says 'yes' to God's decisive act. If, therefore, we wish to determine the theological starting point for all that we must say about Mary, we shall have to begin with this fact, and seek to understand it.

But before we do this, we need to reflect more exactly from particular theological points of view on the starting point that we have established already in Scripture. What have we actually said in saying: 'Mary in faith conceived the Word of God, and in so acting stands at the decisive point in salvation history'? What is the relationship of this deed of hers to that of Christ, in whom alone God reconciles the world to himself? These questions raise many points that are discussed in recent theology, and that we cannot simply leave aside if our starting point is to be fixed sufficiently clearly really to serve our purpose.

What is the relationship between the action of Mary that is significant for salvation history and that of Christ? This question itself contains two further ones. What is the relationship in general between Mary's action and Christ's? And how does this relationship work out in the concrete, once we reflect that we find on the one hand in Scripture Mary's decisive deed at the incarnation, while of course Christ's deed is on the cross?

To answer the first question we must start from the fact that the reality and action of Christ is the event upon which *everything* depends that is important for salvation in the world and in history. No act of faith, no salvific action is possible except through the existence of the dead and risen Christ; for no act of faith is possible except in the power of the Spirit and of the grace which is his and which is present in the world because of him. This then also applies to the events of history and salvation which precede his cross and his resurrection.[7] . . .

Now, as regards our case here of Christ's salvific act having an effect which anticipates it, we can begin by noticing something distinctive about it: here Christ's action has a retroactive effect on *a particular reality* that in turn is the cause or condition of that action of his: Mary brings about through her word of faith the incarnation, the incarnation by which she herself is redeemed and her 'yes' made possible. Meanwhile, as we look at things more closely, it becomes evident that this is a characteristic of salvation history as such: the 'before' occurs through the power of the 'after', and brings about this very 'after'.[8] In so far as such an act is sustained by the grace of Christ and presupposes it (and thereby, in an 'ideal' form, already presupposes the sacrifice of the cross), it belongs to the order of subjective redemption; in so far as at the same time it enables and brings about this objective redemption, there is no reason against counting it within the order of 'objective redemption'. But this point demonstrates only that the two ideas (subjective and objective redemption) are not so unambiguous, and clearly distinguishable from each other, as one often tacitly assumes. And it is not in this, therefore, not in an interpenetration of objective and subjective redemption, that we find anything special about what Mary does in salvation history. Rather, this specialness, over against earlier

---

7.   Cf., for example, Denzinger 1641, *'intuitu meritorum Christi'* as the reason of Mary's immaculate conception. More generally, theologians commonly hold the doctrine that those who were justified before the time of Christ were justified by his grace and thus 'on account of' his redemption. By reason of the doctrine found in the epistle to the Hebrews, and also in Romans 4, among others, this must be considered as a doctrine implicit in Scripture.

8.   This is because all the earlier acts of a positive nature in salvation history are realized in faith, and thus in the grace of Christ; little by little they bring about a historical existence for the Christ-event.

events of salvation, lies in the fact that her deed is a precondition of an event that is no longer 'open'. That is to say, it can no longer progress in a *different* manner, known exclusively to God and dependent upon his unforeseeable 'reaction'. It is an occurrence which is the beginning of God's decisive act; it is an *eschatological* event. Mary says 'yes' to the incarnation of the Son, with which the destiny of the world and of history is already definitively fixed and manifest as one of salvation (and not of judgement and anger). There could not have been a 'co-operation' with such an event before her, because there was no such event. But the fact that her prior deed occurred through the power of the later Christ-event itself does not distinguish it from other salvation events that helped to bring about (even if still in an 'open' dialectic of dialogue between God and humanity) Christ's coming.

At first sight, one thing that distinguishes this act of Mary's is the fact that it *seems* to be different from salvation events occurring '*after*' Christ'. *These* occur – so it seems at first sight at least – in such a manner that they draw their life from the Christ-event's power in a way that they are only its consequences, but in absolutely no way also its cause, whereas Mary's deed conditions the Christ-event itself, however much it also originates in its power. But one could ask if this distinction really works: i.e. one could ask if the events 'after Christ' are not also, at least by God, foreseen in such a way that, foreseen for what they are, they co-condition the earlier Christ-event – thus, in other words, looking at it from God and God's transcendence, it is always the whole which is the salvation of the whole human race that is the first things willed, and within this whole everything depends on everything else, and each individual reality, always in its distinctive way, is the 'cause' in its own place and degree for everything. Within this whole, the Christ event would always remain the irreplaceable and decisive centre, from which in a qualitatively unique way everything else in salvation history would depend and find its direction, meaning and measure. . . . (I)n view of the fact that Christ acts and suffers on the cross precisely as the head of humanity and as the Second Adam, and precisely as such is 'willed' by God, it is perfectly conceivable that his action and suffering was willed, seen, and 'accepted' by God, precisely in that this also forms a unity with the whole of salvation history, in other words in so far as, in conjunction with the salvific acts of all human beings together it is *the one* answer of the world to God's offer of his mercy and his love. If we thought in this way, then every graced 'yes' of every human being at any point in time would be a part of objective redemption, in that God is gracious to the world 'with a view' also to this 'yes' – however much this 'yes' is only possible in so far as it caused by the Son's sacrifice and would be subjective redemption to the extent that it originated from this cross of the Son's. This idea in no way necessarily denies a *qualitative*, indeed infinite, distinction between what Christ and his deed means within this whole and what an individual's 'yes' means within it. Nor does it deny that a human 'yes' *related* to the deed of *Christ* has the character of an acceptance of Christ's deed and of the grace which springs from it. Nor would there be a denial that *between* the Christ-event in itself and human salvific deeds there is a relationship of cause and effect – though obviously in such a way that for God the foreseen salvation of humanity, wrought by humanity in freedom, is the (final) cause for God's willing the Christ-event (obviously precisely as the efficient cause of that final cause) – in other words, God wills 'objective redemption' in view of 'subjective salvation'. All we would be saying is that a human deed wrought in grace, speaking in quite general terms, does not just have the character of an acceptance of a redemption wrought by Christ in a way already fixed and complete; rather, it also participates in its own way in the working of 'objective' redemption. All we would be saying is that God, if we look at things from God's end, wills the salvation that he offers because[9] and in so far as he wills it precisely as this reality to be accepted by humanity. This would not undermine the sovereignty and gratuitousness of the love that is given, because this 'yes' on the part of humanity is itself God's grace. Be all that as it may, the distinction between 'objective' and 'subjective' redemption is not so simple that we can place every salvific event in advance and as a matter of course up against the unambiguous alternative of being one or the other.

It is thus with all due foresight, and recognizing these general problems, that we need to ask whether Mary's 'yes' to the incarnation belongs to objective or subjective redemption. The grace and faith which condition her 'yes' presuppose her subjective redemption as a matter of divine act. Her deed as such itself joins in bringing about, as we have already seen, the incarnation. Thus she is part of objective redemption. She not only passes on to humanity an objectively achieved redemption; she contributes to its constitution in herself.

---

9. Of course, the 'because' here refers to the objective reality caused by God, not to a motivation affecting God. It is just saying this: *in so far as* and only in so far as the object of divine action is also the 'ground' of this action, the 'yes' given by humanity as a whole is *not just* a consequence dependent on Christ's deed. Rather, as an aspect of the one whole of saved creation, it is in a certain sense also the reason why God willed the Christ-event itself, because he wanted precisely *this* event to be successful, and at the deepest level could only will it to be such.

13

IMMACULATE MARY: THE ECCLESIAL
MARIOLOGY OF HANS URS VON BALTHASAR

FRANCESCA MURPHY

HANS URS VON BALTHASAR (1905–88)

Von Balthasar's doctoral thesis was published as *The Apocalypse of the German Soul* (1937–9).[1] This study of nineteenth-century German literature left the Swiss theologian with abiding commitments. In the first place, as against the secular, immanentized eschatology of the German Idealists, which the Nazi Third Reich was implementing at the time his book appeared,[2] von Balthasar made the medieval, Augustinian interpretation of the book of Revelation as an eternal reality continuously played out in human history a root principle of his biblical exegesis. 'Not only', he writes, 'in a future eternity, but now and already, the Church is "the bride without spot or wrinkle, the Immaculate".'[3]

Since nineteenth-century German philosophy makes volition or *power* the driver of human action and thought, von Balthasar entered on a lifelong questioning of the role of power within the Church, and in God. That is, he came away in partial agreement with Nietzsche: 'there is no alternative for gods: *either* they are the will to power . . . or the incapacity for power' (*The Antichrist*, #16). The first thing which will later strike von Balthasar in the Gospel 'narration' of Mary's life is a renunciation of power.[4]

One lesson von Balthasar drew from the literary and the real 'German apocalypse' was that humanity now has to choose between the way indicated by Nietzsche and that proffered by Soren Kierkegaard. A Kierkegaardian bias can be seen in von Balthasar's stress on the darkness of faith, as when he likens the faith and obedience required of Abraham 'on Mount Moria' to that required of Mary at the foot of the cross. Both had to give away 'the son of the fulfilment' and thus Mary's '"Let it be done to me according to your word" is the completed expression of the faith of

---

1. Von Balthasar's PhD thesis, completed in 1928 as *History of the Eschatological Problem in German Literature*, was published between 1937 and 1939 as *The Apocalypse of the German Soul*.
2. Michael Burleigh has recently taken up Eric Voegelin's idea of Nazism as an eschatological 'political religion', in Burleigh 2000: 2–3, 9–10, 258. Voegelin discusses the trajectory from Joachim of Fiore to German Nazism in Voegelin 1986: 42–5; the book was originally printed in Austrian just before the 1938 Anschluss. Voegelin suggests that he owed this notion to von Balthasar's PhD thesis in Voegelin 1968: v.
3. von Balthasar 1987a: 55–6.
4. von Balthasar 1992: 293.

Abraham and of all Israel.'[5] Following Kierkegaard, von Balthasar developed a personalistic philosophy: for him, 'woman is not an abstract principle' but 'a concrete person, and it is from her as a person that the female atmosphere emanates'.[6] In line with this, and with the probing of his friend Karl Barth, his biblical exegesis maintains an existential focus on revealed historical specifics, as when he states that the 'fullness of Israel's faith was a particular human being called Mary'.[7]

'One cannot read these Gospels cautiously enough', observed Nietzsche, the philologist: 'if we *saw* ... these ... synthetic saints', we would see through them; 'because *I* do not read words without seeing gestures, *I make an end of them*'. A Nietzschean urge for mastery will see through Christ himself, an insufficiently masculine 'deity ... gelded in his most virile virtues' (*Antichrist*, #44 and 17). Von Balthasar considers that the gesture of *seeing through* is inhuman. His first great work, *The Glory of the Lord: A Theological Aesthetics* (1961–9) is about beauty and the kind of vision it takes to see the 'glory' or supernatural beauty of Christ. As God's masterpiece, Mary is the image who enables us to envisage human conformity to Christ.[8] Von Balthasar sets *aesthetic contemplation* of biblical images against the Nietzschean 'looking through': the 'havoc which the "historical-critical" method is ... wreaking in the world of faith is possible only in a spiritual sphere from which the Church's Marian dimension has been banished and which has ... forsaken all spiritual senses and their ecclesial communication ... when the *image* of the woman has vanished from the theological realm, an exclusively masculine, imageless conceptuality ... takes over'.[9] As against *seeing through*, Mary's original experience is a tactile faith.

Mary presents what is most human in us, our ability to be persons who are freely receptive and giving. The dramatic structure of free, personal relations is the theme of von Balthasar's *Theodrama* (1973–83). Here, giving the personalism of the religious existentialists an ontological basis, von Balthasar enters the mystery of the relation of human and divine freedoms. The 'dialogue principle', according to which 'a child is awakened to I-consciousness through the instrumentality of a Thou', becomes part of his Christology. Mary is the 'Thou' who nudges Jesus' eternal mission-consciousness into human awareness. The 'child' Jesus' 'inner initiation' into his Jewish milieu takes place 'in harmony' with his eternal self-consciousness:

> Mary's handing on of the religious tradition is the pure, infallible doctrine of the old and new People of God, for this doctrine springs from pure faith and understanding imparted by the Spirit. Without this spiritual handing on, which takes place simultaneously with the bodily gift of mother's milk and motherly care, God's Word would not have really become flesh. For being-in-the-flesh always means receiving from others ... the Incarnation of the Word that brings

5. von Balthasar 1987a: 47–8.
6. von Balthasar 1975: 111.
7. von Balthasar 1987b: 10.
8. Marchesi 2004: 344, 351.
9. von Balthasar 1982: 421–2.

the promised fulfilment, or the 'new and eternal Covenant', has an inherent need of an antecedent history that we call the 'Old Covenant'; in Mary, the (Abrahamic) faith that characterised this Covenant becomes a contributory element in the Incarnation.[10]

Mothers are free to awaken their child or not to do so. Mary's free decision to bear this child makes the incarnation a personal or human event.

> [This] means that the conception of Jesus demands an act of faith which infinitely surpasses that of Abraham ... That the word of God take flesh in Mary requires that a receptive yes be pronounced by the whole person, body and soul ... offering the whole of human nature as the place in which the Incarnation can come about. To receive and let it happen is not necessarily a passive attitude: if they are realised in faith, then, in relation to God, receiving and letting it happen is supremely active. If there is a shade of reserve in Mary's yes, anything of a 'thus far and no further', then the child could not take possession of a human nature in its entirety.

Only an immaculately sinless person has access to such perfect human freedom.[11] Mary's powerlessness is that of one who puts herself at God's disposal:

> The freedom of Mary exhibits an utterly exuberant form of creaturely freedom ... This is the finite freedom that hands itself over to the sphere of infinite freedom ... in so doing, it has attained perfection ... No finite freedom can be freer from constrictions than when giving its consent to infinite freedom.[12]

Having confronted 'post-Christian Pneumatology' in *The Apocalypse of the German Soul*, von Balthasar outflanked the secular millennialist eschatologies, with their dream of a 'third age of the Spirit', by rethinking reality in terms of the property ascribed by Augustinian theology to the Holy Spirit. His *Theo-Logic* (1947 and 1985–7) develops the most important theme in von Balthasar's theology, that beauty, goodness and truth are grounded in love. Mary is the mediatrix of the inner-Trinitarian love.

Von Balthasar repeatedly returns to the problem of love and power, good and evil in the Church in his five-volume *Explorations in Theology*. The historical backdrop to his *Explorations* and to *The Office of Peter and the Structure of the Church* (1974) is the repercussions of the 1870 declaration of papal infallibility, along with the debate about temporal power, at Vatican I, followed by the modernist crisis. The repression of modernism highlighted the philosophical question raised by Nietzsche, that is, whether the Church is just a power structure. Nietzsche's apocalyptic conception of the will to power has given way to the mundane model of social manipulation

---

10. von Balthasar 1992: 175–7.
11. von Balthasar 1987a: 48–9.
12. von Balthasar 1992: 299–300.

through therapy and bureaucratic management. The theological issue raised by the masters of suspicion remains *where we see* a Church which surmounts the drive to domination. A Church which interprets itself as an institution is, von Balthasar thinks, 'far more vulnerable to sociological criticism' than one 'conceived in terms of the ancient *mysterium* vision', conceived, that is, as the 'new Eve', the 'ideal of all that is feminine'. While always insisting that 'the Church is first of all a *mysterium*',[13] anchored, on the human side, in the historical givens of Mary's life, von Balthasar thought long and hard about the co-existence of this 'ideal' Church with the prostituted, manipulative 'Church of Rahab'.[14] Reflecting on Mark 3.31, where Jesus' 'cousins and . . . close relatives' express annoyance at his eccentricities, von Balthasar comments,

> One must imagine Mary among these people. She does not think of contradicting them or of setting herself apart from them as someone who knows better about everything . . . She belongs to the family. The immaculate belongs to the clan of sinners, the seat of wisdom belongs to the bottomless stupidity of humanity.[15]

As *prototype* Mary represents the eschatological Church, whose beauty underwrites the spots and wrinkles (Eph. 5.27) of the historical Church: 'as this *mysterium* she is Christ's Body and his Bride.'[16] The neurotic need for perfection in the visible Church is exhibited in the conviction that *Father* can do no wrong. Better, then, to distinguish the institution and the spirit: 'we have . . . infallible doctrine residing in the apostolic office of Peter and . . . holiness of life within the (Marian) Church of the saints.'[17]

FAITH AND SIGHT

The Curial response to the fideism implied by some modernist writings was to ensure an even tidier separation of faith and reason than that which marked the theological initiation of Alfred Loisy and his cohorts, and a more rigid 'manualization' of theological education, with each topic assigned its separate loci. It is in reference to this that von Balthasar remarks that constructing 'a separate, completely formulated, Mariology' is a less 'potent' way of securing Mary's 'real presence' to Christians than the practice of the 'Eastern Church', where 'a living Marian principle permeates and perfumes the whole life of the Church'.[18] All of his theological and philosophical ideas interlock with his Mariology.

'Faith and reason' is a case in point. Instead of making an act of reason (such as the

---

13. von Balthasar 1986: 184, 24.
14. See particularly 'Casta Meretrix', in von Balthasar 1991a: 193–286.
15. von Balthasar 1987b: 64.
16. von Balthasar 1986: 24.
17. von Balthasar 1982: 212.
18. von Balthasar 1986: 159.

intuition of being) the foundation of his epistemology and metaphysics, atop of which the articles of faith can be added, von Balthasar constructs his ontology around the free engagement of two persons, that of a child's 'I' awakening 'in the experience of a "Thou": in its mother's smile through which it learns that it is contained, affirmed and loved in a relationship which is incomprehensibly encompassing, already actual, sheltering and nourishing'.[19] The smiling mother who recurs in von Balthasar's metaphysical texts is Mary. The mother–child relationship stands for a general, philosophical 'dialogue principle' and is clearly identified with a particular, revealed historical fact, as in von Balthasar's discussion of how 'Jesus owes his self-consciousness to his mother'.[20] Both the nascent structure of reason and that of faith involve a miniature personal drama.

Modernism produced a sequence of rationalist, humanitarian models of the Church (Felix de Lamennais, Alfred Loisy, George Tyrrell); the institutional counter-reaction gave rise to a 'long list of unnecessary human tragedies'.[21] Both were occasioned by the failure to create an ecclesial model of the relation of faith and reason. Von Balthasar's ecclesiology explores how the reasoning, Petrine institutional Church is rooted in the faith of Mary.

The hermeneutical problem which Nietzsche indicated, and into which modernists like Loisy were drawn, is that the New Testament is only as trustworthy as its authors: text and transmission stand and fall together, and with it faith in Jesus Christ. 'In the *mysterium* of the Church no individual member can be successfully isolated from the whole living organism': Jesus Christ 'stands as an indivisible whole within a constellation of his fellow men.' The figures in the constellation around Christ who become 'prototypes' of the institutional Church are Peter, John, James and Paul. The apostolic experience is that of 'eye-witnesses' – people with evidential knowledge of Christ. This is the *rational*, institutional basis of the Church. Von Balthasar contrasts the apostles' experience of Jesus with Mary's experience: 'Their faith begins in the material and the external and then becomes interiorised, while Mary's ... experience of faith begin[s] in her innermost being and gradually attain[s] external form.'[22] The apostles had *faith* in Christ. But their faith was initiated by the evidence offered them, in their daily contact with Jesus, whereas Mary's faith began in the dark. 'Mary's faith', von Balthasar states, 'could accept the unfathomable, not because she did not try to comprehend (Lk. 1.29, 34; 2.19, 51), but because, for her faith, darkness was more essential than clarity. The mission of Peter, as of all who proclaim the gospel ... is different: he must understand, and will, as far as he is able.'[23] Mary's chronological priority over the apostles is the mark of theological priority: 'the Church was already present in her before men were set in office'.[24] The Christ-centred constellation, with Mary and 'the apostolic foursome', looks like this:[25]

---

19. von Balthasar 1991b: 616.
20. von Balthasar 1987a: 46.
21. von Balthasar 1986: 260.
22. von Balthasar 1982: 346.
23. von Balthasar 1986: 233.
24. 'The Marian Principle', in von Balthasar 1975: 113.
25. von Balthasar 1986: 132–6, 148, 310–11. See also von Balthasar 1992: 279.

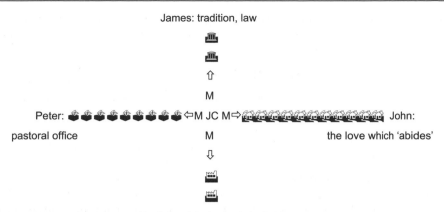

Paul: freedom in the holy Spirit

Faith fertilizes reason in the Marian Church, because the gift of faith can be shared out in a way in which that of being an eye-witness cannot:

> the form of the Marian faith (consenting to God's activity) is offered to the *Catholica* as the model of all being and acting, whereas the catholicity of Peter's pastoral care, though all-embracing in its object, is not communicable in its specific uniqueness ... the Petrine universality is subject to the formative influence of the Marian, but not vice versa.

Mary's 'witness' of faith is the *universally* extensive mission; 'her obedient consent ... has archetypal efficacy for salvation.'

MEMORY

In the Neo-Thomism which dominated Catholic seminary education until Vatican II, mysticism is important, but detachable from the foundations in philosophy. Von Balthasar reverses this because he sees faith-experience as dealing with more concrete and specific objects than those engaged in philosophical enquiry. For him, Mary's faith perceptions make her the 'memory' of the Church: no one else 'has a similar unbroken memory from the first moment of the Incarnation to the Cross, to the taking down from the Cross, to the burial and resurrection'. Von Balthasar ties the significance of Mary's memory to the nineteenth- and twentieth-century apparitions and, almost as frequent in late-twentieth-century Catholicism, to the practice of the rosary.[26] Mary remembers what it means to possess Christ as an object of faith. 'It would be odd if in heaven Mary had denied her earthly experience of faith and had changed over to giving Christians prophetic revelations about the future (the conversion of Russia and so on)';[27] 'under the Cross she also understands that one

---

26.   von Balthasar 1987b: 38, 43–5.
27.   von Balthasar 1987a: 17.

must say Yes to what is most incomprehensible. All this remains steadfastly in her memory.'[28]

THE NUPTIAL PERSONALITY OF THE CHURCH

Catholics have traditionally countenanced the defects in their clergy by distinguishing the person and the objective *role* (deacon, priest, bishop, pope). In the modern world, the model of *impersonal* authority makes the Church feel like a control panel: 'what', von Balthasar asks, 'can the most personal of all relationships and experiences, those of vocation and discipleship, have to do with an authority that can still function substantially despite personal sinfulness?'[29] Does our ordinary language about the Church contain a commonsense grasp of a deeper, personal reality, undergirding the impersonal roles? For we habitually say that the Church rejoices, prays, wills such and such a policy, and suffers such and such results.[30] Since 'God as Creator is a God of form and of the beautiful', even 'impersonal' ecclesial authority devolves upon reception of a 'form': the 'act of surrender under the impulse of grace is ... answered by God with investiture with "the form of Christ" ... formed in the Christian (Gal. 4.19) so that he ... may become a "form" for others (1 Thess. 1.7)'. The Church will remain 'impersonal', in von Balthasar's perspective, so long as we divide 'male' office-running from 'female' spiritual perfectionism. He writes,

> This form of Christ has its source in the, so to speak, material, feminine principle of the surrender of faith, 'leaving all things', and in the formal, male principle of grace giving itself and imprinting itself on the believer, in whom it is a participation in Jesus Christ, in the life of the Trinity. This life of grace is not 'impersonal' ... It is, rather, 'supra-personal' ... a participation in the vitality of the interchange of life between the three Persons.[31]

Humanly speaking, Mary is the 'person-begetting' principle in the Church, the male office-holders her midwives: 'The Church's faith is the womb that can bring to birth, to assist which the Church's functions were framed.'[32]

Von Balthasar was not wholly satisfied by the idea of the Church exposed in Charles Journet's *The Church of the Word Incarnate* (1951). This Thomistic conception sees it as the sacramental-eucharistic *body* of Christ. Journet considered the Church as a single person, with Christ as its head, his grace overflowing through the sacraments onto the members of his human body. A 'formal abstraction' enabled him to slot the Pauline idea of nuptiality into this block: one can formally distinguish the 'bride' from the Head. But taking the Church as a collective neglects the 'subjectivity and

---

28. von Balthasar 1987b: 38.
29. 'Office in the Church', in von Balthasar 1991a: 81.
30. 'Who is the Church?', in ibid.: 143.
31. 'Office in the Church', in ibid.: 106–7.
32. 'Who is the Church?', in ibid.: 159.

personality' of the concrete individuals 'who form the Church'.[33] Von Balthasar gives preference to the nuptial analogy for the Church. The bride who is to be of 'one flesh' with her groom must be spotless, as in Ephesians 5.27.[34] Which of its members is worthy of the Bridegroom?

THE SINLESSNESS OF MARY

What gave divine authority to the *role* was the fact that clerical office comes from God. This imparts what von Balthasar calls 'objective holiness',[35] the power to teach and to consecrate the sacraments. But original sin alone makes it impossible for Peter and his successors to match their 'objective' gift with a corresponding *subjective* holiness. Peter, the successors of each of the apostles and all lay people, in fact, are sinners, never living up to their mission as Christians. How can sanctity rub off on the members of Christ's body if all lack that odour? To be humanized, sanctity must not only be objectively given by God, but also take root in a co-operative personal subject.

Mary is the foundation of the Church in von Balthasar's theology because she is *sinless*. She is therefore the *subject* source of the Church's external or objective holiness. The office-holders are subjectively sanctified by participation in her personal holiness. She is therefore the 'objectivity of the Church'.[36] This is the ecclesial meaning of the doctrine of the immaculate conception, for von Balthasar: 'In Mary ... the Church is not only infallible in the official Sacramental sphere', but also 'personally immaculate and beyond the tension between reality and ideal'. The act of faith which Mary makes as 'an individual believer within the Church community' is the 'subjective ... ground of each personal act of faith within the *communio sanctorum*',[37] standing behind and completing, for instance, each imperfect confession and act of communion.[38]

Since the modernist crisis, there has been a lesion between those Catholics who uphold experience as the basis of Christian faith, and those who regard this as the high road to the subjectivization of doctrine. Von Balthasar's Mariology mediates between the two by describing Mary's sinless relation to God as both 'subjective', the spiritual experience of an historical individual, and also so completely 'objective' as to be the source of grace for others. There is, von Balthasar thinks, an inescapable play-off between the perfection of spiritual *experience* and the objective charism of office: 'this bipolar character of Marian, subjective holiness and Petrine, objective holiness ... constitutes [the] inner dramatic tension' of the Catholic Church, and

---

33. Ibid.: 156–7.
34. von Balthasar 1989: 93.
35. von Balthasar 1992: 356–7.
36. von Balthasar, 'Homo Creatus Est', in *Skizzen zur Theologie V*, Einsiedeln: Johannes Verlag, 1986: 146, cited in an unpublished paper by Hilda Steinhauer, given at the Centenary conference in honour of von Balthasar, Lugano, Switzerland, March 2005. Dr Steinhauer's paper, 'Mariologia e personalità teo-drammatica – l'identità salvifica dell'uomo', alerted me to the centrality of the immaculate conception for von Balthasar's Mariology. I intend to translate it shortly.
37. 'Who is the Church?' in von Balthasar 1991a: 162.
38. von Balthasar 1987b: 41.

makes her the extension (... 'body') of Christ as well as his partner ('Bride'), enabling her to participate in Christ's redemptive mission and ... in his Trinitarian being. There is drama in the encounter between the believer's experiential knowledge, which comes from the fullness of Christ, and authority's official knowledge ... imparted by Christ directly.[39]

What it means to be Christian in relation to God is articulated in Mary. As von Balthasar says, 'The Church flowing forth from Christ finds her personal centre in Mary as well as the full realisation of her idea as Church ... in its womanly openness to the divine, the Divine-human Bridegroom,' her faith

is coextensive with the masculine principle ... of office and Sacrament ... She is ... the adequate response awaited by God from the created sphere ... For this ... a special grace is needed ... which elevates the Marian response of faith to the status of principle and exemplar of the response of the entire Church. Mary's faith, as the fruitful womb of the Word, is privileged on two counts. In respect of its origin, it is a faith proceeding from her 'immaculate conception'; in respect of its end, it is a faith destined to bear the fruit that is not only Christ's body but also himself as Head.[40]

LOVE

Rino Fisichella considers that 'Von Balthasar's theology is a hymn to Mary'.[41] Others, reading that Mary is the human co-creator of the Church in her passionate 'self-surrender', her 'presence' at Christ's 'cross, her agreement to his abandonment of her to the Church in the midst of his dereliction',[42] would rather say that von Balthasar employs Mariology in a manner designed to annoy liberals with its romantic gender essentialism, and more worldly conservatives by what they regard as its transparent fideism. Von Balthasar's notion of Mary is tied to his original ontology, in which being is taken as a supra-personal reality; more precisely, von Balthasar identifies *being* with *love*. Faith is not an ultimate value in his theology. Rather, faith 'means allowing love to have its way'.[43] The transcendental properties of being, that is, truth, beauty and goodness, are held in Thomistic metaphysics to be *convertible* with being. Back of the elasticity of being and its properties, von Balthasar says, 'the hidden ground of the transcendentals and their circumincessive relation',[44] is love. If we do 'not read words', such as *being*, 'without seeing gestures' (Nietzsche), then the *actus purus* is committing the sort of act we ascribe to personalities, which is expressed in its basic gesture: since 'the self-giving of the Father to the Son, and of

39. von Balthasar 1992: 358.
40. 'Who is the Church?', in von Balthasar 1991a: 161.
41. Fisichella 2004: 88.
42. 'Who is the Church?', in von Balthasar 1991a: 165–6.
43. von Balthasar 1989: 401.
44. von Balthasar 2000: 9.

both to the Spirit corresponds ... to God's intimate essence, this ... itself can be ... only love'.[45] It is because he views love as common and garden to all things that von Balthasar claims that it was 'the universality and unrestrictedness' of Mary's *fiat* which became the 'infinitely plastic medium'[46] from which her son would sculpt the 'kind of Christ'.[47] Mary's 'plasticity' expresses the lovingness of reality; since sin isolates, whereas goodness makes us more available to others, the fact that Mary is immaculately conceived does not escalate her above solidarity with sinful humans.[48]

The ascription of 'plasticity' to Mary is paired with a meditation on Christ's 'eucharistic ubiquity', the ability of the risen Christ to make free with his resurrected body. Von Balthasar argues that,

> when we believe that we can call on the saints at any time and in any place ... we are presupposing that the saints have this same eucharistic openness toward us ... This eucharistic 'permeability' of all subjects to one another ... is the very basis of the *communio sanctorum* ... beholding and inwardly participating in the Son in his eucharistic self-giving becomes a beholding and a participating in the life of the Trinity. For when the Son allows himself to be poured out, he directly reveals the love of the Father, who manifests himself in his Son's *eucharistia*.[49]

Even more than truth, goodness, beauty or being, *love* calls conscious personality to mind. This brings Mary's nuptial *personality* to the foreground.

THE ESCHATOLOGICAL CHURCH

It is when the Church perceives 'herself as the outflowing love of the Lord' that she can begin to interpret herself as the Bride of Christ. As the love flowing from the Trinity, and the reciprocated, human love for God, the Church is both 'at two' with God, and desires to be entirely one with him. The Church as 'bride' cannot 'think of herself as definitively "over against" her Lord but only as pressing on to closer union with him, the Source of her being'.[50] The impetus towards unity with God is eschatological. Since 'she is the epitome and embodiment of Israel', 'which as a whole is continually experiencing the birth-pangs of the Messiah', our starting place for understanding Mary should be Revelation 12.[51] So the Church on earth cannot equate herself with Mary. 'Only at the end of time can she hope to reach the level of her most exalted member ... Till then, the Church, in honouring Mary, cannot be honouring herself.'[52] As a *factual individual* Mary's mission effects all human history.

---

45.   von Balthasar 1985: 126–7.
46.   'Who is the Church?', in von Balthasar 1991a: 165–6.
47.   Mary's words to King Alfred in G. K. Chesterton's 'The Ballad of the White Horse': 'You and all the kind of Christ are ignorant and brave.'
48.   von Balthasar 1992: 324.
49.   von Balthasar 1998: 373, 380, 383–4.
50.   'The Contemporary Experience of the Church', in von Balthasar 1991a: 21–2.
51.   von Balthasar 1987b: 29, 23, 9.
52.   'The Contemporary Experience of the Church', in von Balthasar 1991a: 23.

She belongs 'to the Old Covenant, to the time of Christ and to the time of the Church. . ..: she is located between a paradisial (supralapsarian) existence and human life in its fallen state; eschatologically, she exists between the latter state and final fulfilment.'[53]

<h2 style="text-align:center">TRINITY AND THEOTOKOS</h2>

For Thomas Aquinas, it is the Head's 'prerogative to communicate grace' and hence the human 'soul of Christ received grace so that it could be passed on from him to others'. In this sacramental action, 'the human nature of Christ' works 'like an *instrument* of the divinity'.[54] This is how the Church is created. Von Balthasar draws out the notion that the 'virginal man Christ is . . . the generative organ (*instrumentum conjunctum*)' of the Church. Since he considers that Christ's human consciousness is inseparable from his divinity, including the 'whole Trinitarian consciousness', von Balthasar accentuates that the grace thereby given is 'the pouring forth of the Trinitarian life'.[55] Having thus made it explicit that the Church is *Trinitarian*, or a 'being-for-one-another',[56] he correlates this with his own idea of the Church as containing a Bride–Groom opposition.

St Thomas expresses the idea of Mary as *Theotokos*, or Godbearer, by saying that 'grace flowed over from her soul into her body: for through the grace of the Holy Spirit . . . her womb was supernaturally impregnated . . . And so after Gabriel said, "Hail full of grace," he refers at once to the fullness of her womb, adding "the Lord is with you" (Lk. 1.28).'[57] This locating of grace in the physical womb of Mary corresponds to the idea of the Church as the body of Christ. Von Balthasar makes the physical Godbearing of the Virgin reflect the heart of the Trinity. He finds 'the first revelation of the divine Trinity' in the three steps of the Annunciation, where the angel 'communicates the salutation of the "Lord", Yahweh', and then tells Mary that 'she will give birth to "the Son of the Most High"'; this is possible because 'the Holy Spirit will overshadow her': thus is the 'Old Testament faith' fulfilled 'in Mary's own being', since her task is to be 'the archetype of the Church'.[58] Because the 'Spirit of Love, issuing from "the bosom of the Father", becomes the principle of the life of the Son in *the bosom of the Virgin*, Mary conceives in her self the mystery of the Love which binds the three persons of the Trinity, and thus becomes she who is rightly entitled *Theotokos*'.[59] For von Balthasar, 'Mary is the mediatrix of the graces of the Trinity', mediating the Trinity 'in and with the Church'.[60]

Supernaturally, in God, the Church is made trinitarian, peopled with 'personal

53. von Balthasar 1992: 318–19.
54. Thomas Aquinas, in *John*, Caput 1, Lectio 8; *Summa Theologiae* IIIa, q. 7, a. 9; *Summa Theologiae* IIIa, q. 7, a. 1.
55. 'Who is the Church?', in von Balthasar 1991a: 145, 190.
56. 'The Communion of Saints', in von Balthasar 1975: 95.
57. Aquinas, in *John*, Caput 1, Lectio 8.
58. von Balthasar 1987a: 50.
59. Fisichella 2004: 90–1.
60. von Balthasar 1998: 467.

members', 'because the "I" of Christ harbours the Father and the Spirit in circumincession'; humanly, this unity-in-difference comes about through the *Theotokos*, in her bridal relation to God. For the 'Church is not, purely and simply Christ ... not hypostatically united to God', but rather God's creaturely other-half, his opposite. In 'this opposition ... she is receptive to her Head and so has a feminine role. She is Marial ... In this consists the fulfilment of the [human man–woman] opposition that underlies the mystery of love and fecundity in the bodily sphere, a fulfilment ... derived from ... the Trinitarian opposition of persons in identity of nature.'[61] Von Balthasar correlates the contrapuntal unity of the persons of the Trinity with the unity-in-difference of creaturely Bride and supernatural Groom, making it the source and foundation of human erotic love.

WHY MARY?

As rooted in chemical DNA, biological fate, not to mention the fall, gives men and women over to power relationships: Nietzsche spoke for Neo-Darwinism when he advised, 'Thou goest to woman? Do not forget thy whip' (*Thus Spoke Zarathustra*). For von Balthasar, Mariology begins on page 1 of Genesis, when God creates humans in his image as male and female, thereby making the complementarity or 'opposition' of male and female part and parcel of the divine image; Paul's nuptial analogy in Ephesians 5, referring the union of Christ and Church back to the 'union in the flesh' of Adam and Eve, indicates that the form of the human–God relationship follows the pattern of that between man and woman.[62] Why shouldn't a contemporary theology contain either no Mariology (Barth, George Lindbeck) or a compartmentalized one, which makes no impress upon one's presentation of Christian doctrine as a whole? Von Balthasar's answer is that, if we are to believe that the Church composes the Scriptures, not to delude or control, but 'as the spontaneous expression of its experience of the inbreaking of absolute love',[63] our idea of human relationships must flow not from our post-Nietzschean culture, but from the mutual love of Mary and Christ. For von Balthasar claimed, 'the kenosis of Christ, consummated in the death on the Cross, is the ... point of origin of the Church', the nub of the 'generative power of Christ ...'

> As Christ has received from the Father the power to surrender his life, so he breathes forth his spirit on the Cross in an extremity of weakness, so he can also, at Easter, breathe his Spirit into the Church. His weakness unto death is his divine and his human form, his omnipotence, willing to assume the form of utter powerlessness.[64]

---

61. 'Who is the Church?', in von Balthasar 1991a: 168, 187.
62. 'The Marian Principle', in von Balthasar 1975: 105–6. Francis Martin develops this point in Martin 2004: 141–68.
63. von Balthasar 1989: 100.
64. 'The Contemporary Experience of the Church', in von Balthasar 1991a: 27–8.

VON BALTHASAR'S MARIOLOGY IN THE DOCUMENTS OF THE PAPACY OF JOHN PAUL II

Von Balthasar's Mariology has influenced the encyclicals of John Paul II, and is cited in the 1994 *Catechism of the Catholic Church*. John Paul's readiness to think of Mary as 'the *tota pulchra* portrayed by countless artists',[65] together with his image of the rosary as the means by which the believer '*sits at the school of Mary* and is led to contemplate the beauty on the face of Christ and to experience the depths of his love',[66] betrays a careful reading of von Balthasar by an original theologian in his own right. *Mulieris Dignitatis* (*On the Dignity of Women*, 1988) states that

> [the] Marian profile is also – even perhaps more so – fundamental and characteristic for the Church as is the apostolic and Petrine profile to which it is profoundly united ... The Marian dimension of the Church is antecedent to that of the Petrine, without being in any way divided from it or being less complementary. Mary Immaculate precedes all others, including obviously Peter himself and the Apostles. This is so, not only because Peter and the Apostles, being born of the human race under the burden of sin, form part of the Church which is 'holy from out of sinners', but also because their triple function has no other purpose except to form the Church in line with the ideal of sanctity already programmed and prefigured in Mary. A contemporary theologian has rightly stated that Mary is 'Queen of the Apostles without any pretensions to apostolic powers: she has other and greater powers' (H U von Balthasar, *Neue Klarstellungen*).[67]

The *Catechism* states likewise that 'Mary goes before us all in the holiness that is the Church's mystery, as "the bride without spot or wrinkle". This is why the "Marian" dimension of the Church precedes the "Petrine".'[68] The papal injunction '*philosophari in Maria*'[69] is stoutly von Balthasarian and Mariocentric in its understanding of the relation of faith to reason.

Finished as John Paul II received the last rites, 31 March 2005

---

65. John Paul II, 'Letter to Artists', 1999, #16.
66. John Paul II, *Rosarium Virginis Maria* #1. In Fisichella 2004: 87, 91, Fisichella notes John Paul II's use of the rosary-Marian memory theme in the 2002 encyclical *Rosarium Virginis Maria* and argues for an influence of von Balthasar on the Pope's thinking. Although this encyclical was clearly written by someone who admires von Balthasar's thought, direct influence could be difficult to establish, since von Balthasar claims, conversely, that he takes the idea from a 1987 papal homily: see von Balthasar 1987b: 35 and *Rosarium Virginis Maria* #11, 12.
67. John Paul II, *Mulieris Dignitatis*, 1988, #27; cf. also *Redemptoris Mater*, #27, 28.
68. *Catechism of the Catholic Church*, London: Geoffrey Chapman, 1994, no. 773.
69. John Paul II, *Fides et Ratio*, 1998, #108.

BIBLIOGRAPHY

Primary Sources

von Balthasar, Hans Urs (1975) *Elucidations*, trans. John Riches, San Francisco, CA: Ignatius Press.

von Balthasar, Hans Urs (1982) *The Glory of the Lord: A Theological Aesthetics. Volume I: Seeing the Form*, trans. Erasmo Leiva-Merikakis, ed. Joseph Fessio and John Riches, San Francisco, CA: Ignatius Press.

von Balthasar, Hans Urs (1985) *Theologik II*, Einsiedeln: Johannes Verlag.

von Balthasar, Hans Urs (1986) *The Office of Peter and the Structure of the Church*, trans. Andrée Emery, San Francisco, CA: Ignatius Press; German: *Der Antirömische Affekt*, 1974.

von Balthasar, Hans Urs (1987a) 'O Vierge, Mère et Fille de ton Fils', in Hans Urs von Balthasar and Joseph Ratzinger, *Marie première Eglise*, trans. Robert Givord, Paris: Médiaspaul; German: *Maria Kirche im Ursprung*.

von Balthasar, Hans Urs (1987b) *Mary for Today*, trans. Robert Nowell, San Francisco, CA: Ignatius Press.

von Balthasar, Hans Urs (1989) *The Glory of the Lord: A Theological Aesthetics. Volume VII: Theology: The New Covenant*, trans. Brian McNeil, San Francisco, CA: Ignatius Press.

von Balthasar, Hans Urs (1991a) *Explorations in Theology II: Spouse of the Word*, several translators, including A. V. Littledale, Alexander Dru and John Saward, San Francisco, CA: Ignatius Press; German: *Sponsa Verbi: Skizzen zur Theologie II*, 1961, Einsiedeln.

von Balthasar, Hans Urs (1991b) *The Glory of the Lord: A Theological Aesthetics. Volume V: The Realm of Metaphysics in the Modern Age*, trans. Oliver Davies *et al.*, Edinburgh: T&T Clark.

von Balthasar, Hans Urs (1992) *Theodrama. Theological Dramatic Theory III: Dramatis Personae. Persons in Christ*, trans. Graham Harrison, San Francisco, CA: Ignatius Press; see especially Part III B: 'Theological Persons: Woman's Answer': 283–360.

von Balthasar, Hans Urs (1998) *Theodrama: Theological Dramatic Theory V: The Last Act*, trans. Graham Harrison, San Francisco, CA: Ignatius Press.

von Balthasar, Hans Urs (2000) *Theo-Logic. Theological Logical Theory, Volume I: Truth of the World*, trans. Adrian J. Walker, San Francisco, CA: Ignatius Press.

Secondary Sources

Burleigh, Michael (2000) *The Third Reich: A New History*, London: Macmillan.

Fisichella, Rino (2004) 'Marie dans la théologie d'Hans Urs von Balthasar', *Communio*, XXIX.1, January–February: 87–98.

Herbst, Michele Marie (1995) *Christological and Marian Meditation: The Dramatic Integration of Human Freedom into Divine Communion According to Hans Urs von Balthasar*, PhD dissertation, Ann Arbor, MI: U.M.I.

Leahy, Brendan (2000) *The Marian Profile in the Ecclesiology of Hans Urs Von Balthasar*, London and New York: New City.

Marchesi, Giovanni (2004) 'Maria "Splendore della Chiesa" Nell'Estetica Teologica di Hans Urs von Balthasar', *La Civilta Cattolica* 155.3688: 341–53.

Martin, Francis (2004) 'The New Feminism: Biblical Foundations And Some Lines Of Development', in Michele M. Schumacher (ed.), *Women In Christ: Toward A New Feminism*, Grand Rapids, MI: William B. Eerdmans.

Steinhauer, Hilda (2001) *Maria also dramatische Person bei von Balthasar. Zum marianischen Prinzip seines Denkens*, Innsbruck-Wien: Tyrolia Verlag.

Voegelin, Eric (1968) *Science Politics and Gnosticism*, Chicago, IL: Henry Regnery.

Voegelin, Eric (1986) *Political Religions*, trans. T. J. Dinapoli and E. S. Easterly III, New York: Edwin Mellen Press.

14

THE VIRGIN MARY IN ANGLICAN TRADITION[1]

PAUL WILLIAMS

INTRODUCTION

This chapter will sketch the place of the Virgin Mary in Anglican tradition by concentrating on the classic texts of the sixteenth and seventeenth centuries, and then tracing developments in the nineteenth and twentieth centuries. We shall say little about the place of Mary in popular devotion, since the Marian devotions of late medieval Catholicism were, at the advent of the Reformation, sharply excised, though they were to some extent restored in the era of the Caroline Divines and Non-Jurors and significantly reaffirmed by the Anglo-Catholic revival of the nineteenth and twentieth centuries. Further, we shall not attempt to explore, in any detail, the place of Mary in contemporary worldwide Anglicanism. The concern here is with the received 'shape' of Anglican tradition since the Reformation.

The term 'tradition' spans both official doctrine and popular devotion. With respect to popular Marian devotion, even more than official teaching, Anglican and Roman Catholic tradition has differed markedly. In the late Middle Ages there was in Western Europe a whole range of popular expressions of devotion to Mary (among other saints), warmly supported by the Roman Catholic Church. Liturgy, private prayer, the calendar, pilgrimage, iconography, imaginative lives of Mary, lyrical poetry and music were all interwoven in Marian devotions. There were Marian shrines; Marian prayers such as the *Ave Maria*, *Angelus* and *Salve Regina*; Marian statues; Marian guilds and societies. The Dominicans, who promoted the use of the rosary, and the Franciscans, who supported the immaculate conception, each had their distinctive ways of promoting devotion to Mary. The extent to which it took on a life of its own varied hugely. The English Reformers of the sixteenth century reacted strongly against what they saw as the excesses of Marian piety, supported by the Roman Catholic Church, and sought to prune away devotions which obscured the central place of Jesus Christ in Christian belief and practice.[2]

The place of Mary and the saints in Anglican tradition was defined in part by

---

1. Originally prepared by Paul Williams for Nicholas Sagovsky and Michael Nazir-Ali as a background document for the Anglican group in the Anglican/Roman Catholic International Commission's discussion of the Virgin Mary.

2. For some choice examples, selected for the purposes of the Reformers' polemic against unscriptural Marian devotion, see *Foxe's Book of Martyrs* 1881, Book XII, sect. vii: 695–8, quoting 'Our Lady's Matins' and 'Our Lady's Psalter'. Duffy 1992 provides a magisterial and sympathetic account of popular devotion in England at the time of the Reformation.

reaction. The suppression of the guilds, shrines and prayers honouring Mary; the disbanding of the religious Orders which promoted Marian devotion; the pruning of the calendar of the feasts which had been occasions of Marian celebration; and the removal of most Marian statuary[3] cauterized this area of effective Christian belief for more than a generation. Nevertheless, the place of Mary in Anglican doctrine was never in question. The emphasis upon Holy Scripture as containing 'all things necessary to salvation', the reception of the creeds of the early Church; the reception of the teaching of the four Ecumenical Councils (and for some Anglicans as many as seven); and the reception of the tradition of the early centuries of the Church ensured the place of Mary in the Anglican understanding of the scheme of salvation. In addition, the definition of Anglican doctrine by means of the Prayer Book and by articles which simply set boundaries to doctrinal understanding in areas of contemporary controversy left ample space for new growth and continuing variety in the Anglican tradition after the radical, politicized measures of the sixteenth century. Although the 1552 Prayer Book and the 42 Articles of 1559 may be striking for the severe limits they set to Marian devotion, and for their lack of explicit Marian themes, the seventeenth century saw the formation of a broader Anglicanism shaped by further reflection on the tradition of East and West, a process that was renewed and, for some like Newman, tested to the limit in the nineteenth century. There was much to support this recovery: churches dedicated to the Blessed Virgin, Lady Chapels, popular shrines of 'Our Lady' held in folk memory, some Marian statuary, Marian imagery in stained-glass windows, the Marian feasts in the Anglican calendar, such as 'Lady Day'. Anglican tradition, as it spread throughout the world, proved in many places open to much more in the way of Marian devotion than the severer of the Reformers would have tolerated, though there has always been in Anglicanism a reluctance to see that devotion expressed in doctrines and official formularies which would have proved fatally divisive. The place of the Virgin Mary in Anglican tradition is assured because of Mary's place in the Gospel tradition,[4] but the way in which that place is celebrated by Anglicans has varied greatly and it continues to be so.

THE INFLUENCE OF THE CONTINENTAL REFORMERS

English Reformers, such as Latimer (*c.* 1485–1555) and Cranmer (1489–1556), were among the first of those to be influenced by the pioneering work of Luther and Zwingli. It was not, however, until the reign of Queen Mary (1553–8) that English exiles came under the full force of Calvin's teaching, and since the reign of Elizabeth (1558–1603) there has been a tension in Anglicanism between the received theology of Cranmer, which is indebted to the moderate Lutheranism of Bucer,[5] and, on the

---

3. See the third part of the homily 'Against Peril of Idolatry', *The Book of Homilies* (1833): 267.
4. This is particularly evident in Allchin 1993.
5. Cranmer's theological understanding underwent an evolution, and the expression of his views was always moderated by what was politically possible. The 'reading' of Cranmer has thus itself been a matter of controversy, to which the fine biography by Diarmaid MacCulloch (1996) makes an authoritative contribution.

one hand, Puritans like Cartwright (1535–1603) and Perkins (1552–1602) who were indebted to Calvin and, on the other, traditionalists like Laud (1573–1645) and other Caroline Divines in whom there was strong sympathy for Catholic teaching and practice, while maintaining the characteristic Anglican rejection of Roman juridical claims. Since the time of Jewel (1522–71) and Hooker (*c.* 1554–1600), both of whom resisted Puritan demands for further reform after the model of the Church of Geneva, the Calvinist (Presbyterian) tradition was effectively marginalized in the Church of England, whereas the tradition of the Caroline Divines was more firmly integrated in the Book of Common Prayer and the continuing strength of the High Church tradition and the Oxford Movement.

Marian teaching did not, at least in the beginning of the Reformation, belong to the dividing issues. First-generation Reformers, such as Luther and Zwingli, did not immediately question the Marian doctrine in which they had grown up, though they rejected Marian devotion centred on the invocation of Mary to the exclusion of Christ. There were those like Erasmus[6] and Thomas More[7] who criticized the excesses of Marian devotion as fiercely as any Reformer who went out of communion with Rome. The Apology of the Augsburg Confession (1531), drawn up by Melanchthon, rejects the veneration of Mary and the saints.[8] The Smalcald Articles (1537), drawn up by Luther and included in the *Book of Concord* (1580), attack the invocation of saints, but accept the doctrine of Mary as *Theotokos* (following the Council of Ephesus, 431) and as *semper virgo* (following Constantinople II, 553).[9] The Formula of Concord (1577) reaffirms the Lutheran belief in Mary as *Theotokos* and *virgo in partu*.[10]

The Reformers' positive understanding of the place of Mary in salvation history is clear. There could for them be no doubt that Mary was integral to the gospel and consequently to the creed. In 1521 Luther wrote an Exposition of the Magnificat[11] in which he affirmed her perfect virginity, including virginity *in partu*, praising her humility and perfect obedience to God's will and criticizing those who make an 'idol' of her. In a sermon on the feast of the Conception of Mary (1527), he made it clear

---

6. Erasmus (1466/9–1536) visited Walsingham twice in 1512 and 1514. He criticized the Christians of his time because they never seemed to address themselves to God, but only to Our Lady and the saints. Thus in *The Shipwreck*, from his *Familiar Colloquies*, the sailors call on Mary, chanting the *Salve Regina*: 'They implored the Virgin Mother, calling her Star of the Sea, Queen of Heaven, Mistress of the World, Port of Salvation and many other flattering titles which Holy Scripture nowhere applies to her.' See Graef 1965, vol. 2: 3–4.

7. Thomas More wrote in his *Dialogue Concerning Heresies*, 'The people in speaking of our lady: Of al our Ladies, saith one, I love best our Lady of Walsingham, And I, saith the other, our Lady of Ipswich. In whiche woordes what meneth she but her love and her affeccion to the stocke that standeth in the chapel of Walsingham or Ippiswiche? . . . Doth it not plainly appeare that either thei trust in the images of Christes stede and our Ladies, letting Christ and our Lady go, or take at lest wise those ymages that thei wene thei were verily the one Christ, the other our Lady her self'; quoted in *The Two Books of Homilies* (1859): 224n.

8. See Tappert (ed.) 1959: 232–4. Compare Article 21 of the Augsburg Confession (1530), which rejects invocation of the saints without specifically mentioning Mary.

9. The Smalcald Articles: 229, n. 3.

10. Tappert (ed.) 1959: 488, 595.

11. *WA* VII: 538–604; Pelikan (ed.) 1956: 295–358 (esp. 302).

that he still believed in her immaculate conception, saying that 'one believes blessedly that at the very infusion of her soul [Mary] was also purified from original sin'.[12]

Zwingli believed that Mary was '*virgo ante partum, in partu et post partum*'.[13] In 1522 he preached a series of sermons in Zurich on devotion to Mary. He made sure that the great Marian feasts of the Purification, the Annunciation and the Assumption continued to be kept as public holidays in the reformed city. 'How do we properly praise Mary?' he wrote:

> Not with elaborate and high (church) buildings, with processions where canons ride on beautiful horses, and dine with fine ladies ... but rather by using the money otherwise used for bricks and mortar for the welfare of poor daughters and women, whose beauty is endangered by poverty.[14]

In the subsequent generation, Calvin considered all prayers to Mary to be contrary to Scripture: to ask her to obtain grace for us is no less than an 'execrable blasphemy', because God has predestined the measure of grace for every person from all eternity.[15] To call her our hope, life, light and other similar names is to turn her into an idol and detract from God's honour, and to regard her as our 'advocate' is blasphemous, because she needed Christ as much as do all other human beings. Calvin recognized the theological legitimacy of the title 'Mother of God', but in practice never adopted it, unlike Luther and Zwingli, who made frequent use of if for its Christological power.[16] 'I am not able to disguise the fact', he wrote, 'that I find it wrong to have this title ordinarily attributed in sermons about the Virgin, and for my own part I would not think that such language was good or proper or convenient.'[17] Nevertheless, he has the highest regard for the dignity of Mary's divine motherhood. He also teaches her perpetual virginity and wants Christians to venerate and praise her as a teacher who instructs them in the commandments of Christ. In his *Commentary on the Magnificat*, he accepts the Catholic term 'treasurer of grace', explaining that this is because Mary kept all the things about Christ in her heart not for herself but for others. We must learn to praise Mary, but in the proper way, and to imitate her:

> Let us learn to praise the Holy Virgin. When we accord with the Holy Spirit, then there will be genuine praises ... But it is necessary also that with the praise there be imitation ... for our part, let us follow her and understand that God has looked on her in pity; let us contemplate in her person, as in a mirror, the mercy of God ... When we understand that the Virgin Mary is set before us as

---

12.   *WA* 17.2: 288. Graef 1965: 11, n. 6 suggests that from 1528 Luther no longer believed in the immaculate conception, but acknowledges that this is disputed.
13.   Hollenweger 1980: 64.
14.   Quoted in ibid.: 66.
15.   Graef 1965: 12, following Algermissen *et al.* 1957.
16.   Miegge 1955: 67.
17.   Quoted by Mackenzie (1980): 72.

such an example, and confess with her that we are nothing, that we are worth nothing, and that we owe everything to the pure goodness of God, see how we will be disciples of the Virgin Mary and will show that we have retained her doctrine. And what honour are we able to do her greater than that?[18]

In England, the Reformation took a distinctive political and ecclesial form that produced a unique Anglican polity, but England was very much part of Catholic Europe and the theological critique of Marian devotion and teaching that developed in England was much indebted to that of the continental Reformers.

THE ENGLISH REFORMATION

England's sixteenth-century Reformers grew up in a world of rich, if at times overblown, Marian devotion. In their own preaching and devotion, Mary was no longer seen as the Queen of Heaven, the ready intercessor, or abundant source of grace for humanity. The piety they encouraged brought together two perspectives. In one, Mary was seen as sharing fully in human experience: she was a woman, she was a wife, she was a mother; she knew about the care of a household and the nurture of a child; she was rejected at the inn door and she suffered the loss of her son. She was a model of humility and obedience to God's will. In the other perspective, Mary was seen as participating in salvation history: she was a humble, modest maid chosen to be the mother of the Saviour, and thereby a willing participant in God's redemption of the world. The Reformers of the English Church perceived Mary as a woman of humble obedience, called by God to an extraordinary role and rightly deserving of honour.[19]

Hugh Latimer, perhaps the most abrasive of the Anglican Reformers, regarded excessive devotion to Mary as dishonouring to her, since she never exalted herself above her son:

But some are so superstitiously religious, or so religiously superstitious, so preposterously devout towards our lady, as though there could not be too much given to her. Such are zeals without knowledge and judgement to our lady's displeasure.[20]

With reference to Luke 8.19–21, he was seemingly ready to assert that Mary had sinned:

On a time when our Saviour was preaching, his mother came unto him, very desirous to speak with him, insomuch that she made means to speak with him, interrupting his sermon, which was not good manners. Therefore, after St Augustine and St Chrysostom's mind, she was pricked a little with vain-glory

---

18. Ibid.: 74.
19. These two perspectives are exemplified by the quotations from *The Book of Homilies* below.
20. Latimer 1985, vol. 2: 227.

... And here you may perceive that we gave her too much, thinking her to be without any sparkle of sin, which was too much; for no man born into the world is without sin, save Christ only.[21]

Latimer goes on to note[22] that 'The school doctors say she was arrogant.' He himself argues that, since 'the very mother of Christ had sins, and yet was saved, we shall be saved too'.[23] His attitude was:

It hath been said in times past, without sin, that our lady was a sinner; but it was never said, without sin, that our lady was not saved, but a Saviour. I go not about to make our lady a sinner, but to have Christ her Saviour.[24]

Yet he could argue, with some nicety:

They did belie me to have said [that our Lady was a sinner], when I had said nothing [so] but to reprove certain, both priests and beneficed men, which do give so much to our Lady, as though she had not been saved by Christ, a whole Saviour, both of her, and of all that be or shall be saved.[25]

He is typical of the radical early English Reformers in that Mary is seen primarily as a humble and obedient agent of God in the redemption of humankind. Because of its biblical provenance, the *Ave Maria* (in its biblical form) was for him a legitimate devotion. So Latimer could write:

As for the *Ave Maria*, who can think that I would deny it? I said it was a heavenly greeting or saluting of our blessed Lady, wherein the angel Gabriel, sent from the Father of heaven, did annunciate and show unto her the goodwill of God towards her ... I did not speak against the well saying of it, but against the superstitious saying of it, and of the *Pater Noster* too.[26]

---

21.   Ibid., vol. 1: 383; cf.: 515.
22.   Cf. Thomas Aquinas, St III. qXXVii.4, where the authorities Latimer is referring to (Augustine and Chrysostom) are rehearsed. Augustine is quoted on both sides of the argument. Thomas's own opinion is, 'We should therefore simply say that the blessed virgin committed no sin, either mortal or venial.'
23.   Latimer 1985: vol. 2: 117; cf.: 157, 228, 358.
24.   Ibid.: 228.
25.   *Foxe*: 832. The usefulness of a source as polemical as *Foxe* has been disputed, but since Foxe's concern is to distance Latimer from corrupt Catholicism, this lends strength to his record of the honour he says Latimer accorded to Mary. The passage goes on to say: 'If she were a sinner, then she was redeemed or delivered from sin by Christ, as other sinners be; if she was no sinner, then she was preserved from sin by Christ; so that Christ saved her, and was her necessary Saviour, whether she sinned or no ... forasmuch as now it is universally and constantly received and applied that she was no sinner, it becometh every man to stand and agree to the same, "and so will I," quoth I, "nor any man that wise is, will be the contrary. But to my purpose, it is neither to nor from, to prove neither this, nor that; or I will have her saved and Christ her Saviour, whether else she was."'
26.   *Foxe*: 833; cf. Latimer 1985, vol. 2: 228–9.

In 1536, the convocation of the Church of England agreed Ten Articles which were intended to put an end to the 'diversity of opinions' that had sprung up in the realm. They were 'the first official doctrinal formulary of the Church of England'.[27] In them, the 'Four Holy Councils' (including Ephesus at which Mary was proclaimed as *Theotokos*) were commended, and images, especially images of Christ and Our Lady, were approved of as 'kindlers and stirrers of men's minds' – although warnings were given against 'censing of them, and kneeling and offering unto them'.[28] There was cautious encouragement for intercessions to the saints – 'We may pray to our Blessed Lady, to St John the Baptist, to all and every Apostle and to any other saint particularly as our devotion doth serve us, without any vain superstition' – but there is evidence within the text of the Articles of a struggle between those who wished to push forward with reform and, on the other hand, conservative resistance.[29]

In 1535, William Marshall had published '*cum gratia et privilegio regali*' a primer, much indebted to Luther, which omitted the Litany of the Saints and attacked traditional primers 'which have sore deceived the multitude'.[30] Such was the outcry that a second edition was published with the Litany restored, though Marshall insisted that he had made this and other omissions,

> Not of any perverse mynde or opinion, thynking that our blessed lady, and holy sayntes, mighte in no wyse be prayed unto, but rather bicause I was not ignoraunte of the … vayn superstitious maner, that dyverse and many persons have … used in worshypping of them.

Duffy calls Marshall's polemic 'as comprehensive an onslaught on the time-honoured forms of Catholic piety as had yet appeared in England',[31] but it was one which had quasi-official sanction. Whole paragraphs of Marshall's *Primer* were incorporated into the *Bishop's Book* (1537), or *Institution of a Christian Man*, which was intended to be an authoritative guide to the teaching of the Ten Articles for use in preaching and catechizing. In the *Bishop's Book*, the *Ave Maria* is discussed firmly in the context of the incarnation.[32]

In 1543, *The King's Book*, or *A Necessary Doctrine and Erudition for any Christian Man*, was published. Once more, the *Ave Maria* is discussed in the context of the incarnation. In *The Primer set foorth by the Kinges Maiestie and his Clergie* (1545), the *Ave Maria* (in its biblical form, with no petitionary versicle and response) stands in its customary place at the beginning of Matins. As in other primers influenced by the Reformed cause, it is clearly not an invocation of Mary. At Lauds, the '*Maria semper virgo*' is retained:

---

27. Duffy 1992: 392.
28. In Hardwick 1876, Appendix 1, the Ten Articles are given in full.
29. MacCulloch 1996: 162 shows that the text of the Ten Articles represents a compromise between the conservative views of Cuthbert Tunstall, Bishop of Durham, and Cranmer, to whom the last phrase quoted here ('without any vain superstition') may be attributed.
30. Duffy 1992: 382. For the text, see Burton (ed.) 1834. The other primers are *The Manual of Prayers or The Prymer in English* (1539) and *King Henry's Primer* (1545).
31. Duffy 1992: 382.
32. For discussion of *The Bishop's Book*, see MacCulloch 1996: 185–93.

Virgin Mary, rejoice always, which hast borne Christ the Maker of heaven and earth, for out of thy womb thou has brought forth the Saviour of the world. Thanks be to God.

In 1544, the Litany, the first vernacular service, was authorized. The Marian invocation reads, 'Holy Virgin Mary, Mother of God our Saviour Jesus Christ, pray for us.' When the Litany was included in the Prayer Book of 1552, this invocation was removed, together with that of individual saints and biddings invoking 'All holy Angels and Archangels and all holy orders of blessed spirits' and 'All holy Patriarchs and Prophets, Apostles, Martyrs, Confessors, and Virgins: and all the blessed company of heaven'.

In the Prayer Book of 1549 there was a commemoration within the Eucharistic Prayer which ran:

And, here we do give unto thee most high praise and hearty thanks, for the wonderful grace and virtue declared in all thy Saints from the beginning of the world: And chiefly in the glorious and most Blessed Virgin Mary, Mother of thy Son, Jesus Christ, Our Lord and God and in the holy Patriarchs, Prophets, Apostles and Martyrs, whose examples ... and steadfastness in thy faith, and keeping thy holy commandments, grant us to follow.

In writing this paragraph, Cranmer carefully adapted his two main sources.[33] The immediate source is the *Communicantes* from the Roman Rite:

In fellowship with ... and venerating above all the memory of the glorious ever-Virgin Mary, mother of God and our Lord Jesus Christ, and also of your blessed apostles and martyrs ...

The Roman Canon goes on to list a number of saints individually. At this point Cranmer drew closer to the great Prayer from the Liturgy of Saint Basil which asks:

... that we may find mercy and grace with all the saints who have been well pleased to you from of old, forefathers, fathers, patriarchs, prophets, apostles, preachers, evangelists, martyrs, confessors, teachers, and every righteous spirit perfected in faith; especially our all-holy, immaculate, highly blessed, glorious, Lady, Mother of God and ever-Virgin Mary ...

Cranmer simplified the doctrinal and liturgical expression to focus on what God does in his saints. He omitted the '*semper virgo*' and, by breaking up the phrase 'Mother of God' to become 'Mary, mother of thy Son, Jesus Christ, our Lord and God', he emphasized the Christological focus of the term *Theotokos*. Three years later, in 1552, he removed the whole paragraph.

---

33.   Brightman 1915, vol. 2: 690. See also Jasper and Cuming (eds) 1987: 164, 120.

In the Prayer Books of 1549 and 1552, the Calendar was greatly simplified. Of the Marian feasts, only the Annunciation and Purification were retained. The Conception, the Nativity, the Visitation and all mention of the Assumption were omitted. In the Calendar of 1561, the Conception (*sic*) of the Blessed Virgin Mary, the Nativity of the Blessed Virgin Mary and Visitation were all restored to join the Annunciation and the Purification as Marian feasts. The conspicuous continuing omission was the Assumption, which disappeared from Anglican worship in 1549, only partially to return in some twentieth-century Anglican calendars.

The second half of the sixteenth century was an austere period for the celebration of Mary in the Anglican tradition. In the Prayer Books (1549, 1552) the Purification was celebrated with a collect and gospel, to which an epistle was added in 1662; the Annunciation was celebrated with collect, epistle, gospel. In the Litany and the Eucharist there was no specific reference to Mary and the saints. The 39 Articles of Religion (1563)[34] sought to introduce clarity by teaching that 'Holy Scripture containeth all things necessary to salvation: so that whatsoever is not read therein, nor may be proved thereby, is not to be required of any man, that it should be believed as an article of Faith, or be thought necessary to salvation' (Article 6); that Christ alone is 'without Sin' (Article 15),[35] that 'the Romanish Doctrine concerning Purgatory, Pardons, Worshipping and Adoration, as well as of Images as of Reliques, and also invocation of Saintes, is a fond thing vainly invented, and grounded upon no warranty of scripture, but rather repugnant to the Word of God' (Article 22). Article 35 also specifically commended both *Books of Homilies* as containing 'a godly and wholesome doctrine'.

The doctrine about Mary in the *Book of Homilies* is set out in four main passages. In the third part of the 'Homily Against Peril of Idolatry', the worship at Marian shrines is criticized:

And where one Saint hath images in divers places, the same Saint hath divers names thereof, most like to the Gentiles. When you hear of our Lady of Walsingham, our Lady of Ipswich, our Lady of Wilsdon, and such other, what is it but an imitation of the Gentiles idolaters' Diana Agrotera, Diana Coryphea, Diana Ephesia, &tc., Venus Cypria, Venus Paphia, Venus Gnidia? Whereby is evidently meant, that the Saint for the image sake should in those places, yea, in the images themselves, have a dwelling: which is the ground of their idolatry; for where no images be they have no such means.[36]

---

34.   The main steps towards the 39 Articles were: the Ten Articles (1536), *The Bishop's Book* (1537), the Six Articles (1539), the *King's Book* (1543) and the 42 Articles (1553). The 39 Articles of 1563 represented a slight revision of the 42 (1553).

35.   There seems to be an indirect but clear reference to the Mother of our Lord, though authorities differ at this point. E. C. Gibson, *The Thiry Nine Articles* (1904), is strongly of the opinion that the Article does not refer to this subject. On the other hand, C. Hardwick, *The History of the Articles* (1859), and H. Browne, *Exposition of the Thirty Nine Articles* (1850), take the contrary view. It is, at least, noteworthy that the earliest commentator on the Article, T. Rogers, *The Catholic Doctrine of the Church of England: and Explanation of the Thirty Nine Articles* (1607), refers to the subject.

36.   *Book of Homilies*: 244.

In the second part of the 'Sermon Against Wilful Rebellion', Mary is commended as an example of civil obedience:

> In the New Testament the excellent example of the blessed Virgin Mary, the Mother of our Saviour Christ, doth at the first offer itself. When proclamation of commandment was sent in Jewry from Augustus the Emperor of Rome, that the people there should repair unto their own cities and dwelling places, there to be taxed; neither did the blessed Virgin, though both highly in God's favour, and also being of the royal blood of the ancient natural kings of Jewry, disdain to obey the commandment of a heathen and foreign prince, when God had placed such a one over them ... but, all excuses set apart, she obeyed, and came to the appointed place ... this obedience of this most noble and most virtuous lady to a foreign and pagan prince doth well teach us, who in comparison to her are most base and vile, what ready obedience we do owe to our natural and gracious Sovereign.[37]

This ideological use of the example of Mary, culminating in the *double-entendre* ('natural and gracious Sovereign' could refer both to the earthly and the heavenly sovereign whom Christians ought to obey), captures for us exactly the political and theological flavour of the times.

While admitting that the saints in heaven might pray for us, a key passage in the second part of the 'Homily Concerning Prayer' does not mention Mary by name, but once more reiterates the Reformed critique of the invocation of the saints, including, of course, Mary:

> Let us not therefore put our trust or confidence in the Saints or Martyrs that be dead. Let us not call upon them, nor desire help at their hands: but let us always lift up our hearts to God in the name of his dear Son Christ: for whose sake as God hath promised to hear our prayers, so he will truly perform it. Invocation is a thing proper unto God: which if we attribute unto the Saints, it soundeth to their reproach, neither can they well bear it at our hands.[38]

Lastly, we need to note that the homily on 'Repentance, and true Reconciliation' records:

> Jesus Christ, who being true and natural God, equal and of one substance with the Father, did at the same time appointed to take upon him our frail nature, in the blessed Virgin's womb, and that of her undefiled substance, that so he might be a Mediator between God and us, and pacify his wrath.[39]

---

37.   Ibid.: 623f.
38.   Ibid.: 356.
39.   Ibid.: 578.

It should be remembered that *The Book of Homilies* is one of the authoritative Anglican formularies.

Richard Hooker's focus in *The Laws of Ecclesiastical Polity* is such that he says nothing specifically about Mary (for Anglicans who look to Hooker's *Laws* as a major Anglican authority, a significant silence) and his discussion about the Communion of Saints (V.1vi.6–13) is a discussion about the communion of all Christians in Christ. In his 'Answer to Travers', however, he deals with the complaint from a Puritan critic[40] that Hooker is, especially since the Council of Trent, wrong to say of Roman Catholics, 'They acknowledge all men sinners, even the Blessed Virgin, though some of them freed her from sin', and, 'They teach Christ's righteousness to be the only meritorious cause of taking away sin, and differ from us only in applying it.'[41] On the first, Hooker corrects Travers: he actually said, 'They acknowledge all men sinners except the Blessed Virgin.' He goes on to affirm, 'Although they imagine that the Mother of our Lord Jesus Christ were for his honour and by his special protection preserved from all sin, yet *concerning the rest* they teach *as we do*, that all have sinned.'[42] In avoiding any further opening up of the question, Hooker merely follows Article 15, 'Of Christ Alone without Sin', but he does so in such a way as to leave open the possibility that there might be more to be said about the sinlessness of Mary. On Travers' second point, Hooker affirms that Roman Catholics 'teach as we do, that altogether Christ be the only meritorious cause of our justice, yet as a medicine, which made for health, doth not heal by being made, but by being applied; so, by the merits of Christ, there can be no life nor justification, without the application of his merits: but about the manner of applying Christ, about the number and power of means whereby he is applied, we dissent from them.' Even today, this remains a useful corrective of exaggerated Mariology, and of exaggerated accounts of the gulf between Anglicanism and official Roman Catholic teaching, especially as Hooker's position represents the mature Anglicanism of the late sixteenth century.

THE CAROLINE DIVINES AND THE NON-JURORS

The doctrine of the incarnation, the union of the divine and human in Christ, was at the heart of seventeenth-century Anglican theology. From this conviction flowed the celebration of this mystery in the Church's liturgy, the notion that the whole of human nature, including the body, was redeemed, and consequently the place of Mary in the economy as understood by Anglicans was secured. After the 'beating of the theological bounds' in the sixteenth century, there was among Anglican scholars a growing recognition of the place of Mary and the saints in the early Christian tradition, and a willingness to contemplate afresh the significance of Mary for Christian tradition, which was expressed in sermons, devotional writing and poetry.

---

40. When, in 1584, Walter Travers (*c.* 1548–1635) declined to receive Orders in the Church of England, he was passed over for the post of Master of the Temple, which went to Hooker.
41. See 'Travers' Supplication', in Keble (ed.) 1888: 563, and Hooker's 'Answer to Travers': 579–85.
42. Our emphasis.

King James I (1566–1625) was himself a keen theologian. What he wrote about Mary sums up well the Anglican position at the beginning of the seventeenth century:

> And first for the Blessed Virgin Mary, I yield her that which the Angel Gabriel pronounced of her, and which in her Canticle she prophesied of herself, that is, That she is blessed among women, and That all generations shall call her blessed. I reverence her as the Mother of Christ, of whom our Saviour took His flesh, and so The Mother of God, since the divinity and Humanity of Christ are inseparable. And I freely confess that she is in glory both above angels and men, her own Son (that is both God and man) only excepted. But I dare not mock her, and blaspheme against God, calling her not only *Diva* but *Dea*, and praying her to command and control her Son, who is her God and her Saviour. Nor yet not, I think, that she hath no other thing to do in Heaven than to hear every idle man's suit and busy herself in their errands, whiles requesting, whiles commanding her Son, whiles coming down to kiss and make love with priests, and whiles disputing and brawling with devils. In Heaven she is in eternal glory and joy, never to be interrupted with any worldly business; and there I leave her with her blessed Son, our Saviour and hers, in eternal felicity.[43]

Lancelot Andrewes (1555–1626), bishop, preacher and author of the *Preces Privatae*, makes few references to the Blessed Virgin Mary in his sermons, though he preached regularly on the Nativity. In one of his *Two Answers to Cardinal Perron* he protested that Mary was not to be adored nor to be invoked, since each involved *cultu latriae*, which is proper to God alone.[44] However, the inclusion in the *Preces Privatae* of one brief passage, borrowed from the Liturgies of St Chrysostom and St James, clearly shows a warmth of Marian devotion:

> *Sanctissimae, intemeratae, super caeteros benedictae,*
> *Deiparae, et semper Virginis Mariae, cum omnibut Sanctis, memoria habita,*
> *Nos ipsos, et vicissim alios, et omnem vitam nostram,*
> *Christo Deo commendemus.*

> Commemorating the allholy, immaculate, more than blessed mother of God and evervirgin Mary with all saints,
> let us commend ourselves and one another and all our life unto Christ God.[45]

---

43. From King James I, *A Premonition to All Most Might Monarchs, Kings, Free Princes, and States of Christendom*, quoted in More and Cross 1962: p.r. More and Cross's anthology is an invaluable source, but it does have important omissions (e.g. Herbert's poetry and Andrewes' *Precese Privatae*) and must be supplemented by other sources for a balanced picture.
44. Here we are indebted to Reidy 1995: 116.
45. Brightman (ed.) 1903: 85, cf. 59, where Mary is also called 'evervirgin'.

This was precisely the note of joyous communion with Mary and the saints that had been excised from the 1552 Prayer Book, and which Andrewes and other divines rejoiced to find in the liturgies of the East. For him, belief in Mary as *deipara* (*Theotokos*) and *semper virgo* was expressed in private prayers, written in Latin, which were almost a commonplace book of quotation from the early Christian tradition. Andrewes, however, also publicly encouraged people to pray by 'making mention of all the holy, undefiled and more than Blessed Mary, mother of God, and ever virgin, with all the Saints'.[46]

In the formation of Anglican devotion and pastoral ministry, few influences are more powerful than the poetry and prose of George Herbert (1593–1633). In both, Mary is striking by her absence. Herbert's sense of the incarnation as a hallowing of everyday tasks and objects and feelings ('Teach me my God and King / in all things Thee to see') is pervasive. The participation of God in the everyday, especially through the sacraments, is at the very core of his devotion, but this is not a hallowing shared with the saints and Mary, for they are in heaven and the temptation to invoke them by prayer is one which, in obedience to God's 'injunction', must be actively resisted:

> Oh Glorious spirits, who after all your bands
> See the smooth face of God, without a frown,
>   Or strict commands;
> Where every one is king, and hath his crown,
> If not upon his head, yet in his hands.
>
> Not out of envy or maliciousness
> Do I forbear to crave your special aid.
>   I would address
> My vows to thee most gladly, blessed Maid,
> And Mother of my God, in my distress:
>
> Thou art the holy Mine, whence came the Gold,
> The great restorative for all decay
>   In young and old;
> Thou art the cabinet where the jewel lay:
> Chiefly to thee I would my soul unfold.
>
> But now Alas! I dare not; for our King,
> Whom we do all jointly adore and praise,
>   Bid no such thing:
> And where his pleasure no injunction lays,
> ('Tis your own case) ye never move a wing.

---

46.   Andrewes 1841–3, vol. 1: 6.

All worship is prerogative, and a flower
Of his rich crown, from whom lies no appeal
      At the last hour:
Therefore we dare not from his garland steal,
To make a posy for inferior power.

Although then others court you, if ye know
What's done on earth, we shall not fare the worse,
      Who do not so;
Since we are ever ready to disburse,
If any one our Master's hand can show.[47]

Surely, no other Anglican wrote an *apologia* such as this of pity and longing for the mother neglected because of the 'strict commands' of the Son! The ambivalent address to Mary, which is not quite addressed to her, expresses precisely that sense of something precious that has been lost and not quite recovered in Anglicanism ('holy Mine' perhaps alludes euphonically to the *pro me* of Protestantism) which the Caroline Divines set to heal. The tension between the God of 'strict commands' and the God of the incarnation is palpable.

For Mark Frank (1613–44),[48] Master of Pembroke College, Cambridge, the rightful honouring of Mary is never to be confused with the worship due to God alone. He expounds a *via media*, criticizing those who,

> because the Romanists make little less of her than a goddess ... make not so much of her as a good woman: because they bless her too much, these unbless her quite, at least will not suffer her to be blessed as she should.[49]

In one of his sermons for Epiphany, Frank has a remarkable passage, typical of the seventeenth century in its rich development of novel imagery, alluding to the close connection between the incarnation, the Blessed Virgin Mary, the homage of the wise men and the liturgy today:

---

47. 'To all Angels and Saints', from Herbert 1859, vol. 1: 80. The sense of alienation from a heavenly world of colour and human warmth was reinforced by the revival of a somewhat austere philosophic Platonism in mid-seventeenth-century Cambridge (see, e.g., McAdoo 1965: 81–155). It is expressed with great pathos in the poetry of Henry Vaughan (1621/2–95).
    They are all gone into the world of light!
      And I alone sit lingring here;
      Their very memory is fair and bright,
      And my sad thoughts doth clear.
See, H. Gardner (ed), *The Metaphysical Poets* (Harmondsworth: Penguin, 1957), p. 275.
48. Allchin comments, 'Of all the Anglican preachers of this time, [Frank] speaks most fully about Mary'; Allchin 1993: 49.
49. Frank 1849, vol. 2: 35–6.

Gentiles and all; hither they come to worship, hither they come to pay their offerings and their vows; here is the shrine and altar, the glorious Virgin's lap, where the Saviour of the world is laid to be adored and worshipped; here stands the star for tapers to give it light; and here the wise men this day become the priests.[50]

The sustained metaphor is typical of seventeenth-century preaching and meditative poetry in the style of Andrewes and Herbert. The compression of the doctrines of the incarnation and the Eucharist into a Marian image that vividly recalls, in the homeliest language, so many pictorial representations of the Nativity ('the glorious Virgin's lap') invites the participation and the reflection of the hearers; it invites the hearers to make the Epiphany their own.

John Pearson (1612–86), whose commentary on the creed was standard reading for generations of Cambridge students, wrote at some length on 'Born of the Virgin Mary'. He was trenchant:

> We believe the mother of our Lord to have been not only before and after his nativity, but also for ever, the most immaculate and blessed virgin ... The peculiar eminency and unparalleled privilege of that mother, the special honour and reverence due unto that Son, and ever paid by her, the regard of that Holy Ghost who came upon her, and the power of the Highest which overshadowed her, the singular goodness and piety of Joseph, to whom she was espoused, have persuaded the church of God in all ages to believe that she still continued in the same virginity, and therefore is to be acknowledged the ever virgin Mary.[51]

Pearson continued, 'Far be it from any Christian to derogate from that special privilege granted her which is incommunicable to any other. We cannot bear too reverend a regard unto the mother of our Lord, so long as we give her not that worship which is due unto the Lord himself.'

In his *Life of Christ (The Great Exemplar)* of 1649, Jeremy Taylor provides a similarly lengthy meditation on Mary. He attempts, when discussing Mary's virginity, to avoid any slight on marriage:

> When the eternal God meant to stoop so low as to be fixed to our centre, he chose for his mother a holy person and a maid, but yet affianced to a just man, that he might not only be secure in the innocency, but also provided for in the reputation of his holy mother ... And yet her marriage was more mysterious; for as, besides the miracle it was an eternal honour and advancement to the glory of virginity, that he chose a virgin for his mother, so it was in that manner attempered, that the Virgin was betrothed, lest honourable marriage might be

---

50. Ibid., vol. 1: 280.
51. Pearson 1822: 249–61.

disreputed, and seem inglorious, by a positive rejection from any participation of the honour.[52]

In *Ductor Dubitantium* (1660), Taylor discusses the title *Theotokos* together with Mary's virginity when he considers the authority of unbroken tradition for the establishing of doctrine:

> So though the blessed virgin Mary be not in Scripture called *theotokos*, 'the mother of God', yet that she was the mother of Jesus, and Jesus Christ is God, and yet but one person, that we can prove from scripture, and that is sufficient for the appellative ... The scripture no where says that the blessed Virgin was a virgin perpetually to the day of her death: but as therefore it cannot be obtruded as an article of faith, yet there are a great many decencies and probabilities of the thing, beside the great consent of almost all the church of God, which makes it very fit to be entertained.[53]

Thomas Ken (1627–1711) was one of the best-known episcopal writers of this period, and a leading non-juror.[54] Among Ken's devotional verse is a long poem entitled *Sion* or *Philothea*, which includes a long section on Mary that appears to proclaim the immaculate conception. Ken writes of Mary's conception:

> The Holy Ghost, his Temple in her built,
> Cleansed from congenial, kept from mortal guilt,
> And from the moment that her blood was fired,
> Into her heart celestial love inspired.

He goes on, in verses which were taken into the English Hymnal:[55]

> Her Virgin-eyes saw God incarnate born
> When she to bethlem came that happy morn.
> How high her raptures then began to swell,
> None but her own omniscient Son can tell ...
> As Eve, when she her fontal sin reviewed,
> Wept for herself, and all she should include;
> Blessed Mary, with Man's Saviour in embrace,
> Joyed for herself, and for all human race ...

52.   Taylor 1847, vol. 2: 53.
53.   Ibid., vol. 9: 637.
54.   The non-jurors were members of the Church of England who, on conscientious ground, would not take the Oaths of Allegiance and Supremacy to William and Mary after the deposition of James II in 1688, since they had pledged their allegiance to James. Nine bishops, including the Archbishop of Canterbury and Thomas Ken, were deposed. The non-jurors were Anglicans with a high view of the Church as a spiritual society in which the monarch's place as 'supreme governor' was established by 'divine right'.
55.   See *English Hymnal* 217.

> Heaven with transcendent joys her entrance grac'd
> Next to his throne her Son his mother plac'd;
> And her below, now she's of heaven possess'd
> All generations are to call her blest.[56]

While George Hickes (1642–1715) was Dean of Worcester and before he was consecrated (as a non-juror) Bishop of Thetford, he published a pamphlet in which he attempted to defend a middle way. In *Speculum Beatae Virginis: A Discourse of the Due Praise and Honour of the Virgin Mary by a True Catholick of the Church of England* (1689), Hickes wanted to recognize the unique position of Mary within the Christian tradition, but at the same time to avoid the cultus which existed in the Roman Catholic Church of his time:

> It is our duty, who have the benefit of her example, to honour, and celebrate her name, and commemorate her virtues, and set forth her praises. If the names of the other saints are distinguished with miniature, hers ought to shine with gold ... But then we must not let our respect for her commence into worship, not romance her into a deity ... we must not treat her upon the account of her singular relation to Immanuel, as if she were an infinite majesty, or as if her graces were indeed divine attributes ... We ought not to pay such homage and veneration to her under the character of the Queen as is only due to the King of Heaven ... lest transgressing herein, we should fall into those unwarrantable excesses and abuses which a great part of Christendom is too justly chargeable with.[57]

The seventeenth century offers no further development of Anglican doctrine about Mary, but it offers a powerful recovery of interest in Mary's place within the Anglican tradition. Clearly, theologians like Andrewes and Herbert are cautious about this, and the incautious promotion of Catholicism in ritual and devotion by Laud quickly excited anti-Roman suspicion. Anglican caution with respect to the place of Mary and the saints continues to be reflected in mainstream thinking today, but seventeenth-century Anglican preachers, well versed in early Christian thought, and in the liturgies of the Eastern tradition, could not ignore the honoured place held by the *Theotokos*. They remained allergic to invocation of Mary, sympathetic to talk about 'sinlessness', open to Mary being *semper virgo*. The heartland of Anglican devotion lies in wonder at the humanity of Mary, honoured by God in the bearing of divinity, and her attractiveness as an exemplar of obedience, humility and joy. It should not be forgotten that of the two invariable canticles at the daily Evening Prayer of Anglicans, one is the *Magnificat*.

---

56.   *Sion* or *Philothea*, from Ken 1721, vol. 4: 367–73.
57.   Hickes 1686: 9–10.

THE OXFORD MOVEMENT

It was in the nineteenth century that Marian devotion was to come to fruition. Before we consider the Oxford Movement, we need to note the work of Bishop Reginald Heber (1783–1826), missionary, evangelist and hymn-writer. He was closely associated with the Evangelicals of his day, yet consciously disassociated himself from some of their Calvinistic theology. Inspired by the work of Thomas Ken, he wrote:

> Virgin-born, we bow before thee,
> Blessed was the womb that bore thee,
> Mary, mother meek and mild
> Blessed was she in her child.

> Blessed was the breast that fed thee,
> Blessed was the hand that led thee,
> Blessed was the parent's eye
> That watched thy slumbering infancy.

> Blessed she by all creation
> Who brought forth the world's salvation,
> And blessed they, for ever blest
> Who love thee most and serve thee best.

> Virgin-born we bow before thee,
> Blessed was the womb that bore thee,
> Mary, mother meek and mild,
> Blessed was she in her child.

Allchin praises the author by saying, 'There is something remarkable about this hymn which for all its apparent simplicity manages to say so much in so small a space.'[58]

The Oxford Movement's emphasis on patristic studies inevitably led to a fresh appreciation of the role of the *Theotokos* within the Christian tradition. In 1823 John Keble (1792–1866) had written the first stanza of his famous hymn *Ave Maria*. This poem was inspired by his mother's death and was published in the immensely popular *Christian Year*. In it Keble addressed Mary as the 'Blessed Maid, Lily of Eden's fragrant shade ... whose name, all but adoring love may claim'. Interestingly, Keble's friends persuaded him to omit the following verse from a poem significantly entitled 'Mother out of sight':

> Therefore, as kneeling day by day
> We to our Father duteous pray
> so, unforbidden may we speak

---

58.   Allchin 1993: 142.

an Ave to Christ's mother meek;
(as children with 'good morrow' come
to elders in some happy home)
inviting so the saintly host above
with our unworthiness to pray in love.[59]

In 1832, thirteen years before being received into the Roman Catholic Church, John Henry Newman (1800–91) preached a sermon on the Annunciation in which he praised Mary's transcendent purity in such terms that he was accused of teaching the immaculate conception.[60] In 1843, in a sermon on 'The Theory of Development in Religious Doctrine', for the feast of the Purification,[61] Newman called Mary 'our pattern of faith, both in the reception and in the study of divine truth', who 'symbolises to us, not only the faith of the unlearned but of the doctors of the Church also, who have to investigate, and weigh, and define, as well as to profess the Gospel'.

Nevertheless, it is interesting to note that Newman rendered Mary no personal cult and, even three years before being received into the Roman Catholic Church, still regarded her public veneration as incompatible with the worship of God.

Newman was to become a correspondent of E. B. Pusey (1800–82) who, in 1865, published his *Eirenicon: Certain Difficulties Felt by Anglicans in Catholic Teaching*.[62] Pusey's *Eirenicon* was in the form of a letter addressed to Keble in which he considered, among other things, 'the vast system as to the blessed Virgin', as 'the special crux of the Roman System' and one of the principal obstacles for reunion. In the *Eirenicon* Pusey attacked the recently defined dogma of the immaculate conception as a further obstacle to reunion. Pusey's chief objections are directed against the view that Mary is Mediatrix of all graces whose intercession is in some way necessary to salvation,[63] that her mercy is opposed to Christ's vengeance, that she is Co-Redemptrix,[64] that she has authority over Christ,[65] and that she produces Christ in souls.[66]

In 1865, B. F. Westcott (1823–1901), J. B. Lightfoot and E. W. Benson visited the Marian shrine at La Salette. As Allchin records, 'it would be hard to think of more weighty representatives of nineteenth-century Church of England.'[67] Westcott recorded his experience and thoughts in a 16-page pamphlet entitled *La Salette in 1865*. He develops three lines of thought. First, an account of the story of the apparition and of the faith and devotion which it engendered; second, a reflection on the nature of that devotion; and third, a brief discussion of the last two points in relation to the spiritual life of the Church of England. For Westcott, La Salette

59. Keble 1870: 256–9.
60. Newman 1999, vol. 2: 132.
61. Newman 1998, No. 15.
62. Pusey 1892.
63. Ibid.: 101–3.
64. Ibid.: 152.
65. Ibid.: 160.
66. Ibid.
67. Allchin 1993: 159.

... gave expression to an instinct which claims to be recognized. It is perhaps not too much to say that the vitality of a religion may be measured by the intensity of the belief in the immediate working of the divine power which it produces. This is not the place for theological discussion, but very little reflection will show that when the belief in the miraculous – in the action of a special providence as it is called – as an element in common life is destroyed, religion is destroyed at the same time, so far as religion includes the ideas of worship and prayer.[68]

The year 1878 saw the publication of the Bishop of Brechin's commentary on the Thirty Nine Articles. Bishop Forbes, in commenting upon Article 15, has a remarkable passage concerning the Blessed Virgin Mary:

One's first thought with regard to her is a jealousy for the honour of the Lord God of Hosts. Anything that approaches him must be fended off. We cannot endure that the idea of any created thing, however great and holy, shall be compared unto Him. He is supreme, and His honour we must not give unto another ... But on the other hand, viewed rightly and in the analogy of faith, the great honour bestowed upon Mary, the recognition of her place in the order of grace, tends very directly to a proper understanding of the glory of God ... estimate her pure as Eve at the moment of creation, add to that the miraculous fact of divine maternity, exhaust all thought and all positive language in the conception and expression of her august prerogatives, and yet, when you have reached the height, God is still infinitely greater. Thus she becomes a height of created nature, whence to rise to the Divine Humanity of her Son, and thence to the infinitude of God, and the higher ideal we have of her, the more complete is our all-perfect estimate of Him.[69]

Concluding his commentary on the 1854 dogma, Bishop Forbes remarks:

Whether the interests of Christianity have gained by the increase of honour which hereby accrues to the Holy Virgin, and by additional prominence given to the idea of Suprasensual in the mystery of redemption, or have lost by the divorce in sentiment between the past and present Church, by the dissidence between the Old Traditional Faith and the Developed Sentiment of the Living Church, is a question which suggests the gravest consideration, and excites the deepest anxiety.[70]

THE TWENTIETH CENTURY

During the second half of the nineteenth and into the twentieth century the 'ritualistic' phase of the Oxford Movement gathered pace. Through stained glass,

---

68.   Ibid.: 164.
69.   Forbes 1878: 226–7.
70.   Ibid.: 229.

banners, images and shrines, devotion to Mary was significantly revived. Many of the prayers used at this time were either adapted or culled from contemporary Roman Catholic sources,[71] and a number of shrines devoted to the blessed Virgin Mary were re-established.[72] Several books on the Blessed Virgin Mary were written by Anglican theologians at this time – Bede Frost's *Mystery of Mary* (1938) and the symposium *The Mother of God* (1948), edited by E. L. Mascall, who contributed the chapter on 'The Dogmataic Theology of the Mother of God'. In this article, Mascall emphasizes the traditional doctrines of Mary as the Mother of God and also of her as the Mother of the Church. Moreover, he accepts Mary's virginity *in partu* and *post partum*, her immaculate conception and her bodily assumption into heaven, though he does not think any of these doctrines ought to be imposed 'as of faith'. T. Parker, in his contribution on 'Devotion to the Mother of God' in the same work, considers that the Eastern Church has been more faithful to Mariological tradition than the West; the East stresses the honour due to Mary more than her power of intercession.

In 1976 came the publication of *Mary and the Christian Gospel* by John de Satge. The significance of this book is that it is written by an Anglican Evangelical who, in accordance with Article 6, insists that the Holy Scripture is the norm of tradition. Canon de Satge illustrates this by taking *solus Christus*, *sola scriptura* and *sola fide* (*sola gratia*) as means by which to interpret the Marian dogmas. The first of these principles, *solus Christus*, means that any attempt to supplement Christ's sole mediatorship (Mary as Mediatrix or Co-Redemptrix) is rejected as blasphemous; the second, *sola scriptura*, that the two later dogmas (immaculate conception and assumption) are rejected as unscriptural; the third, *sola fide* – *sola gratia*, that any suggestion of Mary possessing any merits of her own which give her a special place and privilege are unacceptable.

It is Canon de Satge's belief that the bad press which the two traditional doctrines (virgin birth and *Theotokos*), and to some extent the ancient tradition of the perpetual virginity, have had among Protestants in recent times is due not to the Reformation principles but to the corruptions of liberalism. Further, the later Roman Catholic dogmas (immaculate conception and assumption) have been largely misunderstood by Protestants and are not really so contrary to Reformation principles as they sound. So Canon de Satge sets out in his book to examine the Marian dogmas and doctrines from the Reformation point of view and to bring them to a sympathetic understanding and appreciation. Because of the importance of this work, it might repay us to examine more closely Canon de Satge's work.

Canon de Satge contends that the virgin birth has, in recent times, been questioned by those liberal Protestants who wish to stress Jesus' 'brotherness' over and against his 'otherness'. This abandonment of traditional Christology, Canon de Satge suggests, is contrary to the Reformation writers who completely accepted this belief. Canon de Satge notes that while the *Theotokos* doctrine is primarily

---

71. The Anglo-Catholic Prayer Book of 1931 contains the Rosary, the *Angelus*, the *Regina Coeli*, the Litany of Loreto and special prayers for Marian feasts.
72. The Shrine of Our Lady of Walsingham, Our Lady of Willesden, Our Lady Undercroft in Canterbury Cathedral and Our Lady of the Pew in Westminster Abbey, to name but a few.

Christological in nature, it also has Mariological implications. Following Newman, de Satge argues that because of the perfect humanity of Jesus there are areas of human life in which we feel we cannot identify with him:

> But it is not so with Mary. She who gave human birth is yet completely human. She is a sinner who is redeemed. It is with her that we may fully identify. It may be for certain reasons due to her uniqueness as the mother of God that she has reached the fullness of human potential sooner than the rest of us, but though she has made the journey more quickly she has still had the same path to tread, a path different from that of the sinless Saviour.[73]

Equally, for de Satge, the *Theotokos* doctrine safeguards God's free choice of Mary to be the human mother of the eternal *Logos* and Mary's free acceptance of that choice. Likewise in considering the perpetual virginity of Mary, Canon de Satge sees nothing to invalidate the generally accepted tradition of both East and West. Instead of undermining the Reformation bulwarks of *solus Christus* and *sola gratia*, Canon de Satge suggests that the dogma of the immaculate conception re-enforces these Reformation principles. For Mary's immunity from original sin was granted as a gift of grace in prospect of the redeeming work of Christ:

> The doctrine of the Immaculate Conception does not suggest that, in itself, Mary was sinless. It was not her merits but those of her Son which were, so to speak, applied to her in advance. As much as any other Christian she was saved by the blood of Jesus.[74]

Noting the lack of direct scriptural authority and maintaining the importance of Article 6, de Satge rejected the idea that the dogma of the assumption is necessary to salvation. However, Canon de Satge does maintain that it is 'congruent' with Scripture, and specifically with St Paul's formula, 'those whom he predestined he also called: and those whom he called he also justified; and those whom he justified he also glorified' (Rom. 8.30).

In his closing chapters de Satge turns his attention to those beliefs, currently developed in theology and devotion, about the Virgin Mary which have not been defined as dogma. De Satge explores the Eve–Mary typology as well as Mary as *mater ecclesiae*. Perhaps the most startling suggestion, coming as it does from an Evangelical, is the hospitality shown to the idea of Mary as Mediatrix. De Satge points out that Christ commonly exercised his mediatorship through subordinate human mediators. Converts are normally won to Christ, and Christ's work is continued in believers, through the witness and intercession of other human beings. If we can see them as mediators under the one true Mediator, why not also the Blessed Virgin?

---

73. de Satge 1976: 51.
74. Ibid.: 69.

Is not the assertion of even a subordinate mediatorship on Mary's part an unwarrantable infringement of the unique mediatorship of her Son? I believe that it is not. My reasons spring from the fact that Mary's mediatorship arises from the ministry she has been given and not from her won virtues. Her role ... is to point not to her self but to her Son. In that respect Mary stands in the line of all genuine Christian ministry. For the fact remains that, though there are notable exceptions to which the Bible societies especially bear witness, in most cases it takes a human being (or a collection of human beings gathered in a 'church') to mediate Christ to those who have not previously realised him as being of any vital concern to themselves. Christ is indeed the only mediator between God and man; but Christian experience shows no limit in the number of mediators needed between Christ and man.[75]

Father Edward Yarnold SJ has suggested that it is a characteristic of the Anglican approach to Mary that it prefers the poetic image to the abstract concept. Conceptual clarity is not something to be despised, but, in this area in particular, there are many things which can be said in images both verbal and visual which can hardly be conveyed in prose. Here, perhaps, is a point where Anglicans have something in common with the East. This particular understanding is taken up in Allchin's *The Joy of All Creation*.

The twentieth century has been marked by a number of revisions of the Anglican liturgy. In the Calendar of the 1662 Prayer Book, 8 December is marked as the 'Conception of the Blessed Virgin Mary'. In Anglican terms this is a 'black letter day', a day for which no liturgical provision, through readings and collect, is provided. In the ill-fated revision of 1928, a collect only is given. It is, however, worded in quite general terms. We have already noted that 15 August was dropped from the 1549 Prayer Book. It has only recently made an appearance in Anglican Calendars. The American, Australian, Canadian and New Zealand Books have made 15 August a principal feast, a trend that seems to have begun with the South African Prayer Book of 1954. The South African Prayer Book describes the feast as 'The Falling Asleep of the Blessed Virgin Mary' and provides a collect that is unmistakably one of Dormition. (The 1960 Prayer Book of the Church of India, Pakistan, Burma and Ceylon also has a feast of this name.) Some[76] might argue that since Prayer Books are not only liturgically, but also theologically, normative for Anglicans, it seems that in a number of provinces of the Anglican Communion, the Dormition now enjoys the status of official teaching.

In the new Common Worship *Calendar, Lectionary and Collects* of the Church of England, readings are given for the Blessed Virgin Mary under the 'Common of the Saints' and a collect and post-Communion prayer is provided for the Conception of the Blessed Virgin Mary on 8 December. A collect and readings for 15 August are provided under the title of 'The Blessed Virgin Mary'. Further, we need to note that

75. Ibid.: 118.
76. A. Williams, unpublished paper, *The Language of Reality: The Mother of God in the Anglican Tradition*, for ARCIC II (Mary) 432/99.

Anne and Joachim, parents of the Blessed Virgin Mary, are commemorated on 26 July with collects and readings. Mary is mentioned by name in the third Eucharistic Prayer of Rite A in the Alternative Service Book and Prayers B and G in Common Worship. Further, Common Worship provides an opportunity to remember particular saints by name in the Eucharistic Prayers B, E, F and G.

ARCIC

Alberic Stacpoole OSB, in his article 'Mary in Ecumenical Dialogue',[77] reminds us of an important paper prepared by Dr R. J. Halliburton on 'The Exercise of Authority: an Anglican Approach to the Dogma of the Immaculate Conception and the Assumption' for an Anglican/Roman Catholic subcommission on 'Church and Authority' in 1970. Dr Halliburton begins by saying that Anglicans, on hearing of the papal pronouncements, suspected Rome of a further corruption of the primitive faith. He continued by noting that Anglican Mariology had the tendency to either stand as a protest against the seeming corruption of the Middle Ages or adopt, wholesale, the Roman theology of Mary. This resulted, he believed, in too much 'extra-ordinary', and not enough 'ordinary' devotion. Halliburton hoped that the modern return to the study of the patristic age might lead to a reappraisal of Mary as a type of the Church, of Mary as the beginning of our redemption and of Mary as prefiguring, in the salvation of her soul and body, all the redeemed. With this approach, Dr Halliburton judged that a large measure of ecumenical agreement in faith could be reached. All it required was that theology be taught first so that faith may be aroused.

The Vatican's response to the final report of ARCIC said that '... the commission has not been able to record any real consensus on the Marian dogmas'. It is true that the final report states:

> ... the dogmas of the Immaculate Conception and the Assumption raise a special problem for those Anglicans who do not consider that the precise definitions given by these dogmas are sufficiently supported by Scripture. For many Anglicans the teaching authority of the Bishop of Rome, independent of a council, is not recommended by the fact that through it these Marian doctrines were proclaimed as dogmas binding on all the faithful. Anglicans would also ask whether, in any future union between our two Churches, they would be required to subscribe to such dogmatic statements.[78]

But is this the whole picture? At the outset we need to acknowledge what has been agreed! First, ARCIC affirmed Mary as *Theotokos* – in fact the commission makes this more precise by adding 'Mother of God Incarnate'. Second, the Final Report places

---

77. Stacpoole (ed.) 1965: 57–78.
78. ARCIC, the Final Report, London, 1982: 96.

Mary's role within the work of Christ and his Church. Third, this leads ARCIC to acknowledge the 'grace and unique vocation of Mary' and 'that she was prepared by divine grace to be the mother of the Redeemer; by whom she herself was redeemed and received into glory'. Lastly, Mary is a model of holiness, obedience and faith for all Christians as well as a prophetic figure of the Church both before and after the incarnation. This statement is further amplified by a footnote which bears repeating in full:

> The affirmation of the Roman Catholic Church that Mary was conceived without original sin is based on recognition of her unique role within the mystery of the Incarnation. By being thus prepared to be the mother of our Redeemer, she also becomes a sign that the salvation won by Christ was operative among all mankind before his birth. The affirmation that her glory in heaven involves full participation in the fruits of salvation expresses and reinforces our faith that the life of the world to come has already broken into the life of our world. It is the conviction of Roman Catholics that the Marian dogmas formulate a faith consonant with Scripture.[79]

The *Emmaus Report* was a preparation document for the Lambeth Conference of 1988. While discussing the notion of 'Reception', the report states:

> A particular instance of the problem of 'reception' in a divided church is the case of the two Marian definitions of the Roman Catholic Church. Several Provinces drew particular attention to this problem.

The Southern Cone said:

> ARCIC accepts that the Marian dogmas are a problem for many Anglicans and says that it should be specifically stated whether the recognition of papal primacy automatically implies subscription by Anglicans to both the dogmas of the Immaculate Conception and the Assumption of our Lady.

The USA noted that the problem concerns both the *content* of the definitions and their *authoritative* status:

> To pose this question is not to deny that some Anglicans believe the Marian dogmas already as doctrines. Further work can and should be done to render them as intelligible as possible to the Anglican communion as a whole. To restate these doctrines as possible *theologoumena* however, does not obviate the dogmatic issue. We would raise the question of the status of these dogmas in the hierarchy of truths recognised by the Roman Catholic Church.[80]

---

79. Ibid.
80. The *Emmaus Report*, A Report of the Anglican Ecumenical Consultation 1987, ACC, 1987: 68f.

BIBLIOGRAPHY

Algermissen, K. *et al.* (1957) *Lexicon der Marienkunde*, Regensburg: Pustet.

Allchin, A. M. (1993) *The Joy of All Creation: An Anglican Meditation on the Place of Mary*, London: Darton, Longman and Todd.

Andrewes, Lancelot (1841–3) *Ninety-Six Sermons*, 5 vols, LACT, Oxford.

The Book of Homilies (1833), London: SPCK.

Brightman, F. E. (ed.) (1903) *The Preces Privatae of Lancelot Andrewes, Bishop of Winchester*, London: Methuen.

Brightman, F. E. (1915) *The English Rite*, 2 vols, London: Rivingtons.

Burton. E. (ed.) (1834) *Three Primers put Forth in the Reign of Henry VIII*, Oxford.

Duffy, E. (1992) *The Stripping of the Altars, Traditional Religion in England 1400–1580*, New Haven, CT, and London: Yale University Press.

Forbes, A. P. (1878) *An Explanation of the Thirty-Nine Articles*, London.

Foxe's Book of Martyrs (1881), new edn, illustrated, London: Morgan & Scott.

Frank, Mark (1849) *Sermons*, 2 vols, LACT, Oxford: Parker.

Graef, Hilda (1965) *Mary: A History of Doctrine and Devotion*, 2 vols, London: Sheed and Ward.

Hardwick, C. (1876) *History of the Articles of Religion*, London: Bell.

Herbert, George (1859) *The Works of George Herbert in Prose and Verse*, 2 vols, London: Bell and Daldy.

Hickes, George (1686) *Speculum Beatae Virginis: A Discourse of the Due Praise and Honour of the Virgin Mary, by a True Chatholick of the Church of England*, 2nd edn, London.

Hollenweger, W. (1980) 'Zwingli's Devotion to Mary', *One in Christ* 16.

Jasper, R. C. D. and Cuming, G. J. (eds) (1987) *Prayers of the Eucharist: Early and Reformed*, 3rd rev. edn, New York: Pueblo.

Keble, John (1870) *Miscellaneous Poems*, Oxford.

Keble, John (ed.) (1888) *Hooker's Works*, vol. 3, Oxford: Clarendon.

Ken, Thomas (1721) *Works*, 4 vols, London.

Latimer, Hugh (1985) *Sermons and Remains*, ed for the Parker Society by G. E. Corri, 2 vols, Cambridge: Cambridge University Press.

MacCulloch, Diarmaid (1996) *Thomas Cranmer*, New Haven and London: Yale University Press.

Mackenzie, A. R. (1980), 'Calvin and the Calvinists on Mary', *One in Christ* 16.

McAdoo, H. R. (1965) *The Spirit of Anglicanism*, London: A. and C. Black.

Miegge, G. (1955) *The Virgin Mary*, London: Lutterworth.

More, P. E. and Cross, F. L. (1962) *Anglicanism, The Thought and Practice of the Church of England illustrated from the Religious Literature of the Seventeenth Century*, London: SPCK.

Newman, John Henry (1999) *Parochial and Plain Sermons*, vol. 2, San Francisco: Ignatius Press.

Newman, John Henry (1998) *Fifteen Sermons Preached Before the University of Oxford*, Notre Dame, IN: University of Notre Dame.

Pearson, John (1822) *Exposition of the Creed*, London: Valpy.

Pelikan, J. (ed.) (1956) *Luther's Works*, vol. 219, Saint Louis, MO: Concordia.

Pusey, E. B. (1892) *Eirenicon: Certain Difficulties Felt by Anglicans in Catholic Teaching*, London.

Reidy, M. F. (1995) *Bishop Lancelot Andrewes*, Chicago, IL: Loyola.

de Satge, J. (1976) *Mary and Christian Gospel*, London: SPCK.

Stacpoole, A. (ed.) (1982) *Mary's Place in Christian Dialogue*, Slough: St Paul Publications.

Tappert, Theodore G. (ed.) (1959) *The Book of Concord: the Confessions of the Evangelical Lutheran Church*, Philadelphia, PA: Fortress Press.

Taylor, Jeremy (1947) *The Whole Works of Jeremy Taylor*, 12 vols, London: Longman *et al.*

The Two Books of Homilies (1859), Oxford: Oxford University Press.

15

MARY IN ECUMENICAL DIALOGUE AND EXCHANGE

DAVID CARTER

Both formal dialogue between Christian communions and informal exchange between individual members of the varying confessions concerning the role of Mary and devotion to her were slow to develop in the early years of the Ecumenical Movement. In part, this was due to the relatively late official entry of the Roman Catholic Church into the movement. It was also due to a widespread belief among Protestants and Catholics that it would prove an emotive and almost intractable problem. The American Protestant ecumenical pioneer Robert McAffee Brown believed that no subject, other than perhaps the role of the papacy, would prove so difficult.[1]

The Orthodox churches with their strong Marian piety were involved in the Ecumenical Movement much earlier; nevertheless, an attempt by an Orthodox at the first World Faith and Order Conference at Lausanne in 1927 to raise the question of the role of Mary within the economy of salvation was ruled out of order.

There is no doubt that for the vast majority of Roman Catholics and Protestants in the first half of the twentieth century, the understanding of the role of Mary and the consequent rightness or otherwise of devotion, particularly public devotion, to her was a neuralgic issue. Many Protestants, even learned leaders as far back as John Wesley, misunderstood the distinction between the *latreia*, or worship, due alone to Almighty God and the *dulia*, or reverence, paid to Mary and, indeed, other saints.[2] They accused Roman Catholics of 'gross superstition', even idolatry, and demonstrations by extreme Protestants at the shrine of Walsingham have been a recurrent feature even in recent years. For both Catholics and Protestants, attitudes to Mary were a touchstone of their negative self-definition against each other. At a time when Roman Catholics were fond of saying '*numquam satis de Maria*' – 'one cannot say too much about Mary' – Protestants tended to ignore her, giving her only (as a

---

1. Cited by Donal Flanagan in his article 'An Ecumenical Future for Roman Catholic Theology of Mary', in Stacpoole (ed.) 1982: 3.
2. For an account of Methodist–Roman Catholic relationships since the time of the Wesleys and their theological critique of the Roman Catholic tradition as they knew it, see Butler 1995.

recent Methodist writer has put it) a walk-on part in the Sunday school Nativity play.[3]

Such attitudes were in contrast to those of several of the first generation of Protestant Reformers who retained a considerable devotion to the Virgin even while decrying aspects of her cult and that of other saints and, in particular, questioning the rightness of the concepts of merit and intercession involved in the late medieval pre-Reformation cults.[4] Protestant antagonism to any veneration of Mary combined with an almost total ignoring even of Scripture's statements about her grew from the second generation of the Reformers onwards. The advent of 'Liberal Protestantism' in the nineteenth century did not make for a markedly more irenic approach, since many liberal Protestants regarded the whole cult of the saints as a relic of medieval superstition not worthy of the rational and simplified form of faith in the fatherhood of God and brotherhood of humanity for which they stood.

Isolated exceptions to the general ignoring of Mary within their own tradition and antagonism to her role within the Roman Catholic one can be found among later Protestants. The famous Congregationalist pastor John Angell James wrote a glowing testimony to the courage and dignity of Mary at the foot of the cross, calling her a 'wondrous woman'.[5] A key feature of the last decades of the previous century and first decade of this has been an increasing degree of interest taken by a minority of Protestant theologians and spiritual writers in Mary; how far their work, some of which will be described later, will be more generally 'received' within their churches remains to be seen.[6]

THEOLOGICAL FACTORS IN THE GULF BETWEEN ROMAN CATHOLICS AND PROTESTANTS CONCERNING MARY

Differences between Roman Catholics and Protestants concerning Mary are related to a whole range of theological factors. The most important ones relate to the authority of Scripture, the legitimacy of varying modes of interpretation of it, interpretation of particular passages within it, the authority of tradition and of the magisterium or teaching office of the Church, the doctrines of grace and the incarnation.

---

3. Michael Hurley argues that much Roman Catholic thought since Trent was coloured by reaction against Protestantism. See his article 'Mary and Ecumenism Today', in McLoughlin and Pinnock (eds) 2002: 185–208. It is interesting in this context also to quote from ch. 30 of the Final Report of ARCIC I: 'One consequence of our separation has been a tendency for Anglicans and Roman Catholics alike to exaggerate the importance of the Marian dogmas in themselves at the expense of other truths more closely related to the foundations of the Christian faith.'

4. For an excellent account of the original Reformers on Mary, see the essay 'Mary and sixteenth century Protestants' by Diarmid MacCulloch, in Swanson (ed.) 2004: 191–217.

5. See his sermon 'Woman's Mission' (1852), reproduced in Wolffe (ed.) 1996: 89–104, esp. 98–9, for his moving meditation on Mary at the foot of the cross. James was minister of the famous Carr's Lane Congregational Church in Birmingham.

6. Two particularly interesting works, both out of a North American context, are Gaventa and Rigby (eds) 2002; and Braaten and Jenson (eds) 2004. The latter contains some contributions from Roman Catholic scholars; both the editors are Lutherans.

Protestants, including Anglicans according to the authority of Article 6 of the Church of England, believe in the perspicuity of Scripture, that is to say its clarity on all essential points, and in its sole sufficiency in matters immediately related to salvation. They do not believe that Christians should be compelled to accept as binding in conscience and faith any doctrine that cannot be clearly evidenced from Scripture. Traditional and evangelical Protestants thus have no difficulty with the doctrine of the virgin birth, since it is clearly taught in Scripture, but they do have difficulty with the doctrines of the perpetual virginity of Mary, which many of them would allege on a literal reading is directly contradicted by Scripture, and with those of the immaculate conception and assumption. Many of them would say the former is contradicted by Paul's teaching that 'all have sinned',[7] and the latter just cannot be proved since Scripture tells us nothing about Mary's life after her presence in the upper room awaiting Pentecost.

Following their insistence of the perspicuity of Scripture, Protestants are usually suspicious of allegorical interpretations of Scripture and thus contest attempts by Roman Catholics to show a biblical foundation for the disputed doctrines from such interpretations – for example, the assumption from the vision of the 'woman clothed with the sun' in Revelation 12, or the perpetual virginity from such a passage as Ezekiel 44.2.[8] They also contest the authority of later tradition except where (as, for example, in their opinion, in trinitarian theology) it can be held to make *explicit* something already *implicit* in the whole general tenor of Scripture. Thus the argument that later tradition clearly came to establish that the brothers and sisters of Jesus referred to in Scripture were either cousins of Jesus or children of Joseph by an earlier marriage carries no compelling weight for Protestant exegetes, even though some of them are prepared to accept that the term 'brothers' *could* have referred to more distant relatives.[9] Roman Catholics believe that Scripture must be read in the light of the tradition of the Church, whereas Protestants believe that Scripture is judge over all later tradition. There has been some softening and nuancing of this opposition in more recent ecumenical dialogue, but by and large the principles remain as stated.

One can easily demonstrate how differently Catholic and Protestant exegetes have approached individual texts. In the case of the famous episode of the marriage feast at Cana, some Protestants have construed Christ's addressing of his mother as 'woman' as a form of distancing himself from her, of showing that he was not going to let his

---

7. Rom. 3.12; 5.12. The recent ARCIC report, *Mary: Grace and Hope in Christ* (2005), specifically deals with the interpretation of Rom. 3.12.

8. 'The gate shall remain shut, it shall not be opened and no one shall enter by it; for the Lord God of Israel has entered by it, therefore it shall remain shut.'

9. For an example of trenchant literalism, see W. Bridcut, 'Did Mary remain a virgin?', in McLoughlin and Pinnock (eds) 1997: 15–20. See especially 17, commenting on Mk 3.31–5 and parallels: 'In speaking like this the Lord Jesus is saying that there are bonds closer than those of blood and his words have force only if the spiritual relationship he speaks about is seen to be as close as the closest of family ties ... The words lose their wonderful meaning if the contrast is not with Mary and the brothers related by blood to each other and to Jesus on the one hand and those who do God's will on the other.'

ministry be determined by anyone, even his mother.[10] Catholics, by contrast, have seen it as a sign of her intercessory power that Christ responded to her concern and request; they have also seen it as a sign of her wisdom and her ability to point people to him – 'do whatever he tells you'.[11] Likewise, the episode of Christ being sought out, in the middle of his ministry, has been construed differently. Again, Protestant scholars have regarded his 'Whoever does the will of my Father is my mother, my sister and my brother' as being a sitting light on the part of Christ to all earthly relationships, including that with his mother, whereas Catholics have argued that Mary was nevertheless commended since she was his mother both physically and through the doing of the Father's will, already proved by her obedience at the incarnation.

Some Protestants have argued that the Church should make relatively little of Mary because Scripture has little, cumulatively, to say about her. However, a prominent Methodist ecumenist, David Butler, has pointed out that Scripture says more about Mary than it does about the Eucharist and that has not prevented Protestants from insisting on the importance of the sacrament.[12] It can be argued that the biblical texts referring to Mary, though few, occur at particularly significant points of the gospel story; even those Protestants who insist most strongly on the extent to which Mark 3.31–5 and parallels seem to distance Jesus from his earthly family accept that the Lukan birth narrative both emphasizes Mary's obedience and attests her statement as to the future memory throughout history of her 'blessedness'.

Perhaps the biggest difference lies in the understanding of grace and the possibility of creaturely co-operation with grace. Both Catholics and Protestants agree that salvation is the gift of God and that human beings cannot be saved by their own unaided efforts. For the classical Protestantism of the Reformation, both Lutheran and 'Reformed', salvation was the totally unmerited gift of God. The later Protestant hymn couplet sums up Protestant conviction about the atoning death of Christ:

> Nothing in my hand I bring,
> Simply to Thy Cross I cling.[13]

The Protestant motto is *soli Deo gloria*. All human beings are simply 'unprofitable' servants and there is a reluctance to honour anyone but God. By contrast, the Roman

---

10. Again, for an example, see W. Bridcut, 'Our Lord's relation with his mother', in Stacpoole (ed.) 1987: 107–13. Commenting on 'Do whatever he tells you' (Jn 2), he says, 'by making her last words those to be spoken at the beginning of Christ's ministry, the gospel writer makes Mary say in effect: "My part in preparing Jesus for his great work is over, and now that he has entered on his ministry you should forget about me and pay attention to him".'

11. An article entitled *'La Beaute de Marie, femme Juive'* by Fr Frederic Manns in the French magazine *Famille Chretienne*, no. 1427 (21 May 2005): 36–8, talks of Mary at Cana as 'mediatrice' (*mediatrix*), comparing her intercession at the inauguration of the new covenant with that of Moses at the beginning of the old covenant.

12. D. Butler, 'The Blessed Virgin Mary in Protestant Tradition', in McLoughlin and Pinnock (eds) 1997: 57–68. On 57, Butler calculates that 129 verses in the New Testament relate to Mary, but only 29 to the Eucharist.

13. From the famous hymn 'Rock of Ages' by Augustus Toplady. Cited in *Methodist Hymn Book* (1933), no. 498, v. 3.

Catholic and Orthodox traditions emphasize that though salvation is entirely dependent upon the divine initiative, it also involves a necessary human response. God respects human freedom and will not save us against our will. Within this framework of understanding, Mary is seen as the one who, supremely, obeyed God. The contrast between classical Reformed Protestantism and the Catholic tradition is well put in an article by Edward Ball, a Methodist, citing the glosses of Karl Barth and von Balthasar on Mary's *fiat*. In this context, Barth talks of faith as 'not an act of reciprocity, but the act of renouncing all reciprocity, the act of acknowledging the one Mediator beside whom there is no other'. Ball comments, 'Mary's response then is the acceptance of the miracle of grace, not the acceptance of a co-operative role.' His quotation of von Balthasar shows a diametrically opposed understanding. 'In Christ human nature is given the chance to co-operate and to serve.'[14]

It should also be noted that, within the Protestant world, the Wesleyan theological tradition also affirms this understanding of responsible grace and, in its doctrine of holiness, stands nearer to the Catholic and Orthodox traditions than to some other Protestant traditions.[15] This point was strongly affirmed in the British Roman Catholic–Methodist dialogue on Mary.

Finally, we should mention that, though Catholics and Protestants both affirm the Christ as the Mediator (1 Tim. 2.5), Catholics also stress the work of co-mediators in the transmission of grace, even while stressing that their mediation is subordinate to and dependent upon that of Christ. Protestant theology and spirituality stress the immediate relationship of the soul with God in Christ and there is a tendency to be suspicious of any priesthood or mediator being seen as an essential 'go-between' in the relationship with Christ. This deeply rooted experience of a direct relationship with the Father through Christ explains the fact that while most Protestants will revere and learn from the example of the saints, many find direct invocation of them problematic and, in a very real sense, redundant in terms of their own spirituality.

THE DAWN OF DIALOGUE: VATICAN II AND THE ESBVM

It was only as a result of the Second Vatican Council (1962–5) that the Roman Catholic Church could enter into, and, indeed, impart a new elan to the Ecumenical Movement. For the future of Marian dialogue as such, the key development was the treatment of Mary in the schema on the Church, thus affirming that her role has to be seen within the Church and the rest of the communion of saints.[16] Within that framework, the emphasis upon her as first and model disciple would prove especially helpful, since Protestants could accept that the emphasis upon her obedience was entirely biblical and could look upon her as an elder sister in faith in a manner that was consistent with Protestant ecclesiology, especially that of the free churches with their emphasis upon church as a mutual fellowship in learning and discipleship.[17]

---

14. E. Ball, 'Mary, Mother of the Lord', in *Epworth Review*, vol. 24, no. 4, Oct. 1997: 25–41.
15. A key standard work is Maddox 1997.
16. *Lumen Gentium*, ch. 8, cited in Abbott (ed.) 1966: 90–6.
17. I have developed this point in my paper 'Mary, Servant of the Word', in McLoughlin and Pinnock (eds) 1997: 157–70.

There was now a good starting point from which dialogue could then progress to examine issues more difficult for the Protestant mindset. The new situation was recognized by McAfee Brown,[18] who wrote:

> Catholics have gone a first mile in trying to re-establish theological rapport on this issue. Protestants have an obligation to go a second mile in opening themselves to an examination of what the New Testament says about the place of Mary in the Christian faith.

Nevertheless, the feeling in general in the dialogues between Catholics and Reformation and post-Reformation traditions that emerged from the late 1960s was that it was better to start with other issues. One prophetic figure, Martin Gillett, a Catholic layman and former Anglican deacon, disputed this and argued that far from being a cause of disunity, common dialogue concerning Mary might actually help to promote unity. To this end, he formed the Ecumenical Society of the Blessed Virgin Mary (ESBVM) in 1967 in England.[19]

Gillett was a tireless activist and soon succeeded in convincing some senior Anglican, Roman Catholic and Methodist leaders of the value of such a society. The society grew to a membership of well over 1,000 with branches in Ireland and the USA as well as several in England. It sponsored both local meetings and national and international conferences. The latter, in particular, attracted the services of many theologians and over the years the society has published many pamphlets on Marian and ecumenical matters, as well as four books of essays, mainly representing conference papers.[20] Its role in bringing Marian themes to the fore in ecumenical discussion has been widely affirmed. The success of the society has, however, been limited to the extent that most of its members are Roman Catholic and most of the remaining members come from the wings of the Church of England and the Methodist Church most favourable to the Catholic and sacramental traditions. There are only a few members from the other free churches. Nevertheless, the society has been very open to the expression of Marian opinions decidedly contrary to those of the bulk of the membership and it has given the floor to speakers who express very traditional Protestant reservations, such as William Bridcut, a minister of the Church of Ireland, whose work has already been quoted.

Several individual pioneering theologians (often though not always in connection with the ESBVM or dialogue groups) have made and continue to make important contributions to the development of an irenic ecumenical understanding of Mary. Outstanding examples are the Taizé brother Max Thurian, in his *Mother of the Lord, Figure of the Church*, the Methodist Neville Ward with his *Five for Sorrow, Ten for Joy*, a

---

18. Cited in ibid.: 11.
19. See Stacpoole (ed.) 1982: xi.
20. The four books of papers are Stacpoole (ed.) 1982, *Mary's Place in Christian Dialogue*; Stacpoole (ed.) 1987, *Mary and the Churches*; McLoughlin and Pinnock (eds) 1997, *Mary is for Everyone*; and McLoughlin and Pinnock (eds) 2002, *Mary for Earth and Heaven*.

book that first brought the spirituality of the rosary to the attention of considerable numbers of British Methodists, the Methodist Pauline Warner whose essay 'Mary, A two edged sword to pierce your heart' was an attempt to commend to Methodists the concept of the immaculate conception in terms of preparation for a unique vocation, and the French Jesuit Bernard Sesboüé.[21] Recently, important work has been produced in America by scholars from the Reformation traditions, particularly, but not exclusively, the Lutheran tradition.

CATHOLICS AND ORTHODOX

Orthodox (including here Oriental Orthodox) Christians do not have the same difficulties with Catholic piety and doctrine as Protestants, though they do have some difficulties with the Marian dogmatic definitions of 1854 and 1950. In general, Marian devotion is central to the Orthodox; indeed, the Mother of God is more frequently mentioned in the official liturgical books of the Orthodox Church than in those of the Catholic Church. The doctrine of her perpetual virginity is affirmed. She is stated to be 'all holy' (*panagia*).

Orthodox difficulties with and criticism of the Roman Catholic teaching of 1854 and 1950 stem partly from differing views on the necessity of dogmatic definition and partly from a different understanding of teaching authority in the Church. Many Orthodox state that they accept the truths undergirding the two definitions, but they do not believe that it was necessary to define them dogmatically. They argue that faith in the assumption, in Mary's bodily presence in heaven, has always been part of the *hope* of the Church, but never part of its *public* preaching, for which reason dogmatic definition was unnecessary. They also argue that solemn dogmas can only be defined by a council of all the bishops; even then, they are still subject to reception by *all* the faithful, who, according to the teaching of the Orthodox, are the final guardians of the faith. Certainly, they do not regard the Roman Catholic Church, on its own, as competent to *add* to the faith.

Orthodox are also critical on two other points. They do not accept the Augustinian teaching on original sin which undergirds the doctrine of the immaculate conception, even though they have no difficulty in believing that Mary never, at any stage of her life, sinned. They also argue that their dogmatic and devotional development stems directly from contemplation of the union of the two natures in Christ and has never become detached from this to the degree that was true of some Marian maximalism before Vatican II. The fear of a 'detached' Mary, exalted for her own sake and considered almost independently both of her Son and of the Holy Spirit that overshadowed her both at her Annunciation and again, in union with the apostles, at Pentecost, is a fear in the minds of some Orthodox. Elizabeth Behr-Sigel emphasizes that certain Fathers of the Church were aware of the risk of 'attributing too great a role to nature and to human will at the expense of divine

---

21. Thurian 1963; Ward 1971; Warner's article is in *Epworth Review*, 1991: 67–78; Sesboue 1990, see chs 18 and 19, '*Marie comblee de grace*': 377–88, and '*Theologie mariale et dialogue oecumenique*': 389–404.

grace' and that they 'insisted on the human weakness of Mary', while seeing her as the 'spirit bearer, pneumatophoros par excellence'.[22] Behr-Sigel also expresses reservation over Paul VI's title 'Mother of the Church' on the grounds that this might seem to put our adoption by Mary on the same level as our adoption in Christ by the Father.[23]

A helpful development since Vatican II has been the increasing recognition by many Catholic scholars that the Roman Catholic and Orthodox churches accept essentially the same faith. Many Catholics now accept that the ancient division over the *filioque* clause in the creed need no longer divide. Cardinal Ratzinger even delivered himself of the view that, in the case of reunion, the Orthodox would not be expected to accept all the dogmatic formulae developed solely in the West. It thus seems that, at least from the Roman Catholic side, differing ways of expressing an essentially common faith and devotion to Mary need no longer be church-dividing.[24]

THE DIALOGUES

So far there have been three official interconfessional dialogues, all involving the Roman Catholic Church, and one unofficial, but extremely influential dialogue in France, this last having been, to date, the most thorough. A few other dialogues have *touched* upon Marian themes, including the Orthodox–Old Catholic dialogue and the Catholic–Pentecostal one.[25]

ARCIC I, in section 30 of the Final Report (1981), touched on several themes, all of which have been taken up, to varying degrees, in the other dialogues. The first fuller-scale dialogue was that of the American Lutherans and Roman Catholics. In the mid-1990s came the British Roman Catholic–Methodist dialogue, resulting in the pamphlet *Mary, Mother of the Lord, Sign of Grace, Faith and Holiness*, written by Michael Evans.[26] At the end of the 1990s, representing the culmination of a long series of consultations, came the report of the Groupe des Dombes, an unofficial but extremely influential group of French Roman Catholics and Protestants.[27] Finally,

---

22.   Behr-Sigel 1991: 201–2.

23.   Ibid.: 204.

24.   In light of the recent Christological agreement between the Roman Catholic Church and the Assyrian Church of the East, it would seem that there should be no problem over this.

25.   A summary of Marian references in these dialogues is given by Kilian McDonald in his article 'Mary in recent ecumenical documents', in Stacpoole (ed.) 1987: 129–32.

26.   Evans 1995. Published jointly by Epworth Press and Catholic Truth Society. Written by Fr (now Bishop) Evans, but incorporating the insights of the many discussions in the committee. Hereafter cited as *Mary*.

27.   The Groupe, consisting of equal teams of French Catholic and Protestant (Lutheran and Reformed) theologians, dates back to an initiative of the French ecumenical pioneer Abbe Paul Couturier in 1937. It pioneered the attempt to move from position-stating in ecumenical dialogue to creative convergence statements and it has now dealt with most of the key points at issue between the Roman Catholic Church and the classical Reformation Churches. The report is entitled *Marie dans le Dessein de Dieu et la Communion des Saints. I Dans l'Histoire et l'Ecriture. II Controverse et Conversion* and was published in Paris, 1997/8. Hereafter cited as *Marie*.

delayed because of complications in Anglican–Catholic relationships, came the report of ARCIC II in May 2005.

The ARCIC I statement of 1981 set the tone for much which was to be discussed in greater detail in the later dialogues, as well as pointing to some of the continuing issues. Section 30 contains these statements:

> Anglicans and Roman Catholics can agree in much of the truth that these two dogmas (i.e. those of the Immaculate Conception and the Assumption) are designed to affirm. We agree that there can be but one mediator between God and man, Jesus Christ and reject any interpretation of the role of Mary that obscures this affirmation. We agree in recognising that Christian understanding of Mary is inseparably linked with the doctrines of Christ and the Church. We agree in recognising the grace and unique vocation of Mary, Mother of God Incarnate, in observing her festivals, and in according her honour in the communion of saints. We agree that she was prepared by divine grace to be the mother of the Redeemer, by whom she herself was redeemed and received into glory. We further agree in recognising in Mary a model of holiness, obedience and faith for all Christians ... Nevertheless, the dogmas of the Immaculate Conception and the Assumption raise a special problem for those Anglicans who do not consider that the precise definitions given by these dogmas are sufficiently supported by Scripture.

All the dialogues share certain common emphases. Primary is the stress that Mary's 'co-operation' with God, her *fiat*, is not an act independent of divine grace, but rather one made possible by it. As Fr Sesboüé, the French Jesuit who has long played a distinguished role in the Groupe des Dombes, puts it, 'her fiat is the purest fruit of grace'.[28] Sesboue points to the way in which Mary had to walk by faith and not by sight, an emphasis that reassures Protestants that Mary is not being divorced or set totally apart from the experience and struggle of other believers.[29] The dialogues all emphasize the sheer gratuitousness of God's regard for Mary. Sesboue prefers the translation *comblée de grace* to the traditional *pleine de Grace* as a more accurate rendering of the Greek *kecharitomene*, his favoured translation being perhaps best rendered in English as 'overwhelmed with grace'. Only Christ can be said to be full of grace, but Mary can be said to be overflowing with the gifts of grace.[30] Sesboue resembles the Presbyterian theologian John Oman in his emphasis upon grace as relational. 'In this term are included amiability, kindness, free friendship, pleasure, even good pleasure.'[31] This last expression resonates with Methodists, accustomed to singing at their Covenant services,

28. Sesboüé 1990: 378.
29. Ibid.: 383.
30. Ibid.: 378.
31. Ibid.: 379. Cf. J. Oman, *Grace and Personality*, Cambridge, 1917.

> And if thou art well pleased to hear,
> Come down and meet us now.[32]

From their side, Roman Catholics have been eager to acknowledge that Mary needed redemption as much as any other human being, the difference being in the Catholic teaching that this was effected in a unique way in view of her unique vocation and in *anticipation* of the merits of Christ's sacrifice on the cross.

The Individual Dialogues

Despite the considerable overlap in their conclusions, each dialogue was differently shaped by its particular context. The first, the American Lutheran–Catholic dialogue, was particularly concerned with its relationship to a prior agreement on justification by faith, that doctrine for Lutherans being the *articulus stantis vel cadentis ecclesiae*, the touchstone of all other Christian teaching. The Lutherans were anxious to see that Catholic teaching and practice and any possible reception of them among Lutherans did not contradict the basic principles of their previous agreement on justification.[33]

The dialogue was thus particularly concerned to explore the present and past practice of both churches with regard to Marian devotion and the cult of the saints in general. It started from a common concern to safeguard the uniqueness of Christ and his justifying grace. Both churches were anxious to disabuse themselves of any misconceptions; thus Lutherans came to accept that Catholic practices in regard to the saints are not idolatrous, while Catholics recorded their appreciation of the very real honour in which Luther and many Lutherans held Mary.[34]

Both churches expounded their convictions in detail, giving weight to contextual factors. The Lutherans explained that their utter trust in the sole sufficiency of the merits of Christ and their belief in the literal *immediacy* of his self-giving to the faithful believer made it difficult for them to see why it should be useful or necessary to place trust *also* in the saints, including Mary. Luther had objected to the cult of the saints on the grounds that it detracted from trust in Christ alone. They did not deny that the saints in heaven prayed for the Church on earth, but they did not see them as playing any essential role in the salvation of others.[35] The Roman Catholics responded by emphasizing that, though Christ is the sole autonomous mediator, he nevertheless empowers his faithful saints to co-operate with him. Though Catholics freely accept that God is free to save whom he will and certainly cannot be bound by the prayers of the saints, they nevertheless have confidence in the communion and mutual aid of the saints as something that continues on either side of death.[36]

For Lutherans, by contrast, the key importance of the saints lies in the example of

---

32. *Hymns and Psalms, a Methodist and Ecumenical Hymn Book*, Peterborough, 1983, no. 649, v. 4.
33. *The One Mediator, the Saints and Mary, Lutherans and Catholics in Dialogue, VII, 1983–90*, reproduced in Burgess and Gros (eds) 1995: 374–484. Hereafter cited as *The One Mediator*. On this initial point, see 374.
34. Ibid.: 375–84, 438–51, 456.
35. Ibid.: 386.
36. Ibid.: 395.

obedience on earth, for which thereafter they are certainly to be honoured and imitated. Mary is in this especially pre-eminent as 'Godbearer and most praiseworthy of the saints'. 'In this sense, Mary is, to Lutherans, a prototype of the Church, obedient to the Spirit, humble in her great calling, and the embodiment of the unmerited grace of God.' Roman Catholics gave Lutherans an assurance that nowhere was invocation of the saints and Mary defined as an *obligatory* practice.[37]

In their study, the Lutherans and Catholics identified 19 'church-uniting convergences', beginning with the basic affirmation that 'our entire hope of justification rests on Christ Jesus ... we do not place our ultimate trust in anything other than God's promise and saving work in Christ'. Point 14 stresses that 'Christians honour saints in at least three ways, by thanking God for them; by having faith strengthened as a result of the saints' response to God's grace; and by imitating in various situations their faith and their virtues'. Christians are neither forbidden nor commanded to ask the departed saints to pray for them. Devotion to Mary and to the other saints should be practised in ways that do not detract from the ultimate trust to be placed in Christ alone as mediator.[38]

In their final reflections, both Catholics and Lutherans accepted that five centuries of separation had led to the development of 'different ways of living out the Gospel'.[39] The Catholics accepted that within 'popular' tradition many Catholics had tended to invoke the saints for temporal favours rather than as exemplars of holiness, a practice that had been deplored more recently by the magisterium. They accepted, possibly with modern feminist as well as Protestant critiques in mind, that Mary had too frequently been portrayed as a submissive rather than responsible woman disciple. Mary needed, rather, to be presented as both responsible disciple and model of the Church.[40] The Lutherans reflected that, through the dialogue, they had come to a deeper appreciation of the doxological dimension of the Church and to a greater appreciation of the legitimate diversity of forms of spirituality; nevertheless, they felt obliged to reiterate the centrality of the doctrine of justification.[41]

The British Catholic–Methodist Dialogue

This dialogue was far less concerned with the problem of justification.[42] The common Catholic and Methodist emphases on sanctification and responsible grace made for a different style of convergence. Methodists are agreed with other classical Protestants in emphasizing the utter gratuitousness of grace and in rejecting any concept of salvation by works.[43] However, they are closer to Tridentine Catholicism than to the classical teaching of the Reformation on the question of the potential for

---

37. Ibid.: 388–9, 462.
38. Ibid.: 405–7.
39. Ibid.: 451.
40. Ibid.: 453.
41. Ibid.: 457–64.
42. Although there is reference to a prior agreement on justification as an essential context for the discussion; see *Mary*, para. 5.
43. In his sermon on salvation by faith, Wesley refers to this as 'the grand doctrine that drove popery from these kingdoms'; see Wesley 1984, vol. 1: 129.

actual sanctification.[44] The term 'faith that sweetly works by love' in the hymnody of Charles Wesley is close to the *fides caritate formata* of Trent. The Wesleyan reconciliation of the Reformation doctrine of justification with a strong doctrine of sanctification receives doxological expression in these two lines of Wesley:

> Joyful from my own works to cease,
> Glad to fulfil all righteousness.[45]

Methodist theology precludes any idea that the redeemed sinner must inevitably always remain *simul iustus et peccator*, while accepting realistically that most of us, perhaps the vast majority, do so. On principle, it sets no limits to the sanctifying power of the Holy Spirit and encourages all believers to 'press on to full salvation'. Granted that Catholics and Methodists are able to concur in such sentiments, the dialogue was able to make the statement that 'Methodists and Catholics recognise the need for human beings to co-operate in the mystery of salvation', subject to the necessary caveat that it is divine grace alone that enables our free response to God and any resultant growth in holiness. From this, it is possible for Catholics and Methodists to share the position that 'Mary "sums up" in herself, the relationship between God's sovereign grace and our free co-operation as individual believers and as the Church of Christ'.[46]

From this, and from the Methodist emphasis upon all divinity as 'practical divinity', concerned primarily with the active living of the Christian life of devotion and discipline, flows a common Catholic and Methodist emphasis upon Mary as model disciple, an emphasis which, of course, also coheres with Catholic teaching at and since Vatican II. The final section of the report, entitled 'Mary and Christians Today', ends on this practical note, starting with the assertion that 'Methodists and Catholics confess together the Communion of Saints as a practical fellowship of mutual aid and care', a point also made from the Catholic side in the US Lutheran–Catholic dialogue. This emphasis, which should especially appeal to Methodists, who are accustomed to thinking of the saints as 'our friends above', as fellow travellers on the way, is placed on Mary as 'our sister in the Church, a fellow disciple'. It is balanced with an emphasis upon Mary as mother, which has always been central to Catholic piety but which is not incompatible with Methodism, which in the nineteenth century revered many of its own female saints and spiritual leaders as true 'mothers in Israel'.[47]

The report dealt in considerable detail with Catholic belief concerning Mary.[48] Methodists of all generations from the Wesleys onwards have frequently been apt to

---

44. The standard work is Lindstrom 1946. For the hymn, see *Hymns and Psalms*, op. cit., no. 788.
45. From Wesley's hymn, 'Behold the servant of the Lord', with its naturally Marian echoes to Catholic ears, though it will often have been sung by Methodists without any consciousness of these echoes. *Hymns and Psalms*, no. 788.
46. *Mary*, paras 5, 17.
47. Ibid., paras 35–6.
48. See ibid., paras 23–6, for the immaculate conception, and 31–4 for the assumption.

dismiss Marian devotion, often very inaccurately understood, as superstitious, even idolatrous, but they have perhaps ignored far more than they have rejected. In these circumstances, Catholics needed to expound Marian teaching in a way most likely to make sense to and appeal to Methodists. They were also in a position to make a challenge to Methodism: Do Methodists respond positively enough to the Scriptural call for all generations to call Mary blessed? Has this scripturally based Church been blind to scriptural teaching? A prominent Methodist member of the dialogue[49] has more than once reminded Methodists that Scripture says more about Mary than it does about the Eucharist, yet Methodists have never doubted the importance of the latter.

The Methodist members of the dialogue accepted that there was a case to be answered and that exploration of Marian devotion was part of their ecumenical duty, integral to 'walking together on the pilgrim journey'.[50] The practical flavour of the dialogue, in contrast to the more purely theological tone of the other dialogues, is seen in the provision of practical questions designed for the faithful to explore together as part of a reception process.[51] Discussion of the Marian dogmas of 1854 and 1950 was not, however, omitted.

Unsurprisingly, the two churches were unable to reach agreement on these. Methodists do not accept them, arguing that they lack any clear basis in Scripture. On the other hand, the Methodists were prepared to concede that they accepted the truths to which they point, that is to say, in the case of the immaculate conception, the availability of a special grace for a unique vocation, and in the case of the assumption, the anticipation of our eschatological destiny in heaven. It is said in the report that Methodists 'safeguard in other ways the faith which they seek to express and symbolise'.[52] The question of the literal truth of the dogmas was left vague. Paragraph 3 pointed to the quest of the historical Mary as being subject to the same problems as the quest of the historical Jesus and for the distinction between Mary, the historical figure, and Mary, the 'figure' or type, to be maintained. It seems to the present writer that, if such distinctions are indeed valid, then the Marian dogmas need no longer be church-dividing as between Methodists and Catholics. Similarly, the belief in Mary as 'ever virgin', accepted by none less than Wesley himself, need create no problem if the emphasis is laid upon the purity and single-mindedness of Mary in her vocation as opposed to a particular historical interpretation of the controverted critical question of the nature of the 'brothers and sisters' of the Lord.[53]

The practical call of the report is clear. It challenges both churches. Catholics are challenged to present their Marian faith as part of a total understanding of the workings of divine grace and human but divinely evoked and enabled response. The

---

49. Rev. Dr David Butler, already cited above in n. 13.

50. *Mary*, Introduction, para. 1.

51. Questions are posed at the end of each section of the report. At the end is a final question, 'How, if at all, has your understanding of and attitude to Mary and the marian doctrines changed during your reflections on this document?'

52. *Mary*, para. 4.

53. Ibid., para. 30. For a recent assessment of the Wesleys on Mary, see the pamphlet by Wallwork 2005.

Catholic Church is also challenged to purify its devotional practice so as to remove any fear that devotion to Mary might obscure her truly creaturely and redeemed status. Catholics are also challenged to ensure that Marian piety does 'justice to a truly Christian image of womanhood'. To Methodism, there is a challenge to develop an authentically Methodist devotion to Mary as elder sister in the faith and model disciple, as pattern of obedience, contemplation, wisdom and faithfulness. The Methodist response will be a true test of Methodism's ecumenical credibility and receptiveness.[54]

Shortly after the publication of *Mary*, two significant assessments of it were written by Methodist scholars. The first, by John Newton, was basically very affirmative, recognizing the traditional Methodist neglect of Mary and asserting, in respect of the dogmas of the perpetual virginity, the immaculate conception and the assumption, that:

> I take it to be an ecumenical principle that what is a vital matter of faith to my Christian brother or sister of another Christian tradition cannot be a matter of indifference to me. I must listen, explore, try to understand.[55]

Newton felt that the report should have said more about the motherhood of Mary from the standpoint of the influence that she must have had in forming the growing Christ.

The second assessment, by Edward Ball, was more critical, evincing a much more robustly Protestant critique of ideas of co-operation and responsible grace. Ball cited Barth's view that Mary's response in her *fiat* was 'the acceptance of a miracle of grace, not the acceptance of a co-operative role'.[56] He argued that the commission had at various points uncritically accepted debatable Catholic interpretations of Scripture – for example, in deriving Mary's spiritual motherhood of believers from Christ's commitment of the beloved disciple to her care. He also felt that they had failed to give full weight to the Markan 'coolness' towards Mary recorded in Mark 3.31–5. He felt that an emphasis upon the assumption as an anticipation of our eschatological destiny had displaced the ascension as an entirely sufficient pledge in itself. He felt that if Mary was to be commended as a model, she should be seen as one in her weakness and failure as well as in her obedience. Ball undoubtedly expressed reservations that would be shared by some Methodists; equally, some other members of the commission felt that he had failed to do justice to the divergence between the Methodist understanding of responsible grace and the views held within the other

---

54. *Mary*, paras 2–4. It is too early to assess the 'reception' of this.
55. J. Newton, 'Mary. Mother of the Lord, sign of grace, faith and holiness; reflections on the Methodist-Roman Catholic Joint Statement', in McLoughlin and Pinnock 1997: 171–80, esp. 179 for this particular quotation.
56. In *Epworth Review*, Oct. 1997, vol. 24, no. 4: 25–41. Ball, a lecturer in Old Testament at the University of Nottingham, is a Methodist local preacher and is now also a member of the British Roman Catholic–Methodist Committee, though he was not on it at the time that Fr Evans compiled the report.

Reformed traditions, while Newton felt that confession of the perfect humanity of Christ necessarily implied something about the mother from whom he derived that humanity.

The Groupe des Dombes

The Groupe is bolder in its conclusions than the other dialogues so far considered. In line with its earlier practice, it was concerned to challenge both Protestants and Catholics to a very specific degree of real convergence.[57] It aimed to set controversies over grace and response in an agreed context. It repudiated the language of co-redemption as used in certain circles in the Catholic Church, noting its intentional abandonment at Vatican II. It recorded its distrust of any language of mediation used of Mary in any way that was not strictly instrumental and subordinate to Christ as sole mediator.[58] It affirmed that there need be no necessary incompatibility between the traditional Catholic language of co-operation and the term 'grateful response to a perfect gift' as used by the French Reformed theologian Jean Bosc.[59] It cited Luther's affirmation of Mary's free works of love and his conclusion, 'after we have been justified by faith, we must do everything for others, freely and gladly'.[60]

An attempt to balance the Protestant emphasis on the sovereignty of God and the Catholic emphasis on the nature of 'engraced response' can be discerned in the following sentences: 'Passivity before grace, the "letting go" of faith in its presence, is the source of a new activity. Availability translates into obedience.'[61]

The challenge to Roman Catholics is to take seriously and act upon legitimate Protestant concerns about the extent to which Marian doctrine and devotion have come dangerously close to losing their moorings in the fundamental truths of grace and Christology. Catholics are warned about the danger of invoking the *sensus fidelium* in defence of new cults or proposed dogmas, since the alleged *sensus fidelium* can rest upon 'religious sentiment rather than Christian faith'. Mariology should be seen as an aspect of Christology, not an independent theological discipline.[62]

The Groupe argues that its consensus on Mary's co-operation should suffice for unity in faith, thereby, incidentally, asserting a resolution to the problem left unresolved in the British Catholic–Methodist dialogue. It argues that submission to the dogmas of 1854 and 1950 should not be required of non-Catholics, not simply because of their definition in separation and without consultation with the other churches, but also because of the repeated requests by popes prior to 1854 that those holding contrary opinions in these matters should not anathematize each other. Protestants should simply be asked to affirm that they 'respect' the content of the dogmas, not judging them as contrary to the faith, but accepting them as 'free and legitimate consequences of the reflection of the Catholic consciousness on the

---

57. *Marie*, paras 289–338.
58. Ibid., para. 210.
59. Ibid., para. 209.
60. Ibid., para. 216.
61. Ibid., para. 219.
62. Ibid., paras 291–4.

coherence of the faith'. Reference is made to the recent progress in Christological dialogue between Rome and the Oriental Orthodox churches, in which it has been agreed that these churches need not be bound to the Christological theses of Chalcedon from which they dissented in 451.[63] Finally, stress is placed on Paul VI's teaching that Marian doctrine and devotion should be biblical, liturgical, ecumenically sensitive and anthropologically related, the key emphasis being upon Mary as active in faith and love.[64]

Protestants are challenged as to whether their silence concerning Mary prejudices their relationship with Christ and does justice to the Reformers and, even more significantly, to Scripture.[65] They are challenged to acknowledge the symbolic value of the Marian dogmas and to affirm that they are not contrary to the basic doctrine of justification. They should recover the celebration of those Marian feasts that have a clear scriptural basis, such as the Annunciation and the Presentation.[66] There is relatively little emphasis upon Mary as model disciple, in contrast to the Catholic–Methodist dialogue, but that is perhaps to be explained by the very different context of French classical Protestantism from that of British Methodism.

ARCIC II on Mary

The recent ARCIC report, *Mary, Grace and Hope in Christ*, represents the highest degree of convergence yet achieved between the Roman Catholic Church and any of its Western ecumenical dialogue partners. The report is quite clear in affirming that 'the teaching about Mary in the two definitions of the Assumption and the Immaculate Conception, understood within the biblical pattern of the economy of hope and grace, can be said to be consonant with the teaching of the Scriptures and the ancient common traditions', and that 'Mary has a continuing ministry which serves the ministry of Christ, our unique mediator'.[67] It will be apparent that the assertion that the doctrines of the assumption and the immaculate conception are 'consonant with Scripture' (and can only be understood in a total scriptural context) goes beyond the more tentative statement of the British Catholic–Methodist dialogue that Methodists could accept many of the truths that the dogmas were meant to undergird, while still not being able to accept them as scriptural. The report is also bold in stating that it is 'impossible to be faithful to Scripture without giving due attention to the person of Mary (paras. 6–30)'. It argues that:

> affirming together unambiguously Christ's unique mediation, which bears fruit in the life of the Church, we do not consider that the practice of asking Mary

63. Ibid., paras 295–9.
64. Ibid., para. 306.
65. Ibid., paras 315–17.
66. Ibid., paras 326, 331.
67. *Mary, Grace and Hope in Christ, The Anglican Roman Catholic International Commission – An Agreed Statement*, London, 2005. Also referred to as the Seattle Statement. For the statements quoted here, see para. 78.

and the saints to pray for us is communion dividing ... we believe there is no continuing theological reason for ecclesial division on these matters.[68]

It accepts, however, that there are still general questions of authority relating to dogmatic definition and reception that need to be settled. It accepts that a recognition by Anglicans of the controverted dogmas of 1854 and 1950 as consonant with Scripture would not necessarily fulfil normal Roman Catholic requirements of the full acceptance of all solemnly defined dogmas as 'revealed by God'. In an important footnote, it points to 'instances in ecumenical agreement in which what one partner has defined as de fide can be expressed by another partner in a different way', citing the examples of accords with the Lutherans and the Assyrian Church of the East.[69]

The report is set out in three main sections. The first, in the spirit of the original ARCIC commitment to seek consensus through a return to the commonly accepted sources of Scripture and early tradition, represents a common re-reading of the scriptural evidence relating to the role of Mary. Paragraph 30 sums up the conclusions of the commission on the role of Mary as attested in Scripture.

> The scriptural witness summons all believers in every generation to call Mary blessed, this Jewish woman of humble status, this daughter of Israel living in hope of justice for the poor, whom God has graced and chosen to become the virgin mother of his Son, through the overshadowing of the Holy Spirit. We are to bless her as the 'handmaid of the Lord' who gave her unqualified assent to the fulfilment of God's saving plan, as the mother who pondered all things in her heart, as the refugee seeking asylum in a foreign land, as the mother pierced by the innocent suffering of her own child, and as the woman to whom Jesus entrusted his friends. We are at one with her and the apostles as they pray for the outpouring of the Spirit on the nascent Church, the eschatological family of Christ. And we may even glimpse in her the final destiny of God's people to share in her son's victory over the powers of evil and death.[70]

The second section looks at Mary within Christian tradition, noting delicately the developing shifts of emphasis within Marian theology and devotion, especially the medieval one from seeing Mary primarily as type of the Church to associating her ever more closely with Christ's work of redemption. 'The centre of attention of believers shifted from Mary as representing the faithful Church, and so also redeemed humanity, to Mary as dispensing Christ's graces to the faithful.'[71] Attention is then given to the reaction of the Reformers against abuses in the contemporary cult of the saints and to the resultant reactions on both sides of the Reformation divide, with

---

68. Ibid., para. 75.
69. Ibid.: 63, n. 13. The agreements mentioned dealt respectively with justification and Christology.
70. It will be noted that the report acknowledges that the 'primary meaning' of the 'woman clothed with the sun' in Rev. 12 is corporate and ecclesial as the people of God, whether of the old covenant or the new, though it accepts the possibility of a Marian interpretation; ibid., paras 28–9.
71. Ibid., para. 42.

Roman Catholics increasingly seeing Marian devotion as a badge of their Catholicism, while Protestants reacted in a negative direction.[72] Emphasis is laid upon the fact that the Anglican Reformers showed reticence in ascribing any sort of sin to Mary.[73] Five feasts of Mary were preserved in the Book of Common Prayer and individual Anglicans preserved a strong devotion to her before as well as after the beginning of the Oxford Movement in 1833.[74] Finally, stress is laid upon the re-reception of Mary's essentially Christological and ecclesiological role in the teaching of Vatican II, and on a 'new prominence' for Mary in Anglican worship 'through the liturgical renewals of the twentieth century'. 'Growing ecumenical exchange has contributed to the process of re-reception in both communions.'[75]

The last section seeks to locate Mary and her role in the history of salvation within the framework of a 'theology of grace and hope'. It adduces Romans 8.30, where Paul sets out a pattern of grace and hope as paradigmatic of God's intended relationship with the human race. 'Those whom God predestined, he also called; those whom he called he also justified; and those whom he justified he also glorified.' It sees God as anticipating in Mary his work in other faithful Christians. The sense of God's calling others from the womb, such as Jeremiah, helps to give credence to the commission's statement that 'we can affirm together that Christ's redeeming work reached "back" in Mary to the very depths of her being, and to her earliest beginnings'.[76] Likewise, the universal hope within the Church of ultimate glorification helps to sustain the affirmation of the teaching that 'God has taken the Blessed Virgin Mary in the fullness of her person into his glory as consonant with Scripture'.[77] Nicholas Sagovsky, an Anglican member of ARCIC II, has since testified to the fruitfulness of the Pauline text in assisting the members of the commission towards a *fresh* understanding of the role of Mary in Christian faith.[78]

It is too early to say exactly how the report will be received. It is likely to meet with some scepticism from the more Protestant wing of the Church of England. On the BBC's *Sunday* programme, David Hilborne, an Anglican priest who is also an official of the Evangelical Alliance, irenically stated that a distinction had to be made between the ability to argue that the doctrines of the immaculate conception and the assumption were *consonant* with Scripture and their being held actually to be '*warranted* by Scripture', thus allowing Evangelicals, Anglicans and others to accept that they had the plain scriptural authority to justify their being enforced as doctrine.[79] Rather less irenically, Rod Thomas of Reform accuses ARCIC of trying to 'shoehorn' the dogmas into Scripture.[80]

---

72. Ibid., paras 44, 47.
73. Ibid., para. 45.
74. Ibid., para. 46. Lancelot Andrewes, Jeremy Taylor and Thomas Ken are specifically mentioned.
75. Ibid., paras 47–50.
76. Ibid., para. 59.
77. Ibid., para. 58.
78. *Tablet*, 21 May 2005: 8.
79. On the morning of Sunday 22 May 2005.
80. Report in *Tablet*, 21 May 2005: 30.

One suspects that some Protestant biblical scholars may be unhappy with the interpretation of Mark 3.31–5 and parallels, with the endorsement of the view that the term 'brothers' in relation to Christ is not to be taken literally and with the special pleading that Romans 3.23 with its stark statement that 'all have sinned' is to be taken in a particular contextual meaning rather than at face value.[81] There will certainly be reservations over the concept of Mary's continuing ministry and over the degree of cautious affirmation of the spiritual value of private revelations.[82]

From the Roman Catholic side, Sarah Boss has commented that the report gives little attention to the identification of Mary as a type of the Church which is so strong in the early Fathers.[83] She also points to the very real difficulties that the report will pose for those Evangelical Anglicans who can accept that Mary was used as an instrument of the divine will, but who are also very unwilling to accept the language of 'co-operation' with God which the report takes for granted.[84]

It is also significant that, though Mary's 'pondering' is recorded, there is no discussion of its significance for the creative development of tradition within the Church. The commission can, of course, reply that the context of Anglican–Roman Catholic relationships has determined the thrust of the report with its emphasis on showing the consonance of Marian doctrine with Scripture, just as, for the Catholic–Methodist dialogue, the context was, in part, the Wesleyan concept of responsible discipleship.

These reservations apart, many Anglicans, Roman Catholics and others will find the report lucid, stimulating and even devotional.

CONCLUSIONS AND FUTURE PROSPECTS

It will be apparent from the above summaries of four key ecumenical dialogue reports that very considerable progress has been made with what was once commonly seen as an intractable issue. It is worth stressing that, even apart from the achievements of the set-piece dialogues, the progress of the dialogue has influenced the way in which Roman Catholic, Orthodox and Protestant theologians have tried to commend their positions in terms that will make sense and appeal to their partners. Particularly notable work in this respect by individual theologians has been done by Bishop Kallistos Ware, in taking an irenic stance vis-à-vis Catholic teaching on the immaculate conception, and by Fr Ted Yarnold, who has commended the same doctrine to Protestants as a particularly important instance of grace alone.[85]

There seems to be a consensus on the following points. First, that Marian doctrine and devotion must be integrated within an understanding of the primacy of the grace and saving mission of the triune God. In calling Mary the Abraham of the new

---

81. *Mary, Grace and Hope*, paras 19–20, para. 59, n. 12.
82. Ibid., para. 73. The commission, though, record the dictum of the Congregation of the Doctrine of the Faith of 2000 that no one is obliged to 'use such help'.
83. *Tablet*, 21 May 2005: 7.
84. Ibid.
85. See, for example, K. Ware, 'The Mother of God in Orthodox Theology', and E. J. Yarnold, 'The Immaculate Conception, the Assumption and Reunion', in Stacpoole (ed.) 1982: 169–81, 125–30.

covenant, the Groupe des Dombes locates her clearly within the context of the Pilgrim Church and identifies her as a pilgrim in faith, a theological approach which will resonate with Protestant emphases while retaining the Roman Catholic emphasis upon her pivotal importance.[86] It can certainly be agreed that Mary, like every faithful Christian, stood constantly in need of grace and, indeed, received all the graces needed for her special and unique vocation. Catholics and Methodists could fruitfully deepen their Marian dialogue by discussing the question of Mary's reception of grace in the light of Wesley's theologoumenon that those who have attained to perfect love stand even more in need of sustaining grace than those who have not yet attained to this perfection. Finally, there is the common emphasis upon Mary as model disciple, sister as well as mother, always within the fellowship, never above it or detached from it, Mother of the Church, as Paul VI taught, but also fellow disciple who travels with us, having gone through her own doubts and periods of darkness, and who teaches through her own profound reflection. If there is one aspect of the scriptural record that might have been more thoroughly examined in the dialogues (and not just by ARCIC as specifically recorded above), it is the significance of the sentence recorded twice by Luke, 'and Mary kept all these things in her heart and pondered on them' (Lk. 2.19, 51).

A possible cloud on the ecumenical Marian horizon came with the request, backed by 40 cardinals and 500 bishops, that the Pope consider the solemn definition of the dogmas of Maria co-redemptrix and Maria mediatrix of all graces.[87] This was vigorously opposed at a Marian congress, at which Anglican and Orthodox observers were present, as likely to create almost insuperable problems. It will be seen that such a definition would certainly go against the spirit of the understanding of Christ as sole mediator and of grace expressed in the dialogues, most particularly that adopted by the Groupe des Dombes. What the future of such Marian maximalism will be within the Catholic Church is difficult to predict. Even more important is the question of the reception of the dialogues already detailed. It is quite clear that this remains the most urgent question for the next generation: how to communicate the agreed insights within the churches, especially the Roman Catholic, Anglican, Lutheran and Methodist churches that have taken the lead.

BIBLIOGRAPHY

Key works on Mary in an ecumenical context include:

Braaten, C. E. and Jenson, R. W. (eds) (2004) *Mary, Mother of God*, Grand Rapids, MI: Eerdmans.
Gaventa, B. R. and Rigby, C. L. (eds) (2002) *Blessed One. Protestant Perspectives on Mary*, Louisville, KY: John Knox Press.
Macquarrie, J. (1991) *Mary for all Christians*, London: HarperCollins.
Thurian, M. (1963) *Mother of the Lord, Figure of the Church*, English translation, London: Faith Press.

---

86. Sesboue 1990: 384–5.
87. For discussion of the issues raised by such a possibility and particularly in the light of the Congress, see the articles in the *Tablet* by E. J. Yarnold, R. Greenacre, R. Laurentin and E. Storkey on 17 January, 24 January, 31 January and 7 February 1998 respectively.

The main volumes of publications by the Ecumenical Society of the Blessed Virgin Mary are:

Stacpoole, A. (ed) (1982) *Mary's Place in Christian Dialogue*, Slough: St Paul Publications.
Stacpoole, A. (ed.) (1987) *Mary and the Churches*, Dublin: Columba Press.
McLoughlin, W. and Pinnock, J. (eds) (1997) *Mary is for Everyone*, Leominster: Gracewing.
McLoughlin, W. and Pinnock, J. (eds) (2002) *Mary for Earth and Heaven. Essays on Mary and Ecumenism*, Leominster: Gracewing.

Additionally, the society has published a wide range of occasional papers, mostly from Anglican, Roman Catholic, Orthodox and Methodist perspectives, but with occasional contributions from Lutheran and Reformed standpoints.

The four dialogues referred to in the text can be referenced as follows:

The One Mediator, the Saints and Mary. Lutherans and Catholics in Dialogue, VIII, 1983–90, cited in J. Burgess and J. Gros (eds) (1995) *Growing Consensus: Church Dialogues in the United States, 1962–1991*, New York: Paulist Press.
Evans, M. (1995) *Mary, Mother of the Lord, Sign of Grace, Faith and Holiness. Towards a Shared Understanding*, London: Epworth Press and Catholic Truth Society.
Groupe des Dombes (1997/8) *Marie dans le Dessein de Dieu et la Communion des Saints, I, Dans l'Histoire et l'Ecriture, II, Controverse et Conversion*, Paris: Bavard/Centurion.
ARCIC II (2005) *Mary, Grace and Hope in Christ, The Anglican Roman Catholic International Commission – An Agreed Statement*, London: Continuum. Also known as the Seattle Statement.

Other works referenced in this essay are as follows:

Abbott, W. M. (ed.) (1966) *Documents of Vatican II*, London: Geoffrey Chapman.
Behr-Sigel, E. (1991) *The Ministry of Women in the Church*, Steven Bigham, trans, New York: Oakwood.
Butler, D. (1995) *Methodists and Papists*, London: Darton, Longman and Todd.
Lindstrom, H. (1946) *Wesley and Sanctification*, London: Epworth.
Maddox, R. (1997) *Responsible Grace*, Nashville, TN: Kingswood Books.
Sesboüé, B. (1990) *Pour Une Theologie Oecumenique*, Paris: Editions du Cerf.
Swanson, R. N. (ed.) (2004) *The Church and Mary*, Studies in Church History 39, Woodbridge: Boydell Press.
Wallwork, N. (2005) *The Blessed Virgin Mary in the Doctrine and Devotion of John and Charles Wesley*, ESBVM.
Ward, N. (1971) *Five for Sorrow, Ten for Joy*, London: Epworth.
Wesley, J. (1984) *Works*, ed. A. Outler, Nashville: Abingdon Books.
Wolffe, J. (ed.) (1996) *Evangelicals, Women and Community in Nineteenth Century Britain*, Milton Keynes: Open University.

PART 4

TRADITIONS OF DEVOTION

16

MARY IN EARLY MODERN EUROPE

TREVOR JOHNSON

In early modern Catholic Europe, long identified as the age of the Counter-Reformation, the Blessed Virgin Mary was ubiquitous. Wherever one looks in the period's religious culture, she is present, even dominant, in image, cult and institution, modelled in Italian street-corner Virgins and South German *Hausmadonnen*, venerated in altarpieces, festivals and pilgrimages, the beloved focus of Marian sodalities, Rosary confraternities or the 'Slaves of Mary'. The Marian piety of the sixteenth, seventeenth and eighteenth centuries has excited less scholarly interest than that of the Middle Ages, which saw the establishment of its basic patterns, or that of the nineteenth and twentieth centuries, with their dogmatic definitions of the immaculate conception and the assumption and the resurgence of a popular Marianism expressed in international pilgrimage sites such as Lourdes. Nonetheless, a glance at early modern Marian devotion, at visual art on Marian themes and at the immense corpus of Baroque Mariological literature, assuming an astonishing variety of genres and attracting authors of the intellectual stature of Suárez, Bellarmine and Canisius, suggests that the sixteenth and seventeenth centuries did make significant contributions to the development of Marian piety.[1] New sensibilities, it has been recently shown, which had been formed against the backdrop of humanism, the Protestant Reformation and changing attitudes to women, in turn led to important shifts in the public portrayal of the Virgin. Above all, leading Catholic apologists began to move away from emphasizing Mary's shared flesh with her son, which had hitherto been stressed as the mystical link which enabled her to participate actively in Christ's life and work and rendered her own body praiseworthy as the source of Christ's suffering body on the cross and of his glorified body received in the Eucharistic host. Instead, Catholic writers increasingly preferred to stress the Virgin's identity as Christ's spiritual mother, united to him much more closely by shared will and affection than by flesh, and portrayed her as silent, distant and obedient.[2] At the same time, the social, political and intellectual climate encouraged a Marian fervour throughout Catholic Europe at both elite and popular levels. As will be suggested in this brief and partial essay, such unprecedented Marian enthusiasm found expression in a key emblem of Counter-Reformation Catholic identity, the devotion to the Virgin of the Immaculate Conception.

---

1. For an overview, see the editors' introduction to de Fiores and Gambero (eds) 2003: 25–54.
2. Ellington 2001. See also Boss 2000, esp. 140–6, on changing attitudes to Mary's physical motherhood as evidenced by early modern debates on the doctrine of the immaculate conception.

Of all external factors, perhaps the most determinative event for the culture of early modern Catholic Christianity was the rise of Protestantism in the sixteenth century. For Reformist divines, the status of the Virgin was not a central concern, being firmly subordinated to essential theological disputes over grace and salvation. Nonetheless, their shared doctrinal positions had immediate implications for Marian devotion. A focus on Christ as the sole mediator between God and humanity, the abandonment of intercessory prayer through the saints and the rejection of the value of cultic imagery, while not uniquely directed against Mary, removed the basis for nearly all the features of her cult as it had developed by the later Middle Ages. At the same time, when Reformers did turn to discuss Mary directly, their approaches and arguments could vary significantly.[3] Luther, in this respect fairly conservative in his religious imagination, honoured the Virgin, while churches in Lutheran cities occasionally retained pre-Reformation Marian iconography, even if it was now discreetly repositioned or screened.[4] Other Reformers were more hostile, fearing the danger of a continued Marian cult. Somewhat paradoxically, all mainstream Reformers defended the doctrine of the Virgin's perpetual virginity, embracing it as one of several 'unwritten verities', or exceptions to the rule that traditions unsupported directly by Scripture were human inventions which could (and usually should) be discarded.[5]

On the Catholic side of what by the middle of the sixteenth century had become an apparently irreversible schism in the Western Church, the Council of Trent (1545–63) had little to say on the Virgin, beyond upholding the value of intercession and the worth of suitably chaste images of her and the other saints as foci of devotion. After Trent, however, Catholic writers, including members of the new religious orders of the sixteenth century such as the Society of Jesus (founded in 1540), took up their pens to discuss and defend Marian propositions, producing, in effect, a novel genre: the specifically Mariological treatise.[6] They wrote primarily to counter Protestant critique, in ways which acknowledged at least in part their opponents' success in ranking scriptural and patristic sources over medieval tradition. In 1577, for example, Peter Canisius published an 800-page work entitled *On the Incomparable Virgin Mary*.[7] It is significant that this first book on an exclusively Marian theme by a Jesuit was penned by a major architect of the Catholic resurgence in the German lands in the decades around 1600. The *Mariale*, as Canisius called his book, was conceived as part of a larger project which aimed to refute the Lutheran ecclesiastical histories known as the *Magdeburg Centuries* and was thoroughly apologetic in tone and purpose. In its pages, the Jesuit sought authority in the patristic as well as the medieval corpus, while demonstrating through exegesis the mutual reinforcement of Scripture and tradition on Mariological questions. He attempted to weaken his

---

3. For the now classic account, see Tappolet and Ebneter 1962.
4. Heal 2004: 218–27.
5. MacCulloch 2004: 191–217.
6. The term 'Mariology', to denote a distinct genre of religious literature, seems to have been coined in a treatise of 1602 by a Sicilian, Placido Nigido (*c.* 1570–1640), although it subsequently fell into disuse before a nineteenth-century revival; de Fiores and Gambero (eds) 2003: 42.
7. *De Maria virgine incomparabili* (Ingolstadt, 1577).

opponents' case by accentuating their own divergence of opinion on the fundamental matter of grace, a divergence exposed by their positions on the apparently secondary question of the Virgin.[8] The approach of Canisius in this regard exemplifies how in the confessional battleground of sixteenth- and seventeenth-century Europe Mariology came to form part of the arsenal of Catholic apologists, at both the sophisticated level of learned treatise and at the more mundane level of popular devotion, on both the front line of interdenominational conflict in northern and central Europe and in the Mediterranean Catholic heartlands.

ELITE AND POPULAR MARIOLOGY

Among elite manifestations of Marian devotion, the political use of the cult of the Virgin by Europe's Catholic rulers, although by no means a new phenomenon, was a key feature of the post-Tridentine age, a period when cultural tropes were self-consciously manipulated by princes to promote proto-absolutist state-building. In the seventeenth century strenuous competition occurred throughout Europe between Catholic dynasties as they rushed to appropriate the Virgin by declaring her the patron of their houses and lands, and consecrating themselves and their peoples to her, as occurred in the kingdoms of France in 1638, Portugal in 1644, in the Austrian lands in 1647 and in Poland in 1656. Expressions of dynastic Marianism often extended to ceremonies in which statues of the Virgin were crowned.[9] In the Holy Roman Empire, a leading role was played by the Wittelsbach dukes of Bavaria, particularly Maximilian I (ruled 1598–1651), who not only developed a rich personal devotion to Mary, consecrating himself to her with a vow written in his own blood, but also adopted the Virgin as the chief emblem of his considerable dynastic and confessional ambitions, such that some historians have attributed to him a 'Marian programme'. In 1601, the duke required all Bavarians by law to carry rosary beads constantly; in 1616 he declared the Virgin patron of Bavaria and in that guise had her sculpted image placed by the entrance of his Munich residence, the prototype for the *Hausmadonnen* which graced the facades of Bavarian dwellings thereafter; in 1638 he oversaw the dedication to Mary of a column, the *Mariensäule*, in Munich's principal square, in fulfilment of a vow inspired by the threat to his duchy from Swedish forces during the Thirty Years War: the sceptred Virgin stands atop her pedestal while at its base angels crush monsters representing heresy. The Munich *Mariensäule* was imitated in other states, not least by the Austrian Habsburgs.[10] Dynastic competition for celestial patronage was not restricted to seeking that of the Virgin Mary and it frequently extended to other saints. However, even in such cases the Virgin's superior rank in the heavenly hierarchy was constantly acknowledged. The Habsburgs claimed as one of their patrons the fifteenth-century Czech martyr Jan Nepomuk, who was canonized in 1729 and whose cult had been deliberately fostered in Bohemia during its re-Catholicization. Nepomuk's cult was associated

8.   Giesberts 1925: 109–36.
9.   de Fiores and Gambero (eds) 2003: 42.
10.   On Maximilian, see Albrecht 1998, esp. 292–7; on Habsburg dynastic piety, see Coreth 1959.

with and to an extent subordinated to that of the Virgin, primarily through the unique iconographic association of the halo of stars shared by both (although Nepomuk only had five stars, each representing a letter of the Latin word *tacui*, meaning 'I was silent' and a reference to the saint's heroic refusal to reveal confessional secrets).[11] In a parallel case of the subordination of local saints to the Virgin at the behest of a ruling house, the Jesuit Matthaeus Rader (1561–1634) composed for Duke Maximilian of Bavaria a four-volume compendium of the lives of all the saints connected in some way with his duchy.[12] The Virgin appeared unambiguously at their head, and the local Bavarian saints, though their lives are illustrated throughout the work in sumptuous engravings, did not adorn the rich frontispiece, which was dominated by Mary herself, accompanied only by St Michael and the angelic guardians of the four Bavarian provinces (Fig. 18).[13]

As polyvalent symbol, the Virgin could exhibit paradox and even contradiction. Rulers and soldiers adopted the innocent *Immaculata* or the nurturing Madonna as a figurehead of the militant (and militaristic) Counter-Reformation. Pius V attributed the defeat of the Turks at Lepanto (1571) to the intercession of the Virgin of the Rosary, and Philip II of Spain presented a lantern taken from one of the Ottoman vessels during the battle to the Hieronymite friary at Guadalupe, where the shrine of the Virgin was already the symbol of the triumph of Christianity over its Muslim opponents.[14] Mary's image decorated Catholic military standards during Europe's sixteenth- and seventeenth-century religious conflicts and the Virgin was nominated *generalissima* of the Imperialist forces during the Thirty Years War. In 1620, during the Bohemian campaign which culminated at the Battle of the White Mountain, the principal banner of the Catholic field army carried an image of the Virgin and the text of Songs 6.10, '*terribilis ut castrorum acies ordenata*' ('terrible as an army with banners'), while the image of the Virgin would long remain on the colours of Bavarian and Austrian regiments. The Spanish Discalced Carmelite friar Domingo à Jesu Maria, papal legate to the Catholic army in the 1620 campaign, retrieved from a torched castle at Strakonitz an icon of the Virgin and Child which had allegedly been mutilated by a Calvinist iconoclast; taking the image into battle at the White Mountain, he attributed the Catholic triumph to its wondrous power. The icon was then sent to Rome to reside in the new Carmelite church of Santa Maria della Vittoria, dedicated to the freshly vindicated cult of 'Our Lady of Victory'.[15]

The Marian enthusiasm of ruling dynasties, whose scions manipulated the Virgin as symbol and instrument of their political projects, was complemented by keen participation by all levels of Catholic society in the Marian cult, a piety which could even run counter to the power claims of lords and princes.[16] There was nothing new

---

11. The basis for the development of distinctive Nepomuk iconography was provided by the Czech Jesuit Bohuslav Balbín, in his *Vita S. Joannis Nepomuceni sigilli sacramentalis Protomartyris* (Augsburg, 1730).

12. *Bavaria sancta et pia* (1615–28).

13. Johnson 2002a: 83–100.

14. Starr-LeBeau 2002: 192–216.

15. Johnson 2002b: 319–35; Chaline 1999.

16. Luebke 1997: 71–106.

Fig. 18. Matthaeus Rader SJ, *Bavaria sancta* (Munich, 1615), frontispiece (Bayerische Staatsbibliothek München).

in the ability of the Virgin to be all things to all men, but traditional practical devotions, represented by the rosary (in its various forms), the office of the Virgin, litanies and attachment to devotional images were fostered and considerably expanded through new institutional frameworks, of which the Jesuits' Marian congregations or sodalities were perhaps the most pervasive, at least in the urban centres of Catholic Europe.[17] Typical of the devotional handbooks used by the Marian sodalities of the seventeenth century, both in its handiness and in its recycling of medieval horticultural metaphors, was that of a Spanish Jesuit, Francisco de la Cruz, entitled *Mary's Garden: or Manual of Varied Devotions to the Blessed Virgin.*[18] Here the devotee of Mary was invited to take a stroll through the five flowerbeds of her garden, each denominated by its symbolic blooms: the violet of humble reverence; the rose of love and confidence; the white lily of purity; the hyacinths of varied devotions; and the heliotrope of perfect imitation. The pious soul was urged to venerate the most holy name of Mary, never to utter it lightly (for even the archangel Gabriel did not use Mary's name) and to bow on hearing it. It was a name to be linked to that of Jesus: 'when you examine your conscience at night,' the Jesuit urged, 'place in the centre of your heart the sweetest names of Jesus and Mary, and you will sleep happily.' De la Cruz recounted stories of miraculous escapes from danger attributed to the wearing of Marian medals, gave tips for pilgrims to Marian shrines and recommended daily recitation of the rosary. This was in spirit a continuation of the piety expressed in medieval books of hours, but print culture and an expanded reading public combined with the institutionalized networks of confraternities to give Marian devotion an identity-sustaining quotidian vigour across swathes of Catholic Europe.

Baroque spiritual writers' enthusiasm for practical meditational exercises encouraged imaginative visualization of the Virgin, a picturing which required some knowledge of Mary's appearance and regard for her physical beauty. In his 900-page *History of the Life and Excellencies of Our Lady the Virgin Mary*, the Spanish Discalced Carmelite José de Jesús María (1562–1629) employed classical categories to deduce the appearance of the Virgin, arguing that physically she must have closely resembled Christ ('for does not Aristotle say "the son is the image of his parents"?') and claiming that her body was the most beautiful that a mortal body could be. Following Epiphanius (as translated by Canisius), he described the Virgin as of average or above-average height, perfectly proportioned, blonde, green-eyed, with curved, 'decently dark' eyebrows, a long nose, soft, red lips, white, even teeth, and a face neither round nor sharp, but quite long. Long too were her hands and fingers. Her complection was excellent and without blemish; her face was a pale pink, the 'most perfect colour for the human body', he claimed, 'because it derives from the balance of the four humours'. Perfect humoral balance explained also the singular fragrance of Mary's body. The friar devoted several chapters to explaining how all this beauty did not give rise to the dangers that normally accompanied God's gift to women of fine appearance, in particular the arousal of concupiscence in their beholders. It was one

---

17. Châtellier 1989.
18. *Jardin de Maria. O practica de devociones varias con la beatissima Virgen* (Salamanca, 1655).

of the qualities of the Virgin's beauty that, by a special grace which had been attributed by Aquinas to her sanctification and by others to her immaculate conception, it infused purity into the hearts of all who saw her, suppressing in them any sensual desires and 'dousing the fire of carnal feeling'.[19] Such descriptions assisted artists in representing the Virgin, besides helping the devout to focus their imaginations in mental prayer. Admittedly, some Reformist spiritual directors expressed caution. François de Sales, for example, warned Jeanne de Chantal in 1606: 'you must neither linger over your images, nor totally disregard them. Neither should you imagine in too much detail, for instance, wondering about the colour of our lady's hair, the shape of her face, details of that sort; but simply and in a general way, imagine her longing for her son, or the like, and only briefly.'[20]

Besides such devotions and their theological supports, the primary (and most intense) popular experience of encounter with the Virgin was before one of her many miraculous images. As the volumes of William Christian, Philip Soergel and Marc Forster, on Castile, Bavaria and Swabia respectively, have shown, local pilgrimage, especially to Marian shrines, was a dominant feature of popular religious culture throughout Catholic Europe, a feature which could be exploited for propagandistic purposes.[21] Marian shrines abounded across the Catholic world, easily outstripping in number and crowd-pulling power those of other saints, and increasingly so post-Trent. This had much to do with official suspicion of the cults of obscure or 'legendary' local holy figures, although to an extent this mitigated against official acceptance of new Marian apparitions as well.[22] Safest all round were established centres of Marian pilgrimage, although in these cases too the Counter-Reformation brought change as well as stability, as the history of the Marian shrine of Scherpenheuvel in the Spanish Netherlands exemplifies. Before the Reformation local pilgrims had sought cures from a small wooden carving of the Virgin resting in the branches of an isolated oak tree on top of the 'Sharp Hill' near Zichem. The statue disappeared when the region came under Calvinist control in the 1580s, but was replaced when the Spanish army re-occupied the area and fresh miracles were enthusiastically reported by the garrison and its Jesuit chaplains. The local clergy organized formal processions and had a small wooden chapel built by the tree. The fame of the shrine rose further when witnesses testified to having seen the statue weep blood, taken as the Virgin's sorrow at the sins of the Netherlanders. However, at this point, the diocesan authorities, alarmed by reports that pilgrims were stripping the oak of its leaves, branches and bark to take away for home-cures, intervened decisively and had the tree chopped down. The image of Mary was transferred to a new stone chapel. Torn from popular grasp in high-handed fashion, the wood from the felled oak was used to make rosary beads and a number of new Marian statues, modelled on the original, some of which in turn wrought miracles. Under the patronage of the regents of the area, the Habsburg Archdukes Albert and Isabella, a

---

19.   José de Jesús María 1652: 172–99.
20.   de Sales, de Chantal, trans. Thibert 1988: 145.
21.   Christian 1981a; Soergel 1993; Forster 2001, esp. 61–105.
22.   Christian 1981b.

grand new basilica was constructed, creating a veritable fortress of the faith and a national shrine for the Spanish Netherlands.[23] The history of Scherpenheuvel illustrates a common Counter-Reformation phenomenon of elite appropriation of a popular shrine, expressed here in the felling of the oak and the remodelling of the site's sacred topography. In this instance, the clerical desire to efface the lay cult of the tree and transfer the focus of devotion unambiguously to the Virgin herself was accompanied by the politicization of the pilgrimage as a reassertion of Habsburg authority.

The ubiquity of Marian pilgrimage was vividly advertised in the popular *Atlas Marianus*, published by a Jesuit, Wilhelm von Gumppenberg (1609–75), in several volumes in the 1650s, a work which presented brief histories of over 1,000 Marian shrines from all over the Catholic world.[24] Each was illustrated with an engraving of its wonder-working image and, as David Freedberg has noted, these depictions carefully delineated the distinctive adornment, clothing and framing of every Madonna, so the result conveyed a sense of great variety, even when the icons or statues fell within a narrow range of basic types.[25] Clearly the distinctive look of each miraculous Madonna was linked to the localization of the Virgin's power. There was no reticence in Gumppenberg, or in other authors and illustrators, when it came to representing the devolution of the universal Virgin into her distinctive localizations. The *Marian Atlas* also broke new ground in rendering a 'searchable' handiness out of extreme classificatory complexity. In a landmark in the history of indexing, Gumppenberg brought out the taxonomic index to the work as a separate volume in 1655.[26] Running to 128 pages, its chapters were divided into indices which were then subdivided into catalogues. In Chapter One, Index Two, Catalogue One, for example, the Jesuit listed twelve species of tree in which miraculous Marian images had been found; in Chapter Three, Index Five, he treated attacks which had been made against Marian images, classifying the weapons used against them, the parts of the images that were 'wounded', the effects of the wounds on the images and the Virgin's various responses to the attacks. In Index Six he gave lists of the various ghastly fates of the iconoclasts, catalogues of the images' modes of self-defence and a classification of the iconoclasts into seven types: Indians, Moors, Saracens, Jews, Turks, heretics and blasphemers.

The cultic significance attached to damaged images of the Virgin, conveying a message of resistance against Protestant iconoclasm, was one feature of post-Tridentine Marian pilgrimage. Another was the proliferation of imitative shrines, with a diffusion of replica images which partook of the sacred and miraculous properties of their originals. Most spectacular were reproductions of the Holy House of Loreto and its Virgin, 18 of which were constructed in Bavaria alone between 1632 and 1675.[27] Antique images, whether Byzantine-style icons or Romanesque

---

23. Duerloo and Wingens 2002.
24. *Atlas Marianus, sive de imaginibus Deiparae per orbem christianum miraculosis* (Ingolstadt, 1657).
25. Freedberg 1989: 113–15.
26. *Idea Atlantis Mariani* (Trent, 1655).
27. On Marian shrines in Baroque Bavaria, see Woeckel 1992.

figures of hieratic, imperial virgins, continued to exercise a strong pull. Best-known and most copied of them was the icon of Our Lady '*Salus Populi Romani*', attributed to St Luke and housed in the Roman basilica of Santa Maria Maggiore, whose likeness, in Gauvin Bailey's words, 'thanks to the Jesuits, probably enjoyed wider currency than any other image on earth by the turn of the seventeenth century'. In 1569 the society gained permission to have copies made of the image and by the early seventeenth century such replicas, as well as pictures exhibiting syncretic blending of the Roman prototype with local styles, could be found across the continents, from Peru to Japan, providing a spectacular emblem of Catholicism's status as the first 'world' religion.[28] Besides images of antique style, new, more naturalistic representations could also feature in the expanding universe of Marian devotion. Freshly fashioned devotional images, conforming to Baroque taste, could become shrine images through the display of miraculous signs, but perhaps the most designedly 'naturalistic' of all Marian images were the processional Madonnas of southern Spain. As more and more confraternities in the peninsula adopted penitential styles and Passion avocations in the years around 1600, artists were employed to create images of unprecedented realism, made to be viewed on the move and in the round and exquisitely crafted to provoke the desired emotional reactions of contrition and compassion. The most popular were the *imágenes de vestir*: life-size dressable mannequins with glass eyes and tears and real hair. Their elaborate vestments, modelled on contemporary court dress, hid the armatures which supported their delicately modelled faces and hands. Such devotional statues fostered a cult of the Passion as a mystical union between Christ and Mary; Son and Mother were, as the sixteenth-century friar Ambrosio de Montesino put it, 'bound up in one love, and suffering one pain, and on one cross entwined'.[29]

The same intimacy was reflected in the way in which, in the post-Tridentine period as in the Middle Ages, the Virgin was enlisted to help not only the living but also the dead. Her importance as the primary intercessor with Christ on behalf of the suffering Holy Souls in Purgatory was reinforced with the reform of the indulgence system in the Counter-Reformation, after the crisis it had experienced in the early sixteenth century. Catholics everywhere could now participate in a democratization of charity towards the dead, through the accessibility offered by the so–called privileged altars at which a single celebration could gain a plenary indulgence. Bypassing the rich person's costly multiplication of Masses for the dead at private altars, the generosity of Pope Gregory XIII (reigned 1572–85) with the Treasury of Merits now placed total remission within everyone's pocket. The sponsorship of new privileged altars was a spur to new iconographies of Purgatory, although traditional representations of the Virgin interceding with her Son on behalf of the Holy Souls, indicating or exposing her own breasts, persisted, a sign that new, spiritualizing sensibilities had not yet eclipsed an older, more fleshly, conceptualization of Mary (Fig. 19). The rise in the number of confraternities dedicated to the Holy Souls in the

28.   Bailey 1999: 8. On New World Marianism, see also Brading 2001.
29.   Webster 1998: 180.

Fig. 19. Pieter van der Borcht (1545–1608), engraving of Christ and the Virgin interceding for the Holy Souls in Purgatory. (Christine Göttler, *Die Kunst des Fegefeuers nach der Reformation. Kirchliche Schenkungen, Ablaß und Almosen in Antwerpen und Bologna um 1600* (Mainz, 1996, Plate 22, p. 83. Orig.: Antwerpen, Stedelijk Prentenkabinet).

seventeenth century, often under the aegis of regular clergy, fostered inter-order rivalry but also further raised the profile of Mary. While the Franciscans promoted St Francis as an intercessor for the Holy Souls, the Dominicans emphasized the Madonna of the Rosary and the Carmelites lauded Our Lady of Carmel, provider of the miraculous scapular.[30]

THE IMMACULIST WAVE

That the doctrine of the immaculate conception became the foremost Mariological theme of the post-Tridentine era might initially surprise. No fundamentally new theology was involved, since the key positions relative to the claim of Mary's preservation from sin at the moment of her conception had emerged long before the Reformation. Moreover, despite some dogged Dominican resistance, by the late sixteenth century there was on this question a broad consensus in the Catholic world.[31] The Council of Trent had reiterated Mary's exemption from sin without actually defining her conception as immaculate. Admittedly, this was just about sufficient to keep anti-Immaculist hopes alive, and it was to silence embarrassing divisions that Pius V tried to prohibit public debate of the issue with the Bull *Super speculum* in 1570, the first substantial papal intervention since Sixtus IV's Bull *Grave nimis* of 1483. Nonetheless, there was an enormous surge of interest in Immaculism in the years around 1600, as a result of which intense pressure was applied to the papacy to pronounce a formal definition of Mary's immaculate conception as dogma. In the continued absence of a definition, devotion to the immaculate conception was increasingly presented as a litmus test of Catholic fervour and fidelity. An Immaculist campaign was waged throughout Catholic Europe, although most intensively in Spain, and led to the notorious 'blood vow'. It produced an unprecedented volume of Marian literature of all kinds, polemical and panegyric, plays, theses, sermons and poetry, in a campaign which rested on rhetorical force rather than theological originality and which also placed great stress on visual representation, establishing a new and lasting iconography.[32]

Crucial to the resurgence of Immaculism was again the impact of the Reformation. Here, clearly, was a Marian dogma too far, even for the most Mariophile Protestants. Their outright rejection of the doctrine echoed the scepticism of some Catholics, but in an era of confessionalism Protestant antipathy was itself perhaps sufficient cause for enthusiastic Catholic espousal. In his above-mentioned treatise, *De Maria virgine incomparabili*, Peter Canisius addressed the doctrine in his early chapters, conceding that the notion posed difficult questions, but defending it against traditional counter-arguments and the new critiques of Protestant divines.[33] Since the doctrine directly addressed the problem of original sin, the nature of its transmission, its consequences and the operation of grace, it went beyond the status of Mary *per se* and into the heart of the Reformation's

---

30. Scaramella 1991; Göttler 1996.
31. Sixteenth-century Dominicans were themselves divided on the question; Preston 2004: 181–90.
32. On Immaculist iconography, see Stratton 1994.
33. Canisius 1577: 33–58.

theological battleground. As indicated above, Canisius's work was emblematic of a shift in the argumentation of such matters, occasioned chiefly by the Reformation. Without rejecting the authority of tradition, it involved a turn to Scripture, plundered now more than ever for approbation for the doctrine and viewed in part through a patristic prism, and a corresponding shift away from apocryphal literature, such as the *Protevangelium of James*. Among other things, this meant discarding any miraculous virginal conception by St Anne; Mary's physical conception, it was now generally agreed, was through the normal means, but attention became focused on the moment of the animation of her soul within her mother's womb. Admittedly, much exegetical approach was traditional. The Angelic Salutation (Lk. 1.28) and the praise of the Shulamite woman in Songs 4.7, '*tota pulchra es, amica mea, et macula non est in te*' ('thou art all fair, my love, and there is no spot in thee'), the latter having been identified with the immaculate conception since the twelfth century, remained the most frequent resorts, if one judges by the scriptural citation index of Pedro de Alva y Astorga's compendium of Immaculist references, the *Militia Immaculatae Conceptionis*, which listed 113 citations of Luke 1.28, 84 of Songs 4.7 and 27 of Genesis 3.15 ('And I will put enmity between thee and the woman'). Psalm 45.5 ('The holy place of the tabernacles of the most high') came fourth with 16 citations.[34]

The frustrating silences of Scripture could tempt divines into ingenious exegetical strategies. In a volume of 21 sermons on the Marian feasts, one seventeenth-century Spanish Augustinian wondered why the Gospel genealogies of Christ made no mention of Mary's parents: a surprising omission, given that Scripture usually publicized the names of those favoured by God. The friar's explanation was that although Anne and Joachim engendered the Virgin, they did not engender her in their own 'fallen' likeness. God made Mary so perfect, so like himself, that he was more worthy to be called her father than her own natural parents. The light, the dawn, that God created on the first day was a portrait (*un dibujo*) of the pure conception of Mary. The evangelist therefore wrote '*Iacob autem genuit Ioseph*', but did not want to apply the word *genuit* to Mary. From this highly spiritualized reading the conclusion was clear: the very silence of Scripture proved that Mary's creation was unique and was thus in itself testimony to her immaculate conception.[35]

Immaculism was far from being the exclusive preoccupation of learned theologians, but had broader cultural and political resonance. The heartland of the seventeenth-century Immaculist campaign was the Iberian peninsula, and if the initial impetus came from the religious orders, and the Franciscans in particular, it was also intimately associated with the Spanish monarchs.[36] This was an old alliance, which had flagged somewhat in the sixteenth century but revived in the seventeenth, the 'century of Immaculist struggles', as one later Spanish historian dubbed it, under Philip III, Philip IV and Charles II.[37] A prelude was provided by the strange affair of

---

34. de Alva y Astorga 1663, Index Three.
35. de San José 1651: 3–5.
36. For an authoritative survey of Spanish Immaculism, see Pérez SJ 1995, *passim*.
37. See, for example, Fernández OFM 1955: 619–866; and Vázquez OFM 1957. The extensive literature on this subject is brilliantly summarized in Stratton 1994.

the 'Lead Books' of the 'Sacro Monte' in Granada, a case of pious fraud perpetrated in the 1590s. Accompanied by Solomonic seals, a number of mysterious Arabic texts were unearthed which purported to substantiate a lively pre-Moorish Christian history for Granada and an apostolic witness for the immaculate conception. Although dismissed by most contemporary scholars, their authenticity was vociferously proclaimed by the archbishop, Pedro de Castro Vaca y Quiñones, who was soon translated to Seville, and the affair served to reignite the local Conceptionist debate.[38] Immaculists looked for ways to circumvent the papal Bull and promote broader acceptance of the doctrine which would make a formal papal definition easier, while the Dominicans continued to oppose it. Attempted censures merely inflamed things further and the sharpest clashes occurred in Seville, Pedro de Castro's new see. Backed by the Franciscans, in 1613 the archbishop and chapter organized a series of public demonstrations to mobilize popular opinion behind the Immaculist cause. The processions were complete with their own slogan ('Mary conceived without original sin!'), banners and a *copla* composed for the occasion by Miguel Cid:

> Everyone in general
> In a clamorous cry, elect Queen,
> Claims that you are conceived
> Without original sin.[39]

These in turn were greeted by satirical verses sung by the opposition, accusing the archbishop of intimidating the Dominican order into silence, of 'muzzling the black-and-white dog', as one of them put it. The entire city seems to have been caught up in the frenzy: one friar reported that Seville's 'mulattoes' celebrated a fiesta in honour of the immaculate conception, the 'Negroes' celebrated two, and the 'Moors' had wanted to celebrate one but were denied permission. The archbishop authorized another procession in 1615, allegedly supported by 40,000 people. It was from Seville too in these years that the calls were first heard for the establishment of what would become a series of *reales juntas*, royal commissions of prelates and theologians who collated Immaculist evidence in support of extraordinary embassies to Rome to secure papal definition of the dogma. These embassies had mixed fortunes and, while enjoying the unalloyed support of Philip III and then Philip IV, they exposed the weakened ability of the Spanish monarchy to influence a papacy which was simultaneously lobbied by France to postpone a definition.[40]

In fact, fortunes tended to swing with the proclivities of particular popes. Paul V, though sympathetic to the cause, did not wish to detract from the authority of the Council of Trent by re-opening a matter which it had discussed. However, he did issue a decretal prohibiting public defence of the Dominican doctrine of sanctification. Gregory XV went so far as to forbid even private assertions that the

---

38. Medina 1996: 5–57; Harris 1999: 945–66.
39. Pérez SJ 1995: 17.
40. Stratton 1994: 72ff. On the Sevillian 'moment', see Bonnefoy OFM 1955: 7–33.

Virgin was conceived in sin. Urban VIII (1623–44) was less willing to accede to Spanish pressure, on Immaculism or anything else. However, in 1624 he authorized the Franciscan establishment of a military order dedicated to the immaculate conception. The Franciscans had moreover been busy establishing Immaculist confraternities and popularizing the so-called 'blood vow', an oath to give their lives in defence of the doctrine. The feast of the Immaculate Conception was adopted throughout the Spanish monarchy, while one after another Spanish cities and universities swore themselves formally to the Virgin under this avocation.[41] These instances of political Marianism were connected to the diplomatic and military situation, which saw rebellions on the imperial periphery and setbacks reaching a nadir in 1643 with the siege of Lerida and the defeat of the Army of Flanders at Rocroi. Urban VIII's parting shot, as he lay dying in 1644, was to allow an Inquisitorial decretal prohibiting use of the word 'immaculate' to describe Mary's conception, but permitting references to the conception of 'Mary Immaculate'. When news of the development reached Seville in 1645, the prohibited words were belligerently posted everywhere and the cathedral defiantly exhibited a canvas of the Virgin by Murillo under the legend 'conceived without sin'.[42] Little was achieved under Innocent X, despite the direct personal appeals of Philip IV, as in a letter dated 17 August 1649:

> Holy Father,
> Having resolved to send the Duke of Infantado as my extraordinary ambassador to Your Holiness and commissioning him to conduct the affairs of his office for the greater good of the Church and the peace of Christendom, I have instructed him, having kissed Your Beatitude's feet in my name, to request a private audience with Your Holiness to give you a letter and to represent to you the keenness with which I desire to render Our Lord and His Blessed Mother a service which I consider most agreeable, particularly at a time when the Catholic faith needs support, to give her all the due exaltation and lustre which her children should desire. To achieve this, my devotion urges Your Holiness to recall my hand-written letter of 23 February 1645, and what was said by the Admiral of Castile and the Count of Siruela, my ambassadors, in begging Your Beatitude to define as a matter of faith the mystery of the Immaculate Conception of Our Lady, the Virgin Mary. And although they have not returned to remind Your Holiness of this, this is not because I have forgotten that cause (which I have always before my eyes), but because of the difficulties, agitation and wars throughout my kingdoms. However, I recognise that the best way of speedily leaving these problems behind which are so damaging for the Holy See is to do this service to the Blessed Virgin. So again I throw myself at the feet of Your Beatitude and beseech you in the strongest possible terms that, since this is in your hands, do not delay the definition any longer. May Your Holiness at the very least begin to deal with it, for there is no

41. Gomez OFM 1955: 867–1045.
42. Stratton 1994: 101.

work accomplished which does not have a beginning and many things at first appear unachievable which when one begins to deal with them are not. Your Beatitude must not be hindered by the current state of the world, as I hope that if Your Holiness begins such a glorious affair, Our Lord will show you the way and smooth out any difficulties ... Most Holy Father, if we are to see this definition, let your Beatitude not delay; gain the fame of performing this service for Our Lord and His Blessed Mother. Do not leave it for your successors to do. May Your Holiness be the one who, in this way, exalts the Catholic faith which we profess. Give some repose to Christendom which has suffered for so many years. Gain from Our Lord a lasting peace to avoid such an effusion of the blood of Christians, and give all us devotees of His Blessed Mother the consolation, which I hold to be infallible, that we will achieve such holy and just ends, if Your Holiness defines this mystery as faith.[43]

Immaculist hopes rose again with the election of Alexander VII in 1655. The following year Philip IV wrote some 50 letters to religious communities and prelates asking them to plead with the Pope for a more permanent solution to the problem. The emphasis in the resulting letters was often less on theological proof than on the widespread nature of the belief, which is interesting in that official rhetoric for once ascribed a role to the common laity, anticipating Pius IX's later appeal to the *sensus fidelium*. 'And what can we say to this?' asked the Bishop of Lerida, 'That all err? That all are deceived? And that God permits it? We can say that the voice of God, which is the voice of the people, cries aloud that His mother was conceived without sin.'[44] Alexander VII's Bull *Sollicitudo* of 1661 renewed the Immaculist decretals of his predecessors, emphasizing both the antiquity of the belief and the fact that there were now few Catholics who did not profess it.[45] The last Habsburg king of Spain, Charles II, contrived to extract from Innocent XII the Bull *In excelsa* of 1696, which made the feast of the Immaculate Conception obligatory throughout the Church as a 'second-class double' solemnity with octave.[46] The final clinch of a dogmatic definition, however, remained elusive.

These oscillations of papal approval or disfavour, alongside local spats, explain the chronology and the scale of the publication of Conceptionist literature.[47] The aforementioned Minim friar, Pedro de Alva y Astorga (c. 1602–67), for example, produced an enormous corpus of work in the mid-century to back the Franciscan campaign to mobilize support for the *reales juntas*. This involved republishing older texts as well as bringing out the *Militia Immaculatae Conceptionis*, the compendium of Immaculist sources which he offered as a 'militia against malice ... a host of nearly six thousand soldiers which, although an army, wields only pens'. Against these 6,000

---

43. Pérez SJ 1995: 147–8.
44. Stratton 1994: 103; see also Abad 1953: 25–63, text cited: 55.
45. Gutiérrez SJ 1955: 13–480.
46. Vázquez 1957: 119–32.
47. The chronology and scale of Spanish Franciscan literature on the subject may be gleaned from the following annotated bibliography: Uribe OFM 1955: 201–495.

paladins the anti-Immaculists could, he claimed, produce only six writers.[48] Admittedly, his definition of authorities was generous, including even Martin Luther, whom he remembered to qualify as '*haeresiarcha damnatus*'. Citing Luther's early Marian texts, the friar concluded: 'one may say that this worst of heretics, when he was a Catholic, had a pious opinion; but then he apostasised from the faith and changed his opinion, and therefore in other places taught the opposite.' The early Luther was used to condemn the later.[49]

Hispanic pre-eminence in Immaculist devotion was a status which the monarchy's apologists relished. In 1616, for example, the Jesuit Pedro de Ojeda enlisted Old Testament prophecy to account for southern Spain's Immaculist vanguardism, specifically Psalm 45.12 ('And the daughter of Tyre shall be there with a gift, Even the rich among the people shall entreat thy favour'). He first established that other verses of the psalm contained Immaculist references. Myrrh, aloes and cassia signified preservation from and cleansing of original and actual sin, the particular Hebrew word used for 'gold' indicated the finest, uncontaminated form of the precious metal, the robes and jewels must be Mary's: 'I do not know what other convincing reason can be given than that the reference to the generation and conception of gold without alloy or dregs was placed here to signify that the jewels and robe pertain solely to her who was engendered and conceived without the dregs of original sin.'[50] The Jesuit then affirmed that the 'daughter of Tyre' was the group of settlements founded by ancient Tyre, the greatest of which could be found now in Spain:

> What difficulty can there be in a legitimate understanding that this prophecy refers to the devotion of Spain to the Blessed Virgin, and especially the mystery of her Immaculate Conception, which has been signalled from the time of St James the Apostle until the present? It is proven. What else can this daughter of Tyre, so dazzling in devotion to the Mother of God and her Immaculate Conception, be? Must we seek her in Thebes? Is she Carthage or Tunis? None of these daughters of Tyre can compete with Spain in this respect and in some of them we will find scarcely any memory of Our Lady. And has Spain been so obscure a part of the Christian Church that we are not worthy for a prophet to accord us his piety or deem us a worthy subject of his prophecy?[51]

Modern scholarship might find the question of why Spain should have been at the forefront of the seventeenth-century Immaculist drive harder to answer. The obsessions of individuals such as Pedro de Castro combined with the political imperatives of the Spanish Habsburgs, but also with the distinctive social relations of southern Spain in particular, where ethnic tensions between 'Old' and 'New' Christians (the latter converted Jews and Moors and their descendants) figured sharply. The linguistic convergence between *limpieza de sangre* (purity of blood), the

---

48. de Alva y Astorga 1663, Preface. On the author, see Eguiluz OFM 1955: 497–594.
49. de Alva y Astorga 1663, Column 1016.
50. de Ojeda SJ 1616: 36v.
51. Ibid.: 38v.

term which notoriously encapsulated Old Christian anxieties about identity, and the use of the adjective *limpia* ('pure') by many seventeenth-century authors to describe the immaculate conception, is striking. Was Immaculism, the cult of the spotless, blonde, fair-skinned Virgin, a way of refining what could so easily become invisible boundaries between Old and New Christians, landing a further blow against Spain's beleaguered *converso* and *morisco* populations (the latter diasporized since the Granada revolt and forcibly expelled by Philip III in 1609)? The 'Lead Books' of Granada point to a desire to expunge the Moorish centuries from collective memory, and the ongoing struggles with Islam in the Mediterranean provided a constant reminder of the threat and a warning not to drop one's guard.[52] Seville, the teeming commercial metropolis of the Spanish empire (the 'Great Babylon', as Góngora called it), felt most acutely the tensions between the various communities. Perhaps, though, Immaculism could serve as a unifying as well as excluding force, symbolically forging an imagined community. Immaculist celebrations by confraternities representing Seville's minority populations have been noted. One can find literary clues too. In Lope de Vega's Immaculist sacred comedy, *Spotless Purity* (*La Limpieza no manchada*), commissioned by the university of Salamanca to celebrate the vow which it had made to defend the immaculate conception, we meet the figures of Germany, France and Spain, who all boast of their Marian festivals. But the play ends with India and Ethiopia presenting dancers from their respective lands, while the rest kneel before an altar of the *Inmaculada*.[53]

It was, though, not Andalucia but the Castilian–Aragonese border which produced the boldest, and, for those inclined to accept the veracity of private revelations, the most authoritative Immaculist statement of the seventeenth century. Penned by a Franciscan Conceptionist nun, Sor María de Jesús (Maria Coronel, 1602–65), in the town of Agreda, the *Mystical City of God* purported to be a life of Mary as revealed by the Virgin herself to Sor María in regular visions over many years.[54] To many Immaculists it was an infallible witness to their favourite doctrine and when it appeared posthumously, in 1670, it came as timely vindication. Sor María is known today in the Hispanic world in part for her career as confidante and unofficial spiritual adviser to Philip IV and for her alleged miraculous bilocations to the New World. However, her reputation mainly rests on the text of her Marian biography. Although investigated by the Holy Office, the nun of Agreda managed to charm her inquisitors and was handled by them lightly, but her book had a more chequered career, slipping on and off the Index, although stubbornly popular: by

---

52.   A Spanish newsbook of 1624 associated fear of Islam with Immaculism in recounting the prodigy of a monstrous fish caught in a German river. 'The main thing about this fish', it declared, 'was that it was unknown until it was caught, just as the Muslims are secret until they creep up on us and strike us. Therefore we need to unite in resistance under the Pope, the Emperor and the Catholic King of Spain, represented by the monster's three crowns; the two crosses in its central crown signify our first line of defense, the ancient Order of St John and the modern Order of the Immaculate Conception'; Bibliotheca Nacional de España, Mss / 2355: 516r–517v.

53.   de Vega, ed. Pelayo 1965: 153–92.

54.   The extensive literature on Sor María de Agreda is best approached through Colahan 1994. See also Colahan 1999: 155–70.

1700 it had gone through 20 editions and by 1740 at least another 37, including translations into Greek and Arabic. The 'Mystical City' of the title was the Virgin herself and the work was both an encomium of her unique place in the economy of salvation and a loving portrait of this most perfect of creatures, a being of supreme intellectual as well as spiritual accomplishment. In Sor María's account, the Virgin performed numerous miracles alongside Christ, governed the Church after his death and by vicarious participation in her son's Passion became humanity's Co-Redemptrix. All her graces and privileges stemmed from her immaculate conception, a point maintained so vigorously and pervasively in the book that Immaculism has been described as its 'paramount doctrine'.[55] The dynamic interuterine life of Mary was depicted expansively by Sor María. 'I see', she wrote of the Virgin's embryonic residence within St Anne, 'the true Ark of the Covenant, fashioned, decorated and placed in the temple of a sterile mother ... I see the altar of the Holy of Holies, where the first sacrifice is offered ... and the making of a new Earth and a new Heaven, being the first the womb of a humble woman, attended by the Blessed Trinity and innumerable courtiers of the old Heaven, with a thousand angels assigned to guard the treasure of this tiny body.'[56]

The great Spanish Immaculist campaign of the seventeenth century, surely one of the most notable examples of systematic lobbying in the history of the Church, failed to gain papal definition of the dogma, although in promoting its favoured devotion with such vigour and imagination and by forcing Rome incrementally to concede such privileges as a universal solemnity it undeniably achieved a partial success. Moreover, the emphasis in Sor María and other writers not just on the beauty, purity and maternal tenderness of the Virgin, but also on her wisdom, knowledge, intellectual ability and practical accomplishment, shows once again the rich possibilities of the Virgin as symbol, one not so easily confined to patriarchal stereotypes as might have been predicted. The keenness of so much of the Immaculist discourse of the seventeenth century to delineate with exactitude the bodily circumstances as well as the spiritual significance of the Virgin's conception, to evoke what St Bernard had called the 'prerogatives of the flesh', underlined the varied and at times even contradictory trajectories of Marian devotion in the Baroque.

CONCLUSION

In the eighteenth century confessional tensions were gradually replaced by the challenges of Enlightenment. In the case of Sor Maria's *Mystical City*, vigorous promotion by its supporters and the enthusiasm of its extensive readership were confronted by formal censure of the work from the Sorbonne in 1696, a systematic rubbishing by the Bavarian Augustinian philosopher and theologian Eusebius Amort (1692–1777), and the dismissal of the nun of Agreda's canonization cause by Pope

---

55. Colahan 1994: 160.
56. de Jesús de Agreda, ed. Solaguren 1970: 102.

Benedict XIV.[57] If belief in Immaculism itself was now so entrenched throughout the Catholic world as to be unassailable, the very strategies which had helped to make it so had lost much of their rationale and lay open to critique. The noted Italian scholar Ludovico Antonio Muratori (1672–1750), for example, attacked the 'blood vow' as imprudent, culpable and inspired by an unenlightened piety: it was not licit, he argued, to expose one's life for an opinion, rather than for a declared dogma.[58] In general the cult of the Virgin was affected by a tendency in elite circles to demand a more interiorized and spiritualized faith and to distance 'respectable' religion from the 'superstitious' excesses of popular piety. The French missioner and ardent devotee of the Virgin, Louis-Marie Grignion de Montfort (1673–1716), advocated a purified and 'true', if nonetheless 'tender' and practical, Marian devotion, which was above all Christocentric and summed up by the watchwords 'Glory to Jesus in Mary! Glory to Mary in Jesus! Glory to God alone!'[59] This is not to argue that the effusiveness of Baroque Marianism was expunged, or that it did not continue to receive embellishment. Perhaps the best-known and best-loved Catholic spiritual writer of the eighteenth century, Alphonsus de Liguori (1696–1787), in his *The Glories of Mary* (1750), highlighted the role of the Virgin in the economy of salvation and her constant intercession for the faithful. He also showed more favour to popular Marian devotion, even defending the blood vow on the grounds that, *pace* Muratori, the consensus of the faithful and the existence of a solemnity meant the immaculate conception was more than a mere 'opinion'.[60]

The eighteenth century therefore preserved many of the Mariological features which had developed in the Counter-Reformation. Inevitably, there was much continuity with the Middle Ages, but in the course of the sixteenth and seventeenth centuries the medieval inheritance was partially reshaped in distinctive ways, above all through a focus on the spiritual motherhood of Mary and on her egregious purity, as underscored in the doctrine of her immaculate conception. This in turn provided fertile ground for the resurgence of choreographed popular devotion and post-revolutionary political Marianism in the industrial age. As ever, the semiotically rich figure of Mary eluded neat classification, but in the texts of early modern Mariologists powerfully evoked tensions between the spiritual and the fleshly, the universal and the local, the transcendent and the immanent.

---

57. Johnson 2004: 259–70.
58. de Fiores and Meo (eds) 1988: 914.
59. de Montfort, trans. Cortinovis 2000: 182.
60. de Ligouri 1989, Part II, First Discourse: 358–9.

BIBLIOGRAPHY

Primary Sources

Manuscript
Bibliotheca Nacional de España, Mss / 2355.

Printed
de Alva y Astorga, Pedro (1663) *Militia Immaculatae Conceptionis Virginis Mariae contra malitiam originalis infecationis Peccati*, Louvain.
Balbín, Bohuslav (1730) *Vita S. Joannis Nepomuceni sigilli sacramentalis Protomartyris*, Augsburg.
Canisius, Peter (1577) *De Maria virgine incomparabili*, Ingolstadt.
de la Cruz SJ, Francisco (1655) *Jardin de Maria. O practica de devociones varias con la beatissima Virgen*, Salamanca.
Gumppenberg SJ, William (1657) *Atlas Marianus, sive de imaginibus Deiparae per orbem christianum miraculosis*, Ingolstadt.
Gumppenberg SJ, William (1655) *Idea Atlantis Mariani*, Trent.
de Jesús de Agreda, Sor María (1970) *Mística Ciudad de Dios. Vida de Maria*, ed. Celestino Solaguren, Madrid: Fareso.
de Jesús María OCD, José (1652) *Historia de la Vida y Exelencias de la Virgen Maria Nuestra Señora*, Antwerp.
de Ligouri, Alfonso (1989) *Le Glorie di Maria*, Verona: Editrice Bettinelli.
de Montfort, Louis-Marie Grignion (2000) *Trattato della vera devozione a Maria*, Italian edn, trans. Battista Cortinovis, Rome: Città Nuova Editrice.
de Ojeda SJ, Pedro (1616) *Informacion Eclesiastica en defensa de la limpia Concepcion de la Madre de Dios*, Cuenca.
Rader SJ, Mattheus (1615–28) *Bavaria sancta et pia*, Munich.
de Sales, Francis, de Chantal, Jane, trans. P. M. Thibert (1988) *Letters of Spiritual Direction*, VHM, New York: Paulist Press.
de San José, Pedro (1651) *Glorias de María Santissima en sermones duplicados para todas sus festividades*, Alcalá.

Secondary Sources

Abad, C. María (1953) 'Preparando una embajada concepcionista en el año 1656. Estudio sobre cartas inéditas al rey Don Felipe IV y al papa Alejandro VII', *Miscelánea Comillas* 20.
Albrecht, Dieter (1998) *Maximilian I. von Bayern 1573–1651*, Munich: Oldenbourg.
Bailey, Gauvin Alexander (1999) *Art on the Jesuit Missions in Asia and Latin America, 1542–1773*, Toronto: University of Toronto.
Bonnefoy OFM, Juan-Fr. (1955) 'Sevilla por la Inmaculada en 1614–1617', *Archivo Ibero-Americano*, época 2, 15: 7–33.
Boss, Sarah Jane (2000) *Empress and Handmaid: On Nature and Gender in the Cult of the Virgin Mary*, London: Cassell.
Brading, D. A. (2001) *Mexican Phoenix. Our Lady of Guadalupe: Image and Tradition across Five Centuries*, Cambridge: Cambridge University Press.
Chaline, Olivier (1999) *La bataille de la Montagne Blanche: un mystique chez le guerriers*, Paris: Noesis.
Châtellier, Louis (1989) *The Europe of the Devout. The Catholic Reformation and the Formation of a New Society*, Cambridge: Cambridge University Press.
Christian, William A. (1981a) *Local Religion in Sixteenth-Century Spain*, Princeton, NJ: Princeton University Press.
Christian, William A. (1981b) *Apparitions in Late Medieval and Renaissance Spain*, Princeton, NJ: Princeton University Press.

Colahan, Clark (1994) *The Visions of Sor María de Agreda. Writing Knowledge and Power*, Tucson, AL, and London: University of Arizona Press.

Colahan, Clark (1999) 'María de Jesús de Agreda: the Sweetheart of the Holy Office', in Mary E. Giles (ed.), *Women in the Inquisition. Spain and the New World*, Baltimore, MD, and London: John Hopkins University Press: 155–70.

Coreth, Anna (1959) *Pietas Austriaca. Ursprung und Entwicklung barocker Frömmigkeit in Österreich*, Munich: Oldenbourg.

Duerloo, Luc and Wingens, Marc (2002) *Scherpenheuvel. Het Jeruzalem van de Lage Landen*, Leuven: ?.

Eguiluz OFM, Antonio (1955) 'El P. Alva y Astorga y sus escritos inmaculistas', *Archivo Ibero-Americano*, época 2, 15: 497–594.

Ellington, Donna Spivey (2001) *From Sacred Body to Angelic Soul: Understanding Mary in Late Medieval and Early Modern Europe*, Washington: The Catholic University of America Press.

Fernández OFM, Juan Meseguer (1955) 'La Real Junta de la Inmaculada Concepción (1616–1817/20)', *Archivo Ibero-Americano*, época 2, 15: 619–866.

de Fiores, Stefano and Gambero, Luigi (eds) (2003) *Testi Mariani del Secondo Millenio*, vol. V, *Autori moderni dell'Occidente, Secoli XVI–XVII*, Rome: Città Nuova Editrice.

de Fiores, Stefano and Meo, Slavatore (eds) (1988) *Nuevo Diccionario de Mariología*, Spanish edn, Madrid: Ediciones Paulinas.

Forster, Marc R. (2001) *Catholic Revival in the Age of the Baroque. Religious Identity in Southwest Germany, 1550–1750*, Cambridge: Cambridge University Press.

Freedberg, David (1989) *The Power of Images: Studies in the History and Theory of Response*, Chicago, IL, and London: University of Chicago Press.

Giesberts, A. (1925) 'De Heilige Petrus Canisius als Marioloog', *Historisch Tijdschrift* 4: 109–36.

Gomez OFM, Odilo (1955) 'Juramentos concepcionistas de las Universidades españolas en el siglo XVII', *Archivo Ibero-Americano*, época 2, 15: 867–1045.

Göttler, Christine (1996) *Die Kunst des Fegefeuers nach der Reformation. Kirchliche Schenkungen, Ablaß und Almosen in Antwerpen und Bologna um 1600*, Mainz: Von Zabern.

Gutiérrez SJ, Constancio (1955) 'España por el Dogma de la Inmaculada. La embajada a Roma de 1659 y la Bula "Sollicitudo" de Alejandro VII', *Miscelánea Comillas* 24: 13–480.

Harris, A. Katie (1999) 'Forging History: The *Plomos* of the Sacromonte of Granada in Francisco Bermúdez de Pedraza's *Historia Eclesiastica*', *The Sixteenth Century Journal*, 30: 945–66.

Heal, Bridget (2004) 'Marian Devotion and Confessional Identity in Sixteenth-Century Germany', in Swanson (ed.), *The Church and Mary*: 218–27.

Johnson, Trevor (2002a) 'Holy Dynasts and Sacred Soil: Politics and Sanctity in Matthaeus Rader's *Bavaria Sancta* (1615–1628)', in Sofia Boesch Gaijano and Raimondo Michetti (eds), *Europa sacra. Raccolte agiografiche e identità politiche in Europa far Medioevo ed Età moderna*, Rome: Carocci: 83–100.

Johnson, Trevor (2002b) '"Victoria a Deo missa?" Living Saints on the Battlefields of the Central European Counter Reformation', in Jürgen Beyer, Albrecht Burkardt, Fred van Lieburg and Marc Wingens (eds), *Confessional Sanctity (c. 1500 – c. 1800)*, Mainz: Von Zabern: 319–35.

Johnson, Trevor (2004) '"That in her the seed of the serpent may have no part": the Agredan visions and the Immaculate Conception of the Virgin in early modern Spain and Germany', in Swanson (ed.), *The Church and Mary*: 259–70.

Luebke, David M. (1997) 'Naïve Monarchism and Marian Veneration in Early Modern Germany', *Past and Present* 154, February: 71–106.

MacCulloch, Diarmaid (2004) 'Mary and Sixteenth-Century Protestants', in Swanson (ed.), *The Church and Mary*: 191–217.

Medina, Francisco Martínez (1996) 'El Sacromonte de Granada y los Discursos Inmaculistas Postridentinos', *Archivo Teológico Granadino* 59: 5–57.

Pérez SJ, Nazario (1995) *Historia Mariana de España*, vol. II, 2nd edn, Toledo: Kadmos.

Preston, Patrick (2004) 'Cardinal Cajetan and Fra Ambrosius Catharinus in the Controversy over the Immaculate Conception of the Virgin in Italy, 1515–51', in Swanson (ed.), *The Church and Mary*: 181–90.

Scaramella, Pierroberto (1991) *Le Madonne del Purgatorio. Iconografia e religione in Campania tra rinascimento e controriforma*, Genoa: Marietti.

Soergel, Philip (1993) *Wondrous in His Saints: Counter-Reformation Propaganda in Bavaria*, Berkeley, CA, London: University of California Press.

Starr-LeBeau, Gretchen D. (2002) ' "The Joyous History of Devotion and Memory of the Grandeur of Spain": The Spanish Virgin of Guadalupe and Religious and Political Memory', *Archive for Reformation History / Archiv für Reformationsgeschichte* 93: 192–216.

Stratton, Suzanne L. (1994) *The Immaculate Conception in Spanish Art*, Cambridge: Cambridge University Press.

Swanson, R. N. (ed.) (2004) *The Church and Mary*, Studies in Church History 39, Woodbridge: Boydell Press.

Tappolet, W. and Ebneter, A. (1962) *Das Marienlob der Reformatoren*, Tübingen: Katzmann.

Uribe OFM, Angel (1955) 'La Inmaculada en la literatura franciscano-española', *Archivo Ibero-Americano*, época 2, 15: 201–495.

Vázquez OFM, Isaac (1957) *Las Negociaciones Inmaculistas en la Curia Romana durante el Reinado de Carlos II de España (1665–1700)*, Madrid: no publ.

de Vega, Lope (1965) *La Limpieza no manchada*, ed. Marcelino Menendez Pelayo, Bibliotheca de Autores Españoles, 187, Madrid: Cervantes.

Webster, Susan Verdi (1998) *Art and Ritual in Golden-Age Spain: Sevillian Confraternities and the Processional Sculpture of Holy Week*, Princeton, NJ: Princeton University Press.

Woeckel, Gerhard P. (1992) *Pietas bavarica: Wallfahrt, Prozession und Ex-Voto-Gabe im Haus Wittelsbach*, Weissenhorn: Anton H. Konrad Verlag.

17

TELLING THE BEADS: THE PRACTICE AND SYMBOLISM OF THE ROSARY

SARAH JANE BOSS

FOUNDATIONS

There are some activities which are so widespread among human cultures that one might almost describe them as 'natural' to the human condition. Praying or meditating with beads may be one such activity. The very word 'bead' is cognate with the German *gebet*, meaning 'prayer', and the English word 'bid', which still has religious connations in the phrase 'bidding prayers'. Thus we can see that beads and prayers are connected to one another from antiquity. Buddhists, Muslims and Catholics across the world meditate with strings of beads, and Orthodox Christians use knotted ropes.[1] The 'worry beads' that Greeks put around their wrists probably have their origin in a similar practice;[2] and the New Age 'power beads' that are sold in the form of bracelets because of the special properties that are supposed to be inherent in the stones from which they are made evidently have an explicitly spiritual function.

In the British Museum there is a string of beads from the Aigina Treasure – Cretan work from about 1,700 to 1,500 years before Christ – in which each bead is carved or moulded in the form of a woman's breast with a hand around it.[3] The identification label displayed next to the beads includes the observation that fertility goddesses in the ancient Near East were often shown holding one breast,[4] and that the beads probably had a religious function. In other words, it looks as though they formed a rosary. The beads are made of carnelian, lapis lazuli and gold, which is to say that their colours are red, blue and gold – the same colours that in the Middle Ages came to be associated with Our Lady, in whose honour the Catholic rosary is dedicated. And – as we shall see below – the motif of the nursing breast is likewise one with strong rosarian associations.

The most widely used modern Catholic rosary consists of meditation upon a circle,

---

1. A brief overview of bead meditation in several religious traditions is given in Henry and Marriott 2002.
2. Wilkins 1969: 57.
3. BM Catalogue: Jewellery 756A. The beads are usually on display.
4. A line drawing of a Cretan seal (*c.* 1500 bce) which shows, among other figures, a woman holding her breast, can be found in Jones and Pennick 1997: 7. The interpretation of the image is disputed.

or *chaplet*, of 50 beads, divided into five groups of ten, or *decades*, with a separating bead between each decade and its neighbour. The meditator passes the beads through the fingers, saying the prayer 'Hail Mary' on each bead of each decade, and beginning each decade by reciting the 'Our Father' on the previous separating bead, and finishing the decade by reciting the 'Glory be' on the bead following. For each decade there is a different subject of meditation, or *mystery*. These are divided into three groups of five, so it takes one round of the rosary to complete one set of mysteries.

The mysteries are as follows. The Joyful Mysteries: the Annunciation, the Visitation, Christ's Nativity, the Presentation in the Temple, and the Finding in the Temple; the Sorrowful Mysteries: the Agony in the Garden, the Scourging at the Pillar, the Crowning with Thorns, the Carrying of the Cross, and the Crucifixion; the Glorious Mysteries: the Resurrection, the Ascension, the Descent of the Holy Spirit at Pentecost, the Assumption of the Virgin, and the Coronation of the Virgin in Heaven. A 'complete' set of rosary beads includes 15 decades with their separating beads, but the shorter form is more commonly used, and is often used for reciting only one set of mysteries at a time.

Pope John Paul II (in the Apostolic Letter *Rosarium Virginis Mariae*) promoted the use of an additional set of mysteries, the Mysteries of Light. These are concerned with Christ's earthly ministry, and are placed between the Joyful and Sorrowful mysteries. They are: the Baptism in the Jordan, the Wedding Feast at Cana, the Proclamation of the Kingdom, the Transfiguration, and the Institution of the Eucharist.

Most rosaries have a pendant of additional beads with a cross or crucifix attached, and there are a various traditions as to what prayers are recited on these and why, although the Apostles' Creed is almost always included.

At this point, the puzzled enquirer may ask, 'What is the point of repeating the same prayer over and over again?' Is it to gain the merit that accrues to each recitation? Well, partly. Is it to help keep one's mind on holy subjects and to stop it from wandering? Yes: that is quite an important function. But most of all, perhaps, the repetition of a prayer over and over again is a technique for lulling the mind into a meditative state in which – to put the thing in Christian terms – it may become attentive to the movement of the Holy Spirit. The more it is used, the easier it becomes to slip into a meditative state. The habitual use of the rosary can turn it into something to which the meditator has recourse at times of panic or other distress. It makes the reassurance of God's presence close at hand: the trust that the meditator is grounded in the divine may be summoned by the movement of a hand or the silent recitation of simple words.

The repetition of the rosary, especially when recited by a group of people, may be compared to the repetition of a sea shanty. The recurrent pattern of verse and response induces a sense of being caught up in the flow of something greater, and thus liberates the meditator to throw him- or herself completely into the task. It is probably the case that the two most ancient forms of song are those used for ritual and those used for work.[5] If the sea shanty retains an ancient manner of working, then the rosary retains a correspondingly ancient manner of praying.

---

5.   A consideration of shanties, and a briefer consideration of ritual songs, is given in Lloyd 1975.

Repetitive incantation is common to the use of prayer beads in all the traditions that employ them. What is more unusual about the Catholic rosary is the practice, which grew up in the Middle Ages and endures to the present, of using the beads to meditate upon a variety of different topics or 'mysteries' in sequence. The grouping together of a number of related topics under a single heading has been a popular religious practice retained until recent times in, for example, English folksong. It acts as a mnemonic device, that is, helping one call to mind sacred mysteries or other points for meditation or devotion. Thus there are the well-known Seven Sorrows of Our Lady – a devotion particularly promoted by the Servite order. The so-called 'dolour rosary' consists of seven groups of seven beads to assist in meditation upon the seven sorrows. Our Lady's Joys have been variously enumerated; one English song recounts ten, and another tells of seven. A common number is five, although these are by no means always the five which are familiar in the modern rosary. One song lists them as the Annunciation, the Nativity, the Crucifixion, the Harrowing of Hell, and the Ascension.[6] It is most interesting that the Crucifixion is included in a list of Our Lady's Joys: it always occurs, of course, in lists of her Sorrows, but its inclusion in the list of Joys reflects the fuller understanding that the mystery of the cross is a paradox. For the instrument of death is simultaneously the instrument of life and salvation, and to see the Crucifixion as one of Our Lady's Joys invites the devotee to meditate upon this central Christian mystery at a much deeper level than that of the human drama.

EARLY CATHOLIC BEADS

The rosary in its current form is a relatively modern invention, having evolved over many centuries. It is likely that Christians from early times counted their prayers by moving pebbles from one pile to another, and subsequently by pulling beads or knots along a string or by turning a prayer wheel a spoke at a time. The devout Lady Godiva, Queen of Mercia, founded the women's monastery of Our Lady at Coventry (the name 'Coventry' is derived from 'convent', after the monastery), and when she died in 1041, in her will she left a string of beads, on which she used to keep a tally of her prayers, to be hung upon the neck of the image of Our Lady.[7] However, the evidence does not indicate that praying with beads was associated especially strongly with Marian devotion; rather, beads were used for prayers of several kinds.

In monasteries, monks and nuns chanted the 150 psalms, and lay brothers and sisters, who were not bound by the obligation to do this, may have said 150 *Pater nosters* instead. By having 150 beads to pass through their fingers, they would have been easily able to keep count of the number of prayers they had said. Here again, it does not seem that the pattern of reciting 150 prayers on 150 beads was anything like

---

6. Manuscript and published references to these and others are given in Dearmer, Vaughan Williams and Shaw (eds) 1964: 157. The full words and melody are given of a seven-joy version: 156–7.
7. Recorded in William of Malmesbury's *Gesta pontificum Anglorum* of 1123. Quoted at length in Waterton 1879, under the catalogue entry for Coventry. Brief quotation in Wilkins 1969: 25.

a universal practice for several hundred years. Beads were strung together in lines as well as circles, and the number could vary quite widely. In London, the streets around St Paul's Cathedral bearing the names Ave Maria Lane, Creed Lane and Pater Noster Row are the streets where the bead-makers lived and worked. The names indicate that the prayers used for bead meditation in the Middle Ages were largely those that are still in use today, but they would not always have been used in the same sequence. For example, the 'Our Father', or *Pater Noster*, has given rise to the English word 'patter', after the sound of the practice of constantly repeating the prayer.

A popular Catholic legend recounts the origin of the rosary as follows. In the twelfth century in southern France there was a group of Christians known as Cathars (or Albigenses, after the town of Albi), who did not subscribe to the teachings of the Catholic Church, but believed that the material creation was evil and taught a world-denying doctrine of the necessity for retreat into a purely spiritual realm. St Dominic tried by his preaching to convert them to Catholicism, but failed. In the year 1214, after much fasting and prayer, and when he was on the point of losing hope, Dominic received a vision of the Blessed Virgin escorted by three queens and 50 maidens. The Virgin gave him the rosary, explaining to him the prayers that were to be said and the mysteries which the devotee should meditate upon when passing the beads through the fingers. The rosary would convert the heretics to the love of Christ in human flesh. The Virgin also pressed milk from her breast, which Dominic drank.[8]

We shall return later to the origins of this legend; for the present, let us attend to the symbolism of the milk pressed from the breast.

The Virgin's milk signifies the real humanity of Christ. His humanity was given by his mother, and her milk fed his dependent human body. In medieval iconography, Mary's bare breast often has connotations of mercy, and these connotations are directly related to the doctrine of the incarnation. It is because the eternal Word of God took human flesh and understands our weaknesses that Christians can trust that he will show mercy to sinful humanity: indeed, he was so much one of us that he even depended upon a mother's milk for his survival. So Mary's breast is the reminder of Christ's humanity and vulnerability, and hence of Christ's mercy. Her breast is sometimes compared in art and literature to the wound in the side of Christ, since both show his human weakness and both point to his pity for the world. Or again, it was because Mary gave Christ his humanity (symbolized by the breast) that he was able to die for the world's salvation (symbolized by the wound). The mysteries of the rosary are centrally concerned with the incarnation, and it is therefore fitting that the motif of Mary's milk should appear in the legend of the rosary's supernatural origin.

St Dominic is not the only saint of whom such a legend is recounted. Most famously, it is St Bernard – noted for his Marian homilies and great devotion to Our Lady – who received from the Virgin's breast drops of milk upon his lips. Roland Bermann, a contemporary French writer on esoteric subjects, suggests that the symbol of the Virgin's milk falling upon St Bernard's lips stands for the mercy of God (made of the Virgin's own substance) falling upon that part of his body with which he

---

8.   Wilkins 1969: 37–8.

speaks, indicating that he is called to transmit (by preaching) the grace that he has received.[9] This interpretation would perhaps be even more appropriate to St Dominic, since he founded the Order of Preachers and in the legend of the rosary is being called to preach this particular form of devotion. Moreover, since the rosary is a devotion conducted not only with the fingers but also with the mouth, or at least the lips, there is the implication that the prayers of the rosary are themselves like drops of the Virgin's milk in their spiritual purity and their capacity to nourish the life of Christ within the devotee.

Yet the image of a nursing breast gains its symbolic power because it evokes a profound emotional reaction. It has often reminded men and women of their dependence upon their own mothers and upon the whole material world that nourishes us, as we transform it into our very selves and participate in it through labour and pleasure – the same world, of course, which can fail to provide us with that nourishment and pleasure.[10] Perhaps the pagan goddess whose breast is represented in the Aigina Treasure personified that world and its divine power. The Blessed Virgin and the mysteries of the rosary point the devotee to the Creator God who makes and sanctifies both the human race and all that sustains or destroys it.

The colours of red, blue and gold – the colours of the Cretan beads – are found on a number of ancient Mediterranean images that seem to be representations of goddesses.[11] When applied to the Virgin Mary in the Middle Ages, people attributed the colours with symbolic meanings. In thirteenth-century Spain, King Alphonsus X ('the Learned') of Castile, or one of his court musicians, wrote a song retelling the story of a monk who illuminated the name of Mary in three colours.[12] Gold, traditionally associated with royalty, was appropriate to the Virgin because it was 'rich, harmonious, noble and very precious'; blue, traditionally symbolic of heaven and of purity, 'resembles the heavens which show her splendours'; and the third colour, vermillion, is also called 'rose', a flower which, as we shall see below, has often been associated with Mary. But since gold may be represented – in heraldry, for example – by yellow, it is surely the case that what we have here are the primary colours: the three colours which underlie all the colours of creation, as well as white and black. The nursing breast, the primary colours and the beads themselves: all are things which are primitive and fundamental to the human condition as something both physical and social. And it is precisely in operating at that most primitive and universal level that the rosary leads the devotee into intimacy with the divine.

---

9.   Bermann 1993: 80–1.
10.   See Boss 2000: 33–79 and references.
11.   These too can be seen in the British Museum, e.g. an enthroned figure from Athens (*c.* 500 BC), catalogue number BM.1966.3-28.19.
12.   Many of the *cantigas* of Alfonso el Sabio are now available on recordings. This *cantiga* is no. 384, and has been recorded by Esther Lamandier, on the album *Alfonso el Sabio: Cantigas de Santa Maria*, on the Astrée label.

THE MODERN ROSARY

Although precedents survive from the beginning of the fourteenth century, it was during the fifteenth century that the rosary became established in the form in which it is most widely used today.[13] Even the prayer the 'Hail Mary' was not used in its modern form until that time, having previously consisted only of the scriptural greetings: 'Hail Mary, full of grace, the Lord is with thee. Blessed art thou among women, and blessed is the fruit of thy womb.' The name most strongly associated with the establishment and promotion of the modern rosary, that is, the sequence of 150 'Hail Mary' beads, with 15 intervening 'Our Fathers', and the corresponding pattern of three joyful, three sorrowful and three glorious mysteries for meditation, is that of the Dominican Alan de la Roche (Alanus de Rupe, 1428–74). It is from him that we first learn the story of Our Lady giving the rosary to St Dominic, and it may be that Alan wrote the story of the Virgin's milk in imitation of the similar story concerning St Bernard. Unfortunately, another point of dubious historical accuracy concerns the conversion of the Albigensians, since this came about not so much through the preaching of the friars as through military force. Yet Alan had struck a winner: through the promotion of the Dominicans, and later of the Jesuits, the modern rosary became hugely popular and quickly supplanted other techniques of bead meditation in the Catholic world.

At a later date, the rosary was associated with another conflict – also partly religious in character. In 1571, the extraordinary victory of European Christians over Ottoman Turks at the battle of Lepanto[14] was attributed by Catholics to the power of the rosary, since large numbers of people had recited rosaries through the streets of Rome, in petition for the success of the European fleet, before the battle was fought.[15] The feast of Our Lady of the Rosary is celebrated on the anniversary of the battle, 7 October.

An image that is sometimes found in church wall-painting of the late Middle Ages is that which art historians term the *Marian psychostasis*. This shows St Michael holding the balances in which souls are weighed for their good and evil deeds on the Day of Judgement. In one pan of the scales is a soul being weighed, and around the other pan there are devils trying to pull it down. If the soul weighs more heavily, then that indicates that it is righteous, and therefore will be saved. But if the soul is sinful, then the devils will pull down their scale-pan and the soul will be damned. The Virgin Mary, however, is throwing weights, or, more often, a string of rosary beads, into the pan on the soul's side, thereby ensuring the soul's salvation.[16] Thus the Virgin's intercession is associated directly with the rosary, and images of this kind may well have been promoted by rosary confraternities – associations of lay people who met to pray the rosary, and in particular to pray for the faithful departed.[17]

---

13. Winston-Allen 1997: 15–17.
14. See Constam 2003.
15. Miller 2001: 28–9; Graef 1985, 2: 17.
16. A discussion of the evolution of this iconography, together with a list of extant examples, can be found in Oakes 2000: 11–36. See also the Marian miracle from Herolt's collection, in this volume: 202.
17. The evolution of these confraternities is discussed in detail in Winston-Allen 1997.

Perhaps the popularity of the modern rosary derives in part from the particular sequence of the mysteries. The first five concern a woman who gives birth for the salvation of the world; the second five concern a man, the son whom she has borne, who dies for the salvation of the world; and the third group concerns the reunion of the man and the woman in the accomplishment of that salvation. The balancing of man and woman and of birth and death, together with the reuniting of the man and the woman in their transcendence of birth and death, is a satisfying pattern.

Yet even since the general establishment of the modern rosary, people have explored other ways of using the beads – a sign that the tradition has remained vibrant. Francis Borgia, for example, the third general of the Society of Jesus, in 1613 wrote a set of meditations that begins with recollection of one's sins, and then moves on to meditation on the immaculate conception, before continuing with other mysteries of the lives of Our Lady and Our Lord.[18]

Another variation in rosary meditation is that promoted by devotees of Our Lady of Fatima. This variation consists in the addition of the prayer 'O my Jesus' after the 'Glory be' at the end of each decade.[19] Indeed, promotion of the rosary has come to be a mainstay of the devotions associated with modern Marian apparitions, and Medjugorje prayer groups, for example, make it an important feature of their meetings, again adding a distinctive touch of their own, in this case by reciting the prayers very slowly in order to allow more time for meditation.

Dolour rosaries, rosary rings (to wear on the finger) and bracelets, and strings of ten *Pater Noster* beads are again becoming more widely available, which suggests that bead meditation is currently alive and well.

NUMBER SYMBOLISM

Numbers tend to acquire a certain significance of their own. The modern rosary has three sets of mysteries – three being the number of the Blessed Trinity – and five mysteries in each set – five being noted supremely as the number of Our Lord's precious wounds, although it is also a 'natural' number in the sense that it is the number of fingers on a human hand. In the fourteenth-century poem *Sir Gawain and the Green Knight*, Sir Gawain is solemnly equipped to set out on his mission to meet the Green Knight in the Green Chapel at New Year.[20] On his shield is painted a gold pentacle on a red ground. The pentacle is the five-pointed star made of a single continuous line. The author explains the symbolism of the pentacle at some length. It was devised by King Solomon and is called 'the endless knot'. This should certainly be read not just as a description of its physical appearance, but as indicating that it is a symbol of eternity – that which has no point of beginning or end: and one might

---

18.   Borgia 1620.
19.   The prayer is usually recited in the form: 'O my Jesus, forgive us our sins, save us from the fires of Hell and lead all souls to Heaven, especially those most in need of thy mercy.' An account of the apparitions and development of the cult of Our Lady of Fatima, including the giving of this prayer, can be found in Johnston 1980.
20.   *Sir Gawain and the Green Knight*, trans. Stone 1974, ll. 619–69: 44–6.

understand the ring of rosary beads in a similar manner. Among the several points signified by the five points of the pentacle, the author of the medieval poem mentions Gawain's trust in the five wounds of Christ and the five Joys of Our Lady, both of which occur in different ways in rosary meditation. The image of Our Lady is painted on the inside of Gawain's shield, so that he might look upon it to give him heart. This constant reminder or evocation of Mary's presence again has a certain correspondence to the repetition of the 'Hail Mary' in rosary recitation.

THE ROSE

The symbol of the rose is another aspect of bead meditation that has been handed down from the Middle Ages. The Tibetan rosary is called a *mala*, which means 'garland', and likewise, the word 'rosary' means 'rose garland' or 'rose garden'. The nursery rhyme 'Ring-a-ring-a-roses' may have its ancestry in a song about the rosary.[21] The rose is a very rich symbol, and doubtless its full significance can be grasped only through meditation rather than explanation. The following, therefore, are merely pointers for further reflection.

When you look at a rose window, such as that in Durham Cathedral or in the Gothic cathedrals of France, you see layers and layers of stained-glass petals radiating around a central image. If you start at the outermost lights, you will usually find saints represented in these petals, and the closer you come to the centre, the holier – the closer to the Lord – are the saints or angels represented in the successive layers. When you come to the centre, there is usually an image of Christ or of the Virgin and Child. In the East Rose of Laon Cathedral, the central image is of the Virgin and Child enthroned, with the Virgin holding up a rose in her right hand. When the Virgin in Majesty holds a flower in her right hand, this is usually taken to be a rod of Jesse (Isa. 11.1), understood typologically: she herself is the shoot, and Christ is the flower. Yet when we look through the layers of rose petals and come at the heart of the flower to the Virgin and Child raising a rose to our gaze, we might sense that something even more mysterious is at work here. It is as though the rose that she holds up to the viewer is an initiatory or revelatory symbol, which they will comprehend only when they have attained a sufficient degree of spiritual maturity and understanding.

In Catholic tradition, Mary herself is the Mystic Rose *par excellence*. She is the noblest flower at whose centre is contained the most precious jewel in the universe, Christ himself. As it says in the English carol:

> There is no rose of such virtue
> As is the rose that bare Jesu.
> *Alleluia.*
> For in that rose contained was
> Heaven and earth in little space:
> Res miranda.

---

21. Wilkins 1969: 81.

Because the Blessed Virgin received the Word of God in her womb, because she was the rose who bore God at the very centre of her being, it is possible for each human person to receive that Word and be transformed by it, and so come to recognize God at the heart of all created things. This is the work which rosary meditation is designed to help the meditator accomplish.

TECHNIQUES

The number of different prayers used in the standard Catholic rosary, together with the number of different subjects for meditation, mean that, whatever method is used, it is an exceptionally complicated technique. There are some people who prefer to repeat one prayer only and to focus on one subject for meditation. This subject may be one of the standard mysteries, or some other scriptural or sacred scene, or it may be more akin to that striving towards God which is described most famously in the *Cloud of Unknowing*. An individual devotee may try different forms of meditation to discover what is most helpful.

Some of the early books of rosary meditations consist of a series of pictures of the mysteries, with the intention that the reader look at the image while passing the beads through the fingers and reciting the prayers. For many people, this is probably a very helpful means of meditation, and in the 1940s Maisie Ward produced a book containing a sequence of prints of paintings by Fra Angelico for this purpose.[22] But rosarians can compile their own collection of favourite images for meditation.

Another method of rosary meditation is to imagine the scene and the drama of each mystery in detail. This is helpful for those who have the kind of visual imagination that can conjure up such a 'stage set', and many Ignatian meditators will fall into this category. For others, it is more helpful to focus on a single image, word or sensation which draws them into the particular mystery.

Of course, even among devout Catholics with a great devotion to the Virgin Mary, there are those for whom bead meditation has little to offer. Having said this, one should not ignore the fact that, for most people, to become at all expert in the technique of rosary meditation demands a good deal of practice. It is like learning a new language or cultivating a new friendship: you really have to devote time and effort to it.

THE BEADS

And what about the beads themselves? Some people feel drawn to beads that are very simple – perhaps made of wood. Others like beads that sparkle or look precious (or, indeed, really are precious!). One can find beads carved or moulded in the shape of stylized roses, or made from crushed rose petals which retain their scent. Traditionally, you should not buy your own rosary, but should be given it or find it. For the devout person, a rosary is not only a lovely thing to receive, but also to give.

---

22. M. Ward 1946.

When the Cretan craftsmen of 3000 BC made their beads of precious stones and gold, those who used the beads must have understood that the beauty of the material world gave them an inkling of heaven. And so it remains with the modern rosary and its mysteries.

BIBLIOGRAPHY

Primary Sources

von Balthasar, Hans Urs (1982) *The Threefold Garland*, trans. Erasmo Leiva-Merikakis, San Francisco, CA: Ignatius Press.

Borgia, Francis (1620) 'Pious Meditations on the Beades: For detestation of Synne; obtayning of Christian Perfection; and dayly Memory of the Life, and Passion of Christ our Sauiour', included in *The Practise of Christian Workes*, written in Spanish and Englished by a Father of the Society of Jesus.

Dearmer, Percy, Vaughan Williams, R. and Shaw, Martin (eds) (1964) *The Oxford Book of Carols*, Oxford: Oxford University Press.

Sir Gawain and the Green Knight, trans. Brian Stone (1974), Harmondsworth: Penguin.

Vail, Anne (1997) *The Rosary: A Way into Prayer*, with wood engravings by David Jones, Norwich: Canterbury Press.

Ward, J. Neville (1985) *Five for Sorrow, Ten for Joy*, London: Darton, Longman & Todd.

Ward, Maisie (1946) *The Splendour of the Rosary*, London: Sheed and Ward.

Waterton, Edmund (1879) *Pietas Mariana Britannica: a history of English devotion to the Blessed Virgin Marye with a catalogue of shrines*, London: St Joseph's Catholic Library.

Secondary Sources

Bermann, Roland (1993) *La Vierge Noire: vierge initiatique*, Paris: Dervy.

Boss, Sarah Jane (2000) *Empress and Handmaid: On Nature and Gender in the Cult of the Virgin Mary*, London: Cassell.

Constam, Angus (2003) *Lepanto 1571: The greatest naval battle of the Renaissance* (Campaign 114), Oxford: Osprey Publishing.

Graef, Hilda (1985) *Mary: A History of Doctrine and Devotion*, combined edn, London: Sheed & Ward.

Henry, Gray and Marriott, Susannah (2002) *Beads of Faith*, London: Carroll and Brown.

Johnston, Francis (1980) *Fatima: The Great Sign*, Chulmleigh, Devon: Augustine Publishing Co.

Jones, Prudence and Pennick, Nigel (1997) *A History of Pagan Europe*, London and New York: Routledge.

Lloyd, A. L. (1975) *Folk Song in England*, London: Paladin.

Miller, John D. (2001) *Beads and Prayers: The Rosary in History and Devotion*, London: Burns & Oates.

Oakes, Catherine (2000) 'The Scales: An iconographic motif of justice, redemption and intercession', in *Maria: A Journal of Marian Studies* 1, August: 11–36.

Thurston, Herbert (1900) 'Our Popular Devotions: II. The Rosary', *The Month* 96: 403–18, 513–27, 620–37.

Thurston, Herbert (1901) 'Our Popular Devotions: II. The Rosary', *The Month* 97: 67–9, 172–88, 286–304.

Wilkins, Eithne (1969) *The Rose-Garden Game: The Symbolic Background to the European Prayer-Beads*, London: Victor Gollancz.

Winston-Allen, Anne (1997) *Stories of the Rose*, University Park, PA: Pennsylvania State University Press.

18

MARY: IMAGES AND OBJECTS

SIMON COLEMAN

Like the figure of the honoured and life-giving cross, the revered and holy images, whether painted or made of mosaic or of other suitable material, are to be exposed in the holy churches of God, on sacred instruments and vestments, on walls and panels, in houses and by public ways; these are the images of our Lord, God and Saviour, Jesus Christ, and of Our Lady without blemish, the holy God-bearer, and of the revered angels and of any of the saintly holy men. The more frequently they are seen in representational art, the more are those who see them drawn to remember and long for those who serve as models, and to pay these images the tribute of salutation and respectful veneration. Certainly this is not the full adoration in accordance with our faith, which is properly paid only to the divine nature, but it resembles that given to the figure of the honoured and life-giving cross, and also to the holy books of the gospels and to other sacred cult objects. Further, people are drawn to honour these images with the offering of incense and lights, as was piously established by ancient custom. Indeed, the honour paid to an image traverses it, reaching the model; and he who venerates the image, venerates the person represented in that image.[1]

These words are taken from a famous if ancient decree, that of the Council of Nicaea held in 787. While the decree explains how to honour the divine through art, it also sounds a sombre note of caution: images are to be venerated and honoured but not adored, since the latter action is suitable for 'divine nature' alone. Such a combination of latitude and restraint was perhaps well suited to a century that had seen numerous campaigns to eradicate the use of images of the holy. At the same time, the decree contains a shrewd version of an inchoate sociology of worship in its assertion that people will be 'drawn' to images and will retain the models they depict in their memory of, and desire for, the divine.

I start this chapter with the Council of Nicaea not only because of its historical significance for the Christian Church, but also because its decree contains in microcosm so many of the recurring aspirations and anxieties associated with the materialization of the divine in the Christian Church. In particular, we see an early formulation of the key question of how image relates to person: does the honour paid

---

1. *Decrees of the Ecumenical Councils*, Tanner and Aberigo (eds) 1990, vol. 1: 135–6.

to an image reach the holy figure represented by that image? Whether or not that is the case, are not material image and the divine being conflated in ways that might seem highly dangerous? And yet, do such dangers justify the proscription of an activity that seems to be so ubiquitous a dimension of human relations with sacred figures? Of course, such worries have biblical precedents. The Old Testament was deeply concerned with the perils of giving adulation to objects produced by human hand, and early Christians suffered martyrdom in expressing their opposition to the worship of Greek and Roman idols.[2]

These questions will reverberate throughout the coming pages. My focus is on how the Virgin Mary, mentioned in the Nicaean decree alongside (though subsequent to) Christ, has indeed acted as an aesthetic as well as a religious inspiration for the Christian Church, even if she has been understood and represented in different ways. While it is easy to see attitudes to the materialization of Mary in stark, binary terms – involving either violent opposition or committed support to the very idea of images – I hope to show how specific historical and contemporary cases provide a much more nuanced and interesting 'picture' of Marian aesthetics.

In making my case, I shall draw on some, though inevitably no more than a fraction, of the best work that has been produced on this topic within the disciplines of anthropology, art history, history and religious studies.[3] Although I do not include long quotations from such works, I draw extensively from them in order to bring out the flavour of their approaches as fully as possible. For the most part, I have chosen to structure the chapter thematically rather than temporally, picking out what I think are some of the more significant ways of thinking about the relationship between material culture and religious practice relating to Mary. However, in order to contextualize my arguments, in the next section I provide a summary of some of the Church's theological attitudes to images, objects and Marianism throughout history.

MATERIALIZING THE SACRED

The anthropologist Jill Dubisch points out that the 'culture' of Mary has not been a constant, even in traditions favourably disposed towards her, such as Catholicism and forms of Orthodoxy.[4] She was not especially prominent in very early Christianity, but the first major impetus towards Marian devotion may have come as the Church gained in respectability with the support of the Emperor Constantine, at the beginning of the fourth century. In 431, the Council of Ephesus referred to Mary as *Theotokos* ('Bearer of God'), and Pope Sixtus III subsequently built the Basilica of Santa Maria Maggiore in Rome, containing a celebrated mosaic of the Annunciation and the Epiphany. In the next century the first relics and miraculous icons of Mary began to appear, with paintings rather than sculptures predominating at first.

Two key points must immediately be borne in mind as we examine such a process

2. Brading 2001: 13.
3. My own disciplinary specialization is anthropology.
4. Dubisch 1995: 233ff.

of consolidating and materializing representations of Mary. First, that – unlike the saints and martyrs – she left no obvious bodily relics on earth. After all, both Orthodox and Catholic believers accepted (albeit in different ways) that Mary had ascended to heaven after her death.[5] Second, that Mary as Mother and 'Bearer of God' nonetheless acted as mediator between the earthly and the divine. Dubisch notes that the cult of Mary developed particular importance in Constantinople, perhaps because the city was believed to possess a number of relics of Mary that had been acquired in the fifth century, including her robe, girdle, shroud, and the swaddling clothes in which Christ rested against her breast.[6] Indeed, such relics took on political significance as they received increasing ceremonial attention in the sixth century, and by 626 an icon of Mary was being carried in procession around the city walls to defend them (successfully, as it happens) against attack. As images appeared and were replicated, so their reputation as workers of miracles was magnified, either on the personal level – typically involving healing – or as protectors of whole communities.

Mary proved a fertile catalyst for artistic representation in part because she evoked a variety of powerful associations. For instance, to her role as *Mediatrix* could be added that of the *Mater Dolorosa*, the sorrowful Mother, a common portrayal in the high Middle Ages. As Pelikan notes, what the poetry of the Middle Ages in both West and East was describing in its verses, the visual arts also portrayed, in effect acting as books for the unlettered.[7] At times, art could be used to express theological points in striking visual terms. Medieval Catholicism often used the idea of the body of Mary to represent the body of the Church, and this idea was illustrated in the genre of the *vierge ouverte* – the 'opening virgin', a statue of Mary that opened to reveal Christ or a church within.[8] At a different level of aesthetic accomplishment, Michelangelo's *Pietà*, produced in the final years of the fifteenth century, captured the depth of the Virgin's grief as she held the broken body of her crucified Son: significantly, however, she was shown not as an older woman, broken in body, but as a young mourner who, because of her unique position as the Virgin full of grace, had not been subject to the ravages of age.[9]

Of course, the veneration of the Virgin needs also to be placed in the context of a rich Christian culture of conjoining the material and the miraculous, with many of the faithful continuing to believe that God could effect healing through saints' bones or such items as *brandea*, cloths that had been in touch with such relics. Yet material culture was also used to express theology in the starkest possible terms at the time of the Reformation. In England, for instance, iconoclasm became an increasing feature of the religious debates of the 1520s, and by 1538 pilgrimage itself – an activity centrally associated with the veneration of major sites and images – was outlawed.[10]

---

5.   This conviction was finally declared a dogma by Pope Pius XII in 1950.
6.   Dubisch 1995: 237.
7.   Pelikan 1996: 128.
8.   Dubisch 1995: 234.
9.   Pelikan 1996: 128.
10. Duffy 1992: 407.

Sixteenth-century Protestant assertions of the omnipresence of the divine led to a rejection of the idea of 'confining' the sacred in material form, and thus were aimed at the veneration of saints' relics and the material cult of the Virgin.[11]

In turn, the Catholic response used the language of materiality to make its point. The Council of Trent in the middle of the sixteenth century reaffirmed the legitimacy of the veneration of holy images, even if its confirmation was accompanied by a warning against superstition and a demand for careful regulation by bishops of all cults of images and relics.[12] Dubisch also argues that the cult of Mary took on a significant role in the Counter-Reformation: in re-exalting the Marian ideal of the mother placed at the centre of the household, the Church appealed not only to women but also to men, attempting to reorientate the latter away from the external and dangerous areas of politics.[13]

While the conflicts between Protestant and Catholic understandings of locating the sacred would continue, and indeed still rage today, it is notable that the supposed age of secularization in the West – from the nineteenth century onwards – saw an increase rather than a decrease in the ascription of miracles to Mary and the creation of visual forms associated with her veneration. As Dubisch remarks, the cult of Mary has increased rather than diminished in southern Europe over the past century or more, even if within the Orthodox tradition independent Marian apparitions are less common than in Catholicism.[14] In the modern era, it seems that apparitions of Mary have not only acted to convey political messages in opposition to the enemies of faith – reaffirming the immaculate conception in the case of Lourdes, or anti-communism at Fatima – but have also worked in concert with the physical production of new pilgrimage sites, whose reach is increasingly trans-national in scope.

We shall revisit many of these points later in this chapter. For the time being, it is worth reflecting upon some of the recurring themes in the materialization of Mary, evident through the many cultural and temporal shifts of the past two millennia. Firstly, we might consider the recurrent issue of divine 'presence' in the image. The early bishop St Basil the Great (329–79) made the influential remark that 'the honour given to the image is transferred to its prototype', and we saw a similar sentiment in the decree from the Council of Nicaea; but the ambiguity remains. The art historian David Freedberg tells a personal anecdote that illustrates the point.[15] In the French town of Rocamadour, there is a much venerated statue of the Virgin that has attracted pilgrims since the Middle Ages. Freedberg notes how a colleague of his visited the site, full of expectation, and was deeply disappointed to encounter what she felt was an apparently insignificant and rather ugly little sculpture. She exclaimed, 'After so long a journey, all I saw was a small ugly Madonna, with a supercilious look on her face. I was so angry with her!' For Freedberg, what is significant about this reaction lies in the final words: not angry with *it*, but with *her*. Even in her complaint,

---

11. Nolan and Nolan 1989: 337.
12. Brading 2001: 30.
13. Dubisch 1995: 235.
14. Ibid.: 238ff.
15. Freedberg 1989: 28ff.

uttered more than one and a half millennia after St Basil's remark, Freedberg's colleague raises the issue of how image relates to prototype. A variant on a similar issue is at stake in an anecdote from a medieval text.[16] In the *Miracles of Our Lady of Chartres* we read of a lady of Audignecourt who is cured of a skin disease by praying to the Virgin. When she sets off for Notre-Dame de Soissons to give thanks, the Virgin appears in a vision to inform her that it was by Notre-Dame de Chartres that she was healed. Here we see how the prototype (the vision of the Virgin) extols the particularity of a single image and a specific place, perhaps indicating the politics of competing sites as much as theological concern over 'presence'.

As our second recurring theme, we might consider the problem of how to bridge the human and the divine worlds in aesthetic as well as material terms. More specifically, how can we assert that an object made by a mere mortal can point us towards the transcendent? In fact, the Church has come up with numerous ingenious means to deal with this issue. One is the phenomenon of so-called 'acheiropoietic' images, ones supposedly not made by human hands.[17] An example of such an image is that of the Virgin of Guadalupe, discussed below, which was supposedly impressed miraculously onto cloth. An alternative route towards the sacralization of production, much invoked in the Middle Ages, was the idea that holy images were carved or painted by St Luke himself.

Third, there is the key issue of multiplication. If an image is powerful, we can be sure that it will spawn numerous copies in a variety of media, diffusing the sacred power either through similarity of design or, alternatively, through having touched the original object. Again, Freedberg provides a powerful illustration of the point in his discussion of a picture that illustrates within itself the very process of replication.[18] Michael Ostendorfer's print of 1519–20 shows the pilgrimage to, and adoration of, the *Schöne Maria* of Regensberg. The picture actually contains a total of four representations of the miraculous figure: the original image located deep in the church; a statue in the foreground; a further version on the huge banner suspended from the tower; and another on the pennant fluttering by the side of the church. It is as if secondary images not only partake of the power of the original (albeit perhaps in diluted form), but also increase its significance through their very replication.

Each of these themes – and there could have been many more – illustrate what Morgan sees as a key aspect of sacred images: their ability to encourage interaction with believers, who may wash, dress, address and study them, incorporating them into their emotional lives and reducing the aesthetic distance between object and believer.[19] Morgan describes how many people in recent years have visited the St George Orthodox Antiochan Church in Cicero, Illinois, to venerate Our Miraculous Lady of Cicero, an icon of the Mother and Child that has been weeping since Easter 1994.[20] The devout are described as genuflecting, praying and lighting

---

16. Ibid.: 120.
17. Ibid.: 110.
18. Ibid.: 103–4.
19. Morgan 1998: 50.
20. Ibid.: 54.

candles before the image of Mary, offering her flowers and money and speaking to her, or gazing intently at the eyes and tears of the weeping Mother. On the one hand, as Morgan points out, we see how this is a 'presence' characterized by change, by a constant exchange between image and humans. Yet one might add that it recalls themes and practices that have had deep resonances within Christian worship since the beginning of the faith itself.

MARY AS MULTI-VOCAL SYMBOL

We have already examined some of the different imagery associated with Mary – she can be conceptualized and represented as young girl, as mediator between heaven and earth, as sorrowful mother, and so on. In social-scientific terms, we might therefore describe her as a powerful symbol that is able to sustain a range of referents within the same form. Thus the famous anthropologist of religion (and convert to Catholicism) Victor Turner argued that symbols acted to 'condense' and bring together different but linked meanings.[21] In the process they sometimes embody what seem at times to be contradictory ideas, ranging from the concrete to the abstract, the emotional to the cognitive. In a famous example, Turner examines how the *mudyi* tree is used in the rituals of the Ndembu of Zambia. The tree exudes a white latex if its bark is scratched, and Turner argues that, according to ritual context, the tree is associated with anything from breast milk to the tracing of descent through women to the very unity of Ndembu society as a whole.

What, we might ask, does this have to do with the materialization of Mary in images and other objects? The objective is to see how, even within a single cultural context, Mary as image and symbol can represent religious and social ideals in complex and multi-layered ways. To illustrate the point, let us examine some specific case studies.

Symbolizing the Nation: Eric Wolf and the Virgin of Guadalupe

In a famous study carried out some 50 years ago, the anthropologist Eric Wolf focused on the Virgin of Guadalupe, patron saint of Mexico.[22] He argued that, as idea and as material form, the Virgin enshrines the major hopes and aspirations of an entire society. According to the origin myth of the image and its shrine at Tepeyac, located in the environs of what is now Mexico City, Mary appeared to Juan Diego, a Christianized Indian of commoner status, and addressed him in the local language, Nahuatl. The encounter took place on a hill in 1531, ten years after the Spanish conquest. In pre-Hispanic times, the location had housed a temple to the earth and a fertility goddess who, like the Virgin of Guadalupe, was associated with the moon. The Virgin commanded Juan Diego to tell the Archbishop of Mexico that she wanted a church to be built in her honour on the hill. When Juan Diego unfolded his cloak before the Archbishop, the image of the Virgin Mary was miraculously stamped on it. The stunned cleric immediately ordered a shrine to be built. The shrine has

21. Turner 1967.
22. Wolf 1958.

been rebuilt several times since, and above the central altar hangs Diego's cloak with the miraculous image.

We shall return to the miraculous origins and history of the image later. For the time being, we need to consider Wolf's argument that the Virgin forms part of the past and present of Mexican culture (at least at the time of his writing). Indeed, during the Mexican War of Independence against Spain, her image preceded the insurgents into battle (an echo here of the seventh-century inhabitants of Constantinople). Zapata and his agrarian rebels also fought under her emblem in the Great Revolution of 1910. Today, her image adorns house fronts and interiors, churches and altars at home, bullrings, taxis, and so on. The shrine at Tepeyac is visited each year by hundreds of thousands of pilgrims, ranging from inhabitants of far-off Indian villages to members of socialist trade unions.

How, then, does the Virgin represent a whole nation? We need to remember that a nation is not like a football team or a single family – it cannot be contained within a small space and viewed in its entirety. Moreover, in common with all complex societies, nations must act as social umbrellas for different groups to pursue their various interests within a roughly co-ordinated framework. Thus the Virgin as national symbol works well, according to Wolf, because she condenses and juxtaposes a wide set of social relations connected with different levels of social grouping. To rural Indians, the image of the Virgin is addressed passionately as the source of warmth and love, and beer drunk on ceremonial occasions is associated with her milk (there are shades here of the *mudyi* tree). For non-Indian Mexicans, in Wolf's account, she is again associated with motherhood, but this time in the context of adult male dominance in the family: she is often associated with rebellion against the father.

More broadly, the Virgin appears to embody major political and religious aspirations. The Spanish conquest signified not only political defeat for Mexico, but also defeat of the old gods and the decline of old rituals. Thus the appearance to an Indian commoner might be taken to represent, at least at a symbolic level, a return to faith in former traditions alongside an acknowledgement that an 'Indian' as much as a 'Spaniard' is capable of being saved.

So the Virgin is seen by Wolf as a dominant symbol, encapsulating physical as well as abstract ideas associated with motherhood, food, hope, health, life, salvation and removal from oppression. There is even the sense of Mexico as a New Israel, with the Virgin from Spain finding a new paradise in Mexico. Wolf sees the Virgin as a way of talking about Mexico, a collective representation of the whole society, and his account is a useful way of considering the 'multi-vocality' of Mary in a given national context. Admittedly, one of the questions it raises is the extent to which symbols always appear to act in unifying ways, and this is an issue we shall examine in a later section. For the time being, I want to continue to explore the idea of Mary as material object that comes to be identified with a specific locality and community. However, my next case study presents a rather more dynamic, changing picture than that provided by Wolf.

An Image in Transition: Robert Orsi and the Madonna of 115th Street

The historian Robert Orsi, in common with Wolf, presents a study of the relationship between the Virgin and her faithful, though in this case the faithful do not comprise a whole country, but rather a community of immigrants, caught between nations. Orsi focuses on the annual *festa* particularly associated with the Madonna of Mount Carmel on East 115th Street in New York between 1880 and 1950, and on the devotion to the Madonna that flourished among Italian immigrants and their American-born children.[23] The *festa* and its procession took place on 16 July each year, in an urban context (Harlem) where Italians competed with members of other ethnic groups – Jews, Irish, Germans – over the physical and cultural borders of local neighbourhoods.

Orsi's fundamental point (writing not as a theologian, but as a social-scientifically aware historian) is that it is not possible to appreciate the significance of the Madonna without understanding the community surrounding her: 'The Madonna ... was ... of the community, unintelligible apart from it and independent of any single member of the community, each of whom was forced to confront her ... as a reality in his or her life.'[24] The story of the devotion began in the summer of 1881, when immigrants from the town of Polla in Salerno formed a mutual aid society in New York named after the Madonna del Carmine.[25] The members of the new society decided to organize a *festa* in honour of their patroness, and this celebration grew larger and larger over the years until it was taken over by the Catholic church on 115th Street. At the centre of the celebration was a lifelike representation of a young Mediterranean peasant woman holding a small child. The statue resembled those found in towns of southern Italy and was in fact obtained from the old country. Indeed, for Orsi *festas* it became the most obvious declaration of what was unique about Italian Catholicism, while bringing together Italians who in their home country might have been rather more conscious of their different regional identities. At one level, processions came to express a kind of community physicality as the Madonna was taken out into the streets – parks, alleyways, traffic – to bless the local area, as the exploration of an ecology of devotion led to the sacralization of Italian Harlem. More generally, the community could be seen as re-establishing a sense of its place in relation to tradition. Orsi notes, for instance, that honouring the Virgin became a way for the younger generation, born in America, to participate in a central event associated with their parents' histories – and to experience a part of Harlem that temporarily gave access to the sense world of southern Italy as it filled with the pungent aromas of sausage, peppers and incense.[26]

Orsi's account also contains an analysis of how attitudes to the Virgin of 115th

---

23.   Orsi 1985.

24.   Ibid.: xxii. Of course, many different forms of Catholicism existed in turn-of-the-century America, and to some of the Catholic clergy and to other lay Catholics, Italian immigrant Catholicism seemed almost like a new religion – almost pagan in some of its practices.

25.   Ibid.: 51ff. Devotion to the Madonna del Carmine had a venerable history in southern Italy, but in America celebration of the Virgin was transformed in significant ways, taking on meanings associated with the new encounters and experiences of the faithful.

26.   Ibid.: 165ff.

Street could be seen as an index of changes in the community itself. The Madonna took a prominent place in the local church just as Italian immigrants and their children were beginning to take control of the political and social life in their part of Harlem. Furthermore, the Virgin came to symbolize community members' wishes for social and economic mobility. Just as people always decorated the Madonna in a manner just beyond their means, so she served to express their hopes for themselves in America. Ironically, the ideas behind such devotion were also those that came to weaken the power of the Virgin in Italian Harlem. After the Second World War the community itself disappeared from the area and the intimate connections between the Madonna and the location were snapped: 'The holy, which had been localized, no longer has a place, a community, and so its power seems broken – it can be listened to on the radio.'[27]

FROM MULTI-VOCALITY TO CONTESTATION

These case studies from Mexico and New York appear to take us far from the question of the connection between 'image' and 'prototype'. But in fact the old ambiguity is still there, if we consider that, in both cases, communities are attempting to 'localize' Mary, to appropriate her imagery and clothe it with specific cultural garb. Of course, it might be argued that such a process is not only inevitable, it is also necessary, since for any image – religious or otherwise – to have resonance in people's lives it must be seen to connect with the specificities of particular societies and cultures. Indeed, a central characteristic of the Virgin as universal symbol might be precisely her ability to take on multiple local guises.

Such multiplicity can act as a suitable symbolic umbrella for differing interests, but it can also lead to social and religious conflict. For instance, competition can occur even among believers who accept the same fundamental attitudes towards Marian imagery. Freedberg tells the story of St Thomas More hearing a conversation between pilgrims: one says, 'Of all Our Ladies, I love best Our Lady of Walsingham'; the other replies, 'And I, Our Lady of Ipswich.'[28] Debates between the particular and the generic, often translated into contradictions between 'popular' and 'official' views, have also often resulted in conflicts around the connections between theology and aesthetics. Ruth Behar writes of a priest in the Cantabrian foothills of Spain burning the wooden image of a saint, to the horror of one of his parishioners.[29] The priest, in the light of reforms introduced by Vatican II in the 1960s, considered the image to be of no artistic merit, and moreover regarded his parishioners as investing too much religiosity in external images – in empty forms.

Here, I want to focus on a different kind of conflict, though it is again one rooted in the materiality of images. I think it is worth exploring the ways in which different images of Mary can be opposed – historically, ideologically, aesthetically – in quite systematic ways. The example I shall give takes us back to Mexico.

---

27. Ibid.: 72.
28. Freedberg 1989: 120.
29. Behar 1990: 76ff.

A Tale of Two Virgins: The Turners on Guadalupe and *Los Remedios*

In their extended discussion of *Image and Pilgrimage in Christian Culture*, Victor and Edith Turner extend our view of the Virgin of Guadalupe by showing how she need not be seen as an 'autonomous' symbol, but instead can be analysed through uncovering an intriguing series of iconographic and ideological oppositions in relation to another great Marian site in Mexico City, Our Lady of the Remedies (*Los Remedios*).[30]

The Turners note that indigenous people's devotion to Our Lady of Guadalupe has historically been connected with the original vision being granted to an Aztec Indian named Juan Diego. Indeed, Guadalupe is sometimes known as 'the little dark one' from her brown colouring, and in her original appearance she was indeed brown and spoke the local language, Nahuatl. By way of contrast, the image of Our Lady of the Remedies was once the saddle Virgin, carried by one of Cortes's conquistadores.

Such oppositions have continued over time. In the Mexican struggle for independence from the Spaniards in 1810, the insurgents fought under a banner of Our Lady of Guadalupe that had been snatched from a country church. On the other hand, the Spanish viceroy made Our Lady of the Remedies the spiritual commander of the Spanish forces and even gave the image a marshal's baton. Guadalupe, as a dark image, is often seen as a *mestiza*, while Remedies is referred to by a slang name for a native of Spain. Guadaupe is undecorated and is believed to be of miraculous origin, whereas Remedies is known to have been carved by a human artist in Spain. Or again, Guadalupe is believed to have saved Mexico City from floods, whereas Remedies has saved the area from droughts.

The list could go on, but the important point is the way the two images and their associated histories provide transformations of parallel themes, with both believed to protect the nation but in rather different ways. Intriguingly, over the long term there is also some evidence that some of the meanings attached to the images can shift, though the oppositional dimension between them can continue. The Turners note that, ironically, there is now a partial reversal of the commoner–high-class division between the two. Guadalupe has become upwardly mobile, as its national significance has attracted ever stricter organization from church and state, whereas Remedies has taken on a more 'popular' hue.

Crossing Religious Boundaries: Paul Younger and the Virgin in South India

The two Virgins in Mexico City have much in common, but are also locked into a set of iconographic oppositions that themselves link in with social and cultural divisions in the Mexican context. We should not always assume, however, that significant cultural 'differences' have to be explicitly articulated in practices associated with Marian or any other religious imagery. Paul Younger provides the intriguing example of Hindu patterns of pilgrimage at a Christian shrine in South India.[31] The Shrine of Velankanni in south India is managed by the Roman Catholic Church, and consists of a huge, European-style church complex with a normal Roman Catholic

---

30. Turner and Turner 1978.
31. Younger 1992.

sanctuary on each level. Back-to-back with the church is a shrine with an image of the Mother and Child, facing the east and the sea. While perhaps a million people visit the shrine in the first week of September each year, many are scarcely aware of the shrine's Christian connections.[32] Younger argues that the religious sensibility expressed in the pilgrimage is deeply rooted in patterns of Hindu goddess worship among the lower classes of south India. The festival lasts ten days, and features a procession of images pulled on carts. For many, worship begins with a shaving of the head. People also bathe in the sea, then join a long queue to see the image. It may be that many do not even notice the child at the shrine, since the goddess is considered to be the important religious persona.

LINKING OBJECTS, IMAGES AND LANDSCAPES

We have seen how adjacent sites can play off each other iconographically and ideologically, but we also need to understand how the different material cultures within a single shrine complex may constitute a multi-layered, mutually reinforcing reflection of the significance of a site: different media of representation can be seen as enmeshing believers in forms of material culture that are none the less eloquent or powerful for being expressed in objects rather than words. Let us follow our policy of illustration by example, by focusing on Our Lady of Walsingham, in Norfolk, England.

Mary in 'England's Nazareth': Susan Morrison and Our Lady of Walsingham

Susan Signe Morrison, in her discussion of women pilgrims in late medieval England, argues that many women went on pilgrimage during the Middle Ages.[33] A good proportion of such women are likely to have travelled for the sake of their family – an institution that was often centred on the woman's body, given the importance of reproduction and providing sustenance for offspring through mother's milk. In a sense, the female body, as symbol of the healthy, functioning family, could be seen as a shared, public responsibility. Undertaking a pilgrimage might seem to be a matter of personal religious piety, and yet it involved the woman moving out of the domestic sphere, searching for forms of physical relief that had social resonances.

Morrison is keen to point out the ways in which art and other forms of material culture were central and mutually reinforcing elements in the performances of such pilgrimages, including the journeys themselves. Walsingham, which claimed to possess a few drops of the Virgin's milk,[34] became an enormously popular shrine in medieval England in the wake of an intensified Marian cult. The symbolism of the shrine involved the depiction of many saints whose legends involved milk, and intriguingly the Milky Way was referred to as the 'Walsingham Way' in late medieval England

---

32. Ibid.: 90ff.
33. Morrison 2000.
34. Returning crusaders had brought back a phial reputedly containing milk from the breast of the Virgin Mary.

because it pointed north to the shrine.[35] The route to Walsingham seems to have catered for women pilgrims, as mother saints were depicted on the north side (the traditionally 'female' side) of pilgrimage churches leading to the shrine. On the one hand, medieval women pilgrims, by moving publicly through space, were sometimes seen as threatening – almost escapees from the domestic sphere.[36] On the other, women on pilgrimage to Walsingham would be encouraged to 'write themselves' as holy mothers owing to the images encountered on the routes to the shrine.[37]

More generally, the association of Walsingham with women originates with the very establishment of the shrine.[38] In 1061, a wealthy aristocratic woman named Richeldis is said to have had visions of the Virgin and to have been led 'in spirit' to Nazareth and the House of the Annunciation. Richeldis was instructed by the Virgin to build a replica of the Holy House. She hesitated about where to site the wooden structure, until she noticed the morning dew covering an adjoining meadow but leaving two dry patches.[39] Richeldis ordered the men to erect the house on the patch nearest to two holy wells, but they could not fasten it properly on its foundations. That night, while Richeldis prayed, angels moved the house to the second patch. Subsequently, she built a stone church some 23 by 13 feet in size around the wooden construction.

The enormous popularity of Walsingham was in part achieved by, and in part reflected in, its material culture.[40] Wax images representing miraculous cures decorated the shrine. Pilgrims could buy ampullae filled with holy water and a drop of Mary's milk, presumably to aid in childbirth or lactation. Badges depicted the Holy House of Walsingham with such images as the Annunciation. It is even possible to see the shrine itself as an expression of the Virgin, a womb-like 'container' both for the Christ child and for the many pilgrims who came to visit the shrine.[41]

MARY IN MODERNITY

Marian imagery has not been rendered anachronistic in the modern world – far from it. For instance, we have already seen how devotion to the Madonna helped Italian immigrants adjust to their new lives in New York at the turn of the last century. Forms of Marianism have expressed opposition to secularizing tendencies, but they have also proved highly adaptable to modern forms of commercialization, commodification and mobility. This observation can be illustrated by sampling from a recent work by Colleen McDannell that examines the role of material culture in American Christianity.[42]

---

35. Medieval medical theories connected milk with menstrual blood; Mary's milk might also have been linked symbolically with the blood of Christ through the Holy Mother's role as Co-Redemptrix.
36. Morrison 2000: 122.
37. Ibid.: 35.
38. Ibid.: 17.
39. See also Adair 1978: 114.
40. Morrison 2000: 23–4.
41. For a contemporary study of Walsingham, see e.g. Coleman and Elsner 1998.
42. McDannell 1995.

Modern Madonnas: Colleen McDannell on 'Material Christianity'

In an argument that has some parallels with that of Orsi discussed above, McDannell argues that the construction and distribution of material culture helped to mediate the translation of Catholicism from Europe to the United States.[43] For instance, in the late nineteenth century the religious community at Notre Dame devised specific methods to spread the veneration of the Virgin throughout the country.[44] In the 1870s the first Lourdes water was shipped to Notre Dame for circulation.[45] The Notre Dame community also produced a Marian devotional journal and organized a National Association of Our Lady of the Sacred Heart. As shrines were built on the campus, Notre Dame became a pilgrimage spot for Catholics. In effect, Notre Dame's outreach programme helped to forge a national Marian piety. The widely distributed Lourdes water and constructed grotto replicas became material reminders of the power and influence of Mary, as well as helping to translate the holy from more ancient religious centres.[46]

Meanwhile, Catholics in such ancient centres were proving well able to adapt to new commercial conditions. McDannell notes that nineteenth-century French companies became expert at selling religious goods.[47] Most Catholics of the time did not deride their mass-produced art, which became known as *l'art Saint-Sulpice*, but rather saw it as modern and technologically sophisticated. Religious goods bought from catalogues of mass producers reflected standard Catholic iconography and were supposedly assured of being free from local heresies. From Ireland to Mexico to India to the United States, local art was therefore replaced by goods either imported from France or copied from French standards. Not until the twentieth century was a sustained effort made to turn Catholics away from such art towards what became known as *l'art sacré*. By the 1950s, Catholic art critics were following the conventions promoted by modernist architects such as Walter Gropius, Le Corbusier, Mies van der Rohe and Adolf Loos, emphasizing the virtues of functionalism and simplicity.[48] Promoters of the modern sacred art insisted that images should not trick people into thinking that representations were anything more than mere representations, and ornamentation was distrusted because it tended to be representational in character: abstract art was seen to be more truthful and powerful than realistic art.

Whatever the differences between *l'art Saint-Sulpice* and *l'art sacré*, in the context of this chapter they share an intriguing – and, one might argue, deeply modernist – characteristic: a search for the generic. In one case mass production is welcomed as it avoids the idiosyncrasies of the local; in the other the idea of the mass is scorned, but it is replaced by a desire for the abstract, and therefore a refusal to become enmeshed in detail. It is going too far to say that both are searching for a way to make the image

---

43.   Generally, Protestants in the nineteenth century could include Mary among their visual images by emphasizing her maternal qualities and downplaying her mediating capacities; ibid.: 61.

44.   Ibid.: 133.

45.   Ibid.: 143.

46.   Ibid.: 155.

47.   Ibid.: 168ff.

48.   Ibid.: 171ff.

conform to some putative prototype, but both are self-consciously appealing to an aesthetic that can transcend locality. We are far here from the world of Our Lady of Ipswich competing with Our Lady of Walsingham.

In a curious sense, such modernist tendencies have been both extended and reversed by the latest developments in Marian imagery. Here, I refer to the explosion over the last decade or so of websites devoted to the Virgin, her visionaries and associated pilgrimage locations. On the one hand, the delocalization of Marian imagery has been promoted precisely by its 'virtualization' and endless replication on the internet; on the other, the fragmentary nature of the internet has allowed any number of idiosyncratic and 'localized' expressions of imagery to gain a forum. Such issues are discussed in a new book by the Italian anthropologist Paolo Apolito.[49]

The Virtual Virgin: Paolo Apolito and Visionary Experience on the Web

Paolo Apolito examines the vast number of websites offering accounts, testimonials, messages and miraculous photos on the subject of the Catholic visionary movement. His argument is that such sites offer a blend of archaic elements with elements of later modernity, but above all embody a pervasive eclecticism 'which blends religious visions and the Internet, weeping icons and television, stigmata oozing blood and high-tech laboratories, wheeling suns and digital video cameras'.[50] Just as vision has long played a role in Catholic and Orthodox religious experience, so it is given new impetus and form by contemporary technology.

A key aspect of the virtualization of Marian imagery is the fact that it is taken away from the ecclesiastical control of the Church: given the ease with which sites can be produced, the internet has a democratizing effect on modes of religious production, even as it might render any one site almost insignificant within the vast market of possible locations to browse: 'The relationship between heaven and earth passes from the ecclesiastical dimension to the technological dimension, which becomes its site of actual experience, the measure of "truth" and the model of reference, breaking sharply away from the control of the ecclesiastical hierarchy.'[51]

We should not, however, see websites as located randomly around the globe. Inevitably, many either emerge from the United States or have an American flavour. Celestial messages on the web are increasingly uttered not in local dialects such as Nahuatl, but in English. For Apolito, the fact that 84 per cent of all web pages on the internet are created in the US can be linked not only to that country's wealth, but also to the weakness of the ideology of the traditional community and the ideological centrality of individualism.[52] Whether or not his interpretation is correct, it is intriguing that visionary Marianism and its associated websites contain certain recurrent themes.[53] In the US in particular, many of the messages attributed to the Virgin Mary and Jesus evoke technological threats, amplifying a more generally

---

49. Apolito 2005.
50. Ibid.: 2–3.
51. Ibid.: 13.
52. Ibid.: 146–7.
53. Ibid.: 7.

apocalyptic attitude that has informed the ideology of modern Marian apparitions, from the nineteenth century to the present.

CONCLUDING COMMENTS

We have moved a long way, from the Council of Nicaea to contemporary websites. The cultural and religious distances traversed should not be underestimated, despite the universalist claims of Christianity. Yet it is at least intriguing that a study of the images and objects associated with the Virgin deals with so many recurring themes: where to locate divine 'presence'; the role of vision in worship; and the relationship between prototype and copy. These, after all, are key not only to an understanding of the aesthetics of Marianism, but also perhaps to an understanding of human religious systems in general.

BIBLIOGRAPHY

Adair, J. (1978) *The Pilgrims' Way: Shrines and Saints in Britain and Ireland*, London: Thames and Hudson.

Apolito, P. (2005) *The Internet and the Madonna: Religious Visionary Experience on the Web*, Chicago, IL: University of Chicago Press.

Behar, R. (1990) 'The Struggle for the Church: Popular Anticlericalism and Religiosity in Post-Franco Spain', in E. Badone (ed.), *Religious Orthodoxy and Popular Faith in European Society*, Princeton, NJ: Princeton University Press: 76–112.

Brading, D. A. (2001) *Mexican Phoenix: Our Lady of Guadalupe: Image and Tradition across Five Centuries*, Cambridge: Cambridge University Press.

Coleman, S. and Elsner, J. (1998) 'Performing Pilgrimage: Walsingham and the Ritual Construction of Irony', in F. Hughes-Freeland (ed.), *Ritual, Performance, Media*, London: Routledge: 46–65.

Dubisch, J. (1995) *In a Different Place: Pilgrimage, Gender, and Politics at a Greek Island Shrine*, Princeton, NJ: Princeton University Press.

Duffy, Eamon (1992) *The Stripping of the Altars: Traditional Religion in England 1400–1580*, New Haven, CT: Yale University Press.

Freedberg, D. (1989) *The Power of Images: Studies in the History and Theory of Response*, Chicago, IL: Chicago University Press.

McDannell, C. (1995) *Material Christianity: Religion and Popular Culture in America*, New Haven, CT: Yale University Press.

Morgan, D. (1998) *Visual Piety: A History and Theory of Popular Religious Images*, Berkeley, CA: University of California Press.

Morrison, S. (2000) *Women Pilgrims in Late Medieval England: Private Piety as Public Performance*, London: Routledge.

Nolan, M. and Nolan, S. (1989) *Christian Pilgrimage in Modern Western Europe*, Chapel Hill, NC: The University of North Carolina Press.

Orsi, R. (1985) *The Madonna of 115th Street: Faith and Community in Italian Harlem, 1880–1950*, New Haven, CT: Yale.

Pelikan, J. (1996) *Mary through the Centuries: Her Place in the History of Culture*, New Haven, CT: Yale University Press.

Tanner, N. and Aberigo, G. (eds) (1990) *Decrees of the Ecumenical Councils*, 2 vols, Washington DC: Georgetown University Press.

Turner, V. (1967) *The Forest of Symbols: Aspect of Ndembu Ritual*, Ithaca, NY: Cornell University Press.

Turner, V. and Turner, E. (1978) *Image and Pilgrimage in Christian Culture: Anthropological Perspectives*, Oxford: Blackwell.

Wolf, E. (1958) 'The Virgin of Guadalupe: A Mexican National Symbol', *Journal of American Folklore* 71(1): 34–9.

Younger, P. (1992) 'Velankanni Calling: Hindu Patterns of Pilgrimage at a Christian Shrine', in A. Morinis (ed.), *Sacred Journeys: The Anthropology of Pilgrimage*, Westport, CT: Greenwood.

19

Marian Consecration in the Contemporary Church

Sarah Jane Boss

INTRODUCTION

Throughout the world, millions of Catholics make a more or less formal act by which they consecrate themselves to Mary, or to God through Mary. The practice has been increasingly widespread since the seventeenth century, and became extremely popular in the twentieth. This article examines what constitutes such an act of consecration, and how it is to be understood.

The term 'consecration' refers to an act or state of separation, whereby the consecrated object is given over totally, or exclusively, to the purpose for which it is separated. That purpose is a sacred one. A common example of such an act would be the consecration of a church, when a special rite sets the building apart for sacred use. Corresponding to the state of consecration is the possibility of *desecration*, that is, the treatment of that which is consecrated in a manner which the consecration specifically forbids. In certain cases, an act of desecration destroys the state of consecration. Violence leading to bloodshed in a church, for example, destroys the building's previous state of ritual sanctity, so that it has to be reconsecrated. By contrast, trampling the elements of the Eucharist underfoot, or cursing them, does not destroy their essential holiness, since that holiness is divine. Actions of this kind are nonetheless deemed to be acts of desecration, and have traditionally carried heavy penalties for those who carry them out.

Periods of time, as well as material objects, can be consecrated. In biblical teaching, the Sabbath is set aside for rest, enjoyment and the praise of God. Work therefore desecrates the Sabbath, as does forcing another person to work on the Sabbath, since it prevents them from Sabbath observance. In the teaching of Exodus, the reason for Sabbath observance is that God himself consecrated the seventh day when he created the world in six days and rested on the seventh. Thus the initial consecration was carried out by God, and human consecration is a continuation and imitation of a divine original. This holds true also for the Eucharist – established by Christ – and for many Christian acts of consecration.

In baptism, it is a human being who is consecrated – in this case, for the Christian life as a whole – and desecration is incurred by serious sin, such as murder or adultery. Karl Rahner has argued that a state of sanctity, bestowed from the outset by the grace with which God makes all people, characterizes human beings regardless of whether or not they are baptized, and that the function of baptism is to elicit, or activate, a holiness that is inherent in the baptismal subject. Further voluntary acts of consecration may be viewed as the baptismal subject's expression of a desire to respond to God's grace by cultivating that holiness by some specific means.[1]

Christians frequently forget or ignore their baptismal consecration, and a broad movement has built up in the Catholic Church since the sixteenth century which re-emphasizes consecration with a view to re-establishing the 'proper interior links'[2] between God and humanity. This may be seen in part as a response to the growing individualism of European culture during the same period, in so far as that individualism has given Christians a sense that their community's identification with the institutional Church is not sufficient for them, and so has inspired the desire to make some personal public gesture of Christian commitment. Such a gesture may be seen as a reappropriation of the baptismal promises that were made on their behalf in infancy.

René Laurentin argues that consecration is a response to increasing secularization, and an expression of resistance to it.[3]

MODERN MARIAN CONSECRATION

Apart from the sacramental consecration of baptism and confirmation, most voluntary lay consecration in the Catholic Church in the past 150 years has been Marian in character, and has incorporated, or been influenced by, the consecration recommended by St Louis-Marie Grignon de Montfort (1673–1716). During the eighteenth century, Louis Grignion's little work known as *The True Devotion to the Blessed Virgin* was lost, and was only rediscovered in 1842, since when it has been widely disseminated. This work includes the recommendation to use the following act of consecration:

ACT OF CONSECRATION
Eternal and Incarnate Wisdom, most lovable and adorable Jesus, true God and true man, only Son of the eternal Father and of Mary always virgin, I adore you profoundly, dwelling in the splendour of your Father from all eternity and in the virginal womb of Mary, your most worthy Mother, at the time of your Incarnation. I thank you for having emptied yourself in assuming the condition of a slave to set me free from the cruel slavery of the evil one. I praise and glorify you for having willingly chosen to obey Mary, your holy Mother, in all things, so that through her I may be your faithful slave of love.

But I must confess that I have not kept the vows and promises which I made to you so solemnly at my baptism. I have not fulfilled my obligations, and I do not deserve to be called your child or even your loving slave. Since I cannot lay claim to anything except what merits your rejection and displeasure, I dare no longer approach the holiness of your majesty on my own. That is why I turn to

---

1. This is explained in Philip Endean's chapter on Rahner in this volume: chapter 12.
2. Laurentin 1992: 32.
3. Ibid.: 13–32 and *passim*.

the intercession and the mercy of your holy Mother, whom you yourself have given me to mediate with you. Through her I hope to obtain from you contrition and pardon for my sins, and that Wisdom whom I desire to dwell in me always.

I turn to you, then, Mary immaculate, living tabernacle of God. The eternal Wisdom, hidden in you, willed to receive the adoration of both men and angels.

I greet you as Queen of heaven and earth. All that is under God has been made subject to your sovereignty.

I call upon you as the unfailing refuge of sinners.

In your mercy you have never forsaken anyone. Grant my desire for divine Wisdom and, in support of my petition, accept the promises and the offering of myself which I now make, conscious of my unworthiness.

I, an unfaithful sinner, renew and ratify today through you my baptismal promises. I renounce for ever Satan, his empty promises and his evil designs, and I give myself completely to Jesus Christ, the Incarnate Wisdom, to carry my cross after him for the rest of my life, and to be more faithful to him than I have been till now.

This day, with the whole court of heaven as witness, I choose you, Mary, as my Mother and Queen. I surrender and consecrate myself to you, body and soul, with all that I possess, both spiritual and material, even including the spiritual value of all my actions, past, present, and to come. I give you the full right to dispose of me and all that belongs to me, without any reservations, in whatever way you please, for the greater glory of God in time and throughout eternity.

Accept, gracious Virgin, this little offering of my slavery to honour and imitate that obedience which the eternal Wisdom willingly chose to have towards you, his Mother. I wish to acknowledge the authority which both of you have over this little worm and pitiful sinner. By it I wish also to thank God for the privileges bestowed on you by the Blessed Trinity. I solemnly declare that for the future I will try to honour and obey you in all things as your true slave of love.

O admirable Mother, present me to your dear Son as his slave now and for always, so that he who redeemed me through you, will now receive me through you.

Mother of mercy, grant me the favour of obtaining the true Wisdom of God, and so make me one of those whom you love, teach and guide, whom you nourish and protect as your children and slaves.

Virgin most faithful, make me in everything so committed a disciple, imitator, and slave of Jesus, your Son, the Incarnate Wisdom, that I may become, through your intercession and example, fully mature with the fulness which Jesus possessed on earth, and with the fulness of his glory in heaven. Amen.[4]

---

4. de Montfort, trans. 1976: 141–3.

HISTORICAL BACKGROUND

René Laurentin writes, 'The essence of the Christian life is to be found in consecration.'[5] This is to be seen in biblical injunctions such as, 'You shall be holy; for I the Lord your God am holy' (Lev. 19.2; 20.26). In the New Testament, the notion of *incorporation* into Christ goes hand in hand with an implied separation of the Church from the world. Acts 2.44 tells us that the earliest Christians held all things in common – a state which simultaneously created solidarity among Church members, and separation from the world around them. Paul's preference for celibacy over marriage also indicates that he intended the Christian to be marked off from his or her surroundings, in order to be given over entirely to Christ (1 Cor. 7.8, 25, 28, 37–8).[6]

The word 'consecration', however, does not seem to have been used until the fourth century, when St Jerome used it to refer to women who were consecrated virgins.[7] Indeed, the consecrated virgin is really the prototype of personal Christian consecration. In the early centuries, the consecrated virgin did not necessarily live apart from her family or the rest of the world; but the practice of the physical separation of those leading the consecrated life gradually emerged, as hermits, consecrated virgins and monastic communities set themselves apart, in order to give themselves more completely to the ascetic or contemplative life.

During the high Middle Ages, the vows of poverty, chastity and obedience were codified, and those taking such vows thereby renounced the world. Monks and nuns typically lived (and still live) in an enclosure which symbolized and facilitated their separation from worldly things. In the later Middle Ages, however, other forms of life became possible for men and women who wished to consecrate themselves to God. The preaching friars; the secular people who comprised the third orders; lay people, such as the beguines, who lived in religious communities; and, from the sixteenth century, religious societies (of which the Society of Jesus was the first): all these were associations of consecrated men or women, who worked in the world, but who were set apart from it by their interior disposition and, to a greater or lesser degree, by their manner of life.

During the medieval period, local guilds flourished, which were lay associations devoted to prayer and almsgiving, usually to some particular end, such as the support of a local hospital. In the Tridentine period, these came to be supplanted by confraternities, which usually had a broader territorial base, or none at all. Associations of this kind did not require members to commit every aspect of their lives to the service of its aims and ideals, but some aspects of their organization laid the basis for later organizations of lay people who were formally consecrated. In 1563, the newly established Society of Jesus set up the Sodality of the Holy Virgin, whose members had to *offer* themselves to Mary in order to achieve a *consecration* to God.[8] Marian sodalities were set up in all Jesuit schools and, during the seventeenth century, in very many schools run by other religious orders as well. The notion of

---

5. Laurentin 1992: 35.
6. Ibid.: 36.
7. *Adversus Jovinianum*, PL 23: 240; quoted in ibid.: 40.
8. Laurentin 1992: 50.

asking the Blessed Virgin for assistance in attaining consecration to God was thus firmly rooted in the Catholic mind for the whole of the Tridentine era.

In 1947, Pope Pius XII made possible the establishment of *secular institutes*, of which the first was Opus Dei, for the consecration of secular life. Typically, a secular institute includes lay people who live in community, and associates who live in whatever circumstances they would if they were not members of the institute – for example, in their families.

The Second Vatican Council (1962–5), however, was keen to reassert the consecrated nature of all Christian life and, rather than seeing the consecrated and secular lives as distinguishable, pointed out that all Christians are consecrated in virtue of their baptism. In fact, Louis de Montfort's Act of Consecration implicitly recognizes the primacy of baptismal vows, and presents the renewed consecration as a means by which the past breach of those vows may in some manner be repaired. There is no evidence that Catholics have broken their baptismal vows less frequently since Vatican II, and so perhaps it is not surprising that, during the closing decades of the twentieth century, the irruption of fervent religiosity across the world has been manifested in Catholicism by, among other things, a certain revival of the practice of personal consecration – a consecration that almost always takes a Marian form.

SLAVERY TO MARY

Perhaps the most striking aspect of Louis de Montfort's Act of Consecration is its pledge of slavery. This takes the form of a play on the paradox of the incarnation – play of a kind that has been beloved of Christian authors since earliest times. Christ himself became a slave, in order to free humanity from slavery to sin, and in thankgiving for this, the devotee now offers him- or herself to be a slave out of love. It needs to be pointed out that, in most previous periods of history, a servant or slave frequently shared in the overall identity of the master or mistress's household – by wearing the master's livery, for example – so that it was a point of pride to be the slave of a highly placed or honourable master, and an embarrassment to be the slave of a man or woman of ill repute. Thus, the psalmist says, 'I had rather be a doorkeeper in the house of the Lord than dwell in the tents of the ungodly' (Ps. 84.10); that is, it is better to be the lowliest servant of the Lord than to be the equal of those who are unrighteous. Paul describes himself as a 'slave' or 'servant' (*doulos*) of Christ (Rom. 1.1), and it seems as if this is something of which he is proud. Likewise, when Mary says, 'Behold the handmaid (*doulē*) of the Lord' (Lk. 1.38, 48), it is probably correct to read this as her welcoming of a state which she deems to be honourable and desirable. She puts herself totally at God's disposal, and by this act of self-abandonment defends and reflects God's glory. Louis de Montfort's writing always presumes a strongly hierarchical view of human society, and so we should probably assume that, in his understanding, to make oneself a slave of the Mother of God is not to enter a condition of debasement, but rather to take on an office of humility which simultaneously ennobles the office holder.[9]

---

9.   See de Montfort 1995; and de Fiores *et al.* (eds) 1994.

By the eighteenth century, the tradition of slavery to Mary was well established. Notable slaves of Mary from a thousand years earlier included Isidore of Seville (*c.* 560–636) and St Germanus of Constantinople (*c.* 635–733). However, the example of entering into slavery to Mary was not much followed for many centuries afterwards. The Council of Trent taught that pastors should exhort the faithful 'to give themselves as nothing other than slaves [*mancipia*] to our Redeemer and Lord in perpetuity', and before the end of the sixteenth century, Sister Ines Bautista had founded the Confraternity of Slaves of the Most Holy Virgin. More confraternities of slaves of Mary were to follow.

During the early decades of the seventeenth century, the practice of consecration as a slave of the Virgin became widespread in Spain, and this movement influenced St Louis de Montfort. Mary's slaves took up the practice of wearing little chains on their clothing to signify their enslavement to her, but in 1673 – the year of St Louis's birth – the Holy Office forbade this practice.

St Louis's own theologial training had occurred at the seminary of St Sulpice, in Paris. It was founded by Jean-Jacques Olier, who, with Pierre de Bérulle (1575–1629), was largely responsible for a great revival of French Catholicism in the seventeenth century. They and their immediate followers are known collectively as the *Ecole française*, or French School. Bérulle, who founded the Oratory movement in France, taught that one should offer oneself to Mary in a state of dependence and servitude – a view which was hotly contested at the time. The Oratory as a whole was pledged to servitude to Christ, and for Bérulle, the purpose of servitude to Mary was that one might in turn become a follower of Christ. Louis de Montfort was a product of the French School, whose tradition he continued.

In the teaching of St Louis, the key element is that it was through Mary that the Wisdom of God became incarnate. For this reason, he believes that an 'age of Mary' will precede the second coming of Christ and the establishment of the kingdom of God. Conversely, and in accordance with a long tradition represented most notably by St Bernard of Clairvaux, he teaches that the route by which the Christian should approach God is the same as that by which God approached humanity, namely, through Mary. Thus to make oneself a slave of Mary is to offer oneself entirely to Christ.

In the twentieth century, promoters of the cults of Our Lady of Fatima and Our Lady of Medjugorje have encouraged devotees to make use of St Louis's formula of consecration, but in their literature more generally, the element of slavery is not emphasized.

THE SCAPULAR

It is common to find the wearing of a scapular as a sign of Marian consecration. In origin, the scapular is a kind of apron – a long strip of cloth with a hole in the middle to go over the head – which was worn in the Middle Ages. Members of religious orders wore (and in some cases still wear) a scapular over the habit, and the colour of the scapular varied according to the order. There is a legend which tells the origin of the brown Carmelite scapular, claiming that it was miraculously given to St Simon

Stock in the year 1251. The tradition teaches that Mary appeared to Simon, a brother of the Order of Our Lady of Mount Carmel, that she gave him a brown scapular and said, 'Receive, my beloved son, this habit of thy order. This shall be to thee and to all Carmelites a privilege that whosoever dies clothed in this shall never suffer eternal fire.' The scapular, then, marks the wearer out as one separated from the power of hell.[10]

Lay members of a religious order – members of 'third orders', known as 'tertiaries' – would sometimes wear the order's scapular over their ordinary clothes as a sign of their religious commitment. Over time, and with changes in styles of clothing, the scapular was reduced to a small scapular-shaped token to be worn around the neck, and this is what the term 'scapular' most commonly refers to today.

The popularity of the brown scapular meant that, eventually, it became possible for a lay person to receive consecration with the brown scapular without formally becoming a member of the Carmelite order. Many modern acts of Marian consecration include investiture with the brown scapular, and in the modern period other scapulars, of various colours, have been introduced and gained official Church approval.[11]

THE IMMACULATE HEART OF MARY[12]

Many acts of consecration are made to Mary's Immaculate Heart, a cult which has its principal origin in Jean Eudes's work *The Admirable Heart of Mary*, which was published in 1680, the year of his death.[13] He had previously published a book on *The Sacred Heart of Jesus*, and devotion to Jesus and Mary together, and in particular to their hearts, was central to his teaching.

In art, the image of the heart had for several centuries been employed to stand for Mary's soul. Luke 2.35 recounts that at the time of Mary's purification, Simeon prophesied that a sword would pierce Mary's soul; and that motif was, and is, found in art in the form of a heart pierced by a sword (Fig. 20). The soul and the heart each stand for the whole person, and this is the sense in which Jean Eudes writes of the Heart of Mary. But although the heart of Mary had been represented and written about in earlier centuries, it had not previously been an object of devotion. That was something new in the seventeenth century, and seems to be modelled in part upon devotion to the Sacred Heart of Jesus, which was already well established, being directed towards a deeper appreciation of the incarnation.[14]

Eudes begins his work with chapters on Mary's heart under three main headings: her 'corporeal heart', her 'spiritual heart' and her 'divine heart'. The corporeal heart,

---

10.   Modern Carmelites are often keen to distance themselves from this tradition. For example, Clarke 1994 does not describe it.
11.   A list is given in Carroll 1986: 69.
12.   For a detailed discussion of this subject, see Boss 2004.
13.   Eudes, trans. Targiani and Hauser 1948.
14.   For example, the sixteenth-century spiritual writer Lanspergius encouraged devotion to the Heart of Jesus. A quotation illustrating this is given in Brodrick 1938: 16.

Fig. 20. *Immaculate Heart of Mary*. Picture on prayer card.

he says, is not only the principle of her own earthly life, but also produced the blood of which Christ's body was formed. It is the source of the material life of Christ in the womb.[15] The spiritual heart is the noblest portion of the soul; it is made in the image of God, and by grace is able to participate in the divine nature.[16] In Mary that image is untarnished, and the participation, or divinization, is as full as possible. And finally, the divine heart is that aspect of Mary which is concerned directly with her divine motherhood – with the fact that she is the Mother of God. Christ, says Eudes, is the heart of God the Father, and he is also the Heart of his earthly mother. That is to say, the Word of God is not only the Son of both God the Father and the human Mary, but is also the Heart of both. He lives in every part of her, both physical and spiritual.[17] The divine Heart therefore ties Mary immediately to the life of the Blessed Trinity.

Now, one aspect of what Eudes is telling us in this is that the Heart of the Virgin Mary is a microcosm of the universe. He outlines an Aristotelian account of the three parts of the human soul: 'the vegetative soul, which is similar in nature to that of

15. Eudes 1948: 14.
16. Ibid.: 19–20.
17. Ibid.: 24.

plants ... the sensitive life, which we have in common with animals ... [and] the intellectual life, like that of angels'.[18] This is already an account of the human person – any human person – as a microcosm which bears the three orders of life. In the case of Mary, howevever, not only does her heart embody these three modes of life in a state of perfection, but that heart is also a microcosm of the whole inanimate universe. For example, her heart corresponds to the heavens, because God went forth from heaven to dwell in his mother's heart, so that it too became a heaven.[19] Yet more significant than this is the claim that Mary's heart corresponds to the sun. Eudes writes:

> The infinite power of God has divided this great universe into three different states or orders, namely, the state of nature, the state of grace and the state of glory ... whatever is in the order of nature is an image of the things belonging to the order of grace, and whatever belongs to the order of nature and grace is a figure of what is to be seen in the state of glory. Hence, the sun, which is truly the heart of the visible world, and the most beautiful and glowing gem of nature, gives us ... only a very faint shadow of our heavenly Sun, the Heart of the Mother of God.[20]

Jean Eudes understands the human person to be a figure that corresponds to the whole order of creation, and the Heart of Mary to be, as it were, the perfection of the microscosm and the archetype of the macrocosm: creation in the state of glory. In her, furthermore, God is fully united to creation, and the purpose of devotion to the Admirable Heart is articulated in words such as the following: 'I would have you realize, dear Reader, that Our Lord Jesus Christ, who is the Heart of the Eternal Father, willed to become the Heart or life-principle of His Most Blessed Mother, and He likewise wills to become the Heart of your own life.'[21]

Eudes employs a large number of adjectives to describe Mary's heart: admirable, lovable, holy, sacred and immaculate, for example; and the term 'Sacred Heart of Mary' was common in the late eighteenth and early nineteenth centuries. But in the middle decades of the nineteenth century, the cult of Mary's heart came to use the adjective 'immaculate' almost exclusively. There were probably a number of different factors influencing this. One, for instance, may have been the development of the cult of Our Lady of the Sacred Heart.[22] This was a devotion which focused upon Mary in relation to the Sacred Heart of Jesus; and it is easy to see that a confusion could have arisen between the Sacred Heart of Mary and Our Lady of the Sacred

---

18. Ibid.: 19.
19. Ibid.: 34–5.
20. Ibid.: 38. Elsewhere Eudes writes of Christ as the sun, and Mary's heart as the mirror which reflects it; e.g. 105–11.
21. Ibid.: 27. 'The Admirable Heart of Mary is the perfect image of the most divine Heart of Jesus. It is the pattern and model for our own hearts; and all our happiness, perfection and glory consists in striving to transform them into so many living images of the sacred Heart of Mary, just as her holy Heart is a consummate likeness of the adorable Heart of Jesus': 265.
22. Chevalier 1895.

Heart, so that the use of a term rarely applied to the Heart of Jesus, namely 'immaculate', would make for ease of comprehension. The most important influence on the choice of the term 'immaculate', however, was certainly the campaign for a papal definition of the dogma of the immaculate conception and the Holy See's promulgation of that dogma in 1854.

In the popular imagination, the Miraculous Medal associated the image of the heart both with the globe and with Mary's immaculate conception (see Fig. 16).[23] At the time of Catherine Labouré's visions and of the initial production of the medal, the parish priest in the Rue du Bac was the Abbé Desgenettes, and he was a great enthusiast for the medal. But in 1832 he was moved to the parish of Notre-Dame des Victoires, in the Place des Grands Augustins, and there he found the parish in a rundown state, with few church attenders. He worked hard to evangelize among the people of the area, but all to no avail; and he started to wonder whether he should not just leave the parish and go somewhere else where his ministry would be more fruitful. However, in 1836, as he was celebrating Mass one day, he heard a voice telling him to 'consecrate [his] parish to the Most Holy and Immaculate Heart of Mary'. The standard accounts narrate that he did this shortly afterwards, and that four or five hundred people appeared, as it were, out of the blue, for the occasion.[24]

A confraternity of lay people was formed under the protection of the Heart of Mary, and in 1838 Pope Gregory XVI 'created and erected in perpetuity in the Church of Our Lady of Victories in Paris, the Archconfraternity of the Holy and Immaculate Heart of Mary for the conversion of sinners'. This was, and is, an association open to Catholics not just in France, but all over the world.[25]

In the twentieth century, the leading movement for devotion to the Immaculate Heart became the cult of Our Lady of Fatima. The history and practices of this cult are so complicated that I shall not attempt to give a thorough account of even the main features.[26] But I can at least draw attention to one or two of them.

In 1917, the Virgin appeared again to three children at Fatima in Portugal. In a series of visions between May and October, she addressed Lucia dos Santos and her cousins, Jacinta and Francisco Martos. Some of the things that Our Lady is reported to have said to the children were recorded at the time and subjected to scrutiny by the official commission of enquiry into the authenticity of the apparitions. Other things seem not to have been revealed until the late 1920s and 1940s, when Lucia — who by this time had become a Carmelite nun — made them known.[27] There has been some dispute as to whether those matters that were told only later should really be counted as part of the visions that were authenticated by the Church; but for most devotees of Our Lady of Fatima, all Lucia's later pronouncements are deemed to be valid.

---

23. See Sarah Jane Boss, 'The Development of the Doctrine of Mary's Immaculate Conception', in this volume: 28–29.
24. Blond 1937: 10–13.
25. Ibid.: 14–15.
26. For a more detailed account, see Zimdars-Swartz 1991: 67–91; for an account by a protagonist for the cult, see Johnston 1980.
27. Zimdars-Swartz 1991: 190–219.

The first apparition was inaugurated by a flash of lightning, which drew the children's attention to the brilliant figure of a 'lady' over a holm-oak tree in the Cova da Iria. During the sequence of monthly visions, the Lady asked the children to pray for the conversion of sinners and an end to the war. She called in particular for recitation of the rosary. In October, she said that if people would amend their lives, then the war would soon be over. Now, 7 October is the feast of Our Lady of the Rosary, and October is the month specially dedicated to the rosary in popular Catholic devotion. It is therefore not surprising that it was during the October apparition that the lady identified herself as 'Our Lady of the Rosary'. What was most remarkable about the October apparition, however, was something experienced not only by the visionaries themselves, but also by the crowd that had gathered around them to witness their ecstasy. When the people arrived, it was pouring with rain, and they all stood with wet clothes and umbrellas. But then the sun came out and seemed to fall from the sky, so that the people were terrified and ran screaming for cover. This lasted for more than ten minutes, before the sun seemed to return to the sky, leaving everyone's clothes and umbrellas, and the ground around them, completely dry.

Some years later, Lucia had a vision in which she saw the Virgin holding her own heart encircled by thorns. The child who accompanied the Virgin told Lucia that the thorns were placed there by ungrateful people; he asked Lucia to have compassion on her Holy Mother's heart, complaining that there was no one to make the reparation that would remove the thorns. He then indicated a series of devotions to be undertaken on the first Saturdays of five consecutive months in order to make this reparation. The devotions consisted principally of confession, reception of Holy Communion and recitation of the rosary.[28]

At a later date, Lucia revealed that Our Lady of Fatima had spoken against the errors of Communist Russia, which, she said, were already spreading across the globe. For this reason, devotion to Our Lady of Fatima was especially adopted by Catholic organizations opposed to Communism, such as the Blue Army in the United States.[29] In 1929 Lucia reported that Our Lady had called for the Pope to consecrate Russia to her Immaculate Heart in order to bring about its conversion. Again, in the 1950s, Lucia said that if the Virgin's message of repentance was not heeded, then many nations in the world would be annihilated, and – apparently following the model of Old Testament prophecies such as those of Amos – she said that God would use Russia as the instrument of his chastisement upon the world. But, Lucia said, Our Lady had reassured her that 'in the end, my Immaculate Heart will triumph', a phrase that is frequently repeated by Fatima devotees (Fig. 21).

The question of what it means for a Pope to consecrate the world to anything – and whether, indeed, he can be deemed by Catholic teaching to have the authority to do so – is one that we shall leave aside here. But there is a certain precedent for such an act in Pope Leo XIII's consecration of the entire human race to the Sacred Heart

---

28.   This practice recalls that of a popular devotion to the Sacred Heart of Jesus, whereby the devotee receives Communion on the first Friday of each month for nine consecutive months.
29.   Cuneo 1997: 134–7.

Gosto
tanto do
Coração
Imaculado
de Maria!
Jacinta

Fig. 21. *Our Lady of Fatima Asks for Devotion to her Immaculate Heart*. Postcard.

of Jesus in 1899.[30] Those who promote Fatima devotions have had some disagreement as to when and whether a Pope has actually accomplished the consecration which Lucia said was demanded. In 1942, Pope Pius XII consecrated the world to the Immaculate Heart of Mary. It is generally asserted that the reason why this consecration did not mention Russia by name was that it would have been politically unwise to do so – which undoubtedly it would. This consecration of the

---

30.   Laurentin 1992: 56–9.

world to the Immaculate Heart was repeated in 1982 by Pope John Paul II. On both these occasions, however, Lucia said that the act did not fulfil the conditions requested by Our Lady, which were that the consecration should be made by the Pope together with the Catholic bishops of the world. The fact that the bishops were not included rendered the consecration invalid. In 1983, however, Pope John Paul wrote to all the bishops of the world requesting that they should join him in making a further act of consecration of the world to the Immaculate Heart. After this further consecration was accomplished in 1984, Lucia said that the Virgin's request had now, at last, been fulfilled.

Now Lucia's claim had been that the consecration of Russia in particular would be to the benefit of the entire planet. Nonetheless, in the light of the global imagery associated with the Immaculate Heart, it is perhaps more in accordance with the logic of the symbols that the universal pontiff should have consecrated the whole world, rather than just one part of it. With the advent of *glasnost* and *perestroika*, and the fall of the Iron Curtain in 1989, many Fatima devotees claimed that it was because of Our Lady and the Pope that these changes had at last come about.

BIBLIOGRAPHY

Blond, Louis (1937) *Notre-Dame des Victoires*, Paris: Aux Editions Franciscaines.

Boss, Sarah Jane (2004) 'The Immaculate Heart of Mary: Visions for the World', in R. N. Swanson (ed.), *The Church and Mary*, Studies in Church History 39, Woodbridge: Boydell Press: 319–48.

Brodrick, James (1938) *Saint Peter Canisius*, London: Sheed & Ward.

Chevalier, Jules (1895) *Notre-Dame du Sacré-Cœur*, Paris: Librairie de l'Œvre de Saint-Paul.

Clarke, Hugh (1994) *Mary and the Brown Scapular*, Aylesford: Carmelite Province of Our Lady of the Assumption; and Oxford: Anglo Irish Province of the Discalced Carmelites.

Carroll, Michael P. (1986) *The Cult of the Virgin Mary: Psychological Origins*, Princeton, NJ: Princeton University Press.

Cuneo, Michael W. (1997) *The Smoke of Satan: Conservative and Traditionalist Dissent in Contemporary American Catholicism*, New York and Oxford: Oxford University Press.

Eudes, St John (1948) *The Admirable Heart of Mary*, trans. Charles di Targiani and Ruth Hauser, New York: P. J. Kennedy and Sons.

de Fiores, Stefano *et al.* (eds) (1994) *Jesus Living in Mary: Handbook of the Spirituality of St Louis Marie de Montfort*, Bay Shore, NY: Montfort Publications.

Johnston, Francis (1980) *Fatima: The Great Sign*, Chulmleigh, Devon: Augustine Publishing Company.

Laurentin, René (1992) *The Meaning of Consecration Today: A Marian Model for a Secularized Age*, trans. Kenneth D. Whitehead, San Francisco, CA: Ignatius Press.

de Montfort, St Louis-Marie (1976) *True Devotion to the Blessed Virgin*, trans. anon., Liverpool: Montfort Press.

de Montfort, St Louis-Marie (1995) *God Alone: The Collected Writings of St Louis Marie de Montfort*, Bay Shore, NY: Montfort Publications.

Zimdars-Swartz, Sandra (1991) *Encountering Mary: From La Salette to Medjugorje*, Princeton, NJ: Princeton University Press.

20

APPARITIONS OF MARY

CHRIS MAUNDER

Apparitions of Mary have been influential throughout Christian history in both East and West; they are particularly prominent in Roman Catholicism in the modern era because of the fame of shrines such as Guadalupe, Lourdes and Fatima. The Catholic community includes many people who are most eager to receive messages, either assurances or warnings, from the supernatural realm – the belief that Christ, Mary or the saints are invisibly present in the community is given substance when there is a report that they have manifested themselves to particular visionaries. Whereas, before the industrial age, most apparition cases were known only in their local context, the global dimension of Marian apparitions today is assured by the ease of communication and travel. Thus one may log onto the internet in mid-west America, hear that visions have been reported in Ireland, Egypt or Bosnia, and arrange travel to the newly emerging shrine. The discomforts that beset the medieval pilgrim are not necessary in the age of jet and hotel.

An apparition, or vision, is the visual perception of a person or object that one knows not to be present in the normal, objective, material sense. In many cases, messages are passed on through the visionary to the wider faith community. Sometimes the perception is aural only, and it is then categorized as a locution. Visions and locutions are very common in the population at large, and certainly among religious people. However, the Marian vision that results in a shrine and lasting devotion will have features that suggest its special importance. It may, for example, be experienced by a group; occur in a series of encounters to the same person(s) or at the same location; address questions that are very urgent for the community (local, national, whole church); occur at a time of crisis – warfare, social conflict or traumatic social change, widespread famine or disease; be accompanied by signs, healings, conversions. Influential Marian apparitions are therefore communal experiences, even if originating in the reports of a person or small group.

Apparitions have always been interesting to theologians; in the Roman Catholic tradition, Augustine, Aquinas and the Carmelite mystics Teresa of Avila and John of the Cross are among those who have written about them, and more recently, Karl Rahner. The persistence of Marian apparition cults into the modern era has also provoked interest among religious studies scholars, who have adopted anthropological, sociological or psychological approaches in attempting to understand them. The readings given here all concern themselves with Marian apparitions in the Roman Catholic world, as these have been the focal point of academic and theological interest. Yet, of course, Marian apparitions also occur in Orthodox societies and, in Egypt in the 1960s and 1970s, were experienced by Copts and Muslims.

AN OVERVIEW OF THE HISTORY OF MARIAN APPARITIONS

It is difficult to be precise as to when apparitions of Mary became a regular, accepted part of the Christian experience of the supernatural. Zaragoza in Spain claims the first Marian apparition: according to the tradition there, Mary appeared within her own lifetime in the year 40 to James, to inspire his missionary journey. Other early apparition sites, according to local claims, include Le Puy in France (fourth century), and Rome (fourth century), where Mary in a dream identified the site where the basilica of St Mary Major was to be built, which would be indicated by a miraculous fall of snow in August.[1] All of these, however, lack historical evidence, and are very likely to be legendary, testifying to the desire for a religious site to have a miraculous origin.[2] Clearly, when these legends emerged, the idea of the Marian apparition had been established. 'Gregory the Wonderworker' was said to have had an apparition of Mary in the third century. Certainly, given the growth of devotion to Mary in the early Church, one can expect apparition claims to have been part of the Marian cult, even if not quite as early as CE 40. We can conclude that Marian apparitions have been regular phenomena in the Christian tradition, at least as far back as the state institutionalization of Christianity in the fourth century.

The importance of Marian visions in the medieval period is undisputed. The seventh-century apparition to Ildephonsus, Archbishop of Toledo, was well known in the medieval period. In England, the beginning of the eighth century saw the first famous English apparition of Mary, when Evesham Abbey was established on the site of the vision experienced by a swineherd, Eoves, who gave his name to the town, and then by a bishop, Egwin. Walsingham claims its origin in a dream vision in 1061, although the actual date of foundation is uncertain. English religious houses with claimed Marian visionary origins included Kirkstall and Jervaulx, in Yorkshire, and Willesden and Thetford were other famous apparition shrines in medieval England.[3] All over Europe, apparition shrines emerged, together with shrines founded to house 'miraculous' statues or because of the existence of important relics. William Christian Jr wrote a classic account in *Apparitions in Late Medieval and Renaissance Spain*, and many of his examples are Marian.[4] In the sixteenth and seventeenth centuries, there were Marian visions in the colonial context; the most-visited Christian shrine in the world is Guadalupe, near Mexico City, which claims an apparition in 1531 to an

---

1. Historical information on apparitions and shrines can be found in, for example, Lee and Nolan 1989: 274–89.
2. Joseph Ratzinger (now Pope Benedict XVI) accepts that many Catholic shrines have founding legends that are dubious historically, and yet this does not devalue the devotion: see Ratzinger 1985: 111–12.
3. For data on shrines in England, including vision founding stories, see Northcote 1868; Waterton 1879; Bridgett 1890; Gillett 1957.
4. Christian Jr 1981.

Indian Catholic, Juan Diego. The cloak on which the vision image is said to have been miraculously imprinted is still displayed at Guadalupe.

During the early modern period, Mary and her visions were integral to the Roman Catholic community's own struggle against its rivals, Protestant and Muslim. Stories circulated in which opponents were converted by visions, and Catholics protected. The theme of visions converting persons whose faith or viewpoint might make them inimical to Catholicism continued later, in the nineteenth century (the Jew Alphonse Ratisbonne in 1842) and the twentieth (the anti-papal atheist Bruno Cornacchiola in 1947), both in Rome.[5]

Despite the view in some circles that the apparitions and shrines of Mary belong to a bygone, superstitious age, the modern period could quite rightly be seen as the great age of such phenomena. In western Europe, the so-called 'Marian Age' began in 1830, with visions to an anonymous nun in Paris, only identified as Catherine Labouré after her death over 40 years later.[6] Nineteenth-century French cases became prototypes for modern apparitions, particularly the most famous of them all, to Bernadette Soubirous at Lourdes. Both Bernadette and Catherine were canonized for their contribution to Catholic devotional life.

Ruth Harris, in her book on Lourdes, *Lourdes: Body and Spirit in the Secular Age*, makes the point very well that nineteenth- and twentieth-century apparitions are not survivals of a superstitious past, rapidly disappearing with the advance of technology, but truly modern phenomena even if set in a centuries-old tradition:

> Bernadette Soubirous's apparitions at the Grotto of Massabielle and the development of the shrine at Lourdes followed in a long tradition of the miraculous in the Pyrenees. At the same time these extraordinary phenomena revealed something particular about the religious aspirations of the nineteenth century. The story of Lourdes demonstrates how the religion of the rural poor and the tale of a shepherdess in a grotto was eagerly embraced by both laity and clergy, rural and urban. They romanticized and sentimentalized its details, contributed to the construction of the sanctuary, embarked on massive pilgrimages and made Lourdes the best-known shrine in modern Christendom.
>
> The history of the shrine shows the mingling of different currents of Catholic belief and also offers a rare glimpse of a France normally hidden from view. For the history of the nineteenth century is still seen as the inevitable triumph of the republican ethos of secularization; even today historians are influenced by a stripped-down version of the model of religious belief and political modernization associated with the German sociologist Max Weber. With notable and growing exceptions, modern history has been understood as a process of 'disenchantment' in which school, ballot box and barracks ultimately triumph over superstition and backwoods provincialism, with peasant belief studied only to see the process of its eradication. In such an

5. For Ratisbonne, see Laurentin 1983; for Cornacchiola, see Alimenti 1987.
6. Laurentin 1983.

overarching scheme, the apparitions at Lourdes seem nothing more than a 'survival', a lingering cultural manifestation of a remote, impoverished and illiterate world. In this guise the development of the sanctuary is nothing more than an example of 'revival', of a mass, 'modernized' form of piety facilitated by package pilgrimage, a view that reduces the phenomenon to a form of right-wing leisure activity and ignores the widespread appeal of its devotional novelty and the unique, psychological dimensions of nineteenth-century Marianism.

This view is wrong, for it was the living and evolving religious tradition of the early cultists of Lourdes that stimulated the world's imagination and transformed the story of their apparitions into the model for contemporary Marian pilgrimage. Their judgement of the miraculous was hardly based on some naïve misunderstanding, or the need to find solace in the supernatural to compensate for the miseries of their daily life. Certainly, the Lourdais *were* comforted by their conviction that the Virgin had chosen their *bourg* as the site for her appearance, but this sense of blessing was matched by the sophistication of the mythical and legendary apparatus they used to assess Bernadette's experience. French peasants were neither gullible nor superstitious; such pejorative adjectives make more difficult the necessary process of understanding a magical and religious universe as much detached from secularism as it often was from orthodoxy. The beliefs of the Lourdais can best be understood as building on the traditions of older centuries and borrowing from more recent nineteenth-century cultural trends. Dismissing them as 'irrational' explains nothing, and perpetuates a complacent and inaccurate assessment of the 'rationality' of the contemporary era.[7]

In the nineteenth century, considerable tension existed between Catholicism and the more rationalist and secular tendencies of post-revolutionary France (which spread its ideas across Catholic Europe). In the twentieth century, the natural enemy of the Catholic Church was republicanism's successor, communism. The spectacular apparitions of Fatima, Portugal, in 1917, where the sun was said to appear to fall to earth and dry out the rain-soaked pilgrims, originally contained messages about the need to pray for peace during the First World War. However, the Fatima cult became the focus for warnings against communism, after later revelations by the surviving visionary, Lucia dos Santos (deceased 2005), from 1929 onwards.[8] William Christian Jr relates how, in the political struggle between communism and Christian democracy in the aftermath of the Second World War, with the concomitant social turmoil, visionary revelations were at their height:

The visions of the 1940s and 1950s were undoubtedly informed by the Fatima story. It remains to be seen why they were paid attention to, what it was in

---

7. Harris 1999: 357–8. Also on Lourdes, see Taylor 2003; on nineteenth-century France, see Kselman 1983.
8. For Fatima, see, for example, Zimdars-Swartz 1991: 67–91, 190–219. See also the description in Sarah Jane Boss, 'Marian Consecration in the Contemporary Church', in this volume: 420–23.

them that spoke to the historical moment of the Cold War. All of them performed the age-old role of providing a sacred place and sacred relics for curing. Those of Spain pointed out sacred trees (as, indeed, had that of Fatima), variously chestnut, ash, olive, pear, almond, and pine trees, whose leaves were used by the public for talismans and cures. In Italy pilgrims especially removed the dirt from the ground above which the Virgin had hovered. At four Spanish sites caves were sacralized as holy places, echoing the visions at Lourdes, and as at Lourdes and many older Spanish shrines, the Virgin pointed out holy springs whose water had curative powers. But in these aspects the postwar visions were indistinguishable from village apparitions in the preceding 500 years.

What does seem to key them in to the Fatima missions, the crusades of Father Lombardi, and the ethos of each nation's particular 'Christian political warfare', is their emphasis on conversion. The conversion theme is most explicit in the countries where the enemy was most salient. It is dramatically evident in the descriptions of East European visions that circulated in Western Europe, quite clear in Italy, and more implicit in Spain.

According to the Spanish magazine *Iris de Paz* (1 March 1948, 101), there had been four sets of visions in Yugoslavia in recent years. Whether or not these visions really took place, especially under the circumstances described, I do not know. But the credence they were given in Spain points to the more general connection of visions and anti-communism.[9]

Despite the end of the Cold War by 1991, the apocalyptic strain in Marian apparitions has continued into the twenty-first century. They express a deep unease about the state of the world, its perceived immorality and lack of spirituality which, it is claimed, are leading humanity to disaster. Yet, for the visionaries and their devotees, God wishes to intervene, through Mary, to remedy the situation on our behalf. The most famous recent instances of this message are the cults of Garabandal (Spain, 1960s) and Medjugorje (Bosnia-Herzegovina, 1980s to date).[10] Ireland is another good example: apparitions in the 1980s expressed a general concern about social change, and in more conservative quarters, they continue to attract devotees there.[11] As René Laurentin observes in *The Apparitions of the Blessed Virgin Mary Today*,[12] the phenomenon is global and widespread, among Catholic and Orthodox. However, although modern media and forms of communication may make it appear that cases are increasing, they have always been a common occurrence.

Ann E. Matter comments on aspects of recent cases in her article 'Apparitions of the Virgin Mary in the Late Twentieth Century'. She reflects on how apparitions

---

9. William Christian Jr, 'Religious Apparitions and the Cold War in Southern Europe', in Wolf (ed.) 1984: 252–3.
10. For Garabandal and Medjugorje, see Zimdars-Swartz 1991: 124–62, 225–33 and 233–44, respectively.
11. For Ireland, see Maunder 2000: 69–85 and 2003: 239–54.
12. Laurentin 1991.

refer to a golden past and an uncertain future; past occurrences are reinterpreted to fit this twentieth-century trend:

> The particularly twentieth-century phenomenon of Marian apparitions is, therefore, a Janus faced expression of Catholic identity. One side looks back, idealising a type of devotion more prominent before Vatican II and the modernising of the Church under Pope John XXIII and Pope Paul VI. But the other face is set in dreadful anticipation towards the unfolding of the new millennium. The force of apocalyptic thought in this movement is so strong that it has even influenced a popular interpretation of non-apocalyptic marian apparitions, such as those at Lourdes. A recent issue of the tabloid *Sun* trumpets the discovery of hidden papers of Bernadette Soubirous that include 'Five Prophecies', including warnings about the year 2000 as the 'Year of Disaster' (see Roller 2000). Apparently, Bernadette did receive three 'secrets', which she refused to reveal to anyone, not even the Pope, since 'the Virgin forbade me to tell any person, and the Pope is a person' (see Harris 1999, p. 162). But the traditional spirituality of Lourdes, although centered on an understanding of reparatory suffering, is not particularly apocalyptic, and has developed along very different lines from Fatima and the Fatima-like cults (see Thellier 1999). By this point, however, it is almost expected that a Marian apparition should include secrets and revelations of disaster, and the tabloid press is only too happy to oblige.[13]

As we have seen, apparitions of Mary have occurred throughout Christian history. While in cases from previous centuries, their origins are often uncertain, the modern visions provide an opportunity for observers to chart their development from as near to the beginning of the experiences as possible. In this chapter, we will be providing some examples of this work. The way in which the Roman Catholic Church engages with its visionaries is of interest, too. It is also important to consider the theological message that apparitions promote, as well as the image that they present of the Virgin Mary herself. These can be edifying for the Catholic community, but also the subject of social and political critique. Therefore, the sections below will consider: the nature of visions in Catholic theology; the visionary image of the Virgin Mary; the evolution of visionary cults; and communal and political dimensions.

THE NATURE OF VISIONS IN CATHOLIC THEOLOGY

The Roman Catholic Church as an institution defines and directs expressions of faith; it establishes canons of practice and belief. Clear examples of this are the books of the Bible (in the Roman Catholic tradition, the Vulgate version); theological doctrines; moral tenets; liturgical forms; life and practice in the religious and secular orders. The biblical canon was established in the fourth century; the other areas have been progressively established through Catholic history with the major decisive

---

13. Matter 2001: 125–53.

moments being the theology of Augustine; Scholasticism, in particular the systematic work of Thomas Aquinas; the Council of Trent; the Second Vatican Council.

The treatment of apparitions, too, has followed this timeline. Augustine categorized three types of vision, arising from the senses, the imagination and the intellect.[14] Later theologians would continue to use this taxonomy: Aquinas speculates as to which of these should be regarded as the most profound when discerning divine revelation. His view – that the vision of the intellect is of a higher order than the pictures of the imagination – has helped to relativize apparitions, which are clearly of the latter type (indeed, according to the experience of the visionary, the apparitions or locutions seem to occur through the senses, although if the visions are seen by a limited number of those present, their sense objectivity is ruled out). Aquinas uses his customary method of proposition and counter-proposition to establish his conclusion: 'hence it follows that the prophecy whereby a supernatural truth is seen by intellectual vision, is more excellent than that in which a supernatural truth is manifested by means of the similitudes of corporeal things in the vision of the imagination.'[15]

As the 'imaginative' vision is the more likely in popular manifestations of faith, then this view privileges the 'intellectual' experience of the mystic and contemplative (often in religious orders) over the ordinary visionary, who emerges spontaneously from the local community. The sixteenth-century Spanish Carmelite mystics St Teresa of Avila and St John of the Cross used such traditional arguments to restrain the passionate movements that followed apparitions in their time;[16] their writings have been used by Catholics in opposition to more recent cases, such as the apparitions in Beauraing, Belgium, in 1932–3.[17] The fact that many approved visionaries have been in religious orders, and that prominent lay seers have been encouraged to enter convents, such as Bernadette of Lourdes and Lucia of Fatima, serves to prove the point that the Catholic tradition wishes to keep control over visionary phenomena, because they are recognized as a normal means of divine communication within it.

Another categorization which helps to keep apparition movements within manageable bounds is the distinction between the 'public revelation' of the gospel, which has been handed down through the history of the Church and is binding upon Catholic belief, and the 'private revelations' of apparitions and other spontaneous phenomena, which are not. Although approving certain cases after careful discernment, and establishing them in the 'canon' of apparitions, the Catholic magisterium is keen to retain this distinction, as in the recent document that revealed and endorsed the so-called 'Third Secret' of Fatima (2000), published by the Congregation for the Doctrine of the Faith. However, the document also points out

---

14. St Augustine wrote about visions in *De Genesi Ad Litteram* ('On the Literal Meaning of Genesis'), Book XII. See Bourke 1945: 242–7.
15. Aquinas, *Summa Theologica 2.2*, trans. 1922: 49, Question CLXXIV, Second Article.
16. St Teresa of Avila 1988, 1990, 1995, see 'The Life of the Holy Mother Teresa of Jesus, ch. XXVIII; John of the Cross 1994, see 'Ascent of Mount Carmel', Book 2.
17. Carmelite publications opposed to Beauraing included Derselle 1933 and de Jésus-Marie *et al.* 1933.

the value of the apparitions in the canon, and how Catholics should understand them:

> The criterion for the truth and value of a private revelation is therefore its orientation to Christ himself. When it leads us away from him, when it becomes independent of him or even presents itself as another and better plan of salvation, more important than the Gospel, then it certainly does not come from the Holy Spirit, who guides us more deeply into the Gospel and not away from it. This does not mean that a private revelation will not offer new emphases or give rise to new devotional forms, or deepen and spread older forms. But in all of this then must be a nurturing of faith, hope and love, which are the unchanging path to salvation for everyone. We might add that private revelations often spring from popular piety and leave their stamp on it, giving it a new impulse and opening the way for new forms of it. Nor does this exclude that they will have an effect even on the liturgy, as we see for instance in the feasts of *Corpus Christi* and of the Sacred Heart of Jesus. From one point of view, the relationship between Revelation and private revelations appears in the relationship between the liturgy and popular piety: the liturgy is the criterion, it is the living form of the Church as a whole, fed directly by the Gospel. Popular piety is a sign that the faith is spreading its roots into the heart of a people in such a way that it reaches into daily life. Popular religiosity is the first and fundamental mode of 'inculturation' of the faith. While it must always take its lead and direction from the liturgy, it in turn enriches the faith by involving the heart.[18]

At the Council of Trent, the discernment of apparitions was formalized. In medieval Catholic Europe, approval of apparitions was often tied to the status of the visionary in the Church (for example, Joan of Arc, Savonarola), according to their political and theological importance. In the Tridentine period and up until today, the local bishop has had the responsibility of deciding whether apparitions can be accepted into the 'canon', and he has been encouraged to use local experts in theology and medicine to help him in his deliberations, using a 'commission of enquiry'. In recent history, and certainly since La Salette (1846),[19] the visions can take on such momentous importance that it has been customary to consult bishops in the country more widely, or the Vatican itself, on the matter. Between the sixteenth and twentieth centuries, national churches have varied in their policy towards official approval: in Italy many local shrines and cults were allowed to flourish, while in Spain the general rule was repression; nineteenth-century France, however, emphasized the commission of enquiry and its decision, and limited approval to four cases.

The criteria for discernment have been manifold, and vary from one apparition event to another. They usually draw upon the conclusions of Cardinal Lambertini

---

18. Bertone and Ratzinger 2000: 35.
19. For La Salette, see Zimdars-Swartz 1991: 27–42, 165–89; Stern 1980, 1984.

(later Pope Benedict XIV) in the eighteenth century, who compiled criteria for the canonization of saints.[20] There is a comprehensive summary of criteria in the volume *Vraies et Fausses Apparitions dans l'Eglise*.[21] Overall, there are four main criteria, commonly employed, that help to summarize the rest, and these were re-emphasized by the Sacred Congregation for the Doctrine of the Faith in 1978:[22]

- the character and comportment of the seers after the visions have occurred;
- the orthodoxy and accuracy of images and messages passed on;
- the lack of an explanation which would render any supernatural interpretation unnecessary (such as proven manipulation or duplicity, or illusion);
- the fruitfulness for those believing in the apparitions, such as increased religiosity, improved morals, or healing.

The process of discernment leads to a judgement which concludes one of three main alternatives: either the apparitions can be said to be of divine origin, and therefore Catholics are permitted (but not constrained) to believe in them; or the case is unproven, but not rejected altogether; or the case is proven to be not of divine origin, and should be shunned by faithful Catholics. The judgement may also indicate pastoral initiatives that are appropriate in the particular instance. Shrines where the apparitions are regarded as unproven may still be the object of pastoral guidance and cautious encouragement of devotion: Medjugorje is the prime example. Previously disqualified apparitions, such as Garabandal and San Damiano (Italy) in the 1960s, have – in the friendlier environment of the papacy of John Paul II – been re-evaluated at least in as far as allowing masses at the shrines and support for pilgrims.

The Mariologian René Laurentin is the most prominent of a number of priests who have become advocates of Marian apparitions, and attempt to establish their importance for the modern Church. In his younger years, Laurentin did much work on the histories of French shrines such as the Rue du Bac, Lourdes and Pontmain; more recently, in the 1980s, he became a supporter of the visionaries at Medjugorje in the face of local episcopal opposition. In his book *The Apparitions of the Blessed Virgin Mary Today*, he grapples with the large number of modern apparitions.[23] He seeks out the common themes, and concludes that part of the problem with apparitions is that, on the pattern of Garabandal and Lourdes, they are regarded as so universally important that they take on a gravity that makes discernment difficult. For Laurentin, the multiplicity of visionary phenomena means that we should regard them as having more limited import. Each case has a local context, and should be cherished there for its local value, without being presented to the universal community as having global significance as part of a co-ordinated divine plan, and

---

20. Lambertini 1852.
21. Alonso *et al.* 1973.
22. Cardinal Seper, *Normae Congregationis pro Doctrina Fidei de Modo Procendi in Diudicandis Praesumtis Apparitionibus ac Revelationibus* (Vatican City: Congregation for the Doctrine of the Faith, 1978). They are given in Laurentin 1990: 15:17–23; 16: 27–33; 17: 20–4; 18: 22–7; 19: 19–24; Reck 1996: 181–92.
23. Laurentin 1991: 9–16.

therefore to stand or fall on large-scale disputes and interests. Laurentin also argues for Church guidance and support; without this, he says, the cults will become unhealthy and schismatic. Furthermore, the cases do not satisfy a single paradigm, but are diverse:

> These facts give the lie to the received wisdom according to which visionaries are always children, young girls or shepherdesses. There is not even one shepherdess among the visionaries listed in this book. The statistics produced by Fr Besutti in respect of Italian visionaries from the thirteenth century onwards already disproved this belief. The majority of them are in fact male adults; but proverbs seem to ignore the facts.
>
> Another factor that leads to diversity is the apparitions' adaptation to each language, culture and country, etc. We have no stereotypical description regarding clothing or age. As in previous apparitions these differences are a sign of the freedom and powers of adaptation of glorified bodies. The signs are extremely varied; they include lights, scents, spiritual and physical cures, particularly at Finca Betania (Venezuela).
>
> The missions are also varied: contemplative, evangelical and ecumenical. From many points of view the fruits are diverse. Again there is no stereotype, but, as always in a living Church, initiatives seem to burgeon and the fruits are structured from within: prayer, mutual help and commitment, adapted to the needs of the time. Sometimes the apparitions give rise to a parochial cult and sometimes they are merely private, but this depends on the extent to which they are welcomed. The very fact of objection to an apparition marginalises the cult. But where priests prudently take this grace on board, with all its uncertainties, there is a better chance of a healthy evolution through the parish environment and the grace of the sacraments. This was one of the admirable features of Medjugorje: though the parish priest was initially sceptical he did all in his power to bring the people from the hill of the apparitions to the church for daily Mass. Little by little the apparitions became part of the daily Mass. The Virgin had led people to the Eucharist, but the skill of the parish priest had contributed enormously.
>
> There are many different reactions. There are two series of alleged apparitions at Split. Both parish priests in question tended to marginalise the events. The first series of apparitions alleged to have taken place at Gala were so successfully marginalised that they are no longer even spoken of. There were other apparitions in another parish. The subject was a young man who was so far removed from the Church that he could scarcely recall the Our Father. During the apparitions a crowd gathered round him spontaneously. They were not able to fit in his house and this naturally drew the attention of the police; in that country religion is permitted only in church. These good Christians requested the parish priest to invite them one way or another into the church. He refused. However, the bishop, who had shown an interest in the events, wrote to the parish priest and asked him to receive the people into the church without any commitment, by way of emergency solution as it were. He then

put a gifted priest in charge of the visionary and the group, who, through their association with him, had rediscovered their faith. At least that bishop understood that it was more important to provide proper pastoral guidance than to set up a commission of inquiry.

The frequency and diversity of the apparitions described would seem to mark a turning point. Lately, whenever there is an apparition that on the face of it looks genuine, the question is immediately raised: will it be a new Lourdes, a new Fatima? Of course the model was established in a certain number of cases where officially approved apparitions tended to become major events in the Church. The biggest sanctuaries in the world (after Rome) are in Guadalupe (Mexico), Lourdes and Fatima. A new apparition seemed to herald a new high-point for the Church. This is an illusion caused by a lack of perspective. There are plenty of small sanctuaries associated with apparitions which have remained regional or local: Laus, Garaison, Pellevoisin, Saint-Bauzille de la Sylve, etc. Thus those apparitions that emerged from the crucible appeared to be of such stature that people automatically thought that every apparition would be of universal importance. But the very frequency of apparitions and the modest stature of some among them shows clearly that we are dealing with rather modest phenomena, many of them private, and that Guadalupe, rue du Bac, Lourdes or Fatima are the exceptions.

So the present multiplicity of apparitions leads us to a proper understanding of their status: small signs from heaven given for the time being in one place or another and by no means always requiring the erection of a sanctuary. Where there are sanctuaries they are frequently small and of local importance. Apparitions have suffered because too much was made of them. The proliferation which has made them popular is in itself healthy. Perhaps we should speak of a democratisation of apparitions?

There is a strongly held view that present-day apparitions are a phase in Our Lady's organic plan which is unfolding from Guadalupe through the Miraculous Medal right up to our own times. According to this view each apparition is like a single piece of a jigsaw puzzle or the single notes of a symphony which need to be put together. This view has always appeared to me to be artificial and even dangerous.

To me apparitions seem like individual cries from heaven, heard in various places at various times without any overall plan. Our Lady's familiarity intervenes to particularise and personalise the Christian message according to our needs.[24]

So Laurentin's view of apparitions, at least those meeting the criteria, is one in which their value is undoubted, but their role and importance has boundaries, and they are best integrated with the sacramental and priestly elements of the Church. Such a perspective is understandable among priests, but Laurentin's balance is not held by all of the clergy, some of whom promote apparitions without discernment, and others reject them out of hand.

---

24.   Ibid.: 117–19.

Laurentin's more famous contemporary among the priests writing at the time of Vatican II and afterwards, Karl Rahner, also attempted to understand apparitions in an orthodox theological perspective. In *Visions and Prophecies* (1963), he unsurprisingly stresses the contextual and limited scope of visionary phenomena, as in all official views.[25] All messages are disseminated via the person of the visionary and their community context; they cannot be guaranteed as the words of Mary in any authoritative or objective sense. Apparitions are private revelations. However, certain cases are deserving of their more public impact.[26]

Yet what is left if we understand the apparitions and their messages as being based in the subjective world of the visionary? Is there anything objective? If the vision is authentic, then Rahner says yes, and for this draws upon the mystical literature of such as St John of the Cross. At the centre of the experience is the encounter with God. Visions 'are relatively unimportant compared with the infused contemplation from which they derive, and compared with faith, charity and the other supernatural Christian virtues'.[27]

Although the messages of the visionaries are open to doubt as to whether they are all profound and of import for the community, and much of their content may be for the visionaries alone (e.g. the 'secrets'), Rahner is prepared to accept that the Church approval of Lourdes, Fatima and the rest does point Catholics to a prophecy that is generally relevant. 'Prophecy is also to be a permanent endowment of the Church and a proof of her supernatural mission.'[28] What of the fact that visionary prophecies are so often warnings of impending disaster due to human immorality or unbelief?

> Divine prophecies will warn us against worldly optimism, against the mania for progress and against the utopian attempt to realise on this earth a kingdom of universal bliss. For this reason they constantly announce a dark future. True prophecies call us to penance, conversion, prayer, trust in the victory of Christ, hope in God eternal.[29]

For Rahner, like John of the Cross centuries before, God's symbolic language in the form of secrets and apocalyptic is not to be taken too literally: it is not like the language of human beings.[30] His work shows, for example, that he does not accept unequivocally the messages of Fatima. Yet he, Laurentin and other theologians tackling this question have to balance two apparently competing factors. One is the cautious theology that declares the apparitions private revelations and puts them in the perspective of the eternal gospel: their temporality, contextuality and subjectivity means that they are relativized. The second is the widespread acceptance in the Catholic tradition of the cases that pass the criteria and are generally recognized, their

---

25.   Rahner 1963: 55–75, 103–4.
26.   Ibid.: 18–30.
27.   Ibid.: 79–80.
28.   Ibid.: 103.
29.   Ibid.: 105.
30.   Ibid.: 73–4, 104–5; John of the Cross 1994, 'Ascent of Mount Carmel', Book 2, ch. XIX.

impact at all levels of the Church and the way in which their message resonates with the Catholic spirit of a particular age. Theologians who achieve this balance are more likely to gain a widespread hearing in the Catholic community.

THE VISIONARY IMAGE OF THE VIRGIN MARY

The classical image of Mary in apparitions is familiar: she wears the long gown and shawl over her head worn by women of all classes through the ages; the clothing is simple, but usually splendid in a way that suggests a very dignified person. Something will mark out the unusual nature of the appearance: light rays emanating from the figure, or the fact that she may hover above the ground or a natural object such as a tree, and ascend into the clouds at the end of the encounter. Other figures may accompany the Virgin: angels perhaps, or the infant Jesus, or one or more of the saints. In Green's and McCreery's book *Apparitions*, they write as researchers of 'psychic phenomena' in general and do not mention Mary.[31] Yet in apparitions of all kinds, the figure in the vision appears real, but certain clues tell the visionary that this is a special experience, and not an everyday one.

In many cases, the vision is identified as the Virgin Mary immediately or at an early point. People in Roman Catholic or Orthodox societies have come to expect that she may 'visit' them in this way. However, it is not always like that, and the two most famous apparitions in modern Catholic Europe, Lourdes and Fatima, are examples of a gradually evolving identification of the figure as Mary. This was because they occurred in rural communities where there was belief in a range of supernatural beings, and encounters with beings in the wild were common. Bernadette referred to her vision as *Aquèro*, 'that thing', showing her own uncertainty of its identity, or at least her reluctance to make the ultimate claim that it was the Virgin Mary.

Ruth Harris describes how the Pyrenean grotto Massabielle at Lourdes was a site associated with the terrors of the unknown: unpredictable and not always benign spiritual beings, the fairies and spirits of the forests, springs and mountains, like the *sidhe* of old Ireland.[32] There were also the spirits of the unquiet dead. In the nineteenth century, peasant societies still glimpsed women in white in the woods, sometimes leading processions of the dead, a strange phenomenon that helped to inspire Wilkie Collins' novel *The Woman in White*. Thus it was not entirely clear to the people of Lourdes what Bernadette had actually seen: it could have been a fairy queen. Bernadette's repeated requests for the vision's identity were reminiscent of the fairy queen's reticence to reveal her name. On the other hand, some suggested it was the spirit of a recently departed young woman, a member of the Enfants de Marie, whose uniform the clothing of the vision closely resembled. Harris describes this ambivalence about the figure in Bernadette's visions:

---

31. Green and McCreery 1989.
32. Harris 1999: 52–4.

Bernadette did not see a fairy, for her apparition was clearly differentiated from the little ladies of the forest by her golden rosary and blue belt. But both the poor and well educated were none the less alerted to this possibility: M. A. Clarens, the director of the Ecole supérieure de Lourdes, for example, recognized the parallels, since *Aquerò* also appeared in a grotto and, with her smallness, beauty, snowy whiteness and especially the yellow roses on her feet, showed several fairy-like attributes.

The parallels were not merely in appearance, however, for saints could behave like fairies and fairies like saints. The Pyrenean vision of the Virgin showed her willingness to engage in the daily affairs of men and women with severe punishments or quick rewards. Bernadette's apparition was also mercurial, for she did not always turn up on time, leaving the visionary bereft and accused of fraud. She could be severe, exacting a penitential devotion that the transgressor would never forget. For example, Jacques Laborde, a cabaret owner and a tailor, known for the way he ignored his religious duties and questioned Bernadette's sanity, was punished swiftly for cursing after the wild rose bush caught his cap. That very night he came down with a terrible diarrhoea and had to wash all his sheets, an act often seen in peasant society as a rite of purification. From that time forward Laborde went to the Grotto every morning, his joined hands holding the rosary. 'When on my way to Lourdes of a morning, I often met him coming down, humbled, eyes lowered. He went like this to the Grotto every morning. One could see from his humble demeanour that he was doing penance.'[33]

The identification of *Aquerò* as the Virgin Mary did occur in various stages after the first apparition of 11 February 1858, and was established on 25 March, when she announced herself as the 'Immaculate Conception'. But even an apparition of the 'Blessed Mother' could be ambivalent:

In the eyes of the poorer Lourdais the Virgin was not the sentimental character of nineteenth-century images of piety, but rather the strong, sometimes harsh mother of peasant society. She hit back hard when slighted or insulted and demanded speedy fulfilment of proper religious observances. An indication of this mentality can be seen in the way they transformed orthodox devotions, much to the annoyance of the clergy. In the June before the apparitions the bishop of Tarbes and Lourdes, Mgr Laurence, wanted to stop the way the standard 'Hail Mary' was followed by a mixture of supplication and a talisman to ward off potential suffering: 'Whoever wears this prayer on their person will not die a sudden death.' Many suggested that great punishments were in store for those who did not recite these inventions with proper care at the moment of death. Thus, the Virgin of the poor required appeasement as much as veneration, and in this resembled the Virgin of Garaison, who 300 years earlier smacked Anglèze de Sagazan despite her piety and humility.

---

33. Ibid.: 78–9.

While Bernadette's lady could be harsh, she could also be infinitely merciful, in keeping with her image as divine mother and as mercurial fairy. From this early moment, before the clerical commissions and medical consultations that were later to surround Lourdes and make it famous, the poor were convinced of the Virgin's miraculous intercession.[34]

Understanding apparition cases like Lourdes in some detail tells against the simple assertion that the Mary of visionary phenomena in Roman Catholic societies is a constant figure, transcending the context, a universal mother figure. This assumption occurs because the process of approval, or canonization, of apparitions in the Church picks out those features that belong to an internationally agreed understanding of Mary, and aspects of folklore and local belief are forgotten or suppressed. Opponents of the recent visions in Medjugorje, Bosnia–Herzegovina (1981 to date)[35] point out the potentially embarrassing links it seems to have with Bosnian-Croatian folklore, while its supporters prefer to stress those elements that are more familiar to outsiders. However, one factor that causes apparitions to tend to universal – rather than distinctive and local – images is the way in which apparition stories are known to succeeding generations, whose own experiences will then contain themes and impressions from earlier cases. However, too close a copying will disqualify an apparition from taking its place among the few approved cases. This was the fate of Marpingen in Germany (1876), where the visions echoed many elements of those at Lourdes, by now famous. David Blackbourn's study of Marpingen, which gives a window into life in Catholic Saarland of the time, shows how the visions came to be doubted by the Church hierarchy despite attracting many thousands of pilgrims to the site. He also paints a picture of how they differed from more worthy counterparts.

> The classic Marian visions of the nineteenth century contained an intense vision of a better world, of peace, hope, or plenty. Even the less spiritually compelling seers reported visions whose beauty contrasted starkly with the realities of everyday life. The Virgin's face was gentle and surrounded by radiant light, her clothes rich and sumptuous. When apparitions took place at times of agricultural crisis, as they so often did, the children told of the plenty that would replace want. A number of these motifs occurred (although not as prophecies) in the Mettenbuch visions. The children described angels carrying the Virgin's train, so that it was possible to see she had 'golden shoes and white stockings'. They had 'seen angels eating grilled fish from a golden table', and they described the Virgin's instructions that they make up and drink daily from a concoction that sounds like a rustic ambrosia. The Marpingen apparitions were, by contrast, remarkably lacking in intensity or a sense of rapture. Drawing on half-remembered fragments from books or catechism classes, prompted by parents and other adults, the girls talked conventionally about the

---

34. Ibid.: 79.
35. Opponents of Medjugorje have included Jones 1998; Sivrič 1988.

beauty of the Blessed Virgin, adding details of familiar Bible stories like the Annunciation. The overriding impression is one of fragmented descriptions lacking any real centre. In other apparitions the Virgin assumed a fixed appearance, graced a particular spot, and delivered a single powerful message. In Marpingen the children described a Virgin in motley who flitted from place to place and had no special message. The exchanges they reported seldom rose above the level of banality, their prophecies concerning missed appointments rather than sublime matters of war, peace and famine.

The apparitions described by the Marpingen children did not so much represent the eruption of the divine into everyday life, as subject the divine to an everyday regimen. We can see this in the lengthy, commonplace exchanges the seers reported having with the Virgin, who sometimes sat, sometimes joined them in their games as they rolled down the hillside. It is even more apparent in the list of places where they claimed to have seen her: in their homes, in the barn and stables, in various houses in Marpingen, and in a shop in Tholey, in the school, the church, the graveyard. This aspect of the apparitions created doubts among some clerical observers, and it is worth exploring what it might have meant to the visionary children. Most obviously, of course, if the apparitions were to continue after the authorities blocked off the Härtelwald, they would have to do so within the village. This inevitably meant a certain domestication of the Virgin. But we can go further than that. In recounting the appearance of Mary in these places, by 'naming' houses and meadows, the children were able to employ familiar village landmarks. There was doubtless a reassuring element to this: a Blessed Virgin who could be associated with Schafer's meadow, or with the large round stone that stood at the edge of the upper village, was rendered benign, placed firmly within a bounded world. At the same time, the visionaries' message that the Virgin Mary had graced these everyday spots cast the places themselves in a new light. It also enhanced the status of the messengers, for the children – through their privileged position – placed their own stamp vicariously on property and places that were normally the concern of adults.

This element of reversal continued what had begun at the original apparition site. Access to the site had been jealously guarded by the seers. Neither the parish priest nor the priest from Heusweiler was to approach it; at one point the children brought Father Neureuter the instruction (*Weisung*) of the Virgin that he should cease his close contact with and observation of them. On several occasions they indicated with a shake of the head that particular individuals were not to approach. The children announced which prayers had to be recited and the spring from which water should be drunk (not the Marienbrunnen near the church, but one in the Härtelwald). In other ways, too, the visionaries underlined their special status. They spoke of secrets, and told pilgrims that celestial omens would be explained. Katharina Hubertus said she had been told to become a nun.[36]

---

36. Blackbourn 1993: 132–4.

The homely Virgin of Marpingen is not the common image of Mary in the more famous apparitions, in which, as at Lourdes and Fatima, she is the sterner and more numinous figure of the other-world, who gives solace only in a context of warning and calls to repentance. As such, she gives voice to the anger of devotees against the moral lapses of their communities and the wider society. The scope of this has increased with the greater international awareness of the last two centuries. While visions arise in a local context and address local issues, they also address a global dimension. The secrets of La Salette (1846) condemned Western European governments, while those of Fatima warned against the international spread of Russian communism. Apparitions since the Second World War have a global import and articulate a cosmic drama, in which Mary is the messenger in a time of extreme crisis for the world. Zimdars-Swartz's book *Encountering Mary* shows how this is portrayed:

> In fact, something like a single, transcultural, apocalyptic ideology based on apparition messages has grown up in recent years around the edge of mainline Roman Catholic institutions which incorporates the messages of various apparitions and to which the majority of supporters of the more recent unrecognized apparitions could be said to subscribe. This ideology is a sort of popular, free-floating apocalyptic worldview, built out of images and themes prominent in the messages of the more recent apparitions and can be seen as anchored in almost any one, or any combination, of these apparitions. To judge from the immense amount of apparition literature published in recent years in various languages which propagates one form or another of this popular apocalyptic ideology or worldview, the themes and images which define this phenomenon merit some attention.
>
> Fundamental to this worldview are the images of intercession and intervention. It is assumed here that a divinely appointed figure may, on the heavenly plane, intercede with God or Christ, and on the earthly plane, intervene in history to change an otherwise predetermined course of events. Most modern apparition devotees assume that the Virgin Mary has been appointed by God as the chief executor of both of these tasks, although she may, on occasion, enlist other heavenly or human figures to assist with her interventions in earthly life. Intercession, as it is understood here, usually involves a dramatic interaction between God, who in the persons of the Father and the Son represents the divine law, and the Virgin, who represents divine mercy.
>
> In this schema, God is portrayed as angry with the world because the sins of humanity have overturned or disrupted the established order, and indeed, he is portrayed as so angry that his justice demands immediate chastisement ...
>
> War, famine, persecution, catastrophic illness, and other calamities are in this worldview understood as both chastisements for sin and admonitions to reform or conversion. At La Salette Mary reportedly told the seers that the failure of the potato crop had been a warning about their sins; because they had not heeded her warning, however, they faced famine and disease. At Fatima, the

Virgin warned in the second part of Lucia's secret of the imminent threat of war, hunger, and persecution of the Church. At Garabandal, according to the seers, the Virgin warned that people needed to lead good lives, and that if they did not, a chastisement would be forthcoming.

Future chastisements are not, however, seen in this worldview as inevitable. Indeed, the major purpose of the Virgin's latter-day appearances is to give the world a last opportunity to restore the disrupted sacred order and the divine-human relationship which this order represents – through repentance or conversion, a return to appropriate devotional practices, and submission to the ordinances of the Church ...

In the messages of the more recent apparitions, particularly in the context of the devotee's question of why she has been appearing so often in recent times, Mary's motherly qualities have been especially emphasized. In most of these apparitions, there have been messages suggesting that it is a mother who is best able to rescue her children from impending disaster ...[37]

The picture of the loving but stern mother who intercedes at a time of crisis for humanity is the abiding image of modern Marian apparitions when the elements regarded as universally relevant are extracted as the case takes its place in the list of those accepted by devotees. The canon circumscribed by Church authorities is not the same as that agreed by the international circle of devotees, who use books, periodicals and the internet to gather information on how the phenomena are developing worldwide. Garabandal (1961–5) and Medjugorje are popularly acclaimed, but not yet recognized by the Church, which nevertheless tolerates the pilgrimages and devotions at these sites, often attended by priests. The apocalyptic messages of these apparitions, with promises of miracles and warnings of chastisements, add to their fame and popularity. Their devotees will be encouraged by the more formal approval given to modern cases outside Europe, like Akita (Japan, 1973); Betania (Venezuela, 1976–84); San Nicolas (Argentina, 1893); Cuapa (Nicaragua, 1980); Kibeho (Rwanda, 1981–9).[38]

THE EVOLUTION OF VISIONARY CULTS

The popular belief about apparitions is that the visionaries pass on a verbatim account of their experience into posterity, and are the sole mediums of their messages and images. Scholarly accounts have cast doubt on this understanding. Before the account is published and finds its way into general knowledge, it is mediated through the local community among whom the visionaries live. The initial devotees come to be active participants in the unfolding of an apparition event. Both priests and lay people may be involved. At some stage, suitable people are chosen to write down the accounts; there may be several editions. During this whole process, members of the

---

37. Zimdars-Swartz 1991: 247–9.
38. See Laurentin 1991: 53–113 for brief accounts.

community (acting in the best interests of the visionaries as they perceive them) may edit the material according to what is regarded as being consonant with Church teaching and popular expectation. Zimdars-Swartz shows how this process occurred at the Lourdes grotto in Mellerary, Ireland (1985):

> There is, of course, no minute-by-minute report of the events at the grotto, nor even of what was heard and seen by the two boys in the apparition itself. Moreover, a comparison of the early unpublished records of the apparition, that is, the transcripts made by Cait Cliffe and Deevy, with the aforementioned brochure makes it clear that a considerable amount of material in the earlier records did not make it into the brochure that was publicly distributed several months later. Some of this material is of a personal nature, pertaining to one or both of the seers or to particular persons in the crowd, and was evidently judged to be of private concern only. Most of the remaining deleted material seems to make little sense and was evidently excluded for that reason. None of this private or enigmatic material, in fact, has been included in any of the accounts distributed to the public at the grotto. Messages that were understood as specifically addressed to the public, however, have not only been included but have been at the core of all three accounts, appearing in the March brochure, for example, in bold type. This brochure, then, like the leaflets that were distributed earlier, was an official account of the apparition that included and emphasized what committee members, looking back over the many events and reported messages, thought to be of public importance and relevance.
>
> In their production of an account of what had happened at their grotto, the Melleray grotto committee went through a process that no doubt reflects what has taken place among the first devotees of most other modern Marian apparitions, but in most cases only a few glimpses of this process may be evident in the available written records. The basic task of such communities is to simplify the complex web of events in which they have participated and to shape it into a meaningful, memorable, and engaging narrative. Public interest in particular aspects of these events, which is influenced by an awareness of previous apparitions and other similar phenomena associated with popular Catholicism, impinges on this process both in formal interviews and in many informal conversations and functions as a touchstone for those who assume the task of constructing the narrative. This interest becomes the guide, as it were, which leads them to select and to highlight some material and to reject other material as irrelevant. While the words and actions of the seers that pertain to what the narrators perceive as the central theme of the apparition are of primary importance in this construction, the testimonies of others who have experienced one or more of the traditional confirmatory signs (sun miracles, healings, conversions) are typically used to supplement the narrative and to reinforce the drama of the encounter with the supernatural that it presents. What has begun as an oral process within a community responding to some unusual experiences thus leads, finally, to a written account, which is usually printed and often widely distributed and which tends to be accepted as

canonical by persons who are subsequently drawn into the believing community. Such accounts are usually devotional, which is to say that they can be used by persons who already accept the apparition to rehearse its drama, and apologetic, which is to say that they present the apparition in terms that will probably be meaningful to other Roman Catholics and that may encourage its recognition by Church authorities.

The task of producing this account typically falls to an educated person, sometimes a member of the local community but more often an outsider. This individual is usually an educated layperson or priest who has an active personal interest in such phenomena, considerable leisure time, and the financial means for travel and for underwriting the costs of publication. While the official account of the apparition may technically be the work of this person and may reflect some of his or her biases, it is more properly understood as the work of the believing community which has gathered around the apparition site.

In June 1986, the Melleray grotto committee with the help of Mr Deevy was negotiating with Mercier Press for the publication of a book that would include both an account of the Melleray apparition and testimonies to other presumably supernatural phenomena witnessed at the grotto. They were also making plans for the production of a videotape. With respect to their goal of obtaining official church recognition for their apparition, members of the committee spoke with both optimism and studied realism. They were prepared to wait, they said, 'as long as it took at Knock'.[39]

In this account, there is a certain control on the phenomenon in that it remains centred upon the two boys as visionaries. Despite community involvement in the editing of the visionaries' accounts, they are still the prominent figures and source of the messages. Official approval requires a clearly identified group of visionaries and a coherent account, and devotees will have this in mind.

The anthropologist Paolo Apolito's book *Apparitions of the Madonna at Oliveto Citra* derives from the rare instance of a scholar being present near the very beginning of an apparition event (at Oliveto Citra, Italy, from 1985).[40] It will not be comfortable reading for those convinced by apparition claims, as Apolito concludes that apparitions are *constructions*, that is, they only become systematic accounts when they are constructed from a great variety of fragmented pieces. Oliveto Citra does not have one, two or a few visionaries, but many, and no one person comes out as the principal seer. Other cases that have multiple visionaries (such as Lourdes and Beauraing, Belgium, 1932–3, in particular) remained focused on the young people who had contributed the original reports. There are also cases that begin with child visionaries, but adults with more compelling, politically aware messages become more prominent (for example, Palmar de Troya, Spain, from 1968; in Ireland, from 1985, Mary Casey and Christina Gallagher eventually took over from the children at

---

39. Zimdars-Swartz 1991: 14–16.
40. Apolito 1998.

Inchigeela and Carns respectively; this was also a tendency at Beauraing, but the emphasis on the children prevailed).[41]

The wisdom for the devotees of keeping a focus on a special person or group as the 'official' seer(s) is illustrated by the Oliveto Citra case. Apolito narrates a confusing story of messages and experiences that runs counter to the logic of the devotional account. Even Laurentin, who accepts the possibility that apparitions are genuine supernatural encounters, says that 'there are many apparitions, perhaps too many, at Oliveto Citra, including those had by pilgrims'.[42] This will have told against Oliveto Citra gaining its place in the canon. Apolito's analysis shows how the dynamics of this event worked in practice, and how the chaos of experiences began to form into something more generally accepted:

> The phenomenon would not have taken hold if all had depended on the credibility of the children. Even when the children were, at first, taken seriously, few people believed in the apparition of the Madonna. In 'It Is Said They Have Seen the Madonna,' I tried to demonstrate that, in spite of their claim to have withheld judgment, the main community leaders contributed decisively to the transformation of the visions from a subjective experience to objective events. In the first place, simply by talking about it, they inevitably endowed the varied and uncertain reconstructions of events that they considered with coherence, even when they addressed them critically. The testimony of the witnesses was almost always fragmentary and often contradictory and incoherent. Drawing them together into the same narrative scheme itself gave the happenings a storylike structure that endowed them with coherence and plausibility. This narrative, imbued with a structural logic, constituted the events all the more since the events themselves were not yet established by the fragmentary testimony of the first protagonists.
>
> The implicit acceptance by the leaders was a decisive act from which, in fact, the phenomena were constituted, while in appearance the phenomena simply gained credibility. The role of the seers was surely important but that of the leaders was much more so. The seers limited themselves to (or were limited by) recounting 'things as I lived them.' The leader, on the other hand, recounted 'the things that occurred.' As a result, the normative power of the leaders was far greater. By situating themselves as the center of meaning and the controllers of the events, the leaders were able to delineate the arena in which people were permitted to have experiences of visions; that is, they decided what was external to visionary experience – spurious, implausible – what simply did not exist. The leaders' control of the word gave them control of the events.
>
> Furthermore, the leaders, especially the parish priest, sought to reduce the importance of the seers as a whole by making a distinction between seers and

41. For Palmar de Troya, see Laurentin 1991: 142–3; for Ireland, see Maunder 2000; for Beauraing, see Thurston 1934 and Charue 1943–6.
42. Laurentin 1991: 95.

visions. Given the hazards of personal subjectivity, the seers might wander into unorthodox terrain at any moment. But the visions could be configured into a coherent, orthodox scheme by the leadership. By distinguishing the human subjects from their experience, the leaders could control the very experience of the seers; that is, the words that defined it and, through the words, the production of the apparitions.

The leaders controlled the production of the events in yet another way. Their prudent 'attention' generated positive expectations among the curious spectators. Given the leaders' lack of hostility toward the events, the spectators adopted attitudes of piety, which the leaders themselves then interpreted as a general faith in the events. In this way, the leaders were affirmed in their attitude of *attention* and, little by little, opened themselves to *acceptance,* however prudent. In a circular process, the increase in their support generated stronger support in the devout, which in turn affected the leaders, increasing their own belief. Hence, in a cyclical feedback, each leader contributed to the growth of the events without realizing that they were seeing in the mirror of others their own growing conviction, yet assuming, to the contrary, that it was the events that were imposing their own evidence.[43]

Apolito's account is an interesting critique of the general Catholic understanding that Church authorities evaluate orthodox piety as a spontaneous occurrence that confirms the genuine nature of the apparitions themselves. The orthodox piety might be a response to the expectations of the authorities as much as they are to the charisma of the visionaries. The channelling of visions using careful canonical criteria will, of course, create a circular process of authentication in which the Church recognizes those cases which conform to its own presuppositions of what constitute appropriate messages, devotions and cultic activities. Therefore, any truly prophetic or unusual phenomena that challenge the status quo are, by definition, ruled out.

Apolito's anthropological approach is an analysis of the interactions and agreements that take place in the evolution of an apparition account. A psychological approach was attempted a few years earlier by Michael P. Carroll, in his *The Cult of the Virgin Mary: Psychological Origins*.[44] Carroll will not convince anyone who finds Freudian theory problematic, but his work does provide detail that will be helpful in understanding the Marian cult and its apparition phenomena. Carroll concentrates on the role of the mother figure in the Christian family, and argues that the image of Mary as merciful counterpart to the wrath of God is based on this. One does not need to be a Freudian to agree with him that there is a strong relationship there, nor to accept that mother deprivation may be an important factor in apparitions of Mary. Visionaries deprived of mothers at an early age include Catherine Labouré, of the Rue du Bac, Paris, 1830, and Ivanka Ivanković of Medjugorje (Pope John Paul II, a

---

43. Apolito 1998: 8–10.
44. Carroll 1986.

promoter of the Marian cult, particularly at Czestochowa and Fatima, likewise lost his mother as a child).

Carroll's theory becomes more problematic in cases where he posits mother deprivation for visionaries whose mothers remain alive and present with them (Maximin Giraud of La Salette, Bernadette Soubirous of Lourdes). It is difficult to see why the vision at Lourdes was a mother figure for Bernadette when she described it as being as young and petite as herself. The cult of Lourdes came to accept *Aquerò* as a mother, it is true, but Bernadette resisted attempts to make the statue look older and more maternal. It is not easy to try, as Carroll does, to identify psychological factors in the life of an individual visionary when, as we have seen, the phenomenon becomes so quickly a communal event.

COMMUNAL AND POLITICAL DIMENSIONS

What do Marian apparitions mean to the communities that espouse them? After the period of acceptance and discernment, they pass into tradition, a tradition handed down through pilgrimage to the apparition site, now a shrine; published literature including stories and interpretations; occasionally, canonization of the seer (St Catherine Labouré; St Bernadette Soubirous; it remains to be seen whether this will be extended to Lucia of Fatima, who died in 2005). They are bearers of meaning, firstly to the local, then to the national, and finally to the international community. In the Roman Catholic tradition, this promotion to the global level is common; in other denominations, such as the Orthodox churches, the canonization process is not so formalized or centralized, and so the importance tends to stay at the local level.

An example of an apparition which is important on a universal scale, but which has particular significance for the national community, is Guadalupe in Mexico (claimed to have occurred in 1531). In recent times, Our Lady of Guadalupe has been declared Patroness of All the Americas by the Pope, but it remains a very important part of Mexican Catholic identity. It has also been adopted by the liberation theologies of Latin America, because the vision occurred during the period of the Conquest, the seer was an Indian, the Madonna was black, and the site was one originally dedicated to the indigenous goddess. As Virgil Elizondo points out in his *Guadalupe: Mother of the New Creation*, these features of the story have a resonance with a movement that proclaims the liberation of the oppressed peoples in the nations of Latin America:

> The story of Our Lady of Guadalupe is the indigenous account of the real new beginnings of the Americas. The story of her appearances and compassion is sacred narrative as remembered by the victim-survivors of the conquest who were equally the firstborn of the new creation. The entire Guadalupe event as recorded in the *Nican Mopohua* is a Nahuatl communication par excellence. It proceeds by way of contrasting images whose full meaning is arrived at only in the final synthesis. The symbolic meaning of the images created by the words is all-important. Each detail had special signification for the Nahuatl peoples. The

story came from their world, and if we are to discover its regenerative signification, we must seek to understand it through their cosmovision.

The whole Guadalupe narrative is a beautiful, delicate, and carefully thought-out Nahuatl poem of contrasting imagery, symbolic communication, tender consolation, radical affirmation, and divine inversion. It is a highly complex mestizo (Nahuatl-European) form of communication in various ways: the image and the narrative are mutually interpretative; there are elements of both Nahuatl and Iberian worldviews in the narrative and the image, and together they say new things that neither alone could have expressed; the image is poetry that is seen while the poem is imagery that is heard, and together they constitute a coherent communication.

While the sacred imagery of the native world was being insulted, discredited, and burned, the sacred imagery of the Christian world was being imposed as the sole representation of that which was good, beautiful, and true. This did not make sense to peoples whose sacred imagery had guided their lives from time immemorial. Furthermore, it was alien to the gospel itself. But now, a new Nahuatl-Christian sacred imagery would erupt from within these tensions.

The full life-giving meaning of Guadalupe can be seen and understood only in the overall context of the confused and painful reality of the postconquest period. The Aztec-Nahuatl Empire, and with it all the native peoples, was defeated in 1531. It was the beginning of the end of their world. Their entire world of meaning had been destroyed and discredited. Had their ancestors been wrong all along and therefore to be disclaimed? Were they now to be ashamed of their parents and ancestors? Were they now to cut off all family tradition and relations? Had their God deceived them for generations? Since the conquering people, who claimed their European God was all-powerful, were white men and women, did that mean that their brown skin was an indication of their inferiority or even of their collective sinful condition? Would grace make them white with blue eyes?

It seemed the sun had been permanently eclipsed, and the innermost darkness of the soul prevailed throughout the land and its native peoples. In the midst of the death cries of a vanquished people, a new light broke through to announce new life. This was the good news of Our Lady of Guadalupe – the gospel through the language and imagery of the conquered people of the Nahuatl world.[45]

The link between apparitions and the self-identity of marginalized people is also one made by Blackbourn. While he is writing in an historical – rather than theological – vein, he too points out how visionary phenomena appeal particularly to people in struggling communities. This can be interpreted by the devotee, such as Elizondo, as Mary's favour for the poor, and by the sceptic as an indication that visions are

---

45.   Elizondo 1997: xviii–xix.

psychologically generated compensations for disadvantage, a conclusion that can be expressed in Marxist theory among other alternatives. For Blackbourn, it is simply an observation that arises from his investigation into Marpingen:

> The Catholic revival in nineteenth-century Europe, only now receiving the attention it deserves from historians, was centred on the figure of the Virgin Mary. Her growing presence could be seen not only in new doctrine (the Immaculate Conception) and the naming of new congregations, but in liturgical changes, Marian hymnals and new popular devotions. Catholic children growing up during the papacy of Pius IX lived in a world permeated by images of the Virgin Mary, and apparitions were one aspect of this. Visions of Mary became increasingly the most common visions of the nineteenth century: that was another distinguishing feature of the period after the French Revolution compared with earlier centuries. This can be ascribed partly to the general Marianization of the church in these years, but even more to the fact that the church chose to authenticate and celebrate a number of apparitions as exemplary. Most notable among them were, of course, the visions of Bernadette Soubirous in 1858, taken by Rome as a vindication of the doctrine of the Immaculate Conception promulgated just four years earlier. The outcome was that Lourdes became a kind of template, a stimulus to future visionaries, however much the church might condemn the frequently unsatisfactory results.

Marpingen provides an excellent illustration of what all this meant in practice. A village in which, up to the 1840s, religious duties were performed without enthusiasm and successive parish priests encountered surly hostility, it became an exemplar of the Catholic revival in the third quarter of the nineteenth century. Throughout the diocese of Trier this religious renewal was strongly associated with the Virgin Mary. In Marpingen a Marian well was restored and a discredited village practice (the oath of 1699) replaced by a brotherhood dedicated to the Sacred and Immaculate Heart of Mary. A new parish priest arrived, who placed his own painting of the Virgin and Child in the church and sermonized enthusiastically to his flock about Lourdes. His message was echoed by a village schoolteacher. None of this drove out popular belief in the mysterious power of certain rocks and trees, or vanquished the idea that poor souls from purgatory walked abroad as ghosts – witness the many 'women in white' in the area during the 1870s. The stories told by priest and teacher about a Virgin Mary who appeared to simple peasant children were more likely to overlay popular belief than to replace it. In this sense, the ground was well prepared by July 1876, when the Marpingen visionaries made their first claims on a day that saw 100,000 Catholics gathered for inaugural celebrations in Lourdes.

Marpingen had in common with other apparition sites not only its new-found and heavily Marianized piety, but its former 'bad reputation' – a point that devotees of La Salette and Lourdes also liked to emphasize. The resemblances did not stop there. Many places that greeted apparitions enthusiastically felt themselves to be in some way overshadowed by their neighbours. Many were located close to powerful religious foundations or long-established pilgrimage centres; others were dominated by the commercial weight or political muscle of a neighbouring town. All of this was true of Lourdes, and it was also true of Marpingen. The village had lived for centuries in the shadow of Tholey abbey, its tithe-lord until French Revolutionary armies arrived. (The abbey of Metten stood in the same relationship to Mettenbuch, the Bavarian apparition site of the 1870s.) The merchants and moneylenders of Tholey continued to play an important but resented part in the economic life of the village. Slightly further away, St Wendel was a regional market centre on whose craftsmen the village was dependent for any substantial project, such as church rebuilding; it was an important pilgrimage centre and the seat of local political power; and unlike Marpingen, it had the railway. Even neighbouring Alsweiler, although smaller in population, gave its name to a local mayoralty. Marpingen was one of the largest villages in the area, but it might be described as 'inert', a place associated with nothing in particular except perhaps a reputation for truculence. It was not the only apparition site that took special pleasure in its new celebrity.

This raises important questions about the geography of apparitions. They are, of course, associated with inaccessible and barren spots. In Latin America the Virgin has favoured landscapes of mesquite, in Europe rocky uplands – areas of sheep and goats, low-yield arable, and quarrying, not the fertile European plains. This apparently clear-cut picture confirmed supporters of the apparitions in their belief that Our Lady sought out the obscure for a sign of special grace; it suggested to opponents that everything could be attributed to the idiocy of rural life. The reality is a little more complicated. Apparition sites were indeed generally poor, but they were hardly cut off from the world. How could they be in an era of state-building, furious diocesan organization, and the encroaching market? By the third quarter of the nineteenth century the railway and the telegraph had arrived close to communities like this, even if they had not yet reached them. The movement of itinerant workers and the trade in wool, animal skins, or quarry stone brought contact with a larger world, even if that contact was not always happy. If we interrogate the cliché of the remote apparition site, we find that they were not always so remote after all, but had been at least partially penetrated by the forces of change. Their problem was not that they were isolated, but that they were marginal. That is what fuelled the sense of being overshadowed by neighbours who were richer or more powerful.[46]

Another close study of a now mostly forgotten apparition site is William Christian Jr's book on Ezquioga (Spain, 1931–4), *Visionaries: the Spanish Republic and the Reign of Christ*.[47] Just as apparitions appeal to marginalized communities, they have also been

---

46. Blackbourn 1993: 396–7.
47. Christian Jr 1996.

very important for communities that perceive themselves to be under threat in a period of rapid, and often violent, social change. As Victor and Edith Turner put it, apparitions 'appear at the point of major stress between contrary cultures and their major definitions of reality',[48] i.e. they often express a political message in a time of conflict between the conservative sections of the Catholic community and strong modernizing forces. This is true of Ezquioga: the conflict was between the secularizing anti-clerical Spanish Second Republic, and Catholics from all regions of Spain. However, as Christian points out, such politically charged apparitions are usually rejected by Church authorities and perceived as an embarrassment in the struggle. This is true of Ezquioga. However, Christian's book runs counter to the tendency of history to select the material that is more comfortable for posterity. The way in which Christian describes how Ezquioga's visions were edited and weeded by devotees themselves recalls the work of Apolito (above), an associate of his. Of course, Ezquioga's historical and political context is very different from, and much more intense than, that of Oliveto Citra in 1980s Italy.

> My inquiries in dioceses and in religious orders about persons involved in the Ezkioga apparitions revealed a certain sensitivity and reticence ... Others had an involvement with Ezkioga that their communities now consider embarrassing.
>
> But these people's stories, and that of Ezkioga as a whole, are necessary and useful. The selective memory that removed this story from church history, Spanish history, and Basque history removed the opportunity for us to learn from the phenomenon. Only through reflection on historical events in all their human detail can we understand a process and avoid the same tragic result. In 1931 Basques, Catalans, and Spaniards seized on people to voice collective hopes. For some of the children especially, the episode hopelessly distorted their lives and confused their family relations. Some lived with fear until their death.
>
> Tens of thousands of older people in the Basque Country were left perplexed by what they saw and heard. The silence the bishop imposed left them ashamed of their own enthusiasm. They too need a historical explanation that makes these events understandable. Hundreds of families of the seers throughout Navarra and Gipuzkoa, especially the rural and small-town families who have not moved have borne the stigma of Ezkioga in total silence for sixty years. Whatever variations the seers themselves introduced, the visions at Ezkioga were a collaborative enterprise of hundreds of thousands of people in search of meaning and direction. At the turn of the century psychologists suggested that crowds responded to skilled persons who manipulated them, the *meneurs*. At Ezkioga the press, the religious and civic elites, and in the last analysis the general public, were the meneurs. How else can we explain an entire Catholic society that delegated its direction to its children and to some of its least prestigious members? These seers gave voice to the society's hope.

---

48. Turner and Turner 1978: 150.

Selective memory is a problem not just for the Basques, the church, churches, or institutions. Remembering and forgetting are equally important for all of us. But we generally conceal the way we accumulate, discard, and distribute meaning. In the rush of grace in time of upset – in the visions of Ezkioga as in the cargo cults of New Guinea or in the ghost dances of the American West – we can see the process at work more easily. The process works by trial and error. From an immense range of alternatives we reject some material even before we know it. By the nature of awareness itself, we are never aware of the alternatives. By the very way we know and perceive, we block out information that we cannot use. What remains as information, news, fact, is the recognizable and believable item.

Before the church even starts to confer or deny holiness, people have been at work, consciously or unconsciously eliminating persons, times, places, and messages they consider inappropriate. At Ezkioga the public never saw certain seers and quickly dismissed others. There were vision sites the press in hundreds of articles never mentioned. Seers did not tell about certain supernatural figures – devils or witches, for example. People ridiculed certain visions and locations. Photographers did not portray bizarre visionary poses. People rejected some messages as demonic or invented. In short, there was a constant, intensive weeding out, the elimination of cultural material that did not fit. Conversely, there were rewards for seers who addressed certain problems – the collective predicament of Catholic Basques, Catalans, or Spaniards or the everyday problems of the dead, the missing, the unforgiven, the unabsolved. Wittingly or not, every person who went to see the visions or merely read a newspaper about them was doing this kind of evaluating and rewarding. Certain selectors and patrons played a powerful role in determining which visions and seers prevailed.[49]

Thus apparitions bear meaning, and meanings relate to local and contextual factors. If the apparition is taken up into wider circles in the Church, national and international, its meanings may evolve and change. Guadalupe is now understood not just as a symbol of Mexican or American Catholic identity, but also as associated with liberation. Lourdes passed through the monarchist–republican tension of the 1870s into a time when this had passed into history, and its sole purpose then became and is until now understood in terms of healing and devotion. Beauraing left behind its nationalist Rexist associations in 1930s Belgium, embarrassing only a few years later. It is better remembered as a place of solace during the German occupation of the Second World War. In the move to the universal appeal of an apparition shrine, some aspects of its original message may be forgotten, as they are no longer perceived to be important to, or edifying for, the wider community. Devotees at Garabandal and San Damiano may want to forget the way in which these shrines were linked to rebellion against the Second Vatican Council, while at Medjugorje the shrine's future

---

49. Christian 1996: 400–1.

popularity may mean a total erasure of the ecclesiastical and nationalist politics associated with its early years. Where an apparition and its messages are regarded as being too tied into the local and temporal context, and nothing of its story is thought able to be taken into a more widely relevant interpretation concerning faith, devotion, pilgrimage and healing, then it is not likely to thrive in the Church. After some years of conflict, argument and suppression, it will be relegated to the footnotes of history (the revelation of 'secrets' with political agendas by the visionaries of La Salette and Fatima occurred only after official Church approval). The interesting aspect of the work by Blackbourn and Christian is the way that they have rediscovered the stories of these now obscure cases. In Christian's case, this work allows elderly people, who remember Ezquioga and its dynamism, the chance to express their memories to a wider audience.

There are also issues which arise regarding social structure and change – to what extent, for example, does the exaltation of the mother figure Mary enhance or restrict the movement for the emancipation of women? Barbara Pope wrote a chapter, 'Immaculate and Powerful: the Marian Revival in the Nineteenth Century', on the way in which the nineteenth-century Marian apparition cults were generally, although not totally, likely to have promoted a conservative agenda on the question of gender roles:

> Mary's high position in the church was obviously a source of female pride. But as powerful as Mary was, her male-defined cult had serious limitations, particularly for women. These become clear when we consider what the nineteenth-century Virgin did *not* represent.
>
> This Virgin had no connection with fertility and sexuality, the two most obvious attributes of any symbol of female divinity. This connection could only belong to an underground interpretation of the Good Mother's role. Although the connection was recognized and utilized in village rituals and local cults, it went unrecognized (officially at least) in the cults of the famous black Virgins, some of whom may have gotten their coloration from their connection with the earth and with pre-Christian goddesses. From the perspective of these earlier images, the blue and white Virgin seems not only immaculate but also bloodless and disconnected from the earth and from the experiences of most women.
>
> The Virgin, who did not have any control over fertility, also had little autonomy within 'her' church. In official interpretations all evidences of her independence were slighted. But they were there. At Pontmain the vision's robes and headdress could be interpreted as priestly. At La Salette the Lady (who never identified herself) made remarkable statements: '*I* gave you six days' work. *I* have reserved the seventh for *myself*.' (Italics mine.) Certainly there was no suggestion that God was a woman! In fact, leaders of the church were not at all troubled by this lapse. They either ignored the first-person pronouns or dismissed them as a common means found often in the Hebrew Bible, whereby God spoke through his prophets.
>
> The Virgin of the apparitions is not the Mary of the Bible, who had doubts

and hesitations during her life. Although she usually appeared alone, she was always cast as an intermediary, who had been given her privileges by a loving Son and prescient Father. Her *active* cooperation was not stressed. She was a vessel rather than the first disciple, who willingly acted out of faith.

This is not surprising. In nineteenth-century Catholicism, discipleship and its historical successor, priesthood, belonged exclusively to males. A female model for sacramental and public leadership roles seemed inconceivable. Any official and public version of the apparitions would have to suit a celibate priesthood's sense of fitness. Mary the pure and passive vessel was an important part of the inherited interpretation.

Finally, if the apparitions had a prophetic mission, it only struck one social and political note. Although the visions appeared to the humble, they never carried a message of social transformation or suggested that the realm of Mary or the coming of Christ meant the overcoming of exploitation or oppression. The political direction they augured was always backward rather than forward: in favor of kings and the old social order, and fearful of change.

This defensive antimodernism may be the most distinct legacy of the church-defined Marian cult of the nineteenth century.[50]

This conclusion – that apparitions have contributed to conservative views, socially and politically – was also one put forward by Perry and Echeverría in their book *Under the Heel of Mary*.[51] The Marian cult in their view always served to promote not only conservative, but also fascist and oppressive regimes. Although there are examples where this is true, the book is far too sweeping in its argument. For instance, Perry and Echeverría argue that Lourdes, under the Vichy regime of the Second World War, was a hotbed of fascist and anti-Semitic sentiment. Yet Franz Werfl, a Jew on the run from the Nazis, wrote his famous novel based on the apparitions of Lourdes, *The Song of Bernadette*, because he managed to find refuge in Lourdes on his way to escaping to America. It is difficult to see how Werfl could have extolled the Lourdes story if it only served to promote the ideology of French fascists. Perry and Echeverría's view is too one-sided to give us helpful information about the role of the Marian apparition cult in politics, which requires a more subtle and thoughtful investigation. Nor, on the other hand, is it helpful to publish material that promotes apparitions only in the cause of a chauvinistic Catholic position, as does Donal Foley's *Marian Apparitions, the Bible and the Modern World*.[52] Here we find a Mary who visits the world whenever the Catholic social world is under threat. Yet the refusal by the author to see any wrong in Catholic history, including the Hispanic conquest of 'Latin' America, or anything of value in the movements with which Catholics have been in conflict at times in history, can only

---

50. Barbara Corrado Pope, 'Immaculate and Powerful: the Marian Revival in the Nineteenth Century', in Atkinson *et al.* (eds) 1985: 194–5.
51. Perry and Echeverría 1988.
52. Foley 2002. Foley has also written the Catholic Truth Society booklet in a similar vein, *Apparitions of Mary: Their Meaning in History* (2000).

serve to fuel the belief that the Marian cult is at the service of a very questionable right-wing Catholic agenda.

A more balanced view will accept that apparition cults are often utilized by conservative and right-wing movements, but that is not the end of the story. Visions articulate social anxiety, it is true, but at the time of the visions, the visionaries themselves would not always have conceived the extreme answers to the social problems promoted by some of the later devotees. Fatima's first messages concerned prayers for peace during the First World War, and there was no mention of the battle against communism that later became the concern of the visionary and, through her, the more right-wing followers of Fatima. Medjugorje's Croat nationalism stands in stark contrast to a Madonna who urged for intercommunity understanding in the early days of the visions. Muslims and the Orthodox were to be respected; she was to be known as the 'Queen of Peace'. And, as we have seen, the Roman Catholic Church tends on the whole to reject messages which support its cause but in a fervent and apocalyptic vein. The fact that there is more to apparitions than conservative agendas is illustrated in the case of Ezquioga, and Christian's study, which has already been quoted above.

The visions at Ezkioga were the first large-scale apparitions of the old talking but invisible type in Spain since the sixteenth century. But they included the innovations of Lourdes: there were many seers, the seers had their visions in public view, and most of the seers entered some kind of altered state. We will see how the social and political situation of Spain and the Basque Country encouraged Catholics to believe the seers.

The reader should know something about nationalism in Spain, the Basque Country, and Catalonia. The less authoritarian and more democratic the central government, the less Spain coheres. At present, in the new freedom after the long dictatorship of Francisco Franco, in the Basque Country and Catalonia in particular, many people are careful to refer to Spain only as a state, not as a nation. When the majority of male voters brought in the Second Republic in April 1931, Spain was a mosaic of cultures that hundreds of years of royal rule had done little to homogenize. The regions with the strongest nationalist movements were those with the most international contacts: the Basques lived on both sides of the border with France and had a major trading partner in Great Britain; Catalonia, also on the border, traded with the Mediterranean countries and the Caribbean. These external contacts meant that some regional elites did not depend entirely on Madrid and resented its taxes, bureaucracy, and language. Eight years of centralized rule by General Miguel Primo de Rivera in the twenties had exacerbated these resentments. Even in regions with virtually no separatist sentiment in 1931, people had a strong sense that they were different culturally. The Navarrese, for instance, had a past that helped them maintain an identity distinct from that as Spaniards. Navarra was once an independent kingdom that spanned the Pyrenees. Those Navarrese who lived in a strip running across the north of the province spoke Basque, and in the distant past most of the region's inhabitants had been

Basque-speaking. Most still had Basque family names and lived in towns with names of Basque origin.

As a mass phenomenon the apparitions at Ezkioga were a kind of dialogue between divinities and the anticlerical left – anarchists and socialists in the Basque coastal cities, socialist farmworkers in Navarra, republican railway officials and schoolteachers in rural areas, anticlerical poor in cities throughout Spain, and socialist and communist movements worldwide. In this aspect Ezkioga was similar to other modern apparitions. As over the years the enemy changed from Freemasons and liberals to communists, the messages seers conveyed changed to maintain the dialogue. But any analysis that reads the last two centuries of Marian visions as a clerical plot to thwart social progress is impoverished, as we shall see. To be sure, visions are easy to manipulate for political purposes. But at Ezkioga people of all classes immediately put the seers to work for other practical and spiritual ends. Apparitions spark little interest without people's general hunger for access to the divine.[53]

CONCLUSION

In this section, there have been no excerpts from the many popular devotional accounts that list and describe the major apparition cases, nor from those which focus on one case in particular.[54] We have stayed with important Catholic theologians, or work from academic, critical, perspectives. This should not be taken to imply that there is nothing of value in such literature, but it is essential to distinguish between the critical and devotional for the purposes of study. The strength of recent academic work on Marian apparitions – such as Blackbourn, Christian, Apolito, Harris – is that the close study made of particular cases avoids the tendency to generalize in unhelpful ways. It is true that there are some themes that seem to run through a variety of apparition events, and all of these authors seek to set the specific object of their study in the wider context of Catholic Marian apparition history. Yet each case demands its own research; it is a microcosm of the greater society in which it is situated; it takes on the personality of its seers, of its early devotees, and the local, regional and national characteristics of its setting. Studies which recognize the rich and diverse layers of understanding and inspiration that apparitions engender; which identify the conflicts over meaning within a Catholic community which knows how important apparition messages can be; which understand the fact that symbolic images are polyvalent and can never be limited to single and simple interpretations – these studies give the greatest insight into the human phenomena that are Marian apparitions. The theologians, particularly those in the Roman Catholic Church, will attempt to discern whether these human phenomena are or are not responses to a divine stimulus.

53. Christian 1996: 6–7.
54. For example, Ashton 1988; Beevers 1953; Delaney 1961; Derobert 1985; Lochet 1960; Odell 1986; Walsh 1904.

BIBLIOGRAPHY

Alimenti, Dante (1987) *The Grotto of Tre Fontane*, trans. Peter Fehlner, Rome: Provincia Romana del Frati Minori Conventuali.

Alonso, J. M., Billet, B., Bobrinskoy, B., Laurentin, R. and Oraison, M. (1973) *Vraies et Fausses Apparitions dans l'Eglise*, Paris: P. Lethielleux.

Apolito, Paolo (1998) *Apparitions of the Madonna at Oliveto Citra: Local Visions and Cosmic Drama*, trans. William A. Christian Jr, University Park, PA: Pennsylvania State University Press.

Aquinas, St Thomas (trans. 1922) *Summa Theologica 2.2 (CLXXI–CLXXXIX)*, trans. Fathers of the English Dominican Province, London: Burns, Oates & Washbourne.

Ashton, Joan (1988) *Mother of Nations: Visions of Mary*, Basingstoke: The Lamp Press.

Atkinson, Clarissa W., Buchanan, Constance H. and Miles, Margaret R. (eds) (1985) *Immaculate and Powerful: The Female in Sacred Image and Social Reality*, Boston, MA: Beacon.

Beevers, John (1953) *The Sun Her Mantle*, Dublin: Browne & Nolan.

Bertone, Tarcisio and Ratzinger, Joseph (2000) *The Message of Fatima*, Vatican City: Congregation for the Doctrine of the Faith.

Blackbourn, David (1993) *Marpingen: Apparitions of the Virgin Mary in Bismarckian Germany*, Oxford: Clarendon.

Bourke, Vernon J. (1945) *Augustine's Quest of Wisdom: Life and Philosophy of the Bishop of Hippo*, Milwaukee, WI: Bruce.

Bridgett, T. E. (1890) *Our Lady's Dowry*, London: Burns and Oates.

Carroll, Michael (1986) *The Cult of the Virgin Mary: Psychological Origins*, Princeton, NJ: Princeton University Press.

Charue, André-Marie (1943–6) *Beauraing: Documents Episcopeaux*, Remy: Diocese of Namur.

Christian Jr, William (1981) *Apparitions in Late Medieval and Renaissance Spain*, Princeton, NJ: Princeton University Press.

Christian Jr, William (1996) *Visionaries: The Spanish Republic and the Reign of Christ*, Berkeley, CA: University of California Press.

Delaney, John J. (1961) *A Woman Clothed with the Sun*, Garden City, ID: Image/Doubleday.

Derobert, P. J. (1985) *L'Ange Puissant qui Descend du Ciel*, Marquain: Jules Hovine.

Derselle, C. (1933) *Beauraing: La Verité en Marche de Nouveau*, Brussels: Etudes Carmelitaines.

Elizondo, Virgin (1997) *Guadalupe: Mother of the New Creation*, Maryknoll, NY: Orbis.

Foley, Donal Anthony (2002) *Marian Apparitions, the Bible, and the Modern World*, Leominster: Gracewing.

Gillett, H. M. (1957) *Shrines of Our Lady in England and Wales*, London: Samuel Walker.

Green, Celia and McCreery, Charles (1989) *Apparitions*, Oxford: Institute of Parapsychological Research.

Harris, Ruth (1999) *Lourdes: Body and Spirit in the Secular Age*, London: Penguin.

de Jésus-Marie, Bruno, de Greeff, E., Janssens, A. and van Gehuchten, P. (1933) *Les Faits Mysterieux de Beauraing: Etudes, Documents, Réponses*, Paris: Desclée de Brouwer.

John of the Cross (1994) *The Collected Works*, trans. Kieran Kavanaugh and Otilio Rodriguez, Washington DC: Institute of Carmelite Studies.

Jones, E. Michael (1998) *The Medjugorje Deception: Queen of Peace, Ethnic Cleansing, Ruined Lives*, South Bend, IN: Fidelity Press.

Kselman, Thomas A. (1983) *Miracles and Prophecies in Nineteenth-Century France*, New Brunswick, NJ: Rutgers University Press.

Lambertini, Cardinal (1852) *Heroic Virtue: A Portion of the Treatise of Benedict XIV on the Beatification and Canonization of the Servants of God*, 3 vols, London: Thomas Richardson.

Laurentin, René (1983) *The Life of Catherine Labouré*, trans. Paul Inwood, London: Collins.

Laurentin, René (1990) 'The Church and Apparitions', *Mir* 15–19.

Laurentin, René (1991) *Apparitions of the Blessed Virgin Mary Today*, trans. Luke Griffin, 2nd edn, Dublin, Veritas.

Lee, Mary and Nolan, Sidney (1989) *Christian Pilgrimage in Modern Western Europe*, Chapel Hill, NC: University of Carolina Press.

Lochet, Louis (1960) *Apparitions of Our Lady: Their Place in the Life of the Church*, trans. John Dingle, Freiburg: Herder.

Matter, Ann E. (2001) 'Apparitions of the Virgin Mary in the Late Twentieth Century: Apocalyptic, Representation, Politics', *Religion* 31: 125–53.

Maunder, Chris (2000) 'Apparitions of the Virgin Mary in Late Twentieth-Century Ireland: Visions and Reflections Part 1', *Maria* 1: 69–85.

Maunder, Chris (2003) 'Apparitions of the Virgin Mary in Late Twentieth-Century Ireland: Visions and Reflections Part 2', *Maria* 3.2: 239–54.

Northcote, J. Spencer (1868) *Celebrated Sanctuaries of the Madonna*, London: Longmans, Green & Co.

Odell, Catherine (1986) *Those Who Saw Her: The Apparitions of Mary*, Huntington, IN: Our Sunday Visitor.

Perry, Nicholas and Echeverría, Loreto (1988) *Under the Heel of Mary*, London: Routledge.

Rahner, Karl (1963) *Visions and Prophecies (Quaestiones Disputatae 8–10)*, trans. Charles Henkey and Richard Strachan, New York: Herder & Herder.

Ratzinger, Joseph with Messori, Vittorio (1985) *The Ratzinger Report*, trans. S. Attanasio and G. Harrison, Leominster: Fowler Wright.

Reck, William A. (1996) *Dear Marian Movement: Let God be God*, Milford: Riehle Foundation.

Sivrič, Ivo (1988) *La Face Cachée de Medjugorje Vol 1: Observations d'un Théologien*, trans. Benoit Bélanger, Saint-Francois-du-Lac: Psilog.

Stern, Jean (1980, 1984) *La Salette: Documents Authentiques, Dossier Chronologique Intégral*, 2 vols, La Salette: Desclée de Brouwer; Paris: du Cerf.

Taylor, Thérèse (2003) *Bernadette of Lourdes: Her Life, Death and Visions*, London: Burns & Oates.

St Teresa of Avila (1988, 1990, 1995) *The Collected Works*, trans. Kieran Kavanaugh and Otilio Rodriguez, 3 vols, Washington DC: Institute of Carmelite Studies.

Thurston, Herbert (1934) *Beauraing and Other Apparitions: An Account of Some Borderline Cases in the Psychology of Mysticism*, London: Burns, Oates & Washbourne.

Turner, Victor and Edith (1978) *Image and Pilgrimage in Christian Culture: Anthropological Perspectives*, New York: Columbia University Press.

Walsh, William J. (1904) *The Apparitions and Shrines of Heaven's Bright Queen in Legend, Poetry and History*, 4 vols, New York: Carey-Stafford.

Waterton, Edmund (1879) *Pietas Mariana Britannica*, London: St Joseph's Catholic Library.

Wolf, Eric R. (ed.) (1984) *Religion, Power and Protest in Local Communities: The Northern Shore of the Mediterranean*, Berlin: Mouton.

Zimdars-Swartz, Sandra (1991) *Encountering Mary: From La Salette to Medjugorje*, Princeton, NJ: Princeton University Press.

21

BLACK MADONNAS[1]

SARAH JANE BOSS

This article examines aspects of the phenomenon of Black Madonnas – their topology, history and mythology.[2] We start with accounts of two shrines, Le Puy and Rocamadour.

OUR LADY OF LE PUY

The shrine of Our Lady of Le Puy (Fig. 22), in the province of Velay in Southern France, is home to one of the most famous of the numerous Black Madonnas that are found in Europe.[3] It is located in a striking natural setting, where peaks of rock emerge out of what were once thick woodlands. Romantic legend maintains that in ancient times there was a sanctuary on each of the rocky peaks, the most important of which was Mount Anis. On its summit was a dolmen, a single megalith, on which sacrifices were offered to 'the Virgin who would bear a son'. The legend of how this place came to be a shrine of the Virgin Mary runs as follows.

A widow with rheumatic fever went to lie on the stone that was there. During the night, the Virgin appeared to the woman in a vision, and said that she wished for a Christian sanctuary to be built on Mount Anis. When the woman awoke from her sleep, she was cured of the rheumatic fever. So the widow went to see the bishop, George, the man who had first brought the Christian gospel to this region of Gaul, and told him what had happened. Together, the bishop and the widow went back to the mountain and, although it was a hot day in July, the summit was covered with snow. As they stood there, a stag leapt out of a thicket and ran around the rock on which the stone lay, leaving hoof marks in the snow. Although the miraculous events confirmed the truth of the widow's vision, Bishop George could not afford to build a church, but he planted a hawthorn hedge in the stag's footprints, to mark out the sacred territory. The next morning the snow was gone, but the hawthorn was in bloom, making a 'snowy crown' on the mountain top. Clearly, this place was sacred to the Virgin Mary. It was consecrated by another bishop, St Martial, who brought there a relic of the Virgin, one of her shoes.

---

1. This article is extracted and edited from Boss 2004: 74–100.
2. A discussion of other aspects of the cults of Black Madonnas, including their roles as protectresses of women in childbirth and as guardians of the dead, can be found in Boss 1999: 95–122.
3. For accounts of the shrine of Our Lady of Le Puy, see Paul 1950; Begg 1996: 212–14; Saillens 1945: 84–95; Gostling 1911: 162–79.

Fig. 22. Our Lady of Le Puy.

Gradually, the hawthorn hedge grew into a grove, and pilgrims would come to spend the night there, sleeping on the sacred stone. Among these, in the year 350, was a paralytic woman to whom the Virgin also appeared in a vision, and who was also healed of her infirmity. She too went to report her experience to the bishop, whose name was Vosy. By this time, the Church had become wealthier, and Vosy was a rich man who was able to build the first Christian church on this site. One tradition maintains that the bishop and his chaplain happened to meet an old man who supplied them with the relics that they would need to place in the church's altar, and that the next day, when no man or woman was present in the building, the church bells rang, its doors were opened and its windows ablaze with light, because its consecration was being undertaken by angels.

For many centuries, the stone stood in front of the church's high altar (presumably because the altar was built by the site where the stone already lay). Steps led directly up to it from outside the building. Nowadays, however, there is an ordinary floor in the nave, and the stone has been placed by the door. The custom of spending the night on the stone was still carried out at least as recently as a hundred years ago. Francis Gostling, an English traveller in France in 1911, wrote of Le Puy:

> And when you have knelt and made your prayer on the stone, you ascend to the Lady of the Stone, the Mother of Health and Healing. A beautiful symbol, is it not, the Druid altar a Marche Pied leading to the Virgin herself? The old religion conducting to the new?[4]

---

4. Gostling 1911: 165.

This is a legend rich in natural symbolism: the sacred mountain in its woodland, the healing stone, the hawthorn grove and the stag are all signs of the divine presence in this chosen place. The idea that this was a prophetically sacred spot even before the advent of Christianity, or a 'Druid' shrine, is also significant, not so much for its historical claim (which is almost certainly awry) as for the importance that it holds as a myth for us today.

But at Le Puy, it is not only the site that is enveloped in sacred mythology, but also the statue of the Virgin and Child. According to tradition, this too is a pre-Christian image prophetic of Christianity. The original statue is said to have been carved by the Hebrew prophet Jeremiah, while he remained in Egypt after fleeing there following the fall of Jerusalem. The statue is thus a visual prophecy of the incarnation. One tradition recounts that King St Louis IX of France, on his way to Palestine to join a Crusade, was captured by the Sultan of Egypt. Whilst he was there awaiting his ransom, the sultan showed him many of the treasures of his country, among which, in the temple, was a black statue of a mother and child. King Louis immediately recognized the image as a statue of the Virgin and Christ. When the king's ransom arrived, the sultan told him that he could choose a gift, from everything he had seen in Egypt, to take back with him to his native land, and the gift that Louis chose was the statue of the mother and child. The sultan was most reluctant to let it go, but, having given his word, he could not go back on it, and so the statue was taken by Louis to France, where it was given to the shrine of Le Puy.

An older version of this story,[5] however, recounts that Jeremiah made the statue in Jerusalem, before the destruction of the Temple by Nebuchadnezzar, and that at the fall of Jerusalem it was taken to the treasury in Babylon. It was eventually brought to France by a Catholic king returning from pilgrimage to the Holy Land, long before the time of the Crusades. The French king received hospitality from the Sultan of Babylon, who asked him to choose a gift before he left, and the king chose the statue of the Virgin and Child. On his outward journey to the East, he had passed through Le Puy, and on his return, he presented the statue to the shrine there.

After the French Revolution, with the desecration of many holy places, the statue of Our Lady of Le Puy was burnt in 1794. The present statue is a copy of the original. Fortunately, at the time of the statue's destruction, a detailed description and drawing of it was made by an antiquarian, Faujas de Saint-Fond. The account by Faujas de Saint-Fond suggests to art historians that the image was a Virgin in Majesty, similar to that of Our Lady of Orcival (frontispiece), probably dating from the twelfth century.[6] Faujas de Saint-Fond, however, believed it to be a statue of the Egyptian goddess Isis with her son Horus, brought to France from Egypt in the mistaken belief that it represented Christ and the Virgin.

A Book of Hours (daily prayer used by lay people) from the end of the fifteenth century contains an illumination depicting the Virgin of Le Puy. She is represented as

5. *La fondacion de la saincte eglise & singulier oratoire de nostre dame du puy* (copy in British Library has lost page containing printer's details, but date in catalogue is given as 1500).
6. A good and well-illustrated discussion of the image is given in Kaeppelin 1997.

black, and this illustration may be the earliest surviving representation of a Black Virgin.[7]

BLACK VIRGINS: THEIR CHARACTER AND ORIGINS

So what is the definition of a Black Virgin? Where are they found? And why are they black?

The first use of the term 'Black Virgin' seems to have occurred in France during the nineteenth century. It referred to those statues of the Virgin Mary that were painted black, even though the local populations – who were predominantly French – were white. And indeed, *an image of the Virgin Mary that is coloured black or dark brown, in a place where the local population is white*, makes quite a good initial definition of a Black Virgin. It is true that there are some 'Black Virgins' in places where the native population is dark skinned, but these usually have some connection to Europe. For example, the famous image of Our Lady of Guadalupe in Mexico City (Fig. 23), who has the features of the local Indian population, is named after the Black Virgin of Guadalupe in Extremadura, Spain.

Our definition has to be qualified, however, by the puzzling fact that there are a few images commonly called 'Black Virgins' that are painted in the flesh tones of the local white inhabitants. Our Lady of Orcival, in the diocese of Clermont in the French province of Auvergne, is one such example (see Fig. 12, page 00). It is as though the word 'black' has some metaphorical meaning that is not bound to the colour of the actual image. The safest definition of a Black Virgin is probably *an image of the Virgin Mary whose devotees commonly refer to her as 'black'*.

Black Virgins are found in many places – the icon of Our Lady of Czestochowa in Poland, for example, is usually thought of as 'the Black Madonna', and the statue of Nossa Señora Aparecida, the patroness of Brazil, is also a Black Madonna. France is particularly rich in Black Virgin statues, and much of the literature on the subject of Black Madonnas maintains that France is the single nation with the largest number, if not an absolute majority, of the world's Black Virgins. However, we need to be a little sceptical of this claim. The French have provided most of the scholarship on this subject and, naturally, French scholars have tended to focus predominantly on the images in their own country. Yet Spain and Italy are certainly not lacking in Black Virgins. However, there seem to be no specialist studies of Black Madonnas in those countries,[8] let alone any thorough international study of the phenomenon.[9]

The most intriguing question, of course, concerns the reason for the images' blackness. 'Why is she black?' asks the surprised visitor to the European shrine. And

---

7.   Vilatte 1997: 12–38 (13). Mary Elizabeth Perry claims that Mary is sometimes represented as black in Spanish illuminated manuscripts from the eighth century onwards; Perry 1990: 109–28 (116), citing evidence from Frederico Delclaux (1973), *Imágenes de la Virgen en los Codices Medievales de España*, Madrid: Patronato Nacional de Museos.

8.   For Italian examples, see Birnbaum 1993.

9.   A very important study that takes account of a certain number of figures from outside France is Durand-Lefebvre 1937.

Fig. 23. Our Lady of Guadalupe, Mexico City. Prayer card.

the answers are many and varied. The traditional answer from clergy or Church officials has tended to be that the image became blackened with candle smoke or other dirt collected over time. Yet even if this account were true in origin, it would not explain why it is that the statue has gone on being painted black, rather than being restored to its original white. This, after all, is what has been done with the statues of other saints – and other Madonnas – when they have become grubby.

One of the most persuasive arguments for the origins of Black Madonnas is that

462

put forward by Sophie Cassagnes-Brouquet,[10] following in the footsteps of the great folklorist Emile Saillens,[11] who points out that the dispersion of Black Virgins in France is most dense in the south-east and the centre, while there are very few Black Virgins in the north and west of the country. This means that Black Virgins occur most commonly in the part of France that was most heavily influenced by classical culture. The trade route from the Mediterranean up the Rhône Valley in ancient times ensured that cultural influences from Africa and the East could always find their way into Gaul, and the influx of wider Mediterranean culture became particularly strong during the period of the Greek colony at Marseilles (founded about 600 BC), followed by the Roman occupation which eventually spread to the whole country. In classical antiquity, black was sometimes used as a colour for statues of people of exceptional importance, and there were some goddesses who could be represented as black – most notably, perhaps, Artemis of the Ephesians. According to the argument promoted by Cassagnes-Brouquet, many shrines of Black Virgins are on sites previously occupied by the shrines of goddesses.[12] Cassagnes-Brouquet contends, therefore, that the blackness of the Virgin in these places represents a tradition of continuity with the pagan past of the same sites.

Another argument concerning the origins of the statues' blackness is put forward by Sylvie Vilatte, who holds that statues which were previously white were deliberately painted black in the fourteenth century, as part of a campaign to revive interest in the Crusades. According to this theory, the representation of Christian saints as black was intended to draw the attention of ordinary Europeans to the possibility of converting dark-skinned Moors to Christianity.[13]

Both these theories have some degree of plausibility with regard to the origins of black-coloured Virgin statues, but neither of them says enough to give the whole story. If the statues were painted black in the fourteenth century, then why did people not return them to their original colour at a later time? What was, and is, the attraction of continuing the statues' blackness? Then again, if the Virgins were coloured black in continuity with pagan precedent, the question is similar: why was black considered an appropriate colour for the goddesses, and why did Christians see their blackness as an attribute that they wished, and still wish, to maintain in their images of the Virgin Mary? Do we not have to suppose that there is some spiritual significance to this colour, and that it is in the realm of the spiritual, and not the historical, that the meaning of the Black Madonnas must be sought?

BLACKNESS AS DARKNESS

In English, 'black' can sometimes be used as a synonym for 'dark'. If I look out of the window on a dark night, I might say, 'It's inky black out there.' Conversely, the words 'dark' and 'dusky' (from *dusk*, meaning twilight) can be used to describe skin

---

10. Cassagnes–Brouquet 1990.
11. Saillens 1945.
12. Cassagnes–Brouqet 1990: 150–9.
13. Vilatte 1997.

colour. In some languages, however, blackness and darkness are quite distinct, and cannot be assimilated to one another in this way: darkness is one thing, and the colour black another. I am going on to suggest that at least some of the significance of Black Madonnas depends upon a confusion of these two concepts.

In Western European culture, blackness has often been associated with evil. We speak of 'black magic' or the 'black arts'. The word 'denigrate', meaning to make something appear bad, comes from the Latin *niger*, meaning 'black'. Indeed, we can speak straightforwardly of 'blackening' someone's character. At the same time, Europeans have had an ambivalent attitude to dark-skinned people – black, Arab and Asian alike – and have frequently seen them as being in several respects inferior to white-skinned people. In European culture, sacred figures are most commonly of fair complection (and note the double meaning of the word 'fair', corresponding to the double meaning of its opposite, 'dark', as in the expression, 'Those were dark days'). This may, of course, be due partly to the fact that in a society in which most people have to spend their time toiling in fields, it is only the privileged who can afford to stay indoors and not get weatherbeaten brown skin. But this reinforces the point: whiteness or fairness is seen as a desirable condition, while blackness or darkness is not.

From this point of view, the representation of the Virgin and Child as black is on the one hand curious, because of the figures' supreme sanctity, yet at the same time may have a Christian rationale. For a constant theme of the Hebrew Scriptures, the Gospels and Christian teaching through the ages has been God's preference for the poor and the humble, that is to say, for those whom human society despises. In the Middle Ages it was taught consistently that the rich could enter heaven only by charity towards the poor, and the prayers of the poor were considered highly desirable to help one on the path to salvation. The free choice of poverty for oneself has been presented in the Catholic Church as one of the delineations of the path of spiritual excellence, down to the present day. Likewise, righteous people who suffer physical ailments, and those who adopt an attitude of humility in any aspect of life, are believed to be especially beloved of God. This philosophy is articulated with particular clarity in the song that Mary sings to her cousin Elizabeth when the two pregnant women meet one another (Lk. 1.46–55). In this song of rejoicing, the *Magnificat*, Mary proclaims that God has 'cast down the mighty from their seats, and exalted the humble and meek'. This is what God has done in bringing about the conception of Christ in Mary's womb. So there is a certain appropriateness about an image of the Virgin and Child being represented as black, especially since, in most Black Virgin statues, the Virgin is enthroned as a queen. It is as though the blackness signifies all that human culture mistakenly despises, and all the people that it rejects, so that in the Black Madonna we see God raising these things and these people up to a place of honour. In becoming human, Christ binds himself to every last part of the human condition and the material world – including the things that we think of as 'black' – and offers it the possibility of redemption and glorification. In the blackness of the regal Virgin and Child, the very humblest are exalted.

Many of the Black Virgin statues were sculpted during the twelfth and thirteenth centuries, and a further clue to their spiritual significance may perhaps be indicated by a contemporary text, the story of *Peredur Son of Efrawg*, which is included in the Welsh collection *The Mabinogion*.[14] The hero, Peredur, is the Arthurian knight who is the Welsh equivalent of Percival, and his story has many points in common with Wolfram von Eschenbach's *Parsifal*, although *Peredur* has the merit of being told in a more primitive and less ornate style. Peredur's adventures include many extraordinary experiences. Early on, he is present at the hall of the Lame King, when two youths proceed through the hall carrying an enormous spear with three streams of blood running along it. After that, two maidens come through carrying a salver on which there is a man's head surrounded by blood.[15] The reader is given no explanation for this, and Peredur does not enquire. Indeed, throughout the whole narrative, strange events occur which seem disconnected from one another. Peredur continues on his way, and does many acts of heroism. Eventually, he goes to seek the hand of the Empress of Constantinople, who desires only the bravest man, and he succeeds in winning her favour. He rules with her for 14 years, before returning to the court of King Arthur.[16] At several points in the narrative, Peredur fights with men who are described as 'black'. The final denouement to the story is at least as strange as everything that has gone before, and one part of it concerns a terrifying woman called the Black Virgin, *y forwyn ddu*. The Black Virgin challenges Peredur as to why, when he was at the court of the Lame King, he did not question the meaning of the blood-dripping spear. She says that if he had only asked what this meant, much bloodshed could have been avoided.[17] But he did not, and his failure to ask the right questions has had terrible consequences. So the Black Virgin makes the hero aware of his sins of omission: she forces him to confront those things in his past which he would prefer to ignore.

Now, the confrontation with past sin is central to the Christian tradition. It is through confession of one's sins and the grace of forgiveness that one breaks one's attachment to the past and is freed to form right relationships with God and one's fellow creatures. The rite of Christian initiation, baptism, is specifically for the forgiveness of sins, and Christ says that we must forgive those who wrong us as many times as they cause us offence. Yet full acknowledgement of past wrongdoing, and even mistakes and other failings, can be painfully difficult, so it is not surprising that the figure who calls the hero to account, the Black Virgin, should be a frightening one.

It may therefore be the case that part of the spiritual meaning of the Black Virgin in Christian devotion is likewise one of recalling sin – of becoming aware of that which is 'black' within us, and of confronting 'dark' events in our lives. Certainly, at one of the most important shrines of a Black Virgin, Our Lady of Rocamadour, in south-western central France, it was once the custom for pilgrims to travel there specifically as an act of penitence. Ecclesiastical courts in Germany would send malefactors to Rocamadour in chains, and when the prisoners had carried out their

---

14.   Trans. G. Jones and T. Jones 1949: 183–227.
15.   Ibid.: 192.
16.   Ibid.: 214–17.
17.   Ibid.: 218.

rites of expiation at the shrine, their chains would be removed and their freedom restored. King Henry II is said to have expiated the murder of Thomas Becket by doing penance in front of his troops at Rocamadour, and it was once the custom for pilgrims to undertake the penitential gesture of climbing up the steps to the shrine on their knees. So the Virgin's blackness may in part signify her frightening function of summoning her devotees to address their own 'blackness'.

Yet if the Virgin calls us to acknowledge the darkness of sin, this is only in order that, by doing so, we become freed from that sin and are brought out of darkness and into the light of Christ. That is to say, the Black Virgin signifies and provokes the process of spiritual enlightenment. This is suggested by a verse of Scripture that is commonly cited in connection with Black Madonnas, namely, Song of Songs 1.5. The Song of Songs is a collection of love poetry, traditionally read as a dialogue between the lover, or groom, and the beloved, or bride. In Jewish tradition it has been interpreted as an allegory for the relationship between the Lord and Israel, while Christians have understood it to signify the loving relationship that exists between Christ and the Church, or Christ and the human soul. Since Mary is a 'type' of both the Church and the soul in its relationship with Christ, it became common to attribute to Mary the words of the Song that are said by and about the Beloved. The Song itself claims to have been written by King Solomon, and tradition has often understood the original Lover to be Solomon and the Beloved to be the Queen of Sheba, a wise monarch who visited King Solomon to discover that his wisdom was even greater than her own (1 Kgs 10.1–13). In Matthew's Gospel, Jesus refers to the Queen of Sheba as the Queen of the South, who will rise up to judge the world at the last day. Her wisdom and judgement tie in well with the function of the Black Madonna as one who calls the soul to account for its failings, and in the Song itself, the Beloved says, 'I am black but beautiful', or, 'I am black *and* beautiful' (1.5) (the Hebrew text will yield either translation). These words are written in Latin over the statue of the Black Madonna at the Italian shrine of Tindari: *Nigra sum sed formosa*.

Now, the Hebrew word that is used here for 'black' is *shechorah*, the feminine form of *shachar*. The etymology of this word relates it to the word for 'dawn', and this association of words exists still in biblical texts, where the word for the 'morning star' is *ben-shachar*, that is, 'son of the dawn'. The Beloved gives as the reason for her dark colour the fact that she has been working in the vineyard and is burnt by the sun; but the word's recollection of the dawn reminds the spiritual reader of the text that darkness precedes light, so that, when read in relation to the Black Virgin, her blackness is the darkness that comes before the daylight of Christ her son. Here again, the Black Virgin is, among other things, a figure for spiritual enlightenment.

The Black Virgin of Paris, Notre-Dame de Bonne Délivrance (Fig. 24), is traditionally attributed with the power to release prisoners from captivity. Indeed, from the sixteenth to the eighteenth centuries, some of her devotees – members of a lay confraternity especially dedicated to her – would collect money with which they would buy the release of captives in the debtors' gaol in Paris.[18] From the time of Christ himself, freedom from bondage to debt has been a powerful metaphor for

---

18. de Bascher 1979: 70–3.

Fig. 24. Notre-Dame île Bonne Délivrance, Neuilly-sur-Seine. (Photo Editions C2L).

liberation from bondage to sin, and to anyone familiar with the Christian tradition, the charitable acts of the Black Virgin's devotees towards debtors resonates immediately at the spiritual level. That the Black Virgin desires to liberate men and women not only from the darkness of the gaol and slavery to debt, but also from spiritual darkness and imprisonment, is attested in a well-known anecdote about St Francis de Sales (1567–1622). It is reported that, as a young man, he fell into the sin of despair – which nowadays, perhaps, we would call depression – and feared that he would not attain salvation. But he went to pray before the Black Virgin of Paris, and she heard his prayer and delivered him from his despair. From that time onwards, Francis never suffered again from that condition.[19]

---

19. Vincent 1952: 991–1004 (995–6).

THE SOUL AND THE EARTH

Many twentieth-century writers on Black Madonnas have noted that their blackness seems to be of spiritual importance, and have tried to fathom its precise significance, often by constructing elaborate theories of esoteric symbolism. These are the sorts of theories that are generally dismissed by 'respectable' academics as unscholarly and unworthy of serious attention. Yet the fact that theories of this sort have a certain popularity suggests that they might tell us something about the spiritual condition of the age in which we live, and the student of religion would do well to pay them some attention. I shall therefore briefly describe one of the better researched and more stimulating of these theories, that of Jacques Bonvin.[20]

Bonvin takes up an existing hypothesis of spiritual energy in the land – something akin to the idea of ley lines – whereby there is supposed to be a grid of energy lines running under the earth's surface. At the points where the lines cross, the energy is disturbed, with the consequence that life at those points on the earth's surface is disrupted: crops will grow less well at these places, and animals and humans living there will be more than usually subject to illness and other misfortune. Bonvin contends that in ancient and medieval times, although people would not have had a theory of an energy grid, they would nonetheless have perceived the special character of these places of intersection, so that at the crossing points they erected monuments – megaliths or statues, for example – to perform a particular function. That function was to channel the disturbed energy from beneath the earth's surface in such a way that it was not merely neutralized, but transformed into energy that would be healing and sacred. These places thus became shrines and places of pilgrimage.

According to Bonvin, the medieval Black Virgins, such as those of Le Puy and Rocamadour, occupy sites of precisely this kind, and the function of the images is the transformation of energy from that which is harmful into that which is healing. Moreover, this transformation of spiritual energy in the earth corresponds to the process of spiritual enlightenment in the human person, by which we move from sin and ignorance to salvation and knowledge. The Virgin's blackness is the point at which our metamorphosis begins, and the Black Virgin has her counterpart in the White Virgin, who signifies the culmination of this process of transformation.

Bonvin believes that at the time when the Black Virgin statues were sculpted, this path of spiritual enlightenment would have been available not merely to a select group of learned monks and nuns, but to the most ordinary men and women. He suggests that although the theories of spiritual transformation would have been known only to the orders of monks in whose churches these statues are often found, the use of these statues for popular devotion, alongside the other religious art, architecture and preaching of the period, would have meant that, by attending liturgies and praying before these images, ordinary worshippers would have been frequently exposed to symbols of spiritual transformation, and by this means brought to a state of enlightenment, even without having any precise language with which to describe their experience.

20.   Bonvin 1988.

Now, whatever the accuracies or inaccuracies of Bonvin's telluric and historical hypotheses, his theory has some interesting points for consideration. First, let us notice his assumption that the human soul is formed in such a way as to correspond to the earth's energy, in its innate capacity to be moved from the bad to the good, understood as a movement from darkness to light. This correspondence recalls the theories of the human person as microcosm. Morevoer, according to Bonvin, the Blessed Virgin is both a symbolic figure for the human soul and the energy of the earth in their respective stages of transformation, and also the agent of those processes of transformation.

Jacques Bonvin thus argues that there is a spiritual correspondence between the material creation and the human person, and contends that Black Virgins embody the point of connection between them.

MARY AS THE WORLD'S FOUNDATION

If we take the correspondence between the human person and the cosmos to its most basic level, then the human soul is like the earth 'without form and void', with 'darkness on the face of the deep', over whom the Spirit of God hovers and whom the Lord calls into light. This is the imagery used in John's Gospel, when Nicodemus, on hearing that he must be 'born anew', asks, 'Can a man enter a second time into his mother's womb and be born?' and Christ replies, 'Truly, truly, I say to you, unless one is born of water and the Spirit, one cannot enter the kingdom of God' (Jn 3.4–5). Water and the Spirit are active forces in the creation of the world, and Christ says that it is necessary to be re-created from one's very foundations. In normal Christian practice, entry into the Church, the body of Christ, is by baptism, which is rebirth by water and the Holy Spirit. On Easter Eve, at the Church's Easter Vigil ceremony, the waters of the font are blessed for baptisms in the coming year, and the font is presented as the 'womb' of the Church, from whom new Christians will be born. At the church of Kilpeck, in Herefordshire, there is an Anglo-Saxon font made in the shape of a pregnant belly, so that the symbol is quite unambiguous. Now, as we have already seen, it is because the Word of God became human in the womb of the Virgin Mary that it is possible for human beings to become united to him in the womb of the Church. The common English word for baptism is 'christening', that is, being 'Christ-ed', or 'made Christ'; and it is as though in baptism the Christian is united to Christ in his conception in Mary's womb – a conception which is at the same time the renewal of the cosmos from its foundations – so that the baptized person, in his or her incorporation into Christ, is likewise entirely re-created. The waters of the deep at the dawn of creation are recapitulated in Mary's womb; and because of the work of her womb, those waters are again recapitulated in the womb of the Church, the baptismal font.

A number of writers on the subject of Black Madonnas have suggested that the abiding significance of their blackness is the evocation of the primal darkness, the chaotic matter, or the earth that is 'without form and void', of which the universe is made. Emile Saillens suggests that this is the meaning of the blackness of both the Black Virgins of Christianity and the black goddesses of other religious traditions,

469

such as Kali in Hinduism.[21] If this is correct – at least with regard to Christianity – then what is being said is that Mary in some way represents that out of which all new life is born and in virtue of which everything that exists shares a common substance. It is the 'deep' of Genesis 1.1.

THE CHAOS OF THE EARTH

In a highly illuminating study of the cultural significance of woodlands for human civilization, the literary scholar Robert Pogue Harrison draws attention to the association that exists between civilization's perception of forests and its idea of untamed nature, or 'chaos', and in particular to the frightening character of the wildwood in the eyes of city-dwellers.[22] This frightening aspect of the natural world may be quite close to the surface in the cults of many Black Madonnas. The anthropologists Leonard Moss and Stephen Cappanari made a study of the cults of Black Madonnas in southern Italy, from which they argued that the cults of these Madonnas supersede those of pagan goddesses of fertility, and that the significance of their blackness is that black is the colour of fertile earth. Black Madonnas, they suggest, are protectresses of the fertility of the soil and share their colour with that soil.[23] But soil has ambiguous connotations. On the one hand, it is a source of life, the giver of plants and therefore of sustenance for both animals and humans, but on the other hand, it is where the dead are buried and decay. Soil gives rise to the bodies of new life, but also consumes the bodies of the lifeless. Some Black Madonnas are attributed with the special power of granting fertility – Our Lady of Montserrat, in Catalonia, for example – while others have presided over burial places – Notre-Dame de Ronzières, in Auvergne, for instance, or Notre-Dame de Bonne Mort, in Clermont Cathedral.

Harrison argues that it is forests which constitute the archetypal places of birth and decay. By looking at the mythology and philosophy of urban peoples, he suggests that human beings see the forest as the place of our origins: in both antiquity and modernity, men and women have believed that we are descended from forest-dwellers. Yet civilization has consisted in the progressive movement away from these origins. It has entailed the cutting down of woodland and a fear of the darkness of tree cover. In the forest, nature is in a state of confusion and disorder, unlike the city, in which all is supposed to be under human control. This silvan confusion of forms and colours, flora and fauna, is the matrix from which all life comes and to which it returns. But civilization tries to cut itself off from its origins and to deny its mortality, and so fears the wildwood.[24]

Harrison takes the view that the whole panoply of the natural processes governing human life was once regarded as sacred and personified as a goddess, or goddesses. The confusion apparently inherent in soil and woods was the divine womb that gave

21. Saillens 1945: 238–44.
22. Harrison 1992.
23. Moss and Cappanari 1982: 53–74.
24. Harrison 1992: 1–58.

life and received it back in death. The Latin word *mater*, meaning 'mother', seems to have a common root with *materia*, meaning 'matter', and in Harrison's reconstruction of cultural history, the goddess's womb was the matrix or chaotic matter from which all things are formed and into which they ultimately disintegrate. It was only at a later time that human society tried to break away from this source of its existence, and from the divine mother. But many ordinary people were unwilling to make this break from the goddess, and this, Harrison suggests, was a strong motive force behind the development of the cult of the Virgin Mary in Christianity.[25]

Whether there is or is not an association between the cult of the Virgin and earlier pagan practices, we can note that a number of shrines of the Virgin, including those of Black Madonnas, do have woodland origins. The cult at Le Puy-en-Velay has already been cited. In Switzerland, the largest pilgrim shrine is that of Our Lady of Einsiedeln, whose foundation legend recounts that the shrine had its origin in a remote woodland hermitage inhabited by a holy man, St Meinrad.[26] Likewise, the once popular shrine of Our Lady of Willesden, now in north London, is said to have begun as the oratory of a small group of monks in the middle of what was then the Middlesex woods. The mythology of the Willesden shrine has other explicit connections with the natural world. There is a healing spring by the church, and in the churchyard there was once an oak tree where the Virgin appeared in a vision to a pilgrim.

Other Black Virgin shrines are located in places that are wild, although not especially forested. Rocamadour, for instance, is on a ledge of a cliff face of the limestone gorge cut by the River Alzou, as it flows through the barren plateau of the Causse de Quercy which rises up between the valleys of the Lot and the Dordogne. Montserrat is also a rock shrine, high on the curiously formed Sierra de Montserrat.

It is as though the irregularity and confusion of forms in the wilderness provide people with a sense not only of their immediate earthly origins, but of the origins of the cosmos itself.

SEPARATION AND AMBIGUITY

Reflecting upon the nature of the city, Robert Pogue Harrison writes:

> Walls, no less than writing, define civilization. They are monuments against time, like writing itself ... Walls protect, divide, distinguish; above all, they *abstract*. The basic activities that sustain life – agriculture and stock breeding, for instance – take place beyond the walls. Within the walls one is within an emporium; one is within the jurisdiction of a bureaucracy; one is within the abstract identity of race, city, and institutionalized religion ... [These are] walls that divide history from prehistory, culture from nature, sky from earth, life from death, memory from oblivion.[27]

25.   Ibid.: 21.
26.   Gustafson 1990: 1–19.
27.   Harrison 1992: 14–15.

The abstraction of which Harrison writes began in antiquity, but has now become so sophisticated that city walls are no longer necessary to maintain it. The walls of a house in remote countryside can provide even greater separation from 'the basic activities that sustain life' if the inhabitants of the house can travel within the walls of an air-conditioned car to a supermarket, within whose walls food from across the world can be acquired, ready-made or ready-cleaned, in polythene wrapping. And when they return home, our shoppers can sit among building materials and fabrics that are so highly processed that only a chemical engineer could tell you what natural substances constitute their base materials.

On Harrison's understanding, exclusion and separation are in the nature (so to speak) of civilization, yet are also a mistake, because they are deceitful. For as a matter of fact, we are – at least in part – material beings who do depend upon natural processes for our existence. And a striking feature of many Marian shrines is the force with which they call people back to the source of our physical life by making them cross over that boundary that divides 'culture from nature'. A common legend of the origin of a shrine is one which tells that a statue of the Virgin was found by an animal, usually a bull or an ox, in a bush or a spring. The herdsman sees the animal pawing at the ground, and when he goes to find out why, he sees that it has discovered the holy image. He runs off to the village to tell what has happened, and the people come out and take the statue into the village in a grand procession, culminating in the statue's being set up in a place of honour in the parish church. The next morning, the statue has disappeared, and has miraculously returned to the spot on which it was found. Typically, the legend says that the people returned the image to the village once or twice more, but each time, the statue returned to its original site. From this, the people understood that Our Lady wished to be honoured in the place of her own choosing. So a shrine is constructed to house the image with the bush or the spring where it was discovered, and the Virgin's devotees must make a pilgrimage away from the world of their own artifice to a site where 'the basic activities that sustain life' take place.[28]

At some shrines, the cult is quite explicitly tied to those basic activities. The Catalan shrine of Our Lady of Nuria, for example, is situated in a high mountain valley where shepherds used to graze their flocks in the summer months of July and August, and the chapel there is said to have been founded by St Gil, who brought the gospel to the shepherds and who lived there as their spiritual guide.[29]

Our Lady of Vassivière, in the diocese of Clermont, is also associated with the summer pasturing of flocks. In her case, however, the cult statue is taken in procession to the shrine in the meadows at Vassivière at the beginning of the summer period, and in September is ceremonially returned to her winter home in the nearby town of Besse-en-Chandesse.

With modern means of communication – the walled-in spaces of trains, planes

---

28. A legend of this kind is associated with the shrine of Nuestra Señora del Rocío, Our Lady of the Dew, at Almonte (Huelva), in Spain; see Cruz 1993: 422–3. Other examples can be found in Cassagnes-Brouquet 1990: 51–4.
29. Herce 2001: 11–21.

and cars – places that were once remote, so that even the fittest pilgrim was brought face to face with his or her physical frailty, can often be reached with relative ease. Yet, since human beings in truth are just as material and just as vulnerable as we have always been, this separation from physical necessity means that the danger of our being deluded by our own cleverness is greater than ever. We therefore urgently need to perceive our dependence upon natural processes, and, through them, upon the God who is the source of our life and to whom we shall return at the end of that life. We need to know and to love the chaos from which we try to separate ourselves, and to know it as made by, and beloved of, God. This, among other things, is what the Black Virgin summons her devotees to do.

There is a further point that needs to be made here. We have been considering civilization as based upon acts of separation and division, and in particular upon an actual and pretended separation of city-dwellers from natural processes. We have also seen that there is an ambiguity about humanity's relationship with these processes, since however much we try to distance ourselves from them, they remain the source and substance of our material existence. We should therefore take account of the fact that, in human culture, the significance of actions and objects that are set apart from everyday life is likewise sometimes ambiguous.

We can find an example of this in the biblical book of Joshua, where we read that, when the Hebrew tribes invade the land of Canaan, the Lord imposes a *cherem* upon many of the possessions of the Canaanites. The word *cherem* is usually translated as 'ban'. It means that the things which belonged to the Canaanites are forbidden to the Hebrews. This is because they are especially devoted to the Lord, but devoted to the Lord specifically for the purpose of destruction (for example, Josh. 6.17). Indeed, the notion of 'that which is devoted to sacred use' is one aspect of the concept of *cherem*, and some objects within the area of the *cherem*, namely vessels made of precious metals, are sacred to the Lord in such a way that they are to be preserved in the Lord's treasury (Josh. 6.19). On the other hand, those Israelites who break faith with the *cherem* by taking objects for themselves render themselves under the *cherem*, in the sense that they too are given over to destruction (Josh. 7.12), with no suggestion that they, having breached the sacred code, are in any way consecrated. *Cherem* means something not unlike *tabu*, that is, set apart from everyday use *either* because of exceptional holiness *or* because of exceptional unholiness.

A well-nigh universal practice of separation in human society is that by which women are forbidden to enter certain places or undertake certain activities during their menstrual bleeding. This too can be ambiguous in its meaning. Is the separation imposed because menstruation is regarded as exceptionally nasty or as exceptionally sacred? It is common to assume the former, but the situation is rarely as clear as this. Paula Weidegger carried out a study of menstrual rites in various cultures of the world, and included in her research a survey of women in the United States. Reporting on these, she writes:

> Among Jewish families ... it is customary to slap a young woman's face on the day that menstruation begins. The women I have met who had this experience say they hadn't the vaguest notion of why their mothers slapped them. Many

believed that it was a unique experience and the product of an aberration or a disturbed mother. Only one woman reported a different experience. She had a sense of tradition and positive feelings about her first menstruation. Her mother had taken her into the living room, and said, 'As my mother did to me, as her mother did to her, so I do to you today.' The mother then slapped her daughter across the face. When this woman grew up she said she felt proud to be menstruating and enjoyed a feeling of connection with her female ancestors – it gave her a sense of generational continuity which she, in turn, passed on to her daughter.[30]

The demarcation of a menstruating woman is here a cause for honour, not shame.

Now, although the separation of cities from their natural surroundings has undoubtedly been connected to a hatred of natural processes, the power and fear which engender that hatred may also have engendered a sense of reverence. Indeed, the frequency with which the ever-popular Virgin Mary has her favoured shrines in wilderness locations suggests that a sense of the holiness of the wild continued to flourish long after the time at which urban culture began to have a major influence upon human society. Here again, then, the act of separation may have a double meaning.

Perhaps a similar sort of ambiguity inheres in the blackness of Black Virgins – image of exceptional sanctity, yet painted in the colour that Europeans have associated, since at least the Middle Ages, with inferiority and evil. The statue of Our Lady of Le Puy was outstandingly sacred, being believed to have been carved by the prophet Jeremiah. Yet it was treasured in Babylon, the city of Israel's captivity, proverbial for all that is ungodly. And in the later version of the legend, according to which the image was recovered during the Crusades, it was Moors who actively fought against Christians who were the statue's guardians and protectors. It is as though the things that seem furthest from God are simultaneously the things which are closest to God. At the heart of the humblest or most despised of creatures is nothing other than the divine Goodness; and darkness is a cipher for light. Seen in this way, the blackness of the Black Madonna may refer precisely to these paradoxes.

BIBLIOGRAPHY

de Bascher, Jacques (1979) *La Vierge Noire de Paris*, Paris: Téqui.

Bayard, Jean-Pierre (2001) *Déesses Mères et Vierges Noires: Répertoire des Vierges noires par département*, Monaco: Editions du Monaco.

Begg, Ean (1996) *The Cult of the Black Virgin*, London: Penguin (Arkana).

Berman, Roland (1993) *La Vierge Noire, Vierge Initiatique*, Paris: Dervy.

Birnbaum, Lucia Chiavola (1993) *Black Madonnas: Feminism, Religion, and Politics in Italy*, Boston, MA: Northeastern University Press.

Bonvin, Jacques (1988) *Vierges Noires: La réponse vient de la terre*, Paris: Dervy.

Boss, Sarah Jane (1999) 'Guardians of the Way', in Martin Warner (ed.), *Say Yes to God: Mary and the Revealing of the Word Made Flesh*, London: Tufton Books: 95–122.

---

30. Weidegger 1978: 163–4.

Boss, Sarah Jane (2004) *Mary*, London: Continuum.

Cruz, J. Carroll (1993) *Miraculous Images of Our Lady*, Rockford, IL: Tan Books.

Cassagnes-Brouquet, Sophie (1990) *Vierges Noires: Regard et fascination*, Rodez: Editions du Rouergue.

Durand-Lefebvre, Marie (1937) *Etude sur l'Origine des Vierges Noires*, Paris: G. Durassié.

La fondacion de la saincte eglise & singulier oratoire de nostre dame du puy (1500).

Gostling, Francis M. (1911) *Auvergne and its People*, London: Methuen.

Gustafson, Fred (1990) *The Black Madonna*, Boston, MA: Sigo Press.

Gustafson, Fred (ed.) (2003) *The Moonlit Path: Reflections on the Dark Feminine*, Berwick, ME: Nicolas-Hays.

Hani, Jean (1995) *La Vierge Noire et le Mystère Marial*, Paris: Guy Trédaniel.

Harrison, Robert Pogue (1992) *Forests: The Shadow of Civilization*, Chicago, IL: The University of Chicago Press.

Herce, Antoni Herce (2001) *Vall de Núria: Libro guía*, FGC/Vall de Núria.

Kaeppelin, Philippe (1997) 'La Sainte Image de Notre-Dame du Puy', *Le Fil de la Borne*, 22, Bains: Centre d'Etude de la Vallée de la Borne.

The Mabinogion (1949), trans. Gwyn Jones and Thomas Jones, London and New York: Dent, Everyman's Library (reprinted 1970).

Moss, Leonard W. and Cappanari, Stephen C. (1982) 'In Quest of the Black Virgin: She is black because she is black', in James J. Preston (ed.), *Mother Worship: Themes and Variations*, Chapel Hill, NC: University of North Carolina Press: 53–74.

Paul, Georges et Pierre (1950) *Notre-Dame du Puy: Essai historique et archéologique*, Le Puy-en-Velay: Cazes-Bonneton.

Perry, Mary Elizabeth (1990) 'The Black Madonna of Montserrat', in Frances Richardson Keller (ed.), *Views of Women's Lives in Western Tradition*, Lampeter: Edwin Mellen Press: 109–28.

Saillens, E. (1945) *Nos Vierges Noires: Leurs origines*, Paris: Les Editions Universelles.

St Victor, Owen (1988) *The Masked Madonna: Studies in the Mystical Symbolism of The Secret Sovereign: The Queen of Heaven*, Leuven: Sancta Sophia.

Vilatte, Sylvie (1997) 'La Question des "Vierges Noires"', in *La Vierge à l'Epoque Romane: Culte et représentations*, that is, *Revue d'Auvergne*, 542, Clermont-Ferrand: Société des Amis des Universités de Clermont-Ferrand: 12–38.

Vincent, Francis (1952) 'Saint François de Sales', in Hubert du Manoir (ed.), *Maria: Etudes sur la Sainte Vierge*, vol. 2, Paris: Beauchesne: 991–1004.

Weidegger, Paula (1978) *Female Cycles*, London: The Women's Press.

PART 5

MARY IN ART AND LITERATURE

22

MARY IN ISLAM

TIM WINTER

The Qur'ān knows Mary by her Syriac name, Maryam. As the spotless though defamed mother of God's prophet, Jesus the Messiah, she is the most conspicuous woman in the Muslim scripture. Here she not only provides the matrix for the Messiah, but is also shown as a woman of considerable integrity, sanctity and autonomy in her own right; in fact, the Muslim Mary is not primarily celebrated as mother of Christ, but as a distinctive archetype of female prayerfulness and patience in adversity. As such she is 'a sign for the worlds'.[1]

In the absence of a doctrine of incarnation, Islam could not develop a Mariology analogous to the rich evolutions in Christian cultures which are documented elsewhere in this volume. Indeed, the Qur'ān itself seems to condemn the excesses of a certain kind of Mariology which had developed among Christians in its day.[2] For Muslim formal theologians (*mutakallimūn*), Mary is therefore a figure of very slight relevance, offering a scriptural basis for the belief in the miracles of the saints,[3] but little more. Rather more significant was Mary's importance for historians and authors of Qur'ānic commentaries, who assembled extensive anecdotes about Mary, the exact ancestry of most of which cannot now be determined. In popular culture, and in mysticism, both sophisticated and rustic, the drama and prayerfulness of the Qur'ānic story generated a Marian culture of considerable richness. While Mary could not function as an immediately helpful model for Muslim women, given that her most characteristic miracle was an unrepeatable virgin birth, she often seemed to rival other 'perfect women', such as the Prophet's daughter Fāṭima, and there thus began an unresolved argument, present already in the *ḥadīth*, which sought to determine whether she was the best of all women.

In modern times, Mary has been a favoured theme for Muslims seeking to explore their faith's intimate connections with the major religion of the now-dominant civilization of the West. She has also sometimes provided a starting point for the religion's lively modern debates over the nature and role of womanhood.[4]

---

1. Qur'ān, 21.91; 23.50.
2. Qur'ān, 5.116, where God asks Jesus whether he had asked his people to regard him and his mother as gods. In the fifth century Nestorius had already anticipated the Reformers by denouncing the term *Theotokos*. The Qur'ānic verse should not be taken as implying a statement about the Christian Trinity; cf. Parrinder 1965: 135.
3. Calverley and Pollock (trans.) 2002, II: 1024.
4. See, for instance, Barlas 2002: 175; cf. also the 2001 Iranian film *Maryam-e moqaddas*, scripted by Muḥammad Bahmanpour, and the Pahlavi text below.

QUR'ĀN 3.35–51: MARY'S BEGINNINGS AND HER YOUTH

This is the first of the two major Marian passages in the Qur'ān. The fine translation by George Sale (1697–1736) conveys something of the lyrical dignity of the original, even though its complex rhythms and rhymes have been lost.

While it is impossible to propose a genealogy for the Qur'ān's Marian passages, it has long been recognized that these not only share some of the motifs and concerns of the canonical infancy narratives, but also resonate with the most important extracanonical source of Marian narratives, the *Protevangelium Jacobi*, or *Infancy Gospel of James*. Notes to the long Qur'ānic passages given in this and the following section point out some of the concordances.

While the claim that the *Protevangelium* is older than the canonical Gospels, or shares a common source with them, has not met with general acceptance,[5] it is widely agreed that the text is early, dating substantially from the middle or late second century, and may include material of a much earlier date.[6]

The Qur'ānic text shares the *Protevangelium*'s emphasis on Mary's purity, her prayerfulness, her miracles and her moral excellence. Although these are charisms of Mary in her own right, they also provide a fitting Islamic preface to the birth of a messianic prophet, who explicitly rejects those who would divinize him. Like his mother, he is only a human, a servant of God (Qur'ān, 5.72–5).

35 *Remember* when the wife of 'Imran[7] said: Lord, verily I have vowed unto thee that which is in my womb, to be dedicated *to thy service*: accept it therefore of me; for thou art he who heareth and knoweth.[8]
36 And when she was delivered of it she said, Lord, verily I have brought forth a female (and God well knew what she had brought forth), and a male is not as a female: I have called her Mary; and I commend her to thy protection, and *also* her issue, against Satan driven away with stones.
37 Therefore her Lord accepted her with a gracious acceptance, and caused her to bear an excellent offspring. And Zacharias took care of *the child*; whenever Zacharias went into the chamber to her, he found provisions with her: *and* he said, O Mary, whence hadst thou this? She answered, This is from God: for God provideth for whom he pleaseth without measure.[9]
38 There Zacharias called on his Lord, *and* said, Lord, give me from thee a good offspring, for thou art the hearer of prayer.

---

5. An influential voice in favour of the former claim has been Conrady 1889: 728–84; for the latter claim, see Resch 1897.
6. Elliott (ed.) 1993: 48–51.
7. This is presumably the Joachim of Christian apocrypha such as the *Protevangelium Jacobi*, trans. Ronald F. Hock, in Miller (ed.) 1992: 383. The Muslim commentators distinguish clearly between him and the 'Imran who was the father of Moses; cf. n. 23.
8. Cf. *Protevangelium* 4.2.
9. Cf. *Protevangelium* 8.3, 'And Mary lived in the temple of the Lord. She was fed there like a dove, receiving her food from the hand of a heavenly messenger.' The miracle, adumbrated by Ibn Kathīr (486 below), has been challenged by modernist interpreters concerned to strip the Qur'ān of 'superstitious' or legendary matter; see Jansen 1974: 26–7.

39 And the angels called to him, while he stood praying in the chamber,[10] *saying*, Verily God promiseth thee *a son named* John, who shall bear witness to a word[11] which cometh from God; an honourable person, chaste, and one of the righteous prophets.

40 He answered: Lord how shall I have a son, when old age hath overtaken me, and my wife is barren? *The angel* said, So God doth that which he pleaseth.

41 *Zacharias* answered, Lord, give me a sign. *The angel* said, Thy sign shall be, that thou shalt speak unto no man for three days, otherwise than by gesture: remember thy Lord often, and praise *him* evening and morning.

42 And when the angels said, O Mary, verily God hath chosen thee, and hath purified thee, and hath chosen thee above *all* the women of the world:

43 O Mary, be devout towards thy Lord, and worship, and bow down with those who bow down.[12]

44 This is a secret history: we reveal it unto thee,[13] although thou wast not present with them when they threw in their rods *to cast lots* which of them should have the education of Mary: neither wast thou with them, when they strove among themselves.[14]

45 When the angels[15] said, O Mary, verily God sendeth thee good tidings, *that thou shalt bear* a word, *proceeding* from himself; his name shall be the Messiah, Jesus, son of Mary, honourable in this world and in the world to come, and one of those who approach near *to the presence of God*;

46 and he shall speak unto men in the cradle, and when he is grown up; and he shall be *one* of the righteous:

47 she answered, Lord, how shall I have a son, since a man hath not touched me? *The angel* said, So God createth that which he pleaseth: when he decreeth a thing, he only saith unto it, Be, and it is:

48 *God* shall teach him the scripture, and wisdom, and the law, and the gospel;[16]

49 and *shall appoint him his* apostle to the children of Israel; *and he shall say*,

---

10. Ar. *miḥrāb*. The commentators vary over its sense here. The event is presented as a kind of annunciation; cf. Thackston 1978: 326.

11. Ar. *kalima*, denoting not a Logos, but God's command that brought about Jesus' creation; Parrinder 1965: 45–8.

12. This seems not to be the Annunciation, which follows, but a separate angelic address which predicts her own greatness, not that of her son.

13. The Prophet. This parenthetic verse stresses that the differences between the Qur'ānic and biblical account should not occasion surprise; the former is the direct revelation of God; Asad 1984: 73.

14. Perhaps paralleled in the *Protevangelium* 8.6–9; 9.1–8; although here staffs and not rods (literally, 'pens', *aqlām*) are mentioned, and it is Joseph who becomes her guardian.

15. Gabriel, referred to with the honorific plural; or Gabriel in a group of angels; ibn Juzayy 1403/ 1983: 80.

16. 'Law' is *Tawrāt* (the Torah); the 'Gospel' is *Injīl*, the book which Muslim tradition believes was revealed to Jesus, not identical with the present-day Gospels; Parrinder 1965: 142–51. For the Muslim image of the origins of Christianity, see (for the early period) Declais 2003: 79–92; for current views, see Maqsood 2000.

481

Verily I come unto you with a sign from your Lord; for I will make before you, of clay, as it were the figure of a bird; then I will breathe thereon, and it shall become a bird, by the permission of God:[17] and I will prophesy unto you what ye eat, and what ye lay up for store in your houses. Verily herein will be a sign unto you, if ye believe.

50 And *I come* to confirm the Law which was *revealed* before me, and to allow unto you as lawful, part of that which hath been forbidden you: and I come unto you with a sign from your Lord; therefore fear God, and obey me.

51 Verily God is my Lord and your Lord: therefore serve Him. This is the right way.

QUR'ĀN 19.16–35: THE ANNUNCIATION AND THE BIRTH OF CHRIST (TRANSLATION BY GEORGE SALE)

16 And remember in the book *of the Koran the story of* Mary; when she retired from her family to a place towards the east,[18]

17 and took a veil *to conceal herself* from them;[19] and we sent our spirit[20] *Gabriel* unto her, and he appeared unto her *in the shape of* a perfect man.

18 She said, I fly for refuge unto the merciful *God, that he may defend me* from thee: if thou fearest *him, thou wilt not approach me.*

19 He answered, Verily, I am the messenger of thy Lord, *and am sent* to give thee a holy son.[21]

20 She said, How shall I have a son, seeing a man hath not touched me, and I am no harlot?

21 *Gabriel* replied, *So shall it be*: thy Lord saith, This is easy with me; and *we will perform it*, that we may ordain him for a sign unto men, and a mercy from us: for it is a thing which is decreed.

---

17. A miracle absent from the canonical Gospels, but recorded in the *Infancy Gospel of Thomas* 2.1–7; Miller (ed.) 1992: 371. See Robinson 1989: 1–13.

18. Often seen as a place in the wilderness; see the commentaries translated in Wheeler 2002: 300–1. Some medieval Muslims believed that Christians pray facing the east for this reason; Robinson 1988, 1–16 (4–5).

19. The 'veil' or 'screen' (*ḥijāb*) has been variously interpreted. Fakhr al-Dīn al-Rāzī (1149–1209), perhaps the most profound of exoteric Sunni interpreters, records five opinions, including the view that *ḥijāb* denotes a place of solitary retreat, or that 'she was thirsty and went to the desert to draw water', or that she withdrew from the Temple because of her menses (cf. Lev. 15.19–24). See Robinson 1988: 4. The *Protevangelium* (8.4) may be the source for the latter view; the same text (10.8) refers to an incident in which Mary withdraws in order to help spin the threads for the Temple veil.

20. Usually understood as Gabriel, whom Islam regards as the angel of revelation (cf. Qur'ān 26.193); but a minority opinion holds that 'the reference is to the spirit who was formed in her womb as a human being (i.e. Jesus)'; Rāzī, in Robinson 1988: 5.

21. 'Holy' is *zakī*, more usually translated as 'pure'. Rāzī asks how she could have recognized the stranger as an angel, and suggests that God inspired her with the relevant knowledge, in which case this is another of her miracles. Alternatively, Zecharias might have taught her how to recognize an angel, and when she had collected herself, she applied this knowledge; Rāzī, in ibid.: 9.

22 Wherefore she conceived him:[22] and she retired aside with him *in her womb* to a distant place;

23 and the pains of childbirth came upon her near the trunk of a palm-tree. She said, Would to God I had died before this, and had become a *thing* forgotten, and lost in oblivion!

24 And he who was beneath her called to her, saying, Be not grieved: now hath God provided a rivulet under thee;

25 and do thou shake the body of the palm-tree, and it shall let fall ripe dates upon thee, ready gathered.

26 And eat, and drink, and calm thy mind. Moreover if thou see any man, *and he question thee*, say, Verily I have vowed a fast unto the Merciful; wherefore I will by no means speak to a man this day.

27 So she brought *the child* to her people, carrying him *in her arms. And* they said *unto her*, O Mary, now hast thou done a strange thing:

28 O sister of Aaron,[23] thy father was not a bad man, neither was thy mother a harlot.

29 But she made signs unto *the child to answer them; and* they said, How shall we speak to him, who is an infant in the cradle?

30 *Whereupon the child* said, Verily I am the servant of God; he hath given me the book *of the gospel,* and hath appointed me a prophet.

31 And he hath made me blessed, wheresoever I shall be; and hath commanded me *to observe* prayer, and *to give* alms, so long as I shall live;

32 and *he hath made me* dutiful towards my mother, and hath not made me proud, *or* unhappy.[24]

32 And peace be on me the day whereon I was born, and the day whereon I shall die, and the day whereon I shall be raised to life.

33 This *was* Jesus, the son of Mary; the word of truth, concerning whom they doubt.

34 It is not *meet* for God, that he should have any son: God forbid. When he decreeth a thing, he only saith unto it, Be; and it is.

35 And verily God is my Lord and your Lord; wherefore serve him: this is the right way.

THREE *ḤADĪTHS* OF THE PROPHET

The *ḥadīths*, reports about the Prophet's words and actions which are not included in the Qur'ān, form the second scripture of Islam. Despite their immense bulk, they do

---

22.   Gabriel, or God (cf. Qur'ān 21.91; 66.12), breathed into her mouth, or the fold or sleeve of her robe, or her generative organs, and so she conceived; Wheeler 2002: 302; Rāzī, in Robinson 1988: 15.

23.   Muḥammad Hamidullah's French translation has 'soeur Aaronide', which gives the sense of the Muslim interpretation that this Qur'ānic expression is not to be taken literally; the exegetes were well aware that 'eighteen centuries' separated Aaron from Mary. As a resident of the Temple she was a kind of honorary priest; Wensinck and Johnstone 1986–, VI: 628–32 (630).

24.   The occasional Gospel suggestions of a coldness between the adult Jesus and his mother (e.g. Lk. 11.27–8) are uncongenial to the Qur'ānic assumption of the perfection of God's prophets.

not contain as much about Mary as her importance in the Qur'ān might lead us to expect. These three texts all concern the debate over the 'queens of heaven' which the new religion will recognize.

> God's messenger said: 'The best woman of her time was Mary daughter of 'Imrān, and the best woman of her time is Khadīja daughter of Khuwailid.' In one version, Abū Kuraib said that Wakī' pointed to the sky and to the earth.[25]
>
> The Prophet said: 'Among the women of the universe Mary daughter of 'Imrān, Khadīja daughter of Khuwailid, Fāṭima daughter of Muḥammad, and Āsiya wife of Pharaoh are enough for you.'[26]
>
> Umm Salama told that in the year of the Conquest God's Messenger called Fāṭima and spoke privately to her and she wept; he then spoke to her and she laughed. When God's Messenger died she asked her about her weeping and her laughing and she replied, 'God's Messenger informed me that he was going to die, so I wept; he then informed me that, with the exception of Mary daughter of 'Imrān, I would be the chief lady among the inhabitants of paradise, so I laughed.'[27]

FROM *THE BEGINNING AND THE END*, A WORLD HISTORY BY IBN KATHĪR (D. 1373)

Ismā'īl ibn 'Umar ibn Kathīr was a historian and *ḥadīth* scholar who served as rector of several colleges in Damascus. He wrote a commentary of the Qur'ān, but is most noteworthy for his *The Beginning and the End* (*al-Bidāya wa'l-Nihāya*), which begins with the creation and ends with details of Muslim eschatology. His description of the life of Mary is drawn from earlier Muslim sources, and may be taken as representative of mainstream medieval views. The treatment here takes the form of a formal commentary on Qur'ānic verses.

> Muḥammad ibn Isḥāq and others state that Mary's mother was barren. One day she saw a bird nuzzling a chick. Longing for a child, she vowed to God that if she conceived she would consecrate it to the service of the Temple. She immediately began menstruating; and when she was pure again, her husband made love to her, and she conceived Mary, upon her be peace.
>
> **And when she was delivered of it she said, Lord, verily I have**

25. Khadīja was the Prophet's first wife. Abū Kuraib and Wakī' are narrators of the *ḥadīth*; the significance of the latter's gesture is said to be that 'Mary was the best in heaven and Khadīja the best on earth'. Narrated by Bukhārī and Muslim; translated in Robson 1970, II: 1360.
26. Āsiya is the believing wife of the Pharaoh of the exodus; see Stowasser 1994: 59–60; Thackston 1978: 213–25. The *ḥadīth* is one of a genre, not always consistent, which enumerates the women who are said to achieved perfection (*kamāl*); for arguments over the hierarchy, see Smith and Haddad 1989: 179. The *ḥadīth* is narrated by Tirmidhī; Robson 1970, II: 1361.
27. Umm Salama was a companion of the Prophet. The 'year of the Conquest' denotes the year in which Mecca was conquered by the Muslims. The *ḥadīth* appears in the collection of Tirmidhī; Robson 1970, II: 1362.

brought forth a female (and God well knew what she had brought forth) – according to a variant reading, this may also be 'what I have brought forth', **and a male is not as a female** in serving the Temple, for in that time they would consecrate only sons as servants of the Temple. **I have called her Mary**: this has been used as a proof-text to show that it is legally preferable to name a child on the day it is born. [. . .]

and I commend her to thy protection, and *also* her issue, against Satan driven away with stones. This prayer of hers was answered, just as the prayer which began her vow. For as narrated by Imam Aḥmad on the authority of 'Abd al-Razzāq, on the authority of Maʻmar on the authority of al-Zuhrī, on the authority of Ibn al-Musayyib, on the authority of Abū Hurayra, the Prophet (may God bless him and grant him peace) said: 'There is no child but that the devil touches him at the time that he is born, so that he cries out from his touch; excepting only Mary and her son.' [. . .]

Therefore her Lord accepted her with a gracious acceptance, and caused her to bear an excellent offspring. And Zacharias took care of *the child*. Many of the commentators state that when her mother gave her birth she wrapped her in rags, and then went out with her to the Temple, where she was given to the ascetics who resided there. Since she was the daughter of their prayer-leader and high priest, they disputed her custody amongst themselves. [. . .] Their prophet at that time, Zacharias, wanted her for himself alone, since his wife was her sister (or her maternal aunt, according to another view). They argued over the matter, and asked him to cast lots. Fate was on his side, and he prevailed in the lottery.

This is a secret history: we reveal it unto thee, although thou wast not present with them when they threw in their rods *to cast lots* which of them should have the education of Mary: neither wast thou with them, when they strove among themselves. Each of them provided his own pen, and they were all placed in a spot, from which a pre-adolescent boy would take one. Zacharias's pen emerged first; so they insisted on drawing lots again, this time by casting their pens in the river, so that whichever pen moved against the current would be the winner. This they did, and again, Zacharias's pen prevailed. At this, they desired to cast lots a third time, on the understanding that the winner would be the pen which flowed with the current, while the others went against it. When they did this, Zacharias's pen was again victorious, so that he was the one who became Mary's guardian. He was, in any case, the one with the greatest legal right to do this, on many grounds.

whenever Zacharias went into the chamber to her, he found provisions with her: *and* he said, O Mary, whence hadst thou this? She answered, This is from God: for God provideth for whom he pleaseth without measure. According to the commentators, Zacharias appointed for her an eminent place in the Temple which was to be entered by none save her. There she worshipped God, and undertook her duties as keeper of the Temple when it was her turn to do so. She would worship day and night, until she became a model for worshippers among the Israelites, and also became famous for miracles and for noble traits of character, to the extent that whenever God's prophet Zacharias came in to visit her in her place of prayer he would find strange and out-of-season fruits. In the winter-time he would find that she had summer fruits; and vice-versa. Hence his question: 'O Mary, whence hadst thou this?' and her reply: 'This is from God.'

At this, Zacharias felt a longing for a son from his descendants; despite his advanced years. So he said, **Lord, give me from thee a good offspring, for thou art the hearer of prayer**. According to some, he prayed: 'O Thou who furnishest Mary with fruits when the season is past, grant me offspring.' The remainder of this tale has been told elsewhere.

And when the angels said, O Mary, verily God hath chosen thee, and hath purified thee, and hath chosen thee above *all* the women of the world. God the Exalted is here stating that the angels were giving Mary the good news that God had chosen her among the women of the world in her time, since He had chosen her for the creation of a son from her who would have no father, and who would be a noble Prophet **who shall speak unto men in the cradle**, while still an infant, calling them to worship God alone, without any partner. He would do the same when an adult, this being a prediction that he would indeed grow to adulthood.

Mary is also enjoined to worship constantly, to submit, to prostrate and to bow, that she might be deserving of this miracle, and might be thankful for this grace. It is said that she used to stand in prayer until her feet bled. May God be pleased with her, and show her His mercy, and her mother and father also!

When the Angel said: **God hath purified thee**, the reference is to base traits of character, while **hath chosen thee above *all* the women of the world** may refer to the women of her age, in the way that God says to Moses: 'Verily I have chosen thee over the people' [7.144], and as He says: 'We have knowingly selected them over mankind' [44.32], although it is known that Abraham was superior to Moses, and that Muḥammad was better than either. [...]

It is also possible that the verse is to be taken at face value, so that she is superior to all the world's women who preceded her, and all who followed her. For if she is a prophet, which is believed by Ibn Ḥazm and others, who also believe in the prophetic status of Isaac's mother Sarah, and the mother of Moses,[28] on the grounds that the angels spoke to them, and that Moses's mother received revelation, this would still not rule out her being superior to Sarah and Moses's mother, since this verse is general in implication and is not in conflict with any other text. But God knows best.

The majority opinion, which is the view of the Sunni Muslims as

---

28. In Qur'ān XXVIII.7, the mother of Moses receives *waḥy*, the usual Qur'ānic term for a revelation granted to a prophet of God. Ibn Ḥazm of Cordoba (d. 1064), a literalist (*ẓāhirī*) jurist, took the view that the Qur'ān indicates that Mary was a prophet; 'Alī ibn Ḥazm, *al-Fiṣal fī'l-milal wa'l-niḥal* (Cairo: Muḥammad Ṣubayḥ, 1347–8/1928–9), V: 12–4; he was followed by a fellow Spaniard, Muḥammad al-Qurṭubī, *al-Jāmi' li-aḥkām al-Qur'ān* (Cairo: Dar al-Kutub al-Miṣriyya, 1933–50), IV: 83; see Schleifer 1997: 73–94; Smith and Haddad 1989: 177–8.

represented by Abu'l-Ḥasan al-Ashʿarī[29] and others, is that prophecy is reserved to men alone, and that there have been no female prophets. Hence Mary's highest degree would be that indicated by God's word, 'The Messiah Jesus is but a messenger; messengers have passed away before him; and his mother was a saint' [5.75], in which case it is permissible to hold that she was the highest of all female saints, before or since. And God knows best.[30]

TWO PASSAGES BY THE SUFI POET JALĀL AL-DĪN RŪMĪ (D. 1273)

(1) The Unborn John Bows to the Messiah

Rūmī is using a Muslim legend as a proof-text to show the error of his literal-minded critics, who cannot understand the world of miracles. His readers may have been aware of the story that Jesus and John were conceived simultaneously.[31]

John, upon him be peace, prostrates himself in his mother's womb to the Messiah.

In a private place, before bearing the child, John's mother said to Mary:

'In all certainty I have seen within you a king,

who is of the 'determined ones',[32] most intelligent.

When I came to meet with you, my own burden prostrated itself at once.

This foetus prostrated itself to that foetus, so that a pain appeared in my body
    from the prostration.'

And Mary replied, 'I too beheld within me a prostration, from that child in my
    belly.'

An objection raised to this tale

The fools say, 'Scratch out this legend, for it is a lie and a falsehood!

During her pregnancy Mary met no one; she didn't return to the city.

From without the city, that sweet enchantress did not return until her womb
    was empty.

When she had given birth to him, she placed him on her hip, and brought him
    to her family.

Where did John's mother see her, that she might utter these words about what
    took place?'

---

29. Eponymous founder of one of the two main schools of Muslim doctrinal orthodoxy, he died in 935 or 936.

30. Ismāʿīl ibn Kathīr, *al-Bidāya wa'l-nihāya* (Cairo: al-Saʿāda, 1351–8/1932–9), II: 56–62.

31. Thackston 1978: 328. For Rūmī's sources for this story, see Badīʿ al-Zamān Furūzanfar, *Maʾākhez̲-i qeṣaṣ u temsīlāt-i Masnavī* (Tehran: Intishārāt-i Daneshgāh-i Tehrān, 1333 solar): 82.

32. A Qurʾānic category seemingly denoting an elite among the prophets; cf. Qurʾān 46.35.

The answer to the objection

Let him know that that which is beyond the horizon is present to he who is fit
to receive inspiration.[33]

John's mother would appear as one present before Mary's eyes, though far from
her sight.

The Friend[34] can be beheld with one's eyes closed, when the skin has been
turned into a window.[35]

2. The Annunciation as an Archetype of Mystical Initiation

This famous passage is discussed by Henry Corbin, who sees it as a representation of
the moment where the ascetic, after a long period of purgation, suddenly confronts
the true guide, who is simultaneously like and unlike the self. The guide has human
form, but is angelic, and hence represents the ideal to which the initiate is
summoned. The response to this encounter is firstly to fear and to flee from this
figure, and then to recognize that he is the seeker's refuge who brings the birth and
liberation of the spirit within the seeker's breast.[36] Rūmī is here adapting the legend
that Gabriel appeared to her when she was en déshabillé, a symbol of helplessness and
of tajrīd, the stripping away of worldly attachments, and when she was carrying out
the ritual ablution required by sacred law following menstruation: another helpful
symbol. The Annunciation reveals to Mary that she, like all of humanity, carries
within herself an imperishable spirit (rūḥ); and while Rūmī, as a Muslim, cannot
sanction the idea of an incarnation, he nonetheless makes much of a saying of God
(ḥadīth qudsī), reported by the Prophet, which runs: 'My heaven and my earth cannot
contain Me; but I am contained by the heart of My believing servant.'[37]

The appearance of the Holy Spirit (Gabriel) in the shape of a man, to Mary when she was undressed and washing herself, and how she took refuge with God.

Before the slipping-away of your possessions, say to the form (of created
things), like Mary, '(I take) refuge from thee with the Merciful (God).'

Mary in her chamber saw a form that gave increase of life – a life-increasing,
heart-ravishing one.

That trusted Spirit rose up before her from the face of the earth, like the moon
and the sun.

Beauty unveiled rose up from the earth (in) such (splendour) as the sun rises
from the East.

---

33.   'Inspiration' here is khāṭir, a general Sufi term denoting any true or false address received by the
soul; Abu'l-Qāsim al-Qushayrī, al-Risāla fī 'ilm al-taṣawwuf, ed. 'Abd al-Ḥalīm Maḥmūd and
Muḥammad al-Sharīf (Cairo, 1385/1966): 263.

34.   That is, God.

35.   Rūmī, ed. Nicholson 1929, Persian text, II: 449–50. I have translated this myself, as Nicholson's
rendering here is sometimes problematic (sujūd becomes 'worship', etc.).

36.   Corbin 1972, IV: 51–3; for the Annunciation as archetype of the encounter between seeker and
spiritual director, see also Winter 1999: 453–4.

37.   For Rūmī's use of this hadith, see Chittick 1983: 39–40.

A trembling came over Mary's limbs, for she was undressed and was afraid of evil.

('Twas) such a form that if Joseph had beheld it plainly, he would have cut his hand in amazement, like the (Egyptian) women.[38]

It blossomed from the earth like a rose before her — like a phantasy which lifts its head from the heart.[39]

Mary became selfless (beside herself), and in her selflessness she said, 'I will leap into the Divine protection.'

Because that pure-bosomed one[40] had made a habit of betaking herself in flight to the Unseen.

Since she deemed the world a kingdom without permanence, she prudently made a fortress of that (Divine) Presence.

In order that in the hour of death she should have a stronghold which the Enemy would find no way to attack.

She saw no better fortress than the protection of God: she chose her abiding-place next to that castle.[41]

[Fifty lines then follow on the beauty and majesty of God's love for the mystic; then we return to Mary.]

The Exemplar of (Divine) Bounty cried out to her, 'I am the trusted (messenger) of the Lord: be not afraid of me.

Do not turn thy head away from the exalted (favourites) of (Divine) Majesty, do not withdraw thyself from such goodly confidants.'[42]

He was saying this, and (meanwhile) from his lips a wick (ray) of pure light was going up to Simák (Arcturus) step by step (uninterruptedly).[43]

'Thou art fleeing from my existence into non-existence (the Unseen World): in non-existence I am a King and standard-bearer.

Verily my home and dwelling-place is in non-existence: solely my (outward) form is before the Lady (Mary).

O Mary, look (well), for I am a difficult form (to apprehend): I am both a new-moon and a phantasy in the heart.

---

38. A familiar reference to Joseph, the most handsome of prophets, at whose beauty Potiphar's wife's companions marvelled, so that they cut their hands in distraction. For Rūmī this is often a symbol of the *sacrificium intellectus*; cf. Rūmī, ed. Nicholson 1929, IV: 350–1.

39. The rose (*gul*) is often a symbol of the mystic's heart, which swells and gives fragrance, which is holiness, in springtime (*bahār*), after receiving the rain of God. Rūmī's poem is playing with a stock tension between spring and autumn, heaven and earth, showing the Annunciation as the figure of the opening of the heart. For Rūmī's garden tropology, see Schimmel 1993: 82–93.

40. Nicholson's rendering of *pāk-jayb*, literally 'pure-sleeved', a reference to the story of how the angel breathed into her sleeve.

41. Rūmī, ed. Nicholson 1929, III: 207–8.

42. *Sār-afrāzān*: the 'eminent ones', angels and other superlunary beings attracted to the divine presence like pilgrims around the Ka'ba; cf. Winter 2004: 144–57 (145–6).

43. Arcturus is the symbol of the highest heaven.

When a phantasy comes into thy heart and settles (there), it is (still) with thee
   wheresoever thou fleest –

Except an unsubstantial and vain phantasy which is one that sinks (and
   disappears) like the false dawn.

I am of the light of the Lord, like the true dawn, for no night prowls around my
   day.

Hark, do not cry *Lá ḥawl*[44] against me, O daughter of 'Imran, for I have
descended hither from *Lá ḥawl*.

Lá ḥawl was my origin and sustenance – the light of that *Lá ḥawl* which was
   prior to the spoken word.

Thou art taking refuge from me with God: I am in eternity the image of (Him
   who is) the (only) refuge.

There is no bane worse than ignorance: thou art with thy Friend and dost not
   know how to make love.[45]

Thou art deeming thy Friend a stranger: upon a joy thou hast bestowed the
   name of a grief.'

Such a date-palm, which is our Friend's favour – since we are robbers, His
   date-palm is our gallows.[46]

Such a musky (fragrant) object, which is the tress of our Prince – since we are
   demented, this (tress) is our chain.[47]

Such a (Divine) grace is flowing like a Nile – since we are Pharaohs, it is
   becoming like blood.[48]

A MORISCO PRAYER

Mary's miracles made her a favourite name for mention in prayer, as in this example
drawn from a much longer supplication in which the merits of many other Qur'ānic
figures are also invoked. The language is a form of Castilian, written, as was common
among Hispanic Muslims following the *reconquista*, in Arabic characters. The text is
thought to originate in sixteenth-century Aragon.

> O God, I ask you by [...] the grace that you set within Mary, upon her be
> peace, whom you named, elected and purified over all women, and by the
> good prayers which she raised to you in her chamber (*almiḥrāb*) and in the Holy

---

44. The phrase *lā ḥawla wa-lā quwwata illā bi'Llāh*, 'there is neither power nor might save in God'
(*ḥadīth*: Bukhāri, Adhān: 7; Muslim, Dhikr: 32), is uttered when resigning oneself to a calamity of
God.
45. '*eshq*: not necessarily 'eros' here.
46. The date-palm is his blessings in the world; which destroy us, since we will not take them
lawfully and with gratitude.
47. The tress (*zulf*) is the world in its ambiguous quality: we love the Beloved's tresses, since they are
of her, but we also detest them, since they may veil her face.
48. The greatest river, symbol of divine effusion (*fayẓ*) and generosity (*karam*), becomes a curse
when, like Pharaoh, we defy God. The Qur'ān alludes to this as one of the plagues of Egypt (7.133).
The lines are Nicholson's translation; Rūmī, ed. Nicholson 1929, III: 211–12.

House, and beneath the palm-tree where she gave birth in great distress and in fear of the Jews who wished to slay her, and by the grace which you set within Jesus, upon him be peace, by saying 'Be!' and he was, breathing your spirit into Mary without being corrupted by any man, by your great power, with great purity [...] O God, support us and forgive us our sins.[49]

AN OTTOMAN HYMN TO FĀṬIMA

Although conspicuous in the Qur'ān, Mary does not figure centrally in Muslim devotion. Intercessory prayers invoking her are not unknown, but the place of honour among Muslim female saints is in practice usually given to the Prophet's only surviving child, his daughter Fāṭima. Devotion to Fāṭima recalls many of the characteristic themes of Christian Marian spirituality. She is celebrated for her poverty, for her miracles, her ceaseless prayer for sinners, her retiring and submissive nature, and for intuiting, during her lifetime, the glorious yet tragic martyrdom of her son, al-Ḥusayn. Her titles, such as 'Mother of Sorrows' (*Umm al-Aḥzān*), the 'Pure' (*al-Batūl*), and the 'Lady of the People of Heaven' (*sayyidat ahl al-janna*), also bear clear Marian resemblances; indeed, her title is sometimes *Maryam al-Kubrā*, the Greater Mary.[50] Whether the correspondence reflects the legacy of the many Christian converts to medieval Islam, or an alleged need of all monotheists for a celestial feminine ideal bearing roughly the same qualities, or, as some Muslims will say, an independent process of the community's guidance by God, is a debate that is unlikely to be settled. However, it seems reasonable to suppose that Fāṭima's greater popularity among Muslims stems from her closeness to the Prophet, and also from her status as wife and mother, perpetual virginity forming no part of the Muslim ideal. That popularity bore fruit in the form of intercessory prayers (*tawassul*), and in the context of Islamic monotheism, it is not surprising that while these were regarded as licit by most theologians, sharp arguments periodically arose which recall Calvin's challenge to Catholicism's distinction between *hyperdulia* and *latria*.[51]

Literary devotion to Fāṭima is very extensive in the major Islamic languages. The following example, in Ottoman Turkish, is by Laylā Hanım (d. 1848), one of the best-known female poets of Istanbul. The daughter of a religious judge, she was tutored in literature by the poet and belle-lettrist 'Izzet Mollā (d. 1829), from whom she acquired a direct and brilliant poetic style. As a modern critic records, 'she is full of fun and cares little for the world's opinion, she is determined to enjoy herself and

49. Hegyi (ed.) 1981: 110–11. For Mary in Morisco literature, see Schleifer 1997: 97–100.

50. For references and further discussion, see Winter, '*Pulchra ut luna*', 449–52.

51. The argument has intensified over the past century with the rise of reformist tendencies, both rationalising and scripturalist. See (for a modernist critique) Elizabeth Sirriyeh, *Sufis and Anti-Sufis: The Defence, Rethinking and Rejection of Sufism in the Modern World* (London: Curzon, 1999), 96-8; see also, for a traditional jurist's defence of the practice against fundamentalist (Wahhābī) criticism, Nuh Ha Mim Keller, *Reliance of the Traveller: The Classic Manual of Islamic Sacred Law* 'Umdat al-Salik *by Ahmad ibn Naqib al-Misri (d.769/1368)* (revised edition, Beltsville, MD: Amana, 1994), 933-40.

let others say what they will;'[52] but she is devout as well, writing poems to celebrate appointments in the religious hierarchy, together with heartfelt elegies for the Prophet and the saints, which have ensured the continued popularity of her verse. The present short ode (*gazel*) is addressed to the soul of the Prophet's daughter, whom she perhaps saw in a vision; the Marian parallels are both clear and intriguing.[53]

O mother of the king of martyrs, O holy radiant one!
O helper of the poor at Judgement, O holy radiant one!

The Lord has sent a grace upon each mortal human slave,
And you comprise that gift for us, O holy radiant one!

Show mercy to the wretched states which to you I have shown,
In dreaming visions of my shame, O holy radiant one!

Far be it from your grace to break a promise that you made.
And you have vowed to care for us, O holy radiant one!

Before the Sultan of the Prophets, your father glorious,
Set this my plea, O Mine of Gifts, O holy radiant one!

Remit my faults, let this be for the sake of martyrs' blood,[54]
Eternity's great sultan's spouse,[55] O holy radiant one!

Deny me not your gate, and may I be your grace's guest,
Grant Laylā now a worthy gift, O holy radiant one![56]

A BALLAD IN EGYPTIAN DIALECT

Songs such as this are still immensely popular throughout the Islamic world. Traditionally they are sung at religious festivals, in coffee-houses, and by men and women engaged in manual labour. This one probably dates from the early twentieth century.

---

52.   E. J. W. Gibb, ed. Edward G. Browne, *A History of Ottoman Poetry* (London: Luzac, 1900-7), IV, 344.
53.   Fahir Iz, 'Laylā Khanım', *Encyclopedia of Islam* (2nd edition), V, 710; Ismail Ünver, 'Leylā Hanım', *Türk Diyanet Vakfı Islam Ansiklopedisi*, XXVII, 157. Ottoman sources for her biography: Bursalı Mehmed Zāhid Efendi, '*Osmānlı müellifleri* (Istanbul: Matba'a-yi 'Āmire, 1333AH), II, 406; Mehmed Zihnī Efendi, *Mesāhīnün-Nisā* (Istanbul: Dārüt-Tibā'etül-'Āmire, 1295AH), II, 195.
54.   Specifically, of her unjustly slain sons, al-Ḥasan and al-Ḥusayn.
55.   'Alī ibn Abī Ṭālib (d. 660) was simultaneously the Prophet's cousin and son-in-law.
56.   Mehmet Aslan (ed.), *Leylā Hanım Divanı* (Istanbul: Kitabevi, 2003), 233.

1. Praised be the Knower of the Unseen,
He created things, without doubt,
Forgiving, Concealer of faults.
He has revealed something about Mary.
2. God's blessings and His grace
Be gifted to Muḥammad the guide,
And to his family and children,
And God's peace be upon Mary.
3. Come and hear, people of sense,
A poem like pure pearls
With true and sound news
Of the tale of Jesus and of Mary.
4. 'Imrān the trusty was her father,
A recognised imam was he,
Honoured in the Aqṣā Mosque,[57]
With great honour in Mary.
5. That clever man took to wife,
A pure girl, Ḥanna by name,
She was got with child, by the Bestower's will,
That child was the virgin lady Mary.
6. Said she: 'O Lord, I vow
To You what is in my belly; and I give it over.
My Lord, I put my trust in You.'
When her time came, she bore Mary.
7. She saw she was a girl like the moon.
She said: 'Knower of secret things,
By Your command she came as a girl,
And I have given her the name Maryam.'
8. She gave her to the Merciful God's keeping,
Away from the devil's whims and ploys,
So the Forgiving One accepted her,
And in His kindness He protected Mary.
9. The noble 'Imrān, he then died,
By the will of the All-Knowing Lord,
The Virgin she was still not weaned,
Her mother alone was her guardian.
10. To Jerusalem did she take her.
She said: 'Who will care for an orphan girl?'
God's servants competed for her sake.
Everyone was arguing about Mary.
11. Then our lord Zacharias called out,
He that was a pleasing prophet,

---

57. The Aqṣā Mosque in Jerusalem is believed to stand upon the site of Solomon's Temple.

'Don't dispute, leave off quarrelling!
I have the most right to guard Mary.'
12. Because he was her aunt's husband.
And the Maker brought about his desire,
He prayed and bowed down at once,
To see a vision which would please Mary.
13. When asleep, he heard a voice calling:
'Write the people's names upon
pens, and throw them all together
in the sea, to see who'll look after Mary.
14. The pen that floats on the water's face,
Shall be the pen of he who'll be Mary's guardian,
The names which sink beneath the surface,
Shall never be guardians of fair Mary.
15. When they threw their pens,
They sank in the water, save the pen
Of Zacharias, and then they knew,
All of them, that he was the guardian of Mary.
16. The Virgin's mother passed away,
Only a few days after that,
Zacharias the noblest became her guardian,
And with love he brought up Mary.[58]
[…]

94. They went back to Jerusalem and believed
In his prophethood, and bore witness to it.
They prostrated themselves to their Lord in gratitude,
Saying, 'Pure indeed is Mary.'
95. When he was weaned, she took him,
to a teacher of children, most learned,
who had studied the scriptures and understood them,
Among them he was placed by Mary.
96. 'In God's name,' he said to [the boy],
'read, you of the beautiful face!'
That handsome one replied by reading everything,
In the presence of pure Mary.
97. He had wished to teach [Jesus] the alphabet,
But found him a doctor of the law without peer,
He was amazed at his great understanding,
And his intelligence was pleasing to Mary.
98. Without rancour, Jesus called to him,
'What is the meaning of the alphabet, O teacher?'

---

58.   Littmann 1951: 16–17. Littmann has transcribed and translated this song from a popular edition
of songs entitled *Maḥāsin al-durar fī dīwān al-dabb wa'l-ḥajar* (Cairo: al-Maktaba al-Mulūkiya, n.d.).

And he replied to him: 'I do not know.
So help me to understand, in the presence of Mary.'
99. He replied, 'I shall not tell you,
Until you have risen with your things,
And I have sat there in your place,
I am Jesus, son of Mary.'
100. The schoolman rose to his feet,
Obedient to the pious one's command,
Amazed he was at the beauty of his speech,
And he said, 'A prophet from Mary!'
101. In his place did Jesus sit,
And of each letter taught the sense,
The doctor cried out, in delight,
'Glory to the Giver, O Mary!'[59]
102. He submitted to God at Jesus's hand,
And handed over his affairs to God,
Saying, 'Now I have gained a great prize,
So take him, and rise, Mary!
103. By God, this is a radiant prophet,
His are signs which cannot be gainsaid,
He will predict Muḥammad the most luminous,[60]
So guard him well, O Mary!'
104. At once she left, rejoicing,
Ennobled by seeing his greatness,
His were signs which became manifest,
Like the sun, witnessed by Mary.
105. He was famed for raising the dead,
By the will of He Who is powerful over us,
The halt and lame he healed and made whole,
At his ministry rejoiced Mary.
106. O Lord, by Muḥammad the chosen one,
Forgive my sins and lift my burdens!
Pardon my slips and my evil deeds,
By the Cave, Ṭāhā, and Maryam![61]
107. Open my heart to Islam!
Grant me the best of blessings!
By Your prophet, O Lord of Majesty,
Who made us know the chapter of Mary!
108. May God's grace rest upon the guide,
With His peace like fresh musk,

---

59. The legend of Jesus teaching the rabbi the meaning of the letters is very ancient; it appears in the *Infancy Gospel of Thomas* 6–8, 14–15, noted by Irenaeus; Harold Attridge, in Miller 1992: 369.
60. One of Jesus' prophetic tasks is to proclaim the advent of the final prophet (Qur'ān, 61.6).
61. The names of the Qur'ānic chapters 18, 20 and 19; here part of an intercessory prayer (*tawassul*).

And upon his family and noble companions,
For as long as at dawn is recited [the chapter of] Mary.
109. And praised be our Powerful Lord,
At our poem's beginning and at its end,
For as long as birds sing in meadows,
Or people read about Mary.[62]

FROM *JESUS CHRIST, MARY'S SON*, A HISTORICAL NOVEL BY 'ABD AL-ḤAMĪD JAWDA AL-SAḤḤĀR (1913–74)

Al-Saḥḥār was a leading academic and cultural critic in mid-twentieth-century Egypt, establishing the University Publishing Council in 1943, which supported young novelists such as Naguib Mahfouz, and ending his career as director of the National Council for Cinema, Theatre and Music. He is remembered primarily for his historical novel *In the Caravan of Time* (*Fī Qāfilat al-Zamān*, Cairo: Lajnat al-Nashr li'l-Jāmiʿiyyīn, 1947), which explores changing relations between the sexes in an Egyptian family challenged by modernity; but he also composed an influential autobiography (*Hādhihī ḥayātī*, Cairo: Maktabat Miṣr, 1975), and a 20-volume biography of the Prophet (*Muḥammad rasūlu'Llāh wa'l-ladhīna maʿah*, Cairo: Maktabat Miṣr, 1965–70). His novel about Christ weaves elements from biblical and Qur'ānic narratives to provide a lyrical modern expression of Islamic piety.[63]

The temple priests noticed the signs of pregnancy appear in her, and were appalled. They could not decide what to do with her. They were horrified that the temple should now be polluted by someone whom they had once believed to be the purest person on earth. They had competed for her custody. She had grown to womanhood amongst them, having never left her prayer-niche for anything other than a call of nature. This development was something which shook them, baffled them, and wrenched their souls in grief. They met to take counsel, to reach a final decision; and they came to the view that she must stand trial. If it emerged that she had been unchaste, they would stone her to death, in faithfulness to Moses's law.

Zacharias intervened to remind them of what he had witnessed in her prayer-niche, and of the fair predictions of the Christ that the prophets had made. The one they were unjustly accusing was his promised mother, whose offspring all Israel had been awaiting. His own wife had only conceived through her blessing, and but for her God would never have bestowed John upon him. On and on he spoke, insisting on her innocence; yet they turned away, with fingers in their ears, saying, 'It is only because he is her guardian, and her mother is his sister-in-law Elizabeth, that he troubles to defend her!'

Darkness descended; and Jerusalem donned her black robes. The priests

---

62. Littmann 1951: 36–40.
63. Jomier 1958: 367–86, esp. 378–86. For an Arabic biography of al-Saḥḥār, see Gharīb 1975. See further Bannerth and Morelon 1977: 5–31.

slept, awaiting the dawn of the day when they would place Mary on trial, and stone her. Joseph too went to bed, but no sooner had he surrendered his body to sleep than he heard a voice calling out to him:

'Joseph, get up! Bring Mary out, for the people are scheming against her!'

He awoke with a start, and prepared his donkey. Cautiously he made his way to the place where Mary dwelt, and there he told her of the revelation that he had received. He set her upon the donkey, and in the still night they made their way along the narrow alleys which lay between the immense, awe-inspiring walls which David had built around the holy city.

Leaving the twisted lanes behind them, they travelled through a landscape of dun hills, finally emerging into the desert. The wind was blowing, and they shivered, for it was a freezing night. The moonlight played on their road, and they could see the immense wilderness spread out like a silver and yellow carpet, whose pattern was defined by the thornbushes.

Night was folded away, and the sun shone upon them, its warmth spreading through their chilled bodies.

They saw a well, and rested beside it. When they had recovered their strength, they resumed their journey, until the sun set on the western horizon. They came to the white road which leads to Bethlehem, and they joined it. Before long they could see the city, its simple houses appearing like white phantoms between the tall cypresses and the olive trees which provide its shade. Bethlehem took shape before their eyes; they could see sheep between the trees, like scattered flakes of snow.

They reached the city gate, beneath the Roman eagle. Roman legionaries stood about, collecting the taxes which Herod was imposing throughout his dominions, and which would be forwarded to his masters in Rome. He was complying with all their wishes, whatever the exactions this imposed upon his people; his only desire was to give satisfaction to his lord Caesar Augustus.[64]

A MODERN IRANIAN PROPOSES A 'LIBERATION MARIOLOGY'

Patrick Ali Pahlavi (b. 1944) is the nephew of the last Shah of Iran, and between 1954 and 1960 was heir to the Iranian throne. Imprisoned by the Shah, and later by Khomeini, he is a philanthropist, peasant activist and campaigner for women's rights. His book *'Imran's Daughter* (*La Fille d'Imran*, 1991) suggests that Mary's autonomy, strength and spirituality should make her the 'prophet of the third millennium'.[65] The inventive retelling of the Qur'ānic story introduces animals, and a new figure, Sakina, a mysterious personification of female wisdom.

One beautiful day, Mary and Sakina, followed by the foxes and preceded by the old owl, left for the well of Tasnim. According to the Holy Book, this spring,

---

64.   'Abd al-Ḥamīd Jawda al-Saḥḥār, *al-Masīḥ 'Īsā ibn Maryam* (Cairo: Dār Miṣr, n.d.): 20–1.
65.   Pahlavi 1991: 104.

although terrestrial, flows also in Paradise.[66] Some even say that it is one of Heaven's mysterious gates, which must exist to supply here and there the principle of the unity of all things.

After walking for several hours, our small group at last arrived at the holy place. This was a small circular valley, filled with scattered shrubs and soft grass. The water sprang from between two rocks near which a fig tree grew, bearing Edenic fruits. The two women knelt beneath the stars and cupped the water of Tasnim in their hands, drinking it in a spirit of meditation. The precious nectar brought Mary an indescribable joy, which ravished her entire body. In a moment of intense communion she realised that all of this allegedly banal world is in fact the expression of a unique and immense mystery which has neither limit nor name.

Sakina and her companion were inexorably drawn towards the degrees of ecstasy [...] Everyone and everything was protected by infinite Love. The moments passed beyond the veil of time.

They witnessed the setting of the stars, then the rising of a sun iridescent with all the colours of the world.

Strangely, although no-one had slept, least of all the owl, not one of our friends felt tired. It was in this state that they began the return journey, full of joy and exuberance.[67] [...]

Mary is infinitely free, and is such because she is the total expression of the Real. [...]

She rejected the imprisoning chains of convention and the social neuroses born of respectability, and, guided by God, pursued a quest for Truth, which she discovered because she began with her own self. This deep and complete expression of one's true self is inherent to all the traditions, and explains why the Qur'ān, in its symbolic system, refers to Mary, and Mary alone, by her first name, among all women.

The message of this radical discontinuity offers a challenge to our age. The message of the Virgin, in the Qur'ānic version, might be summarised as follows:

Life is like the sea: it is not simply a surface broken by thousands of constantly changing waves. For in what way could such a surface matter? No, life is essentially depth. Let us take this depth into account when we frame our laws on society, politics, and the economy. It is this depth alone which can save the world. Let us, then, be windows which open upon this unique essence which is our own.[68]

---

66. Qur'ān, 83.27.
67. Pahlavi 1991: 77–8.
68. Ibid.: 97–9.

A MODERN AMERICAN MUSLIM POET
CONTEMPLATES THE VIRGIN

Daniel Abdel-Hayy Moore was born in Oakland, California, in 1940, converted to Islam in 1970, and is widely considered to be the leading Muslim poet of America. His published collections began with *Dawn Visions* (San Francisco, CA: City Lights, 1964), and have included *The Ramadan Sonnets* (San Francisco, CA: City Lights, 1996) and *The Blind Beekeeper* (Syracuse, NY: Syracuse University Press, 2001). The poems offered here were composed specifically for the present volume.

Four Short Meditations on the Virgin Mary
for Abdal Hakim Murad

1

The Virgin Mary sat on a rock that was not wholly rock
in a world that was not wholly world
in a light that was Light direct
in the echo of a Command that came from God direct
whose womb was now to house a halo more than she could
possibly long for
and which made her fear
and caused her angel messenger to comfort her
as he stood at the door and mentioned how
God had designated her the hallowed hall for His pure breath to enter
to make a child with no seed but Himself
to show mankind His holy fatherhood over all
within the physical
but without physical union

2

The pen is hardly lifted
The penalty for birth is death
But he who would be born without coitus
would slide out of death without its mortal coil
Would be taken up to God without entering death's womb
as he had entered Mary's womb without birth's usual folderol
She clutched a tree to steady herself
and dates fell to the ground around her
And he spoke to her from herself
to steady her
Rings of tumult sang around her
The Garden's tree was now there to strengthen her
her nearing it part of God's ordained structure
to redeem Adam and Eve's descent to earth
by new prophecy through standing under
the virgin birth-tree's sacred agency

499

Adam of no visible parents
Eve of no mother but father Adam's rib-side
being both mother and father
now terrestrialized again in Mary's husbandless pregnancy
though all of us are actually children
of much more than our mere mother's earthly sympathy

3

I saw Mary board a bus at Broad and State
her head covered and her face radiant
small and held within herself
careful and preoccupied
a heaven seeming to be wrapped around her
her cheeks red her lips dry her eyes lowered
interior moisture her preferred cloister
the bus passengers sudden ghosts before her
her shoes small and tattered
her hands carrying a book
If any had spoken to her she might have become lost
If she had spoken to anyone
they might have become saved

4

None can be Mother of God but God
nor Father of flesh but God Himself
Jesus begat in light sat in light and was transformed into light
beyond light's shapes of dark and light
his salutation from where he is continues to excite us
just as Mary's humility brings us home
to where impossible things are true
and true things impossible or possible by our own lights
to submit as purely to God's sheer command of: *Be!*
more than enough to be
in Being's age-long mystery[69]

6–9 June 2005

---

69. **Poet's note:**
Walking in the woods as is my wont in the morning
June 9th 2005 Philadelphia Pennsylvania after strong storms and
all the trees dry now creaking in the heat and humidity
thinking of this poem and the editor of this chapter's request for it
thinking of Mary peace be upon her
walking along the trail
I suddenly hear a crack like horrendous thunder seemingly from
far away but look up above me in time to see a

BIBLIOGRAPHY

Asad, Muḥammad (1984) *The Message of the Qur'ān*, Gibraltar: Dar al-Andalus.

Bannerth, Ernst and Morelon, Régis (1977) 'Al-Saḥḥār: Temoin de la vie populaire', *Mélanges de l'Institut Dominicain d'Études Orientales* 13.

Barlas, Asma (2002) *'Believing Women' in Islam: Unreading Patriarchal Interpretations of the Qur'ān*, Austin, TX: University of Texas Press.

Calverley, Edwin E. and Pollock, James W. (trans.) (2002) *Nature, Man and God in Medieval Islam: 'Abd Allah Baydawi's text Tawali' al-Anwar min Matali' al-Anzar along with Mahmud Isfahani's commentary Matali' al-Anzar Sharh Tawali' al-Anwar*, Leiden: Brill.

Chittick, William C. (1983) *The Sufi Path of Love: The Spiritual Teachings of Rūmī*, Albany, NY: State University of New York Press.

Conrady, L. (1889) 'Das Evangelium Jakob in neuer Beleuchtung', *Theologische Studien und Kritiken* 62.

Corbin, Henry (1972) *En Islam iranien: Aspects spirituals et philosophiques*, Paris: Gallimard.

Declais, Jean-Louis (2003) 'Les origins chrétiennes dans les anciens récits musulmans', *Islamochristiana* 29.

Elliott, J. K. (ed.) (1993) *The Apocryphal New Testament: A Collection of Apocryphal Christian Literature in an English Translation based on M. R. James*, Oxford: Clarendon.

Gharīb, Ma'mūn (1975) *al Saḥḥār wa'l-fikr al-Islāmī*, Cairo: n.p.

Hegyi, Ottmar (ed.) (1981) *Cinco leyendas y otros relatos moriscos*, Madrid: Editorial Gredos.

Jansen, J. J. G. (1974) *The Interpretation of the Koran in Modern Egypt*, Leiden: E. J. Brill.

Jomier, J. (1958) 'Quatre ouvrages en arabe sur le Christ', *Mélanges de l'Institut Dominicain d'Études Orientales* 5.

ibn Juzayy, Muḥammad (1403/1983) *Tafsīr (=al-Tashīl li-'ulūm al-tanzīl)*, Beirut: Dār al-Kitāb al-'Arabī.

Littmann, Enno (1951) *Islamisch-arabische Heiligenlieder*, Wiesbaden: Franz Steiner Verlag.

---

cont.

huge bough break from the top of a tall tree with a giant screech and
hurtle down toward me at seemingly supersonic speed
I step aside yelling '*Allah!*' automatically heart thumping
and the heavy branch crash-lands exactly where I
stood a split second before and breaks into four or five
raw pieces cracked and shattered and me shocked and grateful
thanking Allah over and over thanking Him with all my being
my position just under it one split second before happily not there for it to
crash onto me now safe and sound at the side of the trail
I wonder at the force of it as I continue now to wonder
Allah's full and Awful Power exposed to me direct from the
core of the universe as if sky and earth and mortality itself were
opened up in the blink of an eye
and my life actually only a literal hair's breadth away
from death

At the Thursday night Sufi meeting I describe it in detail
to Baji our Pakistani shaykha and first thing she asks is
'*What were you thinking just before the bough broke and fell?*'
and when I tell her I was thinking of the Virgin Mary
she says without a moment's pause
'*Just as Allah protected and saved Mariam*
so Mariam protected you
and saved you!'

Maqsood, Ruqaiyyah Waris (2000) *The Mysteries of Jesus: A Muslim study of the origins and doctrines of the Christian church*, Oxford: Sakina.

Miller, Robert J. (ed.) (1992) *The Complete Gospels: Annotated Scholars Version*, 3rd edn, San Francisco, CA: HarperSanFrancisco.

Pahlavi, Patrick Ali (1991) *La Fille d'Imran*, Paris: PAW Editions.

Parrinder, Geoffrey (1965) *Jesus in the Qur'ān*, London: Faber and Faber.

Resch, Alfred (1897) *Das Kindheitsevangelium nach Lucas und Matthaeus unter Herbeziehung her aussercanonischen Paralleltexte*, Leipzig: J. C. Hinrichs.

Robinson, Neal (1988) 'Al-Râzî and the Virginal Conception', *Islamochristiana* 14.

Robinson, Neal (1989) 'Creating Birds from Clay: A miracle of Jesus in the Qur'ān and in Classical Muslim Exegesis', *The Muslim World* 79.

Robson, James (1970) (tr.) *Mishkat al-Masabih*, Lahore: Sh. Muḥammad Ashraf.

Rūmī, Jalāl al-Dīn (1929) *Mathnawī*, ed. R. A. Nicholson, London: Luzac.

Schimmel, Annemarie (1993) *The Triumphal Sun: A Study of the Works of Jalāloddīn Rūmī*, Albany, NY: State University of New York Press.

Schleifer, Aliah (1997) *Mary the Blessed Virgin of Islam*, Louisville, KY: Fons Vitae.

Smith, Jane I. and Haddad, Yvonne Y. (1989) 'The Virgin Mary in Islamic Tradition and Commentary', *The Muslim World* 79.

Stowasser, Barbara Freyer (1994) *Women in the Qur'ān, Traditions, and Interpretation*, Oxford: Oxford University Press.

Thackston, W. M. (1978) *The Tales of the Prophets of al-Kisa'i*, Boston, MA: Twayne.

Wensinck, A. J. and Johnstone, Penelope (1986–) 'Maryam', *Encyclopedia of Islam*, new edn, Leiden: E. J. Brill.

Wheeler, Brannon (2002) *Prophets in the Quran: An Introduction to the Quran and Muslim Exegesis*, London and New York: Continuum.

Winter, Tim (1999) '*Pulchra ut luna*: some reflections on the Marian theme in Muslim–Catholic dialogue', *Journal of Ecumenical Studies* 36.

Winter, Tim (2004) 'The Chador of God on Earth: the metaphysics of the Muslim veil', *New Blackfriars* 58.

23

MARY IN NINETEENTH-CENTURY ENGLISH AND AMERICAN POETRY

NANCY DE FLON

The development of poetry about Mary is inextricably bound up with the Catholic Revival that England experienced in the nineteenth century. After centuries of suppression, many restrictions against Roman Catholics were lifted with the passage of the Catholic Emancipation Act in 1829 and the restoration of the Roman Catholic hierarchy in 1851. Many new converts, including some well-known ones in addition to John Henry Newman, entered the Church of Rome under the influence of this revival.

While it may seem natural to think of these converts as a homogenous group, in fact there are as many different conversion stories as there were converts. Each was unique; each brought his own family background and religious tradition, his own issues and expectations that led to the submission to Rome, and his own individual life post-conversion. A number of these converts were prolific poets, and all these were factors that influenced the form and content of each one's poetry.

If the Anglican Divine John Keble was correct in defining poetry as the indirect expression of some overpowering emotion, then it can well be said that the converts to Catholicism used the poetic medium as an outlet for articulating their enthusiasms and concerns about their new religion. One of these enthusiasms, inevitably, was Mary, the mother of God, and the Catholic tradition of devotion to her. While this chapter, in treating nineteenth-century poetry about Mary, will not limit itself to a discussion of English poets who were converts to Roman Catholicism, in view of their numbers and the extent of their poetic output – as well as their theological and devotional writings that underpinned their poetry – such poets will receive the most extensive attention. They include John Henry Newman (1801–90) and three younger poets who converted to the Church of Rome as a direct or indirect result of Newman's influence.

Frederick William Faber (1814–63) was born into a 'rising but not distinguished'[1] Yorkshire family, the grandson of a vicar and the son of a businessman from Leeds who became secretary to the Bishop of Durham shortly after Frederick's birth. In 1832 Faber matriculated at Oxford University and took a second-class degree in Classics four years later. He was ordained deacon in the Church of England in 1837 and priest in 1839. An Evangelical by temperament, he flirted with Tractarianism

---

1.   Chapman 1961: 1.

during the heady days of the Oxford Movement, which coincided with his period as a student at the university, but never connected with it on an emotional level. After much painful soul-searching, Faber converted to Roman Catholicism in 1845, one month after Newman. In 1848 he joined the Oratory community that Newman was in the process of forming in Birmingham, but soon left to assume leadership of the new Oratory in London.

Edward Caswall (1814–78) was born into a large, closely knit, staunchly High Church family in which service to Church and country ran strong. His great-uncle on his mother's side was Dr Thomas Burgess, Bishop of St David's and later of Salisbury and a prolific author of theological treatises, and his oldest brother, Henry, was a clergyman and well-known authority on the Mormon Church in America. An exact contemporary of Faber's at Oxford who took a Classics degree in 1836, Caswall considered pursuing a literary career, but decided to become a clergyman, being ordained deacon in the Church of England in 1838 and priest in 1839. His religious allegiance was to the High Church Anglicanism of his birth until he began to develop an interest in Roman Catholicism early in the 1840s. After an intensive spiritual and intellectual journey that involved copious reading and the meticulous keeping of a journal, Caswall converted to Roman Catholicism in 1847.

Gerard Manley Hopkins (1844–89), a native of Stratford in East London, came from a well-to-do Anglican family. His father, a marine insurance adjustor, was a minor poet by avocation. Hopkins entered Oxford University in 1863 and distinguished himself as a brilliant Classics scholar. The second generation of what was left of the Oxford Movement still exerted a strong influence, and in 1866 Hopkins was received into the Church of Rome by Newman, thereby becoming, in effect, the first Roman Catholic student at Oxford. Despite Newman's caution to wait and give careful consideration to his next move, Hopkins entered the Society of Jesus within two years after his conversion and was ordained priest in 1877. He spent the remainder of his life in various parish and teaching posts, and wrote poetry that was largely unappreciated by his contemporaries, although his great classic, *The Wreck of the Deutschland*, was written at the suggestion of one of his religious superiors.

In general, the following observations can be made about nineteenth-century English poetry about Mary:

- These poems sometimes served a polemical purpose and thus reflected the poet's situation in a society still hostile to Roman Catholicism.
- Catholic belief in the immaculate conception figures strongly in polemical as well as other Marian poems.
- Poets sensitive to non-Catholic charges against Catholics of Mariolatry were often at pains to stress Mary's significance in the incarnation – and the liturgical implications of this.
- Nature symbolism is frequently an integral feature of poems about Mary; this includes the importance attributed to the month of May as Mary's month.
- Medieval poetic forms, especially the ballad, were popular.
- The influence of the Victorian ideal of womanhood is sometimes discernible in the theology and the poetry.

504

- These various features do not appear individually, but are often intertwined; for example, nature imagery might figure strongly in a polemical poem.

POETRY AND POLEMICS

Roman Catholics in nineteenth-century England lived in a state of tension between future expectation and present reality – between the belief that the ongoing revival of Catholicism would bring about the return of their country to the true faith, and awareness that they lived in a land that was still hostile to their Catholic beliefs. This hostility manifested itself not only on a general societal level, but also, and especially poignantly, in terms of suspicion and even broken relationships with friends, family and (in the case of clerics and academics) former colleagues. Poetry sometimes reflected the poet's situation and served a polemical purpose: for example, a convert might write verses that exposed the 'falsity' of Anglican doctrine, gave voice to the anticipation of an England restored to Roman Catholicism, or pointedly articulated certain Catholic beliefs or doctrinal practices, sometimes in a tone approaching the triumphalistic. Thus Roman Catholic polemical poetry can be defined as poetry emphasizing Roman Catholic distinctiveness over against the Established Church. Because devotion to Mary was a feature of Roman Catholicism that distinguished it from Protestantism, Mary figured prominently in these polemical verses. A retrospective look at their former religion, for example, would accuse it of 'falsity' because of its neglect of Mary. Thus Edward Caswall, in 'A Convert's Lament to Mary', expresses deep regret for his neglect of Mary during his years as an Anglican, when, 'Blinded by native heresy, / I thought so light of thee.' Similarly, Frederick William Faber, in his hymn 'To Our Blessed Lady', recalls that 'scornful men have coldly said / Thy love was leading me from God'.

John Henry Newman picks up the association of the 'cold' motif with neglect of Mary in 'The Pilgrim Queen'. When the Reformation abolished devotion to Mary, the result was that her Son was placed in a 'palace of ice' – cold, hard, but ephemeral, and prone to 'melt away' at the first sign of summer.

'The Pilgrim Queen' articulates the most important theme of the Catholic Revival: the expectation that England, after several centuries of languishing in error, would soon be restored to the Roman Catholic faith. Catholics in England had been looking forward to this day ever since the Reformation, but never did the time for its fulfilment appear so ripe as it did in the middle of the nineteenth century. That this return of Roman Catholicism was closely linked with Mary was due to England's tradition of devotion to her and to England's historic reputation as 'Our Lady's dowry'. In 1849 Newman composed this 'song' (as he called it) of dethronement and vindication, framing it as a ballad that harks back to medieval chivalry. The Middle Ages, regarded by the Catholic revivalists as the 'golden age' of the Church, were followed by the Reformation. But the time was soon coming when England would return to the true faith, and Mary, the Queen dethroned by the Reformers, promises:

> I am coming to rescue
> my home and my reign

And Peter and Philip
are close in my train.

Of course, Peter is St Peter – the first Pope – and Philip is St Philip Neri, founder of the Congregation of the Oratory. Newman regarded his Oratorian mission – he established England's first Oratory, in Birmingham, in 1848 – as a key instrument in the (re)evangelizing of England for the Church of Rome.[2]

Caswall, too, foresaw a key role for Mary in England's reconversion.[3] He devoted two major Marian poems to an explication of this theme. One of them, the lengthy verse drama 'A May Pageant', centres around a vision of Mary experienced by the protagonist, a holy Franciscan priest named Euthanase.[4] Returning from a cottage in the depths of an ancient wood known as 'Our Lady's Wood',[5] to which he has been summoned to attend a deathbed, Euthanase falls on his knees and becomes 'rapt at once in ecstasy of prayer'.

While in this state, he hears and sees a solemn procession approaching. A young man named Theodore ('gift of God') detaches himself from the procession and ferries Euthanase down the River Severn past several ruined monasteries to Tintern Abbey. Originally dedicated to Mary,[6] Tintern is the goal of this royal procession in which Mary, the Queen, is attended by a train of saints and angels, who participate in a ceremony of homage to Our Lady, held each May in this hallowed spot. Every year Mary visits England and receives a report from St Michael on the status of every ruin – 'the sad memorials of a former day'.

'A May Pageant' affirms the claim of the Roman Catholic Church to be the true Catholic Church on English soil. After three centuries of persecution in England, the Roman Catholic Church is destined to reclaim its rightful place and England will be restored to its traditional identity as 'Mary's dowry'.

The second poem of Caswall that owes its inspiration to the expectation that England would be restored to the Roman Catholic faith is 'The Easter Ship'.[7] This definitive title – he had originally called it 'The Vision and Prophecy of the Hermit of

---

2. The procession in Caswall's poem 'A May Pageant' (see below) is led by St Augustine and St Philip Neri, 'our Isle's new guest', who then shared the same feast day. This was a happy coincidence for Oratorians, for whom St Philip was the new Augustine under whose patronage the true faith would be reintroduced to England.

3. In his hymn 'Faith of Our Fathers', Faber also anticipates that 'Mary's prayers / shall win our country back to thee'; Faber 1880: 313–14.

4. The name means 'happy death'. Caswall undoubtedly made the priest a Franciscan because of that order's tradition of promoting belief in the immaculate conception, which, as we shall see, played a significant part in the Catholic Revival.

5. Coincidentally (?), the area of Birmingham immediately to the north of Edgbaston, where the Oratory is located, is called Ladywood.

6. Caswall took this information from Sir William Dugdale, *Monasticon Anglicanum*, vol. 5, London, 1846: 265.

7. Caswall's notes for this poem indicate that he began work on it shortly after Pius IX had defined the dogma of the immaculate conception; he refers to and quotes from the encyclical of proclamation 'which appeared last year', i.e. 1854.

Finisterre' – highlights the rich ecclesiastical symbolism of the ship as the Church,[8] in conjunction with the resurrection motif pertaining to England's rescue from '[t]he black Satanic deep / Of heresy's awful flood'.

A hermit – a Cistercian monk forced to flee from England when Henry VIII dissolved the monasteries – has a vision 'concerning the Immaculate Conception and the Restoration of England to the Catholic Faith'. One Easter morning the hermit sees a ship, becalmed and apparently without a crew. A storm 'from Satan's breath' sinks the ship, so that nothing of it is visible except the 'topmost spar', from which 'Old England's Catholic ensign' still waves. No sooner has this touched the waters than the ship begins to rise again and to steer 'for England's shore'. Now the hermit sees that the ship's crew consists of England's native saints and that Mary is at the helm.

Inspired by this vision, the hermit prophesies that for three centuries the Catholic Church will languish in virtual lifelessness in England; but then a pope will formally define the dogma of the immaculate conception and Our Lady, in gratitude, will 'restore ... the Isle of the Saints' to the true faith. The 'Easter Ship' is a Coleridgean 'A May Pageant',[9] incorporating the same themes but organizing them around the central image of the ship – clearly a symbol of the barque of Peter – and indeed an *Easter* ship, one that typifies the resurrection of the English Catholic Church from the grave of oppression.

At the climax of the great festival in 'A May Pageant', St Edward the Confessor presents to Mary 'the Sceptre of our Isle' in anticipation of the 'happy days to come', when she will once more rule as defender of the hierarchy and crusher of heresy. The identification of Mary as Queen was replete with meaning for the Catholic poets of this age. An important concept in Newman's Mariology was that of Mary as the Second Eve, which for him was intrinsically bound up with the Church's teaching on the immaculate conception (to be discussed below). As Eve helped to bring sin into the world, so Mary reverses that by bringing into the world Jesus, who would save humankind from its sins.

But an important corollary in this notion of 'reversal', related to the portrayal of Mary as a dethroned queen in Newman's poem 'The Pilgrim Queen', was the idea of Mary the Queen reclaiming her rightful place in England and reversing the Reformation – in other words, replacing Queen Elizabeth I, who definitively established Protestantism in England. It is difficult to say with certainty to what extent this operated on a conscious level with the poets, but Caswall, who wrote extensively, and with distaste, about Elizabeth in the journal he kept before his conversion, comes close to being explicit when he pointedly refers to her as 'false Elizabeth' in 'A May Pageant'.

Caswall exploits, this time quite consciously, a still more contemporary royal parallel. Citing, in his conversion journal, an author named Bennet[10] who criticized a

---

8. Margaret Johnson refers to Tractarian use of the ship 'as an image of spiritual journeying'; Johnson 1997: 209.
9. It has many similarities with 'The Rime of the Ancient Mariner', including the metre and the hermit as a major figure.
10. Caswall alludes only to Bennet's writing 'on the errors of Romanism' and gives no further information.

Roman cardinal for applying the psalms to the Virgin Mary, Caswall counters that Anglicans do the same in their service for the accession of Queen Victoria. 'Here we apply various prophecies of Christ as King to Queen Victoria,' he observes; 'how then can we blame an individual in the Roman Church for applying the same to Christ's own Mother?'[11] The frontispiece to *A May Pageant and Other Poems* features a line-drawing of Mary as a young woman wearing a crown, and the accompanying text reads, '*Regina Coeli, accipe coronam, quam tibi Dominus praeparavit in aeternum.*' Clearly Caswall was taking advantage of the devotion of the English to their Queen, by subtly identifying Victoria with Mary in order to foster devotion to the latter.

Caswall was being doubly polemical in his popular 'Children's Hymn before Our Lady's Image in the Month of May'.[12] Probably written to accompany the Oratory's May processions, this hymn is well known by its first line, 'This is the image of the Queen.' The text is very consciously Roman Catholic, with its pointed reference not only to the Queen but also to the *image* – the accusation that Catholics worship images was something Caswall had to contend with in his journey towards Rome.

The image of Mary as Queen accorded well with the idea of her immaculate conception, which was closely associated with the anticipation of England's return to the true faith. Catherine Labouré's vision of the Virgin treading on a snake, as immortalized on the Miraculous Medal, shows Mary the Immaculate Conception as a militant and defiant figure, powerful symbol of and catalyst for the Church's defeat of encroaching secularism as well as of religious heresy.[13] Intriguingly, Catholic converts were not the only poets writing verses that referred to the immaculate conception. In 'The Virgin', William Wordsworth hailed Mary as 'Above all women glorified, / Our tainted nature's solitary boast.'

The chief purpose of Caswall's 'May Pageant' is for the 'saints of Britain's Isle' to gather annually at Tintern to 'hold festival', 'In [Mary's] Immaculate Conception's praise, / The late-defined Belief of earlier days'. This second line refers to the fact that, although the dogma had been formally defined only in 1854, belief in it could be traced back to earlier centuries. It was crucial for Caswall to establish this connection from the present to the early Church and thereby highlight the Church of Rome's claim to the true apostolic succession and, thus, to rightful authority. Another of Caswall's poems,[14] 'Old Testament Types of Our Lady', apostrophizes Mary under the types of her that appear in the Hebrew Scriptures – the Altar of Incense, Aaron's Rod, the Urn of Manna, the Golden Candlestick – and thereby makes the point that, because Mary is thus anticipated in the Jewish tradition, veneration of her can claim a noble ancestry and is not some mere Roman Catholic invention.

Frederick William Faber's hymn 'The Immaculate Conception', commonly known by its opening line 'O purest of creatures! Sweet Mother! Sweet Maid!', hails Mary as the light shining on the Church in troubled times, and especially as the light

---

11. Caswall, *Journal*: 64.
12. Caswall 1858: 265.
13. See Pope 1985: 173–200. Also de Flon 2004.
14. Caswall 1873: 284.

that gave God a home on earth. Mary's light reflects Christ's light: 'And He shone in thy shining, sweet Star of the Sea!'[15] The title of Immaculate Conception, which had now been officially conferred on Mary, confirms and magnifies her shining.

MARY AND THE MYSTERY OF THE REDEMPTION

Defiant polemicism was not the only stance taken by English Catholics *vis-à-vis* society at large, however. Sensitive to accusations that Catholics worshipped Mary, preachers and authors frequently took care to emphasize the fact that Mary's significance lay solely in her role in the mystery of the redemption: the incarnation of the Saviour, God-made-human, on earth could not have happened without Mary's *fiat*. Newman, who was devoted to Mary even while in the Church of England, continually stresses in both his Anglican and Catholic sermons that everything about Mary is relative to Jesus; he insists 'that the glories of Mary are for the sake of Jesus'.[16] The confession that Mary is mother of God, says Newman, 'declares that [Jesus] is God; it implies that He is man'.[17]

Newman is very specific about the physical implications of the incarnation. Observing that the Eternal Word, in decreeing to come on earth, did nothing by halves, he declared that 'He came to be a man like any of us, to take a human soul and body':[18]

> no heavenly body ... fashioned by the angels ...: no; He imbibed, He absorbed into His Divine Person, [Mary's] blood and the substance of her flesh; by becoming man of her, He received her lineaments and features, as the appropriate character in which He was to manifest Himself to mankind. The child is like the parent, and we may well suppose that by His likeness to her was manifested by her relationship to Him [*sic*].[19]

It was Faber, not Newman, who took up this theme in his poetry. Faber was fixated on the motherhood of Mary, and there was no end to his imagination when it came to developing this in his poems.[20] In 'The Precious Blood' (actually an indulgenced prayer translated from the Italian) he hails Jesus as he 'who for my sake / Sweet Blood from Mary's veins didst take, / And shed it all for me'.[21]

A remarkable hymn on Our Lady's coronation combines a flowery mode of expression typical of Faber with a very basic reference to the physical consequences of the incarnation: God looks just like his mother! 'Her form He bears, / Her look he wears'; Jesus is 'God, with His Mother's face and eye!'[22]

---

15. 'Star of the Sea' (*maris stella* in Latin) is an ancient appellation for Mary.
16. 'The Glories of Mary for the Sake of Her Son', in Newman, ed. Boyce 2001: 131.
17. *Discourses to Mixed Congregations*: 347–8, quoted in ibid.: 70.
18. 'The Glories of Mary for the Sake of her Son', in ibid.: 132.
19. 'On the Fitness of the Glories of Mary', in ibid.: 158.
20. This will be considered in greater detail below.
21. Faber 1880: 116.
22. 'Mary, our Mother, reigns on high', in ibid.: 182.

Given Mary's intimate connection with the incarnation of God on earth, it follows that Mary's feasts are relative to the mystery of the redemption. In his Anglican sermon 'The Reverence due to the Virgin Mary', Newman observes that 'this is the rule of our own Church, which has set apart only such Festivals in honour of the Blessed Mary, as may also be Festivals in honour of our Lord; the Purification commemorating His presentation in the Temple, and the Annunciation commemorating His Incarnation'.[23]

MARY, MAY AND MOTHER NATURE

In light of these Christological implications of Mary's feasts, Newman found it necessary to explain the dedication of the month of May to Mary – a devotion long known on the continent, but only just introduced into England by Fr Luigi Gentili around 1840[24] – in light of the lack of any obvious liturgical reason for this.

In order to understand the importance of the connection between May and Mary, and thus the poets' reasons for treating this theme explicitly, one must appreciate the importance of the month of May and, with it, nature, in the Northern European psyche. Except perhaps for regions blessed with a beautiful autumn foliage season, May is a month unparalleled for awareness of nature, due to the signs of its return to life after winter's dormancy being most obvious at this time. Thus, in pre-Christian times, on May Day one celebrated a spring fertility festival – known to the ancients as Floralia, because it was marked with fires and flowers.[25] Even up to the time of the Reformation there were many May festivities not overtly associated with Mary; as David Cressy notes, 'May games, May bowers, May fires and maypoles enjoyed a popular vigour',[26] and even after the Reformation, the authorities in some areas had a difficult time in attempting to suppress these celebrations.

Given the ancient popular significance of May and its connection with nature, along with the importance of Mary in Catholic devotion, it was inevitable that these things would be conflated in the Catholic poetic mind. Thus, for example, Gerard Manley Hopkins, in 'The May Magnificat', considering the reasons for devoting the month of May to Mary, could offer the advice: 'Ask of her, the mighty mother.' Does he mean Mother Nature or Mary, mother of God? The ambiguity seems deliberate.

As we have just noted, however, it was Newman who first tackled the question of 'Why May?' Already in his Anglican sermon 'The Reverence due to the Virgin Mary' he emphasizes that Mary's feasts are relative to the mystery of the redemption: 'this is the rule of our own Church, which has set apart only such Festivals in honour of the Blessed Mary, as may also be Festivals in honour of our Lord; the Purification commemorating His presentation in the Temple, and the Annunciation commem-

23. Newman, ed. Boyce 2001: 125.
24. Mackenzie 1981: 105.
25. Cressy 1989: 21. On the night between 30 April and 1 May Germans celebrated Walpurgisnacht, and Swedes its counterpart Valborgsmässoafton.
26. Ibid.: 22.

orating His Incarnation.'[27] In light of this fact, then, on becoming a Catholic he meditated on the question, 'Why is May chosen as the month in which we exercise a special devotion to the Blessed Virgin?'[28] First, he offers an explanation based on nature: May is, quite simply, an extraordinarily beautiful month. Earth bursts forth in fresh foliage and green grass, the days become longer – 'such gladness and joyousness of external Nature is a fit attendant on our devotion to her who is the Mystical Rose and the House of Gold'.[29] Second, he adduces quasi-liturgical reasons why May, by default, is Mary's month: it is a joyous time of year. February, March and April (Lent), along with December (Advent), are months of penance. But May comes during the Easter season with the feasts of Ascension and Pentecost; it is a time of 'frequent Alleluias, because Christ has risen'. Thus it is fitting to dedicate to Mary, as the 'first of creatures', a month 'in which we especially glory and rejoice in [God's] great Providence to us, in our redemption and sanctification'. Also – and here Newman the Oratorian is speaking – Mary is Queen of all Saints, including, 'above all, and nearest to us in this Church [i.e. the Oratory], our own holy Patron and Father, St Philip, [who] occupies, with his Novena and Octave, fifteen out of the whole thirty-one days of the month'.[30]

But what if the May weather fails to live up to its promise? Not only in his meditation, but also in a poem devoted to the subject, Newman answers the question: how can we appropriately celebrate Mary in May if it is not bright and beautiful – if the weather lets us down so that the flowers are drooping and their colours do not look their best? In 'The Queen of Seasons (A Song for an Inclement May)',[31] Newman replies that we dedicate May to Mary 'not because it is best, / But because it comes first, / and is pledge of the rest'. By 'first' he means, as he explains in his meditation, that, even if the weather is bad, May is still 'the month that begins and heralds in the summer'[32] – thus May is the month of promise, hence its dedication to Mary. And here Newman makes use of the nature metaphor in Isaiah: 'A shoot shall come from the root of Jesse, and a flower shall rise out of his root': Mary is this beautiful plant out of which this flower grows; Mary holds the promise of the coming Saviour.[33]

Hopkins, looking for the rationale for the connection between May and Mary, finds it in nature for his poem 'The May Magnificat' and comes up with an explanation that differs from Newman's. During May nature is in its high-powered reproductive mode: Spring is 'Growth in everything – / Flesh and fleece, fur and feather, / Grass and greenworld all together'.[34] It is a time when 'bird and blossom

---

27. Newman, ed. Boyce 2001: 125.
28. 'Meditations on the Litany of Loreto for the Month of May', in ibid.: 358. The editor of this volume surmises that these meditations were probably meant to represent one month in a 'Year-Book of Devotion' that Newman began to write but never finished (358).
29. Ibid.: 359.
30. Ibid.: 360–2. Recall the association of St Philip with Mary in Newman's poem 'The Pilgrim Queen'.
31. *Verses on Various Occasions*, London, 1910: 287–9, quoted in ibid.: 355–7.
32. Newman, ed. Boyce 2001: 359.
33. Ibid.
34. 'The May Magnificat', in Phillips (ed.) 1991: 139–40.

swell / In sod or sheath or shell'. Hopkins asserts that the world in May recalls Mary pregnant with Christ, and that Mary, in turn, observing and delighting in nature's reproductive activity, recalls 'How she did in her stored / Magnify the Lord'.

By singling out the thrush as an example of this reproductive activity, Hopkins makes explicit the connection between 'Nature's motherhood' and that of Mary: the thrush – the poet calls her by the old English word *throstle* – lays a 'Cluster of bugle blue eggs'. Blue is Mary's colour, a fact to which Hopkins also refers in his sermon notes for 5 October 1879: she is like 'blue sky, which for its richness of colour does not stain the sunlight'[35] – something that he incorporates into his other well-known Marian poem, 'The Blessed Virgin Compared to the Air we Breathe'. Nature's motherhood is a sacrament – a revelation – of Mary's motherhood. But, he observes, there is 'more than this' to 'Spring's universal bliss': it is about mirth and ecstacy:

> This ecstacy all through mothering earth
> Tells Mary her mirth till Christ's birth
> To remember and exultation
> In God who was her salvation.

Hopkins, obviously more comfortable than Newman with the world and language of sensuality, could more easily come up with such an interpretation of the association of May with Mary than could Newman, who never quite got free of his Calvinist beginnings. In mentioning that the dedication of May to Mary was indulgenced by Popes Pius VII and Pius IX, Norman Mackenzie states that this custom, unlike such Marian feasts as Candlemas and the Annunciation that are intrinsically connected to the life of Christ, 'had no such ancient and rational justification'.[36] I would disagree: the ancient justification is rooted in folk tradition and thus in the Western psyche, and Hopkins has eloquently voiced it in this poem.

In his later great poem about Mary, Hopkins compares her to the most unlikely of natural elements – air. Blue-as-colour-of-the-sky allows him to weave throughout the poem this association with Mary. Air is 'wild ... world-mothering', and so is Mary, 'wild web, wondrous robe, [who] mantles the guilty globe'.[37] Just as air swirls between each of our eyelashes, each of our hairs, each frail snowflake, so too are we 'wound / With mercy round and round' – and it is Mary who, by God's providence, is dispenser of that mercy.

Leo Manglaviti points out that just as air supports physical being, so Mary as air 'is essential to the human spirit, for her mediation nourishes and makes possible the spiritual life in Christ'.[38] There is an intriguing parallel here with Hildegard of Bingen's concept of greenness (*viriditas*): just as sap is the life force for greening plants, so is the Holy Spirit the life force for human beings. Another of Manglaviti's

---

35. Ibid.: 275.
36. Mackenzie 1981: 106.
37. 'The Blessed Virgin Compared to the Air we Breathe', in Phillips (ed.) 1991: 158–61. Hopkins observes in his sermon notes for 5 October 1879 that Mary is 'the universal mother' (ibid.: 275).
38. Manglaviti SJ 2000: 45.

comments suggests a parallel with fellow Jesuit Karl Rahner: 'Comprising *more than simply air inhaled*, Mary is that essential medium which sustains life itself.'[39] In Rahner's concept of different levels of symbol, water as H_2O represents the physical reality, but on a symbolic level water is rich in meaning, such as its association with baptism. For Hopkins an important aspect of the incarnation was its inherent paradox: the Son of God is dependent on a human mother. As he puts it succinctly in the poem, Mary, the 'universal mother', as he calls her elsewhere,[40]

> Gave God's infinity
> Dwindled to infancy
> Welcome in womb and breast,
> Birth, milk, and all the rest.[41]

Even his reference to Mary as 'Merely a woman' should be taken not as denigrating, but as expressing another aspect of that paradox – she is yet one 'Whose presence, power is / Great as no goddess's / Was deemèd, dreamèd'.[42]

In these three brief lines Hopkins achieves two things: first, he states clearly that Mary is not a goddess and thereby counters non-Catholic accusations of Mariolatry. Second, he implies a pre-Christian association with goddesses and thereby a basis for comparing Mary with them – and it is, specifically, 'Mary Immaculate' who comes out on top.

An intriguing twist on the association of Mary with nature is offered in 'Vigil of the Immaculate Conception' by Maurice Francis Egan (1852–1924),[43] an American layman and professor of English at the Catholic University of America. This time we are not in May, but on a brightly moonlit, frigidly cold night in December.[44] A 'sword of silver' – a frozen lake that runs through the fields ('cuts [them] asunder') – anticipates the sword that will pierce Mary's heart, as Simeon prophesied. The paradox of the incarnation is reflected in the juxtaposition of heat and cold – 'how glowing [the] frozen rains [of this December night] upon our warm hearts lie', because God is 'bestowing / A thousand graces' on this vigil.

The poet reverses the usual association of Marian devotion with warmth by developing the Marian symbolism of a cold winter night. He presents yet another original twist, this time on the traditional association of cold, snow-bedecked December with Christmas – yet he also anticipates praise of Mary throughout the year and its close connection with the natural seasons, for he knows that 'from all seasons shall we new jewels borrow / to deck the Mother born Immaculate'.

Hopkins' early 'Rosa Mystica' makes use of Mary's title 'Mystical Rose', the rose

39. Ibid.: 46 (italics mine).
40. Sermon notes for 5 October 1879, in Phillips (ed.) 1991: 275.
41. 'The Blessed Virgin Compared to the Air we Breathe', in ibid.: 158.
42. Ibid.
43. In Walsh 1939.
44. Wordsworth, in 'The Virgin', describes Mary as 'Brighter ... than the unblemished moon / Before her wane begins on heaven's blue coast'.

without thorns that symbolizes the innocent human condition before the fall. Newman, in his meditation on the Mystical Rose, follows convention in identifying Mary as the Rose;[45] for Hopkins, however, Christ is the blossom[46] and Mary the tree that gives birth to it. Hopkins and Newman have in common a focus on the garden in which the flower grows: Newman meditates on the garden as a special place of 'spiritual repose, stillness, peace, refreshment and delight', a 'Paradise' in which Mary was 'sheltered and nurtured' in childhood to be the mother of God.[47] For Hopkins, too, the 'gardens of God' are a place in which to meet Mary and her Son.

Like Newman's 'The Pilgrim Queen', 'Rosa Mystica' is a poem in ballad style, with a two-line refrain in which line 2 differs slightly each time. It is interesting to speculate whether Hopkins actually intended it to be sung. He was a musician himself and may even have composed, or thought of composing, music for it. The ballad is meant to evoke a medieval atmosphere. The Middle Ages were important for the Tractarians and for English Catholics at this time; it was an age they regarded as a 'golden age' of culture and for the Church. It was also an age of chivalry, important in poetry that venerated Mary, the greatest Lady of all. Another of Hopkins' poems in medieval ballad style is '*Angelus ad virginem*', which retells the story of the Annunciation and the incarnation of God-made-human, and concludes by invoking Mary's prayers. This poem is, in fact, Hopkins' modern rendering of a thirteenth-century hymn to our Lady.[48] Interestingly, the tradition of Marian poems in ballad style can be traced at least as far back as the Reformation era, when a 'Ballad of Walsingham' lamented the loss of England to the Catholic faith.[49]

In 'A May Pageant' Caswall expands the concept of nature symbolism to encompass the notion of sacred space. 'Sacred space' in the Tractarian ethos began with the holy shrines and wells, once revered but, as a consequence of the Reformation, officially neglected.[50] A consequence of the Tractarian sacramental world view, which held that any created thing could potentially offer a revelation of God, was that Tractarian poetry extended the concept of 'sacred space' to include any place that offered an encounter with the numinous.

The Tractarian 'sacred space' poem has its roots in the eighteenth-century topographical poem, which would typically begin by describing the elements of nature in a scene and conclude by drawing a moral or 'higher meaning' from the nature observed.[51] From topographical poetry developed the art of the Romantic nature poets, an outstanding example of which, in the 'sacred space' genre, was Wordsworth's 'Lines Written above Tintern Abbey', an important source of inspiration for 'A May Pageant'.

---

45. Newman, ed. Boyce 2001: 372.
46. This harks back to the Anglo-Saxon tradition; cf. the *Blickling Homilies*, the author of which refers to Christ as the 'Golden-blossom' who received his human body from Mary; Dales 2001: 116.
47. Newman, ed. Boyce 2001: 372.
48. Phillips (ed.) 1991: 153–4. The original medieval manuscript, complete with music, is in the British Library.
49. Pearce 1999: 35.
50. Tennyson 1981: 178.
51. See Aubin 1936.

To prepare for 'A May Pageant' Caswall kept a notebook in which much of the information, obviously jotted down in the course of walks through the Severn Valley countryside, consists of names and descriptive phrases of such natural phenomena as birds, flowers, landscape features and words connected with water.[52] His purpose was to establish a definite sense of place by depicting a quintessentially English landscape – indeed, specifically a landscape typical of the Welsh Marches. For much of its length the River Severn more or less straddles the Welsh–English border, and it is such liminal spaces that are typically associated with the numinous. It is here that Euthanase, Caswall's priest-protagonist, encounters the invisible procession in Mary's honour. On their way to Tintern, Euthanase and Theodore pass abbeys and other hallowed sites that recall England's monastic heritage and their Marian connections. They include 'ancient Shrewsbury', 'fair Bildas Abbey', where they stop to chant Mary's litany, and Evesham, famous for an eighth-century Marian apparition.[53] And at Tintern Abbey – eponymous site of Wordsworth's poem – they see Mary herself and the ceremony that honours her. Whether he was conscious of it or not, Caswall is tapping into a concept of sacred space that harks back to pre-Christian traditions – the same traditions in which May and the burgeoning of nature were associated – in which a local goddess, during the month of May, would emerge from the holy mountain that was her usual residence to wander through the countryside made beautiful in this season.[54]

THE VICTORIAN IDEAL OF WOMAN

At the beginning of this chapter it was pointed out that each conversion story was unique in terms of family background and earlier religious traditions, spiritual and intellectual issues and expectations that culminated in the conversion, and post-conversion life, and that, for the poets, these factors all influenced their poetry. Caswall had two major obstacles to contend with in his journey to Rome: family pressures and the resolution of certain theological issues. These obstacles were not unrelated. The chief moving force behind the family pressures was the strong family tradition in the established Church. Caswall's family would have regarded defection to Rome as a traitorous action. While he was touring Ireland in 1846 to witness and experience Roman Catholicism at first hand, his father fell ill, and since he was not

---

52. Caswall incorporated several of these jottings verbatim into the poem.

53. According to the founder's charter of endowment, dated 714, St Egwin, third Bishop of Worcester and founder of Evesham Abbey, and one of his herdsmen, Eoves, each had a vision of the Virgin Mary on the future site of Evesham Abbey. The Virgin commanded Egwin to build a monastery there in her honour; 'Evesham Abbey', in *The Catholic Encyclopedia*, ed. Charles G. Herbermann *et al.*, New York, 1909, vol. 5: 648, col. 1.

54. Richard Wagner, in his opera *Tannhäuser*, captures this in the song of the Shepherd Boy about Frau Holda, a German equivalent of Venus, the opera's female antagonist:

> *Frau Holda kam aus der Berg hervor*
> *Zu zieh'n durch Fluren und Auen.*
> *Gar süssen Klang vernahm da mein Ohr,*
> *Mein Auge begehrte zu schauen.*

expected to survive, Caswall was summoned home. This further intensified family pressure on him to remain in the Church of England. His mother made clear that any conversion to Rome at that point would be regarded as contributing to his father's death.

Early in his process of investigating the truth claims of Roman Catholicism, Caswall realized that one of the chief theological issues to which he must particularly pay attention was 'to ascertain whether the mass of the Roman Catholic people invoke [*sic*] the Blessed Virgin in such a way as to obscure her Eternal Son'.[55] One of the Caswall family's main objections was the misconception that Roman Catholics were idolaters: that they adored images and paid divine worship to Mary and the saints. For his own sake, then – 'I was perpetually suspecting that in the Invocation of the blessed Virgin there must be some latent spirit of idolatry'[56] – and in order to satisfy his family, he paid particular attention to this matter, taking every opportunity to observe carefully and question Roman Catholics about their devotion to Mary. It was literally at the eleventh hour, during a trip to Rome he undertook that would be decisive in resolving his issues, and, in particular, a conversation he had with Newman during this trip, that he became satisfied that worship of Mary plays no part in Catholic devotion.

Caswall's hymns and poems about Mary thus witness to the influence of his family situation and, consequently, to his painstaking examination of 'Mariolatry' during his conversion journey. His primary concerns in relation to Mary are, first, to establish her as someone whom God prepared from all time for her role in salvation history. Her foreshadowing in Old Testament typology gives proof of this.[57] Thus Caswall aims to demonstrate – to his family? – that devotion to Mary is a legitimate part of Christian tradition and not a recent 'idolatrous' accretion devised by Roman Catholics. Second, he was intent on recalling England's devotion to Mary as Queen, an important part of England's Catholic heritage. By deliberately applying to Mary the title 'Virgin Queen', a traditional epithet for Elizabeth I, Caswall asserts that devotion to Mary cancels out the Protestantizing carried out by this 'false Elizabeth', as he calls her in 'A May Pageant'.[58]

Hopkins' poetry was free of polemic content and, indeed, relatively free of any overt references to Roman Catholic doctrine and devotion. As a member of the next generation that came after Newman, and then after Caswall and Faber's generation, he was able to articulate Marian devotion in his poems without having to be overly conscious of a need to 'defend' himself and his decision to convert to the Church of Rome. Moreover, Hopkins did not meet with the wrenching personal hostility that dogged the earlier generations of converts.

Among these poets, Faber is, for all intents and purposes, in a class by himself in

---

55. Unpublished conversion journal, entry for 29 June 1845: 301.
56. Letter to 'George', 15 March 1847, reproduced in *The Oratory Parish Magazine*, n.d.: 6–7. The magazine claims that the letter was addressed to Caswall's brother, but none of his brothers was named George. Most likely the addressee was George Copeland, a lifelong friend from school days.
57. See discussion of 'Old Testament Types of Mary' above.
58. 'La Corona', in *A May Pageant*: 75.

revealing consistent, overt influence by one other factor of his era – the Victorian ideal of womanhood that held up women as pure, domestic and passive; women were to find their fulfilment, above all, in motherhood. Mary, 'immaculate virgin', was the perfect icon that reconciled virginity (equated with purity) and motherhood. In assessing Faber's poetic contribution to extolling this ideal, his family of origin must be taken into account. Faber's next oldest sibling was a brother seven years older than him. The parents had had two children in between, both of whom died the year before Frederick's birth. Thus Frederick was especially close to his mother, who regarded him as a special gift from God. She idolized him and he 'loved her deeply in return'.[59]

When Faber was 15 years old, his mother died. This devastating blow left its mark on Faber and precipitated a religious crisis that exerted a lifelong influence on him. The person who helped him through the crisis was the Evangelical vicar of Harrow, John Cunningham, who 'reinforced the religion Faber had learnt at home ... and gave it an Evangelical colour'[60] – in other words, a strongly emotional orientation. In 1833, just as Faber had begun his studies at Oxford, his father died.

Of Faber's 22 Marian hymns, 15 address Mary or refer to her as (our) mother. Five of these hymns have Mary's motherhood (of us) as their main theme; two have as their main theme Mary's motherhood of God and at the end elide into a reference to her motherhood of all. In focusing on Mary as mother, Faber attempted to retrieve the beloved mother he had lost in his youth. His Marian poetry is informed, above all, by his sentimental attachment to Mary as mother figure. Unlike the other poets we have been considering, Faber is not concerned with establishing that Mary's 'prerogatives' or the honour due her have anything to do with her role in the incarnation and the mystery of the redemption; more than anything else, she is mother – God's/Jesus' mother, but, notably, *our* mother. The only hint that Mary is in any way connected with the incarnation and redemption is that the hymns on her in Part 3 of his book of hymns, 'Our Blessed Lady, St Joseph, and the Holy Family', are arranged according to the chronological order of their occurrence, and thus to the liturgical year.

In Part 2 of Faber's hymn book, 'The Sacred Humanity of Jesus', a number of the events are recounted as if the poet/reader were standing with Mary. 'Christmas Night'[61] presents a typically saccharine view of motherhood, while the baby described in 'The Infant Jesus' is no paradoxical God, no King of the Universe emptied into a manger, but Mary's helpless baby. 'Pentecost'[62] refers to the physical resemblance between Jesus and Mary, not to stress the latter's key role in the incarnation, but to give the apostles gathered in the Upper Room the opportunity for a sentimental recollection of their ascended Master: 'They gaze on her with raptured eyes, / Her features are like His.'

---

59.   Chapman 1961: 11.
60.   Ibid.: 14.
61.   Faber 1880: 95–7.
62.   Ibid.: 135–9.

Among the poems in Part 3 of the book, 'Our Lady's Expectation'[63] views the season of Advent through the sentimental lens of a 'pure' (and therefore idealized) pregnancy (a word Faber would never have thought of using), while 'The Assumption'[64] portrays Jesus taking his mother by the hand and leading her up to heaven; although she is Queen, Mary will still be, we (and especially the poet himself) are assured, 'Man's Mother'.

Faber's naturally passionate nature was more suited to Evangelicalism and ultimately to Roman Catholicism than to Tractarianism, and the exuberant Italianate Catholic devotions he discovered during his continental travels perfectly suited his temperament. In 'To Our Blessed Lady',[65] which begins, 'Mother of mercy! day by day / My love of thee grows more and more', he points out, countering those who claimed that devotion to Mary detracted from devotion to Christ, that in loving Mary he is merely imitating her Son: 'For what did Jesus love on earth / One half so tenderly as thee?' Here Faber not only finds a new mother to love, but he also takes comfort in the fact that in so doing he is imitating Christ. Indeed, he asks, considering that Jesus bequeathed Mary to him from the cross, 'how can I love thy Son, / Sweet Mother! if I love not thee?' And the hymn on 'Our Lady's Coronation' that comes at the end of a group of hymns devoted to Mary's life and Marian doctrines does not honour Mary as Queen of Heaven so much as it celebrates the fact that 'Mary, our Mother, reigns on high'.[66]

LATER POETS

By the later nineteenth century many of the religious issues that had occupied the earlier generations were no longer so pressing, and poets began looking at Mary with fresh eyes, indeed even through lenses that anticipated a post-Vatican II vantage point. The Annunciation had been, and remains, a subject of fascination for visual artists as well as poets – one thinks of the paintings by Dante Gabriel Rossetti and William Henry Tanner and, in our own time, Robert Morneau's poem written as a response to seeing the latter – and Oscar Wilde (1854–1900), in 'Ave Maria Gratia Plena',[67] writes as if he had entered the mind of old Simeon and the encounter between Simeon and the baby Jesus had been moved back in time to the conception of Jesus – the angel's annunciation to Mary. The poet has anticipated the Lord's coming; he has looked forward to it and has obviously expected something quite different – something more appropriate for the gods of classical mythology, 'A scene of wondrous glory'. Instead he beholds 'Some kneeling girl with passionless pale face, / An angel with a lily in his hand, / And over both the white wings of a Dove'. In other words, he beholds something quite different from what he had expected. One wonders whether Simeon had also expected something different – but in both cases,

---

63. Ibid.: 172–4.
64. Ibid.: 178–81.
65. Ibid.: 155–6.
66. Ibid.: 181–2.
67. In Walsh 1939: 313.

Simeon's and this poet's, the attitude is one of openness, of willingness to be surprised, because the poet looks on this 'with wondering eyes and heart' and sees a scene that he realizes is a 'supreme mystery of Love'.

'Our Lady' by Mary Coleridge (1861–1907),[68] a cousin of Samuel Taylor Coleridge and a non-Catholic, is quite forward-looking in its outlook on Mary. The poem's title is quite deliberate and purposely ironic: the poet emphasizes that Mary was no 'lady', in the sense of being a woman from the upper classes or the nobility, but 'a maid of low degree' – after all, who else would Christ, 'A common man of the common earth', have chosen for his mother? The irony is that 'The noblest lady in the land' would have given her right hand to bear Mary's child. The poem concludes by pointedly reminding 'lords and ladies' of Mary's song: 'He hath filled the hungry with good things / And the rich He hath sent empty away.' In Mary Coleridge's hands the *Magnificat* becomes the song of reversal as we interpret it in our own age – a hymn to the God who turns the world upside down by liberating the oppressed, with Mary, God's mother, leading us in that song.

BIBLIOGRAPHY

Aubin, Robert Arnold (1936) *Topographical Poetry in XVIII-Century England*, New York: The Modern Language Association of America (reprinted 1966).

Caswall, Edward (1873) *Hymns and Poems Original and Translated*, 2nd edn, London: Burns, Oates & Co.

Caswall, Edward (1858) *The Masque of Mary and Other Poems*, London: Burns and Oates Ltd.

Chapman, Ronald (1961) *Father Faber*, Westminster, MD: The Newman Press.

Cressy, David (1989) *Bonfires and Bells: National Memory and the Protestant Calendar in Elizabethan and Stuart England*, Berkeley and Los Angeles, CA: University of California Press.

Dales, Douglas (2001) *Christ the Golden-Blossom: A Treasury of Anglo-Saxon Prayer*, Norwich: Canterbury Press.

de Flon, Nancy M. (2004) 'Mary and Roman Catholicism in Mid Nineteenth-Century England: The Poetry of Edward Caswall', in R. N. Swanson (ed.), *The Church and Mary*, Studies in Church History 39, Woodbridge: Boydell Press.

Faber, Frederick William (1880) *Hymns*, 1st American edn, Baltimore: Murphy & Co.

Johnson, Margaret (1997) *Gerard Manley Hopkins and Tractarian Poetry*, Aldershot: Ashgate.

Mackenzie, Norman H. (1981) *A Reader's Guide to Gerard Manley Hopkins*, Ithaca, NY: Cornell University Press.

Manglaviti SJ, Leo M. (2000) ' "World-Mothering Air": The Virgin Mary as Poetic Image', in *The Hopkins Quarterly* 27.1–2, Winter–Spring.

Newman, John Henry (2001) *Mary: The Virgin Mary in the Life and Writings of John Henry Newman*, ed. Philip Boyce, Leominster, UK: Gracewing; Grand Rapids, MI: Wm. B. Eerdmans.

Pearce, Joseph (1999) *Flowers of Heaven: One Thousand Years of Christian Verse*, London: Hodder & Stoughton.

Phillips, Catherine (ed.) (1991) *Gerard Manley Hopkins*, The Oxford Authors, Oxford: Oxford University Press (reprint).

Pope, Barbara Corrado (1985) 'Immaculate and Powerful: The Marian Revival in the Nineteenth Century', in Clarissa W. Atkinson, Constance H. Buchanan and Margaret R.

---

68. In ibid.: 471.

Miles (eds.), *Immaculate and Powerful: The Female in Sacred Image and Social Reality*, Harvard Women's Studies in Religion Series, Boston, MA: Beacon.

Tennyson, G. B. (1981) *Victorian Devotional Poetry: The Tractarian Mode*, Cambridge, MA: Harvard University Press.

Walsh, Thomas (1939) *The Catholic Anthology: The World's Great Catholic Poetry*, rev. edn, New York: Macmillan.

24

MARY IN MODERN EUROPEAN LITERATURE

CATHERINE O'BRIEN

A fascination with the Virgin Mary as an independent person began in the early Church and has continued throughout literary history. The tenth-century *Vita* told Mary's story anew in poetic form, embellishing and transforming the biblical text,[1] and this tradition has been handed down across the centuries, attracting European writers with varying agendas. It is unsurprising that Catholic poets such as Paul Claudel or Gerard Manley Hopkins found inspiration in Marian devotion; but there is a certain irony in the fact that Mariologist Fr René Laurentin chooses an extract from *Bariona*, the Nativity play written by atheist Jean-Paul Sartre during his imprisonment, as one of the most beautiful texts about the Virgin of the last 2,000 years.[2]

Unlike theologians and biblical historians who must defend their theories before Church and academic authorities, secular artists are at liberty to follow their individual beliefs and creativity within the restrictions of censorship. After nineteenth-century Romanticism brought religious themes to the forefront in literature following the barren years of the Age of Enlightenment, writers projected their personal devotion and contemporary ideology onto the outline of the Madonna. As Thomas Merton wrote:

> What people find to say about her sometimes tells us more about their own selves than it does about Our Lady. For since God has revealed very little to us about her, men who know nothing of who and what she was tend to reveal themselves when they try to add something to what God has told us about her.[3]

Consequently, the Virgin Mary is a testament to the 'marshmallow effect': as an iconic figure without a complete biographical history, she has been pressed into a variety of cultural schema.[4]

The following overview identifies two approaches to Mariology in European literary works: the first charts the narrative of the mortal Mary of Nazareth, exploring the wider repercussions of the Marian model; and the second perspective reflects on the Virgin's iconic status and intercessory role.

---

1. See J. H. Kirchberger, 'Mary in Literature', in Ebertshauser *et al.* 1998: 72.
2. Laurentin 1984: 276.
3. Merton 1972: 167.
4. See Roten SM 1999: 167.

MARY OF NAZARETH

The main material on the life of the Virgin is taken from the infancy narratives in the Gospels of Matthew and Luke, the scenes at Cana and the crucifixion in the Gospel of John, and selections from the Apocrypha. Although the apocryphal *Book of James*, which recounts Mary's birth and betrothal to Joseph, has been dismissed by scholars as 'inventive hagiography', it has been influential in the development of a Marian biography.[5]

Despite the noticeable gaps, the biography of the Virgin recorded in the New Testament contains elements with which writers and their readers can identify: virginity, pregnancy (out of wedlock), marriage, motherhood, exile, suffering and the death of a son. European literature offers texts that concentrate on specific biblical scenes (with the Annunciation, Nativity and Crucifixion being particularly favoured), as well as more sweeping narratives that exceed the limitations of the evangelists' texts.

In most overarching attempts to write the story of Mary, the events related in the Gospels are harmonized to form a coherent narrative and the discrepancies are removed. There are reflections on the life of Jesus – of which the Greek Nikos Kazantzakis's *The Last Temptation* is a notably controversial example – in which Mary plays a more minor, although subversive, role. However, there are several texts in which Mary is a major protagonist, including the Yiddish writer Sholem Asch's *Mary*, which relates Mary's life from her betrothal to Joseph until the resurrection; Rainer Maria Rilke's *Das Marien-Leben* (*The Life of the Virgin Mary*), which captures incidents from Mary's birth to the assumption in 13 poems; Sarah Boss's illustrated children's book *Mary's Story*, which draws together events from the Apocrypha and New Testament; and Jean-Claude Darrigaud's *L'Evangile selon Marie de Nazareth*, which reflects on the New Testament through Mary's first-person narrative.

The story of Mary has received an ambivalent assessment from feminist commentators. The Virgin Mary was repudiated by Simone de Beauvoir, who argues that the Marian story reflects a woman's submission within a patriarchal Church: 'If Mary's status as spouse be denied her, it is for the purpose of exalting the Woman Mother more purely in her. But she will be glorified only in accepting the subordinate role assigned to her. "I am the servant of the Lord." '[6] In *La Femme gelée* (*A Frozen Woman*) the French novelist Annie Ernaux despises the Marian role model espoused during her Catholic education, while Elisabeth Burmeister rejects Mary's image as detrimental to women:

> Mary,
> keep your smooth face,
> the false humility,
> the false renunciation,
> the false obedience, the false duty,
> the false patience till the Last Judgement.[7]

---

5. See Brown *et al.* 1978: 248–9.
6. de Beauvoir 1953: 203.
7. Quoted in Ebertshauser *et al.* 1998: 120.

Mary has been seen 'as a subservient woman, impossible model to other women, for she is both mother and virgin'.[8]

The positioning of Mary as a symbol of domesticated humility is witnessed in certain literary works, which emphasize the beauty of God's handmaid while underlining her trembling acquiescence or silence. The angel brings fear in W. B. Yeats's poem 'The Mother of God',[9] while Louis Mercier[10] and Rilke end their Annunciation poems with the angelic salutation and Mary is offered no space to enter into dialogue with the messenger. Yet the Virgin does not accept her role unquestioningly, as the Lukan verses confirm, and Mary's ultimate words – 'I am the handmaid of the Lord. Let what you have said be done to me' (Lk. 1.26–38) – cannot be explained as part of a typical five-stage biblical Annunciation schema, for it is not a step found in the usual Annunciation pattern.[11]

The repercussions of Mary's 'yes' at the Annunciation are treated in greater depth in Jacqueline Saveria Huré's Marian 'autobiography' *Marie de Nazareth, fille d'Israël* (*I Mary, daughter of Israel*), whose location within Jewish tradition reminds the reader of Mary's ancestry; Norah Loft's novel *How far to Bethlehem?*, which focuses on the period from the Annunciation to the Nativity; and Paul Claudel's allegorical play *L'Annonce faite à Marie* (*The Tidings brought to Mary*), in which the central female protagonist, Violaine, experiences her own *fiat* when she reacts with compassion to the suffering of Pierre de Craon, a leper.

In praise of the Virgin Mary, Therese of Lisieux once exclaimed, 'She is spoken of as unapproachable, whereas she should be represented as imitable'.[12] This issue is at the heart of Claudel's drama. Violaine cures Pierre (taking his leprosy upon herself by means of a kiss) and, by a circuitous path, saves her sister from suicide and restores a baby to life through a type of virgin birth on Christmas Eve. Violaine's father uses the words of the Annunciation to describe his daughter's actions: 'Behold the handmaid of the Lord.' Here Mary is regarded as a 'pattern' for the faithful through the 'response that put her totally at the service of Christ and His brothers and sisters'.[13] While Claudel's play has been rejected by some feminist critics as the story of a sacrificial victim in an ecclesiastical society gone awry,[14] the work has been reviewed as an example of Hans Urs von Balthasar's concept of the 'freedom to attain authentic selfhood and authentic humanity'.[15]

In reflecting on the repercussions of the Annunciation, Norah Lofts and Paul Claudel consider the effect of Mary's *fiat* on her relationship with Joseph, as does the British-born W. H. Auden in 'The Temptation of St Joseph', that forms part of the Christmas Oratorio *For the Time Being*:

---

8.   Carroll 1994: 49–62 (51).
9.   Yeats 1958: 281–2.
10.   Quoted in Chandavoine 1993: 162.
11.   Brown 1993: 316.
12.   Backhouse (ed.) 1994: 207.
13.   *Dictionary of Mary* 1997: 450.
14.   Lambert 1990: 162.
15.   See Pelikan 1996: 86.

> All I ask is one
> Important and elegant proof
> That what my Love had done
> Was really at your will
> And that your will is Love.[16]

The texts explore the sexual politics, including the 'liberation Mariologist' view (to use a term coined by Rosemary Radford Ruether) that, through the virginal conception of Jesus, Mary achieved her full realization as a person independent of any man.[17] The psychoanalyst Françoise Dolto has argued, 'The human density of every couple is thus found in the story of the couple composed by Joseph and Mary. But, in return, this extraordinary couple helps us to discover the depth of any encounter between an ordinary man and woman.'[18]

One of the suggested re-visionings of the Marian cult is a revalorization of the bonds between women, as epitomized by Mary's independent journey to visit her cousin Elizabeth, and the sisterly affinity that exists between the cousins. In Paul Claudel's 'La Visitation'[19] and Marie Noël's 'Magnificat',[20] there is an unspoken connection between two women united in the apparent miraculousness of their respective pregnancies – Elizabeth because of her previous infertility, and Mary because of her virginity. Catholic anti-abortionists have looked to the Visitation scene for support for their stance, regarding Elizabeth's words to Mary, 'Blessed is the fruit of your womb', as relevant to every unborn child.[21] It is notable that Marie Nöel leaves the children in the womb to communicate while the mothers themselves remain silent.

As Catholic feminist theologians have pointed out that the Marian tradition, for all its faults, offers Christians a female-focused symbol, liberation Mariologists have gone further by representing the Virgin Mary in an empowering manner as a self-defining woman who announces the end of the patriarchal order, proclaiming the good news in her *Magnificat*. The canticle has been embraced as the words of 'a woman of unshakeable faith, unwavering hope, and uncommon love'.[22] The Marxist writer Wolf Biermann sees Mary as a revolutionary figure;[23] and Marceline Desbordes-Valmore's 'Cantique des mères' ('Canticle of the Mothers') reworks the Lukan verses in a manner that pre-dates the preoccupations of liberation theology by more than a century.[24]

The humble setting of the Nativity scene evokes the common bond with women

---

16. Auden 1966: 79.
17. See Hamington 1995: 106.
18. Quoted in S. Laugier, 'The Holy Family', in Locke and Warren 1993: 27–38 (33).
19. Quoted in Chandavoine 1993: 146.
20. Noël 1983: 167–8.
21. *Dictionary of Mary*: 127.
22. *Dictionary of Mary*: 500.
23. See K. J. Kuschel, 'Maria in der deutschen Literatur des 20. Jahrhunderts', in Beinert and Petri (eds) 1997, vol. 2: 262–3.
24. Bertrand 1997: 91.

living in poverty rather than the singularity of Mary's role. It is a theme taken up in a number of poems, including Jehan Rictus's 'La Charlotte', in which a poor homeless girl who is freezing on the streets on Christmas Eve compares her situation to that of Mary and Jesus;[25] and Berthold Brecht's 'Maria' locates the birth of Jesus in a context of hardship.[26] Emphasis on the impoverishment of the protagonists finds an echo in Latin American liberation theology, where, as Victor Codina explains, Mary 'has known, with the People, suffering and oppression'.[27]

Mary's comprehension of human suffering is a favoured theme in literature dealing with the question of mortality. Bertrand Bouvier has studied the role of the Virgin Mary in the funeral songs composed and sung by women in Greece,[28] where the Marian story provides a vehicle for lamentation. In Rudyard Kipling's 'Hymn before Action', it is the Mother of God who is the source of comfort:

> Ah, Mary pierced with sorrow,
> Remember, reach and save
> The soul that comes to-morrow
> Before the God that gave![29]

Women's war literature also uses the image of the sorrowful mother to express suffering at the death of a soldier. Just as Christological themes are traditionally found in male war poetry, in which a soldier lays down his life for his fellow men, so the theme of the *mater dolorosa* allows female protagonists to express their agony: 'Mary, mother of God, / All women tread where thy feet have trod,' writes Mary H. J. Henderson in 'An Incident'.[30] The German pacifist writer Claire Studer evokes the women praying before invisible crosses on which they visualize that their sons are hanging on the battlegrounds of the First World War;[31] and Ilse Boy-Ed exploits the image of the *mater dolorosa* in her wartime novel *Die Opferschale*, when the Protestant heroine Katharina considers the cult of the Virgin Mary and 'the seven swords in the heart of the Virgin' – the traditional image of the sword piercing the heart of the Madonna is multiplied by the depiction of the woman's pain,[32] as evoked in the title of G. K. Chesterton's *The Queen of Seven Swords*. Edith Stein, who died in Auschwitz, took the theme of the *Stabat Mater* in her poem '*Juxta crucem tecum stare*':

> Today I have stood under the cross with you
> And felt it more clearly than ever before,
> That under the cross you become our mother.[33]

---

25. Quoted in Chandavoine 1993: 130.
26. Brecht 1965: 64–5.
27. Victor Codina, quoted in de Margerie 1987: 47–62 (48).
28. Bouvier 1976.
29. Kipling 1940: 326.
30. Quoted in Reilly (ed.) 1981: 52.
31. Studer 1918: 90.
32. Boy-Ed 1916: 87.
33. Quoted in Ebertshauser *et al.* 1998: 117.

ICON AND INTERCESSOR

While negative feminist interpretations of the Marian cult have rejected an emphasis on women's primary vocation as motherhood, other critics have underlined the continuing significance of the Marian dimension. Exploring the writings of Anna Jameson and George Eliot, Kimberly Van Esveld Adams argues that their desire to harmonize a religious tradition with their feminist principles led them towards 'the Virgin Mother of Christianity, who became their Lady of Victorian Feminism'.[34] In *Tales of Love*, Julia Kristeva has warned that a decline in Mariology would leave motherhood 'without a discourse';[35] a survey of Italian feminist writers demonstrates the importance of this maternal discourse in literature;[36] and Luce Irigaray's *Le souffle des femmes* offers a collection of writings by women searching for the sacred within an egalitarian society.

Consequently, European writers turn to the Virgin as icon and intercessor, and laud this role in their poetry and prose. François-René de Chateaubriand wrote lines in praise of the Virgin in *The Genius of Christianity* in France;[37] the religious orders were the home of a number of Marian poets in Hungary, including the Jesuit Kálmán Rosty and the Cistercian Alán Kalocsay;[38] and the Italian Alessandro Manzoni celebrated his conversion to Catholicism in his poems, of which 'Il Nome di Maria' is of particular note.[39] In Seville the poets at the Academy of Literature under the patronage of the Immaculate Conception dedicated poetry to the Virgin; and José Zorrilla y Moral wrote a Marian tribute entitled *Maria, Poetic Crown of the Virgin* which, although uncompleted, numbered 2,187 verses.[40]

The Anglican poets of the New Oxford movement and the Pre-Raphaelite Brotherhood were responsible for a revival in Marian poetry in England. In the writings of John Henry Newman, for example, Mary is seen as the Mother of God and the Second Eve.[41] English poets wrote verse in honour of Mary, including Lord Byron and William Wordsworth;[42] and Arthur Mastrolia reveals a 'Marian attitude' in the work of C. S. Lewis, despite the writer's explanation of his silence on Mary in *Mere Christianity*.[43]

In the Germanic language, the Swiss Gottfried Keller's *Seven Legends* gave new life

---

34.   Adams 2001: 226.
35.   J. Kristeva, 'Stabat Mater', in Moi (ed.) 1986: 184.
36.   S. Wood, 'Feminist writing in the twentieth century', in Bondanello and Ciccarelli (eds) 2003: 151–67.
37.   For an overview of Marian literature in France, see A. Garreau, 'La Sainte Vierge dans les lettres françaises modernes et contemporaines', in du Manoir (ed.) 1952: 47–66.
38.   See A. Csavossy SJ, 'La Vierge Marie dans la littérature hongraise', in ibid.: 141–61.
39.   See D. Mondrone SJ, 'La Madone dans la poésie italienne', in ibid.: 163–95; and 'The Age of Romanticism 1800–1870', in Brand and Pertile (eds) 1996: 397–456.
40.   Perez and Ihrie (eds) 2002: 696. For a survey of Marian literature in Spain, see N. Perez SJ, 'Marie dans la littérature espagnole', in du Manoir (ed.) 1952: 125–40; and Herrán 1979.
41.   Barry 1970: 11.
42.   See 'Mary in Poetry', in Tavard 1996: 153–67. See also C. Martindale SJ, 'Notre Dame dans la littérature anglaise. Piété mariale en Angleterre', in du Manoir (ed.) 1952: 95–123.
43.   Mastrolia 2000: 149.

to medieval Marian sagas,[44] while the fairy tales of the Brothers Grimm, such as 'Our Lady's Child', contain Marian references.[45] Devotion to the Virgin Mary was influenced by Luther in Germany, but the Catholic/Protestant divide did not prevent writers of various denominations from finding inspiration in Marian themes. There are works that laud the Virgin by Friedrich Hölderlin, Clemens Brentano (the secretary of Blessed Anne Catherine Emmerich), Max von Schenkendorf, Joseph von Eichendorff, Annette von Droste-Hülshoff, Ernst Moritz Arndt, Friedrich Hebbel and Hermann Hesse.[46] Novalis famously wrote:

> I see you in a thousand pictures,
> Mary, lovingly expressed,
> Yet none of them can portray you,
> As my soul looks upon you.[47]

Marian shrines have provided ample material for literary works, with the nineteenth-century apparitions in France providing fresh subject matter. While arguments over the merits of La Salette caused contention on the printed page in the works of French writers Léon Bloy and Joris-Karl Huysmans,[48] the events at Lourdes in 1858 reached a larger audience. Emile Zola's controversial novel *Lourdes* conflicted with the work of Henri Lasserre, Fr Léonard Cros and Huysmans, who added their own perspectives on the shrine;[49] and the Jew Franz Werfl, who sought refuge from Nazi persecution in the Pyrenean village and kept his vow to publish the story of the apparitions by way of gratitude, increased the fame of Bernadette when his book *Song of Bernadette* was transformed into an award-winning Hollywood film.

One-time decadent writer Huysmans expressed his devotion to the Virgin in his novel *The Cathedral*, where it is claimed that Mary manifests a political awareness of her effect upon the visionaries: 'The Virgin is, as far as possible, considerate of the temperament and individual character of the persons She appears to. She places Herself on the level of their intellect, is incarnate in the only material form that they can conceive of.'[50]

St Bernadette had a vision of the Virgin of the Immaculate Conception, and her youthful appearance is evoked in the famous passage in Georges Bernanos's novel *Diary of a Country Priest*, when the priest of Torcy describes Mary as 'younger than sin, younger than the race from which she sprang, and though a mother, by grace, Mother of all grace, our little youngest sister'.[51] French poets draw on the battle

---

44. Keller 1987.

45. http://www.ucs.mun.ca/~wbarker/fairies/grimm/003.html; accessed 30 March 2005.

46. See P. Lorson SJ, 'Notre Dame dans la littérature allemande', in du Manoir (ed.) 1952: 67–93; and K. J. Kuschel, 'Maria in der deutschen Literatur des 20. Jahrhunderts', in Beinert and Petri (eds) 1997, vol. 2: 215–69.

47. Quoted in Ebertshauser *et al.* 1998: 104.

48. See Angelier and Langlois (eds) 2000.

49. See ch. 6, 'The Battle of the Books', in Harris 1999.

50. Huysmans 1989: 13.

51. Bernanos 1977: 181.

between the Virgin and the devil in Louis Le Cardonnel's 'Prière du soir d'été'[52] and Germain Nouveau's 'Cantique à la Reine', in which Mary crushes the serpent beneath her foot.[53]

Heinrich Heine, a Jew who converted to Christianity, wrote a poem about a pilgrimage to Kevelaer (the German Lourdes of its day) in which a mother takes her son to the shrine in the hope of helping him recover after the death of his fiancée. When he dies at the shrine, the mother accepts the outcome peacefully: 'She softly sang devoutly: / "Hail Mary, praised be thou!" '[54] In Heinrich Böll's short story 'Kerzen für Maria', the first-person narrator finds a sense of peace from his earthly woes before a dilapidated statue of the Madonna in a church.[55] By contrast, Muriel Spark's story 'The Black Madonna' tells how a white childless couple pray before the eponymous statue for help, but when the woman gives birth to a black baby, the new arrival is not welcomed and the parents' hypocrisy is underlined.[56]

In the practice of intercession, there is 'the projection of the patriarchal model of the human family into the heavenly sphere' and reflections of the 'medieval aberrations which envisioned Mary as the zone of mercy over against Christ or God the Father, angry and just judges needing to be placated'.[57] Theologians claim that this relationship should not be a question 'of having the Mother appease the anger of her Son', for such responses visualize the deity 'as an intractable despot but one whose decisions can be modified through maneuvers of one kind or another'.[58]

Yet a number of French poets find inspiration in this very idea, as expressed by Thomas Aquinas: 'When the Blessed Virgin conceived the Eternal Word in her womb and gave Him birth, she obtained half the Kingdom of God. She became Queen of *Mercy* and her Son remained King of *Justice*.'[59] The Virgin is asked to plead to her son for the cause of the suppliant in Guy Chastel's 'Humble et si belle Notre-Dame',[60] Charles Nodier's 'Hymne à la Vierge',[61] and Edouard Turquety's 'Rosa mystica';[62] François Coppée's 'En égrenant le chapelet' has Mary as a lawyer defending a sinner before God's judgement;[63] and Charles Péguy makes the distinction between the justice of God and the mercy of Mary in 'L'Enfant'.[64]

As Maurice Hamington points out, in Catholicism 'prayers directed to someone other than God are not considered polytheistic because they seek communal support and mediation to the one true God'.[65] Andrew Greely argues that 'Mary's poetic

52. Quoted in Chandavoine 1993: 125.
53. Quoted in Lefouin 1998: 183.
54. Quoted in Ebertshauser *et al.* 1998: 108.
55. 'Kerzen für Maria', in Ley (ed.) 1970: 68–79.
56. 'The Black Madonna', in Spark 1984.
57. Johnson 1985: 116–35 (128).
58. *Dictionary of Mary*: 210.
59. Quoted in ibid.: 298.
60. Quoted in Chandavoine 1993: 217.
61. Quoted in Lefouin 1998: 129.
62. Quoted in ibid.: 132.
63. Quoted in Chandavoine 1993: 106.
64. Quoted in ibid.: 186–7.
65. Hamington 1995: 90.

function in the Catholic tradition, as one can see in many great poems and paintings, is to represent the womanliness of God – the life-giving, nurturing, healing aspects of God's love'.[66]

In his celebrated poetic work, *Le Porche du Mystère de la deuxième vertu* (*The Portal of the Mystery of Hope*), Charles Péguy writes:

> To she who is infinitely queen
> Because she is the most humble of creatures.
> Because she was a poor woman, a miserable woman, a poor Jewess
> from Judea.
> To she who is infinitely distant
> Because she is infinitely near.
> To she who is the highest princess
> Because she is the most humble woman.
> To she who is the nearest to God
> Because she is the nearest to men.
> To she who is infinitely saved
> Because in her turn she saves infinitely.[67]

According to the liberationist scholars Gebara and Bingemer, Mary should not be made 'into an eternal model, or way of being'; rather 'this historical figure of Mary must always enter into dialogue with the time, space, culture, problems and actual people who relate to her'.[68] European literature has taken up this challenge. Across the centuries that have witnessed the Golden Age of Mary, the reduction of Marian devotion in the wake of the Second Vatican Council, and the rise of feminism and liberation theology, literature has pre-empted, and continues to transpose, theological debates surrounding the life and intercessory role of the Virgin Mary.

BIBLIOGRAPHY

Adams, K. Van Esveld (2001) *Our Lady of Victorian Feminism: the Madonna in the work of Anna Jameson, Margaret Fuller and George Eliot*, Athens, GA: Ohio University Press.

Angelier, F. and Langlois, C. (eds) (2000) *La Salette: Apocalypse, pèlerinage et littérature 1856–1996*, Grenoble: Jérôme Millon.

Asch, S. (1949) *Mary*, New York: G. P. Putnam's Sons.

Auden, W. H. (1966) *For the Time Being*, London: Faber and Faber.

Backhouse, R. (ed.) (1994) *The Autobiography of Therese of Lisieux*, London: Hodder and Stoughton.

Barry, P. J. (1970) *Mary in Hopkins' Writings and Life*, Rome: Catholic Book Agency.

de Beauvoir, S. (1953) *The Second Sex*, trans. H. M. Parshley, London: Penguin Books.

Beinert, W. and Petri, H. (eds) (1997) *Handbuch der Marienkunde*, 2 vols, Regensburg: Verlag Friedrich Pustet.

Bernanos, G. (1977) *Diary of a Country Priest*, trans. Pamela Morris, London: Fount Paperbacks.

---

66.   Greeley and Greeley Durkin 1984: xix.
67.   Péguy 1996: 44.
68.   Quoted in Cunneen 1996: 23.

Bertrand, M. (1997) *Une femme à l'écoute de son temps: Marceline Desbordes-Valmore*, Lyon: La cigogne Editions.

Bondanello, P. and Ciccarelli, A. (eds) (2003) *The Cambridge Companion to the Italian Novel*, Cambridge: Cambridge University Press.

Boss, S. (1999) *Mary's Story*, Bath: Barefoot Books.

Bouvier, B. (1976) *Le Mirologue de la Vierge. Chansons et Poèmes grecs sur la passion du Christ*, Rome: Bibliotheca Helvetica Romana, XVI.

Boy-Ed, I. (1916) *Die Opferschale*, Berlin: August Scherl.

Brand, P. and Pertile, L. (eds) (1996) *The Cambridge History of Italian Literature*, Cambridge: Cambridge University Press.

Brecht, B. (1965) *Selected Poems*, Oxford: Oxford University Press.

Brown, R. E. (1993) *The Birth of the Messiah: A Commentary on the Infancy Narratives in the Gospels of Matthew and Luke*, New York: Doubleday.

Brown, R. E. *et al.* (1978) *Mary in the New Testament*, New York/Mahwah: Paulist Press.

Carroll, E. R. (1994) 'The Virgin Mary and Feminist Writers', *Carmelus*, vol. 41.

Chandavoine, H. (1993) *Anthologie de la poésie mariale*, Paris: Les Éditions du Cerf.

Claudel, P. (1960) *The Tidings brought to Mary*, trans. W. Fowlie, Chicago, IL: Henry Regnery Company.

Claudel, P. (1998) *Le Poète et la Bible*, Paris: NRF.

Cunneen, S. (1996) *In Search of Mary*, New York: Ballantine Books.

Darrigaud, J.-C. (1999) *L'Evangile selon Marie de Nazareth*, Bondy: Les Éditions Sakramento.

Dictionary of Mary (1997), New Jersey: Catholic Book Publishing Co.

Ebertshauser, C. H. *et al.* (1998) *Mary: Art, Culture, and Religion through the Ages*, New York: Crossroad.

Ernaux, A. (1996) *A Frozen Woman*, trans. L. Coverdale, New York: Seven Stories Press.

Greeley, A. M. and Greeley Durkin, M. (1984) *How to save the Catholic Church*, New York: Viking.

Hamington, M. (1995) *Hail Mary? The Struggle for Ultimate Womanhood in Catholicism*, New York: Routledge.

Harris, R. (1999) *Lourdes: Body and Spirit in the Secular Age*, London: Penguin.

Herrán, L. M. (1979) *Santa María en las literaturas hispánicas*, Pamplona: Eunsa.

Hopkins, G. M. (1970) *The Poems of Gerard Manley Hopkins*, London: Oxford University Press.

Huysmans, J.-K. (1989) *The Cathedral*, trans. Clara Bell, Sawtry: Deladus.

Irigaray, L. (1996) *Le Souffle des femmes*, Paris: AGCF.

Johnson, E. A. (1985) 'The Marian Tradition and the Reality of Women', *Horizons*, vol. 12/1, Spring.

Kazantzakis, N. (1975) *The Last Temptation*, London: Faber and Faber.

Keller, G. (1987) *Sieben Legenden*, Berlin: Verlag der Nation.

Kipling, R. (1940) *Verse: Definitive Edition*, London: Hodder and Stoughton.

Kristeva, J. (1987) *Tales of Love*, trans. L. S. Roudiez, New York: Columbia University Press.

Lambert, C. J. (1990) *The Empty Cross: Medieval Hopes, Modern Futility in the Theatre of Maurice Maeterlinck, Paul Claudel, August Strindberg and Georg Kaiser*, New York: Garland.

Laurentin, R. (1984) *Marie, mère du Seigneur: Les plus beaux textes depuis deux millénaires*, Paris: Desclée.

Lefouin, C. (1998) *Marie dans la littérature française*, Paris: Pierre Téqui.

Ley, R. (ed.) (1970) *Böll für Zeitgenossen*, New York: Harper and Row.

Locke, M. and Warren, C. (1993) *Jean-Luc Godard's Hail Mary: Women and the Sacred in Film*, Carbondale and Edwardsville, IL: Southern Illinois University Press.

Lofts, N. (1965) *How Far to Bethlehem?*, London: Hutchinson.

du Manoir, H. (ed.) (1952) *Maria: Etudes sur la Sainte Vierge*, vol. 2, Paris: Beauchesne.

de Margerie, B. (1987) 'Mary in Latin American Liberation Theologies', in *Marian Studies*, vol. 48.

Mastrolia, A. (2000) *C. S. Lewis and the Blessed Virgin Mary: Uncovering a 'Marian Attitude'*, Lima, OH: Fairway Press.

Merton, T. (1972) *New Seeds of Contemplation*, New York: New Directions.

Moi, T. (ed.) (1986) *The Kristeva Reader*, Oxford: Blackwell.

Noël, Marie (1983) *Les Chansons et les Heures et Le Rosaire des joies*, Paris: Gallimard.

Péguy, C. (1996) *The Portal of the Mystery of Hope*, trans. David Louis Schindler, Edinburgh: T&T Clark.

Pelikan, J. (1996) *Mary through the Centuries: Her Place in the History of Culture*, New Haven, CT: Yale University Press.

Perez, J. and Ihrie, M. (eds) (2002) *The Feminist Encyclopedia of Spanish Literature*, Westport, CT: Greenwood Press.

Reilly, C. (ed.) (1981) *Scars upon my Heart*, London: Virgao.

Rilke, R. M. (2003) *The Life of the Virgin Mary*, trans. Christine McNeill, Dublin: The Dedalus Press.

Roten SM, J. G. (1999) 'Marian Studies – Doctrine', *Marian Studies* 50.

Saveria Huré, J. (1987) *I Mary, Daughter of Israel*, trans. Nina de Voogd, London: Weidenfeld and Nicolson.

Spark, M. (1984) *The Go-away Bird and Other Stories*, London: Penguin.

Studer, C. (1918) *Die Frauen erwachen*, Frauenfeld: Huber & Co.

Tavard, G. H. (1996) *The Thousand Faces of the Virgin Mary*, Collegeville, MN: The Liturgical Press.

Werfl, F. (1988) *Song of Bernadette*, New York: Phoenix Press.

Ycats, W. B. (1958) *The Collected Poems*, London: Macmillan and Co. Ltd.

Zola, E. (1998) *Lourdes*, Paris: Omnibus.

25

MARY IN FILM

CATHERINE O'BRIEN

Since the invention of the moving image, religion has offered thematic ideas to cinema directors, beginning with the filming of passion plays in the pioneering era of the late nineteenth century. While the depiction of Jesus Christ on screen may provide the greatest opportunity for controversy, the role of the Virgin Mary offers its own particular challenges. The variety of Marian images available is illustrated by the extensive database held at the International Marian Research Institute in Dayton, Ohio, which catalogues films and videos with Marian references, including traditional biblical epics, parodies, documentaries and lectures on Marian subjects, traces of Marian symbolic figures, and glimpses of statues and rosary beads in Hollywood movies.[1]

In D. W. Griffith's *Intolerance* (1916), which interweaves New Testament scenes with three stories from different historical eras, Lillian Gish represents 'The Woman Who Rocks the Cradle/The Eternal Mother', whose image appears at intervals throughout the film; and Lillian Langdon plays 'Mary the Mother', appearing as a witness at the wedding of Cana. These performances indicate two dominant approaches to the Virgin in the history of feature film: the iconic dimension, which presents the Virgin as a recognizable symbolic figure beyond the biblical context; and the narrative response, which relates incidents from Mary's earthly biography within the overarching story of Jesus of Nazareth.

An iconic reference is found in early cinema in Alice Guy's *My Madonna* (1915), in which a painter tries to find a human model capable of capturing the beauty of his Marian vision. The reported apparitions of the Virgin in Europe and Mexico have also inspired film-makers with both devotional and political agendas, including *Le Miracle de Lourdes* (1926), *La Virgen de Guadalupe* (1976) and Jean-Pierre Mocky's controversial parody *Le Miraculé* (1986), which centres on an insurance fraud that exploits the shrine at Lourdes. John Brahm's *The Miracle of Our Lady of Fatima* (1952) carried an anti-communist message that would have found favour within the House Un-American Activities Committee in the 1950s; and in the 1990s, the apparitions at Medjugorje provided the impetus for a political story of conflict between communism and the Catholic Church in Jakov Sedlar's *Gospa* (1995).

---

1. See http://www.udayton.edu/mary/resources/researchdatabase.html. This research tool is complemented by the work of Michael Duricy, who has examined over 1,000 films for his study *Mary in Film*; Duricy 2000. Other important overviews of the subject are Roten 2001: 102–28; and R. Zwick, 'Maria im Film', in Beinert and Petri (eds) 1997, vol. 2: 270–317.

Mary of Nazareth has appeared as a secondary figure in Life of Christ films from the early days of silent cinema, including Sidney Olcott's *From the Manger to the Cross* (1912), Robert Wiene's *I.N.R.I* (1923), and Cecil B. DeMille's epic *The King of Kings* (1927). A number of questions arise when the Virgin is made visible on screen. Each actress adds an extratextual dimension to the role of Mary through her physicality and celebrity. The problem was illustrated by the disputed (although uncredited) casting of Linda Darnell as the Virgin of the apparitions at Lourdes in Henry King's *Song of Bernadette* (1943). The French director Jean Delannoy was sensitive to this issue when he chose the unknown Myriam Muller to play the eponymous protagonist of *Marie de Nazareth* (1994), so that no outside events would detract from her credibility as the mother of Jesus.

Ethnicity is a contentious subject when the image of a blue-eyed, fair-haired Mary of Nazareth is found in Western culture, so that the Jewishness of Jesus' mother is frequently disregarded. The fact that biblical historians indicate that Mary would have been aged about 13 or 14 at the Annunciation is also often overlooked in keeping with Western sensibilities. In the two New Testament Hollywood epics of the 1960s, Mary is played by the Irish actress Siobhan McKenna in Nicholas Ray's *King of Kings* (1961), while the American Dorothy McGuire takes the role in George Stevens' *The Greatest Story Ever Told* (1965), with both actresses bringing Western features and a mature perspective to the Nativity scenes. When the Marxist and atheist Pier Paolo Pasolini was motivated to make *The Gospel according to Matthew* (1964), he circumnavigated the latter problem by having Margherita Caruso interpret the young Mary of the Annunciation and Nativity; and choosing Susanna Pasolini, the director's own mother, to play the older Mary of the time of Jesus' ministry. Nevertheless, the question of Mary's Jewish heritage is often unresolved.

There were a number of biblical interpretations in the 1970s, including Roberto Rossellini's *The Messiah* (1976) and Franco Zeffirelli's television mini-series *Jesus of Nazareth* (1977), but the 1980s proved to be a more polemical decade and not all of the resulting output pleased the Vatican. There were demonstrations against Jean-Luc Godard's *Je vous salue, Marie* (1984), which updates the story of Mary and Joseph to twentieth-century Switzerland; Martin Scorsese's *The Last Temptation of Christ* (1988), based on the novel by Nikos Kazantzakis, included a Mary (Verna Bloom) who appears unsupportive of her son's mission;[2] and Denys Arcand's *Jesus of Montreal*, in which a fashion model (played by Catherine Wilkening) takes the role of Mary/Magdalene in an unorthodox passion play, met with conflicting reviews.

In the 1940s Roberto Rossellini's *The Miracle* (1948), in which a peasant girl mistakenly believes that she is undergoing a virgin birth, caused scandal. As a sign of the changing times, in the 1990s the Christmas television schedules included Ralph Howard and Katharina Otto's *The Second Greatest Story Ever Told* (1994), which relates the tale of Mary Weinstein (Mira Sorvino), who receives an unexpected visit

---

2. See M. Locke, 'A History of the Public Controversy', in Locke and Warren 1993: 1–9; and Riley 2003.

from the angel Gabriel (Malcolm McDowell) in a public toilet on Coney Island and is called upon to raise a modern Messiah in New York in the 1960s.

It is clear that the *lacunae* in the New Testament leave space for the screenwriter's imagination, for there are only a few scriptural lines of text on which to draw for Mary's dialogue. Mary remains silent in Pasolini's film, with both actresses expressing their emotions through facial expression. The young Mary lowers her eyes when she sees Joseph's troubled reaction to her visibly pregnant body, and she smiles happily when Joseph returns to her after the revelation by the angel has vanquished his doubts. The older Mary is present for the 'mothers and brothers' pericope (Mt. 12.46–50), but, in a reaction shot, she smiles at Jesus' words, so that they are not interpreted as a rejection. Other film-makers extend Mary's role by inventing scenes that exceed the work of the evangelists. This strategy is found in Ray's *King of Kings*, when Mary relates the parable of the Lost Sheep (Lk. 15.4–7) to welcome a former prostitute into her home; and in Mel Gibson's *The Passion of the Christ* (2004) Mary's role is enhanced via flashbacks to Jesus' life during the Hidden Years and through events inspired by the visions of Blessed Anne Catherine Emmerich.

Throughout the twentieth century there were only a small number of attempts to present Mary as a chief focus of the action, such as Don Emilio Cordeo's *Mater Dei* (1950), Bernard Kowalski's *The Nativity* (1978), Eric Till's *Mary and Joseph, A story of faith* (1979), and Jean Delannoy's *Marie de Nazareth* (1994). Making Mary the central protagonist is a project that creates its own dilemmas, both on a theological and on a plot-related level.

While the titular Mary is clearly the heroine in the first half of Delannoy's *Marie de Nazareth*, which draws on the infancy narratives of Matthew and Luke, the director struggles to prevent Mary's story from becoming a minor adjunct to Jesus' mission and, in one of the more disputed additions, manifests blood upon her forehead during the Passion – a stigmata reference which is in keeping with the iconic translation of the mystery of the co-redemption.

Whether Mary is a primary or secondary figure within the diegesis, directors must decide how to formulate her character: from the humble handmaiden beloved of patriarchy to the independent woman heralded by feminist Mariologists. In Zeffirelli's *Jesus of Nazareth*, Joseph is a more commanding figure than the shy and hesitant suitor in *Marie de Nazareth*, allowing Delannoy's Mary to take on a more assertive role.

In assessing the aspect of Mary's autonomous response, the treatment of the Annunciation is a determining factor. It is notable that a number of the Hollywood epics, including the films of Ray and Stevens, avoid the Annunciation, thereby depriving Mary of a key scene while avoiding the problematics of filming divine intervention.

When the Lukan scene is depicted, the angelic messenger is transposed into secular culture in a variety of ways, from the unkempt 'Uncle Gabriel', who arrives by aeroplane in *Je vous salue, Marie*, to the disembodied male voice (accompanied by light and wind effects) favoured by Delannoy. In Zeffirelli's *Jesus of Nazareth* there is no visible angel and the audience (placed in the position of Anna, who observes her daughter's startled reaction from across the room) watches Mary (Olivia Hussey) as she gazes towards light streaming through the window. The animal noises in the background demonstrate how normal life continues outside.

In *Jesus of Nazareth* Mary's body language changes from fear to humility as she says 'Behold the handmaid of the Lord', while Delannoy's Mary opens her arms in a gesture of acceptance, indicating a spirit of co-operation that Godard's reluctant twentieth-century Mary figure (her concluding words are: 'I am of the Virgin and I didn't want this being') fails to manifest. However, Zeffirelli and Delannoy avoid the possible political dimension of the *Magnificat*. Mary travels in a caravan to visit her cousin Elizabeth in *Jesus of Nazareth* – a mode of transport that seems more probable than Mary's solitary donkey ride in *Marie de Nazareth* – but in both films Mary's canticle is curtailed before it reaches the verses lauded by liberation theologians.

Mary's role as the *mater dolorosa* finds poignant expression in *Jesus of Nazareth*, in which Mary visually and audibly expresses her distress in the *Pietà* scene in the rain. However, it is Gibson's *The Passion of the Christ* that has focused the attention on the significance of Jesus' mother. While the accusations of anti-Semitism and excessive on-screen violence have caught the attention, Gibson's Mary (Maia Morgenstern) has won acclaim as a suffering human figure who breaks the cinematic 'fourth wall' by looking towards the camera and drawing the audience into the action at the deposition. As Robert Johnson argues, 'Not only do we see Jesus' agony through her eyes; her maternal instincts become our own. We identify spiritually with this mother watching her own child suffer. And her suffering vicariously becomes our own.'[3]

The New Testament has inspired directors ranging from non-believers to committed Christians. The Marxist and atheist Pasolini responded to the call for a new dialogue with non-Catholic artists in the spirit of the Second Vatican Council, shooting his low-budget, neo-realist *Gospel according to Matthew* in Matera in Italy and dedicating the film to Pope John XXIII. Forty years later the same location was used by Mel Gibson for *The Passion of the Christ* – a film that earned over $300 million at the box office in the United States during the first year of its release. It is a demonstration of the visual power of the story of the Passion, and of Mary's role within it.

FILMOGRAPHY

Ferdinand Zecca and Lucien Nonguet, *La Vie et La Passion de Jésus-Christ* (France 1905)
Sidney Olcott, *From the Manger to the Cross* (US 1912)
Alice Guy, *My Madonna* (France 1915)
D. W. Griffiths, *Intolerance* (US 1916)
Robert Wiene, *I.N.R.I* (Germany 1923)
B. Simon, *Miracle de Lourdes* (France 1926)
Cecil B. DeMille, *The King of Kings* (US 1927)
George Pallu, *La Vie merveilleuse de Bernadette* (France 1929)
Rino Lupo, *Fátima Milagrosa* (Portugal 1929)
Julien Duvivier, *Golgotha* (France 1935)

---

3. R. K. Johnston, 'The Passion as Dynamic Icon', in Plate (ed.) 2004: 68.

Gabriel Soria, *La Vírgen morena* (Mexico 1942)
Julio Bracho, *La Vírgen que forjó una patria* (Mexico 1942)
Henry King, *The Song of Bernadette* (US 1943)
Don Emilio Cordero, *Mater Dei* (Italy 1950)
Miguel Morayta, *El Mártir del Calvario* (Mexico 1952)
John Brahm, *The Miracle of Our Lady of Fatima* (US 1952)
Nicholas Ray, *The King of Kings* (US 1961)
Pier Paolo Pasolini, *The Gospel according to Matthew* (Italy 1964)
George Stevens, *The Greatest Story Ever Told* (US 1965)
Luis Bunuel, *The Milky Way* (France/Germany/Italy 1969)
Roberto Rossellini, *The Messiah* (Italy/France 1976)
Alfredo Salazar, *La Virgen de Guadalupe* (Mexico 1976)
Franco Zeffirelli, *Jesus of Nazareth* (Italy/UK 1977)
Bernard L. Kowalski, *The Nativity* (US TV movie, 1978)
Eric Till, *Mary and Joseph, A story of faith* (Canada/Germany/Israel 1979)
Jean-Luc Godard, *Je vous salue, Marie* (France/Switzerland/UK 1984)
Jean-Pierre Mocky, *Le Miraculé* (France 1986)
Franco Rossi, *A Child Called Jesus* (Italy/Germany TV mini-series 1987)
Jean Delannoy, *Bernadette* (France 1988)
Martin Scorsese, *The Last Temptation of Christ* (US 1988)
Denys Arcand, *Jesus of Montreal* (Canada/France 1989)
Giovanni Veronesi, *Per amore, solo per amore* (For Love, Only For Love) (Italy 1993)
Ralph Howard and Katharina Otto, *The Second Greatest Story Ever Told* (US TV movie 1994)
Jean Delannoy, *Marie de Nazareth* (France 1994)
Jakov Sedlar, *Gospa* (Croatia/Canada/US 1995)
Kevin Connor, *Mary, mother of Jesus* (US TV movie, 1999)
Goffredo Lombardo, *Maria, daughter of her son* (Italy TV movie, 2000)
Mel Gibson, *The Passion of the Christ* (US 2004)
Catherine Hardwicke, *The Nativity Story* (US 2006)

BIBLIOGRAPHY

Beinert, W. and Petri, H. (eds) (1997) *Handbuch der Marienkunde*, 2 vols, Regensburg: Verlag Friedrich Pustet.

Duricy, M. P. (2000) *Mary in Film: An Analysis of Cinematic Presentations of the Virgin Mary From 1897–1999, A Theological Appraisal of a Socio-Cultural Reality*, unpublished STL thesis, Dayton, OH: International Marian Research Institute.

Duricy, M. P. (2003) 'The Life of the Virgin Mary in Film', *Ephemerides Mariologicae*, vol. LIII – Fasc. III–IV, Julio-Diciembre: 479–88.

Locke, M. and Warren, C. (1993) *Jean-Luc Godard's Hail Mary: Women and the Sacred in Film*, Carbondale and Edwardsville, IL: Southern Illinois University Press.

du Manoir, H. (ed.) (1952) *Maria: Etudes sur la Sainte Vierge*, vol. 5, Paris: Beauchesne.

Plate, S. B. (ed.) (2004) *Re-viewing the Passion: Mel Gibson's Film and Its Critics*, New York: Palgrave Macmillan.

Riley, R. (2003) *Film, Faith and Cultural Conflict: The Case of Martin Scorsese's 'The Last Temptation of Christ'*, Westport, CT: Greenwood Press.

Roten, J. G. (2001) 'Marie dans le Cinéma', *Études Mariales: Bulletin de la Société Française d'Études Mariales* 58: 102–28.

26

THE ICONOGRAPHIC TYPES OF THE VIRGIN IN WESTERN ART[1]

MAURICE VLOBERG

EDITOR'S INTRODUCTION

People sometimes make comments about 'Mary in art'. In response to such generalizations, art historians are inclined to throw up their hands in horror, and point out that the variety of types of representation of the Virgin, and of the media through which she is represented, are so enormous that one cannot even begin to think about such a vast category. Art historians usually study representations of the Virgin at particular times and places, or in particular media. Maurice Vloberg, however, adopted a thematic approach to much of his work, studying a variety of representations of the Virgin, from numerous periods of history. So perhaps only he could have produced such an erudite paper on such an enormous topic as is presented here. Some of the material included in this paper has been superseded by more recent research, such as that described by Geri Parlby.[2] Nonetheless, as a piece of descriptive writing on this subject, it is unsurpassed.

CONTENTS

1. The Virgin Mother and Virgin Orant of the catacombs.
2. The triumphal art of the fifth and sixth centuries. Roman representations of the Virgin Queen.
3. The majestic and tender Virgin of the Middle Ages and early Renaissance.
4. The maternal Virgin of the Renaissance.
5. Dogmatic themes of the seventeenth century.
6. Representations and formulas from the nineteenth century to the present.
7. General bibliography.

* * *

While Marian art cannot be said to constitute a specific genre, the theme of the Virgin Mary occupies a unique position in the annals of art. No subject has been

---

1. Translated by Imogen Forster Associates, from 'Les Types Iconographiques de la Vierge dans l'Art Occidental', in Hubert du Manoir (ed.) *Maria: Etudes sur la Sainte Vierge*, vol. II, Paris: Beauchesne, 1952: 106–29.
2. 'The Origins of Marian Art', in this volume: 106–29.

Fig. 25. *Ivory Virgin*. Beginning of the 14th century. Museum of Villeneuve-lès-Avignon. (Copyright Photo Daspet).

Fig. 26. *Marienklage*. South German. Second quarter of 14th century. Suermondt-Museum, Aachen.

treated with greater sympathy, fervour or success. Her iconographic representation has, of course, followed the fortunes of styles and schools. It has been influenced by a variety of formulas and techniques, and frequently by the vagaries of taste and fashion. Nevertheless, Mary always emerges as a unique and magnificent sacred figure, an image bound by the inescapable demands of dogma. This constraint has been as rewarding as it has been rigorous, for it has enabled art to aspire to the sublime and thus to grow.

539

The style and structure of the present study should therefore already be apparent. It does not set out to rewrite the history of Marian art, but to grasp the spiritual dimension of Mary's image as it was conceived in the great periods of artistic creation. The image, especially in its religious aspect, gains as much if not more value from idea and emotion as it does from professional skill. An aesthetic critique is certainly important, and the details of the way artists have handled the theme are not without interest. Extensive research, often extremely meticulous, has been conducted into the paternity of works and the relationship between them in order to ensure their correct attribution and categorization. The direction and spirit of this study have demanded greater attention to the didactic element. It places more emphasis on the moral portrait and evidence of faith than on formal conventions, and traces the parallel development of doctrinal currents and artistic endeavour.

Lathoud has rightly observed that 'iconography is above all a matter of religious symbolism. The representation was often conceived in the mind of the "master of divine sciences", rather than by the person who executed it.'[3] In fact, while history, tradition and legend offer an initial explanation for the works of antiquity, many of them reveal the influence and contribution of dogma, liturgy, mysticism and devotion. This is the best lesson we can learn from images. When plastic value is added, that lesson can only gain in power.

The riches of the Marian theme throughout the centuries are inexhaustible. Our aim is to summarize the most important elements of the *figurative Mariology* that Western schools have employed from the very beginning. Their struggles to depict the pre-eminence of the Mother of God with beauty, grandeur and the most affecting clarity have thus contributed to the realization of her dictum: *Beatam me dicent omnes generationes*.

* * *

1

THE VIRGIN MOTHER AND THE VIRGIN ORANT
OF THE CATACOMBS

The controversies surrounding Roman funerary paintings involved apologetics more than art. Confessional preoccupations played a far greater role than objective analysis and led to the arbitrary dismissal of the significance of certain works. For example, Roller, a Protestant, claimed that 'In the sense that she is the object of a specific cult, there is no Madonna as such in the crypts of the catacombs.'[4]

---

3. D. Lathoud, 'Le theme iconographique du "Pokrov" de la Vierge', in *L'Art byzantin chez les Slaves*, Theodore Uspenskij, Paris, 1932, 2nd anthology: 311.
4. Roller, *Les Catacombs de Rome*, Paris, 1881, vol. II: 354. Before Roller, Coquerel had claimed, 'The Mother of the Redeemer is never depicted alone [in the catacombs], and is always a completely secondary figure.' *Des Beaux-Arts en Italie au point de vue religieux*, Paris, 1857: 147.

Roller's view was not shared by the most knowledgeable investigator of subterranean Rome, nor by the archaeologists who added to his discoveries. Giovanni Battista de' Rossi (1822–94) and his peers uncovered many frescoes which clearly and unequivocally depict the Virgin as the Mother of the Saviour rather than as a passive figure. This enables us legitimately to acknowledge evidence of the primitive cult of Mary. Mgr Wilpert, one of the foremost experts on catacomb art, claims: 'Better than any document written during the centuries of persecution, these paintings express, in a few powerful brushstrokes, the position Mary occupied in the church of the first four centuries, and show that, as far as substance is concerned, she was then what she would be later.'[5]

The earliest of these representations also has the greatest artistic merit.

The *Madonna with Child and Prophet* painted on the vault of a *loculus* in a funeral chamber (*cubiculum*) in the catacomb of Priscilla (Via Salaria Nova) dates back to the interval between the Flavians and the first Antonines, thus to the early second century. It is therefore close to the time of the apostles, and despite its considerable age and poor condition today, the fluent brushwork in the Graeco-Roman style known as 'Pompeian' is still clearly distinguishable. The technique is naturalistic and but for the eight-pointed star – a sign of divinity – which shines above Mary's head, the subject could be taken for a simple portrayal of mother and child. The seated Virgin holds the naked Infant to her breast; he is a lively child with a rounded, muscular brown back; his head is turned towards us and his great black eyes seem full of wonder. Standing before the Mother, a clean-shaven man clad in a pallium holds a scroll (*volumen*) in his left hand, while his right hand points to the star. The most likely explanation for this small fresco is that it represents Isaiah's prophecy of the virginal conception of Christ, whose gospel would illuminate the world:

> Behold, a virgin shall conceive, and bear a son,
> and shall call his name Immanuel.

This interpretation fits the composition perfectly. If it is correct, it is likely that the teaching of the image escaped neither the artist who painted it nor the Christians who contemplated it: it avoids symbolism and attests to the mystery of the incarnation. The dignified, maternal Virgin and her alert, naked infant in the catacomb of Priscilla represent a clear profession of the truth that second-century apologists so fiercely defended against the various Docetistic heresies claiming that Christ had only apparently taken on human form. The *Virgin with Child and Prophet*, a pictorial reflection of the doctrine, confirms the belief in divine maternity three centuries before the dogma was laid down at the Council of Ephesus.

The meaning of another important painting in the catacomb of Priscilla, this time from the third century, is more problematic. Some critics hesitate over the identity of the young mother it represents, but others see her as the Mother of Christ rather than a figure of motherhood in general. This Virgin and Child – called the *Velatio* (the

---

5.   *Die Malerein der Katakomben Roms*, vol. I: 197.

Veiling) since this may be the theme of the enigmatic group of which it is part – is derived from Hellenistic models. There is a similar mother figure in the Jewish hypogeum in Palmyra, but the grave and beautiful image in the catacomb of Priscilla has a grace and meaning surpassing that of a conventional scene. Despite certain indications – the posture and nudity of the infant recall the *Virgin with Child and Prophet* – we cannot be sure that it represents the divine motherhood of the Virgin.

A series of at least fourteen paintings depicts the Adoration of the Magi. The earliest of these Epiphanies adorns an arch of the *Cappella Greca*, the crypt adjoining the cubiculum containing the Virgin with Isaiah. The most remarkable examples date from the third century, and are found in the catacombs of Domitilla (Via Ardeatina) and Sts Marcellinus and Peter (Via Labicana). Bas-reliefs on sarcophagi depict a tender yet dignified Mary standing between two Magi intent upon offering their gifts, and similar scenes appear on engraved funerary tablets like that of *Severa*, also from the third century, in which the pace of the three Magi is so eager that their fluttering mantles resemble outspread wings (Lateran museum: from the Priscilla cemetery).

Some Protestant archaeologists claim that Mary has no personal role in these Epiphanies, but is simply an instrumental figure. But this deliberately extended series of paintings tells us something quite different. Their artists were emphasizing the fact that the tributes of the Magi were offered to both Son and Mother. In the catacomb of Sts Marcellinus and Peter, Mary occupies the centre of the composition, as if to emphasize her role in the election of the Gentiles. Would the early Church have had less knowledge of all this mystery than the Church of today?

It is striking that the art of the first three centuries after Christ represents Mary in a 'literal' fashion: the images are drawn from the Gospels and are free of any apocryphal feature. The fact and glory of her maternity are placed at the centre of the divine story; there is no attempt to turn her into the abstract, theological figure that Byzantium would later prefer. The catacomb painters did not resort to symbolism and responded directly to the dogma of the incarnation.

Yet symbolism was one of the fundamental characteristics of catacomb art. Many images were conceived with the idea of veiling from profane eyes beliefs that would be immediately comprehensible to the initiated. The orant figure is a common example of this type. A Christian transposition of a Hellenistic creation, it combines the naturalistic and the figurative in order to express either the act or the idea of prayer, *oratio*, and is admirably suited to depict the fervour of the union between Mary and God. However, we cannot be sure that this was the intention of the artists who painted the 53 orants in the catacombs, the most perfect of which, stylized and ethereal, decorate the ceilings of the crypts of Lucina. Were they trying to offer the Mother of the Saviour in this posture as the ideal model of prayer and adoration?

In all probability, some orants represent the Virgin in her intercessory function, particularly those which alternate with or are linked to images of the Good Shepherd, as in the crypts of Lucina. But to be certain, the subject would need to be identified by an explicit name or emblem. Now, such a sign does exist and is found on small artefacts – glass vases with gilded bases.

The manufacture of these vessels or chalices stopped at around 410. The base of the object was composed of two pieces of glass which had been fused in a kiln after the insertion of a sheet of gold leaf on which a subject had been etched. We do not know their exact purpose, but there is no doubt that these round vessels were used to identify particular tombs – among so many almost identical *loculi*, the little patch of gold would stand out clearly in the darkness. Large numbers of shards from these cups, dating from the middle of the third century to the end of the fourth century, have been recovered from the mortar. Several feature a young orant identified as MARIA or MARA. On one of them, she stands beside Agnes, another figure of innocence. On others, she stands between two columns or between two trees of Paradise in which doves perch. But the two most significant examples bear her name and show her standing between the apostles Peter and Paul.

It seems beyond doubt that the Virgin is represented on these fragments as a figure of the Church. But we should be wary of taking the interpretation further and claiming that this image represents the Mediatrix of the Church Militant. We will simply note that a later example seems to establish an iconographic tradition. During the seventh century, a mosaicist working under Pope John IV (640–2) and his successor Theodore, in the oratory of San Venanzo adjoining the Lateran baptistery, returned to the theme depicted on the bases of the cups. The blue-clad orant, wearing the pallium and a gold cross on her breast, extends one arm towards St Peter, who stands on her left and clasps the keys and a staff surmounted by a cross, and the other towards St Paul, who stands on her right holding the book of his epistles.

A new type of orant appeared during the reign of Constantine. Influenced by Syrian traditions, it stressed the intercessional element that figures so prominently in Mary's prayer. In one of the chapels in the *Coemeterium Maius* (Via Nomentana, Rome), the head and shoulders of a young patrician woman adorn the central arch of an arcosolium. Her arms are raised, her hands held widespread, and a small child nestles against her breast. Like his mother's, his gaze is directed outward and he seems completely still. The Chrismon, the Sacred Monogram symbolizing Christ which appeared to Constantine in a vision, is inscribed to left and right of the fresco.

This precious iconographic document evokes the glory and prerogatives of the Mother of God, the effectiveness of her entreaty and perhaps also the gift she makes of her Son. This interpretation is supported by other authorities who have observed that the idea is consistent with the series of Adorations of the Magi mentioned above. Leclercq, for example, writes: 'The two ways of representing the Virgin – in the dignity of her divine motherhood and in the attitude of intercession – are combined in this fresco. For this very reason, it is one of the most interesting works in the catacombs.'[6]

When seeking to establish the identity of the orant depicted here and on the gilded vessels, we should bear in mind that Byzantine art had always reserved it for an explicit image of the intercessional Virgin. It is unlikely that artists would have portrayed the *Theotokos*-Advocate in the orant posture if the tradition had not gone back centuries. Those who agree with Duhr[7] that 'it would be a mistake to see in the

---

6. *Dictionnaire d'Archéologie chrétienne, fasc.* 112–13, vol. X, 1932, col. 2001.
7. 'La Vierge de Marie à travers les siècles dans l'art chrétien', in *La Nouvelle Revue Théologique*, May–June 1946: 288.

image of Mary-Orant an allusion to her role as Intercessor' must at least admit that the figure rapidly evolved in that direction. We could venture further and support those archaeologists who tentatively suggest a continuity of iconographic thinking rather than an evolution. The Byzantine Virgin of Intercession, the *Blachernitissa*, of which the model on the *Coemetereum Maius* fresco is an exact copy, takes the theme to its full expression; it helps us to complete the description and to define the meaning of the orants identified as MARIA on the bases of the cups.[8]

We should also note that the figure of the Virgin Orant had a longer existence than the image of the mystical Shepherd. The comforting but oversimplified figure of the Good Shepherd – which Tertullian disapproved of on the grounds that such a vision of mercy would encourage weakness of every sort – gave way to the triumphal figure of an imperious Christ, the *Pantocrator*. Moreover, the Marian and Christological subjects developed in parallel. The Virgin with outstretched arms would survive for centuries in Byzantine art, but would be joined by another and equally popular type – the Virgin enthroned in majesty. We will discuss this image elsewhere.

In addition to a lesson in catechesis, the art of the Roman cemetery painters provides further evidence of devotion. As Mgr Wilpert has observed, 'the reason why the faithful embellished the catacombs, the resting places of the dead, with paintings, has much more to do with religion than with the desire for decoration. This is borne out in both inscriptions and texts. The people who had these paintings executed used this particular medium to express their faith and their hope. For visitors to the cemeteries, it was an invitation to pray for those who reposed there.'

The Virgin of the Epiphany and the Virgin Orant therefore represented the promise of succour. She was probably seen as keeping a tender vigil over those young Christian women 'of an admirable innocence and wisdom whose lives were happy, but whose deaths were happier still' (*Felix vita puellae, felicior exitus ipse*), as their epitaphs record. A plaque in the Lateran museum, probably a seal from a third-century *loculus* in the catacomb of Priscilla, bears the incised epitaph *Severa, in Deo vivas!* A frontal bust of Severa appears on the left, while on the right the seated Virgin receives the Magi.

Scenes found on fourth- and fifth-century sarcophagi, carved in the style of the painters of the Roman hypogea, seem to suggest that the Virgin guards the Church of the dead as well as the Church of the living. They depict both the Orant and the Mother; and the gesture is either one of prayer or of welcome for the soul that has risen to the Lord. She appears to present the Infant Saviour as much to the departed soul as to the Magi. She holds the child to her breast with great dignity, as we see on a marble sarcophagus in the Lateran museum, or nurses him, as on a fragment of bas-relief from the cemetery of San Sebastian, or raises the little swaddled body to her face in ecstatic contemplation, as on another fragment of late-fourth-century sculpture in the Campo Santo Teutonico museum.

---

8. Apart from the argument for the iconographic continuity of the Orant figure in Byzantine art, Wilpert justly points to the supporting evidence provided by early texts: two centuries before the fresco was painted in the *Coemeterium Maius*, St Irenaeus had given the Mother of God the title of *Advocate*.

The custom of inhumation in the catacombs continued long after the triumph of the Church. The deceased would attest, by means of an inscription or an image placed on the tomb, to their trust in the Mother of God. A well-preserved sixth-century fresco in the catacomb of Commodilla depicts the Virgin seated on a jewelled throne; she wears a crimson robe and shoes, and the Child on her lap, wrapped in a sumptuous gold cloth, clutches a sealed scroll. St Felix stands on the right and St Audactus on the left; the latter presents a matron also dressed in crimson, a widow, as indicated by the white fillet retaining her hair. The epitaph lauds the woman's exemplary life during a widowhood that lasted from the ages of 24 to 60. This inscription, composed by her son or perhaps ordered from a panegyrist, plays on her name – *Turtura* – and the belief, widespread in the Middle Ages, that the turtle-dove (*turtur*) was an exemplar of conjugal fidelity:

> *Turtura nomen abis, sed turtur vera fuisti*
> *Cui conjux moriens non fuit alter amor.*

> Your name was Turtura, and truly you were the turtledove
> Who having lost her mate, would not love again.

The paintings executed during of the era of persecution were frequently even more profoundly moving than this late work, and demonstrate the extent to which the cult of the Virgin had become one of the strengths of the confessors of Christ. Pope Sixtus III acknowledged this honour in an epigraph, now lost, that he ordered to be inscribed above the inside of the entrance to Santa Maria Maggiore. It described the file of Christ's witnesses processing towards his Mother and their Queen, each displaying the instruments and suffering of his martyrdom:

> *Ecce tui testes uteri sibi premia portant,*
> *Sub pedibus jacet passio cuique sua . . .*

As Emile Mâle writes, most of the catacomb paintings are little more than 'pale sketches which now float like a dream about to fade. But nothing makes us more aware of the innocence, purity and gentle sweetness of early Christianity than these patches of colour, half-erased by time.'[9]

It may be that God ensured that these infinitely venerable relics were preserved underground in order for us to benefit from their teaching, and protect them from the erosion and destruction suffered by monuments above ground.

BIBLIOGRAPHY

Belvederi, Mgr G. (1931) *Maria 'Mater Dei' nelle Catacombe e nelle Basilica Liberiana*, Rome.
Belvederi, Mgr G. (1931) 'La "Fides Romana" en la maternité divine de la Vierge avant le concile d'Ephèse', in *Le Bulletin des Amis des Catacombes romaines*, no. 6: 164–72.

---

9. *L'Art Religieux du XIIe en France*, 3rd edn, 1928: 49–50.

Besson, Mgr M. (1942) *La Sainte Vierge*, Geneva, 2nd edn (excellent colour reproductions of cemetery paintings).

Conde, L. (1905) *La Iconografia Mariana en las Catacumbas de Roma*, Madrid.

de Fleury, Rohault (1878) *La Sainte Vierge, Etudes archéologiques et iconographiques*, Paris.

Duhr, J. (1946) 'Le visage de Marie à travers les siècles dans l'art chrétien', in *La Nouvelle Revue Théologique*, Lessianum Museum, May–June: 284–8.

Garrucci, Rafaelle (1858) *Vetri ornate di figure in oro trovati nei cimiteri dei Cristiani primitivi di Roma*, Rome, 2nd edn, 1864.

Lathoud, D. (1925) 'Le type égyptien des icones mariales dans l'antiquité chrétienne', in *Notre-Dame*, July–August.

von Lehner, F. A. (1886) *Die Marienverehrung in den ersten Jahrhunderten*, Stuttgart.

Liell, H. F. J. (1887) *Die Darstellungen der Allerseligten Jungfraü und Gottesgabarerin Maria auf den Kuntstdenkmälern der Katakomben*, Freiburg im Breisgau.

Rossi, J. B. de (1863) *Immagini scelte della beata Vergine Maria tratte delle Catacombe romane*, Rome.

Sartoris, G. (1940) 'La più antica pittura di Maria SS. La Madonna di Priscilla', in *Marianum*, April: 109–13.

Vloberg, Maurice (1938) 'La Vierge d'intercession dans l'iconographie ancienne', in *La Vie spirituelle*, May, part 2: 105–27.

Wilpert, J. (1895) 'De Imaginibus B. M. Virginis in coemeteriis', in *Ephemerides Liturgicae*, Rome: 321–7.

Wilpert, J. (1899) 'Madonnenbilder aus den Katakomben', in *Römische Quartalschrift*, III: 290–8.

Wilpert, J. (1900) 'Maria als Fürsprecherin und mit dem sesuknaben auf einem Fresko der Ostrianischer Katakombe', in *Römische Quartalschrift*, XIV: 309–15.

Wilpert, J. (1903) *Die Malereien der Katakomben Roms*, Freiburg im Breisgau.

See also the articles by Dom H. Leclercq in *Le Dictionnaire d'Archéologie chrétienne et de Liturgie*, headings 'Commodille' (vol. III, 1914), 'Fonds de coupes' (vol. V, 1923), 'Marie, Mère de Dieu' (vol. X, 1932), 'Orant, Orante' (1936) and *passim*.

2

THE TRIUMPHAL ART OF THE FIFTH AND SIXTH CENTURIES. THE ROMAN TYPE OF THE VIRGIN QUEEN

The decision of the Council of Ephesus (431) had a significance beyond the accidents of time and space and ensured that the radiance of divine Motherhood would shine throughout the world. As the teaching of the Fathers and the Doctors of the Church revealed more and more of its infinite aspects, art, like liturgy and devotional practice, endeavoured to express it with glory.

Henceforth, the cult of the Mother of God would attract every talent and would establish itself in a triumphal visual style. In Rome, the heart of Catholicism, monuments became of great significance. The popes erected so many magnificent churches that it seemed as if they were trying to turn Peter's city into Mary's.

In 432, the Roman See, seeking as much to associate itself with Christianity's official recognition of the *Theotokos* as to emphasize its authority in the council, decided to embellish the Liberian basilica, Santa Maria Maggiore, with something worthy of the event. Its masterstroke was the erection of a triumphal arch. The city had once raised such monuments to the glory of its victorious leaders; it was felt even more appropriate to erect a monument to the Woman of Ephesus, to her whom the

Church lauded for having vanquished every heresy: *Gaude, Maria Virgo, cunctas haereses interemisti in universo mundo.*

The arch frames the back of the apse and presents scenes of the divine motherhood in mosaics admired as much in early times as they are today. The inscription at the top – *Xystus Episcopus plebi Dei* – shows that the pontiff commissioned the cycle of images to teach the Christian people. This teaching is centred on the Marian theme and illustrates the definition of Ephesus: it proclaims Mary as the *Theotokos* and depicts her role in the mysteries of Christ's Childhood, from the Annunciation to the flight into Egypt. It retraces episodes from the canonical Gospels and from apocryphal texts. That artists working to papal commissions drew inspiration from these legends is evidence of the extent to which they were accepted in Rome.

Although the compositions are typical of Roman art, the sumptuous costumes and formal settings reveal the influence of the Byzantine court. But the luxuriant treatment of the Virgin Mother is specifically intended to emphasize her prerogatives. Mary is endowed with the features and attire of a princess; she wears jewelled collars, a tunic embroidered with pearls and a diagonal dalmatic cinched at the waist by a belt studded with precious stones. Always guarded by tall angels dressed in key-patterned tunics, she is depicted engaged in various activities: unwinding a skein of purple wool from the distaff tucked under her arm, at the moment of the Annunciation, presenting her Son at the Temple, witnessing the adoration of the Magi, seated to the right of the jewelled throne on which the infant rests in the noble posture of a young porphyrogenite (a curious and unique example of this type of Epiphany), and finally in exile in Egypt, where King Affrodosius receives the Holy Family at the city gates.

Another similarly inspired work extolled the Virgin's pre-eminence in a different form. Inside Santa Maria Maggiore, it is still possible to make out an inscription above the entrance. Composed by the same Sixtus III who made the embellishment of the basilica the key work of his pontificate, this brief panegyric recalls his devotion to the project and also refers to images that are now lost. They probably appeared in the mosaic mentioned above – the line of confessors of the faith bearing palms or crowns and processing towards the Virgin, with the instruments of their martyrdom at their feet.

But another dominant image found in Roman churches and elsewhere deserves our attention. From the seventh century onwards, the popes became increasingly preoccupied with the pre-eminence of the Mother of God and had themselves depicted in glittering golden mosaics, standing or kneeling before a sovereign Virgin wearing a massive crown.

This precise, definitive and truly regal type, with the attributes of supreme majesty, appears several times on frescoes in Santa Maria Antiqua, a venerable basilica constructed in the sixth century in the old library of the Temple of Augustus and excavated among the ruins of the Forum in 1900. Thanks to the coating on its walls, a series of paintings executed by Graeco-Roman artists between the sixth and eighth centuries has been preserved. The Eastern influence is understandable, given that popes of Greek and Syrian origin were particularly attached to this church. Monks from those countries acted as deacons, and the church was the authorized place of worship for the Byzantine officers who lived on the Palatine hill.

The earliest of this basilica's Virgin Queens dates from the end of the sixth century. Although the stucco is in poor condition, the surviving fragments give us some idea of its nobility of style and design. The Virgin, with Jesus on her lap, sits on a richly adorned throne. Her attitude could not be more august. Her sumptuous costume is a precise illustration of imperial fashion at the time of Justinian. Her crown, the *stemma*, is of the mural type, *corona muralis*. She is flanked by the archangels Gabriel and Michael, each of whom leans towards his Queen and offers the infant Jesus an object held in the fold of his cloak – a crown and a sceptre, the symbols of imperial power.

As noted above, the *Theotokos* in the regalia and splendour of a *Basilissa* is a clear example of Byzantine influence on Roman art. The idea may not be entirely new, but it is at the very least the culmination of a development whose stages can easily be traced. The point of departure is located in the cemetery Epiphanies, where the eminence of the Mother springs from her association with the tributes offered to her Son by the Gentiles. Examples of sixth-century enthroned Virgins at San Apollinare (Ravenna), the Roman catacomb of Commodilla and at Parenzo (Istria) all derive from this catacomb archetype. Their details are essentially alike: Mary sits on a gem-encrusted throne flanked by angels or saints; she wears garments of a classical simplicity and has a patrician air; the *palla* or mantle – which covers her head but partially reveals her matron's white coif – falls over her key-patterned tunic. The Virgin presents her Son for the adoration of the Church, an act sometimes symbolized by the traditional allegory of the procession of 12 ewes from Bethlehem and Jerusalem.

Despite her noble demeanour and classical dress, these examples of the enthroned *Theotokos* are still not truly majestic in character. The Virgin attains supreme imperial dignity in a fresco in Santa Maria Antiqua. This is important both in terms of iconography and in the history of Marian devotion. According to Grisar, 'This type of Madonna is of even greater significance because it was the first to be introduced into the Church of Rome, from where it passed to more distant churches.' However, it should be noted that it did not appear elsewhere until much later, and the Virgin Queen of Heaven in Santa Maria Antiqua remained unique throughout the sixth century. W. de Grüneisen, a scholar who made a detailed study of the basilica, suggested that the fresco's design, technique and colours enable us to attribute it to the same Roman artist who painted the Virgin in the tomb of the matron Turtura in the catacomb of Commodilla.

The figure of the Virgin Empress, remarkable in its sumptuous originality, also owes its existence to the popes. As we have already said, certain popes chose to be represented before her in an attitude of supplication. They often appear as tiny figures by comparison with the Virgin. This disproportion, an iconographic feature found elsewhere, is meant to emphasize the distance between the Advocate and her terrestrial supplicants.

The popes' predilection for the theme of the Virgin Queen of Heaven explains its continuity in the Roman art of the seventh and eighth centuries. The Greek-born

John VII marked his brief pontificate (705–7) with examples of ardent devotion to the Mother of God, and commissioned for the chapel of the Virgin in St Peter's a mosaic of cubes that were hammered rather than being polished on a grindstone. The central section survives and is now in St Mark's in Florence. It represents, life-size and against a gold background, the Virgin as both Orant and Empress; the crown and the cataseista (a diadem hung with pearls) frame her face in gold and gemstones. In another surviving fragment, now in the cellars of the Vatican, the pontiff stands on the right of the majestic Orant, while the dedication reads: *Johannes, indignus Episcopus fecit, Beatae Dei Genitricis servus.*

An eleventh-century fresco painted by an artist of the Monte Cassino school in the atrium of Sant'Angelo in Formis features a bust of the Virgin in the same imperial dress and attitude of prayer.

There are two eighth-century frescoes, unfortunately in a very poor condition, in Santa Maria Antiqua. The inscription on one of these, *Maria Regina*, is an explicit statement of the theme. The fresco replicates the composition of an earlier painting in which the surviving fragment of the enthroned Virgin (the upper part is missing) suggests that the raised right forearm once supported a long, pearl-encrusted lance surmounted by a cross, a gesture inspired by that of the gods of antiquity and the allegorical figures representing cities, who carried a sceptre in this way in works of sculpture and on coins.

The earliest Virgin with a cross-surmounted staff is carved in relief on the lid of a sixth-century silver reliquary now in the basilica of Grado (Aquiléia). The cruciform lance must have been considered appropriate for the Virgin Queen, and in fact she carries it as a sceptre from the eighth century onwards. It appears on a badly damaged ninth-century fresco in San Clemente in Rome, and also on a twelfth-century mosaic (of which no trace remains) in the ancient oratory of St Nicholas in the Lateran Palace. The latter work contained two references to Mary's sovereign glory: the jewelled crown held above her head by the divine hand and the inscription *Praesidet aethereis pia Virgo Maria choreis.*

We may assume that the *Imago Dei Genitricis antiqua* dating from the reign of Pope Gregory III (731–41) was of the enthroned type. In the following century, Roman art offered another example of the Virgin in majesty with a pope at her feet. Paschal I (817–24), who restored the basilica of Santa Maria in Domnica, had himself depicted on the mosaic decorating the cupola of the apse. This work clearly indicates the decadence of the era, as well as the weakness of a technique that was already in rapid decline. Mosaic art would not flourish again in Italy until 1066, when Abbot Desiderius, the future Victor III, commissioned Byzantine masters to decorate his new church at Monte Cassino.

Concurrently with this renaissance, the old image of the crowned Virgin reappeared on the conches and walls of churches. The composition in Santa Maria Nova (Santa Francesca Romana), executed between 1159 and 1161, recalls the sixth-century fresco in Santa Maria Antiqua. But despite her imperial dress, the Virgin does not seem as majestic as before: the Infant Jesus has lost the solemn posture of the young Pantocrator and stands in intimate proximity to his mother, who is massive and heavy like a strongly built princess.

However, another twelfth-century work heralds the emergence of a new way of portraying the Virgin's magnificence. The enamel mosaic commissioned (*c.* 1140) by Pope Innocent II for the apse of Santa Maria in Trastevere depicts the Christ and Virgin sitting on a single throne. Mary is dressed as an empress, and her son's right arm embraces her shoulder in a tender and noble gesture illustrating the accompanying inscription from the Song of Solomon: *Laeva ejus sub capite meo et dextera illius amplexabitur me.*[10] The grace and intimacy of this gesture echo the line from an old Christian hymn, possibly from the second century: 'Your yoke, he said to Christ, is the groom's arm around the bride's neck.'

To the right of the central group and in close proximity to the figure of Jeremiah, we observe a caged bird, an extremely uncommon symbol in Marian iconography. The inscription which accompanies this curious motif – *Christus Dominus captus est in peccatis nostris* – explains it: the caged bird symbolizes the incarnation of the Word in Mary's breast.

This novel creation breaks with the traditional superposed arrangement of Christ and the Virgin on Byzantine apses. The figures no longer occupy two separate areas, but appear together, emphasizing their association in celestial glory. The emotional beauty of this theme would later be fully exploited in the fresh and radiant art of France. The artists who decorated the French cathedrals would be the first to sculpt it in the noble style that culminated in the representations of the Queen of Heaven at Senlis and Paris.

The Trastevere basilica also houses a late version of the theme of the Virgin Queen of Heaven. Her image is venerated there as the *Madonna della Clemenza*. The cruciform lance in the Virgin's right hand has become the gem-studded pontifical cross with a double traverse. The pope kneeling before the severely beautiful Virgin is either Innocent II (1130–43), who rebuilt the basilica, or Innocent III (1198–1216). The aperture in the base of the throne is a reference to the legendary *Fons olei*, the natural oil spring said to have appeared at this spot in the year of Christ's Nativity. Mgr Wilpert dates this painting on wood to the late thirteenth century and attributes it to a mediocre predecessor of Cavallini.

As we have seen, an entire cycle of Roman paintings and mosaics executed between the fourth and the ninth centuries depicted the Mother of God as a figure of regal splendour. The *Maria Regina*, as the inscriptions refer to her, evolved at the very centre of the faith and was especially favoured by the popes, who invested the type with exceptional significance and ensured that it became an essentially Catholic subject. Theologians would later appreciate the doctrinal value conferred on the image through the cult of devotion the popes paid to it. *Maria Regina* expressed not only their trust, but also their faith and authority.

---

10.   Innocent II may have taken the idea for this composition from the abbey at Saint-Denis, where he had been Suger's guest in 1131 (see E. Mâle, *L'art religieux du XIIe siècle en France*). But it is just as likely that the mosaic painter of the Transtiberine basilica followed the old Byzantino-Roman style of the enthroned and crowned Virgin.

BIBLIOGRAPHY

Berchem, M. van and Clouzot, E. (1924) *Mosaïques chrétiennes du IVe au Xe siècle*, Geneva.

Bertaux, E. (1904) *L'Art dans l'Italie méridionale*, Paris.

Gruneisen, W. de (1911) *Sainte-Maria Antique*, Rome.

Lavagnino, E. and Moschini, V. (1924) *S. Maria Maggiore*, Rome.

Vloberg, Maurice (1938) 'Le Type romain de la Vierge Reine', in *L'Art sacré*, June.

Wilpert, J. (1906) 'L'Immagine della Madonna, detta della Clemenza in Santa Maria in Trastevere', in *L'Arte*, vol. IX: 161–4.

Wilpert, J. (1917) *Die römischen Mosaiken und Malereien der Kirchlichen Bauten vom IV bis XIII Jahrhundert*, Freiburg im Breisgau.

For further information on Santa Maria Maggiore, see the magnificent work with colour plates by J. P. Richter and C. Taylor.

See also:

Leclercq, H. (1932) 'Maria, Mère de Dieu', in *Le Dictionnaire d'archéologie Chrétienne et de Liturgie*, vol. X.

Marucchi, H. (n.d.) *Eléments d'archéologie chrétienne*, vol. III.

3

THE MAJESTIC AND TENDER VIRGIN OF THE MIDDLE AGES AND EARLY RENAISSANCE

In subsequent periods, the image of the Virgin would be treated with greater sophistication elsewhere. During the thirteenth century, the apogee of the Middle Ages, French art excelled in the faithful, noble and tender interpretation of the words written in the preceding century by Anselm and Bernard, the most inspired panegyrists of Our Lady. 'Oh Virgin,' exclaimed Anselm, 'you alone are sweet to contemplate, you alone are delightful to adore, you alone deserve our ecstasy!'

Very few works of genius are spontaneously generated; most are the result of a long process of experimentation and advance. In France, we can discern its precursors as early as the Carolingian renaissance, in the work of the artists who laboured to match the achievements of Alcuin and Hincmar, who celebrated the Virgin in Latin distichs. The artists' opportunities were limited and chiefly confined to illuminating manuscripts. They drew scenes from the Childhood inspired by apocryphal texts, or sketched curious symbolic figures such as the *Vierge à l'encensoir* in Gellone's *Sacramentaire* (eighth-century, Latin manuscript 12048, Bibliothèque Nationale, Paris). Mary stands erect holding a cross in her raised left hand and a thurible in her extended right hand. This rudimentary liturgical image is related to a line from the Arabic Apocryphal text *The Passing of Mary Written by John*: 'On Friday the Virgin Mary fell ill, and having taken up incense and censer, she prayed …'[11]

---

11. See W. Gruneisen, *Saint-Marie Antique*: 324, and the 'Gellone' entry in *Le Dictionnaire d'Archéologie chrétienne*, vol. VI, 1924: 777–81. However, the Comte de Bastard (*Rapport sur la crosse de Tiron*) disputes this identification and claims that the words *Sea Maria* beside the figure were added at a later date; *Le Bulletin du Comité de la langue, de l'histoire et des arts de la France*, vol. IV, 1857: 695.

But this type of subject is quite uncommon. Artists preferred the type of the Virgin in majesty, the 'Seat of Wisdom'; adhering to the Romano-Byzantine formula, they depicted her enthroned, cradling her blessed Son. This is how she appears in Luithard's *Psautier de Charles le Chauve* (842), and in the chapter headings of the *Sacramentaire* of Drogon, Bishop of Metz. The formula would also be used for the model of the Virgin on the gold plaque on the front of the altar erected by Hincmar in Rheims Cathedral. And it was certainly applied to the famous gilded Reliquary-Virgin which Etienne II, Bishop of Clermont, commissioned shortly after his cathedral was consecrated in 946 (see Fig. 10: 162). This innovative work was received with great astonishment and admiration. We cannot be sure that it is the prototype for the carved Romanesque Virgins, but it does seem to have stimulated the production of copies and replicas in neighbouring regions.

Our discussion of this rich period would not be complete without mention of the inscribed miniatures which honour the Virgin and acknowledge her prerogatives. An example from a ninth-century episcopal missal (Paris, Bibliothèque de l'Arsenal) asserts her power of intercession in four lines of golden uncials inscribed above a scene in which she beseeches the enthroned Christ. Its crude execution corroborates its date and the Latin inscription may be translated as:

> The golden star of the sea, the stem
> Of the royal flower is She, the Virgin Mary,
> Who here entreats her Son so that he may deign
> Through clemency to accord us the very precious
> Gifts of salvation, in reverence to his Mother.

While the concept and substance of these works are of interest in terms of the Marian cult, they are of scant artistic value. It would be some time before they became less crude, more skilfully executed, and before France, in a glorious awakening, donned a 'vestment of white churches', in the words of the chronicler Raul Glaber. Once this had happened, the proliferation of images of Our Lady would both reflect and inspire the increasingly refined techniques of miniaturists, fresco painters, glassmakers, and not least the Romanesque sculptors responsible for the revival of statuary.

Art always responds to upheavals that have profoundly shaken the human soul; its monuments are the traces of such upheavals. Many of these monuments survive on French soil, the legacy of a twelfth century that the voices of St Bernard and a hundred others had exhorted to honour the 'Haute Dame de Courtoisie'. This was the period during which Notre-Dame du Puy (see Fig. 22: 459), Notre-Dame du Port (Clermont) and Notre-Dame la Grande (Poitiers) were erected to her glory. Within a few years, the first essays in the new Gothic style, brilliantly successful, would erect incredibly high naves and towers to the Mother of God. A magnificent series of Notre-Dames ensued, including those in Paris (1163), Chartres (after the fire of 1196), Laon, Senlis, Soissons, Coutances and many other parts of the country. The cathedrals are testaments to the power of human creativity, but above all they reveal the deep source from which the gifts of poetry and encyclopaedic knowledge expressed in their stones burst forth: *Et lapides locuti sunt*. Charles Péguy, who was particularly sensitive to this aspect, included cathedrals in the Paradise he dreamed of painting;[12] it would accommodate objects as well as souls, or 'everything that is fully realised, the Notre-Dames, for example'.

Lack of space forbids our expanding on the cult of beauty which the twelfth and thirteenth centuries devoted to the Virgin. Its art aspired to celebrate her in language as magnificent as that of the liturgy. Its creations were fundamentally doctrinal; they placed the Mother of God at the centre of the Infinite, depicted in her the plenitude of the beautiful and the good; and made full use of the resources of symbolism to illustrate every aspect of her glory.

Like the catacomb artists, the twelfth-century sculptors of Burgundy and southern France were drawn to the mystery of the Epiphany. Some, like the stone-carver of Moissac, depicted the Virgin in an attitude of pride and tenderness. But the artists who worked on the cathedrals of Paris and Chartres detached her from the traditional group and presented her in a rather different but equally noble style at the centre of the tympanum, where she sits erect and holds her Son in her lap, both in a frontal composition. Enthroned in majesty, this Mother cannot smile for she is aware of being the Seat of Wisdom, and that the Child 'holds the world in his hand' – *mundum in pugillo continens*. This doctrinal idea is emphasized by the adoration of angels holding thuribles. The Virgin of the Chartres tympanum, carved around 1145 and replicated at Notre-Dame de Paris and Notre-Dame du Pré at Donzy (Nièvre), is itself wonderfully paralleled in Chartres in the limpid colours of *Notre-Dame de la Belle Verrière*.

Stained-glass windows and bas-reliefs sometimes bear references to the Virgin's extraordinary goodness. The abundant literature dedicated to the *Miracles de Notre Dame* was a rich source of inspiration. This vast repertoire of her favours was extremely popular. Anyone who consulted it would recognize something of his own physical and spiritual troubles and take comfort from the Intercessor's power to heal and from its profuse expressions of gratitude for the miracles she had wrought. These collections of legends were more persuasive than any theology. They form a popular commentary on St Bernard's doctrine of Mercy made Woman, the clemency of her who freely dispenses the treasures of the kingdom of God. There was a fashion for depicting the most famous of these miracles, that of the renegade Theophilus, which was carved on the portal of the inner door of Sainte-Marie (Souillac) and portrayed on windows in the cathedral of Le Mans and the church of Saint-Julien-du-Sault (Yonne).

In the latter half of the twelfth century, sculptors began to decorate tympana with representations of Mary's death and glorious assumption. At Senlis, between 1185 and 1191, the resurrection of the virginal body through the ministry of angels was carved with graceful, naturalistic grandeur. The sculptor responsible for the coronation scene above this lintel may have been following an iconographic style invented by Suger 50 years earlier. The same theme appears in a mosaic (*c*. 1140) in Santa Maria in Trastevere (Rome). As belief in the resurrection and enthronement of

---

12.   *Le Porche du Mystère de la Deuxième Vertu.*

Mary in Heaven became established, this imposing and poetic subject would be taken up by the painters of the thirteenth century and rendered in a triumphal style.

Under the chisels of the great anonymous artists of the century of St Louis, the twelfth-century image of the Majestic Virgin completely shed the last traces of the hieratic quality – the impersonal abstraction – of the icons. She would now be more approachable: she descends from the tympanum and adorns the piers of doorways, where she offers a closer view of her Child. She retains her crown and distinction, but smiles and radiates warmth. This innovative relocation appears to have originated in Burgundy, home of St Bernard, for the earliest example is carved on the portal of Moutier-Saint-Jean (Côte d'Or). These proud yet benign Virgins, whose features and charm were modelled on those of the most noble women in France, stand at the pinnacle of medieval art.

These regal conventions, which conveyed the unique gifts of the nature and grace of the Mother of God to the fullest extent, were followed by a shift in emphasis to the depiction of her human qualities, although she lost nothing of her dignity. The fourteenth century presents her curving gracefully over the infant and laughing as she amuses or caresses him. Sometimes she hesitates between gravity and delight, solemnity and relaxation, adoration and intimacy. When she smiles at Jesus, the smile is often the harbinger of tears. This sweet, happy Mother, who suddenly seems to foresee the suffering and crucifixion, is the first embodiment of the *Mater Dolorosa*, the *Pietà* of the fifteenth and sixteenth centuries.

The *Visitation* in Rheims cathedral is but one of the many expressive and wonderfully carved thirteenth-century examples which echo the ideas and feeling of classical sculpture. However, there are limits to our study. Summarizing everything that might be discussed in this chapter, Gillet wisely concludes that "French Christian sculpture was born and perfected in a long dialogue with the Virgin."

Gillet's observation also applies to French painting. During the twelfth century, the art of the fresco was revived in the service of Our Lady. It depicted her either in the mysterious vision of the Apocalypse, as at Saint-Savin, or with a mother's tender gesture, as at Montmorillon, where she kisses the Infant's hand. But it was primarily the delicate masterpieces of miniaturism which prepared the ground for the rise of great painting. From the fourteenth to the sixteenth centuries, the golden age of this minor art, the life of Mary unfolded in the sumptuous books of hours which established the reputations of the three Limburg brothers – Dutch artists working for the Duc de Berry – and three painters with the same forename: Jean Pucelle, Jean Fouquet and Jean Bourdichon. Kings, queens, members of the nobility and persons of great wealth commissioned them to depict themselves kneeling before Our Lady. A mere glance at these prayer books, illustrated with so many 'Virgins with donors' or 'Virgins with donors at prayer' (subjects also represented in sculpture, stained glass and tapestry), enables us to draw up an iconology of the kings and aristocracy of France and to trace the practice of their cult of Our Lady.

As the Middle Ages unfolded, the employment of Marian symbolism reached an extreme point. It was considered both correct and transcendent to present Mary as the 'mirror of the world', a common title for the compilations then in fashion. Despite the profusion of biblical symbols prefiguring the virtues and privileges of the Predestined Woman – the burning bush, Gideon's fleece, Aaron's rod, Ezekiel's gate, etc. – the most curious analogies were sought in nature and its wonders. Illustrated treatises such as herbals, lapidaries and bestiaries all contributed to this trend, while mythical texts inspired new types such as the Virgin and the Unicorn. However, the meaning of most of these mystical themes remained clear and traditional. It was apparent to all that the image of the seven doves converging on the Virgin[13] represented the plenitude of the gifts bestowed upon her by the Holy Spirit, and that the serpent or winged dragon beneath her feet recalled the prophecy in the Book of Genesis.

During the late fifteenth and early sixteenth centuries, the iconography of the immaculate conception, which had previously been restricted to a narrative image of the meeting of Joachim and Anne at the Golden Gate, acquired a mystical dimension. The employment of this legend was ambiguous, for it could lead to the mistaken interpretation that the Virgin had been conceived from her parents' chaste kiss. The new theme – *Tota pulchra es* (the words from the Song of Solomon usually inscribed on these compositions) – while itself not entirely satisfactory, was distinguished by its decorum and by an idealism that could be rendered visually intelligible by the use of sacred signs and symbols. The Virgin, placed at the centre of the composition, stands between earth and heaven, from where God contemplates her as a perfect realization of his most cherished thoughts. She is surrounded by symbols, sometimes arranged in a hierarchy, drawn from the Scriptures. As the accumulation of so many symbols could lead to confusion, some artists, including the great Flemish miniaturist who decorated the *Grimani Breviary* (c. 1475), adopted a landscape setting in order to achieve a less cumbersome and more natural distribution of the emblems: the rose garden, the walled garden, the sealed fountain, the well of living water, etc. This evocative treatment of the immaculate conception, represented countless times in sculpture and stained-glass windows, survived until the seventeenth century.

Meanwhile, the theme of Mary's freedom from all stain of original sin became an explicit dogma. In addition to visual metaphors, Doctors of the Church and defenders of the faith were depicted reading from texts, as in the 1521 canvas which Jan Bellegambe of Douai executed in accordance with the wishes of the dying Marguerite Pottier, who was recalled to God on the eve of her marriage.

We have barely touched upon a subject that would fill a whole volume. Marian symbolism would later be exaggerated by the Picardy school which, under the influence of the Puy de Palinod d'Amiens confraternity, indulged in a form of casuistry that verged on absurdity. Whereas cathedral art had infused dogma with beauty, the puns and witticisms of an increasingly decadent sixteenth-century art reduced the mystery to a matter of puzzle and enigma.

* * *

---

13.   A thirteenth-century stained-glass window in Chartres Cathedral shows only six doves, but the haloed Jesus at Mary's breast represents the seventh gift – Wisdom Incarnate.

In Italy, as in France, the springtime of art was marked by a development of the type of the Virgin. Moreover, the two countries borrowed styles and iconography from each other. But if we concentrate on the way this subject developed initially, we can see how the Italian Primitives shed the restraints of the past and thus produced work of great originality. Between the thirteenth and fifteenth centuries, there was hardly an artist whose surviving oeuvre does not include at least one Madonna which reveals his personal style. Most of these paintings are of interest only to art historians. Many of them are now preserved in museums, exposed to the sterile homage of the aesthete or the covetous gaze of a dealer. The hordes of visitors who stream indifferently past are blind to the fact that they are still imbued with the faith and devotion of past ages.

In Italy, therefore, the replacement of the Byzantine model of the Virgin in majesty by the figure of a mother totally absorbed with her child occurred even more rapidly than it did in France. It is fitting that the transformation occurred in Tuscany and Umbria, a region shaken to its foundations by the teaching of St Francis of Assisi.

The Madonnas of the trecento, whether Sienese or Florentine, whether painted by Duccio, Cimabue or earlier masters, gradually emerged from the rigid archaism which favoured the inclusion of angels supporting the throne, as in Cimabue's *Virgin Enthroned with Angels* (Louvre and the Rucellai chapel, Santa Maria Novella, Florence). The nose is aquiline, the mouth turned down and sad; the figure allows itself to lean forward slightly as it turns its head toward Jesus, but the half-closed eyes are full of sweetness. The kindly gaze, which seems to answer the supplicant's prayer, explains the enthusiasm with which these powerful yet benevolent Madonnas were initially received in churches and chapels. In 1310, Duccio's recently completed *Maestà*, executed for the 'devout of the city of Siena', was borne in triumph through the flag-bedecked streets that led from the painter's studio to the Duomo.

Two masters, one a Florentine and one a Sienese, evinced a greater individuality, although the Virgin retains something of her original gravity. Giotto (d. 1337) painted the walls of the Arena chapel in Padua with scenes from the life of Mary; they have those spiritual and pictorial qualities for which he created the model. Simone Martini (d. 1344), who worked in Avignon, anticipated Fra Angelico in the graceful and reserved expression of the Virgin of the Annunciation, while his slender angel crowned with a wreath of olive leaves (Florence, Uffizi) heralds the fresh, spring-like figures of Botticelli.

Many fourteenth-century works bring out Mary's maternal role and depict her as a nursing mother. The theme of *Maria Lactans*, which had already appeared in a mosaic (1145–53) on the façade of Santa Maria in Trastevere, dates back to sixth-century Egypt, (monastery of Baouit and Sakkara necropolis), and there are also seventh-century examples in Palestine. It was popular in Italian and French art, where its mystery is treated with the same sensitivity and respect as in the liturgy.

Florence finally gained ascendancy over Siena in its representations of the Madonna and the saints thanks to Fra Angelico (d. 1455), the most mystical interpreter of its spirit. Angelico has been taken to task for his miniaturist style, a certain disdain for realism and an ignorance of female anatomy; in short, for an excessively monastic conception of art. However, we must agree with Hourticq that 'the art of painting has never come closer to devotion', a quality which also earned him the approbation of the general public. His Annunciations and depictions of the Madonna and Child exude the tranquillity and incense of the cloisters; our prayers and praise seem to rise up to her, even without urging by an inscription such as the one in St Mark's:

> *Virginis intactae cum veneris ante figuram*
> *Praetereundo, cave ne sileatur Ave.*

Moreover, critics are unanimous in asserting the primacy of Angelico's ability to express the spiritual. While sterner judges have noted flaws in his technique, they ignore the fact that it raised devotional painting to new heights. His work is far removed from the impersonal Madonnas of the Sienese and Florentine primitives. With Cimabue – and even with Giotto – they were liberated, as if reluctantly, from the hieratic conventions of Byzantine art, whereas the ranks of angels surrounding the throne (an arrangement devised by the Luccan artist Berlinghieri) were still stubbornly portrayed as rigid sentries. Fra Angelico's creations were very different. He excelled at doubling the force of Mary's supreme grace by reflecting its intensity in the ecstatic appearance of her celestial guard. These cherubs with their flaming hair and speckled wings, clad in loose dalmatics, play musical instruments or carry baskets of lilies and roses, flowers they might have picked from the garden of the Fiesole monastery as the painter sat there in blissful contemplation. The artist-monk, angelic by name, conduct and technique, is unrivalled in depicting these pure and shining spirits, who seem to have offered him a brotherly invitation to join their winged dances around the Virgin Mother.

Müntz claims that 'Fra Angelico plays only a secondary role in the development of Italian painting, as he recalls the past rather than prepares the ground for the future',[14] but even so, we must at least acknowledge that his merit lies elsewhere – and on a higher plane. Angelico attracts us less through his doctrinal knowledge than through the depth of his feeling for his subject: his work possesses that spiritual grace which is the fruit of mystical experience. He expressed this himself in a famous statement that would later be repeated by Michelangelo: *Chi fa cose di Christo, con Christo deve star sempre* (he who makes the things of Christ must always be with Christ). His art also represents the pinnacle of medieval idealism. When he strives to depict Mary's very soul, no one can match him in raising to the highest level of beauty the holiness that only God fully comprehends.

This spiritual quality, the expression of faith through the most delicate nuances of feeling, is also evident in the work of a family of Florentine ceramicists, the Della Robbia, the originators of the glazed terracotta bas-relief. In particular, the white Virgins on a blue background created by Luca della Robbia (d. 1482), who drew inspiration from the Franciscan poet Jacopone da Todi,[15] manifest a diaphanous

---

14. *Florence et la Toscane*, Paris, 1901: 310.
15. The Bibliotheque Nationale (Paris) contains a manuscript by Jacopone da Todi. Its pages are still maculated with a glaze on which the marks of Luca's fingers can be detected. See Jean de Foville, *Les della Robbia*, Paris, n.d.: 11–12.

beauty beneath the glaze. Fra Angelico achieved the same smoothness by setting his Virgins against a gold background on which angels make music or strew flowers. Luca della Robbia also adorns his Madonnas with lavish garlands of flowers, fruits and leaves, but the floral motif probably came from da Todi's paean to the *Flower of Nazareth* 'born in the field of virginity in the season of flowers'. Luca's nephew Andrea (d. 1525) produced an impassioned treatment of the first moment of Mary's maternity; his Annunciation in the monastery at Alverno is unforgettably fresh and true to its subject. This is how Mary must have appeared 'when the Son of God most high vouchsafed to assume the burden of our clay'.[16]

* * *

In Flanders, where a more advanced technique of mixing colours[17] led to painting of an extraordinary brilliance and translucency, artists invested the Virgin with an intimate northern charm mediated through the idealized features of a living model from Bruges or Ghent. The transformation was further emphasized by the treatment of landscape and horizon: the figure has something of the calm of her surroundings; far from the sounds of the town with its belfries, she seems attentive to the silence of one of those peaceful Beguinages with its quite courtyards and stilled fountains.

The earliest masters of the Flemish school, the Van Eyck brothers and Hans Memlinc, set the standard for the depiction of the female type. Jan van Eyck – who signed his work with the statement 'Als ich can' ('As I can') – strove above all for the grace and ingenuousness of youth, and captured these qualities in faces distinguished by smooth, rounded brows, slightly slanting eyes, thin red-lipped mouths and tresses of wavy, blond hair. Memlinc (d. 1494) used one model in particular whose air of refinement made up for her lack of conventional beauty. He elongated her face and refined her hands with a skill comparable to that of Van Eyck, who painted the most beautiful women. Memlinc preferred sloping shoulders wrapped in a close-fitting cloak, the upper folds of which form a hood at the back. However, the solemnity of his figures is relieved by the harmony and delicacy of his colours, although these are often thinly applied. Rogier van der Weyden (d. 1464) was more concerned with pathos than with the attractions of his models, who were not always wisely chosen. These tall, dry, full-lipped bourgeois matrons, unappealing and even somewhat coarse, do nothing to flatter the Virgin. But Van der Weyden would occasionally redress the balance and endow Mary with charming features, as in the *Braque Triptych* (1457, Louvre), in which she is shown in head and shoulders facing the Redeemer, and may be reciting the *Magnificat*.

Let us examine what this Flemish female type, whether attractive or not, the

---

16. Dante, *Paradiso*, XXXII: 114.

17. Contrary to the opinion held since Vasari, Jan van Eyck did not invent oil painting, which was known before his time. It was by the judicious use of an agglutinate, 'the mixing of the whole egg, the yolk as well as the white, with a natural colour derived from a mineral source, and also by its skilful application, that Jan van Eyck and others after him were able radically to improve the technique'; Leo van Puyvelde, *Les Primitifs Flamands*, Paris, 1941: 18–20.

envelope of the spiritual, is trying to convey about God's Elect. The masters of Bruges emphasized the power of intercession that brought supplicants and their families to kneel before her throne. These people were wealthy enough to commission a painting, but were also pious enough to give such indulgence a noble motive: it was a means of ensuring that their prayer would endure. The theme inspired two of Van Eyck's masterpieces – the *Virgin of Chancellor Nicolas Rollin* (Louvre) and the *Madonna with Canon van der Paele* (Bruges, Musée Communal), one of those wonders of art through which ugliness is transfigured. Memlinc's supplicants include nuns (Bruges, Chasse de Sainte Ursule), Jacques Floreins and his family (Louvre) and Martin van Nieuwenhoven (Bruges, Hôpital Saint-Jean), who is portrayed in a celebrated diptych in head and shoulders facing the Virgin. These confidently executed commissions tell us that the Marian cult flourished in Flanders. But the Flemish masters raised the idea of the relative to the absolute and made the point that the Intercessor's protection was not confined to a single privileged class. Mercy for all is the essential attribute of her royalty. This is conveyed by Van Eyck's accentuation of the Virgin's regal character and power: her youthful air never detracts from her sovereign gravity. A Latin inscription (the provenance is uncertain, but it may have been written by the artist himself) above the figure of the Virgin on the altarpiece of the *Adoration of the Lamb* (1432, Ghent Cathedral) attests to his predilection for Mary as a figure of grandeur. The same text appears on the *Madonna with Canon van der Paele* (1436), and may be translated as:

> She is more brilliant than the sun and the constellations. Their light is as nothing compared with hers, for she is the radiance of Eternal Light, the spotless Mirror of Divine Majesty.

Van Eyck, in order to enhance the regal element, used the symbolism of the crown. The Virgin of the Ghent altarpiece wears a sumptuous gem-studded crown blooming with gilded lilies and pearl flowers. In the *Virgin of Chancellor Nicolas Rollin*, her brow is too delicate for the massive crown, which has to be supported above her head by two cherubs. But the message is clear in both paintings: the crown is not as heavy or as magnificent as the infinite virtues of the Mother of God, or the treasures she freely dispenses. The same symbolism and arrangement appear in Memlinc's *Marriage of Saint Catherine* (Bruges, Hôpital Saint-Jean), while Martin Schongauer adopted the coronation motif for his *Madonna of the Roses*.

Schongauer and other masters of the fifteenth-century Alsatian school popularized the theme of the *Madonna im Rosenhag*, or *Paradiesgarten*. The painters of the Cologne Madonnas were probably influenced by the paean addressed to Mary by the mystic Suso (d. 1366): *O vernalis Rosula*. Their images of the Virgin are of an unfading purity; they are flowers that have yielded their fruit while remaining flowers. The innocence of their childlike blue eyes conveys the calm acceptance of the fact of motherhood. There is scarcely a hint of melancholy in their serenity, a vague foreboding of the events that await the enchanting *Gottkind*. Their peaceful meditation in the shade of the fragrant flower garden is as yet undisturbed.

This atmosphere recalling the 'walled garden' of the Song of Solomon is diffused in the golden background to the *Madonna of the Rose Bower* by Stefan Lochner (d. 1451), a Swabian painter who settled in Cologne in 1430. A similar treatment by Martin Schöngauer (d. 1491) in the church of St Martin (Colmar) – in which the features of the Child are more graceful than those of the mother, whose nose is too long, her brow too high and her fingers too slender – is of particular interest given the rarity of his painted works. Dubbed the father of engraving, Schongauer taught Albrecht Dürer (d. 1528), whose art shows a wide variety of sources and influences. Born in southern Germany, the son of a Hungarian goldsmith and a Franconian mother, Dürer was captivated by Venice and produced many elaborate images of the Virgin that are interesting for their attributes. Taine found them more honest than those of Raphael, for whom his lack of sympathy often amounted to prejudice: 'Unlike Raphael, Dürer would not have dreamed of depicting his Madonnas unclothed. The most licentious hand would not dare disturb a single fold of their garments.'[18] Despite this testimony to their virtue, Dürer's Virgins remain what they are – well fed and very maternal bourgeois women. While in Venice, he completed his celebrated *Madonna of the Rose Garlands* (1506, Prague, Premontstratensian Monastery of Strahov. Is it still there?). But there we must leave it, for with Dürer we have reached the High Renaissance and the final abandonment of the naïve and youthful spirit of the Primitives.

BIBLIOGRAPHY

Beissel, S. (1895) *Fra Giovanni Angelico da Fiesole, Sein Leben und seine Worke*, Freiburg im Breisgau (French translation by J. Helbig in *La Revue de l'Art chrétienne*, 1897 and subsequent years).

Halm, M. (1904) 'Les figures symboliques de Marie à la fin du Moyen Age', in *Zeitschrift für Christliche Kunst*, fasc. 4, 6, 7.

Haug, H. (1938) *Martin Schöngauer et Hans Burgkmair. Etude sur une Vierge inconnue*, Strasbourg.

Hautecoeur, L. (1931) *Les Primitifs italiens*, Paris.

Lorenz (1904) *Madonnendarstellungen Dürer's*.

Mâle, Emile (1923) *L'Art religieux du XIIe siècle en France*, Paris.

Mâle, Emile (1906) *L'Art religieux du XIIIe siècle en France*, Paris.

Mâle, Emile (1910) *L'Art religieux de la fin du Moyen Age en France*, Paris.

Reau, L. (1910) *Les Primitifs allemands*, Paris.

Vloberg, Maurice (1930) *La Madone aux Roses*, Paris.

Vloberg, Maurice (1933) *La Vierge et L'Enfant dans l'Art français*, Grenoble.

Wackenroder, W. H. (n.d.) *Albrecht Durer's Marienbilder*, Nuremberg.

---

18. *Histoire de la Littérature Anglaise*, vol. II: 277. Taine could have applied the same criticism to his favourite artist, Leonardo da Vinci. One of the sketches from life for the celebrated *Saint Anne* (Louvre) displays a similar liberty.

4

THE VIRGIN MOTHER OF THE RENAISSANCE

By the Renaissance, the taste for compendiums of theology and mysticism had passed. This was not for want of talent or lack of faith, as dogmatic critics of the period have claimed. The development of religious themes was influenced by the new spirit of the times, and artists depicted them as they were described and celebrated by humanists. Scholarship went hand in hand with imagination, mythology and the Gospels became blended, and many quattrocento portrayals of the Annunciation could be summed up in the words of the poet Jacopo Sannazaro (1458–1530), whose love of antiquity had earned him the name of the 'Christian Virgil' of his day:

> Muses, I thus invoke, patrons of poets,
> Your caves, your streams and your secret forests;
> Daughters of the fields, cradle of divinity,
> You love innocence and virginity ...[19]

Since humanism had sprung from pagan roots, the image of the Virgin was not always represented with the necessary purity and splendour: her divinity diminished and her features were often coarsened. Botticelli (1444–1510) did not at first consider it indecent to portray her as if she were a cousin of his Venus or Pallas Athene, and imbued her with the same attitudes and languorous smiles. Savonarola fulminated against such impiety:

> You painters, you act badly. Your saints are nothing but portraits of this or that person drawn by foolish young people who then snigger: 'Look, this is Saint John! And this is Mary Magdalene!' It is an abominable contempt of God's work. And the most pure Mary, how do you deck her out! I tell you that she was dressed simply. But you clothe the Virgin of virgins in the garments of a courtesan.

Botticelli took this stinging criticism to heart and burned the objects of the preacher's wrath. His repentance was as profound as that of the *piagnoni* ('snivellers') artists who, under the influence of Savonarola, had destroyed their own profane works. His Madonna would now be serious, with a sadder smile: burdened by foreknowledge, her intimate communion with the Infant Jesus would express the sorrows of maternal love rather than its joys.

Botticelli, like most artists of the day, was profoundly religious. Many of his colleagues agreed with the words inscribed by Sodoma (d. 1549) on a tomb embellished with an Assumption in the Oratory of San Bernadino in Siena: *Si cor non*

---

19. *De Partu Virginis*, trans. Marquis de Valori, Paris, 1838: 119–21.

orat, in vanum lingua laborat. Perhaps 'brush' would have been more appropriate than 'tongue', but the point is clear. Similar inscriptions attest to the piety of other masters. Giovanni Bellini (d. 1516), whose Madonnas reflect the timeless gravity of the icons, followed the Byzantine mosaicists[20] and added in capitals a prayer or line of praise to his subject. The words *Ave, Virginei Flos intemerate pudoris* appear on the vault of the semi-cupola beneath which the Virgin is enthroned between Sts Job and Sebastian (Venice, Galleria dell'Accademia). Two angels dressed in short tunics appear to be providing flute and mandolin accompaniment to the petition addressed to his Madonna of 1488 (Venice, Santa Maria dei Frari): *Janua certa poli, duc mentem, dirige vitam, quae peragam commissa tuae sint omnia curae.*

These artists were probably carrying out commissions, but their work was inspired by their own devotional preoccupations. However, it is certain that they were no longer constructing syntheses of grandeur – their perspectives do not extend into the infinite. Although their frescoes still recounted the mysteries of the Virgin's life, they preferred the intimacy of Mother and Child, the joy and tenderness of the Holy Family. There were thousands of paintings, sculptures and engravings of this type. It is clear from the choice of subject that artists were now less inclined towards the model of the Virgin of Compassion. The earliest of Michelangelo's masterpieces on this theme, the magnificent *Pietà* (Rome, St Peter's), is endowed with a distinctly serene expression.

Did the artists of the fifteenth and sixteenth centuries treat a subject as profound and compassionate as the Mother and divine Bambino with all the care and veneration it demanded? We can only resort to the commonplace that Renaissance religious painting was marred by a naturalism that would eventually bring about its decline, and note that it is now fashionable to compare it unfavourably with the genius of the Middle Ages. The preference of the masters owed much more to art and sentiment than to religious fervour. They sacrificed concept to formal beauty, and restricted meaning to a kind of idyllic poem on motherhood. There is no reflection of divinity in the barely transfigured healthy and fecund Italian women whom they chose as models. In short, as the most sensitive critics have remarked, the type of the Virgin had lost her nobility to the point where she was rendered with greater fidelity to female beauty, an approach that almost always implies an appeal to the baser senses.

On this matter, therefore, sanctity was in conflict with art; strictly religious painting was confined to the abstract, to mysticism or to austere representation. This tendency has been defended. The Abbot Bremond pointedly remarked that the artist had no more right than the saint to create an angel. In other words, he should not resort to excessive spirituality to the detriment of observation and the study of physical beauty. The claim to portray the soul is the product of delusion or idleness, and often a combination of both weaknesses.[21]

---

20. At Murano, a fine twelfth-century mosaic depicting the Virgin with arms raised in the gesture of intercession has an inscription describing the role of the Co-Redeemer: *Quos Eva contrivit, pia Virgo Maria redemit. Hunc cuncti laudent qui Christi munere gaudent.*
21. 'Le Mysticisme dans l'art', in *Etudes*, 1901.

Some commentators went as far as the Abbot Broussolle, who observed: 'I would be content if the artist displayed a minimum of religion. I even believe that I would sacrifice something more if it led to an increase in the potency of art.'[22] This paradoxical statement is a striking denial of the facts: experience shows that a minimum of religion usually produces a minimum of religious art, and that art alone, however powerful, cannot render the essence of Christian Beauty. That is why the Council of Trent (1563) reacted to the excesses perpetrated in the name of art and banned the practice of endowing saints with 'provocative facial features'. However, error and misunderstanding will inevitably occur when the charm and splendour of forms are deliberately rejected in favour of an old-fashioned hieratic approach or an arbitrary taste for symbolism.

The case of Raphael above all provides an opportunity to explore the root of the argument between mystics and naturalists. Their respective positions are quite clear, and the panegyrics and indictments are equally passionate. Taine thought that Raphael's Madonnas were 'nothing more than placid Infants; their dormant souls have not known life'.[23] Gruyer, who possessed greater knowledge of Raphael's work and had subjected his religious painting to detailed analysis, took the opposite view: 'These Virgins are the most beautiful souls in the world in the most beautiful bodies that one could imagine.'[24]

Nobody would deny Gruyer's claim. Human grace attains its ideal in these paintings, in which Mary is depicted either alone with the Bambino, or in the company of the little Precursor and members of the Holy Family, or exalted in glory as the Virgin Mother with Jesus by her side. These Madonnas are not all perfect, but inequality is normal when there is progress. And Raphael's progression was as rapid as it was intense in a brief but dazzling career (1483–1520).

Having shed the religious mannerism of Perugino (d. 1523) – who did, however, produce some pure images of the Virgin, notably the *Madonna and Child Enthroned with St John the Baptist and St Sebastian* (Uffizi) and the *Madonna of the Nativity* (National Gallery), which could only spur him to do better – Raphael went on to confirm his own genius, first in Florence and later in Rome. Of the many Madonnas executed during these periods, we shall mention the most famous, giving their established or probable dates. The early Florentine *Madonna of the Grand Duke* (1505, Florence, Pitti), reveals Raphael's precocious mastery in all its freshness. The artist was 22 when he painted this essentially virginal figure, whose maternity is acknowledged only by the apple-cheeked Infant in her arms. This was followed by the *Tempi Madonna* (1505, Munich), the *Madonna of the Goldfinch* (1506, Uffizi), the *Madonna of Orléans* (1507, Chantilly), *La Belle Jardinière* (1507, Louvre) and the *Colonna Madonna* (1508, Berlin). Then came the Roman sequence, which would rarely be equalled thereafter: the *Alba Madonna* (1509, Leningrad, Hermitage), the *Veiled Virgin* (1510, Louvre), the *Madonna of Foligno* (1511, Vatican), the *Madonna of the Fish* (1513, Madrid, Prado), the *Madonna of the Candelabra* (London, National

---

22.   *La Jeunesse de Pérugin*: 496.
23.   *Voyage en Italie*, vol. I: 408.
24.   *Les Vierges de Raphaël*, vol. I, Introduction: viii.

Gallery), the popular *Madonna of the Chair* (1515, Pitti), the *Madonna della Tenda* (1516, Munich) and the *Madonna of St Sixtus* (1516, Dresden).

Berenson's view that 'no representation of the Virgin is without importance in the work of a master'[25] is corroborated in the case of Raphael, whose Madonnas constitute the most wonderful efflorescence of his gifts. Raphael followed the cycle of the mysteries of Mary, from the *Sposalizio* (Milan, Brero), Visitation and Compassion to the Assumption and Coronation (Vatican), but the most affecting vision remains that of the Virgin Mother as she fondly ministers to the Holy Infant born of her flesh. In the *Tempi Madonna* and the *Madonna of the Chair*, she passionately presses her cheek against his; in the *Madonna of Orléans* and the *Colonna Madonna,* she turns from the book she is reading and devotes her attention to the Bambino, who puts his tiny hand inside her bodice as he seeks the breast. Even when not working to commission, Raphael constantly returned to these subjects, which give scope for the fullest expression of his feminine sensibilities. He made numerous drawings, sometimes using young men as models, before transferring his observations to canvas.

Because they possess such charm, because their maternity sometimes verges on the idyllic, because they are so healthy and happy and so reminiscent of attractive Florentine or Roman women, Raphael's Madonnas have not met with universal approval. Huysmans, whose partisan myopia did not extend beyond the Middle Ages and its plagiarists, sounds more ridiculous than unjust when he speaks of 'the odious Raphael, his sickly-sweet matrons and purely human wet nurses'.[26] Let us leave aside these coarse remarks and consider the more subtle rebukes of other critics. 'These Madonnas', they suggest, 'do not inspire prayer, for they are ambiguous; they mix veneration of the Virgin with the cult of womanhood.'

There is an odd rancour here. In order to render the inimitable Virgin in the best possible way, is it always necessary to revert to arid and outdated formulas, to abstraction, to the conventions of suffering, to emaciated, disembodied figures? Are physical beauty and the supernatural therefore incompatible?

Raphael had no doubts on this matter; the question was settled. When he imbued his Madonnas with the purest reflections of the beauty he had glimpsed on a woman's face, devotion lost nothing and art gained a great deal, for he was intent on portraying the most blessed and perfect of women, the absolute Beauty celebrated by the Doctors of the Church, that which sent the saints into ecstasy. Moreover, if we accept the entirely orthodox view that something in Mary's motherhood links her to all human mothers, why should an artist not attempt to accentuate this link? Why should he not indulgently depict not only her physical perfection but also the joys, games and anxieties, the time of tenderness and intimacy Mary knew in Nazareth, that period in the life of the Holy Infant which was her only experience of happiness?

Moreover, Raphael offered abundant proof that his inspiration conformed with doctrine and never lost sight of the uniqueness of this Motherhood. He would often emphasize the truth of the incarnation through a visual expression of the adage *Filii*

---

25. 'Un Antiphonaire avec miniatures par Lippo Vanni', in *La Gazette des Beaux-Arts*, May 1924: 269.
26. Preface to Broussolle's *Pérugin*.

matrizant. There is a striking resemblance between the Bambino and his mother; when we look at one, we recognize the features of the other. Raphael doubtless recalled the words spoken by St Bernard as he directed Dante's gaze towards the Queen of Heaven: *Riguarda omai nella Faccia ch'a Cristo più si somiglia* ('Now to the face which most resembles Christ direct thine eyes').[27]

And is not the tenderness of the embrace between Mother and Child the most compelling representation of what theology has to teach us about the inseparability of Jesus and Mary?

Raphael's depiction of 'maternal love throughout time and space in its most pure and noble form' (Müntz) would alone have been sufficient to allow him to claim supremacy. But he gave us more, for his thought developed in parallel with his style. The *Madonna of St Sixtus* marks the pinnacle of this double achievement. None of his other glorious Virgins – the *Madonna of Sant'Antonio*, the *Madonna of the Baldacchino*, the *Madonna of Foligno* – appears so intensely conscious of being the Mother of the Son of God.[28]

For a great many people, whether they belong to an elite or are steeped in popular culture (the intuition of the latter group very often equals the erudition of doctrinaire critics), Raphael's fame and talent are associated first and foremost with his reputation as the painter of the Virgin Mother. He was the poet par excellence of this subject, which represents what is immortal in his oeuvre.

* * *

Two other artists made highly individual contributions to the subject of Mary's motherhood, although they could not equal Raphael's work.

Michelangelo (1475–1564) interpreted the subject with his unwavering faith, but also with his customary freedom and power of style and expression, as a painter, and even more so as a sculptor. The robustness and oddly cheerful posture of the Virgin in the *Holy Family* (Uffizi), a mother who is healthy and buxom rather than graceful, are somewhat disconcerting. On the other hand, his marble Madonnas rival the finest creations of antiquity and have a grave dignity. The *Virgin and Child* – a magnificent marble donated to Notre-Dame de Bruges by Jean Mouscron in 1514 – is every bit as proud as the mother of the Gracchi. The wonderful *Medici Madonna* (Florence, San Lorenzo) is almost severe, even before the joyous gift of life. Let us compare this nursing Virgin with the superhuman *Pietà* at St Peter's in Rome. Michelangelo was just 25 when he completed the *Medici Madonna* (1498–1500), and would not begin work on the *Pietà* until 1521. Despite this interval, it is only natural to assume that, given such complete mastery of form and profound knowledge of theology, there is a deliberate parallelism between the two works. The latter is a response to the former: the Precious Blood had been prepared by the virginal milk;

---

27. *Paradiso*, XXXII: 85–6.
28. No painting provides a better illustration of Raphael's gift for transfiguring his living model. We may confirm this by comparing the Dresden Madonna with the Veiled Woman in the Pitti gallery: the one is the ideal animation of the other.

the elongated body gasping in the Mother's lap had suckled her breast as a tiny baby, only to become a victim. Has art ever expressed more effectively the tragedy of the Mother's pain?

Nothing in the work of Leonardo da Vinci (1452–1519) suggests a connection of this kind between two works. There is no sense of foreboding in the *Benois* and *Litta* Madonnas (both in the Hermitage), nor in the *Madonna of the Rocks* (Louvre), which all show Mary playing with the Infant. In the *St Anne* (Louvre), she is like any young mother enjoying the company of her child. We are forced to wonder how Taine[29] could detect so much thought in these Madonnas, whose plucked brows and lashes conform to the fashion favoured by sixteenth-century Florentine beauties,[30] and rank them above those of Raphael. Nonetheless, the power of their smile, which is sometimes as enigmatic as that of *La Gioconda*, is hard to resist.

The Lombardy school, dominated by Leonardo, produced many such serenely untroubled Virgins. The stereotyped charm of the smile is so common that it is difficult to distinguish the style of Luini (d. *c.* 1547) from that of, say, Cesare da Sesto (d. 1527). However, an exception can be made for certain portrayals which retain the smile's original innocence while eschewing the conventionality and knowing accentuation practised by da Vinci and his disciples. I refer to the work of a late primitive, Ambrogio da Fossano (d. 1523 or 1535?), the Fra Angelico of Lombardy. Ambrogio conceived his delicate and ingenuous Virgins, of an astonishing simplicity, while executing a commission for the Carthusian convent at Pavia. The face is plump, the brow smooth and rounded; the eyes are half-closed, but their oblique gaze is as soft as a caress, while the thin mouth permits itself no more than a hint of happiness. Moreover, da Fossano, like Angelico and Botticelli, did not usually depict the Bambino unclothed, but dressed him in the charming little garment worn by well-behaved children of the day.

* * *

Da Fossano's soubriquet – il Borgognone (the Burgundian) – indicates some identification with France and French art. Indeed, his Madonnas are imbued with the sentiment and features typical of French Gothic representations of the Virgin. Moreover, the finest French Renaissance sculptors remained loyal to the traditions established between the twelfth and fourteenth centuries. Their faith was equally demanding and would countenance no self-indulgent exaggeration of the sacred theme.

The Loire school should be credited for facilitating a successful transition. Its master, Michel Colombe, belonged to the Middle Ages, but he found his place in the development of French art without altering or sacrificing dogma, and he created detailed and moving interpretations. His studio, later taken over by his pupil and collaborator Guillaume Regnault, was responsible for the magnificent *Olivet* and *Ecouen* marble Virgins now housed in the Louvre. In the same tradition, if not from

---

29. *Voyage en Italie*, vol. II: 408.
30. See A. Venturi, 'Vasari', in *La Gazette des Beaux-Arts*, 1924: 308.

the same studio (we can detect several details of regional style), there are three examples of the Virgin and Child in the Forez region: Saint-Galmier, l'Hôpital-sous-Rochefort and the Chira chapel at Saint-Marcel d'Urfe.

But the two outstanding masterpieces of the sixteenth century are Virgins of the Epiphany. The first, with her frank, luminous smile, is the crowning glory of the ambulatory in Chartres Cathedral (*c*. 1530). The second, equally refined, showing Mary's restrained reception of the tributes to her fertile virginity, is the jewel of Saint-Paterne, a simple country church in the Indre-et-Loire department. It is of painted terracotta, as are the anonymous but fine *Nursing Virgins* in the Château de La Carte (Indre-et-Loire) and in the École Saint-Aubin collection (Angers). We can, however, identify the great artist who sculpted the group in Notre-Dame-de-la-Couture (Le Mans): the painted eyes of Jesus and Mary meet in sweet communication in an emotionally intense and beautifully carved marble (*c*. 1570) by Gemain Pilon.

These sixteenth-century images of the Virgin – and many, many others – are poised between adoration and intimacy, between gravity and relaxation. Such fluctuations indicate the efforts French Renaissance sculptors made to capture the aspects of a unique maternal love, and testify to the spiritual bond they maintained with the artists of former times.

* * *

Having discussed the finest examples of Marian art, we are forced to mention the abuses perpetrated in its name. At a time when depictions of carnal beauty ('in animal dress', as Montaigne put it) were greatly admired, some artists ceased to portray the sacred theme as respectfully as before.

Bad taste in art was hardly unknown in the fifteenth century. We could cite many examples of so-called mysticism which were nothing more than pointless exercises. But the veil of symbolism gave way to a brazenly exaggerated naturalism. In France, Jean Fouquet carried indecency to the point of painting a Virgin with the features and décolleté of the courtesan Agnès Sorel (*c*. 1450, Antwerp, Musée des Beaux-Arts). Italian artists pursued a similar course and did not hesitate to sanctify their mistresses in this tawdry way. Some of the Virgins painted by Filippo Lippi (d. 1469) bear a distinct resemblance to Lucrezia Buti, a nun he had seduced. Was Raphael guilty of the same profanation? It has been claimed that La Fornarina posed for the *Madonna of the Chair*. Gruyer notes that 'even if La Fornarina was the model for this Madonna, they are still a world apart. Moreover, the faces are not alike. This image of the Virgin is purely impersonal.'[31]

Another provocative but perhaps less reprehensible practice, which continued until well after the Renaissance, involved flattering a queen, a lady of high standing or even a relative by depicting her as the Mother of God and adding a halo to her faithfully painted portrait. In 1646, Ribera chose the youngest and most cherished of his daughters as the model for a Virgin commissioned by a convent in Madrid. The

---

31. *Les Vierges de Raphaël*, vol. III: 242.

risks of such presumption were revealed when the girl was abducted to Naples by John of Austria, the illegitimate son of Philip IV. When the nuns heard the news, they had the Virgin's features altered by Claudio Coello (d. 1694).[32] After Queen Christina of Sweden converted to Catholicism, she had herself painted as a Madonna by Luca Giordano. In the painting by Van Dyck (d. 1641) in the National Gallery, the Virgin and Child before whom the Abbé Scaglia stands in prayer are reputed to be portraits of the Duchess of Arenberg and her son. Lastly, Antoine Talcourt depicted Mme de Montespan as the Virgin of the Annunciation, a canvas now preserved in the church of Beaufort (Maine-et-Loire).[33]

Leaving aside the unseemly practices mentioned above, we may find it easier to forgive François Lemoyne (d. 1737), whose filial piety led him to glorify his mother as the Virgin of the Assumption (1718). The canvas, in the church of Saint-Julien-de-Chapteuil (Haute-Loire), was to torment the respectable artist when he lost his mind. Lemoyne was convinced that he had committed an act of sacrilege, and that this usurpation was responsible for his mother's suffering in the flames of Purgatory.[34] While his obsession was doubtless a manifestation of his insanity, intact minds had their qualms of conscience to guide them. The Church forbade endowing the saints with the features of recognizable individuals who had no right to this canonical title. But it waxed especially indignant over the outrageous behaviour of artists who used creatures with unsavoury reputations as models for the inviolable Virgin. We are not deceived, of course, but they offend us as much as they dishonour themselves: by insulting the purest of the pure in this way, they demonstrate a lack of tact that stems from a lack of simple faith.[35]

BIBLIOGRAPHY

Braschi, Antonia Calderara (1914) *Ambrogio da Fossano, dit Bergognone, et les peintures primitifs de la Lombardie*, French trans. A. Pichon, Paris (see also *La Revue de l'Art ancien et moderne*, 1920: 26).

Fabre, A. (1920) 'Les Madones de Raphaël', in *Pages d'art Chrétien*, Paris: 425–40.

Grenier, A. (1907) 'Une Pietà inconnue de Michel-Ange à Palestrina', in *La Gazette des Beaux-Arts*, March.

Gruyer, G. (1869) *Les Vierges de Raphaël*, Paris.

Keppler, P. W. von (1885) 'Raffaels Madonnen', in *Historischpolitische Blätter*, vol. XCVI: 19–37, 81–102.

Steinmann, E. (May 1896, October 1897) 'Michel Ange et ses Madones', in *Zeitschrift für bildende Kunst*.

Vloberg, Maurice (1933) *La Vierge et l'Enfant dans l'art français*, Grenoble.

32. *La Gazette des Beaux-Arts*, 1888: 445.
33. J. Denais, 'Antoine Talcourt et Nicolas Lagoux', in *Réunion des Beaux-Arts des Départements*, vol. XIV, 1890: 259–60.
34. L. Giron, 'Une Assomption de François Lemoyne, 1718', in *Réunion des Beaux-Arts des Départements*, 1898: 645.
35. See Montalambert, *Du catholicisme et du vandalisme dans l'art*. See also n. 45: 533.

5

SEVENTEENTH CENTURY: DOGMATIC THEMES

The religious crisis of the sixteenth century gave rise to the violent Catholic reaction known as the Counter-Reformation. Art was to play its part in this struggle: it returned to dogma or, more precisely, to apologetics, and often illustrated controversies more persuasively than written texts, thus making them intelligible to all through the beauty of their depiction.

This upsurge of orthodoxy marshalled all the forces of the Church in a righteous and impassioned defence of the beliefs most threatened by Protestantism, particularly the doctrine of Mary's exemption from the stain of original sin. Art proclaimed this prerogative in a sequence of outstanding works. There had been many representations of the immaculate conception during the sixteenth century, but the artists of the following century would largely surmount the difficulties of transposing the mystery in an appropriately sensitive way.

In terms of its ambition and the scale of its achievements, Spain eclipsed the schools of Italy and other countries. The Iberian masters worked in a climate of exceptional fervour; the privilege of Mary's exemption was not simply a shared national belief, but a matter of honour for princes and subjects alike. Philip III had dedicated his realm to the Virgin of the Immaculate Conception in 1614. Devoted like all of Spain to this cult, El Greco (d. 1614), Ribera (d. 1622), Velásquez (d. 1660), Zurbarán (d. 1662) and especially Murillo (d. 1682) gave the object of devotion an aesthetic realization which remains unsurpassed.

We have already commented on how fifteenth-century France created a dogmatic image of the immaculate conception, the Virgin conceived in the thought and predilection of God, the theme indicated iconographically by words from the Song of Songs: *Tota pulchra es.* Although its meaning was rendered intelligible enough through the use of familiar signs and symbols, the figure was still too graphic and abstract. The Spanish masters emphasized the concept by using a new and expanded style that invested it with the purest aspects of female youth and beauty.

Biblical emblems were now no more than accessories, often reduced and sometimes omitted entirely. Art channelled its energy into the portrayal of the Virgin's expression and posture. She stands as if poised for flight or remains motionless, suspended in space and bathed in light. Given the difficulties inherent in representing so sublime a mystery, this was perhaps the best way of suggesting it.

There are fine images of the immaculate conception by Ribera (Salamanca), Zurbarán – a simple and pious representation with the picturesque addition of cherubs' heads emerging from the hem of Mary's robe (Budapest, Museum of Fine Arts) – and Velásquez, who sets his subject against a vast sky (Laurie Collection). However, these white-clad Virgins in a heaven dotted with symbols, with the crescent beneath their feet, still do not seem to be very far beyond the material world. If the immaculate conception is the first moment of the Virgin's existence, then a profound artistry is required to suggest that in this moment she belongs more to the mind of the Creator than to the earth.

No painter was more successful in expressing this aspect than Murillo, the master of visions, ecstasies and the miracles of the saints. He simplified the symbolism favoured by French artists, replacing it with a formal eloquence and a radiant splendour. His *Purisima* is still an idea, but she has assumed a body whose substance and beauty are as pure as the ethereal light that envelops her. Murillo drew the elements of this ideal figure from various sources. He was doubtless aware of St Theresa's loving description of the Virgin's resemblance to a *niña*, a little girl. And his contemporary Maria de Jésus, mother superior of the Franciscan convent of Agreda in Old Castille, had drawn a minutely detailed portrait of the Virgin in her celebrated *Mystica Ciudad de Dios*, a vision of her own supported by theological arguments. Pacheco, who had taught Murillo and had been influenced by these mystics, had laid down these guidelines in *El Arte de la Pintura*, published in Seville in 1649:

> Our Lady should be painted as a beautiful young girl, 12 or 13 years old, in the flower of her youth, with pretty but serious eyes, a perfect nose and mouth, pink cheeks and very fine, loose golden hair. In short, she should be as perfect as a brush wielded by a human hand can make her.

Murillo's visionary temperament and creative powers could happily ignore Pacheco's rather vague and dated commonplaces. No other artist could have expressed with greater intensity a belief that was so dear to Spain. His brush incarnates it in soft visions created from the magic and fluidity of warm, diaphanous colours. This is dazzling painting in which inspiration, driven by the desire to render the supernatural, soars to incredible heights. St Theresa of Avila liked to imagine the Virgin as an adolescent; Murillo contemplated her in her eternal youth. He visualized her in the fulfilment of her sublime predestination; she is the masterpiece as conceived by the Supreme Artist himself, pre-existing any spiritual and physical creation: *ab aeterno ordinata sum*. The Immaculate Virgin stands between heaven and earth, between God who created her and the mortal beings who joyfully await her coming. Hands crossed or arms extended, her large eyes already accustomed to the sweetness of ecstasy, she is less a flawlessly beautiful body than an infinitely fulfilled soul. She descends on streams of sunbeams and golden clouds. She has not yet touched our sphere, and pauses, her feet resting on the moon, in the limpid and mysterious immensity that seems to be her element, as if she is already acquainted with this world of evil and darkness, although contact with it cannot sully her.

Concentrating his genius on this figure, the only element which counted, Murillo ignored the customary garland of symbols and replaced it by groups of wide-awake or sleepy cherubs of a grace that mothers always dream of. Some critics, who may have lacked the insight to interpret these cherubs as anything other than affectionate children, and the Virgin as some delightful Andalusian Carmen, approved only of Murillo's religiosity. Whatever the case, the contemporary aesthetic view was distinctly unfavourable to the master.

The *Purisima* is usually dressed in a white tunic and a blue cloak which, like her long hair, streams behind her in the vastness of infinite space. Italian painters tended to depict the Virgin in blue and red, hence the claim that Murillo was the first to depict her in blue and white. Earlier examples undermine this assertion. Lorenzo Monaco, the Camaldule painter from Florence, dressed Mary in a white robe and blue veil in his fine *Coronation of the Virgin* (1413, Uffizi).

Murillo's vision was certainly popular; he was constantly asked to re-create it and complied with astonishing facility. He painted about 60 versions of the immaculate conception; 18 are better known and four or five of those are greatly admired. The two portrayals in the Prado, the *Aranjuez Conception* and the *Chasuble of St Idelfonso*, are said to be in his early style, as is the vast canvas (2.5 metres) executed for the Franciscans of Seville, which is distinguished more by its vigour than its charm, as it was intended to be viewed from below. There is another style, which includes the popular *Immaculate Conception* formerly in the Louvre, a less intense vision than the so-called Walpole *Immaculate Conception* (Leningrad), but perfect in gesture and expression. It is thought the sitter was one of the artist's daughters.

Opinions and tastes differ as to which *Purísima* is the finest. However, the two examples in the Prado attract the most support. According to the poet José Velardo, Murillo 'sought in the sky the miracle of light' that infuses the *Aranjuez Conception*. But perhaps the slender *Idelfonso* Virgin is the better work, if not for its technique, at least for its remarkable ingenuous charm.

It is hardly surprising that Murillo was able to reach such heights, given his enormous sympathy for the ragged poor and the gypsy boys he so often depicted as they enjoyed their meagre feasts. When genius is thus allied to compassion, it is capable of even greater sublimity. Furthermore, this exceptional artist also possessed the gifts of the poet and the mystic. In terms of expression, he even surpasses most bards and visionaries. While they can only find confused clichés to describe their relationship with the invisible, Murillo captures something of the ineffable in the ecstatic features of the Immaculate Virgin. He quickens our faith, encourages our prayers and raises us to a state of ecstatic contemplation of her who is the joy of God. As Mâle notes: 'Here the Virgin rises far above controversy, she appears to have entered a region in which she is safe from the attacks of innovators. She has the sublimity of an eternal ideal, and not even medieval art could conceive of anything higher.'[36]

The theme of the immaculate conception predominates in Murillo's prolific Marian oeuvre. It is far superior to his representations of the Virgin and Child, although these have such an appealing humanity. Angelico is the painter of Annunciations; Raphael is the poet of the delights and joys of the Virgin Mother; but no one penetrated the mystery of the *Purísima* with greater artistry than Murillo.

What other great master could replace any one of these three giants, who could be said to make up the triumvirate of Marian painting?

* * *

---

36.   *L'art religieux après le concile de Trente*: 48.

571

The Louvre contains another of Murillo's canvases exalting Mary's immaculacy. An exemplar of purity, she extends her arms to a group of lay people, perhaps students in a university such as Salamanca, where they swore an oath to defend the immaculate conception.[37] If this hypothesis is correct, the painting shows the Virgin helping her learned servitors to avenge the denials and insults of heresy.

Besides grappling with this particular heresy, painters offered a Catholic response to other controversies. On the matter of Mary's predestination, Luther had written: 'It cannot be doubted that Christ existed before the beginning of the world, but to say the same of the Virgin is a pure lie, a blasphemy against God.' Artists responded by depicting scenes in which the purported blasphemers were simply saints and scholars. Doctors of the Church and theologians convene as it were in council, determined to affirm the doctrine. Some hold forth while others meditate, their gaze turned to the figure they have gathered to defend, the glorious Virgin conceived before primordial chaos. This is how the subject is rendered by Ippolito Scarsella (Milan, Brera Museum), Domenichino (Hermitage), Carlo Maratta (Rome, Santa Maria del Popolo) and Dosso Dossi (*Dispute over the Immaculate Conception*, Dresden Museum).

Artists also depicted less controversial ideas. Like the theologians who guided them, they were interested in the way such arguments related to the mystery of the incarnation. They were thus confronted with the problem of the test of angels' faith. The antagonism between the Virgin Mother and Satan is said to have come before the beginning of time, when Mary was simply an idea in the Creator's mind. So that angels could earn their bliss through an act of faith, God showed them an intellectual vision of the Word Incarnate, an Infant in the arms of his Mother, and called upon them to adore him in the lesser, human form he was willing to assume. The angels were divided: some prostrated themselves in adoration, while others flaunted their contempt; Lucifer's cry of revolt was met with the archangel Michael's *Quis ut Deus?* This episode, from a story that had not been explicitly revealed, but inferred from a passage in the book of Revelation (12.3–4), was not confined to the realm of scholarship. Art took its inspiration from it, and there are notable representations of the theme in Santa Maria Aracoeli and St Peter's in Rome. Tintoretto (d. 1594) depicted it on a canvas now housed in the Dresden Museum: the arrogant spirits who refuse to pay tribute are given boars' heads and monstrous masks. It was also engraved, notably in the *Pium Oratorium* (1634) by de Briver, a Jesuit. Another image from this collection suggests that the Virgin oversees the allocation of the seats of glory left vacant by the rebel angels.

In the seventeenth century, the masters returned to the theme of the Virgin trampling the serpent or dragon in order to stress her triumph over the many creeping guises that sin could assume. This idea forms the sub-text to a painting by Francesco Vanni (d. 1609). It also reminds us that the fall heralds redemption: the Virgin Mother soars to the top of the Tree of Eden, crushing the head of the serpent

---

37. I have before me the sermon that Ponce de León preached at this university to celebrate its anniversary in 1619 – *del juramento que por server à la Virgen hizo de defender la pureza de su Côcepcion*, Salamanca, 1620.

coiled around the trunk; at its base the two victims of his lie take new hope from this vision (Louvre).[38] In the following century, Tiepolo (d. 1770) painted a magnificently defiant and confident Virgin settling accounts with Satan: proud, noble, calm and invincible, she barely bends her right leg to break the spine of the monster, who holds the apple of perdition between his jaws (Madrid, Prado).

To be sure, seventeenth-century religious art was not exclusively dedicated to the expression of central doctrines and beliefs, or even of mere ideas. But it is appropriate to stress its role as an auxiliary of the Counter-Reformation. Although not all of the works inspired by this movement were equally successful or could be described as masterpieces, they form an historico-doctrinal genre that at least is proof of a serious interest. Following in the footsteps of theologians and mystics, art reacted sharply to Protestant attacks and often exploited all aesthetic possibilities as it strove to assert the prerogatives of the Mother of God. It has thus left us with evidence of its devotion to the Marian cult and of its profoundly Catholic sensibilities.

Moreover, we can see how the persistence of medieval iconographic traditions and the idealist spirit that informed them went hand in hand with seventeenth-century religious commitment. Many artists were assiduous in taking the sacraments. They may be mocked for dipping their brushes in holy water before applying them to the canvas, but it cannot be denied that they often produced work of outstanding quality. The painter Juan de Juanes and the sculptor Montañes, each of whom created a *Purísima*, frequently confessed their sins and took communion. Bernini, Guercino, Carlo Dolci and the French artists Callot and Michel Serre attended morning Mass several times a week. They all knew that religious art is itself a sacrament which cannot be approached except with grace and sincerity.

Can we therefore claim that the discipline of faith led infallibly to the creation of masterpieces? The piety of Rubens (1577–1640) is well known, but is not always reflected in his canvases, even those depicting religious subjects. Despite his virtuosity and occasional bombast, and the aristocratic elegance of his pupil Van Dyke (1599–1641), neither artist achieved Marian painting of the same standard as Fra Angelico, Raphael or Murillo. But even if their contributions to the popular and charming genre of mother and child seem too carnal in the case of Rubens, or too courtly as in that of Van Dyke, we should not underestimate the quality of some of their compositions which show the Mother of God in a scene from the Gospels, history or legend.[39]

We need not linger on an equally illustrious name from the Northern schools. The Protestantism of Rembrandt (1606–74) made him little inclined to meet the

---

38.   This painting, and others based on the same subject, seems to be inspired by St Bernard's second homily on the *Super Missus est* (II, 3): 'Rejoice, Adam our father, and especially you, Eve our mother. You were our murderers before being our parents. You may both take consolation from your daughter, from such a daughter, but you above all, from whom our wretchedness stemmed, the shame of which has tainted all womankind.'

39.   For example, the wonderful canvas by Van Dyck in the Vienna museum, *The Vision of the Blessed Herman Joseph*, a thirteenth-century Premonstratensian monk from the Steinfeld monastery. The subject was painted for a Marian congregation in Antwerp, of which the artist was a member.

demands of the subject. His engravings of biblical themes were of variable quality, some brilliant, others cold. Neither his remarkable skill as an engraver nor the magic of chiaroscuro were sufficient to depict the mystery of the Virgin with the necessary emotion or splendour. The Dutch master lacked the characteristic serenity, sympathy and warmth of a cult repudiated by the Reformation.[40]

If the spirit of the old masters had been maintained, the eighteenth century – in France at least – would not have been the most barren period for Christian art. Religious art went into a complete decline in the era of the *philosophes* and the *libertines*. Fragonard may have painted a *Holy Family* and an *Education of the Virgin*, but the greater part of his oeuvre was secular. And of what value are the Nativity scenes Boucher executed in the same style as he applied to his amorous pastoral scenes? This frivolous and worldly century had lost the ability to understand or appreciate the sublime vision of the Queen of Heaven:

> ... such beauty smiling, that for joyousness
> no eye but sparkled in that blest array.[41]

BIBLIOGRAPHY

Lafond P. (1930) *Murillo*, Paris.
Mâle, Emile (1932) *L'Art religieux après le Concile de Trente*, Paris: 10 ff., 43–8.
Nicolay SJ, J. de (1932) 'Murillo, peintre de l'Immaculée Conception', in *Cahiers Notre Dame*, February: 85–94.
Tormo, Elias (1915) *La Immaculada y el Arte Español*, Madrid.
Vloberg, Maurice (1938) *La Vierge notre Médiatrice*, Grenoble.

6

TYPES AND FORMULAS FROM THE NINETEENTH CENTURY TO THE PRESENT

The flame of religious art, which had almost gone out during the eighteenth century, burned a little more brightly in the nineteenth. But what did this revival amount to? What links did it maintain with tradition? Did it add anything of value to what had gone before? Given the concentration on specific themes and the variety of treatments, an overview cannot easily provide answers to such questions. Further complications would ensue if we were to extend our enquiry to schools outside France. As we are less informed about the latter, we shall focus on the way the Virgin

---

40. As for Rembrandt's evangelical paintings, his *Presentation at the Temple* (1631, Hague Museum) is a masterly evocation, but there is a painful vulgarity to the *Holy Family* (Munich Museum), painted the same year.
41. Paradise, XXXI: 134–5. Our harsh criticism of eighteenth-century art is directed more at painting than at sculpture. The Virgins of Pigalle (d. 1785) in the Parisian churches of Saint-Sulpice and Saint-Eustache are noble and pure examples which deserve the candles and prayers offered to them just as much as venerated statues.

was represented in the successive and often conflicting techniques developed in France.

One reason for this rapid and protean evolution stemmed from the preoccupation with innovation, the desire to produce totally new forms by being in the vanguard at any cost, even to the point of outrageousness. However, as Baudelaire remarked, modernity is only half of art; it does not necessarily imply talent and there is no guarantee that audacity or the fruits of theory will incite admiration. The outcome may even be paradoxical, for under the guise of renewal, artists imitate and produce pastiche, a sure sign of decadence. Nineteenth-century tastes and fashions were dominated by an academicism that copied antiquity and a romanticism that replicated the conventions of the Middle Ages.

The English Pre-Raphaelites, who claimed to draw their inspiration from Botticelli and the quattrocento, tried to show that beauty was the most inviting route to virtue and happiness – an idea advocated by the followers of Ruskin in accordance with Platonic principles of morality.[42] This school employed a subtle symbolism in which supernatural truths underlay ambiguous appearances. The Pre-Raphaelite Virgins, seductive and often strange authentic Celtic or Anglo-Saxon studies in beauty, seem troubled by the joy whose secret they seek in the aura of the dream. They are worthy daughters of English romanticism, sisters of Ophelia and of the heroines of the ancient legends that were being revived at the time. Sometimes certain subjects exude an ambiguous religiosity. Dante-Gabriel Rossetti (d. 1882) painted a *Girlhood of Mary Virgin* and went on to depict an *Annunciation* (1850, National Gallery, London) that seems to suggest a young girl awakened in terror by the appearance in her bedroom of a gentleman from the beyond. Burnes-Jones (d. 1898), the most accomplished artist of this school and the painter of the nostalgic *Golden Staircase*, situates scenes from the childhood of Jesus in a dreamlike landscape in which the pensive, sad young Mother is surrounded by respectful angels.

Despite its taste for fantasy and convention, this English art is vibrant, human and sympathetic, unlike the output of the German school which took primitivism to extremes and claimed a kinship with Simone Martini and the masters of the trecento. Scorning convention and the live model, disdainful of Raphael and Michelangelo, whom they blamed for the decadence of religious art, Overbeck (d. 1869) and his disciples affected biblical hairstyles – hence the name 'Nazarenes' – and claimed to depict only souls. Flandrin subjected this systematic mysticism to a perceptive critique after a visit to Overbeck in 1833. At the time, Overbeck was working on his major project, the *Triumph of Religion in the Arts* (Frankfurt, Staedel Museum), a confused and grandiloquent allegory on a theme in itself truthful and noble: the Virgin Mother, the ideal source for Christian talents. 'I find the idea beautiful and well conceived,' wrote Flandrin, 'but in expressing it, Overbeck employs means he does not possess and simply has the outer appearance of the old masters ... Besides, he does not paint, he simply renders his ideas, writes them.'

Flandrin's criticism would have been even more relevant to another German

---

42. As we know, Plato considered the Stoics' *abstine et sustine* insufficient and suggested a different moral rule: weaken the fascination of evil by demonstrating the attraction of the good.

school which owed much to the Nazarenes. Its theory was purely cerebral and the elements of its style were borrowed from archaeological scholarship. The French artist Victor Orsel, a mystic to whom we shall return, dreamed of 'baptizing Greek art'. The Beuron School in the province of Hohenzollern, founded in 1870 by the Benedictine artist-monk Peter Lenz (Father Desiderius), took it upon itself to 'baptize' Assyrian and Egyptian art and selected Fra Angelico as the baptizer. Lenz and his colleagues attempted to introduce the spirit of Angelico into incredibly rigid and stylized images of Virgins set against a background of lotus flowers which nonetheless conformed to mathematical rules. Syncretism of this order amounts to abnegation: it clips talent's wings and paralyses it. However, it is less shocking when applied directly to cold stone, like the frescoes depicting the *Life of Mary* at the Emmaüs monastery in Prague.

Another form of archaism, the orientalism of Bida, Tissot, Joseph Aubert and William Hole, is more easily defensible. These artists returned Christ and his Mother to a Palestinian setting. However, the quest for historical accuracy seems to have been conducted at the expense of emotional expression, while the higher purposes of art seem to have been sacrificed to the erudite and painstaking reconstruction of places and customs.

Apart from the tendencies discussed above, what can be said of the mass of works which, to a greater or lesser degree, followed the dictates of tradition? Most were mediocre and displayed none of the power, revelation or compositional splendour achieved in earlier centuries. Ambition and inspiration were reduced to treatments ranging from the insipid Madonnas of Ingres to the comforting familiarity of Virgins engaged in domestic activities or surrounded by Sunday school children, so fashionable today. To be fair, we should note that the enfeebled state of religious art was a symptom of a more general decadence. 'Have there been more good Venuses than good Virgins, fewer secular platitudes than sacred platitudes, less boredom and bad painting on one side than the other?' asked Louis Gillet.[43]

We should also bear in mind the moral climate of the nineteenth century. Manifestations of the Virgin may have purified the air and brought forth springs to refresh the faith of many believers, but the masses were corrupted by materialism. Public opinion was under the sway of sceptics; the bourgeoisie railed with Renan just as the eighteenth-century aristocracy had sniggered alongside Voltaire. Art was not immune to such pressures. Although it could claim some success in aesthetic terms, from the spiritual point of view it either continued to stagnate or plumbed new depths. A few talents did manage to prevent themselves from sliding down the slope.

Following a revolution that had erased the past, art was markedly timid in returning to religious themes. Ingres (d. 1867) confessed that he disliked them. This is apparent in his academic treatment of the *Virgin of the Host*, from its technique and emotionless grace, a Raphael without a soul. Classicism shed this coldness in the hands of Victor Orsel (d. 1850), whose work is almost entirely Marian and decorates a chapel of Notre-Dame de Lorette in Paris. The painted area is not extensive, but it

---

43.   'L'Exposition de l'Art Chrétien au Pavillon de Marsan', in *La Revue Hebdomadaire*, 9 December 1911: 212.

is sufficient to reveal the artist's grasp of the subject and his decorative sense of symbolism. Orsel's Virgin has the nobility of line and canonical perfection typical of the Ingres school, but he adds the essential element, for his faith has taught him the grandeur of the Mother of God. We arrive at a better understanding of Ingres's gifts when we compare his *Voeu de Louis XIII* (Caen museum) with the *Voue de la Ville de Lyon* (Fourvière), Orsel's treatment of the same episode.

Orsel was not the only painter to be guided by higher principles. The observations of other great artists are worth quoting, for they indicate the source from which they drew their finest inspiration. Delacroix (d. 1863), whose oeuvre included an *Education of the Virgin*, a *Virgin of the Harvest* (Orcement Church), a *Virgin of the Sacred Heart* (Ajaccio Museum) and several *Pietàs*, wrote: 'God is within us. It is this presence which enables us to admire beauty, and to rejoice when we have done good things.' Gustave Moreau (d. 1898) came to share this view towards the end of his life. Once exclusively devoted to the cult and myths of Olympus, he buried them in his unfinished *Lyres Mortes*, which is adorned with the sign of life and truth, the cross of Christ.[44] The brilliant engraver Ferdinand Gaillard (d. 1887), whose burin sensitively represented Raphael's *Madonna d'Orleans*, also believed that 'faith inspires art and art is the servant of faith'.

While the impressionists were either strangers to this spirit, or remained indifferent to it, their work took nothing from its gravity and even less from its sense of the ideal. 'What this dazzling school lacks', wrote Gillet, referring to the spiritual realism of artists like Manet or Degas, 'is perhaps nothing so much as the moral and emotional qualities without which the finest observation will always be marked by dryness and worldly frivolity. Nothing has been more harmful to this school than its indifference to the highest interests in life.'[45]

Conversely, there is an appreciable receptivity to mystery and a perception of the invisible in the landscapes of Millet and Corot, both of whom died in 1875. How could Corot have failed to discover God in nature, since he always recognized him in poor people – although he neglected to seek him in the Church and the sacraments? 'My work', he declared, 'is finer and more successful when I have given. My brush expresses my joy in relieving poverty.'[46] As for Millet, his masterpiece is an example of Marian art. The Virgin is not depicted, but the *Angelus* (Louvre) is entirely constructed around her. No one was better equipped to portray the religious poetry of the daily tribute to Mary and assert its contribution to the spiritual life of the countryside than Millet, a poet in the biblical sense who brought to life the immensity of the fields where humanity labours in misery. The peasant and his wife interrupt their potato-picking at the first note of the distant bell; the triple peal takes flight in the light of the setting sun and soars across the vastness of sky and landscape like a benediction, an acknowledgement of the harsh toil completed, but above all a reminder of the one vital necessity.

---

44. See the article by Georges Desvallières, 'L'Evolution de la pensée chrétienne dans l'oeuvre de Gustave Moreau', in *La Vie Catholique*, 3 April 1926.
45. *La Revue Hebdomadaire*, 210–11.
46. V. Dumax and P. Ferrand, *Souvenirs de Notre-Dame des Victoires et du grand peintre Corot*, Paris, 1894: 14.

Luc-Olivier Merson (d. 1920) also evoked the enchantment and salutary power of the rural Angelus in a painting showing an encounter between the Virgin and a medieval peasant at a crossroads; he takes off his hat and says the 'Hail Mary'. There may be less profundity here, and more picturesque romanticism, but there is a similar attempt to match the visible with the invisible. Merson would have greater success in later works, finding aspects of truth that encouraged contemplation, as in the *Arrival of Mary and Joseph in Bethlehem*, and especially in his *Flight into Egypt*, in which the Virgin resting between the paws of the Sphinx is a lesson in perfect trust.

The *Flight into Egypt* could have been marred by an excess of orientalism; the pyramids, blurred by distance and darkness, offer a mere hint of it. However, Tissot and Hunter, both of whom illustrated lives of Christ, were concerned with re-creating the 'time of Jesus'. Joseph Aubert's murals for Notre-Dame des Champs (Paris) were also influenced by orientalism, although we may prefer his larger and more classical depiction of the ranks of the blessed advancing towards the Queen of Heaven (Notre-Dame de Besançon).

The combination of compassion and craftsmanship is perhaps found more frequently among sculptors than among painters. Statuary, it is true, was more strongly stimulated by church commissions. Fabish, who topped the bell tower of the old church in Fourvière with a Virgin, faithfully followed Bernadette's description when he carved the marble Apparition of Massabielle. Bonnassieux (d. 1892), was more successful, judging by the quality of his many Virgins in marble, stone or clay. The image which dominates the Corneille rock at Le Puy, the colossal *Notre-Dame de France*, cast from the cannons of Sebastopol, was the result of 'seven years of work, countless difficulties and problems of every kind'.

Sculptors populated sanctuaries, cloisters, valleys and high places with Madonnas in a variety of styles. These figures often commemorate battles or keep a vigil over wartime cemeteries, like the *Vierge à l'offrande* by Bourdelle (d. 1929) on a summit in the Vosges. Contemporary artists such as Henri Bouchard, Henri Charlier, Roger de Villiers, Charles Jacob and Jacques Martin have gone back to the sculptural theology of the Middle Ages and follow its example of direct carving.

Art, like faith, acknowledges no borders, and the union between the two extended to countries other than France. While Italy seemed exhausted after centuries of dedication to the creation of beauty, the Düsseldorf school, which was led by Ernest Deger (d. 1885) and attracted artists like Ittenbach (d. 1879) and the Müller brothers, excelled at investing the Virgin with an air of meditative innocence that sometimes gave way to a much more serious mien as the young Mother foresees the tragedy of Golgotha. In 1879, Karl Müller produced an exquisite and magnificent vision of the *Immaculate Conception* in which the Virgin appears against a vast sky, before the ages of the world and their accompanying perils. This Rhineland school rediscovered the sensitivity that had so distinguished the work of the Cologne primitives; its attachment to the achievements of its predecessors was more productive than the hieratic aesthetic developed by Father Desiderius and the artists of the Beuron School.

As our study has been confined to a rapid overview of the more outstanding examples of Marian art, it would seem appropriate to ignore other late-nineteenth-century contributions to the theme. In these works, as abundant as they were mediocre, sentimentality vies with ignorance. But we should say a little about them, if only to alert artists and public to their insincerity and rebarbative nature.

Although Dagnan Bouveret's Virgins are devoid of spirituality, they are still acceptable as peaceful evocations of the tenderness and gestures of the mother (*Madone à la treille*, Bartet Collection). However, Hébert, and especially Bouguereau, Dubufe and Elisabeth Sonrel, reduce the Madonna to a travesty; a worldly, flighty bourgeois woman; a tragic actress; a psychiatric patient afflicted with neurasthenia, the fashionable ailment of the day. Without being excessively harsh, we are entitled to ask what demon drives artists to profane the celestial model, to match it to their own pettiness of mind, to endow her with a misty, morbid charm which even the halo cannot imbue with sanctity. We approve, of course, of the fact that the Mother of Mercy descends to the level of our sad reality in order to relieve our troubles, but it is unacceptable that we imbue her with the very signs of our decline. When the artist reduces the Marian theme to a matter of whim, daring innovation or studio technique, he demonstrates that he is unworthy of approaching it.

Christianity cannot be used as a testing ground for the dissoluteness of art.[47] Anarchic experimentation must seek another outlet for its games, fantasies and vulgarity. Faith is a precondition of respect. Prayer is necessary to purify and illuminate, before anyone can paint, carve or shape an image of the Virgin in whom infinite beauty is embodied, a single ray or even a glimmer of which is a source of ecstasy for saints and shepherds alike. The work must be brought into being, as it were, through prayer and meditation, before its execution begins. An artist cannot produce with love if he does not first experience it. Before attempting any representation of God's Elect, logic and piety demand a study of her life and its mysteries, so that the mind conceives a truthful image of her beauty. The more constant the artist's inner dialogue with her, the less unfaithfully will he wish to portray her appearance (in fact, like her grandeur, inexpressible), and the greater will be his success.

At the beginning of the twentieth century, Maurice Denis (d. 1943) and Georges Desvallières, aware that the reputation of a Christian artist, like any glorious reputation, entails a burden of obligation, set themselves the task of recovery and renovation. Their goals were similar but their temperaments were very different. Denis preferred a conventional softness and limpidity and an intimate and sometimes liturgical setting, as in his Florentine Annunciations. He varied his style and some of his Madonnas have strong features and heavy bones, a humanization in which he was careful to maintain the proportions. Desvallières was more inclined towards austere contemplation: torment is accentuated in a profusion of streaks and hatching, where his vision is finally fixed in an incisive line, as in his watercolour illustrations for Jean

---

47. Unfortunately, there is always an opportunity to remind artists of a basic duty. In December 1947, the Congregation of the Holy Office ordered Mgr Constantini, President of the Pontifical Commission on Sacred Art in Italy, to send its directives to Italian bishops. The document condemns 'certain works of religious art which are truly blasphemous'. It also states: 'The Holy Church has never tolerated art that offends against the doctrine and dignity of the cult, and that is why the Supreme

Ravennes's fine *Marie de Jérusalem*.[48] However, he softened his style to such an extent that one of his Annunciations has a domestic charm. Desvillières and Denis are united here by the same high purpose: their observation and depiction of life are realistic, but they value that which is higher than life. They link the Virgin with the events of our daily existence, and assure us that her loving and helpful presence is available to each of us throughout our lives. Both painters go beyond the ephemeral, the contingent and the fashionable, and create lucid interpretations of the universal and essential bounty of the Mother of Christ and humankind.

While acknowledging that such art strives for deeper thought, and thus for a better representation, we would once again be misusing the word 'genius' if we were to apply it to the leading figures of this renewal. The Christological and Marian theme is so pre-eminent that its expression requires remarkable gifts. Despite some commendable efforts, the exceptional quality by which we recognize a 'masterpiece' has so far remained elusive.

There was a possibility that art could renew its inspiration through the new types and models suggested by the apparitions and great Marian devotions of the nineteenth century. But nothing of the sort occurred. Through indifference or inability, this precious source has merely resulted in mediocre images. And yet the superhuman event at Lourdes – its setting and phases, the ethereal light of the Apparition – should surely have tempted the brush of a Christian artist, someone whose internal vision was capable of approaching the object of Bernadette's ecstatic contemplation. Léon Bloy said that in expressing the mystery of the immaculate conception, 'every word should inspire fear'.[49] We could say the same, with greater reason, of the forms and colours used to paint her. But if the dogma as defined by Pius IX in 1854 (an event with which that of Lourdes in 1858 is connected and to which it mysteriously responds), if the sublimity of this dogma was inaccessible to art and has thus discouraged it, it is still possible to portray it by using the material and supernatural evidence provided by the Virgin herself when she appeared at Massabielle. Let us take the exquisite youth of the apparition as a single example. Bernadette insisted on describing the Lady as 'a little girl no taller than me'. What a resource for an artist in the shepherd girl's naïve sketch, provided that he contemplates this deliberate appearance of extreme youth and discovers a profound reason for it, like the one clearly expressed by Colette Yver: 'We believe that Bernadette saw the Virgin Mary as she was at the time of the Annunciation. Would it not be that age of divine motherhood that Heaven eternalised in her glorious person?'[50]

---

cont.

Sacred Congregation of the Holy Office, in the same way that it forbids books which attack the truths of faith, remains vigilant so that sacred art does not offend the dignity of the sacred liturgy and the Christian sensitivities of the faithful'; see *La Croix*, 31 December 1947.

48.   *La Vie de Marie* by Jean Ravennes is illustrated with 60 watercolours by George Desvallières and colour woodcuts by P. Gusman. The series was exhibited at the 1927 autumn Salon.

49.   *Vie de Mélanie, Bergère de la Salette*, Paris, 1919, Introduction.

50.   *L'humble sainte Bernadette*, Paris, 1934: 86.

The forms and themes of the apparition of the Virgin were more difficult to represent in sculpture, which has no recourse to the miracle of light and colour. Despite such limitations, modern sculptors have been often more effective than painters in idealizing the Madonnas they created for churches or donors. They have interpreted some symbolic or mystical aspect – the Cause of our Joy, Fisherman's Refuge, Queen of Peace – or highlighted her role in pilgrimages or as patron of a group – Our Lady of the Waves (sailors), Our Lady of the Fields, Our Lady of the Snows, Our Lady of the Wings (scouting movement), Our Lady of the Airwaves (broadcasting).

Many of these fine statues also reflected the devout intentions of the clients who commissioned them. Their sculptors knew they had to create an image which would win the hearts of the public and inspire prayer and thanksgiving. For the thousands of believers whose simplicity enabled them to easily crystallize visual forms, the features of the Virgin would be those the sculptor had given her. And there is no doubt that this statue, in wood, marble or bronze, would be taken as a channel for countless benefits, perhaps even miracles. To think such thoughts in order to produce finer work is the essence of Christian art.

Lastly, we should mention the novelty of missionary art, which adapts the iconography of our worship to the ancestral techniques of host countries, particularly those where major civilizations once flourished. There has been a proliferation of paintings, sculptures and coloured lithographs depicting the Virgin as Chinese, Japanese or Indonesian, although such images preserve the postures and attributes consecrated by Western tradition. This new form of syncretism has its partisans and its critics: the latter may respect its effectiveness in the ministry but point to its emphasis on the picturesque and the exotic, which casts doubt on its vitality and value as art. The complex problem of missionary art is best approached through Father Merveille's study of the psychological, religious and artistic difficulties involved in its application, particularly in China.[51]

* * *

Of all the works of the Supreme Artist, Mary is his eternal masterpiece; even after having brought her into temporal being, he will not reveal her secrets. It is therefore futile to hope for a painting worthy of the original. The situation is exacerbated by the fact that the language of painting and sculpture is even more deficient than written language. If poets, like the saints, admit that they cannot find adequate words

51.   E. Merveille SJ, 'Art Chrétien et art chinois', in *Rythmes du monde*, March 1947: 45–8. See also the article by L. Van den Bossche in *Le Bulletin des Missions*, Lophem, vol. XIV, 1935, fasc. 3: 'Possibilités chrétiennes de l'art nègre', and other observations by the same author in the same journal, vol. XVI, 1937: 60. See also *L'Art Sacré*, January 1938: 14–17; March–April 1938: 88–9.

52.   Dante confessed as much in *Paradiso*, XXXI: 136–8:

> *E s'io avessi in dir tanta divizia*
> *Quanta ad imaginar, non ordirei*
> *Lo minimo tentar di sua delizia.*

to praise her grandeur,[52] artists are still less well equipped to do so. They only have material means: their lines and colours are too humble to capture what cannot be grasped, to take some measure of the full perfection of the Mother of God.

However, some aspects of that plenitude are easier to communicate, those in which we can see humankind shining radiantly in this privileged creature. Her election does indeed raise her to the limits of divinity; it does indeed 'lack nothing if not truly to be God himself', as Péguy interpreted the thought of St Thomas. But she remains the Daughter of Adam, the Flower, honour and hope of fallen humanity. And Mary never loses sight of this; she constantly reveals herself as Dante celebrates her:

> Mercy, compassion, bounty without let,
> whate'er of good created being may boast,
> in thee, have all in thee, together met.[53]

Artists have preferred to concentrate on the tenderness and infinite sweetness of the Ideal Figure. They have been particularly drawn towards her because, as Claudel aptly put it, she has never shown anger towards humankind. She has enchanted men of genius in the past. In the future, she will summon the energy and inspiration of the best of those who choose a career in the noble craft.

Moreover, they will play a very effective part in the general renovation of art which, despite its sound and fury, continues to degenerate. In order to help it emerge from its banality, its mediocrity and the mire in which it finds itself, we can do no better than offer it the absolute Exemplar of beauty, the incomparable Woman, the Virgin Mother for whom God exhausted his grace and power in becoming her Son.

BIBLIOGRAPHY

Armagnac, L. (1897) *Bonnassieux, statuaire (1810–1892)*, Paris.
Arnaud d'Agnel, G. (1936) *L'art religieux moderne*, Grenoble.
Brillant, M. (1927) *L'Art chrétien en France au XXᵉ siècle*, Paris.
Brillant, M. (1945) *Portrait de Maurice Denis*, Paris.
Calvet, Mgr (1922) *Le Cortège de la Vierge. Peintures par J. Aubert à l'église N.-D. de Besançon*, Paris.
Calvet, Mgr (1926) *Un Artiste Chrétien, Joseph Aubert (1849–1924)*, Paris.
Dupré, H. (1921) *Un Italien d'Angleterre, le poète peintre Dante-Gabriel Rossetti*, Paris.
Emerson, E. (1930) 'The Madonna in East Christian Art', in *Asia*, New York.
Fabré, A. (1920) 'Overbeck et l'Ecole de Beuron', in *Pages d'Art chrétien*, Paris: 568–82.
Merveille, E. (1947) 'Art Chrétien et Art Chinois', in *Rythmes du monde*, March: 45–55.
Mourey, G. (n.d.) *D. G. Rossetti et les Préraphaelites anglais*, Paris.
Oeuvres diverses de Victor Orsel (1795–1850) (1852–78) edited and presented by A. Perin, Paris, 2 vols.
Schüller, Sepp (1937) *La Vierge Marie à travers les missions*, Paris.
Schüller, Sepp (1937) 'L'art Chrétien chinois du VIIIᵉ au XVᵉ siècle', in *Le Bulletin des Missions*, Lophem-lez-Bruges, vol. XVI: 101–13.

---

53. *Paradiso*, XXXIII: 19–21:

> *In te misericordia, in te pietate,*
> *In te magnificenza, in te s'aduna*
> *Quantunque in creatura è di bontate.*

Skrudlik, Dr M. (1929) 'Nouveaux modèles pour l'iconographie de la Sainte Vierge', in *Notre-Dame*, Sept–Oct: 709–12.

GENERAL BIBLIOGRAPHY

General Works and Studies of Marian Iconography

Ayala, Jean Interian de (Mercedaire order) (1730) *Pictor Christianus eruditus*, Madrid, I. IV: 'De Imaginibus Sacrae atque Inteme ratae Deiparae'.

Basquin, Dom A. (1912) *Les Peintres de Marie*, Brussels.

Bournand, F. (1896) *La Sainte Vierge dans les arts*, Paris, 15th edn, 1933.

Bourassé, J. J. (ed.) (1886) 'Iconographia Beatae Virginis Mariae', in *Summa Aurea*, vol. II, col. 915–68.

Cahier SJ, C. (1880) 'Iconographie de la Sainte Vierge', in *Les Etudes Religieuses*, 6th series, vol. V: 917–25.

Cecchelli, C. (1946–8) *Mater Christi*, Rome.

Chaine, L. (1906) 'L'Evolution de l'Art Marial pendant les XIVe et XVe siècles', in *Les Etudes*, 5–20 May, 5 June.

Clément, J. H. (1909) *La Représentation de la Madone à travers les âges*, Paris.

Duhr, J. (1946) 'Le Visage de Marie à travers les siècles dans l'art chrétien', in *La Nouvelle Revue Théologique*, Lessianum Museum, May–June: 282–304.

Ferrigni, M. (1912) *Madonne Fiorentine*, Milan.

Gruyer, F. A. (1869) *Les Vierges de Raphaël et l'iconographie de la Vierge*, Paris.

Hurll, E. (1898) *The Madonna in Art*, London.

Jeglot, C. (1924) *La Vierge dans l'Art*, Paris.

Jenner, Mrs. (1905) *Our Lady in Art*, London.

Laforge, E. (1864) *La Vierge Marie, type de l'Art Chrétien. Histoire, Monuments, Légendes*, Lyon.

Leblanc, M-L. (1939) *La Vierge à l'enfant chez les Primitifs néerlandais*, manuscript thesis presented to l'Ecole du Louvre, 10 July.

Leclercq, Dom H. (1932) 'Marie Mère de Dieu', in *Le Dictionnaire d'Archéologie chrétienne et de Liturgie*, vol. X, col. 1928–2043.

Lépicier, A. (1930 and subsequent years) 'L'Iconographie Mariale', draft index published in *Le Messager de la Très Sainte Vierge*.

Munoz, A. (1905) *Iconografia della Madonna. Studio delle rappresentazioni della Vergine nei monumenti artistici d'Oriente e d'Occidente*, Florence.

Nicodemi, G. (1924) *La Sainte Vierge: I. Des origins à la Renaissance; II. Dans la Renaissance et le Baroque*, Turin.

Rohault de Fleury, G. (1878) *La Sainte Vierge. Etudes archéologiques et iconographiques*, Paris.

Rossi, J. B. de (1863) *Immagine scelte della beata Vergine Maria tratte delle Catacombe Romane*, Rome.

Rothes, W. (1905) *Die Madonna in ihrer Verherrlichung durch die bildende Kunst aller Jahrhunderte*, Cologne, 2nd edn, 1909.

Taccone-Gallucci (1870) *La Vergine Madre e l'Arte christiane*, Naples.

Trens, C. (1946) *Iconografia de la Virgen*, Madrid.

Venturi, A. (1900) *La Madonna, Svolgimento artistico delle rappresentazioni della Vergine*, Milan, French translation, Paris, 1902.

Vloberg, Maurice (1933) *La Vierge et l'Enfant dans l'art français*, Grenoble.

Iconography of the Life and Mysteries of the Virgin

Broussolle, J. C. (1908) *De la Conception Immaculée à l'Annonciation Angélique*, Paris.

Broussolle, J. C. (1909) *De la Visitation à la Passion*, Paris.

Jeglot, C. (1927) *La Vie de la Vierge dans l'Art*, Paris.

On the Immaculate Conception

Crosnier, Abbé (1857) 'L'Immaculée Conception de Marie proclamée par les iconographes du moyen âge', in *Le Bulletin Monumental*, vol. XXIII: 57ff.

Hucher, E. (1855) 'L'Immaculée Conception figurée sur les monuments du moyen âge et de la Renaissance', in *Le Bulletin Monumental*, vol. XXI.

Leonard, P., 'L'Immaculée Comception dans l'art. Esquisse d'iconographie', in *Les Cahiers Notre-Dame*: 22ff.

Malou, Mgr (1856) *Iconographie de l'Immaculée Conception de la Très Sainte Vierge Marie, ou de la meilleure manière de représenter ce mystère*, Brussels. (The appendix to Pastor Coquerel's *Des beaux-arts en Italie au point de vue religieux*, Paris, 1857: 253–90, contains an almost entirely worthless critique of Malou's book. Coquerel's own work is little more than a diatribe against the Church of Rome.)

Maxe-Werly, L. (1903) *L'Iconographie de l'Immaculée Conception de la Sainte Vierge depuis le milieu du XVe siècle jusqu'à la fin du XVIe* , Moutiers. (See also *Les Notes d'Art et d'Archéologie*, September, October, November 1902.)

Nicolay, J. de (1932) 'Murillo, peintre de l'Immaculée Conception', in *Les Cahiers Notre-Dame*, February: 85–94.

Tormo, E. (1915) *La Immaculada y el Arte Español*, Madrid.

On the Annunciation

Lépicier, A. M. (1943) *L'Annonciation. Essai d'iconographie Mariale*, S.I.

Malègue, J. (1935) *De l'Annonciation à la Nativité*, Paris.

Pamprolini (1939) *L'Annunziata nei pittori primitive italiani*, Milan.

On the Compassion

Lépicier, A. M. (1948) *Mater Dolorosa. Notes d'histoire, de liturgie et d'iconographie sur le culte de Notre-Dame des Douleurs*, Spa.

Marini, Cardinal N. (1924) *L'Esthétique du Stabat*, French trans. J. C. Brousolle, Paris.

On the Death and Assumption of Mary

Duhr, J. (1946) 'L'Evolution iconographique de l'Assomption', in *La Nouvelle Revue Théologique*, October: 671–82.

Duhr's bibliography may be enlarged by the following works:

Dumont, A. (1870–71) 'Sur quelques représentations de la mort de la Vierge', in *La Revue Archéologique*: 337–44. Reprinted in *Les Mélanges d'Archéologie et d'Epigraphie*, 1892: 652ff.

Ffoulkes, C. J. (1898) 'Le Couronnement de la Sainte Vierge. Notes sur le développement de ce sujet et sur diverses manières de la représenter, particulièrement en Italie', in *La Revue de l'Art Chrétien*: 42–50, 117–27.

Kubler, W. (1906) *Die Legende vom Tode und der Himmelfahrt Maria*, Wurzburg.

Sinding, O. (1903) *Mariae Tod und Himmelfahrt*, Christiana.

Vratislaw-Mitrovic, L. and Okunev, N. (1931) 'La Dormition de la Sainte Vierge dans la peinture médiévale orthodoxe', in *Byzantinoslavica*, vol. III (1), Prague: 134–73.

Monographs and Special Themes

Beissel, S. (1909) *Geschichte der Verehrung Marias in Deutschland während des Mittelalters in Deutschland*, Freiburg im Breisgau.

Beissel, S. (1910) *Geschichte der Verehrung Marias in 16 und 17 Jahrhundert*, Freiburg im Breisgau.

Bertaud, E. (1947) *Etudes de symbolisme dans le culte de la Vierge*, Paris (on the image of Notre-Dame de Perpétuel Secours).

Durand-Lefevre, M. (1937) *Etude sur l'origine des Vierges Noires*, Paris.

Fabre, A. (1920) 'La Vierge Mère', in *Pages d'Art Chrétien*, Paris: 316–35.

Hoppenot, J. (1904) *La Sainte Vierge dans la tradition, dans l'art, dans l'âme des saints et dans notre vie*, Lille.

Jameson, Mrs. (1852) *The Legend of the Madonna as Represented in the Fine Arts*, London.

Joly, E. (1932) *Theotokos. La Mère de Dieu dans la pensée, l'art et la vie*, Paris.

Perdrizet, P. (1908) *La Vierge de Miséricorde. Etude d'un theme iconographique*, Paris.

Porée, Canon, *L'Iconographie de la Sainte Vierge, particulièrement dans la statuaire française du XIIe au XVIe siècle*, Evreux.

Sarrete, J. (1913) *Vierges ouvertes, Vierges ouvrantes et la Vierge de Palau-del-Vidre*, S.I..

Vloberg, Maurice (1938) *La Vierge notre Médiatrice*, Grenoble.

Albums

Borchgrave d'Altena, J. de (1943) *Madones anciennes conserves en Belgique, 1025–1425*, Brussels, 32 plates.

Borchgrave d'Altena, J. de (1939) *Marie, Mère de Dieu*, Paris, 128 plates, introductory note by H. Ghéon.

Perez y Pando, J. (1930) *Iconografia Mariana Española*, Vergara, 206 representations of sculpture.

Podlaha, Dr A. (1904) *Sochy a Skulptury Marianske u Gechach odd ob nejstarsich as do stoleti XVI* [*Marian Statuary and Sculpture in Bohemia from Antiquity to the 16th Century*], Prague, 18 plates.

Podlaha, Dr A. (1904) *Obrazy Marianske u Gechach ze Stoleti XIV-XVI* [*Paintings of the Virgin in Bohemia from the 14th to the 16th Centuries*], Prague, 20 plates.

Vierges Romanes d'Auvergne, Le Point, no. 25, June 1943, Lanzac, by Souillac, Lot, 58 representations.

Wagner, F. (1847) *Nurnberger Bildhanerwerke des Mittelalters. I, Marienbilder*, Nuremburg, 9 engraved plates.

INDEX

Page numbers in *italic* refer to illustrations.

Adam of St Victor   168
Adams, Henry   150–1
Adams, John   44
Adams, K. Van Esveld   526
Adelphia sarcophagus   119–20
Adoration of the Magi   120–2, *124*, 125–6, 161, 163–4, 542
Ælfric   194
Agreda   379
Akita   441
Al-Saḥḥâr, Abd Al-Ḥamīd J.   496–7
Alan de la Roche (Alanus de Rupe)   390
Alan of Lille   198, 199
Alcuin of York   169
Alexander of Alexandria   56, 57
Alexander VII   377
Alexandrian School   76; Alexandrian Christology   53–4
Allchin, A. M.   331, 332, 336
Amadeus of Lausanne   183
Ambrogio da Fossano   566
Ambrose   57, 79, 91–2, 121; and Mary as model of virginity   98–9, 122; and Mary as type of the Church   93–5, 122–3, 159; reliquary casket   122–3
Ambrosio de Montesino   371
Amort, Eusebius   380
Andrewes, Lancelot   325–6, 330
Angelico, Fra Giovanni   393, 556–7, 566
Anglican views of Mary: the 39 Articles   322; ARCIC I   337–8, 347, 348; ARCIC II   355–8; *Book of Homilies*   242, 322–4; the Caroline divines and the non-jurors   324–30; the English reformers   238–54, 318–24; influence of the continental reformers   315–18; Litany   254, 320, 321; overview of Mary's place in Anglican tradition   314–15; the Oxford Movement   331–3; prayer books   253–4, 321–2; the Ten Articles (of 1536)   320; in the twentieth century   333–8

Anne, mother of Mary: conception of Mary *see* conception of Mary; Immaculate Conception; cult of St Anne   267; embrace of Joachim at the Golden Gate   47, 208, 221–2, 227, 555; scriptural silence about   374
Annunciation: film treatment   534–5; frescos   118–19; Lukan account   3, 118; Mary's free response to   158–9, 258–61, 289–90; mosaic tableau in St Maria Maggiore   123, *124*; in *Protevangelium of James*   48–9, 118; Qur'ânic account   482; Rûmî's treatment   488–90; as subject of fascination in the arts   518, 523–4
Anselm of Canterbury   182, 194, 209, 551; Anselmian doctrine of original sin   209, 213–14, 219–20; influence on Suárez   260
anthropology: human glorification   273–5; of the Immaculate Conception   214–21, 230
Antiochene theology: Formulary of Union   60–1; opposition to title *Theotokos*   53–4
Aparecida, Nossa Senhora   228, 461
Apocalypse (Book of Revelation)   224–5, 252; in von Balthasar's thought   300, 309
Apocalypse of Paul   135
apocrypha: absorption of narratives into mainstream Christian thought   188–94; Dormition apocrypha   130, 135, 137–8; Gospel of James *see Protevangelium of James*; Six Books apocryphon   136–8; as source of cult of the Virgin in Middle Ages   188–94; texts in which Mary appears   39–44; *see also individual books*
Apolito, Paolo   408–9, 443–5
Apollinarius   57
apparitions of Mary: to Bernadette Soubirous (Lourdes)   229, 398, 426–7, 429, 436–8, 446, 580; in early Church   131–2,

apparitions of Mary:, *cont.*
136–7, 425; and the evolution of visionary cults 441–6; at Fatima 230, 398, 420–3, 427–8, 440–1, 454; at Guadalupe *see* Guadalupe, Our Lady of; historical overview 424–9; to Labouré 228, 420, 426; at Le Puy 425, 458–61; nature of visions in Catholic theology 429–36; political and communal dimensions of 446–55; political and trans-national dimensions of 398, 440; and promotion of the rosary 391; at Rome 425; to Sor María de Jesús 379–80, 569; visionary experience on the Web 408–9; visionary image of 436–41

Arabic Infancy Gospel 43–4
Arcand, Denys 533
Archconfraternity of the Holy and Immaculate Heart of Mary 420
ARCIC I 337–8, 347, 348
ARCIC II 355–8
Arianism 78
Aristotle 260–1, 269, 368, 418
Arius 78
Ark of the Covenant 2–3, 285, 380
Armenian Lectionary 139, 140, 141
Arndt, Ernst Moritz 527
art: Byzantine 112, 543–4, 549, 561; catacomb paintings 110–22, 152, 540–5; cathedral art *see* cathedral art; early representations of Mary in churches 122–7; films 532–5; frescos of Mary 110n15, 111, 114–22, 541–54, 562, 575; iconoclastic dispute 151–4 *see also* iconoclasm; iconography *see* iconography; *l'art Saint-Sulpice* and *l'art sacré* 407–8; legendary portraits of Mary 106–10; literature *see* literature; *Mappa Mundi* 149, *150*; Mary as a mult-vocal symbol 397, 400–3; medieval ear imagery for Eve and Mary 89; and physical appearance of Mary 368–9; the Pietà 187, 397, *539*, 554, 562 *see also* Mater Dolorosa; Roman 546–50; statues *see* statues; Western art of the high Middle Ages 154–6; Western 'low' theory of sacred art 155; *see also* images of Mary
asceticism 78
Asch, Sholem 522
Assumption of Mary: celebration developed from Memory of Mary feast 141; earliest tradition 70–1, 134; English reformers' views 251; human glorification and 273–5, 286; in Latin *Transitus*

texts 192–4; *Munificentissimus Deus* 281–3; in patristic theology 79; Rahner on Mariology and 292–9; Suárez on 264; *see also* Dormition of Mary
Athanasius of Alexandria 57, 77, 84, 88–9, 100
Atticus 58–9, 138–9
Attis 112–13
Aubert, Joseph 575, 577
Auden, W. H. 523–4
Augsburgh Confession 316
Augustine of Hippo 79–80, 92–3, 94, 99–100, 430; doctrine of the Immaculate Conception 208–9, 249; influence on Suárez 264
Ave Maria 241, 319, 320; Keble's hymn 331

Bailey, Gauvin 371
Balasuriya, Tissa 36
Baldovin, John 140
Bale, John 252
Ball, Edward 353
Balthasar, Hans Urs von *see* von Balthasar, Hans Urs
Barker, Margaret 2
Basel, Council of 207, 211, 279
Basil of Caesarea ('the Great') 79, 97–8, 100–1, 398
Bautista, Ines 416
Bavaria sancta et pia 366, *367*
Beatrice de Silva 227
Beattie, Tina 37
Beauraing 430, 443, 451
Beauvoir, Simone de 522
Becon, Thomas 249
Behar, Ruth 403
Behr-Sigel, E. 347
Beinert, Wolfgang 286
Bellagambe, Jan 555
Bellarmine, Robert 218
Bellini, Giovanni 561
Bembo, Pietro 241–2
Benedict XIV 381
Benson, E. W. 332
Berchmans, John 219
Bernadette, St *see* Soubirous, Bernadette
Bernann, Roland 388–9
Bernanos, George 527
Bernard of Clairvaux 159, 178, 179, 181, 190; on Mary's virginity and humility 259; rejection of Immaculate Conception 194, 210; *Sermons on the Song of Songs* 198; veneration of Mary as

Bernard of Clairvaux, *cont.*
  the grieving mother 182, 183; and the
  Virgin's milk 388–9
Bernardino of Busti 187
Bernini, Gian L. 573
Bertram of Minden: icon of the Virgin's
  conception *222*
Bérulle, Pierre de 416
Betania 441
Beuron School of art 575
Bible, New Testament *see* New Testament
biblical criticism 14
Bida 575
Biermann, Wolf 524
Black Death 186
Black Madonnas: character and origins
  of 461–3; Our Lady of Le Puy
  458–61; symbolism of blackness
  463–74; 'The Black Madonna' by
  Spark 528
Blackbourn, David 438–9, 447–9
Blanche of Castile 180, 181
Bloy, Léon 527, 579–80
Bonaventura 241
Bonne Mort, Notre-Dame de 470
Bonvin, Jacques 468–9
Book of Common Prayer 253–4, 321—2
Borcht, Pieter van der 372
Borgeaud, Philippe 5
Borgia, Francis 391
Bosc, Jean 354
Bosio, Antonio 114
Boss, Sarah 358, 522
Botticelli, Sandro 561
Bouchard, Henri 578
Bouguereau, Adolphe W. 578
Bourdelle, Émile A. 578
Bourdichon, Jean 554
Bouveret, Dagnan 578
Bouvier, Bertrand 525
Boy-Ed, Ilse 525
Brahm, John 532
Brecht, Berthold 525
Bremond, Abbot 562
Brenk, Beat 125–6
Brentano, Clemens 527
Bridcut, William 342n10, 343n11, 345
Bridget of Sweden 186, 215–16, 218, 220
Brown, Dan: *Da Vinci Code* 111
Brown, Raymond E. 16–17, 285; *et
  al.* 18, 19–20
Buby SM, Bertrand 82, 496–7
Bucer, Martin 315
Bullinger, Heinrich 252

Burmeister, Elisabeth 522
Burne-Jones, Sir Edward C. 575
Butler, David 343
Byron, Lord 526

Callot, Jacques 573
Calvin, John 317
Calvinism 315–16
Cameron, Averil 106
Cana wedding feast 30–1, 63, 66–7
Canisius, Peter 364–5, 373–4
canon criticism 15
Cappadocian Fathers 79, 97–8; *see also* Basil
  of Caesarea; Gregory of Nazianzus (the
  Theologian); Gregory of Nyssa
Cappanari, Stephen 470
Carroll, Michael P. 445–6
Cartwright, Thomas 316
Casey, Mary 443
Cassagnes-Brouquet, Sophie 463
Caswall, Edward 504, 505, 506–8, 514–16
catacomb paintings 110–22, 152, 540–5,
  548
cathedral art 126n59, 180–1, 392, 550,
  552–5, 566
Catta, Etienne 170
Chadwick, Henry 76
Chalcedon, Council of 54, 65, 80, 263
Charlemagne 155
Charles the Bald 1–2, 157
Charlier, Henri 578
Chartres Cathedral 180, 181, 399, 552,
  553, 566
Chastel, Guy 528
chastity 78; *see also* virginity of Mary
Chateaubriand, François-René de 526
Chesterton, G. K. 525
Christian, William A. 369, 425, 427–8,
  449–51, 452, 454–5
Christology 51–5; Arianism 78; of
  Council of Chalcedon 54, 65, 263; of
  Council of Ephesus 60–3, 78; Nestorian
  controversy 54, 57–8, 61, 78
Chrysippus of Jerusalem 140
Chrysologus, Peter 95–6
Church: Anglican views of Mary *see* Anglican
  views of Mary; Calendar 253, 322,
  336–7; ecumenism *see* ecumenism;
  eschatological 309–10; liturgy *see*
  liturgy; Mary and the tradition of
  celibacy 190–2; Mary/Church as Bride
  of Christ 198–9, 265, 267; Mary, Eve
  and the Church 93–5; Mary's
  identification with 4–5, 19, 93–5,

Church, *cont.*
122–3, 159, 179–81, 300–12; Mary's
status in early Church 18–23, 27–8;
Modernist models 304; nuptial
personality of the Church 306–7; post-
Vatican II understanding of Mary 19,
285–312; von Balthasar's ecclesial
Mariology 300–12
Cicero, Our Miraculous Lady of 399–400
Cid, Miguel 375
Cimabue, Giovanni 556, 557
cinema 532–5
Claudel, Paul 523, 524
Clayton, Mary 189
Clement of Alexandria 4, 21, 75–6, 77, 96
Cleopas 23
Clopas 22–3
co-redemption 534; Mary as Co-
Redemptrix 290, 332, 334, 359, 380;
Pusey's attack on doctrine of Mary as Co-
Redemptrix 332
Coathalem, H. 93
Codina, Victor 525
Coello, Claudio 567
Coemeterium Maius fresco 115, *116*
Coleridge, Mark 32–3
Coleridge, Mary 519
Colombe, Michel 566
communism, opposition to 421, 427, 428,
440, 532
conception of Mary: immaculate *see*
Immaculate Conception; in *Protevangelium
of James* 47–8
conception, theories of 260–1
Concord, Formula of 316
Confraternity of Slaves of the Most Holy
Virgin 416
Confrérie de Notre Dame de Sept-
Douleurs 187
consecration to Mary 411–16; to the
Immaculate Heart 417–23; signified by
the scapular 416–17
Constantine the Great 122
Constantinople 57–60, 70; apparitions of
Mary 131–2; feast of the Memory of
Mary 138–9
Constas, Nicholas 102, 138–9
Coppée, François 528
Corbin, Henry 488
Cordeo, Don Emilio 534
Corot, Jean B. 577
Coverdale, Miles 243
Coyle, Kathleen 231
Cranmer, Thomas 243, 250, 251, 315, 321

creation 2, 3–4; glorification of 272–5;
Mary as the world's foundation 469–70;
Mary, May and Mother Nature 510–15;
typology of creation and Mary as the New
Eve 86–90, 192
Cressy, David 510
Cros, Léonard 527
crucifixion of Jesus in John's Gospel: Cyril of
Alexandria's reading of Mary's
involvement 64–5; feminist patriarchal
readings of Mary's involvement 31;
Mary's vigil at the cross 179, 181–5
Cuapa 441
cult of Our Lady of the Sacred Heart 419
cult of St Anne 267
cult of St Joseph 267
cult of the martyrs 57, 69, 110, 121
cult of the saints 69, 71, 131, 133–4, 142;
devotion to images 156; Mary's
supereminence among the saints 68,
156, 159; *see also* cult of the Virgin Mary
cult of the Virgin Mary: apparitions of Mary
see apparitions of Mary; assimilation of
pagan cults to 78; Atticus on 59;
centred on divine maternity 71; in
Constantinople 58–60, 70; in Counter-
Reformation Europe 363–80, 398; in
early Christianity 69–72, 130–42; in
Egypt 57; in eighteenth century
Europe 380–1; forms of devotion *see*
Marian devotion; in high Middle
Ages 149–70; in Latin West in later
Middle Ages 177–99; liturgy *see* liturgy;
Marian feasts *see* Marian feasts; Mary as
mother of Christians 160; political use
of 365–6, 374–6; queenship of Mary *see*
queenship of Mary; in reign of Charles the
Bald 1–2; Virgin's milk 388–9, 405
Cybele 112–13
Cyprian of Antioch 131
Cyril of Alexandria 52, 53, 54, 58, 61–3; on
the Cana marriage story 66;
Christological orthodoxy 65; on
Johannine account of Mary at the foot of
the cross 64–5; letter to John of
Antioch 60–1; on title *Theotokos* in *Third
Letter to Nestorius* 74
Cyril of Jerusalem 90–1
Czestochowa 461

da Fossano, Ambrogio 566
Dahlberg, Andrea 232–3
Damian, Peter *see* Peter Damian
Dante Alighieri 581

Darrigaud, Jean-Claude 522
de Alva y Astorga 374, 377–8
de la Cruz, Franciso 368
de Ligouri, Alphonsus 381
de Montfort, Louis-Marie G. 381, 416; *The True Devotion to the Blessed Virgin* 412–13, 415
de Ojeda SJ, Pedro 378
de Rossi, Giovanni B. 114
de Satge, John 334
de Vega, Lope 379
death, conquest of 95–6
Deger, Ernest 578
deification 65–9
Delacroix, Eugène 576
Delannoy, Jean 533, 534, 535
Della Robbia artists 557–8
DeMille, Cecil B. 533
Denis, Maurice 579
Desgenettes, Abbé 420
Desvallières, Georges 579
Dialogue of the Saviour 39
Diana of Ephesus 113
Diego, Juan 400–1, 426
discipleship of Mary 18–20, 285–6
Discourse of St John the Theologian 43
Docetism 82
doctrine of Mary *see* Mariology
Dolci, Carlo 573
Dolto, Françoise 524
Domenichino 571
Domingo à Jesu Maria 366
Dominic, St 388
Dormition apocrypha 130, 135, 137–8; Latin *Transitus* texts 192–4
Dormition of Mary 43, 136–7; apocryphal sources *see* Dormition apocrypha; earliest tradition 134, 135–6; Feast of Dormition 70, 80, 141; *see also* Assumption of Mary
Dossi, Dosso 572
Droste-Hülshoff, Annette von 527
Dubisch, Jill 396–7, 398
Dubufe, Claude-Marie 578
Duhr, J. 543–4
Duns Scotus, Johannes 212–14, 215, 221, 261; influence on Suárez 258
Dürer, Albrecht 559–60

Eadmer of Canterbury 164–5, 194, 210–11
Ebionites 82
ecclesiology *see* Church
Ecumenical Society of the Blessed Virgin Mary (ESBVM) 345–6

ecumenism: American Lutheran–Catholic dialogue 347, 349–50; ARCIC I 337–8, 347, 348; ARCIC II 355–8; British Catholic–Methodist dialogue 347, 350–4; Catholic/Protestant divide over Mariology 341–4; Catholic–Orthodox 346–7; consensus on Marian doctrine and devotion 358–9; early years of Ecumenical Movement 340–1; eclipse of Marian rhetoric 286; Groupe des Dombes dialogue 347, 354–5, 359; Vatican II and the ESBVM 344–6
Egan, Maurice F. 513
Egeria 69, 140
Egwin 425
Egyptian cult of Mary 57, 111
Eichendorff, Joseph von 527
Einsiedeln, Our Lady of 471
El Greco 569
Eliot, George 526
Elizabeth, cousin of Mary 3
Elizondo, Virgil 446–7
Elvira, Councils of 152
Emmerich, Anne C. 534
Eoves 425
Ephesus 113
Ephesus, Council of 53, 58, 60–3, 69–70, 78, 141–2; effects on art 546
Ephrem of Syria 79, 84–5, 89–90, 101–2
Epiphanius of Salamis 79, 132–4, 138
Erasmus 239, 316
Ernaux, Annie 522
Etheria *see* Egeria
Eucharist 54, 158, 265, 363, 433; Eucharistic prayers of Church of England 336–7; Mass of the Immaculate Conception 231
Eudes, Jean 417–19
Eudocia 108
Eusebius of Caesarea 21, 56, 108
Eutyches 80
Evans, Michael 347
Eve: Mary as the new Eve 77, 80, 86–90, 192, 195–8; Mary, Eve and the Church 93–5; Mary, Eve and the salvation of women 90–3
Eyck, Jan van 558–9
Eynsham Abbey Seat of Wisdom illumination 162, *163*, 168
Ezquioga 449–51, 454–5

Faber, Frederick W. 503–4, 508–9, 516–18
Fabish (sculptor) 577

faith 32–3

Fatima, Our Lady of 230, 427–8, 440–1,
454; consecration of devotees 416;
devotion to Immaculate Heart 420—3,
422; 'O my Jesus' rosary prayer of
devotees 391

Faujas de Saint-Fond 460

feasts *see* Marian feasts

Fehribach, Adeline 30–1, 33

feminist critical analysis: dualistic imagery in
idea of Mary as new Eve 90; liberation
theology and 36–7; Mary as female role
model 38; Mary as Lady of Victorian
Feminism 526; Mary's virginity 16,
26–7; patriarchal readings of John's
Gospel 30–1, 33; sexual difference and
gender power relationships 270–1; status
and experience of women in early
Church 23–8; stories of women behind
the New Testament texts 25

films 532–5

Fiorenza, Elisabeth S. 23–4, 36–7

Fitzmyer, Joseph 19

flagellants 186–7

Foley, Donal 453–4

Forbes, A. P. 333

form criticism 14

Foskett, Mary F. 5

Fouquet, Jean 554, 567

Fragonard, Jean H. 573

Francis de Sales 369, 467

Francis of Assisi 182, 183

Franciscans 183–4, 217

Frank, Mark 327–8

Frankfurt, Council of 155

Freedberg, David 398–9, 403

frescos of Mary 110n15, 111, 114–22,
541–54, 562, 575; *see also* catacomb
paintings

Fulke, William 241, 248

Fulton, Rachel 199

Gabriel, angel 3, 13, 118, 158, 195, 548;
Annunciation by *see* Annunciation; in
Islamic literature 488

Gaillard, Ferdinand 576

Galaktotrophousa image 111–12

Galen (Claudius Galenus) 260–1

Gallagher, Christina 443

Gambero, Luigi 77

Garabandal 428, 432, 441, 451

Gaventa, Beverly R. 28–30, 33

Gebara, Ivone and Bingemer, Maria C.
35–6, 529

gender ideology 267–72

Germanus of Constantinople 71, 154, 416

Gibson, Mel 534, 535

Gillet, Louis 576–7

Gillett, Martin 345, 554

Giordano, Luca 567

Giotto (di Bondone) 556, 557

Girard, René 37–8

Glaber, Raul: *see also* 'Seat of Wisdom' (Virgin
in Majesty) image

Gnosticism 81–2

Godard, Jean-Luc 533

'Godbearer' 1, 50, 53; *see also* 'Mother of
God'; *Theotokos*

goddess worship 77, 111–13, 469–70;
Roman temple to goddess Juno 78

Godiva, Lady 387

Golden Legend, The 194

Gospel of Bartholomew 42

Gospel of James *see Protevangelium of James*

Gospel of Mary 39

Gospel of Philip 42

Gospel of the Ebionites 41

Gospel of the Hebrews 41–2

Gospel of Thomas 21, 39; *see also Infancy
Gospel of Thomas*

Gostling, Francis 459

Graef, Hilda 77, 78

Greely, Andrew 528–9

Green, Celia and McCreery, Charles 436

Gregory of Nazianzus (the Theologian) 57,
79, 131–2

Gregory of Nyssa 79, 85–6, 95, 131–2

Gregory of Tours 70

Gregory Thaumaturgus 131

Gregory XIII 371

Gregory XV 375–6

Gregory XVI 420

Griffith, D. W. 532

Grimm Brothers (Jacob L. and Wilhelm
C.) 527

Grindal, E. 242

Groupe des Dombes 347, 354–5, 359

Grüneisen, W. de 548

Gruyer, G. 563, 567

Guadalupe, Our Lady of 425–6, 461, *462*;
acheiropoietic images 399; images of the
Immaculate Conception and 228; and
liberation 446–7, 451; *Los Remedios*
and 404; and Mexican Catholic
identity 446–7; shrine as symbol of
triumphant Christianity 366; study by
Eric Wolf 400–1

Guercino 573

Guibert of Nogent 181
Gumppenberg SJ, William 370
Guy, Alice 532

'Hail Mary' prayer 386, 390, 577
Halliburton, R. J. 337
Hamington, Maurice 528
Harpocrates 111, *113*
Harris, Ruth 426–7, 436
Harrison, Robert P. 470–2
healings 136–7, 232–3, 399
Hebbel, Friedrich 527
Heber, Reginald 331
Hébert 578
Hegisippus 21, 22
Heine, Heinrich 528
Henderson, Mary H. J. 525
Herbert, George 326–7, 330
Herolt, Johannes (Discipulus) 202–3
Hesse, Hermann 527
Hesychius 91, 140
Hickes, George 330
Hilary of Poitiers 79
Hilborne, David 357
Hildegard of Bingen 178, 191–2, 195–8, 512
Hirn, Yrjö 157
Hodegetria icon 108–9, 111–12
Hölderlin, Friedrich 527
Hole, William 575
Holum, Kenneth G. 142
Holy Spirit: in the apocrypha 41, 42; and conception of Jesus 13, 52, 80, 91, 310; Gabriel identified with (Rūmī) 488–9; Mary's fullness of 66; Mary's holiness through 68–9, 222, 248; overshadowing of Mary 3, 32, 82, 210, 310, 346
Hooker, Richard 316, 324
Hooper, John 243–4
Hopkins, Gerard Manley 51, 284–5, 289, 291, 504, 516; on Mary, May and Mother Nature 510, 511–12, 513–14
Horus 111, *112*
Howard, Ralph and Otto, Katharina 533–4
Hroswitha of Gandersheim 186, 193–4
Huré, Jacqueline S. 523
Hutchinson, Roger 252
Huysmans, Joris-Karl 527

Ibn Kathīr, Ismâ'îl 484–7
iconoclasm 109, 110n13, 151–4, 370, 397, 397–8
iconography: of the Adoration of the Magi 120–2, *124*, 125–6, 161, 163–4,

542; of the Annunciation 118–19, 123, *124*; of the catacombs *see* catacomb paintings; dogmatic themes of the seventeenth century 568–73; of high Middle Ages 151–4, 161–9; of the Holy Kinship 267; icons at St Catherine's Monastery on Sinai 70, *107*; of the Immaculate Conception 221–8, 555, 569–71; influence of pagan goddess art 111–14; legendary portraits of Mary 106–9; of the Majestic Virgin 551–5 *see also* 'Seat of Wisdom' (Virgin in Majesty) image; *Maria Regina* inscriptions 549, 550; Mary as icon in modern European literature 526–8; mosaics of St Maria Maggiore 123–7, 396, 546–7; the Pietà 187, 397, *539*, 554, 562; of Purgatory 371, *372*; Renaissance art of the Virgin Mother 555–68; Roman representations of the Virgin Queen 546–50; *Salus Populi Romani* icon 371; of the Tender Virgin 556–60; '*tota pulchra*' images of Mary 225–7, 555, 569; types and formulas from the nineteenth century 574–81; of Virgin holding the child Jesus 115–18; Virgin of the Epiphany 542, 544, 566–7 *see also* Adoration of the Magi; Virgin Orant 542–4; *see also* iconoclasm; images of Mary
Ignatius of Antioch 77, 82–3
Ildephonsus 425
images of Mary: acheiropoietic 399; in catacombs *see* catacomb paintings; contestation over 403–5 *see also* iconoclasm; Council of Nicaea 395–6; frescos *see* frescos of Mary; iconoclastic dispute in high Middle Ages 151–4; iconography *see* iconography; imagery in Modernity 406–9; links with objects and landscapes 405–6; Mary as a mult-vocal symbol 397, 400–3; materializing the sacred through 396–400, 407–8; virtualization of 408–9; visionary 36–41 *see also* apparitions of Mary; *see also* art
Immaculate Conception: Anglican reformer views 245–50; and corruption of Vulgate in Genesis 3.15 246–7; doctrine in nineteenth and twentieth centuries 228–33; Duns Scotus's doctrinal defence 212–15; feast of the Conception 194–5, 208, 210–12, 376;

Immaculate Conception, *cont.*
  foundations of doctrine 208–9;
  iconography 221–8, 555, 569—71, 578;
  Immaculism 214–21, 373–81;
  Immaculists' theological
  anthropology 214–21; *Ineffabilis Deus*
  (papal Bull) 229, 230, 279–80, 288, 580;
  liturgy 221, 231; Luther on 317;
  Mary's bodily conception 217–20; and
  Mary's predestination to divine
  motherhood 220–1, 289–90; Medal of
  (the 'Miraculous Medal') *228*, 228–9;
  Our Lady of Lourdes' identification
  with 437; overview of doctrine 207;
  Rahner on 230, 288–90, 292–3; and
  transmission of apocrypha on
  Mary 194–5; *see also* sinlessness of Mary
Immaculate Heart 230, 417—23, *418, 422*
incarnation, doctrine of: and belief in Virgin
  Mary as Mother of God 50 *see also*
  'Mother of God'; *Theotokos*; Mary's free
  co-operation in the incarnation 158–9,
  258–61, 289–90; as movement of descent
  and glorification 274–5; redemption
  and 51–2; virginity of Mary as focal
  point for reflection on 84–5
indulgence system 371–3
Ineffabilis Deus (papal Bull) 229, 230,
  279–80, 288, 580
Infancy Gospel of Thomas 41
Ingres, Jean A. 576
Innocent II 550
Innocent III 160, 550
Innocent X 376–7
Innocent XII 377
intercession: for the dead 371–3;
  intercessory prayer to Mary 130–2,
  135–6, 317; by Mary in early
  tradition 69, 70–1, 135–7; by Mary in
  Middle Ages tradition 149–50, 185–6;
  and the Mary-Orant image 543–4; in
  modern European literature 528–9;
  Reformation/Tridentine divide 364; *see
  also* mediation
internet 408–9
Iogna-Prat, Dominique 1
Irenaeus 77, 79, 100; Genesis typology and
  Mary as the new Eve 86–8
Irigaray, Luce 270, 526
Isis 111, *112, 113*
Islamic treatment of Mary: historical 484–7;
  Marian parallels to the Prophet's daughter
  Fāṭima 496–7; poetic 487–96,
  499–500; in prayer 490–1; proposal of a

'liberation Mariology' 497–8;
  scriptural 479, 480–3
Ittenbach 578
Ivankoviæ, Ivanka 445; *see also* Medjugorje

Jacob, Charles 578
Jacobus de Voragine 194
Jalâl al-Dīn Rûmī 487–90
James I 325
James and the family of Jesus 20–3
James, Gospel of *see Protevangelium of James*
James, John A. 341
Jameson, Anna 526
Jeffreys, Sheila 270–1
Jerome 21, 79, 99, 189, 414
Jerusalem: bringing the Ark of the Covenant
  to 2–3; feast of the Memory of
  Mary 139–41; Temple cult 2
Jervaulx 425
Jesuits *see* Society of Jesus
Jesus Christ: cross of *see* crucifixion of Jesus in
  John's Gospel; distancing of Jesus from
  Mary in the Gospels 18–19, 23; James
  and the family of Jesus 20–3; *see also*
  incarnation, doctrine of
Jewel, John 239–40, 244–5, 316
Joachim, father of Mary: and the conception
  of Mary *see* conception of Mary;
  Immaculate Conception; embrace of
  Anne at the Golden Gate 47, 208,
  221–2, 227, 555; scriptural silence
  about 374
Johannine tradition: a feminist patriarchal
  reading of texts relating to Mary 30–1,
  33; Gaventa on 29; vigil at foot of
  cross 31, 64–5, 179, 181–5; of water and
  Spirit 469; women's leadership in
  Johannine community 25
John Chrysostom 58, 79, 101, 248–9
John Damascene 153
John of Segovia 211, 218
John of the Cross 430, 435
John Paul II 34–5, 386, 423, 432, 445–6;
  influence of von Balthasar's
  Mariology 312
John Rylands Papyrus 470 56, 57
John VII 548–9
Johnson, Elizabeth A. 24, 286
Johnson, Robert 535
José de Jesús María 368
Joseph cult 267
Josephus 21
Joses 22
Journet, Charles 306

Juanes, Juan de 573
Julian of Norwich 290
Juno, goddess 78, 113
Justin Martyr 75–6, 77, 83–4, 86
Justina 131

Kali 470
Kalocsay, Alán 526
Kathisma, church of 139–40
Kazantzakis, Nikos 522, 533
Keble, John 331–2, 503
Keller, Gottfried 526–7
Ken, Thomas 329–30
Kibeho 441
Kierkegaard, Soren 300–1
kin relations 267–8, 273–5
King, Henry 533
King's Book, The 252, 320
Kipling, Rudyard 525
Kirkstall 425
Kollyridians 132–4, 137–8
Kowalski, Bernard 534
Kristeva, Julia 526

La Salette 332–3, 440–1
Labouré, Catherine 228, 420, 426, 445, 446
Lambertini, Cardinal 431–2
Laqueur, Thomas 271
Lassere, Henri 527
Lathoud, D. 540
Latimer, Hugh 239, 241, 247, 248–9, 250, 315, 318–19
Latin Infancy Gospel 44
Laud, William 316, 330
Laurentin, René 414, 428, 432–4, 444, 521
Law of God 2
Le Cardonnel, Louis 528
Le Puy 425, 458—61, *459*
'Lead Books' of Granada 375, 379
Lemoyne, François 567–8
Lenz, Peter 575
Leo I (Leo the Great) 80
Leo III (Leo the Isaurian) 152–3, 154
Leo XIII 421–2
Leonardo da Vinci 565–6
Lewis, C. S. 526
Liber Requiei 135–6
liberation theology 35–7, 446–7, 525; 'liberation Mariology' 497–8, 524
Libri Carolini 110, 155
Life of St Stephen the Younger 70
Lightfoot, J. B. 332
Liguori, Alphonsus 230

Limburg brothers 554
Lippi, Filippo 567
literature: American poetry 499–501, 513; ballads 492–6, 514; based on *Transitus* narratives 193–4; Islamic *see* Islamic treatment of Mary; of Middle Ages in *Mater Dolorasa* tradition 184–6; modern European 521–9; nineteenth-century English poetry 51, 284–5, 291, 503–19; *see also individual authors and poets*
liturgy: Anglican 253–4, 336–7; of the conception 221; feasts *see* Marian feasts; *Kontakion* 182; Marian liturgies in early Christianity 137–41; Mass of the Immaculate Conception 231; relationship between Mary and Church's liturgy 34; Stations of the Cross 183–4
Llull, Ramon 216
Lochner, Stefan 559
Lofts, Norah 523
Loire school of art 566
Loisy, Alfred 303, 304
Lombardy school of art 565–6
Loreto, Holy House of 370
Lourdes, Our Lady of *229*, 232–3, 426–7, 429, 436–8, 446, 580; evolving meanings of the cult of 451
love 308–9
Lucia dos Santos 230, 420–1, 423, 446
Ludulphus of Saxony 186
Lukan tradition 17, 29, 177–8; feminist readings 26; legendary portraits of Mary 106–9; Luke as patron saint of painters 109; reading of Mary as model of faith 32–3; Simeon's prophecy and *Mater Dolorosa* 182–5
Lumen Gentium 90
Luther, Martin 315, 316–17, 364, 378

MacCulloch, Diarmaid 253
Mackenzie, Norman 512
Magi 109, 119; representations of Adoration of the Magi 120–2, *124*, 125–6, 161, 163–4, 542
Magnificat 3, 16, 464, 519, 524
Mâle, Emile 545, 571
Manglaviti, Leo 512–13
Manzoni, Alessandro 526
Mappa Mundi 149, *150*
Maratta, Carlo 571
María de Jesús (Maria Coronel) 379–81, 569
Marialis cultus 34, 285–6
Marian art *see* art

Marian devotion: in Anglican
tradition 324–37 *see also* Anglican views
of Mary; and apparitions of Mary *see*
apparitions of Mary; through art *see* art;
consecration *see* consecration to Mary;
ecumenical dialogue *see* ecumenism; feasts
see Marian feasts; following Vatican
II 285–6; by historical period and place
see cult of the Virgin Mary;
hyperdoulia 156; images of Mary *see*
images of Mary; to the Immaculate
Heart 230, 417–23; Immaculism
373–81; intercession of Mary *see*
intercession; Islamic *see* Islamic treatment
of Mary; of Jesuit Marian sodalities 368,
414; life of Mary *see* Mary's story: the
popular picture; in literature *see* literature;
liturgy *see* liturgy; Mary and
deification 65–9; Mary and feminine
weakness 63–5; Mary's supereminence
among the saints 68, 156, 159; to *Mater
Dolorosa see Mater Dolorosa*; papal
clarifications of Church status 34–5; to
physical beauty of Mary 368–9;
pilgrimage 369–71; to Queen of Heaven
see queenship of Mary; reactions of
English reformers to 238–54;
Reformation effects on 364, 373–4;
rosary 242, 368, 385–94; slavery to
Mary 415–16
Marian feasts 137–41; in Anglican
calendar 253, 322, 357; celebrated by
continental reformers 317; Feast of
Dormition 70, 80, 141; Feast of Our
Lady of Sorrows 187; Feast of Our Lady
of the Rosary 390; Feast of the
Immaculate Conception 194–5, 208,
210–12, 376; May and Mother
Nature 510–15; and the mystery of
redemption 510
Mariology: and the Anglican tradition *see*
Anglican views of Mary; apocryphal
sources *see* apocrypha; Assumption *see*
Assumption of Mary; biblical sources *see*
New Testament; Christocentric readings
of the Gospels 33; Christocentricity in
Nestorian controversy 65; continental
reformers and 315–18; in Counter-
Reformation Europe 364–5;
ecclesiotypical 4–5, 19, 93–5, 122–3,
159, 179–81, 300–12; in ecumenism *see*
ecumenism; faith and reason 303–5;
feminist *see* feminist critical analysis;
gender ideology and 267–72; and the

glorification of creation and
humanity 272–5; Immaculate
Conception *see* Immaculate Conception;
'liberation Mariology' 497–8, 524;
liberation theology and 35–7, 446–7,
525; literary approaches to *see* literature;
love and 308–9; Mary and
deification 65–9; Mary and the scandal
of the Gospel 28–30; Mary and
Wisdom 166–70 *see also* Wisdom; Mary
as Bride of Christ 198–9, 265, 267;
Mary as Co-Redemptrix 290, 332, 334,
359, 380 *see also* co-redemption; Mary as
Godbearer *see* 'Mother of God'; *Theotokos*;
Mary as the 'memory' of the
Church 305–6; Mary as the new
Eve 77, 80, 86–90, 192, 195–8; Mary's
faith and discipleship 18–20, 285–6;
Mary's predestination to divine
motherhood 220–1, 258–61, 289–90;
maternal Mariology of Suárez 257–69,
271–6; mediation *see* mediation; modern
ideas of kinship and gender in 264–72;
papal discussions of Mary's role in
Christian faith 34–5; in patristic
theology *see* patristic theology; of perfect
discipleship 285–6; of Rahner 230,
288–90, 292–9; and theological
anthropology *see* anthropology;
theological context of post-conciliar
changes 287–8; theology of
visions 429–36; of von Balthasar
300–12
Mark, Secret Gospel of 41
Marpingen 438–40, 448–9
Marshall, William 320
Martin, Jacques 578
Martini, Simone 556
martyrs, cult of 57, 69, 110, 121
Mary Magdalen 1, 12, 23, 30, 39, 42
Marys identified in the apocrypha 39, 42
Marys identified in the New Testament
11–12, 22–3
Mary's story: the popular picture 13, 522; in
modern European literature 521–5
Mascall, E. L. 334
Mass *see* Eucharist
Massabielle apparition *see* Lourdes, Our Lady
of
Mastrolia, Arthur 526
Mater Dolorosa 179, 182–5, 186–7, 397,
535, 554
Matter, Anne E. 428–9
Matthean tradition 17, 29, 161, 177–8

Maximilian I   365
May, as month of Mary   510–15
McAfee Brown, Robert   340, 345
McDannell, Colleen   407–8
McVey, Kathleen   84
mediation: as attribute signified by Mary's
   virginity   5; de Satge on   335–6;
   ecumenical divide over   344; through
   intercession *see* intercession; Mary and
   deification   65–9; Mary as *Mediatrix see*
   Mediatrix function of Mary
Mediatrix function of Mary   181, 302, 310,
   334, 359, 397; attacked by Pusey   332;
   de Satge on   335–6; intercession
   and   185–6
meditation   368; with the rosary   385–94
Medjugorje: consecration of devotees   416;
   Croat nationalism   438, 454; cult
   of   428, 432, 441, 451–2; prayer
   groups   391; visionary image at   438,
   532
Mellenary   442–3
Memlinc, Hans   558, 559
Memory of Mary feast   138–41
Mercier, Louis   523
Merson, Luc-Olivier   577
Merton, Thomas   521
Merveille, E.   580
Mexico City: *Los Remedios*   404; Virgin of
   Guadalupe *see* Guadalupe, Our Lady of
Michelangelo   397, 562, 565
Miegge, Giovanni   216
Milan, edict of   78
Millet, Jean F.   577
Mimouni, Simon   138
miracles   186, 398; of healing   136–7,
   232–3, 399; *Miracles of Our Lady of*
   Chartres   399; *Miracles of the Blessed Virgin*
   Mary (Herolt)   202–3; paintings of
   Miracles of the Virgin, Eton
   College   268
'Miraculous Medal'   *228*, 228–9, 420
Mocky, Jean-Pierre   532
Modernism   303, 304
Monaco, Lorenzo   570
Monophysitism   80
Montañes   573
Montserrat, Our Lady of   470, 471
Moore, Daniel A.   499–501
Moral, José Z. y   526
More, Thomas   239, 316, 403
Moreau, Gustave   576
Morgan, D.   399–400
Morneau, Robert   518

Morrison, Susan   405–6
Moschus, John   70
Moss, Leonard   470
'Mother of God': in Mariology of
   Suárez   257–61, 262–3, 264–5, 268;
   Mary's predestination to divine
   motherhood   220–1, 258–61, 289–90;
   Mary's queenship as   157–60, 164–6 *see*
   also queenship of Mary; Renaissance art of
   the Virgin Mother   555–68; Roman art
   and the cult of   546–50; *Theotokos* title *see*
   Theotokos; views of continental reformers
   on   317
Müller, Karl   578
Munificentissimus Deus   281–3
Muratori, Ludovico A.   381
Murillo, Bartolomé E.   224, 376, 569, 570–1

Nasr, Seyyed H.   275
National Association of Our Lady of the
   Sacred Heart   407
Nepomuk, Jan   365–6
Nestorianism: influence on patristic
   theology   79; Nestorian
   controversy   54, 57–8, 61, 78
Nestorius   54, 57–9, 60, 61, 69n24, 78;
   Cyril's *Third Letter* to   74
New Testament: approaches to critical
   analysis   13–16; historical approach to
   texts concerning Mary   16–28; identity
   of the Marys   11–12, 22–3; list of texts
   relating to Mary, mother of Jesus   12;
   literary approach to texts concerning
   Mary   28–33; Mary and the woman in
   Revelation chapter 12   224–5, 252, 309;
   the popular story of Mary   13, 522; as
   source of cult of the Virgin in Middle
   Ages   177–9; theological approaches to
   texts concerning Mary   34–8; *see also*
   Johannine tradition; Lukan tradition;
   Matthean tradition
New York, Madonna of 115th Street   402–3
Newman, John Henry   80–1, 332, 503,
   505–6, 509, 526; on Mary, May and
   Mother Nature   510–11, 514
Newton, John   353
Nicaea, First Council of (325)   53n6, 78
Nicaea, Second Council of (787)   154, 395–6
Nicholas of Cusa   272
Nietzsche, Friedrich W.   300, 301, 304, 311
Nodier, Charles   528
Noël, Marie   524
Notre Dame, Paris   181, 407; The Black
   Virgin of Paris   466–7

Nouveau, Germain 528
Novalis 527
Nowell, Alexander: *Catechism* 248
number symbolism 391–2
Nuria, Our Lady of 472

Obsequies of the Virgin 135–6
Odes of Solomon 40
Olcott, Sidney 533
Olier, Jean-Jacques 220, 261–2, 268, 416
Oliveto Citra 443–5
Opus Dei 415
Oratory movement 416
Orcival, Our Lady of (statue) 164, *165*,
    168–9, 461
Origen 56, 76, 77, 90, 97, 160
original sin 50–1, 209, 213–14, 219–20
Orsel, Victor 575, 576
Orsi, Robert 402–3
Orthodox Church 80, 106, 108;
    ecumenical Marian dialogue 346–7
Ostendorfer, Michael 399
Overbeck, Johann F. 575
Oxford Movement 331–3, 504; *see also*
    Tractarianism

Pacheco, Francisco 227, 569–70
Pahlavi, Patrick A. 497–8
paintings *see* art; catacomb paintings; frescos
    of Mary
Palm of the Tree of Life narratives 135
Palmar de Troya 443
Paredes, Joseph 231
Parker, T. 334
Pasolini, Pier P. 533, 534, 535
Passion plays 184
patristic theology: and the emergence of
    Marian theology 75–81; Mary, death
    and redemption 95–6; Mary, Eve and
    the Church 93–5; Mary, Eve and the
    salvation of women 90–3; the new
    Eve 86–90; perpetual virginity 96–9;
    sinlessness of Mary 80, 99–102; virginal
    motherhood 81–6
Paul V 375
Paul VI 34, 285–6, 355, 359
Pearson, John 328
Pedro de Castro Vaca y Quiñones 375, 378
Péguy, Charles 528, 529, 552, 581
Pelagianism 209, 216–17
Pelikan, Jaroslav 142, 152–3, 397
Peredur Son of Efrawg 465
Perkins, William 316
perpetual virginity of Mary 13, 96–9,

189–92, 250–1, 317, 364
Perry, Nicholas and Echeverría, Loreto 453
Perugino 563
Peter Damian 166, 168, 178–9, 181, 190;
    quoted by Suárez 263–4
Peter Lombard 195
Peter of Alexandria 97
Philip, Gospel of 42
Philip II of Spain 366
Philip of Harvengt 198
piety, Marian *see* Marian devotion
pilgrimage 369–71; relation of story of
    Mary to the 'pilgrim people of God' 35
Pilon, Gemain 566
Pistis Sophia 39, 42–3
Pius V 366, 373
Pius IX: Bull *Ineffabilis Deus* 229, 230, 279–
    80, 288, 580
Pius XII 415; *Munificentissimus Deus*
    281–3
Pope, Barbara C. 452–3
portraits of Mary 106–10
prayer to Mary 130–2, 135–6; *see also* 'Hail
    Mary' prayer
presence of the Lord 2–3; mediated through
    the Church 5
Presentation in the Temple 123;
    Presentation of Mary feast 44, 141
Priscilla, catacomb of 115–18, 119, 541–2,
    544
Proclus 59, 91, 102–3, 138–9
prophecy 5
Protevangelium of James: account of Mary's
    conception 47–8, 208; account of the
    Annunciation 48–9, 118; birthplace of
    Christ 139; incorporation into Roman
    Catholic and Orthodox views of
    Mary 16; influence on patristic
    writings 76; Mary's association with
    scandal 28; view of Mary's relationship
    to James 21; perpetual virginity of
    Mary 189–90; treatment of the Mary
    story 13, 39–40, 188
Pseudo-Matthew 43, 188–9
Pseudo-Melito, Transitus of 192–3
Pucelle, Jean 554
Pulcheria, St 58, 60, 127
Pusey, E. B. 332

queenship of Mary 156–66; Black
    Madonnas and 464; in cult of *Maria
    Ecclesia* 180; Roman representations of
    the Virgin Queen 546–50
Qur'ân 479, 480–3

Rader, Matthaeus 366
Rahner, Karl: on the Assumption and
Mariology 292–9; on
consecration 411–12; on the
Immaculate Conception 230, 288–90,
292–3; on symbolism 513; on visions
and apparitions 435
Raphael 563–5, 567
Ratzinger, Joseph 265
Ray, Nicholas 533, 534
redaction criticism 14
redemption: Black Madonnas and 464–7;
English nineteenth-century literature on
mystery of 509–10; Mary as Co-
Redemptrix 290, 332, 334, 359, 380 *see
also* co-redemption; Mary, death and
redemption 95–6; Proclus on
redemptive significance of Mary 102–3;
and theology of incarnation 51–2; *see also*
soteriology
Regensberg 399
Reinhartz, Adele 25
relics 70, 108n4, 155, 161, 396–8;
secondary 186
Rembrandt 573
Remedies, Our Lady of the 404
Ribera, Jusepe de *223*, 567, 569
Richard of St Victory 179
Richeldis 406
Rictus, Jehan 525
Rieger, Eva 270
Rilke, Rainer M. 522, 523
Robbia, Luca della 557
Robert's vision (monk Robert) 173–6
Rocamadour, Our Lady of 465–6, 471
Rogers, Thomas 241, 246
Roller: *Les Catacombs de Rome* 540–1
Roman art 540–1, 546–50
Rome: catacomb paintings 540–1; fourth
century apparition of Mary 425;
toleration of Christianity 78; worship of
goddess Juno 78, 113
Ronzières, Notre-Dame de 470
rosary 242, 368, 385–94
rose symbolism 392–3, 513–14
Rossellini, Roberto 533
Rossetti, Dante G. 518, 574–5
Rosty, Kálmán 526
Rubens, Peter P. 573
Rubio, William 217
Rue du Bac, Paris 228, 420, 434, 445
Ruether, Rosemary R. 92
Rūmī 487–90
Rupert of Deutz 160, 198–9

sacred space 514
Sagovsky, Nicholas 357
Saillens, Emile 463, 469–70
saints, cult of *see* cult of the saints
salvation *see* redemption; soteriology
Salve Regina 160
San Damiano 432, 451
San Nicolas 441
Sannazaro, Jacopo 561
Santa Maria Antiqua 547–8, 549
Santa Maria Maggiore, Rome 70, 78, 371,
425, 545; Marian mosaics 123–7, 396,
546–7
sarcophagi carvings 119–20
Sartre, Jean-Paul 521
Savonarola, Girolamo 561
scapulars 416–17
Scarsella, Ippolito 571
Schaberg, Jane 26–7
Scheeben, Matthias 264–5, 270
Scheffczyk, Leo 160
Schenkendorf, Max von 527
Scherpenhuevel, shrine of 369–70
Schongauer, Martin 559
Scorsese, Martin 533
'Seat of Wisdom' (Virgin in Majesty)
image 160, 161–9, 551–2
Secret Gospel of Mark 41
Sedlar, Jakov 532
Seim, Turid K. 26
Semmelroth, Otto 265
Serre, Michel 573
Servites, Order of 187
Sesboüé, Bernard 346, 348
Severus of Antioch 65–9
Seville 375, 376, 379
Simon Stock 416–17
sin, original 50–1, 209, 213–14, 219–20
sinlessness of Mary 80, 99–102, 231,
07–8; Anglican reformer views 245–50;
human freedom and 301–2; *see also*
Immaculate Conception
Six Books apocrypha 136–8
Sixtus III 78, 123, 396, 545
Smalcald Articles 316
Society of Jesus 219, 364, 414; Marian
sodalities 368, 414
Sodoma II 561
Song of Songs 122, 188, 198–9, 466, 550,
569; and '*tota pulchra*' images of
Mary 225–7, 555, 569
Sonrel, Elisabeth 578
soteriology: doctrine of the Immaculate
Conception *see* Immaculate Conception;

soteriology, *cont.*
ecumenical divide in 343–4; Mary, Eve and the salvation of women 90–3; Mary's free co-operation in the incarnation 158–9, 258–61, 289–90; post-conciliar changes of ideas about Jesus, Mary and salvation history 287–8; *see also* co-redemption; redemption
Soubirous, Bernadette 229, 426, 429, 436–8, 446, 527, 580
source criticism 14
Southwell, Robert 219
Sozomen 131–2
Spark, Muriel 528
St Catherine's Monastery, Sinai 70; miniature of St Luke painting icon of the Virgin and Child *107*
St Mary Major *see* Santa Maria Maggiore, Rome
St Nazaro Maggiore, Milan 122
Stations of the Cross 183–4
statues 155–6, 160, 161–9, 577–8, 580; Black Madonnas 458–74; *imágenes de vestir* 371; Our Lady of Lourdes *229*; vision of the monk Robert 173–6
Stein, Edith 525
Stevens, George 533
Stratton, Suzanne 225–7
Stuart, Elizabeth 271
Studer, Claire 525
Suárez, Francisco: life and influence 256; Mariology 257–69, 271–6; Mary and the glorification of creation 272–5
Suger 178, 180–1, 553
Symeon, son of Clopas 22–3

Tabernacle 2, 4
Talbert, Charles H. 31–2, 33
Talcourt, Antoine 567
Tanner, William H. 518
Taylor, Jeremy 328–9
Tellus Mater 113
Temple cult, Jerusalem 2
Temple Presentation 123
Tepeyac shrine 400–1; *see also* Guadalupe, Our Lady of
Teresa of Avila 430
Tertullian 76, 77, 96–7, 100; on Mary as the new Eve 88
Thecla, St 69
Theodore of Mopsuestia 63
Theodoret of Cyrrhus 61–2, 65
theology of Mary *see* Mariology
Theophano 180

Theophilus 185–6
Theotecnus of Livias 70–1
Theotokos 50–5; ARCIC I affirmation 337; Council of Ephesus 53, 58, 60–3, 74; and the cult of the Virgin 69–72; de Satge on 334–5; early uses of the title 56–7; imagery appropriate to title 126, 547–50; Isis and 111; Jeremy Taylor on 329; Jewel's defence of title 245; Mary and deification 65–9; Nestorian controversy 54, 57–8, 61, 74; Oxford Movement and 331; and the Trinity (von Balthasar) 310–11; *see also* 'Mother of God'; queenship of Mary
Theresa of Avila 424, 430, 570
Therese of Lisieux 523
Thetford 425
Thomas Aquinas: Christology 263; view of conception 260–1, 269; on following literal sense of Scripture 265–6; and intercession 528; opposition to doctrine of the Immaculate Conception 195, 212, 245; view of visions 430
Thomas, Gospel of *see Gospel of Thomas*; *Infancy Gospel of Thomas*
Thomas, Rod 357
Thurian, Max 345
Tiepolo, Giovanni B. 572
Till, Eric 534
Tintoretto 572
Tissot, James 575, 577
'*tota pulchra*' images of Mary 225–7, *226*, 555, 569
Tractarianism 503–4, 514; *see also* Oxford Movement
Travers, Walter 324
Trent, Council of 246, 364, 373, 398, 416, 431; curb on art 562
trinitarian theology 51–2
Turner, Edith 404
Turner, Victor 400, 404
Turquety, Edouard 528
Tyndale, William 241, 248, 250, 251

Urban VIII 376

Van Dyck 567, 573
van Esbroeck, Michel 135
Van Eyck, Jan 558–9
Vanni, Franceso 572
Vassivière, Our Lady of 472
Vatican Council I 279, 302

Vatican Council II: on consecration 415;
context of changes in Mariology 287–8;
downplaying of Marian devotion 285–6;
and the ESBVM 344–6; *Lumen
Gentium* 90
Velankanni shrine 404–5
Velardo, José 570–1
Velàzquez, Diego 224, 569
Vesta 113
Vilatte, Sylvie 463
Villiers, Roger de 578
virgin birth: to be hidden from the devil 77,
82; de Satge on 334; Hildegard's vision
of 192; historicity of the tradition 4,
17–18; in medieval Jewish–Christian
polemic 190; Qur'ânic account 482–3
'Virgin in Majesty' (Seat of Wisdom)
image 160, 161–9, 551–2
virginity of Mary: to be hidden from the
devil 77, 82; and celebacy tradition of
the Church 190–2; and Christ's
conquest of death 95–6; 'Ever Virgin'
tradition 13, 96–9, 189–92, 250–1, 317,
364; in feminist criticism 16, 26–7;
humility and 259; mediation and 5; as
model for the ascetic life 78; Old
Testament typology and 85–90; as proof
of Christ's divinity 84; tradition of
Mary's vow of virginity 189; virginal
motherhood in patristic theology 81–6
Virgin's festival 59–60; *see also* Marian feasts
visions of Mary *see* apparitions of Mary
Vloberg, Maurice 225, 227
von Balthasar, Hans Urs 265, 300–12, 344,
523

Walsingham shrine 340, 405–6, 425
Ward, Benedicta 186
Ward, Maisie 393
Ward, Neville 345–6
Ware, Kallistos 358
Warner, Marina 179, 181

Warner, Pauline 346
Weaver, Mary J. 38
Wenger, Antoine 135
Werfl, Franz 453, 527
Wesley, Charles 351
Westcott, B. F. 332–3
Weyden, Rogier van der 558
Whitaker (1849) 245–7, 250, 251
Wiene, Robert 533
Wilde, Oscar 518–19
Willesden 425, 471
William of Ware 212, 217, 218
Wilpert, J. 115, 541, 544
Wisdom: Mary's identification with 4, 160,
169–70, *223*, 224; 'Seat of Wisdom'
image 160, 161–9, 551–2; Temple cult
association with 2
Witherington III, Ben 18–19, 20
Wolf, Eric 400–1
women: emergent ideals of Christian
womanhood 99; Kollyridians 132–4;
Mary, Eve and the salvation of
women 90–3; role and place in first-
century Israel/Palestine 19, 24; status
and experience in early Church 23–8;
stories of women behind the New
Testament texts 25; Victorian ideal of
woman in literature 515–18
Wordsworth, William 514, 526

Yarnold, Edward J. 336, 358
Yeats, W. B. 523
Young, Frances 87
Younger, Paul 404–5
Yver, Colette 580

Zaragoza 425
Zeffirelli, Franco 533, 534–5
Zimdars-Swartz, Sandra 440, 442–3
Zola, Emile 527
Zurbarán 569
Zwingli, Ulrich 315, 316, 317